THE HODDER

POCKET
NIV
CONCORDANCE

THE HODDER POCKET NIV CONCORDANCE

CONTAINS OVER 2000 ENTRY WORDS AND OVER 15000 BIBLE VERSES

Martin H Manser

Hodder & Stoughton
LONDON SYDNEY AUCKLAND

First published as The NIV Shorter Concordance
in Great Britain in 1997
This edition first published in 2001

10 9 8 7 6 5 4 3 2

British Library Cataloguing in Publication Data
A record for this book is available from the British Library

ISBN 0 340 78589 6

Printed and bound in Great Britain by
Clays Ltd, St Ives plc

Hodder & Stoughton
A Division of Hodder Headline Ltd
338 Euston Road
London NW1 3BH

A Shorter Concordance to the New International Version

Introduction

A concordance is an alphabetical list of Bible words. It is useful when you cannot remember the exact words of a passage or where in the Bible a particular passage is.

For example, you may only be able to remember some of the words in the phrase "My grace is sufficient for you, for my power is made perfect in weakness", or you may want to know in which Bible book it comes. By looking in the concordance under the entry words *grace*, *power*, *perfect* or *weak*, you will find extracts of this verse and its location at 2 Corinthians 12:9.

This concordance gives you over 2,000 entry words and over 15,500 Bible passages in which they can be found. The entry words include such key theological terms as *faith*, *fellowship*, *grace* and *holy*, as well as other more general words. Under each entry word the most significant passages are given.

It is important to remember that the Bible passages included are only very brief extracts. You must look up these extracts in their fuller context in order to understand their meaning.

This concordance also has over 200 entries on people, such as Moses, Joshua, Jesus and Paul. The most important aspects of their lives are noted, with Bible references.

How to use this concordance

1. Main entry words are in alphabetical order. Under the main entry word, Bible extracts are listed in Bible-book order.
2. Where the main entry word appears in a Bible extract, it is replaced by the first letter of that word in italics. For example, under the entry word **perfect** appears: for my power is made *p* in weakness. Here *p* stands for *perfect*.
3. Different grammatical forms of the same word are shown next to the main entry word. For example, after the entry word day comes **-s**. The **-s** stands for the plural *days*. In the Bible extracts this appears as *d-s*. The tenses of a verb are shown similarly, e.g., after the entry word **glorify** comes **-ies**, **-ing**. The **-ies**, **-ing**

stands for *glorifies* and *glorifying*. In the Bible extracts these appear as *g-ies* and *g-ing*.

4. A few main entry words have the same spelling but very different meanings. These words are given as separate entries. For example, **bow**[1] lists Bible extracts where the meaning is "a weapon for shooting arrows"; **bow**[2] lists extracts where the meaning is "to bend the body as a sign of respect".
5. A capital letter in the extract line indicates a capital letter in the Bible text. For example, under the entry word **father** appears: yet your heavenly *F* feeds them. Here *F* stands for *Father*.
6. In a Bible extract "..." is used to show that some words have been left out.
7. At entries on people, the use of numbers indicates different people with the same name, e.g., **Mary 1** mother of Jesus; **Mary 2** Mary Magdalene; **Mary 3** sister of Martha and Lazarus.

We hope that you will find this concordance useful and that it will help you not only to read the Bible but also to understand and respond to its message.

MARTIN H. MANSER
GARY BENFOLD
ROSALIND J. S. DESMOND
FRANK J. HARPER
BRIAN E. KELLY
ROBIN L. ROUTLEDGE
ARTHUR J. ROWE

Abbreviations of Bible Books

Genesis	Ge	Nahum	Na
Exodus	Ex	Habakkuk	Hab
Leviticus	Lev	Zephaniah	Zep
Numbers	Nu	Haggai	Hag
Deuteronomy	Dt	Zechariah	Zec
Joshua	Jos	Malachi	Mal
Judges	Jdg	Matthew	Mt
Ruth	Ru	Mark	Mk
1 Samuel	1Sa	Luke	Lk
2 Samuel	2Sa	John	Jn
1 Kings	1Ki	Acts	Ac
2 Kings	2Ki	Romans	Ro
1 Chronicles	1Ch	1 Corinthians	1Co
2 Chronicles	2Ch	2 Corinthians	2Co
Ezra	Ezr	Galatians	Gal
Nehemiah	Ne	Ephesians	Eph
Esther	Est	Philippians	Php
Job	Job	Colossians	Col
Psalms	Ps	1 Thessalonians	1Th
Proverbs	Pr	2 Thessalonians	2Th
Ecclesiastes	Ecc	1 Timothy	1Ti
Song of Songs	SS	2 Timothy	2Ti
Isaiah	Isa	Titus	Tit
Jeremiah	Jer	Philemon	Phm
Lamentations	La	Hebrews	Heb
Ezekiel	Eze	James	Jas
Daniel	Da	1 Peter	1Pe
Hosea	Hos	2 Peter	2Pe
Joel	Joel	1 John	1Jn
Amos	Am	2 John	2Jn
Obadiah	Ob	3 John	3Jn
Jonah	Jhn	Jude	Jude
Micah	Mic	Revelation	Rev

A

Aaron
Brother of Moses; appointed as his spokesman (Ex 4:14–16; 7:1–2). Held up Moses' hands in battle (Ex 17:12). Consecrated as priest (Ex 28:1–4; 29; Lev 8; Heb 5:4). Made golden calf (Ex 32); opposed Moses (Nu 12:1–3). Priesthood challenged (Nu 16); staff budded as confirmation of his call (Nu 17). With Moses, excluded from Canaan (Nu 20:12). Death (Nu 20:22–29).

abandon, -ed
2Ch 12:5	have *a-ed* me; therefore I now *a*
Ps 16:10	you will not *a* me to the grave,
Ac 2:27	you will not *a* me to the grave,

Abba
Mk 14:36	"*A*, Father," he said,
Ro 8:15	by him we cry, "*A*, Father.
Gal 4:6	the Spirit who calls out, "*A*,

Abednego
Formerly Azariah; member of Jewish nobility taken to Babylon with Daniel, Meshach and Shadrach (Da 1:3–7). Refused unclean food (Da 1:8–16); appointed as administrator (Da 2:49). Refused to worship golden image; kept safe in fiery furnace (Da 3).

Abel
Second son of Adam. Shepherd (Ge 4:2); offered sacrifice acceptable to God (Ge 4:4; Heb 11:4); killed by his brother Cain (Ge 4:8).

abhor, -s
Ps 119:163	I hate and *a* falsehood
Pr 11:1	The LORD *a-s* dishonest scales,

Abiathar
Son of Ahimelech; priest in time of Saul and David. Escaped Saul's massacre of priests who helped David (1Sa 22:20–23). Faithful to David (1Sa 23:6; 2Sa 15:24–29;). Supported Adonijah (1Ki 1:7); deposed by Solomon (1Ki 2:26).

Abigail
1. David's sister (1Ch 2:16–17). **2.** Wife of Nabal (1Sa 25:3); entreated David to spare his life (1Sa 25:14–35). Married David after Nabal's death (1Sa 25:40–43); mother of Kiliab (Daniel) (2Sa 3:3; 1Ch 3:1).

ability
Dt 8:18	he who gives you the *a* to produce
Mt 25:15	one talent, each according to his *a*.
Ac 11:29	each according to his *a*,

Abimelech
1. King of Gerar in time of Abraham. Took Sarah, Abraham's wife, thinking she was his sister (Ge 20). Made covenant with Abraham (Ge 21:22–34). **2.** King of Gerar in time of Isaac. Rebuked Isaac for deceit (Ge 26:8–10); later made covenant with him (Ge 26:26–31). **3.** Son of Gideon (Jdg 8:31). Murdered brothers (Jdg 9:5); crowned king at Shechem (Jdg 9:6). Death (Jdg 9:54).

Abishai
Son of David's sister, Zeruiah; brother of Joab (1Sa 26:6; 1Ch 2:16). One of David's leading warriors (1Ch 11:15–21; 18:12; 2Sa 18:2; 20:6). Wanted to kill Saul (1Sa 26:7–8), Shimei (2Sa 16:9; 19:21).

able
Da 3:17	the God we serve is *a* to save us
Mt 9:28	"Do you believe that I am *a*
Ro 14:4	the Lord is *a* to make him stand
Eph 3:20	Now to him who is *a* to do
2Ti 3:15	Scriptures, which are *a* to make you
Heb 2:18	*a* to help those ... being tempted
7:25	he is *a* to save completely
Jude :24	who is *a* to keep you from falling

Abner
Saul's cousin and commander of his army (1Sa 14:50; 17:55). Made Ishbosheth king after Saul's death (2Sa 2:8–9). Killed Asahel, Joab's brother (2Sa 2:18–25). Defected to David (2Sa 3:6–21). Murdered by Joab and Abishai to avenge Asahel's death (2Sa 3:26–30).

abolish
Mt 5:17	that I have come to *a* the Law

abomination
Mt 24:15	*a* that causes desolation',

abound, -ing

Ex 34:6 slow to anger, *a-ing* in love and
Jnh 4:2 slow to anger and *a-ing* in love,
2Co 9:8 God is able to make all grace *a*
Php 1:9 that your love may *a* more and more

Abraham

Formerly Abram ("exalted father"). Descendant of Shem and son of Terah (Ge 11:10–27); married to Sarah (Ge 11:29). With Terah, travelled from Ur to Haran. Obeyed God's call to continue journey to Canaan (Ge 12:1–5). In Egypt (Ge 12:10), passed Sarah off as his sister (Ge 12:11–20). Divided the land with his nephew, Lot (Ge 13:5–17); settled at Hebron (Ge 13:18). Rescued Lot (Ge 14:1–16); blessed by Melchizedek (Ge 14:18–20). Name changed to Abraham ("father of many") (Ge 17:5; Ne 9:7). Father of Ishmael by Hagar (Ge 16). Entertained angelic visitors (Ge 18:1–8); promised a son by Sarah (Ge 18:9–15; 17:16). Pleaded for Sodom (Ge 18:22–32). In Gerar (Ge 20:1), passed Sarah off as his sister (Ge 20:2–18). Father of Isaac (Ge 21:1–7); dismissed Hagar and Ishmael (Ge 21:8–14). Made treaty with Abimelech (Ge 21:22–34). Tested by God's command to sacrifice Isaac (Ge 22). Secured wife for Isaac (Ge 24). Death (Ge 25:7–11). God's covenant with (Ge 12:1–3; 15; 17; 22:15–18; Ex 2:24; Lk 1:72–73; Heb 6:13–15). Example of faith (Heb 11:8–12); faith credited as righteousness (Ge 15:6; Ro 4:3; Gal 3:6–9). Described as father of God's people (Isa 51:2; Ac 13:26; Gal 3:26–29); God's servant (Ge 26:24); God's friend (2Ch 20:7; Isa 41:8; Jas 2:23).

Absalom

Son of David (2Sa 3:3). Had Amnon killed for raping his sister, Tamar (2Sa 13:23–29); fled from David (2Sa 13:37–38). Returned (2Sa 14:21–23); reconciled to David (2Sa 14:33). Conspired against David (2Sa 15:1–12); proclaimed king (2Sa 16:15–22). Defeated, killed by Joab (2Sa 18:6–10); mourned by David (2Sa 18:33).

abstain

Ac 15:20 to *a* from food polluted by idols,

abundant, -nce

Ge 41:29 Seven years of great *a-nce*
Dt 28:11 will grant you *a* prosperity—
Ps 145:7 celebrate your *a* goodness
Lk 12:15 in the *a-nce* of his possessions.
1Pe 1:2 Grace and peace be yours in *a-nce*
2Pe 1:2 Grace and peace be yours in *a-nce*

accept, -s, -ed, -able, -ance

Ex 23:8 "Do not *a* a bribe,
Job 42:9 the LORD *a-ed* Job's prayer
Pr 19:20 Listen to advice and *a* instruction,
Jn 13:20 whoever *a-s* anyone I send *a-s* me;
Ro 15:7 *A* one another ... just as Christ
Php 4:18 *a-able* sacrifice, pleasing to God
1Th 2:13 you *a-ed* it not as the word of men,
1Ti 1:15 saying that deserves full *a-ance*:
Jas 1:21 humbly *a* the word planted in you,
1Pe 2:5 spiritual sacrifices *a-able* to God

access

Ro 5:2 we have gained *a* by faith
Eph 2:18 we both have *a* to the Father

accomplish

Isa 55:11 but will *a* what I desire

account

Ge 2:4 the *a* of the heavens and the earth
Mt 12:36 give *a* on the day of judgment
Lk 1:3 to write an orderly *a* for you,
16:2 Give an *a* of your management,
Ro 14:12 each of us will give an *a*
Heb 4:13 to whom we must give *a*.

accuse, -r

Lk 3:14 don't *a* people falsely—
6:7 looking for a reason to *a* Jesus,
Rev 12:10 the *a-r* of our brothers,

Achan

Sinned by keeping spoils after conquest of Jericho thus causing Israel's defeat at Ai; stoned as punishment (Jos 7).

achieve

Isa 55:11 *a* the purpose for which I sent it

Achish
King of Gath, with whom David sought refuge and feigned insanity (1Sa 21:10–15), and later feigned loyal service (1Sa 27:2–12).

acknowledge, -s
Pr 3:6 in all your ways *a* him,
Mt 10:32 "Whoever *a-s* me before men, I will
1Jn 2:23 whoever *a-s* the Son has the Father
4:3 every spirit that does not *a* Jesus

acquit
Ex 23:7 for I will not *a* the guilty.

act, -s, -ion, -ions, -ive
1Ch 16:9 tell of all his wonderful *a-s*
Isa 64:6 our righteous *a-s* are like filthy
Mic 6:8 To *a* justly and to love mercy
Mt 11:19 is proved right by her *a-ions*.
Php 2:13 who works in you to will and to *a*
Phm :6 be *a-ive* in sharing your faith,
Heb 4:12 the word of God is living and *a-ive*
Jas 2:17 if it is not accompanied by *a-ion*,
1Pe 1:13 prepare your minds for *a-ion*;

Adam
First man. Created by God (Ge 1:27); placed in Eden (Ge 2:15); given Eve as helper (Ge 2:19–24). Disobeyed God (Ge 3; Ro 5:14) and so brought sin into world (Ro 5:12,15–19). Jesus is described as "the last Adam" (1Co 15:45).

add, -s, -ed
Dt 4:2 Do not *a* to what I command you
Mt 6:27 by worrying can *a* a single hour
Ac 2:47 the Lord *a-ed* to their number
Ro 5:20 The law was *a-ed* so that
Rev 22:18 If anyone *a-s* anything to them, God

administration
1Co 12:28 those with gifts of *a*

admonish
Col 3:16 *a* one another with all wisdom,

Adonijah
1. Son of David, by Haggith (2Sa 3:4; 1Ch 3:2). Attempted to succeed David as king (1Ki 1); killed by Solomon's order after he requested Abishag for his wife (1Ki 2). **2.** Levite and teacher of the Law (2Ch 17:8–9).

adopt, -ed, -ion
Ro 8:23 as we wait eagerly for our *a-ion*
Eph 1:5 he predestined us to be *a-ed*

adorn, -ment
1Pe 3:3 should not come from outward *a-ment*

adultery
Ex 20:14 "You shall not commit *a*
Mt 5:28 committed *a* with her in his heart.
15:19 evil thoughts, murder, *a*,
Jn 8:3 brought in a woman caught in *a*.

adults
1Co 14:20 in your thinking be *a*

adversary
Mt 5:25 "Settle matters ... with your *a*

advice
1Ki 12:8 rejected the *a* the elders gave him
Pr 12:5 the *a* of the wicked is deceitful
12:15 a wise man listens to *a*
20:18 Make plans by seeking *a*;

afflict, -ed, -ion, -ions
Ps 119:67 Before I was *a-ed* I went astray,
Isa 48:10 tested you in the furnace of *a-ion*
53:7 He was oppressed and *a-ed*,
La 3:33 he does not willingly bring *a-ion*
Ro 12:12 Be joyful in hope, patient in *a-ion*
Col 1:24 in regard to Christ's *a-ions*,

afraid
Ge 15:1 "Do not be *a*, Abram.
26:24 Do not be *a*, for I am with you;
Ex 3:6 because he was *a* to look at God
14:13 "Do not be *a*. Stand firm
Ps 56:4 in God I trust; I will not be *a*.
Isa 43:5 Do not be *a*, for I am with you;
Mt 1:20 "Joseph son of David, do not be *a*

10:31	So don't be *a*;
Mk 5:36	"Don't be *a*; just believe.
6:50	"Take courage! It is I. Don't be *a*.
Lk 1:13	"Do not be *a*, Zechariah;
1:30	"Do not be *a*, Mary,
2:10	"Do not be *a*. I bring you good
12:32	"Do not be *a*, little flock,
Jn 14:27	hearts be troubled and do not be *a*
Heb 13:6	Lord is my helper; I will not be *a*.

age, -s

Mt 13:49	how it will be at the end of the *a*.
1Co 10:11	the fulfilment of the *a-s* has come
Eph 2:7	in the coming *a-s* he might show
3:9	which for *a-s* past was kept hidden
1Ti 6:19	a firm foundation for the coming *a*,
Heb 6:5	the powers of the coming *a*

agony

Lk 16:24	because I am in *a* in this fire.
Ac 2:24	freeing him from the *a* of death,

agree

Mt 18:19	two of you ... *a* about anything
Php 4:2	with Syntyche to *a* with each other

Agrippa

1. Herod Agrippa I, grandson of Herod the Great. Jewish king, killed apostle James and imprisoned Peter (Ac 12:1–4); sudden death (Ac 12:20–23). **2.** Herod Agrippa II, son of Herod Agrippa I, before whom Paul appeared at Caesarea (Ac 25:13–26:32).

Ahab

1. Son of Omri; evil king of Israel (1Ki 16:29–30). Married Jezebel; encouraged worship of Baal (1Ki 16:31–33). Opposed by Elijah (1Ki 17:1; 18:17–20). Defeated Arameans (1Ki 20); condemned for sparing Ben-Hadad (1Ki 20:42). Murdered Naboth and stole his vineyard (1Ki 21). Opposed by Micaiah (1Ki 22:1–28); killed (1Ki 22:34–38). **2.** False prophet (Jer 29:21–22).

Ahaz

Son of Jotham; king of Judah (2Ki 16). Worshipped foreign gods (2Ki 16:3–4, 10–18; 2Ch 28:2–4,22–25). Attacked by Aram and Israel (2Ki 16:5–6; 2Ch 28:5–8). Turned for help to Assyria rather than God (2Ki 16:7–9; 2Ch 28:16; Isa 7:3–17).

Ahimelech

1. Priest at Nob who helped David (1Sa 21:1–9); killed by Saul (1Sa 22:9–19). **2.** One of David's soldiers (1Sa 26:6).

Ahithophel

David's counsellor; gave support to Absalom (2Sa 15:12; 16:21–23). Hanged himself when his advice was ignored (2Sa 17).

air

Mt 8:20	and birds of the *a* have nests,
1Co 9:26	not fight like a man beating the *a*
Eph 2:2	the kingdom of the *a*,
1Th 4:17	to meet the Lord in the *a*.

alabaster

Mt 26:7	an *a* jar of very expensive perfume,
Mk 14:3	a woman came with an *a* jar
Lk 7:37	she brought an *a* jar of perfume

alert

Eph 6:18	be *a* and always keep on praying
1Pe 5:8	Be self-controlled and *a*.

alien, -s, -ated

Ex 18:3	Moses said, "I have become an *a*
22:21	"Do not ill-treat an *a* or oppress
Ps 81:9	shall not bow down to an *a* god
146:9	The LORD watches over the *a*
Gal 5:4	have been *a-ated* from Christ;
Eph 2:19	no longer foreigners and *a-s*,
1Pe 2:11	as *a-s* and strangers in the world,

alive

Lk 15:24	son of mine was dead and is *a* again;
Ro 6:11	dead to sin but *a* to God in Christ
1Co 15:22	so in Christ all will be made *a*
Eph 2:5	made us *a* with Christ

Rev 3:1 a reputation of being *a*,

Almighty

Ge 17:1 "I am God *A*; walk before me
Ex 6:3 to Isaac and to Jacob as God *A*,
Ru 1:20 the *A* has made my life very bitter
Job 33:4 the breath of the *A* gives me life
Ps 24:10 The LORD *A*—he is the King of glory.
89:8 O LORD God *A*, who is like you?
91:1 rest in the shadow of the *A*
Isa 6:3 "Holy, holy, holy is the LORD *A*;
47:4 Our Redeemer—the LORD *A* is his
Rev 4:8 "Holy, ... holy is the Lord God *A*,
15:3 "Great ... your deeds, Lord God *A*.

Alpha

Rev 1:8 "I am the *A* and the Omega,"
21:6 I am the *A* and the Omega,

altar

Ge 8:20 Then Noah built an *a* to the LORD
12:8 There he built an *a* to the LORD
22:9 Abraham built an *a* there
26:25 Isaac built an *a* there and called
Ex 17:15 Moses built an *a* and called it
Jdg 6:24 Gideon built an *a* to the LORD there
2Sa 24:25 David built an *a* to the LORD there
2Ch 33:16 Then he restored the *a* of the LORD
Ezr 3:2 to build the *a* of the God of Israel
Isa 6:6 he had taken with tongs from the *a*
Mt 5:24 your gift there in front of the *a*.
23:18 'If anyone swears by the *a*,
Ac 17:23 found an *a* with this inscription:
Heb 13:10 We have an *a* from which those who
Jas 2:21 he offered his son Isaac on the *a*
Rev 6:9 I saw under the *a* the souls

always

Ps 16:8 I have set the LORD *a* before me.
105:4 seek his face *a*
Mt 26:11 The poor you will *a* have with you,
28:20 And surely I am with you *a*,
1Co 13:7 *a* protects, *a* trusts, *a* hopes
Php 4:4 Rejoice in the Lord *a*.
1Pe 3:15 *A* be prepared to give an answer

Amasa

David's nephew (1Ch 2:17). In charge of Absalom's army (2Sa 17:24–25); made commander of David's army (2Sa 19:13); treacherously killed by Joab his cousin (2Sa 20:9–10; 1Ki 2:5).

amaze, -d

Mt 7:28 the crowds were *a-d* at his teaching
Mk 6:6 he was *a-d* at their lack of faith.
Lk 2:18 *a-d* at what the shepherds
Ac 2:7 Utterly *a-d*, they asked: "Are not

ambassador, -s

2Co 5:20 We are therefore Christ's *a-s*,

ambition

Ro 15:20 my *a* to preach the gospel
Php 2:3 Do nothing out of selfish *a*
1Th 4:11 Make it your *a* to lead a quiet

Amnon

David's firstborn son (2Sa 3:2). Raped Absalom's sister, Tamar (2Sa 13:1–22); killed by Absalom's men (2Sa 13:23–29).

Amos

1. Prophet from Tekoa (Am 1:1); spoke against Israel (Am 7:10–17). **2.** Ancestor of Jesus. (Lk 3:25).

Ananias

1. With wife Sapphira, died for lying to God (Ac 5:1–11). **2.** Disciple, sent to heal and baptise Saul (Paul) in Damascus (Ac 9:10–19). **3.** High priest before whom Paul appeared (Ac 22:30–23:5; 24:1).

anchor

Heb 6:19 this hope as an *a* for the soul,

ancient

Ps 24:9 lift them up, you *a* doors,
Jer 6:16 ask for the *a* paths,
Da 7:13 He approached the *A* of Days

Andrew

Apostle; brother of Simon Peter (Mt 4:18–20; 10:2; Mk 1:16–18,29); introduced boy with loaves and fish to Jesus (Jn 6:8–9); brought Greeks to Jesus (Jn 12:22). Former disciple of John the Baptist (Jn 1:35–40); brought Simon to Jesus (Jn 1:41).

angel, -s

Ge 22:15 The *a* of the LORD called to Abraham
Ex 23:20 I am sending an *a* ahead of you
Ps 34:7 The *a* of the LORD encamps around
Mt 2:13 an *a* of the Lord appeared to Joseph
18:10 their *a-s* in heaven always see
25:41 prepared for the devil and his *a-s*
Lk 1:26 God sent the *a* Gabriel to Nazareth,
2:9 An *a* of the Lord appeared to them,
Ac 6:15 his face was like the face of an *a*
1Co 6:3 know that we will judge *a-s*?
13:1 in the tongues of men and of *a-s*,
2Co 11:14 Satan himself masquerades as an *a*
Heb 1:4 as much superior to the *a-s*
1:6 "Let all God's *a-s* worship him.
1:7 "He makes his *a-s* winds,
2:9 made a little lower than the *a-s*,
12:22 thousands of *a-s* in joyful assembly
13:2 entertained *a-s* without knowing it
1Pe 1:12 *a-s* long to look into these things
2Pe 2:4 For if God did not spare *a-s*
Rev 12:7 Michael and his *a-s* fought against

anger, -ed

Ex 32:11 "why should your *a* burn against
34:6 slow to *a*, abounding in love
2Ki 22:13 Great is the LORD's *a* that burns
Ps 4:4 In your *a* do not sin;
30:5 For his *a* lasts only a moment,
90:11 Who knows the power of your *a*?
Pr 22:24 do not associate with one easily *a-ed*
29:11 A fool gives full vent to his *a*,
1Co 13:5 it is not easily *a-ed*,
Eph 4:26 "In your *a* do not sin": Do not let
Jas 1:20 man's *a* does not bring about

angry

Ps 2:12 Kiss the Son, lest he be *a*
95:10 For forty years I was *a*
Pr 29:22 An *a* man stirs up dissension,
Mt 5:22 anyone who is *a* with his brother
Eph 4:26 sun go down while you are still *a*
Jas 1:19 slow to speak and slow to become *a*

Anna

Widow; prophetess of the tribe of Asher; recognised the baby Jesus as the Messiah when he was brought into the temple (Lk 2:36–38).

Annas

High priest (Lk 3:2). Questioned Jesus (Jn 18:13,19–24); questioned Peter and John (Ac 4:5–7).

annual

2Ch 8:13 New Moons and the three *a* feasts—
Heb 10:3 an *a* reminder of sins

anoint, -ed, -ing

Ex 30:30 "*A* Aaron and his sons
1Sa 15:1 *a* you king over his people Israel;
Ps 23:5 You *a* my head with oil;
45:7 by *a-ing* you with the oil of joy
Isa 61:1 LORD has *a-ed* me to preach good
Mk 6:13 and *a-ed* many sick people with oil
Lk 4:18 he has *a-ed* me to preach good news
Ac 10:38 how God *a-ed* Jesus of Nazareth
Heb 1:9 by *a-ing* you with the oil of joy.
Jas 5:14 to pray over him and *a* him with oil
1Jn 2:20 have an *a-ing* from the Holy One,

answer, -s, -ed

1Ki 10:3 Solomon *a-ed* all her questions;
18:24 The god who *a-s* by fire—he is God
Job 38:1 the LORD *a-ed* Job out of the storm.

Ps 34:4 I sought the LORD, and he *a-ed* me
38:15 I wait for you, O LORD; you will *a*
69:13 God, *a* me with your sure salvation
69:17 *a* me quickly, for I am in trouble
86:1 and *a* me, for I am poor and needy
119:145 *a* me, O LORD, and I will obey
143:7 *A* me quickly, O LORD; my spirit
Pr 15:1 A gentle *a* turns away wrath,
24:26 An honest *a* is like a kiss
26:5 *A* a fool according to his folly,
Isa 65:24 Before they call I will *a*;
Jnh 2:2 I called to the LORD, and he *a-ed*
Jn 19:9 but Jesus gave him no *a*
1Pe 3:15 be prepared to give an *a* to

ant
Pr 6:6 Go to the *a*, you sluggard;

antichrist
1Jn 2:18 have heard that the *a* is coming,
2:22 Such a man is the *a*—he denies
4:3 This is the spirit of the *a*,
2Jn :7 person is the deceiver and the *a*

Antioch
Ac 11:26 were called Christians first at *A*

anxiety, -ies
Ps 94:19 When *a* was great within me,
Lk 21:34 drunkenness and the *a-ies* of life,
1Pe 5:7 Cast all your *a* on him

anxious
Ps 139:23 test me and know my *a* thoughts
Pr 12:25 An *a* heart weighs a man down,
Php 4:6 Do not be *a* about anything,

Apollos
Disciple from Alexandria, well versed in the Scriptures (Ac 18:24–25); instructed by Priscilla and Aquila in Ephesus (Ac 18:26). Ministered in Corinth (Ac 18:27–19:1; 1Co 1:12; 3:5–9) and on Crete (Tit 3:13).

apostle, -s
Mk 3:14 twelve—designating them *a-s*—
Ac 1:26 so he was added to the eleven *a-s*
2:43 signs were done by the *a-s*
Ro 11:13 I am the *a* to the Gentiles,
1Co 15:9 For I am the least of the *a-s*
2Co 11:13 masquerading as *a-s* of Christ
Eph 2:20 built on the foundation of the *a-s*
4:11 It was he who gave some to be *a-s*,
1Ti 2:7 I was appointed a herald and an *a*—
Heb 3:1 Jesus, the *a* and high priest

appeal
Ac 25:11 I *a* to Caesar!
2Co 5:20 making his *a* through us.
Phm :9 I *a* to you on the basis of love.

appear, -s, -ing, -ed, -ance
1Sa 16:7 Man looks at the outward *a-ance*,
2Ch 1:7 That night God *a-ed* to Solomon
Mal 3:2 Who can stand when he *a-s*?
Mt 1:20 an angel of the Lord *a-ed* to him
24:30 the sign of the Son of Man will *a*
Lk 2:9 An angel of the Lord *a-ed* to them,
24:34 The Lord has risen and has *a-ed*
Ac 1:3 He *a-ed* to them over a period
1Co 15:6 he *a-ed* to more than five hundred
2Co 5:10 we must all *a* before the judgment
Col 3:4 When Christ, who is your life, *a-s*,
1Ti 6:14 until the *a-ing* of our Lord Jesus
2Ti 4:8 all who have longed for his *a-ing*.
Tit 2:13 the glorious *a-ing* of our great God
Heb 9:24 now to *a* for us in God's presence
9:28 and he will *a* a second time,
1Pe 5:4 And when the Chief Shepherd *a-s*,
1Jn 3:2 when he *a-s*, we shall be like him,

appoint, -ed
Ezr 1:2 he has *a-ed* me to build a temple
Mt 26:18 My *a-ed* time is near.
Jn 15:16 I chose you and *a-ed* you
Ac 13:48 all who were *a-ed* for eternal life
14:23 Paul and Barnabas *a-ed* elders
1Co 4:5 judge nothing before the *a-ed* time;
12:28 God has *a-ed* first of all apostles,

Eph 1:22 *a-ed* him to be head over everything
1Th 5:9 God did not *a* us to suffer wrath
Tit 1:5 and *a* elders in every town,
Heb 1:2 his Son, whom he *a-ed* heir of all

approach, -ing, -ed
Ex 24:2 Moses alone is to *a* the LORD;
Lk 9:51 time *a-ed* for him to be taken up
Eph 3:12 through faith in him we may *a* God
Heb 4:16 Let us then *a* the throne of grace
10:25 as you see the Day *a-ing*
1Jn 5:14 confidence we have in *a-ing* God:

approve, -d, -al
Ro 12:2 to test and *a* what God's will is—
14:18 pleasing to God and *a-d* by men
1Co 11:19 show which of you have God's *a-al*
Gal 1:10 to win the *a-al* of men, or of God?
1Th 2:4 we speak as men *a-d* by God
2Ti 2:15 present yourself to God as one *a-d*,

Aquila
Husband of *Priscilla*.

Arabia
Gal 1:17 I went immediately into *A*

Ararat
Ge 8:4 came to rest on the mountains of *A*

arbiter
Lk 12:14 a judge or an *a* between you?

archangel
1Th 4:16 with the voice of the *a*
Jude :9 *a* Michael, when he was disputing

architect
Heb 11:10 whose *a* and builder is God

Areopagus
Ac 17:22 stood up in the meeting of the *A*

arise
Ps 68:1 May God *a*, may his enemies
SS 2:10 "*A*, my darling, my beautiful one,
Isa 60:1 "*A*, shine, for your light has come,

ark[1]
Ge 6:14 make yourself an *a* of cypress wood;
Mt 24:38 up to the day Noah entered the *a*
Heb 11:7 in holy fear built an *a*
1Pe 3:20 while the *a* was being built.

ark[2]
Ex 25:21 Place the cover on top of the *a*
Dt 10:5 and put the tablets in the *a*
1Sa 4:11 The *a* of God was captured;
7:2 the *a* remained at Kiriath Jearim,
2Sa 6:6 reached out and took hold of the *a*
1Ki 8:9 There was nothing in the *a* except
1Ch 13:10 put his hand on the *a*. So he died
2Ch 35:3 "Put the sacred *a* in the temple
Heb 9:4 the gold-covered *a* of the covenant.
Rev 11:19 within his temple was seen the *a*

arm, -s
Nu 11:23 "Is the LORD's *a* too short?
Dt 33:27 underneath are the everlasting *a-s*.
SS 8:6 like a seal on your *a*;
Isa 40:11 He gathers the lambs in his *a-s*
Mk 10:16 he took the children in his *a-s*,
Lk 15:20 threw his *a-s* around him
Heb 12:12 strengthen your feeble *a-s*
1Pe 4:1 *a* yourselves also with the same

Armageddon
Rev 16:16 place that in Hebrew is called *A*

armour
Ro 13:12 put on the *a* of light
Eph 6:13 Therefore put on the full *a* of God,

army, -ies
Jos 5:14 as commander of the *a* of the LORD
1Sa 17:36 defied the *a-ies* of the living God

17:45	the God of the *a-ies* of Israel,
1Ch 12:22	a great *a*, like the army of God
2Ch 14:11	we have come against this vast *a*.
20:12	no power to face this vast *a*
32:7	the king of Assyria and the vast *a*
Ps 33:16	king is saved by the size of his *a*;
44:9	you no longer go out with our *a-ies*
Rev 19:14	*a-ies* of heaven were following him,
19:19	and their *a-ies* gathered together

aroma

Ge 8:21	The LORD smelled the pleasing *a*
Ex 29:18	offering to the LORD, a pleasing *a*,
Nu 28:8	made by fire, an *a* pleasing
2Co 2:15	we are to God the *a* of Christ

arrogant, -nce

Mk 7:22	envy, slander, *a-nce* and folly
Ro 11:20	Do not be *a*, but be afraid
2Co 12:20	factions, slander, gossip, *a-nce*
1Ti 6:17	in this present world not to be *a*

arrow, -s

Job 6:4	The *a-s* of the Almighty are in me,
Ps 64:7	But God will shoot them with *a-s*;
Eph 6:16	extinguish all the flaming *a-s*

Artaxerxes

King of Persia. Stopped work on walls of Jerusalem (Ezr 4:17–23). Provided resources for Temple worship under Ezra (Ezr 7); reversed earlier decision to allow rebuilding of walls under Nehemiah (Ne 2:1–10).

Asa

King of Judah (1Ki 15:9–10). Removed idols and reformed worship (1Ki 15:11–15; 2Ch 14:2–5; 15). Rebuilt Judah's cities (2Ch 14:6–7). Relied on God against the Cushites (2Ch 14:9–15); relied on Aram, instead of God, against Israel, rebuked by Hanani the seer (1Ki 15:15–22; 2Ch 16). Death (2Ch 16:12–14).

Asahel

David's nephew; brother of Joab and Abishai (1Ch 2:16). One of David's leading warriors (2Sa 23:24; 1Ch 11:26; 27:7). Killed by Abner after a rash pursuit (2Sa 2:18–23); avenged by Joab (2Sa 3:26–27).

Asaph

1. Levite, in charge of music in the tabernacle and temple (1Ch 6:39; 15:17–19; 16:4–7,37; 1Ch 25:6; Ne 12:46). Composed several psalms (2Ch 29:30; Ps 50; 73–83). His sons set apart for musical and prophetic ministry (1Ch 25; 2Ch 20:14; 35:15; Ezr 2:41; 3:10; Ne 11:17). **2.** Keeper of the king's forest (Ne 2:8). **3.** Hezekiah's recorder (2Ki 18:18,37; Isa 36:3,22).

ascend, -ed

Dt 30:12	"Who will *a* into heaven to get it
Ps 24:3	Who may *a* the hill of the LORD?
68:18	When you *a-ed* on high,
Ac 2:34	For David did not *a* to heaven,
Eph 4:8	"When he *a-ed* on high,

ascribe

1Ch 16:28	*a* to the LORD glory and strength
Job 36:3	I will *a* justice to my Maker
Ps 29:1	*A* to the LORD, O mighty ones,

ashamed

Mk 8:38	If anyone is *a* of me and my words
Ro 1:16	I am not *a* of the gospel,
2Ti 1:8	So do not be *a* to testify about our
2:15	a workman who does not need to be *a*

Asher

1. Son of Jacob by Zilpah (Ge 30:12–13; 35:26; Ex 1:4; 1Ch 2:2); blessed by Jacob (Ge 49:20). **2.** Tribe descended from Asher. Blessed by Moses (Dt 33:24–25). Included in census (Nu 1:40–41; 26:44–47); apportioned land (Jos 19:24–31; Eze 48:2). Supported Gideon (Jdg 6:35; 7:23) and David (1Ch 12:36) but not Deborah (Jdg 5:17).

ashes

Ge 18:27	though I am nothing but dust and *a*
Job 42:6	and repent in dust and *a*.
Ps 102:9	For I eat *a* as my food

Mt 11:21	long ago in sackcloth and *a*

ask, -s, -ing, -ed

Ex 8:13	And the LORD did what Moses *a-ed.*
1Ki 3:11	you have *a-ed* for this and not
Ps 27:4	One thing I *a* of the LORD,
Isa 7:11	"*A* the LORD your God for a sign,
65:1	to those who did not *a* for me;
Jer 6:16	*a* for the ancient paths,
Mt 6:8	knows what you need before you *a*
7:7	"*A* and it will be given to you;
7:8	For everyone who *a-s* receives;
7:11	give good gifts to those who *a* him
9:38	*A* the Lord of the harvest,
18:19	agree about anything you *a* for,
21:22	whatever you *a* for in prayer.
Mk 10:35	do for us whatever we *a.*
10:38	don't know what you are *a-ing,*"
11:29	"I will *a* you one question.
Lk 6:30	Give to everyone who *a-s* you,
11:13	give the Holy Spirit to those who *a*
20:3	"I will also *a* you a question.
Jn 9:21	*A* him. He is of age; he will speak
11:22	God will give you whatever you *a.*
14:13	will do whatever you *a* in my name,
14:16	And I will *a* the Father,
15:7	*a* whatever you wish,
16:23	you will no longer *a* me anything.
21:17	Jesus *a-ed* him the third time,
Ro 10:20	to those who did not *a* for me.
Eph 3:20	immeasurably more than all we *a*
Jas 1:5	should *a* God, who gives generously
1:6	But when he *a-s,* he must believe
4:2	because you do not *a* God
1Pe 3:15	give an answer to everyone who *a-s*
1Jn 5:14	if we *a* anything according

asleep

Mk 5:39	The child is not dead but *a.*
1Co 15:18	who have fallen *a* in Christ
1Th 4:13	ignorant about those who fall *a,*
5:10	whether we are awake or *a,*

associate

Pr 22:24	do not *a* with one easily angered
Jn 4:9	Jews do not *a* with Samaritans.
Ro 12:16	*a* with people of low position.
1Co 5:9	not to *a* with sexually immoral

assure, -ance

1Ti 3:13	and great *a-ance* in their faith
Heb 10:22	in full *a-ance* of faith,

astonished

Mt 8:10	When Jesus heard this, he was *a*
12:23	All the people were *a* and said,
19:25	they were greatly *a* and asked,
22:33	they were *a* at his teaching
Lk 5:9	he and all his companions were *a*
Gal 1:6	I am *a* that you are so quickly

astray

Ps 119:67	Before I was afflicted I went *a,*
Jn 16:1	so that you will not go *a*
1Pe 2:25	you were like sheep going *a,*
1Jn 3:7	do not let anyone lead you *a.*

astrologer

Da 2:10	The *a-s* answered the king,

ate

Ge 3:6	she took some and *a* it.
Ex 24:11	they saw God, and they *a* and drank
2Sa 9:11	Mephibosheth *a* at David's table
Ps 78:25	Men *a* the bread of angels;
Jer 15:16	When your words came, I *a* them;
Mt 14:20	They all *a* and were satisfied,
1Co 10:3	They all *a* the same spiritual food

Athaliah

Daughter of Ahab; wife of Jehoram, king of Judah; mother of Ahaziah (2Ki 8:18,26; 2Ch 22:2). Encouraged idolatry (2Ki 8:18,27). After Ahaziah's death, killed royal family (except Joash) and reigned for six years (2Ki 11:1–3; 2Ch 22:10–12). Killed by order of Jehoida, who made Joash king (2Ki 11:4–16; 2Ch 23:1–15).

athlete

2Ti 2:5	if anyone competes as an *a,*

atone, -ing, -d, -ment
Ex 30:10 Once a year Aaron shall make *a-ment*
Lev 17:11 it is the blood that makes *a-ment*
Pr 16:6 faithfulness sin is *a-d* for;
Isa 6:7 guilt is taken away ... sin *a-d*
Ro 3:25 sacrifice of *a-ment*, through faith
Heb 2:17 he might make *a-ment* for the sins
1Jn 2:2 He is the *a-ing* sacrifice
4:10 sent his Son as an *a-ing* sacrifice

attention
1Ki 8:28 Yet give *a* to your servant's prayer
Pr 5:1 My son, pay *a* to my wisdom,
Jer 13:15 Hear and pay *a*, do not be arrogant,
Ac 6:4 our *a* to prayer and the ministry
Tit 1:14 and will pay no *a* to Jewish myths
Heb 2:1 We must pay more careful *a*,

attitude, -s
Eph 4:23 made new in the *a* of your minds
Php 2:5 Your *a* should be the same
Heb 4:12 it judges the thoughts and *a-s*
1Pe 4:1 arm yourselves also with the same *a*,

authority, -ies
Mt 7:29 because he taught as one who had *a*,
28:18 "All *a* in heaven and on earth
Mk 2:10 know that the Son of Man has *a*
Jn 17:2 you granted him *a* over all people
Ro 13:1 submit ... to the governing *a-ies*
13:5 necessary to submit to the *a-ies*,
1Co 11:10 a sign of *a* on her head
Col 2:15 disarmed the powers and *a-ies*,
1Ti 2:12 to teach or to have *a* over a man;

avenge, -s, -r
Dt 19:12 hand him over to the *a-r* of blood
32:35 It is mine to *a*; I will repay.
Ps 94:1 O LORD, the God who *a-s*,
Ro 12:19 it is written: "It is mine to *a*;

avoid
Pr 20:3 It is to a man's honour to *a* strife,
20:19 so *a* a man who talks too much
1Th 4:3 that you should *a* sexual immorality
5:22 *A* every kind of evil
2Ti 2:16 *A* godless chatter,
Tit 3:9 But *a* foolish controversies

await, -s
Ps 65:1 Praise *a-s* you, O God, in Zion;
Pr 15:10 Stern discipline *a-s* him who leaves
Gal 5:5 we eagerly *a* through the Spirit
Php 3:20 we eagerly *a* a Saviour from there,

awake
Ps 139:18 When I *a*, I am still with you
Pr 6:22 when you *a*, they will speak to you
20:13 stay *a* and you will have food
1Th 5:10 whether we are *a* or asleep,
Rev 16:15 Blessed is he who stays *a*

awe, -some
Ge 28:17 "How *a-some* is this place!
Ps 47:2 How *a-some* is the LORD Most High,
Lk 5:26 They were filled with *a* and said,
Ac 2:43 Everyone was filled with *a*,
Heb 12:28 worship God acceptably with ... *a*

Azariah
See *Uzziah*.

B

Baal
1Ki 19:18 knees have not bowed down to *B*
Jer 11:13 incense to that shameful god *B*
Ro 11:4 who have not bowed the knee to *B*.

babble, -ing, -r
Mt 6:7 when you pray, do not keep on *b-ing*
Ac 17:18 "What is this *b-r* trying to say?

Babel

Ge 11:9 That is why it was called *B*—

baby, -ies

Ex 2:6 She opened it and saw the *b*.
Isa 49:15 "Can a mother forget the *b*
Lk 1:44 the *b* in my womb leaped for joy
2:12 You will find a *b* wrapped in cloths
18:15 bringing *b-ies* to Jesus
Jn 16:21 but when her *b* is born she forgets
1Pe 2:2 Like newborn *b-ies*, crave pure

Babylon

Ps 87:4 *B* among those who acknowledge me—
137:1 By the rivers of *B* we sat and wept
Isa 48:14 carry out his purpose against *B*;
Jer 25:11 the king of *B* for seventy years
27:17 Serve the king of *B*, and you will
29:15 has raised up prophets for us in *B*
Da 2:48 ruler over the entire province of *B*
Rev 14:8 "Fallen! Fallen is *B* the Great,
17:5 on her forehead: MYSTERY *B*

backsliding, -s

Jer 2:19 your *b* will rebuke you.
3:22 I will cure you of *b*."
5:6 and their *b-s* many
14:7 For our *b* is great;
15:6 keep on *b*. So I will lay hands
Eze 37:23 from all their sinful *b*,

baker

Ge 40:1 the *b* of the king of Egypt
Hos 7:4 oven whose fire the *b* need not

Balaam

Prophet, requested by Balak to curse Israel (Nu 22:4–11; 2Pe 2:15); forbidden by God (Nu 22:12); rebuked by his donkey (Nu 22:21–34). Curse turned to blessing (Nu 23–24; Dt 23:4–5; Jos 24:9–10). Advice led to Israel's seduction (Nu 31:15–16). Killed in Israel's defeat of Midianites (Nu 31:8; Jos 13:22).

baldhead

2Ki 2:23 jeered at him. "Go on up, you *b*!

balm

Jer 8:22 Is there no *b* in Gilead?
46:11 "Go up to Gilead and get *b*,

banner

Ex 17:15 and called it The LORD is my *B*
SS 2:4 and his *b* over me is love
Isa 11:10 the Root of Jesse will stand as a *b*

banquet, -s

SS 2:4 He has taken me to the *b* hall,
Mt 22:4 Come to the wedding *b*.
23:6 love the place of honour at *b-s*
Lk 5:29 Levi held a great *b* for Jesus
14:13 when you give a *b*, invite the poor,

baptise, -ing, -d

Mt 3:11 He will *b* you with the Holy Spirit
3:16 As soon as Jesus was *b-d*,
28:19 *b-ing* them in the name of the
Mk 1:8 I *b* you with water, but he will
16:16 believes and is *b-d* will be saved,
Ac 1:5 For John *b-d* with water,
2:38 "Repent and be *b-d*, every one
2:41 who accepted his message were *b-d*,
1Co 12:13 For we were all *b-d* by one Spirit

baptism

Mt 21:25 John's *b*—where did it come from?
Ac 18:25 though he knew only the *b* of John
Ro 6:4 buried with him ... *b* into death
Eph 4:5 one Lord, one faith, one *b*
Col 2:12 buried with him in *b* and raised
1Pe 3:21 this water symbolises *b* that now

Barabbas

Criminal, released by Pilate instead of Jesus (Mt 27:15–26; Mk 15:6–15; Lk 23:18–25; Jn 18:40).

Barak

Summoned by Deborah to lead Israel against Canaanites (Jdg 4–5; 1Sa 12:11; Heb 11:32).

barn, -s

Mt 6:26 sow or reap or store away in *b-s*,
Lk 12:18 I will tear down my *b-s* and build

Barnabas

Name (meaning "son of encouragement") given to Joseph, a disciple from Cyprus (Ac 4:36). Apostle (Ac 14:14) and missionary (Gal 2:9). Introduced Paul to Jerusalem apostles (Ac 9:27). Sent to Antioch where he worked with Paul (Ac 11:22–26). With Paul on first missionary journey (Ac 13–14) and at Council of Jerusalem (Ac 15:2–35); parted company over his cousin John Mark (Ac 15:36–40).

barren

Ge 11:30 Sarai was *b*; she had no children
Ps 113:9 He settles the *b* woman in her home
Lk 1:7 because Elizabeth was *b*;
Gal 4:27 is written: "Be glad, O *b* woman,
Heb 11:11 and Sarah herself was *b*—

Bartholomew

One of the twelve apostles (Mt 10:2–3; Mk 3:16–18; Lk 6:13–14; Ac 1:13). May also have been known as Nathanael.

Bartimaeus

Blind beggar healed by Jesus (Mk 10:46–52; Lk 19:35–43; Mt 20:29–34).

Baruch

Secretary and companion of Jeremiah. Wrote down Jeremiah's prophecies and read them to the people (Jer 36). Jeremiah gave him deeds of field in Anathoth (Jer 32:12–16). Accused of influencing Jeremiah; taken with him to Egypt (Jer 43:1–7). God's word to (Jer 45).

basin

Ex 30:18 "Make a bronze *b*,
Jn 13:5 he poured water into a *b* and began

basket, -fuls

Ex 2:3 she got a papyrus *b* for him
Mt 14:20 twelve *b-fuls* of broken pieces
2Co 11:33 I was lowered in a *b* from a window

batch

Ro 11:16 then the whole *b* is holy;
1Co 5:7 you may be a new *b* without yeast—
Gal 5:9 through the whole *b* of dough.

bathe, -ing

2Sa 11:2 From the roof he saw a woman *b-ing*.

Bathsheba

Wife of Uriah; committed adultery with David and became his wife (2Sa 11). Secured succession for her son, Solomon (1Ki 1:11–40). Included in Jesus' genealogy (Mt 1:6).

battle, -s

1Sa 17:47 for the *b* is the LORD's,
2Sa 1:25 "How the mighty have fallen in *b*!
22:35 He trains my hands for *b*;
2Ch 20:15 For the *b* is not yours, but God's
32:8 God to help us and to fight our *b-s*
Ps 18:39 You armed me with strength for *b*;
24:8 the LORD mighty in *b*
144:1 my hands for war, my fingers for *b*
Ecc 9:11 or the *b* to the strong,
Isa 31:4 Almighty will come down to do *b*
Eze 13:5 stand firm in the *b* on the day
Jas 4:1 your desires that *b* within you
Rev 16:14 for the *b* on the great day
20:8 Gog and Magog—to gather them for *b*

bear[1], -s, -ing

1Ki 8:43 house I have built *b-s* your Name
Isa 53:11 and he will *b* their iniquities
Mt 7:18 A good tree cannot *b* bad fruit,
Jn 15:16 appointed you to go and *b* fruit
Ro 7:4 that we might *b* fruit to God
1Co 10:13 tempted beyond what you can *b*.
Gal 6:17 I *b* on my body the marks of Jesus
Eph 4:2 *b-ing* with one another in love
Col 1:10 *b-ing* fruit in every good work,
3:13 *B* with each other and forgive

Heb 13:13 *b-ing* the disgrace he bore

bear², -s
1Sa 17:36 has killed both the lion and the *b*;
2Ki 2:24 Then two *b-s* came out of the woods
Isa 11:7 The cow will feed with the *b*,

beast, -s
Ge 2:20 and all the *b-s* of the field.
Ps 73:22 I was a brute *b* before you
Da 7:17 four great *b-s* are four kingdoms
1Co 15:32 If I fought wild *b-s* in Ephesus
2Pe 2:12 brute *b-s*, creatures of instinct,
Rev 13:18 him calculate the number of the *b*,
16:2 people who had the mark of the *b*

beat, -ing, -en
Isa 2:4 *b* their swords into ploughshares
50:6 I offered my back to those who *b* me,
Mk 14:65 And the guards took him and *b* him
Lk 18:13 look up to heaven, but *b* his breast
1Co 9:26 not fight like a man *b-ing* the air
2Co 11:25 Three times I was *b-en* with rods,

beauty, -iful
Ps 27:4 to gaze upon the *b* of the LORD
48:2 It is *b-iful* in its loftiness,
SS 1:15 How *b-iful* you are, my darling!
Isa 52:7 How *b-iful* on the mountains are
53:2 He had not *b* or majesty to attract
Mk 14:6 She has done a *b-iful* thing to me
Lk 21:5 adorned with *b-iful* stones
Ac 3:10 at the temple gate called *B-iful*,
Ro 10:15 As it is written, "How *b-iful* are
1Pe 3:4 *b* of a gentle and quiet spirit,

bed
Ps 63:6 On my *b* I remember you;
139:8 if I make my *b* in the depths,
Pr 26:14 so a sluggard turns on his *b*
Lk 11:7 and my children are with me in *b*.
17:34 two people will be in one *b*;
Heb 13:4 and the marriage *b* kept pure,

Beelzebub
Mt 12:24 "It is only by *B*, the prince of
12:27 if I drive out demons by *B*,

beg, -ging, -ged
Ps 37:25 or their children *b-ging* bread
Mt 8:31 The demons *b-ged* Jesus,
Lk 16:3 and I'm ashamed to *b*
Jn 4:47 *b-ged* him to come and heal his son,

beggar
Lk 16:20 was laid a *b* named Lazarus,
Ac 3:11 While the *b* held on to Peter

beginning
Ge 1:1 In the *b* God created the heavens
Ps 111:10 of the LORD is the *b* of wisdom
Isa 40:21 it not been told you from the *b*?
Jn 1:1 In the *b* was the Word,
1Jn 1:1 That which was from the *b*,
Rev 21:6 Alpha ... Omega, the *B* and the End.

behave, -iour
Ro 13:13 *b* decently, as in the daytime,
1Pe 3:16 against your good *b-iour* in Christ

believe, -s, -ing, -d
Ge 15:6 Abram *b-d* the LORD,
Isa 53:1 Who has *b-d* our message and to whom
Mt 21:22 If you *b*, you will receive
Mk 1:15 Repent and *b* the good news!
9:24 do *b*; help me overcome my unbelief
Lk 8:50 "Don't be afraid; just *b*,
Jn 1:12 to those who *b-d* in his name,
3:16 whoever *b-s* in him shall not perish
3:18 Whoever *b-s* in him is not condemned
3:36 Whoever *b-s* in the Son has eternal
6:35 who *b-s* in me will never be thirsty
6:47 he who *b-s* has everlasting life
11:25 He who *b-s* in me will live,
11:27 "I *b* that you are the Christ,
12:38 "Lord, who has *b-d* our message
14:11 *b* on the evidence of the miracles

20:27	Stop doubting and *b*."
20:31	and that by *b-ing* you may have life
Ac 16:31	"*B* in the Lord Jesus, and you
Ro 1:16	the salvation of everyone who *b-s*:
4:11	he is the father of all who *b*
4:11	he is the father of all who *b*
10:4	righteousness for everyone who *b-s*
10:9	*b* in your heart that God raised him
Gal 3:6	Consider Abraham: "He *b-d* God,
1Th 4:14	We *b* that Jesus died and rose again
1Ti 4:10	and especially of those who *b*
2Ti 1:12	because I know whom I have *b-d*,
Heb 11:6	comes to him must *b* that he exists
Jas 1:6	But when he asks, he must *b*
2:19	Even the demons *b* that—
1Jn 4:1	Dear friends, do not *b* every spirit
5:1	Everyone who *b-s* that Jesus is the

believer, -s

Ac 4:32	the *b-s* were one in heart and mind.
Gal 6:10	who belong to the family of *b-s*
1Th 1:7	you became a model to all the *b-s*
1Ti 4:12	but set an example for the *b-s*
Jas 2:1	as *b-s* in our glorious Lord Jesus
1Pe 2:17	Love the brotherhood of *b-s*,

belong, -s, -ing

Ge 40:8	"Do not interpretations *b* to God?
Dt 5:21	anything that *b-s* to your neighbour
29:29	The secret things *b* to the LORD
Ps 47:9	for the kings of the earth *b* to God
Mk 10:14	kingdom of God *b-s* to such as these
Jn 8:47	*b-s* to God hears what God says.
15:19	you do not *b* to the world,
Ro 7:4	that you might *b* to another, to him
12:5	each member *b-s* to all the others
14:8	live or die, we *b* to the Lord
1Co 12:15	Because I am not a hand, I do not *b*
Gal 3:29	If you *b* to Christ, then you are
Col 3:5	whatever *b-s* to your earthly nature
1Th 5:8	But since we *b* to the day, let us
1Pe 2:9	holy nation, a people *b-ing* to God,
1Jn 2:19	but they did not really *b* to us.

Belshazzar

King of Babylon at time of its overthrow by Darius. Downfall announced by Daniel, who interpreted writing on the wall (Da 5).

belt

Ex 12:11	with your cloak tucked into your *b*,
Isa 11:5	Righteousness will be his *b*
Jer 13:1	"Go and buy a linen *b* and put it
Mt 3:4	he had a leather *b* round his waist
Ac 21:11	took Paul's *b*, tied his own hands
Eph 6:14	*b* of truth buckled round your waist

Belteshazzar

Name given to Daniel in Babylon (Da 1:7).

beneficial

1Co 6:12	but not everything is *b*.

benefit, -s

Ps 103:2	and forget not all his *b-s*
Jn 12:30	"This voice was for your *b*,
Ro 6:22	the *b* you reap leads to holiness,
2Co 4:15	All this is for your *b*,
Eph 4:29	that it may *b* those who listen

Benjamin

1. Jacob's youngest son; second by Rachel, who died in childbirth (Ge 35:16–18,24; 46:19). Jacob's favourite after loss of Joseph. Father reluctant to allow him to go to Egypt (Ge 42:38; 43); brothers' concern about led Joseph to make himself known (Ge 44–45). Blessed by Jacob (Ge 49:27). **2.** Tribe descended from Benjamin. Blessed by Moses (Dt 33:12). Included in census (Nu 1:36–37; 26:38–41). Apportioned land (Jos 18:11–28; Eze 48:23); did not take full possession (Jdg 1:21). Almost destroyed by other tribes (Jdg 20–21). Tribe of Saul (1Sa 9:1); followed Ishbosheth (2Sa 2:8–9); later gave support to David (1Ch 12:29; 1Ki 12:21). Tribe of Esther (Est 2:5) and Paul (Php 3:5).

best

Jn 2:10 but you have saved the *b* till now.
1Th 3:1 we thought it *b* to be left
2Ti 2:15 Do your *b* to present yourself

Bethany

Mt 21:17 to *B*, where he spent the night
26:6 While Jesus was in *B* in the home
Lk 24:50 led them out to the vicinity of *B*,
Jn 1:28 *B* on the other side of the Jordan,
11:1 Lazarus was sick. He was from *B*,

Bethel

Ge 28:19 He called that place *B*,
31:13 I am the God of *B*,
35:7 and he called the place El *B*,
1Ki 12:33 the altar he had built at *B*.
Am 4:4 "Go to *B* and sin;

Bethlehem

Ru 1:19 women went on until they came to *B*.
Mic 5:2 "But you, *B* Ephrathah, though you
Mt 2:6 you, *B*, in the land of Judah,
Lk 2:15 "Let's go to *B* and see this thing

betray, -s, -ed, -er

Ps 89:33 nor will I ever *b* my faithfulness
Pr 11:13 A gossip *b-s* a confidence,
Mt 26:21 the truth, one of you will *b* me.
26:46 Here comes my *b-er*!"
27:4 "for I have *b-ed* innocent blood."

better

1Sa 15:22 To obey is *b* than sacrifice,
Ecc 2:24 nothing *b* than to eat and drink
Mt 5:29 It is *b* for you to lose one part
Lk 10:42 Mary has chosen what is *b*,
Eph 1:17 so that you may know him *b*
Php 1:23 be with Christ, which is *b* by far
2:3 consider others *b* than yourselves
Heb 11:16 they were longing for a *b* country
11:40 God had planned something *b* for us

Bezalel

Craftsman of the tribe of Judah (1Ch 2:20; 2Ch1:5) chosen, with Oholiab, to organise building of the tabernacle (Ex 31:1–6; 35:30–36:7). Credited with making the ark (Ex 37:1–9).

bidding

Ps 103:20 you mighty ones who do his *b*,
148:8 stormy winds that do his *b*

Bildad

See *Job 2*.

bind

Dt 6:8 *b* them on your foreheads.
11:18 and *b* them on your foreheads
Pr 6:21 *B* them upon your heart for ever;
Isa 61:1 to *b* up the broken-hearted,
Hos 6:1 but he will *b* up our wounds
Mt 16:19 whatever you *b* on earth

bird, -s

Ge 1:20 and let *b-s* fly above the earth
Da 4:21 its branches for the *b-s* of the air
Mt 6:26 Look at the *b-s* of the air;
8:20 Foxes have holes and *b-s* of the air
13:4 and the *b-s* came and ate it up
13:32 the *b-s* of the air come and perch

birth

Dt 32:18 you forgot the God who gave you *b*
Ps 51:5 Surely I was sinful at *b*,
71:6 From my *b* I have relied on you;
Mt 1:18 This is how the *b* of Jesus Christ
Lk 1:15 with the Holy Spirit even from *b*
Jn 3:6 Flesh gives *b* to flesh,
Gal 1:15 when God, who set me apart from *b*
Jas 1:15 conceived, it gives *b* to sin;
1:18 He chose to give us *b*
1Pe 1:3 he has given us new *b* into a living

birthright

Ge 25:34 So Esau despised his *b*

bitter, -ness

Ru 1:20	Almighty has made my life very *b*
Eph 4:31	Get rid of all *b-ness*,
Heb 12:15	no *b* root grows up to cause trouble
Jas 3:14	But if you harbour *b* envy

blameless

Ge 17:1	walk before me and be *b*
Job 1:1	This man was *b* and upright;
1Co 1:8	*b* on the day of our Lord Jesus
Eph 1:4	to be holy and *b* in his sight.
Php 1:10	pure and *b* until the day of Christ
1Th 5:23	spirit, soul and body be kept *b*
Tit 1:6	An elder must be *b*,
Heb 7:26	one who is holy, *b*, pure, set apart
2Pe 3:14	spotless, *b* and at peace with him

blaspheme, -s, -ing, -d, -r

Ex 22:28	"Do not *b* God or curse the ruler
Mk 2:7	fellow talk like that? He's *b-ing*!
3:29	whoever *b-s* against the Holy Spirit
Ro 2:24	it is written: "God's name is *b-d*
1Ti 1:13	I was once a *b-r* and a persecutor
1:20	over to Satan to be taught not to *b*

blasphemy, -ies

Ne 9:26	they committed awful *b-ies*
Mk 3:28	*b-ies* of men will be forgiven them
14:64	"You have heard the *b*.
Jn 10:36	Why then do you accuse me of *b*
Ac 6:11	words of *b* against Moses
Rev 13:5	to utter proud words and *b-ies*

bleating

1Sa 15:14	"What then is this *b* of sheep

bleeding

Mt 9:20	a woman who had been subject to *b*

blemish, -es

Lev 22:21	it must be without defect or *b*
Eph 5:27	stain or wrinkle or any other *b*,
Col 1:22	without *b* and free from accusation
1Pe 1:19	Christ, a lamb without *b* or defect
Jude :12	*b-es* at your love feasts,

bless, -ing, -ed

Ge 1:22	God *b-ed* them and said, "Be
2:3	And God *b-ed* the seventh day
12:3	all peoples on earth will be *b-ed*
Nu 6:24	The LORD *b* you and keep you
Ps 32:2	*B-ed* is the man whose sin the LORD
Pr 3:13	*B-ed* is the man who finds wisdom,
16:20	*b-ed* is he who trusts in the LORD
31:28	Her children ... call her *b-ed*;
Eze 34:26	there will be showers of *b-ing*
Mt 5:3	"*B-ed* are the poor in spirit,
5:4	*B-ed* are those who mourn,
5:5	*B-ed* are the meek,
5:6	*B-ed* are those who hunger
5:7	*B-ed* are the merciful,
5:8	*B-ed* are the pure in heart,
5:9	*B-ed* are the peacemakers,
5:10	*B-ed* are those who are persecuted
21:9	"*B-ed* is he who comes in the name
Mk 10:16	put his hands on them and *b-ed* them
Lk 1:42	"*B-ed* are you among women,
1:48	all generations will call me *b-ed*
6:28	*b* those who curse you,
Jn 20:29	*b-ed* are those who have not seen
Ac 3:25	all peoples on earth will be *b-ed*.
20:35	more *b-ed* to give than to receive.'
Ro 4:8	*B-ed* is the man whose sin the Lord
12:14	*B* those who persecute you;
Gal 3:8	"All nations will be *b-ed*
Eph 1:3	every spiritual *b-ing* in Christ.
Tit 2:13	while we wait for the *b-ed* hope—
Rev 1:3	*B-ed* is the one who reads the words
14:13	*B-ed* are the dead who die in the

blind, -ed

Mt 11:5	The *b* receive sight, the lame walk,
23:16	"Woe to you, *b* guides!
Lk 4:18	and recovery of sight for the *b*,
Jn 9:25	I was *b* but now I see!
Ac 9:9	For three days he was *b*,

2Co 4:4 has *b-ed* the minds of unbelievers,

blood

Ge 4:10 Your brother's *b* cries out to me
9:6 "Whoever sheds the *b* of man,
Ex 7:20 all the water was changed into *b*
12:13 when I see the *b*, I will pass over
Lev 16:15 and take its *b* behind the curtain
17:11 the life of a creature is in the *b*,
Dt 12:16 But you must not eat the *b*;
Joel 2:31 to darkness and the moon to *b*
Mt 26:28 This is my *b* of the covenant,
27:4 "for I have betrayed innocent *b*.
27:8 it has been called the Field of *B*
27:24 "I am innocent of this man's *b*,
Lk 22:44 and his sweat was like drops of *b*
Jn 6:54 and drinks my *b* has eternal life,
Ac 2:20 to darkness and the moon to *b*
15:20 of strangled animals and from *b*
20:28 which he bought with his own *b*
22:20 the *b* of your martyr Stephen
Ro 3:25 atonement, through faith in his *b*.
5:9 we have now been justified by his *b*
1Co 11:25 cup is the new covenant in my *b*;
Eph 1:7 we have redemption through his *b*,
Col 1:20 by making peace through his *b*,
Heb 9:12 once for all by his own *b*
9:22 of *b* there is no forgiveness.
10:4 it is impossible for the *b* of bulls
12:24 *b* that speaks a better word
13:20 the *b* of the eternal covenant
1Pe 1:19 but with the precious *b* of Christ,
1Jn 1:7 the *b* of Jesus, his Son, purifies
Rev 1:5 freed us from our sins by his *b*
5:9 and with your *b* you purchased men
7:14 white in the *b* of the Lamb
12:11 him by the *b* of the Lamb

bloodthirsty

Ps 5:6 *b* and deceitful men the LORD abhors
59:2 and save me from *b* men
139:19 Away from me, you *b* men

blot, -ted

Ex 32:32 then *b* me out of the book you have
Ps 51:9 and *b* out all my iniquity
69:28 *b-ted* out of the book of life
Rev 3:5 I will never *b* out his name

blown

Eph 4:14 and *b* here and there by every wind
Jas 1:6 a wave of the sea, *b* and tossed
Jude :12 clouds without rain, *b* along

boast, -s

Ps 34:2 My soul will *b* in the LORD;
Jer 9:24 let him who *b-s b* about this:
1Co 1:31 "Let him who *b-s b* in the Lord
13:4 It does not envy, it does not *b*,
Gal 6:14 May I never *b* except in the cross
Eph 2:9 not by works, so that no-one can *b*

boat

Mt 4:21 They were in a *b* with their father
14:22 made the disciples get into the *b*
14:29 Then Peter got down out of the *b*,
Jn 6:19 they saw Jesus approaching the *b*,

Boaz

Wealthy and benevolent landowner from Bethlehem; married Ruth, the widow of a relative, fulfilling the responsibility of kinsman-redeemer (Ru 2–4). Ancestor of David (Ru 4:17–22; 1Ch 2:5–15) and of Jesus (Mt 1:5).

body, -ies, -ily

Dt 21:23 must not leave his *b* on the tree
Mt 6:22 "The eye is the lamp of the *b*.
26:26 "Take and eat; this is my *b*.
26:41 is willing, but the *b* is weak.
Jn 2:21 temple he had spoken of was his *b*
Ac 2:31 nor did his *b* see decay
Ro 8:11 give life to your mortal *b-ies*
12:1 your *b-ies* as living sacrifices,
1Co 6:19 *b* is a temple of the Holy Spirit,
9:27 I beat my *b* and make it my slave
11:24 "This is my *b*, which is for you;

12:12 The *b* is a unit, though it is made
12:13 baptised by one Spirit into one *b*—
12:27 Now you are the *b* of Christ,
13:3 and surrender my *b* to the flames,
15:44 natural *b*, it is raised a spiritual
Gal 6:17 I bear on my *b* the marks of Jesus
Php 3:21 will transform our lowly *b-ies*
Col 1:18 the head of the *b*, the church;
2:9 of the Deity lives in *b-ily* form
1Th 4:4 should learn to control his own *b*
Heb 10:5 but a *b* you prepared for me
Jas 2:26 the *b* without the spirit is dead,
1Pe 2:24 bore our sins in his *b* on the tree,

boils
Ex 9:10 and festering *b* broke out on men

bold, -ly, -ness
Ps 138:3 you made me *b* and stout-hearted
Pr 28:1 the righteous are as *b* as a lion
Lk 11:8 because of the man's *b-ness*
Ac 4:29 speak your word with great *b-ness*
4:31 and spoke the word of God *b-ly*
2Co 3:12 we have such a hope, we are very *b*

bondage
Ezr 9:9 God has not deserted us in our *b*.
Ro 8:21 liberated from its *b* to decay

bones
Ge 2:23 "This is now bone of my *b*
Ex 12:46 Do not break any of the *b*
Job 19:20 I am nothing but skin and *b*;
Ps 22:14 and all my *b* are out of joint.
Pr 15:30 good news gives health to the *b*
Eze 37:3 "Son of man, can these *b* live?"
Jn 19:36 "Not one of his *b* will be broken,

book, -s
Ex 32:33 against me I will blot out of my *b*
Dt 29:21 covenant ... in this *B* of the Law
31:26 Take this *B* of the Law and place it
2Ki 22:8 "I have found the *B* of the Law
Ne 13:1 the *B* of Moses was read aloud
Ecc 12:12 Of making many *b-s* there is no end,
Jn 20:30 which are not recorded in this *b*
Gal 3:10 written in the *B* of the Law.
Php 4:3 whose names are in the *b* of life
Rev 21:27 written in the Lamb's *b* of life

bore
Isa 53:12 For he *b* the sin of many,
Lk 23:29 the wombs that never *b*
Ro 7:5 so that we *b* fruit for death
1Pe 2:24 He himself *b* our sins in his body
Rev 17:6 those who *b* testimony to Jesus.

born
Ps 87:6 "This one was *b* in Zion."
90:2 Before the mountains were *b*
Ecc 3:2 a time to be *b* and a time to die,
Isa 9:6 For to us a child is *b*,
Lk 2:11 a Saviour has been *b* to you;
Jn 3:3 unless he is *b* again.
3:7 'You must be *b* again.
18:37 for this reason I was *b*,
Ac 22:28 "But I was *b* a citizen,"
Gal 4:4 God sent his Son, *b* of a woman,
1Pe 1:23 For you have been *b* again,
1Jn 3:9 because he has been *b* of God
5:4 for everyone *b* of God overcomes

borrow
Ps 37:21 The wicked *b* and do not repay,
Mt 5:42 the one who wants to *b* from you

bought
Mt 13:44 sold all he had and *b* that field
Lk 14:19 'I have just *b* five yoke of oxen,
Ac 20:28 the church of God, which he *b*

1Co 6:20 you were *b* at a price.

bound
Ge 22:9 He *b* his son Isaac and laid him
Mt 16:19 bind on earth will be *b* in heaven,
Mk 15:1 They *b* Jesus, led him away
1Co 7:39 A woman is *b* to her husband
Rev 20:2 and *b* him for a thousand years

boundary
Dt 19:14 Do not move your neighbour's *b*
Ps 16:6 The *b* lines have fallen for me
Pr 8:29 when he gave the sea its *b*
23:10 Do not move an ancient *b* stone

bow[1]
1Ki 22:34 But someone drew his *b* at random
Ps 18:34 my arms can bend a *b* of bronze
44:6 I do not trust in my *b*,

bow[2], -ed
Dt 5:9 You shall not *b* down to them
Ps 72:11 All kings will *b* down to him
95:6 Come, let us *b* down in worship,
Isa 45:23 Before me every knee will *b*;
Mt 2:11 they *b-ed* down and worshipped him.
4:9 if you will *b* down and worship me.
Ro 14:11 'Every knee will *b* before me;
Php 2:10 name of Jesus every knee should *b*,

bowl, -s
Mt 5:15 light a lamp and put it under a *b*.
26:23 dipped his hand into the *b* with me
Rev 16:1 the seven *b-s* of God's wrath

boy, -'s, -s
Ge 21:17 God heard the *b* crying,
38:27 there were twin *b-s* in her womb
1Sa 2:11 the *b* ministered before the LORD
3:8 the LORD was calling the *b*
1Ki 17:22 the *b-'s* life returned to him,
Mt 2:16 he gave orders to kill all the *b-s*
Jn 6:9 a *b* with five small barley loaves

branch, -es
Isa 4:2 In that day the *B* of the LORD will
Jer 33:15 a righteous *B* sprout from David's
Jn 12:13 They took palm *b-es* and went out
15:5 "I am the vine; you are the *b-es*.
Ro 11:16 the root is holy, so are the *b-es*
11:21 God did not spare the natural *b-es*,

brave
2Sa 2:7 Now then, be strong and *b*,

bread
Ex 12:18 to eat *b* made without yeast,
16:4 "I will rain down *b* from heaven
Dt 8:3 man does not live on *b* alone
Ps 41:9 he who shared my *b*, has lifted up
Pr 31:27 and does not eat the *b* of idleness
Ecc 11:1 Cast your *b* upon the waters,
Mt 4:3 tell these stones to become *b*.
4:4 'Man does not live on *b* alone,
6:11 Give us today our daily *b*
7:9 if his son asks for *b*,
14:17 only five loaves of *b* and two fish
26:26 Jesus took *b*, gave thanks and broke
Jn 6:31 'He gave them *b* from heaven to eat.
6:33 the *b* of God is he who comes down
6:35 "I am the *b* of life.
13:18 'He who shares my *b* has lifted up
Ac 2:46 They broke *b* in their homes
20:7 we came together to break *b*.
1Co 11:23 the night he was betrayed, took *b*

break, -s
Jdg 2:1 I will never *b* my covenant with you
Isa 42:3 A bruised reed he will not *b*,
45:2 I will *b* down gates of bronze
Mal 2:15 do not *b* faith with the wife

Mt 6:20	where thieves do not *b* in and steal
12:20	A bruised reed he will not *b*,
Jn 19:33	they did not *b* his legs
Ac 20:7	we came together to *b* bread.
1Co 10:16	the bread that we *b* a participation
1Jn 3:4	Everyone who sins *b-s* the law;

breast, -s, -plate

Lk 18:13	look up to heaven, but beat his *b*
23:29	and the *b-s* that never nursed!
23:48	they beat their *b-s* and went away
Eph 6:14	the *b-plate* of righteousness
1Th 5:8	faith and love as a *b-plate*,

breath

Ge 2:7	into his nostrils the *b* of life,
Ps 33:6	starry host by the *b* of his mouth
Ac 17:25	he himself gives all men life and *b*
2Th 2:8	overthrow with the *b* of his mouth

breathe, -ing, -d

Ge 2:7	ground and *b-d* into his nostrils
Eze 37:9	O breath, and *b* into these slain,
Mk 15:37	With a loud cry, Jesus *b-d* his last
Jn 20:22	he *b-d* on them and said, "Receive
Ac 9:1	still *b-ing* out murderous threats

bribe, -s

Ex 23:8	a *b* blinds those who see and twists
Dt 10:17	no partiality and accepts no *b-s*
27:25	"Cursed is the man who accepts a *b*
Ecc 7:7	and a *b* corrupts the heart
Isa 5:23	who acquit the guilty for a *b*,

bride

Ps 45:9	at your right hand is the royal *b*
SS 4:9	stolen my heart, my sister, my *b*;
Jn 3:29	The *b* belongs to the bridegroom.
Rev 21:2	prepared as a *b* beautifully dressed
22:17	The Spirit and the *b* say, "Come!"

bridegroom

Ps 19:5	which is like a *b* coming forth
Mt 25:1	and went out to meet the *b*
25:5	The *b* was a long time in coming,
Mk 2:20	the *b* will be taken from them,

bridle

Ps 32:9	but must be controlled by bit and *b*

bright, -ly, -ness

Pr 13:9	light of the righteous shines *b-ly*
Isa 60:3	kings to the *b-ness* of your dawn
Ac 22:6	suddenly a *b* light from heaven
Rev 22:16	and the *b* Morning Star.

broad

Mt 7:13	wide is the gate and *b* is the road
2Pe 2:13	to carouse in *b* daylight.

broke, -n

Ps 34:20	not one of them will be *b-n*
51:17	sacrifices of God are a *b-n* spirit
Ecc 4:12	three strands is not quickly *b-n*
12:6	severed, or the golden bowl is *b-n*;
Mt 21:44	who falls on this stone will be *b-n*
26:26	took bread, gave thanks and *b* it,
Mk 6:41	he gave thanks and *b* the loaves.
Lk 24:35	was recognised by them when he *b*
Jn 10:35	and the Scripture cannot be *b-n*
19:36	"Not one of his bones will be *b-n*,
Ac 2:46	They *b* bread in their homes and ate
Ro 11:20	were *b-n* off because of unbelief,

broken-hearted
Ps 34:18 The LORD is close to the *b*
147:3 He heals the *b* and binds up
Isa 61:1 He has sent me to bind up the *b*,

bronze
Ex 27:2 overlay the altar with *b*
Nu 21:9 So Moses made a *b* snake and put it
Isa 60:17 Instead of *b* I will bring you gold
Da 2:39 third kingdom, one of *b*, will rule
Rev 1:15 His feet were like *b* glowing
2:18 whose feet are like burnished *b*

brother, -'s, -s, -ly
Ge 4:9 he replied. "Am I my *b-'s* keeper?
Dt 15:3 cancel any debt your *b*
Ps 22:22 I will declare your name to my *b-s*
133:1 when *b-s* live together in unity
Pr 17:17 and a *b* is born for adversity
18:24 a friend who sticks closer than a *b*
Mt 5:22 anyone who is angry with his *b*
5:24 go and be reconciled to your *b*;
5:47 And if you greet only your *b-s*,
12:48 and who are my *b-s*?
18:35 forgive your *b* from your heart.
19:29 *b-s* or sisters or father or mother
22:25 Now there were seven *b-s* among us.
23:8 only one Master and you are all *b-s*
25:40 the least of these *b-s* of mine,
Mk 3:35 Whoever does God's will is my *b*
6:3 *b* of James, Joseph, Judas and Simon
Lk 15:32 *b* of yours was dead and is alive
17:3 "If your *b* sins, rebuke him,
Jn 7:5 his own *b-s* did not believe in him
Ac 15:32 to encourage and strengthen the *b-s*
Ro 8:29 the firstborn among many *b-s*
12:10 to one another in *b-ly* love.
14:10 why do you judge your *b*?
14:13 obstacle in your *b-'s* way
14:21 that will cause your *b* to fall
1Co 6:6 one *b* goes to law against another
8:12 When you sin against your *b-s*
8:13 if what I eat causes my *b*
Gal 2:4 false *b-s* had infiltrated our ranks
Col 1:2 the holy and faithful *b-s* in Christ
1Th 3:2 our *b* and God's fellow-worker
4:10 in fact, you do love all the *b-s*
5:25 *B-s*, pray for us.
5:26 Greet all the *b-s* with a holy kiss
1Ti 4:6 point these things out to the *b-s*,
5:1 Treat younger men as *b-s*
Phm :16 better than a slave, as a dear *b*.
Heb 2:11 is not ashamed to call them *b-s*
2:17 made like his *b-s* in every way,
13:1 Keep on loving each other as *b-s*
Jas 2:15 a *b* or sister is without clothes
4:11 Anyone who speaks against his *b*
1Pe 1:22 you have sincere love for your *b-s*,
3:8 be sympathetic, love as *b-s*,
2Pe 1:7 and to godliness, *b-ly* kindness;
1Jn 2:10 Whoever loves his *b* lives
2:11 But whoever hates his *b*
3:10 anyone who does not love his *b*
3:14 to life, because we love our *b-s*.
3:16 to lay down our lives for our *b-s*
3:17 possessions and sees his *b* in need
4:21 loves God must also love his *b*
5:16 If anyone sees his *b* commit a sin
3Jn :10 he refuses to welcome the *b-s*.
Rev 12:10 For the accuser of our *b-s*,

bruise, -d
Isa 42:3 A *b-d* reed he will not break,
Mt 12:20 A *b-d* reed he will not break,

bucket
Isa 40:15 the nations are like a drop in a *b*

build, -s, -ing

2Sa 7:5 Are you the one to *b* me a house
1Ki 6:1 he began to *b* the temple
2Ch 36:23 he has appointed me to *b* a temple
Ezr 1:3 and *b* the temple of the LORD,
Ps 127:1 Unless the LORD *b-s* the house,
Pr 14:1 The wise woman *b-s* her house,
Ecc 3:3 a time to tear down and a time to *b*
Jer 31:4 I will *b* you up again
Mt 16:18 and on this rock I will *b* my church
Ac 20:32 his grace, which can *b* you up
Ro 15:2 for his good, to *b* him up
1Co 3:9 you are God's field, God's *b-ing*
3:10 one should be careful how he *b-s*
14:12 excel in gifts that *b* up the church
2Co 10:8 for *b-ing* you up rather than
Eph 4:16 grows and *b-s* itself up in love,
4:29 what is helpful for *b-ing* others up
Jude :20 *b* yourselves up in your most holy

builder, -s

Ps 127:1 the house, its *b-s* labour in vain.
Mt 21:42 " 'The stone the *b-s* rejected
Ac 4:11 is " 'the stone you *b-s* rejected
1Co 3:10 I laid a foundation as an expert *b*,
Heb 11:10 whose architect and *b* is God
1Pe 2:7 "The stone the *b-s* rejected

built

1Ki 6:14 So Solomon *b* the temple
8:27 How much less this temple I have *b*
Pr 24:3 By wisdom a house is *b*,
Hag 1:2 for the LORD's house to be *b*.'
Mt 7:24 like a wise man who *b* his house
7:26 like a foolish man who *b* his house
Ac 17:24 does not live in temples *b* by hands
1Co 3:14 If what he has *b* survives,
2Co 5:1 in heaven, not *b* by human hands
Eph 2:20 *b* on the foundation of the apostles
2:22 in him you too are being *b* together
4:12 that the body of Christ may be *b* up
Col 2:7 rooted and *b* up in him,
1Pe 2:5 are being *b* into a spiritual house

bull, -s

1Ki 18:33 He arranged the wood, cut the *b*
Ps 22:12 strong *b-s* of Bashan encircle me
Heb 10:4 impossible for the blood of *b-s*

burden, -s, -ed, -some

Ps 68:19 Saviour, who daily bears our *b-s*.
Mt 11:28 all you who are weary and *b-ed*,
11:30 my yoke is easy and my *b* is light.
20:12 who have borne the *b* of the work
Gal 6:2 Carry each other's *b-s*,
1Th 2:9 in order not to be a *b* to anyone
Heb 13:17 their work will be a joy, not a *b*,
1Jn 5:3 And his commands are not *b-some*

burial

Ge 23:4 Sell me some property for a *b* site
Mt 26:12 she did it to prepare me for *b*
Jn 19:40 in accordance with Jewish *b* customs

burn, -ing, -ed, -t

Ge 19:24 rained down *b-ing* sulphur on Sodom
Lev 6:9 regulations for the *b-t* offering:
Dt 7:5 and *b* their idols in the fire
2Sa 6:7 The LORD's anger *b-ed* against Uzzah
24:22 Here are oxen for the *b-t* offering,
1Ki 9:25 Solomon sacrificed *b-t* offerings

10:5	*b-t* offerings he made at the temple
Ps 18:28	You, O LORD, keep my lamp *b-ing*;
Pr 25:22	heap *b-ing* coals on his head,
Mt 13:30	and tie them in bundles to be *b-ed*;
Lk 3:17	but he will *b* up the chaff
12:35	and keep your lamps *b-ing*
24:32	Were not our hearts *b-ing* within us
Ac 19:19	scrolls together and *b-ed* them
Ro 12:20	heap *b-ing* coals on his head.
1Co 3:15	If it is *b-ed* up, he will suffer
7:9	to marry than to *b* with passion
Heb 6:8	In the end it will be *b-ed*
Rev 8:7	A third of the earth was *b-ed* up,
19:20	the fiery lake of *b-ing* sulphur

burnished

Da 10:6	legs like the gleam of *b* bronze,
Rev 2:18	and whose feet are like *b* bronze

bury, -ied

Ge 25:10	Abraham was *b-ied* with his wife
Dt 21:23	Be sure to *b* him that same day,
Mt 8:21	first let me go and *b* my father.
8:22	let the dead *b* their own dead.
Ac 8:2	Godly men *b-ied* Stephen
Ro 6:4	*b-ied* with him through baptism
1Co 15:4	he was *b-ied*, that he was raised

bush

Ex 3:3	why the *b* does not burn up.
Mk 12:26	in the account of the *b*,
Ac 7:35	angel who appeared to him in the *b*

busy, -iness

Jn 15:15	does not know his master's *b-iness*.
Tit 2:5	to be *b* at home, to be kind,

busybodies

2Th 3:11	They are not busy; they are *b*
1Ti 5:13	gossips and *b*, saying things

buy, -s

Pr 23:23	*B* the truth and do not sell it;
31:16	She considers a field and *b-s* it;
Isa 55:1	Come, *b* wine and milk without money
Rev 3:18	*b* from me gold refined in the fire,

C

Caesar, -'s

Mt 22:21	"Give to *C* what is *C-'s*,
Lk 2:1	*C* Augustus issued a decree
23:2	taxes to *C* and claims to be Christ,
Jn 19:15	"We have no king but *C*,"
Ac 25:11	I appeal to *C*!

Caiaphas

High priest at time of Jesus' arrest (Mt 26:57–68; Jn 18:13,24). Unknowingly foretold the significance of Jesus' death (Jn 11:49–52; 18:14). Questioned Peter and John (Ac 4:5–7).

Cain

Eldest son of Adam and Eve (Ge 4:1). Farmer (Ge 4:2; murdered his brother, Abel, when sacrifice not accepted by God (Ge 4:3–8; 1Jn 3:12). Given mark of protection to limit punishment (Ge 4:9–16).

Caleb

One of spies sent to explore Canaan (Nu 13:6); with Joshua encouraged the people to go in (Nu 13:30; 14:6–9). Allowed to enter land because of his faith (Nu 26:65; 32:12; Dt 1:36). Given possession of Hebron (Jos 14:6–15; 15:13–19).

calf, -ves

Ex 32:19	approached the camp and saw the *c*
1Ki 12:28	the king made two golden *c-ves*.
Lk 15:23	Bring the fattened *c* and kill it.
Heb 9:12	of the blood of goats and *c-ves*;

call, -s, -ing, -ed

Ge 13:4	Abram *c-ed* on the name of the LORD
26:25	altar there and *c-ed* on the name of
1Sa 3:4	LORD *c-ed* Samuel. Samuel answered,
2Sa 22:7	In my distress I *c-ed* to the LORD;

2Ch 7:14 my people, who are *c-ed* by my name,
Ps 50:15 *c* upon me in the day of trouble; I
Isa 40:3 voice of one *c-ing*: "In the desert
55:6 while he may be found; *c* on him
65:24 Before they *c* I will answer; while
Joel 2:32 who *c-s* on the name of the LORD
Mt 26:53 think I cannot *c* on my Father, and
Mk 12:37 David himself *c-s* him 'Lord'. How
Lk 1;32 be *c-ed* the Son of the Most High.
5:32 I have not come to *c* the righteous,
15:19 longer worthy to be *c-ed* your son
Jn 1:23 "I am the voice of one *c-ing* in
10:3 sheep listen to his voice. He *c-s*
11:43 *c-ed* in a loud voice, "Lazarus,
Ac 2:21 And everyone who *c-s* on the name
11:26 were *c-ed* Christians first
Ro 8:30 those he predestined, he also *c-ed*;
10:13 Everyone who *c-s* on the name of the
11:29 gifts and his *c* are irrevocable.
1Co 1:1 Paul, *c-ed* to be an apostle of
1:2 Jesus and *c-ed* to be holy, together
1:24 God has *c-ed*, both Jews and Greeks,
1:26 of what you were when you were *c-ed*
7:20 which he was in when God *c-ed* him
15:9 even deserve to be *c-ed* an apostle,
Gal 1:6 quickly deserting the one who *c-ed*
1:15 set me apart from birth and *c-ed* me
Eph 1:18 the hope to which he has *c-ed* you,
4:1 live a life worthy of the *c-ing* you
4:4 just as you were *c-ed* to one hope
1Th 2:12 live lives worthy of God, who *c-s*
4:16 the trumpet *c* of God, and the dead
5:24 The one who *c-s* you is faithful
2Th 1:11 may count you worthy of his *c-ing*,
2:14 *c-ed* you to this through our gospel
1Ti 6:12 eternal life to which you were *c-ed*
2Ti 1:9 saved us and *c-ed* us to a holy
Heb 2:11 is not ashamed to *c* them brothers
1Pe 1:15 But just as he who *c-ed* you is holy
1:17 Since you *c* on a Father who judges
2:9 declare the praises of him who *c-ed*
3:9 to this you were *c-ed* so that you
5:10 the God of all grace, who *c-ed* you
2Pe 1:3 of him who *c-ed* us by his own glory
1:10 make your *c-ing* and election sure.
Rev 6:16 *c-ed* to the mountains and the rocks

callous, -ed

Isa 6:10 Make the heart of this people *c-ed*;
Mt 13:15 people's heart has become *c-ed*;
Ac 28:27 people's heart has become *c-ed*;

calm

Jnh 1:12 he replied, "and it will become *c*.
Mt 8:26 the waves, and it was completely *c*

camel

Ge 24:64 saw Isaac. She got down from her *c*
Mt 23:24 strain out a gnat but swallow a *c*
Lk 18:25 *c* to go through the eye of a needle

camp
Ex 19:17 out of the *c* to meet with God,
32:26 at the entrance to the *c* and said,
Lev 14:3 to go outside the *c* and examine him
Heb 13:11 bodies are burned outside the *c*
13:13 go to him outside the *c*, bearing

Cana
Jn 2:1 a wedding took place at *C*

Canaan
Ex 6:4 to give them the land of *C*,
Lev 14:34 "When you enter the land of *C*,
1Ch 16:18 "To you I will give the land of *C*
Ac 7:11 a famine struck all Egypt and *C*,

cancel, -led
Dt 15:1 every seven years you must *c* debts
Ne 10:31 forgo working the land and will *c*
Mt 18:32 'I *c-led* all that debt of yours
Lk 7:42 so he *c-led* the debts of both.
Col 2:14 having *c-led* the written code,

Capernaum
Mt 8:5 *C*, a centurion came to him,
11:23 *C*, will you be lifted up
Jn 2:12 went down to *C* with his mother
6:24 went to *C* in search of Jesus
6:59 teaching in the synagogue in *C*

capstone
Ps 118:22 builders rejected has become the *c*
Zec 4:7 the *c* to shouts of 'God bless it!
Mt 21:42 builders rejected has become the *c*;
Ac 4:11 rejected, which has become the *c*.
1Pe 2:7 builders rejected has become the *c*,

captain
Ge 37:36 one of Pharaoh's officials, the *c*
2Ki 1:10 *c*, "If I am a man of God, may fire
Ac 4:1 The priests and the *c* of the temple
5:24 report, the *c* of the temple guard

captive, -s
1Ch 9:1 Judah were taken *c* to Babylon
Ps 68:18 ascended on high, you led *c-s* in
126:1 LORD brought back the *c-s* to Zion,
Ac 8:23 are full of bitterness and *c* to sin
2Co 10:5 *c* every thought to make it obedient
Eph 4:8 ascended on high, he led *c-s* in his
Col 2:8 no-one takes you *c* through hollow
2Ti 2:26 who has taken them *c* to do his will

captivity
Ps 78:61 sent {the ark of} his might into *c*,
Jer 29:14 "and will bring you back from *c*. I
Eze 29:14 I will bring them back from *c* and
Rev 13:10 is to go into *c*, into captivity he

capture, -d
1Sa 4:11 ark of God was *c-d*, and Eli's two
19:14 When Saul sent the men to *c* David,
Mt 26:55 out with swords and clubs to *c* me?
Rev 19:20 the beast was *c-d*, and with him the

care, -s
Ps 55:22 Cast your *c-s* on the LORD and he
144:3 O LORD, what is man that you *c* for
Mk 4:38 "Teacher, don't you *c* if we drown?
Lk 10:34 brought him to an inn and took *c* of
10:40 "Lord, don't you *c* that my sister
Jn 10:13 because he is a hired hand and *c-s*

Ac 13:40	Take *c* that what the prophets have
1Co 4:3	*c* very little if I am judged by you
1Ti 3:5	how can he take *c* of God's church?
6:20	what has been entrusted to your *c*.
Heb 2:6	him, the son of man that you *c* for
1Pe 5:2	God's flock that is under your *c*,
5:7	anxiety on him because he *c-s* for

careful, -ly

Ex 23:22	If you listen *c-ly* to what he says
1Ch 28:8	Be *c* to follow all the commands of
Mt 6:1	"Be *c* not to do your 'acts of
Lk 1:3	Therefore, since I myself have *c-ly*
8:18	consider *c-ly* how you listen.
1Co 10:12	think you are standing firm, be *c*
Eph 5:15	Be very *c*, then, how you live—not
Heb 2:1	pay more *c* attention, therefore,
4:1	let us be *c* that none of you be

careless

Mt 12:36	day of judgment for every *c* word

Carmel

1Ki 18:20	assembled the prophets on Mount *C*
2Ki 4:25	to the man of God at Mount *C*.

carpenter, -'s

Mt 13:55	"Isn't this the *c-'s* son?
Mk 6:3	Isn't this the *c*? Isn't this Mary's

carry, -ies, -ied

Ex 19:4	I *c-ied* you on eagles' wings
Nu 11:14	I cannot *c* all these people
Dt 1:31	as a father *c-ies* his son,
1Ki 18:12	the Spirit of the LORD may *c* you
Isa 40:11	*c-ies* them close to his heart;
53:4	and *c-ied* our sorrows,
Mt 3:11	whose sandals I am not fit to *c*.
8:17	took up our infirmities and *c-ied*
12:29	a strong man's house and *c* off
Mk 15:21	they forced him to *c* the cross
Lk 14:27	anyone who does not *c* his cross
Jn 8:44	to *c* out your father's desire.
19:17	*C-ing* his own cross, he went out
20:15	"Sir, if you have *c-ied* him away,
Ac 5:9	they will *c* you out also.
Ro 7:18	I cannot *c* it out
2Co 4:10	We always *c* around in our body
Gal 6:2	*C* each other's burdens,
Php 1:6	will *c* it on to completion
Heb 13:9	Do not be *c-ied* away
2Pe 1:21	*c-ied* along by the Holy Spirit

cast, -ing

Ex 32:4	an idol *c* in the shape of a calf,
Ps 22:18	my garments among them and *c* lots
51:11	Do not *c* me from your presence
55:22	*C* your cares on the LORD
Jnh 1:7	let us *c* lots to find out who
Mt 27:35	up his clothes by *c-ing* lots
Ac 1:26	they *c* lots, and the lot fell to
1Pe 5:7	*C* all your anxiety on him because

catch, -es

Job 5:13	*c-es* the wise in their craftiness,
Lk 5:9	astonished at the *c* of fish they
5:10	from now on you will *c* men.
1Co 3:19	it is written: "He *c-es* the wise

cattle

1Sa 15:14	What is this lowing of *c*
Ps 50:10	and the *c* on a thousand hills.
Da 4:25	you will eat grass like *c* and
Mt 22:4	My oxen and fattened *c* have
Jn 2:14	he found men selling *c*, sheep and

caught

1Sa 15:27	Saul *c* hold of the hem of his robe,
Jn 8:3	brought in a woman *c* in adultery.
2Co 12:2	*c* up to the third heaven.
Gal 6:1	if someone is *c* in a sin,

1Th 4:17 will be *c* up together with them

cause, -s, -d

Ge 2:21 God *c-d* the man to fall into a deep
Ex 33:19 "I will *c* all my goodness to pass
Isa 8:14 a stone that *c-s* men to stumble
53:10 the LORD's will to crush him and *c*
La 3:52 Those who were my enemies without *c*
Da 11:31 abomination that *c-s* desolation
Mt 5:29 If your right eye *c-s* you to sin,
18:8 hand or your foot *c-s* you to sin,
24:15 abomination that *c-s* desolation',
Ro 9:33 I lay in Zion a stone that *c-s* men
1Co 8:13 if what I eat *c-s* my brother to
Jas 4:1 What *c-s* fights and quarrels among
1Pe 2:8 "A stone that *c-s* men to stumble

cave, -s

1Sa 22:1 escaped to the *c* of Adullam.
1Ki 18:4 and hidden them in two *c-s*,
Isa 2:19 Men will flee to *c-s* in the rocks
Heb 11:38 and in *c-s* and holes in the ground

cease

Ge 8:22 day and night will never *c*.
Ps 46:9 He makes wars *c* to the ends
Jer 31:36 Israel ever *c* to be a nation
1Co 12:15 *c* to be part of the body
13:8 there are prophecies, they will *c*;

cedar

2Sa 7:2 Here I am, living in a palace of *c*
2Ki 14:9 sent a message to a *c* in Lebanon,
Job 40:17 His tail sways like a *c*;
Eze 17:3 Taking hold of the top of a *c*
31:3 Assyria, once a *c* in Lebanon,

celebrate, -ing, -ion

Ex 12:17 "*C* the Feast of Unleavened Bread,
1Ch 15:29 saw King David dancing and *c-ing*,
Mt 26:18 I am going to *c* the Passover
Lk 15:23 kill it. Let's have a feast and *c*
Col 2:16 a New Moon *c-ion* or a Sabbath day

censer, -s

Lev 10:1 Nadab and Abihu took their *c-s*,
Nu 16:38 the *c-s* of the men who sinned
2Ch 26:19 Uzziah, who had a *c* in his hand
Rev 8:3 Another angel, who had a golden *c*,

census

2Sa 24:1 "Go and take a *c* of Israel
Lk 2:1 Augustus issued a decree that a *c*
Ac 5:37 appeared in the days of the *c*

centurion

Mt 8:13 Then Jesus said to the *c*, "Go!
27:54 When the *c* and those with him
Lk 7:6 the *c* sent friends to say to him:
Ac 10:1 a man named Cornelius, a *c*

ceremonial, -ly

Lev 12:2 birth to a son will be *c-ly* unclean
Mk 7:3 they give their hands a *c* washing,
Jn 2:6 kind used by the Jews for *c* washing
Ac 24:18 I was *c-ly* clean when they found me
Heb 13:9 strengthened by grace, not by *c*

ceremony

Ex 12:26 'What does this *c* mean to you?

certain, -ty

Lk 1:4 you may know the *c-ty* of the things
Heb 11:1 sure of what we hope for and *c* of
2Pe 1:19 word of the prophets made more *c*,

certificate

Dt 24:1	he writes her a *c* of divorce,
Isa 50:1	Where is your mother's *c* of divorce
Jer 3:8	faithless Israel her *c* of divorce
Mt 5:31	must give her a *c* of divorce.
19:7	a man give his wife a *c* of divorce

chaff

Ps 1:4	like *c* that the wind blows away
35:5	May they be like *c* before the wind,
83:13	O my God, like *c* before the wind
Da 2:35	became like *c* on a threshing-floor
Mt 3:12	burning up the *c* with unquenchable

chain, -s, -ed

Ps 2:3	Let us break their *c-s*," they say,
Mk 5:3	not even with a *c*
Ac 12:6	bound with two *c-s*, and sentries
26:29	except for these *c-s*.
Eph 6:20	I am an ambassador in *c-s*.
Php 1:13	I am in *c-s* for Christ
2Ti 1:16	and was not ashamed of my *c-s*
Heb 11:36	others were *c-ed* and put in prison

champion

1Sa 17:4	A *c* named Goliath,
Ps 19:5	a *c* rejoicing to run his course

change, -s, -d

Ex 7:15	staff that was *c-d* into a snake
Ps 110:4	The LORD has sworn and will not *c*
Da 2:21	He *c-s* times and seasons;
4:16	his mind be *c-d* from that of a man
Mal 3:6	"I the LORD do not *c*.
Mt 18:3	unless you *c* and become like
Lk 9:29	the appearance of his face *c-d*,
Ac 6:14	*c* the customs Moses handed down
1Co 15:51	sleep, but we will all be *c-d*
Heb 1:12	like a garment they will be *c-d*
7:12	there is a *c* of the priesthood,
7:21	has sworn and will not *c* his mind:
12:17	He could bring about no *c* of mind,
Jas 1:17	does not *c* like shifting shadows

character

Pr 31:10	A wife of noble *c* who can find?
Ac 17:11	the Bereans were of more noble *c*
Ro 5:4	perseverance, *c*; and *c*, hope.
1Co 15:33	"Bad company corrupts good *c*.

charge, -s

Job 13:19	Can anyone bring *c-s* against me?
Isa 50:8	Who then will bring *c-s* against me?
Da 2:48	placed him in *c* of all its wise men
Mt 24:47	him in *c* of all his possessions
25:21	I will put you in *c* of many things.
26:63	*c* you under oath by the living God
Mk 15:26	The written notice of the *c*
Jn 13:29	Since Judas had *c* of the money,
Ac 25:20	stand trial there on these *c-s*
Ro 8:33	bring any *c* against those whom God
1Co 9:18	the gospel I may offer it free of *c*
Gal 3:24	the law was put in *c* to lead us to
1Ti 5:21	I *c* you, in the sight of God
6:13	made the good confession, I *c* you

chariot, -s

2Ki 6:17	*c-s* of fire all round Elisha
13:14	"The *c-s* and horsemen of Israel!
Ps 20:7	Some trust in *c-s* and some
68:17	*c-s* of God are tens of thousands
Isa 31:1	trust in the multitude of their *c-s*
66:15	is coming with fire, and his *c-s*
Ac 8:28	in his *c* reading the book of Isaiah
Rev 9:9	horses and *c-s* rushing into battle

chasm
Lk 16:26 a great *c* has been fixed,

chatter, -ing
Pr 10:8 a *c-ing* fool comes to ruin
1Ti 6:20 Turn away from godless *c*
2Ti 2:16 Avoid godless *c*, because

cheat, -ing, -ed
Ge 31:7 *c-ed* me by changing my wages ten
Am 8:5 *c-ing* with dishonest scales
Mal 1:14 "Cursed is the *c* who has
Lk 19:8 if I have *c-ed* anybody
1Co 6:7 Why not rather be *c-ed*
6:8 you yourselves *c* and do wrong,

cheek, -s
Isa 50:6 my *c-s* to those who pulled out
La 3:30 Let him offer his *c* to one
Mt 5:39 strikes you on the right *c*, turn

cheer, -s, -ed, -ful, -fully
Pr 12:25 but a kind word *c-s* him up
17:22 A *c-ful* heart is good medicine,
Mk 10:49 blind man, "*C* up! On your feet!
Ro 12:8 mercy, let him do it *c-fully*
2Co 9:7 for God loves a *c-ful* giver
Php 2:19 I also may be *c-ed* when I receive

cherish, -es, -ed
Ps 66:18 If I had *c-ed* sin in my heart,
Pr 19:8 he who *c-es* understanding prospers

chest
Ex 25:10 Have them make a *c* of acacia wood—
1Sa 6:11 the *c* containing the gold rats
Da 2:32 its *c* and arms of silver, its belly
Rev 1:13 with a golden sash round his *c*

chew, -s, -ed
Lev 11:3 and that *c-s* the cud
Dt 14:6 hoof divided in two and that *c-s*
Jnh 4:7 a worm, which *c-ed* the vine

chief
2Sa 23:13 thirty *c* men came down to David
Da 10:13 Michael, one of the *c* princes,
Mt 20:18 will be betrayed to the *c* priests
27:20 But the *c* priests and the elders
Jn 12:10 So the *c* priests made plans to kill
Ac 9:14 with authority from the *c* priests
14:12 because he was the *c* speaker
Eph 2:20 Jesus himself as the *c* cornerstone
1Pe 5:4 when the *C* Shepherd appears,

child, -ren, -ren's
Ge 17:17 Will Sarah bear a *c* at the age
Dt 4:9 Teach them to your *c-ren*
4:40 may go well with you and your *c-ren*
Ps 8:2 from the lips of *c-ren* and infants
37:25 or their *c-ren* begging bread
103:13 father has compassion on his *c-ren*,
127:3 a heritage from the LORD, *c-ren*
Pr 17:6 *C-ren's c-ren* are a crown
22:6 Train a *c* in the way he should go,
Isa 7:14 The virgin will be with *c* and will
9:6 For to us a *c* is born, to us a son
11:6 and a little *c* will lead them
Jer 1:6 I am only a *c*.
31:29 the *c-ren's* teeth are set on edge.
Hos 11:1 "When Israel was a *c*, I loved him,
Mal 4:6 of the fathers to their *c-ren*,
Mt 1:18 be with *c* through the Holy Spirit
1:23 "The virgin will be with *c*
2:18 Rachel weeping for her *c-ren*
7:11 to give good gifts to your *c-ren*,
11:25 and revealed them to little *c-ren*
15:26 not right to take the *c-ren's* bread
18:2 He called a little *c*
18:3 change and become like little *c-ren*
19:29 or *c-ren* or fields for my sake

23:37 I have longed to gather your *c-ren*
27:25 blood be on us and on our *c-ren*!
Lk 1:17 to their *c-ren* and the disobedient
2:5 and was expecting a *c*
14:26 his wife and *c-ren*, his brothers
Jn 1:12 the right to become *c-ren* of God
8:39 "If you were Abraham's *c-ren*,"
16:21 woman giving birth to a *c* has pain
Ac 2:39 promise is for you and your *c-ren*
13:10 "You are a *c* of the devil
Ro 8:16 our spirit that we are God's *c-ren*
8:17 if we are *c-ren*, then we are heirs—
8:21 glorious freedom of the *c-ren*
9:7 are they all Abraham's *c-ren*.
1Co 13:11 When I was a *c*, I talked like a
Gal 3:7 who believe are *c-ren* of Abraham
Eph 6:1 *C-ren*, obey your parents in the
6:4 do not exasperate your *c-ren*;
Php 2:15 blameless and pure, *c-ren* of God
1Ti 3:12 manage his *c-ren* and his household
Heb 11:23 they saw he was no ordinary *c*,
12:8 then you are illegitimate *c-ren*
1Jn 3:1 we should be called *c-ren* of God!

childbearing
Ge 3:16 greatly increase your pains in *c*;
1Ti 2:15 But women will be saved through *c*—

childbirth
Isa 42:14 like a woman in *c*, I cry out,
Ro 8:22 groaning as in the pains of *c*
Gal 4:19 I am again in the pains of *c*

choke, -d
Mt 13:7 grew up and *c-d* the plants
13:22 the deceitfulness of wealth *c* it,

choose, -s, -ing
Dt 7:7 set his affection on you and *c* you
30:19 Now *c* life, so that you
Jos 24:15 *c* for yourselves this day whom
Mt 11:27 to whom the Son *c-s* to reveal him
Jn 15:16 You did not *c* me, but I chose you
Ac 1:21 it is necessary to *c* one of the men
Ro 9:22 God, *c-ing* to show his wrath
2Co 12:6 Even if I should *c* to boast,
Jas 4:4 *c-s* to be a friend of the world

chose, -n
Dt 7:6 The LORD your God has *c-n* you
Isa 41:9 You are my servant'; I have *c-n* you
Mt 22:14 many are invited, but few are *c-n*.
Lk 9:35 "This is my Son, whom I have *c-n*;
10:42 Mary has *c-n* what is better,
Jn 6:70 "Have I not *c-n* you, the Twelve?
15:16 You did not choose me, but I *c* you
Ac 9:15 "Go! This man is my *c-n* instrument
Ro 8:33 against those whom God has *c-n*?
11:5 there is a remnant *c-n* by grace
1Co 1:27 God *c* the foolish things
Eph 1:4 he *c* us in him before the creation
1:11 also *c-n*, having been predestined
1Th 1:4 loved by God, that he has *c-n* you
2Th 2:13 from the beginning God *c* you
Jas 1:18 He *c* to give us birth
2:5 Has not God *c-n* those who are poor
1Pe 1:2 *c-n* according to the foreknowledge
1:20 He was *c-n* before the creation
2:9 a *c-n* people, a royal priesthood,

Christ, -'s
Mt 2:4 where the *C* was to be born
16:16 "You are the *C*, the Son of
24:5 claiming, 'I am the *C*,'
Lk 2:11 he is *C* the Lord
24:26 Did not the *C* have to suffer
Jn 1:20 confessed freely, "I am not the *C*.

1:41 found the Messiah" (that is, the *C*
11:27 "I believe that you are the *C*,
17:3 the only true God, and Jesus *C*,
Ac 2:36 whom you crucified, both Lord and *C*
17:3 proving that the *C* had to suffer
Ro 3:24 redemption that came by *C* Jesus.
5:1 with God through our Lord Jesus *C*
6:3 baptised into *C* Jesus
8:1 no condemnation ... who are in *C*
8:35 separate us from the love of *C*?
13:14 yourselves with the Lord Jesus *C*,
1Co 1:13 Is *C* divided?
1:23 we preach *C* crucified:
2:2 except Jesus *C* and him crucified.
8:6 there is but one Lord, Jesus *C*,
10:4 that rock was *C*
2Co 4:5 not preach ourselves, but Jesus *C*
5:17 if anyone is in *C*, he is
Gal 2:20 I have been crucified with *C*
3:28 you are all one in *C* Jesus.
Eph 2:6 God raised us up with *C*
2:10 created in *C* Jesus to do good works
2:20 *C* Jesus himself as the chief
3:8 the unsearchable riches of *C*,
5:23 head of the wife as *C* is the head
Php 1:6 until the day of *C* Jesus
1:21 to live is *C* and to die is gain
2:5 be the same as that of *C* Jesus:
2:11 confess that Jesus *C* is Lord,
3:10 to know *C* and the power of his
Col 1:22 reconciled you by *C-'s* physical
1:27 *C* in you, the hope of glory.
2:10 you have been given fulness in *C*,
1Th 4:16 the dead in *C* will rise first
1Ti 1:15 *C* Jesus came into the world to save
2:5 the man *C* Jesus
2Ti 2:3 like a good soldier of *C* Jesus.
Heb 9:14 *C*, who through the eternal Spirit
1Pe 1:19 the precious blood of *C*, a lamb
3:15 set apart *C* as Lord.
2Pe 1:16 coming of our Lord Jesus *C*,
1Jn 2:1 in our defence—Jesus *C*,
2:22 denies that Jesus is the *C*.
Rev 1:1 The revelation of Jesus *C*,
20:4 reigned with *C* for a thousand years

Christian, -s

Ac 11:26 called *C-s* first at Antioch
26:28 you can persuade me to be a *C*?
1Pe 4:16 suffer as a *C*, do not be ashamed,

church

Mt 16:18 on this rock I will build my *c*,
18:17 tell it to the *c*;
Ac 14:23 appointed elders for them in each *c*
20:28 Be shepherds of the *c* of God,
1Co 4:17 I teach everywhere in every *c*
5:12 to judge those outside the *c*?
14:4 he who prophesies edifies the *c*.
Eph 3:10 through the *c*, the manifold wisdom
5:23 Christ is the head of the *c*,
5:25 Christ loved the *c* and gave
Col 1:24 sake of his body, which is the *c*.
1Ti 3:5 how can he take care of God's *c*?
Heb 12:23 the *c* of the firstborn,

circumcise, -d

Ge 17:10 Every male among you shall be *c-d*
Dt 10:16 *C* your hearts,
Ac 15:1 "Unless you are *c-d*,
Ro 3:30 who will justify the *c-d* by faith
Gal 5:2 if you let yourselves be *c-d*,
Col 3:11 no Greek or Jew, *c-d* or

circumcision

Ro 2:29 *c* is *c* of the heart,
1Co 7:19 *C* is nothing and uncircumcision
Gal 5:11 if I am still preaching *c*,
Php 3:3 it is we who are the *c*, we who
Col 2:11 not with a *c* done by the hands

circumstances

Php 4:11 to be content whatever the *c*
1Th 5:18 give thanks in all *c*,

Jas 1:9	The brother in humble *c*

citizen, -s, -ship

Ac 16:37	even though we are Roman *c-s*,
Eph 2:12	excluded from *c-ship* in Israel
Php 3:20	But our *c-ship* is in heaven.

city, -ies

Ps 46:4	streams make glad the *c* of God,
48:2	Zion, the *c* of the Great King
Pr 31:23	husband is respected at the *c* gate,
Isa 24:12	The *c* is left in ruins,
Mt 5:14	A *c* on a hill cannot be hidden.
10:23	finish going through the *c-ies*
Lk 19:17	take charge of ten *c-ies*.
Heb 13:14	looking for the *c* that is to come.
2Pe 2:6	he condemned the *c-ies* of Sodom

civilian

2Ti 2:4	soldier gets involved in *c* affairs—

claim, -s, -ed

Jn 10:33	you, a mere man, *c* to be God.
Ro 1:22	Although they *c-ed* to be wise,
Jas 2:14	if a man *c-s* to have faith
1Jn 1:6	If we *c* to have fellowship
1:8	If we *c* to be without sin,
1:10	If we *c* we have not sinned,

clap

Ps 47:1	*C* your hands, all you nations;
98:8	Let the rivers *c* their hands,
Isa 55:12	all the trees of the field will *c*

clay

Isa 45:9	Does the *c* say to the potter,
64:8	We are the *c*, you are the potter;
Jer 18:4	pot he was shaping from the *c*
Da 2:33	of iron and partly of baked *c*
Ro 9:21	make out of the same lump of *c*
2Co 4:7	this treasure in jars of *c*
2Ti 2:20	*c*; some are for noble purposes

clean

Ps 24:4	He who has *c* hands and
51:7	I shall be *c*; wash me,
Eze 36:25	I will sprinkle *c* water on you,
Mt 8:2	you can make me *c*.
12:44	swept *c* and put in order
23:25	You *c* the outside of the cup
Jn 13:10	his whole body is *c*.
Ac 10:15	impure that God has made *c*.

cleanse, -ing, -d

Ps 51:7	*C* me with hyssop,
Lk 17:14	as they went, they were *c-d*
Eph 5:26	to make her holy, *c-ing* her
Heb 10:22	our hearts sprinkled to *c* us
2Pe 1:9	forgotten that he has been *c-d*

cleft

Ex 33:22	I will put you in a *c* in the rock

cling, -s

Ps 63:8	My soul *c-s* to you;
137:6	tongue *c* to the roof of my mouth
Ro 12:9	*c* to what is good

cloak, -s

Ge 39:12	She caught him by his *c* and said,
Ex 22:26	take your neighbour's *c* as a pledge
2Ki 2:8	Elijah took his *c*, rolled it up
Mt 5:40	let him have your *c* as well
9:20	touched the edge of his *c*
21:7	colt, placed their *c-s* on them,

close[1], -r, -ly

Ps 41:9	my *c* friend, whom I trusted,
Pr 16:28	gossip separates *c* friends
18:24	who sticks *c-r* than a brother
1Ti 4:16	Watch your life and doctrine *c-ly*.

close[2], -d

1Sa 1:5	the LORD had *c-d* her womb
Isa 6:10	their ears dull and *c* their eyes.
Mt 6:6	*c* the door and pray to your Father
13:15	they have *c-d* their eyes.

cloth, -s

Mt 9:16	No-one sews a patch of unshrunk *c*
Lk 2:12	You will find a baby wrapped in *c-s*
Jn 11:44	and a *c* around his face.

Ac 16:14 Lydia, a dealer in purple *c*

clothe, -d
Isa 61:10 *c-d* me with garments of salvation
Mt 25:36 I needed clothes and you *c-d* me,
Jn 19:2 They *c-d* him in a purple robe
Ro 13:14 *c* yourselves with the Lord Jesus
1Co 15:53 the perishable must *c* itself
2Co 5:2 we groan, longing to be *c-d*
Gal 3:27 baptised into Christ have *c-d*

clothes
Ge 27:27 Isaac caught the smell of his *c*,
Dt 8:4 Your *c* did not wear out
Mt 6:30 If that is how God *c* the grass
22:11 who was not wearing wedding *c*
25:36 I needed *c* and you clothed me,
28:3 and his *c* were white as snow
Ac 7:58 the witnesses laid their *c*
14:14 they tore their *c* and rushed out
1Ti 2:9 gold or pearls or expensive *c*
Jas 2:2 wearing a gold ring and fine *c*,
1Pe 3:3 gold jewellery and fine *c*
Rev 3:18 and white *c* to wear,

clothing
Ps 22:18 cast lots for my *c*
102:26 wear out like a garment. Like *c*
Mt 7:15 They come to you in sheep's *c*,
Jn 19:24 cast lots for my *c*."
1Ti 6:8 food and *c*, we will be content
Jude :23 hating even the *c* stained

cloud, -s
Ex 13:21 in a pillar of *c* to guide them
1Ki 18:44 "A *c* as small as a man's hand
Pr 25:14 Like *c-s* and wind without rain
Da 7:13 coming with the *c-s* of heaven.
Mt 24:30 the Son of Man coming on the *c-s*
Lk 9:35 A voice came from the *c*, saying,
1Th 4:17 in the *c-s* to meet the Lord
Heb 12:1 such a great *c* of witnesses,
Jude :12 They are *c-s* without rain,
Rev 1:7 Look, he is coming with the *c-s*,

co-heirs
Ro 8:17 heirs of God and *c* with Christ,

coal, -s
Pr 25:22 heap burning *c-s* on his head,
Isa 6:6 flew to me with a live *c*
Ro 12:20 heap burning *c-s* on his head.

cock
Mt 26:34 before the *c* crows, you will disown
26:74 Immediately a *c* crowed

code
Ro 2:29 not by the written *c*.
7:6 in the old way of the written *c*
Col 2:14 having cancelled the written *c*,

coin, -s
Mt 22:19 the *c* used for paying the tax."
26:15 for him thirty silver *c-s*
Mk 12:42 put in two very small copper *c-s*,
Lk 10:35 *c-s* and gave them to the innkeeper.
15:9 I have found my lost *c*.
Jn 2:15 the *c-s* of the money-changers

cold
Ge 8:22 seedtime and harvest, *c* and heat,
Pr 25:25 Like *c* water to a weary soul
Mt 10:42 gives even a cup of *c* water
24:12 the love of most will grow *c*
2Co 11:27 I have been *c* and naked
Rev 3:15 that you are neither *c* nor hot.

collect, -ed, -ion
Ge 41:48 Joseph *c-ed* all the food produced
Lk 3:13 *c* any more than you are required
1Co 16:1 about the *c-ion* for God's people:

Colosse
Col 1:2 faithful brothers in Christ at *C*:

colt
Zec 9:9 on a *c*, the foal of a donkey
Mt 21:2 a donkey tied there, with her *c*
21:5 on a *c*, the foal of a donkey.'

comb
Ps 19:10 than honey from the *c*

come, -s, -ing

Ge 17:6 kings will *c* from you
39:12 "*C* to bed with me!"
Ex 3:5 "Do not *c* any closer," God said.
Job 1:7 to Satan, "Where have you *c* from?
Ps 19:5 like a bridegroom *c-ing* forth
24:7 the King of glory may *c* in
40:7 I have *c*—it is written about me
91:7 it will not *c* near you
121:1 where does my help *c* from?
Ecc 5:15 a man *c-s* from his mother's womb,
Isa 1:18 "*C* now, let us reason together,
11:1 A shoot will *c* up from the stump
37:32 out of Jerusalem will *c* a remnant,
55:1 thirsty, *c* to the waters;
60:1 Arise, shine, for your light has *c*
62:11 'See, your Saviour *c-s*!
64:1 rend the heavens and *c* down,
Da 7:13 son of man, *c-ing* with the clouds
Hos 6:1 "*C*, let us return to the LORD.
Mic 5:2 *c* for me one who will be ruler
Zec 9:9 See, your king *c-s* to you,
Mal 3:1 will *c* to his temple;
3:2 can endure the day of his *c-ing*?
Mt 2:2 east and have *c* to worship him.
2:6 out of you will *c* a ruler
3:11 will *c* one who is more powerful
4:4 that *c-s* from the mouth of God.'
4:19 "*C*, follow me," Jesus said,
6:10 your kingdom *c*, your will be done
7:15 They *c* to you in sheep's clothing,
10:34 I have *c* to bring peace
11:28 "*C* to me, all you who are weary
15:11 'unclean', but what *c-s* out
16:24 "If anyone would *c* after me,
19:14 "Let the little children *c* to me,
20:28 Son of Man did not *c* to be served,
21:5 'See, your king *c-s* to you,
23:39 who *c-s* in the name of the Lord.'
24:30 the Son of Man *c-ing* on the clouds
Mk 6:31 "*C* with me by yourselves
Jn 1:15 'He who *c-s* after me has surpassed
1:32 I saw the Spirit *c* down from heaven
1:39 "*C*," he replied, "and you will
4:29 *C*, see a man who told me everything
5:25 has now *c* when the dead will hear
5:40 you refuse to *c* to me to have life
6:37 *c-s* to me I will never drive away
10:10 The thief *c-s* only to steal
11:43 "Lazarus, *c* out!
12:15 your king is *c-ing*, seated
14:6 No-one *c-s* to the Father
Ac 1:11 will *c* back in the same way
3:19 refreshing may *c* from the Lord
16:9 "*C* over to Macedonia and help us.
Ro 1:5 the obedience that *c-s* from faith
10:17 faith *c-s* from hearing the message,
1Co 2:1 I did not *c* with eloquence
11:26 the Lord's death until he *c-s*
16:22 a curse be on him. *C*, O Lord
2Co 1:22 guaranteeing what is to *c*
5:17 the old has gone, the new has *c*
6:17 *c* out from them and be separate,
Gal 4:4 when the time had fully *c*,
Eph 5:6 God's wrath *c-s* on those
Col 2:17 the things that were to *c*;
1Th 4:16 the Lord himself will *c* down
5:2 will *c* like a thief in the night
2Th 2:3 for (that day will not *c*) until
Heb 10:7 I have *c* to do your will, O God.'
11:7 righteousness that *c-s* by faith
12:22 you have *c* to Mount Zion,
13:14 looking for the city that is to *c*
Jas 4:8 to God and he will *c* near to you.
2Pe 1:16 the power and *c-ing* of our Lord
1Jn 2:18 many antichrists have *c*.
Rev 1:7 he is *c-ing* with the clouds,
3:3 I will *c* like a thief,
3:11 I am *c-ing* soon.
3:20 I will *c* in and eat with him,

16:15 “Behold, I *c* like a thief!
19:7 the wedding of the Lamb has *c*,
22:17 Whoever is thirsty, let him *c*;
22:20 “Yes, I am *c-ing* soon.”
22:20 Amen. *C*, Lord Jesus.

comfort, -s, -ed, -ers

Job 16:2 miserable *c-ers* are you all!
Ps 23:4 rod and your staff, they *c* me
Isa 40:1 *c* my people, says your God
Mt 5:4 for they will be *c-ed*
Lk 6:24 have already received your *c*
16:25 is *c-ed* here and you are in agony
2Co 1:4 who *c-s* us in all our troubles,

command, -s, -ed

Ge 2:16 And the LORD God *c-ed* the man,
Ex 7:2 You are to say everything I *c* you,
Dt 5:32 the LORD your God has *c-ed* you;
30:16 I *c* you today to love the LORD
Jos 1:9 Have I not *c-ed* you? Be strong
Ps 19:8 The *c-s* of the LORD are radiant,
91:11 he will *c* his angels concerning
112:1 finds great delight in his *c-s*
119:98 Your *c-s* make me wiser than
Pr 3:1 but keep my *c-s* in your heart
Mt 4:6 ‘He will *c* his angels concerning
15:3 do you break the *c* of God
28:20 obey everything I have *c-ed* you.
Mk 7:8 You have let go of the *c-s* of God
7:9 setting aside the *c-s* of God
10:3 “What did Moses *c* you?”
Lk 8:25 He *c-s* even the winds
Jn 10:18 This *c* I received from my Father.
13:34 “A new *c* I give you: Love
14:15 love me, you will obey what I *c*
15:14 my friends if you do what I *c*
Ac 17:30 now he *c-s* all people everywhere
1Co 7:10 To the married I give this *c*
9:14 Lord has *c-ed* that those who preach
14:37 writing to you is the Lord’s *c*
Gal 5:14 summed up in a single *c*:
1Th 4:16 with a loud *c*, with the voice
1Ti 1:5 The goal of this *c* is love,
6:17 *C* those who are rich
Heb 11:3 the universe was formed at God’s *c*,
1Jn 2:3 to know him if we obey his *c-s*
Rev 3:10 have kept my *c* to endure patiently,

commander

Jos 5:14 “but as *c* of the army of the LORD

commandment, -s

Dt 5:22 These are the *c-s* the LORD
Mt 5:19 one of the least of these *c-s*
22:36 the greatest *c* in the Law?
Ro 7:10 *c* that was intended to bring life
13:9 The *c-s*, “Do not commit adultery,
Eph 6:2 the first *c* with a promise

commend, -s, -ed

Ps 145:4 One generation will *c* your works
Lk 16:8 “The master *c-ed* the dishonest
Ro 13:3 do what is right and he will *c* you
2Co 10:18 it is not the one who *c-s* himself
Heb 11:39 all *c-ed* for their faith,

commit, -s, -ted

Ex 20:14 “You shall not *c* adultery
1Ki 8:61 your hearts must be fully *c-ted*
Ps 31:5 Into your hands I *c* my spirit;
37:5 *C* your way to the LORD;
Mt 5:27 ‘Do not *c* adultery.
11:27 “All things have been *c-ted* to me
27:23 “Why? What crime has he *c-ted*?”
Mk 10:11 marries another woman *c-s* adultery
Ac 14:23 *c-ted* them to the Lord,
20:32 I *c* you to God and to the word
Ro 1:27 *c-ted* indecent acts with other men,
1Co 10:8 We should not *c* sexual immorality,
2Co 5:19 he has *c-ted* to us the message
Heb 9:7 for the sins the people had *c-ted*
1Pe 2:22 “He *c-ted* no sin, and no deceit
1Jn 5:16 If anyone sees his brother *c* a sin

common

Pr 22:2 Rich and poor have this in *c*:
Ac 2:44 together and had everything in *c*
Ro 9:21 noble purposes and some for *c* use
1Co 10:13 you except what is *c* to man.
2Co 6:15 What does a believer have in *c*

companion, -s

Ps 45:7 God, has set you above your *c-s*
Pr 13:20 but a *c* of fools suffers harm
Mt 12:3 David did when he and his *c-s*
Heb 1:9 God, has set you above your *c-s*

company

Ps 68:11 the *c* of those who proclaimed it
Lk 2:13 a great *c* of the heavenly host
Ac 15:39 they parted *c*. Barnabas took Mark
1Co 15:33 "Bad *c* corrupts good character.

compare, -d, -ison

Isa 40:25 "To whom will you *c* me?
Mt 11:16 "To what can I *c* this generation?
2Co 3:10 has no glory now in *c-ison* with
Php 3:8 I consider everything a loss *c-d*

compassion, -s, -ate

Ex 33:19 *c* on whom I will have *c*
34:6 LORD, the *c-ate* and gracious God,
Ps 103:8 The LORD is *c-ate* and gracious,
La 3:22 for his *c-s* never fail
Mt 9:36 saw the crowds, he had *c* on them,
Lk 15:20 filled with *c* for him;
Ro 9:15 I will have *c* on whom I have *c*
Eph 4:32 Be kind and *c-ate* to one another,
Col 3:12 clothe yourselves with *c*,
Jas 5:11 The Lord is full of *c* and mercy

compel, -s, -led

Ac 20:22 "And now, *c-led* by the Spirit,
1Co 9:16 I am *c-led* to preach. Woe to me
2Co 5:14 For Christ's love *c-s* us,

compete, -s

Jer 12:5 how can you *c* with horses?
1Co 9:25 Everyone who *c-s* in the games
2Ti 2:5 if anyone *c-s* as an athlete,

competent, -nce

Ro 15:14 *c* to instruct one another
1Co 6:2 are you not *c* to judge trivial
2Co 3:5 but our *c-nce* comes from God
3:6 *c* as ministers of a new covenant—

complacent

Am 6:1 Woe to you who are *c* in Zion,

complain, -ing, -ed, -t

Job 9:27 'I will forget my *c-t*,
Ps 142:2 I pour out my *c-t* before him;
La 3:39 *c* when punished for his sins
Ac 6:1 the Grecian Jews among them *c-ed*
18:14 a *c-t* about some misdemeanour
Php 2:14 Do everything without *c-ing*

complete

Jn 15:11 that your joy may be *c*
Ac 20:24 finish the race and *c* the task
Php 2:2 make my joy *c*
1Jn 1:4 We write this to make our joy *c*
2:5 God's love is truly made *c* in him.

compulsion

1Co 7:37 who is under no *c* but has control
2Co 9:7 *c*, for God loves a cheerful giver

conceal, -s, -ed

Pr 10:18 who *c-s* his hatred has lying lips,
25:2 It is the glory of God to *c*
28:13 who *c-s* his sins does not prosper,
Jer 16:17 nor is their sin *c-ed* from my eyes
Mt 10:26 There is nothing *c-ed* that will not

conceit, -ed
Ro 12:16 low position. Do not be *c-ed*
2Co 12:7 To keep me from becoming *c-ed*
Gal 5:26 Let us not become *c-ed*,
Php 2:3 selfish ambition or vain *c*,
1Ti 3:6 he may become *c-ed* and fall

conceive, -d
1Sa 1:20 in the course of time Hannah *c-d*
Ps 51:5 from the time my mother *c-d* me
Mt 1:20 *c-d* in her is from the Holy Spirit
Lk 2:21 given him before he had been *c-d*
1Co 2:9 no mind has *c-d* what God
Jas 1:15 after desire has *c-d*,

concern, -ed
Ge 39:8 "my master does not *c* himself with
Ex 3:7 I am *c-ed* about their suffering
Jnh 4:11 Should I not be *c-ed* about
1Co 7:32 I would like you to be free from *c*.
2Co 11:28 of my *c* for all the churches

concubine, -s
Jdg 19:24 my virgin daughter, and his *c*.
20:6 I took my *c*, cut her into pieces
2Sa 16:21 "Lie with your father's *c-s*
1Ki 11:3 three hundred *c-s*, and his wives

condemn, -s, -ing, -ed, -ation
Pr 17:15 Acquitting the guilty and *c-ing*
Isa 50:9 Who is he who will *c* me?
Mt 12:41 with this generation and *c* it;
Jn 3:17 Son into the world to *c* the world,
3:18 believes in him is not *c-ed*,
5:24 life and will not be *c-ed*;
5:29 done evil will rise to be *c-ed*
Ro 3:7 why am I still *c-ed* as a sinner?
5:16 one sin and brought *c-ation*,
8:1 there is now no *c-ation* for those
8:34 Who is he that *c-s*?
14:22 *c* himself by what he approves
Gal 1:8 let him be eternally *c-ed*
1Jn 3:20 whenever our hearts *c* us.

confess, -es, -ing
Ps 32:5 "I will *c* my transgressions
Pr 28:13 whoever *c-es* and renounces them
Mt 3:6 *C-ing* their sins,
Ro 10:10 mouth that you *c* and are saved
14:11 every tongue will *c* to God.'
Php 2:11 *c* that Jesus Christ is Lord,
Jas 5:16 *c* your sins to each other
1Jn 1:9 If we *c* our sins, he is faithful

confident, -nce
Ps 27:13 I am still *c* of this:
Pr 11:13 A gossip betrays a *c-nce*,
Lk 18:9 *c* of their own righteousness
2Co 5:6 Therefore we are always *c*
10:7 *c* that he belongs to Christ,
Php 3:3 who put no *c-nce* in the flesh
Heb 4:16 throne of grace with *c-nce*,
10:19 *c-nce* to enter the Most Holy
1Jn 3:21 we have *c-nce* before God

confirm, -s, -ed
Ge 17:2 I will *c* my covenant
Dt 4:31 which he *c-ed* to them by oath
Ro 9:1 not lying, my conscience *c-s* it
1Co 1:6 about Christ was *c-ed* in you
Heb 2:3 *c-ed* to us by those who heard him

conflict, -s
2Co 7:5 *c-s* on the outside, fears within
Gal 5:17 They are in *c* with each other,

conform, -s, -ed, -ity
Ro 8:29 he also predestined to be *c-ed*
12:2 Do not *c* any longer
Eph 1:11 who works out everything in *c-ity*
1Ti 1:11 *c-s* to the glorious gospel
1Pe 1:14 do not *c* to the evil desires

congregation, -s
Ps 22:22 in the *c* I will praise you
68:26 Praise God in the great *c*;
1Co 14:33 As in all the *c-s* of the saints
Heb 2:12 presence of the *c* I will sing

conqueror, -s
Ro 8:37 we are more than *c-s*

conscience, -s

Ac 24:16 always to keep my *c* clear
Ro 2:15 their *c-s* also bearing witness,
9:1 I am not lying, my *c* confirms it
1Co 4:4 My *c* is clear, but that does not
10:25 without raising questions of *c*
1Ti 1:19 faith and a good *c*.
4:2 whose *c-s* have been seared
2Ti 1:3 forefathers did, with a clear *c*,
Heb 9:14 cleanse our *c-s* from acts that
10:22 to cleanse us from a guilty *c*
13:18 sure that we have a clear *c*
1Pe 3:16 keeping a clear *c*,
3:21 a good *c* towards God.

conscious

Ro 3:20 through the law we become *c* of sin
1Pe 2:19 suffering because he is *c* of God

consecrate, -d

Ex 13:2 "*C* to me every firstborn male.
Lev 11:44 *c* yourselves and be holy, because
Jos 3:5 "*C* yourselves, for tomorrow
Mt 12:4 his companions ate the *c-d* bread-
Lk 2:23 "Every firstborn male is to be *c-d*
1Ti 4:5 it is *c-d* by the word of God
Heb 9:2 the table and the *c-d* bread;

consent, -ed

Job 39:9 "Will the wild ox *c* to serve you?
Hos 8:4 They set up kings without my *c*;
Mt 3:15 all righteousness." Then John *c-ed*
Lk 23:51 had not *c-ed* to their decision
1Co 7:5 by mutual *c* and for a time,

consider, -ed

1Sa 16:7 'Do not *c* his appearance or
Job 1:8 "Have you *c-ed* my servant Job?
Ps 8:3 When I *c* your heavens,
Lk 12:27 "*C* how the lilies grow.
Ac 20:24 I *c* my life worth nothing to me,
Php 2:3 in humility *c* others better
2:6 did not *c* equality with God
3:7 *c* loss for the sake of Christ
1Ti 1:12 he *c-ed* me faithful, appointing me
Heb 10:24 *c* how we may spur one another on
12:3 *C* him who endured such
Jas 1:2 *C* it pure joy, my brothers,

considerate

Tit 3:2 to be peaceable and *c*,
Jas 3:17 then peace-loving, *c*, submissive,
1Pe 2:18 to those who are good and *c*,
3:7 Husbands, in the same way be *c*

conspire, -acy

Ps 2:1 Why do the nations *c*
Ac 4:27 *c* against your holy servant Jesus,
23:12 the Jews formed a *c-acy* and bound

constant, -ly

Pr 19:13 quarrelsome wife is like a *c*
Ro 1:9 witness how *c-ly* I remember you
2Th 1:11 we *c-ly* pray for you,
Heb 5:14 by *c* use have trained themselves

consult, -s, -ed

Dt 18:11 or who *c-s* the dead
2Ki 1:6 sending men to *c* Baal-Zebub,
1Ch 10:13 even *c-ed* a medium for guidance
Isa 40:14 Whom did the LORD *c* to enlighten
Gal 1:16 the Gentiles, I did not *c* any man,

consume, -s, -ing, -d

Dt 4:24 God is a *c-ing* fire, a jealous God.
Ps 18:8 *c-ing* fire came from his mouth,
69:9 zeal for your house *c-s* me,
119:20 *c-d* with longing for your laws
Isa 30:27 his tongue is a *c-ing* fire
Jn 2:17 "Zeal for your house will *c* me.
Heb 12:29 for our "God is a *c-ing* fire.

contain, -ing

1Ki 8:27 highest heaven, cannot *c* you.
Jer 36:27 *c-ing* the words that Baruch

2Pe 3:16 *c* some things that are hard

contempt

Da 12:2 others to shame and everlasting *c*
Mal 1:6 who show *c* for my name.
Ro 2:4 *c* for the riches of his kindness,
1Th 5:20 do not treat prophecies with *c*

contend, -ing, -ed

Ge 6:3 "My Spirit will not *c* with man
Php 1:27 *c-ing* as one man for the faith
4:3 help these women who have *c-ed*
Jude :3 urge you to *c* for the faith

content, -ment

Pr 13:25 righteous eat to their hearts' *c*,
Lk 3:14 be *c* with your pay.
Php 4:11 I have learned to be *c* whatever
4:12 learned the secret of being *c*
1Ti 6:6 godliness with *c-ment* is great gain
6:8 clothing, we will be *c* with that
Heb 13:5 be *c* with what you have,

continue, -s, -d

Ps 78:17 But they *c-d* to sin against him,
119:90 Your faithfulness *c-s* through all
2Co 10:15 as your faith *c-s* to grow,
Gal 2:10 we should *c* to remember the poor,
Php 2:12 *c* to work out your salvation
Col 1:23 if you *c* in your faith,
2:6 Jesus as Lord, *c* to live in him
2Ti 3:14 *c* in what you have learned
1Jn 3:6 No-one who *c-s* to sin
Rev 22:11 let him who is holy *c* to be holy.

contribute, -ing, -ion

Lev 7:14 a *c-ion* to the LORD;
Ro 12:8 *c-ing* to the needs of others,
15:26 to make a *c-ion* for the poor

contrite

Ps 51:17 a broken and *c* heart, O God,
Isa 57:15 *c* and lowly in spirit,
66:2 he who is humble and *c* in spirit,

control

1Co 7:9 *c* themselves, they should marry,
14:32 subject to the *c* of prophets
Php 3:21 bring everything under his *c*,
1Jn 5:19 under the *c* of the evil one

controversies

Ac 26:3 all the Jewish customs and *c*.
1Ti 1:4 promote *c* rather than God's work—
6:4 an unhealthy interest in *c*
Tit 3:9 avoid foolish *c* and genealogies

conversation

Col 4:6 Let your *c* be always full of grace

convert, -s, -ed

Mt 23:15 land and sea to win a single *c*,
Ac 13:43 Jews and devout *c-s* to Judaism
15:3 how the Gentiles had been *c-ed*.
Ro 16:5 who was the first *c* to Christ
1Co 16:15 the first *c-s* in Achaia,
1Ti 3:6 He must not be a recent *c*,

convict, -ion

Dt 19:15 One witness is not enough to *c*
Pr 24:25 with those who *c* the guilty,
Jn 16:8 he will *c* the world of guilt
1Th 1:5 Holy Spirit and with deep *c-ion*.

convince, -d

Lk 16:31 *c-d* even if someone rises
Ro 8:38 *c-d* that neither death nor life,
1Co 14:24 prophesying, he will be *c-d* by all
2Co 5:14 we are *c-d* that one died for all,
Php 1:25 *C-d* of this, I know that
2Ti 1:12 I have believed, and am *c-d*

convulsion

Mk 9:20 threw the boy into a *c*.

copy

Dt 17:18 on a scroll a *c* of this law,
2Ch 23:11 *c* of the covenant and proclaimed
Heb 8:5 *c* and shadow of what is in heaven.
9:24 that was only a *c* of the true one;

Corban

Mk 7:11 *C* (that is, a gift devoted to God)

cord, -s

Job 38:31 Can you loose the *c-s* of Orion
Ps 116:3 The *c-s* of death entangled me,
Ecc 4:12 A *c* of three strands is not quickly
Isa 54:2 lengthen your *c-s*, strengthen
Jn 2:15 So he made a whip out of *c-s*,

Corinth

Ac 18:1 Paul left Athens and went to *C*
1Co 1:2 To the church of God in *C*,
2Co 1:1 To the church of God in *C*,

Cornelius

God-fearing Roman centurion stationed at Caesarea (Ac 10:1–2). Sent for Peter (Ac 10:1–8,19–33); heard gospel, received Holy Spirit, baptised (Ac 10:34–48); first Gentile convert.

cornerstone

Job 38:6 or who laid its *c*
Isa 28:16 a tested stone, a precious *c*
Eph 2:20 Jesus himself as the chief *c*
1Pe 2:6 a chosen and precious *c*,

correct, -ing, -ion

Job 40:2 contends with the Almighty *c* him?
Pr 10:17 whoever ignores *c-ion* leads others
Jer 10:24 *C* me, LORD, but only with
2Ti 3:16 for teaching, rebuking, *c-ing*
4:2 out of season; *c*, rebuke and

corrupt, -s, -ed, -ion

Ge 6:11 Now the earth was *c* in God's sight
Ac 2:40 "Save yourselves from this *c*
1Co 15:33 "Bad company *c-s* good character.
Eph 4:22 your old self, which is being *c-ed*
Jas 3:6 It *c-s* the whole person,
2Pe 1:4 escape the *c-ion* in the world

cost

2Sa 24:24 burnt offerings that *c* me nothing."
Pr 4:7 get wisdom. Though it *c* all
7:23 knowing it will *c* him his life
Isa 55:1 milk without money and without *c*
Lk 14:28 first sit down and estimate the *c*
Rev 21:6 drink without *c* from the spring

council, -s

Ps 89:7 In the *c* of the holy ones God
Jer 23:18 which of them has stood in the *c*
Mt 10:17 hand you over to the local *c-s*
Lk 23:50 named Joseph, a member of the *C*,
Jn 3:1 a member of the Jewish ruling *c*

counsel, -lor

Isa 9:6 be called Wonderful *C-lor*,
Jn 14:16 another *C-lor* to be with you
15:26 *C-lor* comes, whom I will send
Rev 3:18 *c* you to buy from me gold refined

count, -s, -ing, -ed

Ps 32:2 whose sin the LORD does not *c*
Ac 5:41 been *c-ed* worthy of suffering
Ro 4:8 whose sin the Lord will never *c*
6:11 *c* yourselves dead to sin but alive
1Co 7:19 Keeping God's commands is what *c-s*
2Co 5:19 not *c-ing* men's sins against them.
Gal 5:6 The only thing that *c-s* is faith
2Th 1:5 will be *c-ed* worthy of the kingdom

country, -men

Ge 12:1 "Leave your *c*, your people
15:13 strangers in a *c* not their own,
Pr 29:4 a king gives a *c* stability,
Mt 2:12 returned to their *c* by another
Lk 15:13 a distant *c* and there squandered
Jn 4:44 has no honour in his own *c*.
2Co 11:26 in danger from my own *c-men*,
1Th 2:14 You suffered from your own *c-men*

Heb 11:16 longing for a better *c*—

courage, -ous

Dt 31:23 "Be strong and *c-ous*,
Jos 1:9 commanded you? Be strong and *c-ous*.
Mt 14:27 "Take *c*! It is I.
Ac 4:13 When they saw the *c* of Peter and
23:11 "Take *c*! As you have testified
1Co 16:13 be men of *c*; be strong

court, -s

Ps 84:2 faints, for the *c-s* of the LORD;
84:10 Better is one day in your *c-s*
100:4 and his *c-s* with praise;
Am 5:15 maintain justice in the *c-s*.
Mt 5:25 adversary who is taking you to *c*.
26:55 Every day I sat in the temple *c-s*
Lk 2:46 they found him in the temple *c-s*,
Jn 2:14 *c-s* he found men selling cattle,
Ac 3:2 those going into the temple *c-s*
Jas 2:6 ones who are dragging you into *c*

covenant, -s

Ge 6:18 I will establish my *c* with you,
9:12 "This is the sign of the *c*
17:7 my *c* as an everlasting covenant
Ex 2:24 he remembered his *c* with Abraham,
Dt 4:13 his *c*, the Ten Commandments,
Job 31:1 "I made a *c* with my eyes
Jer 31:31 I will make a new *c* with the house
Mal 2:14 the wife of your marriage *c*
Mk 14:24 "This is my blood of the *c*,
Ro 9:4 theirs the divine glory, the *c-s*,
1Co 11:25 the new *c* in my blood;
2Co 3:6 ministers of a new *c*—
3:14 when the old *c* is read.
Gal 4:24 the women represent two *c-s*.
Eph 2:12 foreigners to the *c-s* of
Heb 7:22 the guarantee of a better *c*
9:18 first *c* was not put into effect
12:24 Jesus the mediator of a new *c*,

cover, -s, -ing, -ings, -ed, -up

Ge 3:7 made *c-ings* for themselves
Ex 25:17 "Make an atonement *c* of pure gold
33:22 in a cleft in the rock and *c* you
40:34 the cloud *c-ed* the Tent of Meeting,
Ps 32:1 whose sins are *c-ed*
Isa 6:2 two wings they *c-ed* their faces,
Lk 23:30 and to the hills "*C* us!"
Ro 4:7 whose sins are *c-ed*
1Co 11:15 hair is given to her as a *c-ing*
Jas 5:20 *c* over a multitude of sins
1Pe 2:16 do not use your freedom as a *c-up*
4:8 love *c-s* over a multitude of sins

covet, -ing, -ed

Ex 20:17 not *c* your neighbour's house.
Dt 5:21 not *c* your neighbour's wife.
Ac 20:33 not *c-ed* anyone's silver or gold
Ro 7:7 not have known what *c-ing* really
13:9 "Do not *c*," and whatever other
Jas 4:2 kill and *c*, but you cannot have

cowardly

Rev 21:8 the *c*, the unbelieving, the vile,

crafty, -iness

Ge 3:1 the serpent was more *c* than any
Job 5:13 catches the wise in their *c-iness*,
1Co 3:19 catches the wise in their *c-iness*"
Eph 4:14 *c-iness* of men in their deceitful

crave, -s, -ings, -d

Nu 11:34 the people who had *c-d* other food
Pr 13:4 The sluggard *c-s* and gets nothing,
Eph 2:3 the *c-ings* of our sinful nature
1Pe 2:2 *c* pure spiritual milk,

crawl

Ge 3:14 You will *c* on your belly
Mic 7:17 creatures that *c* on the ground.

create, -d

Ge 1:27 God *c-d* man in his own image,
Ps 51:10 *C* in me a pure heart, O God,
Isa 40:26 the heavens: Who *c-d* all these?

Mk 13:19 when God *c-d* the world,
Ro 1:25 worshipped and served *c-d* things
Eph 2:10 God's workmanship, *c-d* in Christ
Col 1:16 by him all things were *c-d*:
Rev 4:11 *c-d* all things, and by your will

creation
Mt 13:35 hidden since the *c* of the world.
Ro 1:20 since the *c* of the world God's
8:19 The *c* waits in eager expectation
8:39 all *c*, will be able to separate us
2Co 5:17 in Christ, he is a new *c*;
Gal 6:15 what counts is a new *c*
Eph 1:4 he chose us in him before the *c*
Col 1:15 the firstborn over all *c*
Heb 4:13 Nothing in all *c* is hidden
1Pe 1:20 He was chosen before the *c*
Rev 13:8 slain from the *c* of the world

Creator
Ge 14:19 Most High, *C* of heaven and earth
Ecc 12:1 *C* in the days of your youth,
Isa 40:28 the *C* of the ends of the earth.
Ro 1:25 created things rather than the *C*—
Col 3:10 knowledge in the image of its *C*

creature, -s
Ge 1:20 Let the water teem with living *c-s*
6:19 ark two of all living *c-s*,
Ps 104:24 the earth is full of your *c-s*
145:21 Let every *c* praise his holy name
Eze 1:13 The appearance of the living *c-s*
Rev 4:6 were four living *c-s*,

credit, -ed
Ge 15:6 he *c-ed* it to him as righteousness
Ro 4:3 *c-ed* to him as righteousness.
1Pe 2:20 your *c* if you receive a beating

Cretans
Tit 1:12 "*C* are always liars, evil brutes,

crime
Mt 27:23 "Why? What *c* has he committed?"
Ac 28:18 guilty of any *c* deserving death

criminal, -s
Lk 23:32 Two other men, both *c-s*, were also
Jn 18:30 "If he were not a *c*," they replied,
1Pe 4:15 thief or any other kind of *c*,

crimson
Isa 1:18 red as *c*, they shall be like wool

cripple, -d
2Sa 4:4 *c-d*. His name was Mephibosheth.
Mal 1:13 you bring injured, *c-d* or diseased
Mt 15:30 the blind, the *c-d*, the mute
18:8 to enter life maimed or *c-d*
Lk 13:11 *c-d* by a spirit for eighteen years.
Ac 3:2 Now a man *c-d* from birth

crooked
Dt 32:5 a warped and *c* generation
Ecc 7:13 straighten what he has made *c*
Lk 3:5 The *c* roads shall become straight,
Php 2:15 in a *c* and depraved generation,

crop, -s
Pr 10:5 He who gathers *c-s* in summer
Mt 13:8 produced a *c*—a hundred,
21:41 share of the *c* at harvest time.
2Ti 2:6 first to receive a share of the *c-s*
Heb 6:7 produces a *c* useful to those

cross
Mt 10:38 anyone who does not take his *c*
27:40 Come down from the *c*, if
Jn 19:17 Carrying his own *c*, he went out
Ac 2:23 by nailing him to the *c*
1Co 1:18 message of the *c* is foolishness
Gal 6:12 persecuted for the *c* of Christ
6:14 May I never boast except in the *c*
Php 2:8 to death—even death on a *c*
Col 1:20 his blood, shed on the *c*
Heb 12:2 joy set before him endured the *c*,

crouch, -ing

Ge 4:7 sin is *c-ing* at your door;

crow, -s, -ed

Mt 26:34 before the cock *c-s*,
26:74 Immediately a cock *c-ed*

crowd, -s

Ex 23:2 not follow the *c* in doing wrong.
Mt 11:7 began to speak to the *c* about John:
13:34 these things to the *c* in parables;
Ac 13:45 When the Jews saw the *c-s*,

crown, -ed

Pr 16:31 Grey hair is a *c* of splendour;
Mt 27:29 twisted together a *c* of thorns
2Ti 2:5 he does not receive the victor's *c*
2Ti 4:8 for me the *c* of righteousness,
Heb 2:7 you *c-ed* him with glory and honour
1Pe 5:4 you will receive the *c* of glory
Rev 2:10 I will give you the *c* of life

crucify, -ied

Mt 20:19 mocked and flogged and *c-ied*.
27:26 and handed him over to be *c-ied*
28:5 Jesus, who was *c-ied*
Jn 19:15 Take him away! *C* him!"
Ro 6:6 our old self was *c-ied* with him
1Co 1:23 we preach Christ *c-ied*:
2:2 except Jesus Christ and him *c-ied*
2:8 not have *c-ied* the Lord of glory
Gal 2:20 I have been *c-ied* with Christ
Rev 11:8 where also their Lord was *c-ied*

crumbs

Mt 15:27 even the dogs eat the *c* that fall

crush, -ed

Ge 3:15 he will *c* your head,
Ps 34:18 saves those who are *c-ed* in spirit
Isa 53:5 he was *c-ed* for our iniquities;
53:10 it was the LORD's will to *c* him
Ro 16:20 The God of peace will soon *c* Satan

cry, -ies, -ing, -ied

Ex 2:23 in their slavery and *c-ied* out,
Ps 22:2 O my God, I *c* out by day,
84:2 my flesh *c* out for the living God
107:13 *c-ied* to the LORD in their trouble,
130:1 Out of the depths I *c* to you,
Pr 21:13 shuts his ears to the *c* of the poor
Isa 6:5 "Woe to me!" I *c-ied*.
Mt 12:19 He will not quarrel or *c* out;
27:50 when Jesus had *c-ied* out again
Lk 19:40 the stones will *c* out.
Jn 20:11 Mary stood outside the tomb *c-ing*.
Ro 8:15 And by him we *c*, "Abba, Father.
Heb 5:7 with loud *c-ies* and tears
Jas 5:4 The *c-ies* of the harvesters have
Rev 21:4 no more death or mourning or *c-ing*

cup

Ps 23:5 my *c* overflows
Pr 23:31 when it sparkles in the *c*,
Mt 10:42 gives even a *c* of cold water
23:25 clean the outside of the *c* and dish
26:39 if it is possible, may this *c*
1Co 11:25 after supper he took the *c*,
Rev 14:10 the *c* of his wrath.

cupbearer

Ge 40:1 the *c* and the baker of the king
Ne 1:11 I was *c* to the king

cure, -d

2Ki 5:6 that you may *c* him of his leprosy.
Jer 3:22 I will *c* you of backsliding."
17:9 above all things and beyond *c*.
Mt 8:3 he was *c-d* of his leprosy
11:5 those who have leprosy are *c-d*,
Lk 9:1 all demons and to *c* diseases

curse, -ing, -d

Ge 3:14 *C-d* are you above all the livestock
3:17 "*C-d* is the ground because of you;
Ex 22:28 Do not blaspheme God or *c* the ruler

Job 2:9	*C* God and die!
Mt 25:41	'Depart from me, you who are *c-d*,
Lk 6:28	bless those who *c* you,
Ro 9:3	wish that I myself were *c-d*
12:14	bless and do not *c*
1Co 12:3	Spirit of God says, "Jesus be *c-d*
Gal 3:10	observing the law are under a *c*,
Jas 3:10	same mouth come praise and *c-ing*.

curtain

Ex 26:33	The *c* will separate the Holy Place
Mt 27:51	the *c* of the temple was torn in two
Heb 10:20	opened for us through the *c*,

custom, -s

Mt 27:15	*c* at the Feast to release
Lk 4:16	into the synagogue, as was his *c*.
Jn 18:39	your *c* for me to release to you
Ac 15:1	according to the *c* taught by Moses,
Gal 2:14	Gentiles to follow Jewish *c-s*

cut, -ting

1Sa 24:11	I *c* off the corner of your robe
1Ki 3:25	"*C* the living child in two
Isa 53:8	*c* off from the land of the living;
Da 9:26	the Anointed One will be *c* off
Mt 3:10	*c* down and thrown into the fire
5:30	*c* it off and throw it away.
24:22	If those days had not been *c* short,
Lk 12:46	*c* him to pieces and assign
13:9	If not, then *c* it down.'
Jn 18:10	*c-ting* off his right ear.
Ac 3:23	*c* off from among his people.
18:18	he had his hair *c* off at Cenchrea
Ro 9:3	I myself were cursed and *c* off
11:22	you also will be *c* off
1Co 11:6	she should have her hair *c* off;
Gal 5:7	Who *c* in on you and kept you

cymbal, -s

Ps 150:5	praise him with the clash of *c-s*,
1Co 13:1	a resounding gong or a clanging *c*

Cyrus

King of Persia. Issued edict to allow exiles to return to rebuild Jerusalem temple (2Ch 36:22–23; Ezr 1:1–4; 5:13; 6:3); gave back articles taken from temple (Ezr 1:7–11; 5:14–15; 6:5) and provided funds for building work (Ezr 3:7; 6:4). Place in God's purpose foretold by Isaiah (Isa 44:28–45:7,13).

D

Damascus

Ac 9:3	As he neared *D* on his journey,

Dan

1. Son of Jacob by Bilhah (Ge 30:4–6; 35:25); blessed by Jacob (Ge 49:16–17). **2.** Tribe descended from Dan. Blessed by Moses (Dt 33:22). Included in census (Nu 1:38–39); 26:42–43). Apportioned land (Jos 19:40–48; Eze 48:1); unable to take full possession (Jdg 1:34), most of tribe migrated northwards to Laish (Jdg 18). Tribe of Samson (Jdg 13).

dance, -ing, -d

2Sa 6:16	leaping and *d-ing* before the LORD,
Ps 30:11	You turned my wailing into *d-ing*;
Ecc 3:4	a time to mourn and a time to *d*
Mt 11:17	flute for you, and you did not *d*;
14:6	daughter of Herodias *d-d* for them

danger

Pr 27:12	The prudent see *d* and take refuge,
Mt 5:22	who says, 'You fool!' will be in *d*
Lk 8:23	swamped, and they were in great *d*
Ro 8:35	famine or nakedness or *d* or sword
2Co 11:26	I have been in *d* from rivers,

Daniel

1. Son of David and Abigail (1Ch 3:1). **2.** Ancient figure regarded as an outstanding example of righteousness and wisdom

(Eze 14:14,20; 28:3). **3.** Hebrew of noble descent among those taken as captives to Babylon to be trained in the king's service (Da 1:3–6); renamed Belteshazzar (Da 1:7); refused to eat unclean food (Da 1:8–16). Possessed great understanding (Da 1:17,20); interpreted Nebuchadnezzar's dreams (Da 2:24–45; 4:19–27), writing on wall (Da 5:13–29). Held government posts under Nebuchadnezzar (Da 2:48), Belshazzar (Da 5:29), Darius (Da 6:1–2). Refused to obey king's decree; thrown into lions' den (Da 6). Visions predicting coming of Messianic kingdom (Da 7–12).

Darius

1. Mede, who became ruler of Babylon (Da 5:31; 9:1). Appointed Daniel as leading official (Da 6:2,28). Possibly to be identified with Cyrus. **2.** Darius the Great, king of Persia (Hag 1:1; Zec 1:1); revived Cyrus' edict allowing work on rebuilding temple to continue (Ezr 4:24–6:15). **3.** Darius II, king of Persia (Ne 12:22).

dark, -ness

Ge 1:2	*d-ness* was over the surface
1:4	separated the light from the *d-ness*
Ex 20:21	the thick *d-ness* where God was
2Sa 22:29	the LORD turns my *d-ness* into light
Ps 139:12	the *d-ness* will not be dark to you
SS 1:5	*D* am I, yet lovely, O daughters
Isa 9:2	people walking in *d-ness* have seen
Joel 2:31	The sun will be turned to *d-ness*
Mt 4:16	people living in *d-ness* have seen
8:12	thrown outside, into the *d-ness*,
27:45	*d-ness* came over all the land
Jn 1:5	The light shines in the *d-ness*,
3:19	men loved *d-ness* instead of light
Eph 5:8	For you were once *d-ness*, but now
Col 1:13	from the dominion of *d-ness*
1Jn 1:5	in him there is no *d-ness* at all
2:11	hates his brother is in the *d-ness*

darken, -s

Job 38:2	"Who is this that *d-s* my counsel

daughter, -s

Ge 6:2	that the *d-s* of men were beautiful,
19:30	Lot and his two *d-s* left Zoar
Ex 2:10	she took him to Pharaoh's *d*
Ps 45:10	Listen, O *d*, consider and give ear
137:8	*D* of Babylon, doomed to destruction
SS 1:5	O *d-s* of Jerusalem,
Isa 62:11	"Say to the *D* of Zion, 'See,
Joel 2:28	Your sons and *d-s* will prophesy,
Zec 9:9	Rejoice greatly, O *D* of Zion!
Mt 21:5	"Say to the *D* of Zion, 'See,
Lk 13:16	this woman, a *d* of Abraham,
23:28	"*D-s* of Jerusalem, do not weep
Ac 2:17	Your sons and *d-s* will prophesy,
21:9	four unmarried *d-s* who prophesied
2Co 6:18	and you will be my sons and *d-s*,

David

Israel's second and greatest king; ancestor of Jesus (Mt 1:1; Ro 1:3; Rev 22:16); type of promised Messiah (Isa 11:1; Eze 34:23–24; 37:24–25).

Singer of psalms and songs (2Sa 23:1; Am 6:5). Son of Jesse of Bethlehem (Ru 4:17; 1Sa 17:12). Anointed king by Samuel (1Sa 16:1–13). Entered Saul's service as musician (1Sa 16:14–23). Killed Goliath (1Sa 17:32–54). Friendship with Jonathan (1Sa 18:1–4; 19:1–7; 20; 23:16–18; 2Sa 1:25–26). Fled because of Saul's hostility (1Sa 19; 21–23). Spared Saul's life (1Sa 24; 26). Among the Philistines (1Sa 21:10–15; 27–29). Lament for Saul and Jonathan (2Sa 1).

Anointed king of Judah at Hebron (2Sa 2:1–7). War with Saul's family (2Sa 2–4). United northern and southern tribes as king over all Israel (2Sa 5:1–4; 1Ch 11:1–3; 12:38–40). Captured Jerusalem from Jebusites (2Sa 5:6–10; 1Ch 11:4–9); installed ark there (2Sa 6; 1Ch 15–16). Promised lasting dynasty by God (2Sa 7; 1Ch 17; Ps 89; 132). Established empire: defeated Philistines (2Sa 5:17–25;

1Ch 14:8–17; 2Sa 21:15–22; 1Ch 20:4–8), Moabites, Arameans, Edomites (2Sa 8:1–14; 1Ch 18:1–13), Ammonites (2Sa 10; 1Ch 19). Committed adultery with Bathsheba; murdered Uriah (2Sa 11); rebuked by Nathan (2Sa 12:1–14); repented (Ps 51). Married Bathsheba and other wives (1Sa 18:27; 25:39–43; 2Sa 5:13; 11:27); father of Solomon, Absalom, Adonijah, etc. (2Sa 3:2–5; 1Ch 3:1–9). Absalom's revolt (2Sa 15–18). Preparations for temple (1Ch 22; 28–29). Appointment of Solomon as successor (1Ki 1:28–48). Death (1Ki 2:10–12; 1Ch 29:26–28).

dawn, -ed

Ps 57:8 harp and lyre! I will awaken the *d*
139:9 If I rise on the wings of the *d*,
Isa 9:2 shadow of death a light has *d-ed*
Mt 4:16 shadow of death a light has *d-ed*.

day, -s

Ge 1:5 God called the light "*d*",
1:14 to separate the *d* from the night,
2:3 And God blessed the seventh *d*
Ex 16:26 Six *d-s* you are to gather it,
16:30 the people rested on the seventh *d*
20:8 "Remember the Sabbath *d*
Nu 14:14 in a pillar of cloud by *d*
Dt 17:19 to read it all the *d-s* of his life
32:7 Remember the *d-s* of old;
33:25 your strength will equal your *d-s*
Jos 1:8 meditate on it *d* and night,
5:12 The manna stopped the *d* after
1Ki 17:14 until the *d* the LORD gives rain
19:8 forty *d-s* and forty nights
2Ki 7:9 This is a *d* of good news
1Ch 29:15 Our *d-s* on earth are like a shadow
2Ch 15:5 In those *d-s* it was not safe
Ne 8:17 From the *d-s* of Joshua son of Nun
Est 3:4 *D* after *d* they spoke to him
Job 3:1 cursed the *d* of his birth
8:9 our *d-s* on earth are but a shadow
14:1 "Man born of woman is of few *d-s*
Ps 21:4 length of *d-s*, for ever and ever
23:6 all the *d-s* of my life,
46:5 God will help her at break of *d*
84:10 Better is one *d* in your courts
90:4 in your sight are like a *d*
90:9 All our *d-s* pass away
90:10 length of our *d-s* is seventy years—
90:12 Teach us to number our *d-s* aright,
103:15 As for man, his *d-s* are like grass,
118:24 This is the *d* the LORD has made;
119:97 I meditate on it all *d* long
119:164 Seven times a *d* I praise you
121:6 the sun will not harm you by *d*,
139:12 the night will shine like the *d*,
144:4 his *d-s* are like a fleeting shadow
Pr 27:1 you do not know what a *d* may bring
Ecc 9:9 the *d-s* of this meaningless life
12:1 Creator in the *d-s* of your youth,
Isa 13:9 See, the *d* of the LORD is coming—
38:20 all the *d-s* of our lives
43:13 Yes, and from ancient *d-s* I am he.
49:8 in the *d* of salvation I will help
Jer 46:10 But that *d* belongs to the Lord,
Da 7:9 the Ancient of *D-s* took his seat.
7:22 until the Ancient of *D-s* came
Joel 2:29 pour out my Spirit in those *d-s*
2:31 great and dreadful *d* of the LORD
Ob :15 "The *d* of the LORD is near
Jnh 1:17 three *d-s* and three nights
Zec 14:1 A *d* of the LORD is coming
Mal 4:5 dreadful *d* of the LORD comes
Mt 4:2 for forty *d-s* and forty nights,
6:34 Each *d* has enough trouble
7:22 Many will say to me on that *d*,
24:38 For in the *d-s* before the flood,
27:63 'After three *d-s* I will rise again.
Lk 11:3 Give us each *d* our daily bread
Jn 5:17 always at his work to this very *d*,
6:40 I will raise him up at the last *d*.
9:4 As long as it is *d*,
Ac 2:17 "'In the last *d-s*, God says,
5:42 *D* after *d*, in the temple courts

17:11 examined the Scriptures every *d*
17:17 as in the market-place *d* by *d*
2Co 4:16 we are being renewed *d* by *d*
Eph 4:30 sealed for the *d* of redemption
Php 1:6 until the *d* of Christ Jesus
1Th 5:2 the *d* of the Lord will come like
5:4 so that this *d* should surprise
5:8 But since we belong to the *d*,
2Th 2:2 the *d* of the Lord has already come
2Ti 3:1 terrible times in the last *d-s*
Heb 1:2 these last *d-s* he has spoken to us
7:27 need to offer sacrifices *d* after *d*
2Pe 3:3 in the last *d-s* scoffers will come,
3:8 With the Lord a *d* is like
3:10 *d* of the Lord will come like a
1Jn 4:17 confidence on the *d* of judgment,
Rev 1:10 On the Lord's *D* I was in the Spirit
4:8 *D* and night they never stop saying:
6:17 For the great *d* of their wrath
7:15 serve him *d* and night in his temple
16:14 on the great *d* of God Almighty

deacon, -s
Php 1:1 together with the overseers and *d-s*
1Ti 3:8 *D-s*, likewise, are to be men worthy
3:10 let them serve as *d-s*
3:12 A *d* must be the husband of

dead
Dt 18:11 or spiritist or who consults the *d*
2Sa 9:8 you should notice a *d* dog like me?
Ecc 9:4 dog is better off than a *d* lion
10:1 *d* flies give perfume a bad smell,
Isa 8:19 Why consult the *d* on behalf of
Mt 8:22 and let the *d* bury their own dead.
9:24 The girl is not *d* but asleep."
10:8 Heal the sick, raise the *d*,
11:5 the deaf hear, the *d* are raised,
Mk 12:27 He is not the God of the *d*,
Lk 15:24 this son of mine was *d* and is alive
Jn 20:9 that Jesus had to rise from the *d*.
Ac 10:42 as judge of the living and the *d*
Ro 6:11 count yourselves *d* to sin but alive
8:11 who raised Christ from the *d*
1Co 15:16 For if the *d* are not raised,
15:52 the *d* will be raised imperishable,
Eph 2:1 you were *d* in your transgressions
Col 2:13 When you were *d* in your sins
1Th 4:16 and the *d* in Christ will rise first
Jas 2:26 so faith without deeds is *d*
Rev 14:13 Blessed are the *d* who die
20:13 The sea gave up the *d*

deaf
Lev 19:14 " 'Do not curse the *d*
Ps 39:12 be not *d* to my weeping.
Isa 42:18 "Hear, you *d*; look, you blind,
Mt 11:5 the *d* hear, the dead are raised,

death
Dt 30:19 I have set before you life and *d*,
Ps 23:4 the valley of the shadow of *d*,
44:22 for your sake we face *d* all day
56:13 For you have delivered me from *d*
116:15 is the *d* of his saints
Ecc 7:2 *d* is the destiny of every man;
SS 8:6 for love is as strong as *d*,
Isa 53:12 he poured out his life unto *d*,
Jer 21:8 the way of life and the way of *d*
Eze 18:23 pleasure in the *d* of the wicked?
Hos 13:14 Where, O *d*, are your plagues?
Jn 5:24 he has crossed over from *d* to life
8:51 he will never see *d*."
Ro 4:25 delivered over to *d* for our sins
5:14 *d* reigned from the time of Adam
6:23 For the wages of sin is *d*,
7:24 rescue me from this body of *d*
8:13 put to *d* the misdeeds of the body,
8:36 "For your sake we face *d* all day
1Co 15:21 since *d* came through a man
15:26 The last enemy to be destroyed is *d*

15:55	"Where, O *d*, is your victory?
Php 3:10	becoming like him in his *d*
Col 3:5	Put to *d*, therefore, whatever
2Ti 1:10	Christ Jesus, who has destroyed *d*
Heb 2:14	him who holds the power of *d*
1Jn 3:14	we have passed from *d* to life,
5:16	There is a sin that leads to *d*.
Rev 1:18	And I hold the keys of *d* and Hades
2:10	Be faithful, even to the point of *d*
20:14	Then *d* and Hades were thrown into
21:4	There will be no more *d*

debauchery

Ro 13:13	not in sexual immorality and *d*,
2Co 12:21	impurity, sexual sin and *d*
Gal 5:19	sexual immorality, impurity and *d*
Eph 5:18	drunk on wine, which leads to *d*.

Deborah

1. Prophetess, one of Israel's judges. Appointed Barak to lead Israel against Canaanites (Jdg 4–5). **2.** Rebekah's nurse (Ge 35:8).

debt, -s, -ors

Dt 15:2	the LORD's time for cancelling *d-s*
Mt 6:12	Forgive us our *d-s*,
6:12	as we also have forgiven our *d-ors*
18:32	'I cancelled all that *d* of yours
Lk 7:42	so he cancelled the *d-s* of both.
16:5	each one of his master's *d-ors*.
Ro 13:8	Let no *d* remain outstanding,

decay

Ps 16:10	will you let your Holy One see *d*
Ac 2:27	will you let your Holy One see *d*
13:35	will not let your Holy One see *d*.
Ro 8:21	liberated from its bondage to *d*

deceit, -ful, -fulness

Ps 119:29	Keep me from *d-ful* ways;
Isa 53:9	nor was any *d* in his mouth
Jer 17:9	The heart is *d-ful* above all things
Mk 4:19	*d-fulness* of wealth and the desires
1Pe 2:22	and no *d* was found in his mouth.

deceive, -d

Ge 3:13	The woman said, "The serpent *d-d* me,
Mt 24:5	'I am the Christ,' and will *d* many
Gal 6:7	Do not be *d-d*: God cannot be mocked
Eph 5:6	Let no-one *d* you with empty words,
1Jn 1:8	to be without sin, we *d* ourselves
Rev 20:10	the devil, who *d-d* them, was thrown

deception, -ive

Jer 7:4	Do not trust in *d-ive* words
2Co 4:2	we do not use *d*, nor do we distort
Col 2:8	through hollow and *d-ive* philosophy

declare, -d

1Ch 16:24	*D* his glory among the nations,
Ps 19:1	The heavens *d* the glory of God;
22:22	I will *d* your name to my brothers;
51:15	and my mouth will *d* your praise
96:3	*D* his glory among the nations,
Mk 7:19	Jesus *d-d* all foods "clean".
Ro 1:4	*d-d* with power to be the Son of God
Heb 2:12	"I will *d* your name to my brothers;

decree, -s, -d

Lev 18:26	you must keep my *d-s* and my laws.
Ps 119:8	I will obey your *d-s*;
119:16	I delight in your *d-s*;
119:48	and I meditate on your *d-s*
119:112	My heart is set on keeping your *d-s*
Lk 2:1	Caesar Augustus issued a *d*
22:22	of Man will go as it has been *d-d*,

Ro 1:32 they know God's righteous *d*

dedicate, -d, -ion

Nu 6:12 He must *d* himself to the LORD
2Ch 7:5 the people *d-d* the temple of God
Jn 10:22 the Feast of *D-ion* at Jerusalem.
1Ti 5:11 desires overcome their *d-ion*

deeds

Ps 72:18 who alone does marvellous *d*
75:1 men tell of your wonderful *d*
96:3 his marvellous *d* among all peoples
Mt 5:16 they may see your good *d* and praise
1Ti 6:18 to do good, to be rich in good *d*,
Heb 10:24 another on towards love and good *d*
Jas 2:26 so faith without *d* is dead
Rev 2:19 I know your *d*, your love and faith,

deep, -ly

Ge 1:2 over the surface of the *d*,
Ps 42:7 *D* calls to *d*
Lk 6:48 dug down *d* and laid the foundation
Jn 4:11 to draw with and the well is *d*.
Ro 10:7 "or 'Who will descend into the *d*?'
Eph 3:18 high and *d* is the love of Christ
1Th 1:5 Holy Spirit and with *d* conviction.
1Ti 3:9 the *d* truths of the faith
1Pe 4:8 Above all, love each other *d-ly*,

deer

Ps 18:33 makes my feet like the feet of a *d*;
42:1 As the *d* pants for streams
Isa 35:6 Then will the lame leap like a *d*,

defend, -s, -ing

Dt 10:18 He *d-s* the cause of the fatherless
Ps 82:2 "How long will you *d* the unjust
Pr 31:9 *d* the rights of the poor and needy.
Isa 1:17 *D* the cause of the fatherless,
Php 1:7 *d-ing* and confirming the gospel,

defile, -d

Lev 19:31 spiritists, for you will be *d-d*
Nu 35:34 Do not *d* the land where you live
Ps 74:7 they *d-d* the dwelling-place
Da 1:8 Daniel resolved not to *d* himself
1Co 8:7 their conscience is weak, it is *d-d*
Rev 14:4 who did not *d* themselves with women

defraud

Lev 19:13 Do not *d* your neighbour or rob him.
Mic 2:2 They *d* a man of his home,
Mal 3:5 against those who *d* labourers
Mk 10:19 do not *d*, honour your father

defy, -ied

1Sa 17:36 because he has *d-ied* the armies of
1Ki 13:21 You have *d-ied* the word of the LORD
Jer 50:29 she *d-ied* the LORD, the Holy One
Da 3:28 and *d-ied* the king's command

deity

Col 2:9 in Christ all the fulness of the *D*

delay

Ps 70:5 my deliverer; O LORD, do not *d*
119:60 and not *d* to obey your commands
Hab 2:3 will certainly come and will not *d*
Heb 10:37 will come and will not *d*
Rev 10:6 and said, "There will be no more *d*

delight, -s

Ps 1:2 But his *d* is in the law of the LORD
22:8 deliver him, since he *d-s* in him.
37:4 *D* yourself in the LORD
43:4 to God, my joy and my *d*.
Isa 42:1 my chosen one in whom I *d*;
61:10 I *d* greatly in the LORD;
Zep 3:17 He will take great *d* in you,
Mt 12:18 the one I love, in whom I *d*;

1Co 13:6	Love does not *d* in evil

Delilah

Betrayed Samson (Jdg 16:4–22).

deliver, -ed, -er, -ance

Ex 14:13	the *d-ance* the LORD will bring you
2Sa 22:2	my rock, my fortress and my *d-er*
2Ch 20:17	see the *d-ance* the LORD will give
Ps 3:8	From the LORD comes *d-ance.*
18:2	my rock, my fortress and my *d-er;*
32:7	surround me with songs of *d-ance.*
34:4	he *d-ed* me from all my fears
40:17	You are my help and my *d-er;*
72:12	For he will *d* the needy who cry out
140:7	O Sovereign LORD, my strong *d-er,*
Mt 6:13	but *d* us from the evil one.
Lk 24:7	*d-ed* into the hands of sinful men,
Ro 4:25	*d-ed* over to death for our sins
11:26	"The *d-er* will come from Zion;
2Co 1:10	he will continue to *d* us,

demand, -ed

Lk 6:30	belongs to you, do not *d* it back
12:20	your life will be *d-ed* from you.
12:48	been given much, much will be *d-ed;*
23:24	So Pilate decided to grant their *d*
1Co 1:22	Jews *d* miraculous signs

Demas

Fellow-worker with Paul (Col 4:14; Phm 24), who later deserted him (2Ti 4:10).

Demetrius

1. Christian commended by John (3Jn 12).
2. Silversmith who stirred up a riot against Paul in Ephesus (Ac 19:23–41).

demolish

2Co 10:4	divine power to *d* strongholds
10:5	We *d* arguments and every pretension

demon, -s

Dt 32:17	to *d-s,* which are not God—
Ps 106:37	sons and their daughters to *d-s*
Mt 7:22	and in your name drive out *d-s*
8:31	The *d-s* begged Jesus,
12:27	And if I drive out *d-s* by Beelzebub
Jn 8:49	"I am not possessed by a *d,*"
Ro 8:38	neither angels nor *d-s,*
1Co 10:20	are offered to *d-s,* not to God,
1Ti 4:1	spirits and things taught by *d-s*
Jas 2:19	Good! Even the *d-s* believe that—

demon-possessed

Mt 4:24	those suffering severe pain, the *d,*
8:28	two *d* men coming from the tombs
9:32	a man who was *d* and could not talk
Lk 8:27	he was met by a *d* man from the town
Jn 7:20	"You are *d,*" the crowd answered.
Ac 19:13	Lord Jesus over those who were *d.*

demonstrate, -s, -ion

Ro 3:25	He did this to *d* his justice,
5:8	God *d-s* his own love for us in this
1Co 2:4	with a *d-ion* of the Spirit's power

den

Da 6:16	and threw him into the lions' *d.*
Mt 21:13	you are making it a '*d* of robbers'.

deny, -ies, -ied

Ex 23:6	"Do not *d* justice to your poor
Mt 16:24	he must *d* himself and take up
26:70	But he *d-ied* it before them all.
Lk 22:34	will *d* three times that you know me
1Ti 5:8	he has *d-ied* the faith and is worse
Tit 1:16	but by their actions they *d* him.
1Jn 2:22	who *d-ies* that Jesus is the Christ
Rev 3:8	my word and have not *d-ied* my name

depart, -ed, -ure

1Sa 4:21 “The glory has *d-ed* from Israel
Ps 119:102 I have not *d-ed* from your laws,
Mt 25:41 ‘*D* from me, you who are cursed,
Lk 9:31 They spoke about his *d-ure*,
Php 1:23 I desire to *d* and be with Christ,

deposit

Mt 25:27 you should have put my money on *d*
2Co 1:22 put his Spirit in our hearts as a *d*
5:5 and has given us the Spirit as a *d*,
Eph 1:14 a *d* guaranteeing our inheritance
2Ti 1:14 Guard the good *d* that was entrusted

depraved

Ro 1:28 he gave them over to a *d* mind,
Php 2:15 in a crooked and *d* generation,
2Ti 3:8 oppose the truth—men of *d* minds,

deprive

Dt 24:17 Do not *d* the alien
Am 5:12 you *d* the poor of justice
1Co 7:5 Do not *d* each other

descend, -ing, -ed

Ge 28:12 were ascending and *d-ing* on it
Ex 19:20 The Lord *d-ed* to the top of Mount
Mt 3:16 the Spirit of God *d-ing* like a dove
Eph 4:9 he also *d-ed* to the lower, earthly
Heb 7:14 our Lord *d-ed* from Judah,

desert

Ex 3:18 take a three-day journey into the *d*
16:32 bread I gave you to eat in the *d*
Nu 32:13 wander in the *d* for forty years,
Dt 8:16 He gave you manna to eat in the *d*,
Ps 78:19 “Can God spread a table in the *d*
107:4 Some wandered in *d* wastelands,
107:35 He turned the *d* into pools of water
Isa 32:2 like streams of water in the *d*
40:3 A voice of one calling: “In the *d*
Mt 3:1 Baptist came, preaching in the *D*
3:3 “A voice of one calling in the *d*,
4:1 led by the Spirit into the *d*
Jn 3:14 Moses lifted up the snake in the *d*
1Co 10:5 bodies were scattered over the *d*
Heb 3:8 during the time of testing in the *d*
Rev 12:6 The woman fled into the *d*

deserve, -s, -d

2Sa 12:5 the man who did this *d-s* to die
Ezr 9:13 less than our sins have *d-d*
Ps 103:10 does not treat us as our sins *d*
Mt 8:8 “Lord, I do not *d* to have you come
Lk 23:15 he has done nothing to *d* death
1Co 15:9 not even *d* to be called an apostle,
1Ti 1:15 saying that *d-s* full acceptance:
5:18 “The worker *d-s* his wages.

desire, -s, -d

Ge 3:16 Your *d* will be for your husband,
Ps 20:4 May he give you the *d* of your heart
73:25 earth has nothing I *d* besides you
103:5 satisfies your *d-s* with good things
Pr 19:22 What a man *d-s* is unfailing love;
Hos 6:6 For I *d* mercy, not sacrifice,
Hag 2:7 the *d-d* of all nations will come,
Mt 9:13 learn what this means: ‘I *d* mercy,
Ro 8:5 minds set on what the Spirit *d-s*
1Co 12:31 But eagerly *d* the greater gifts.
Gal 5:16 not gratify the *d-s* of the sinful
Php 1:23 I *d* to depart and be with Christ,
Col 3:5 impurity, lust, evil *d-s* and greed,
2Ti 2:22 Flee the evil *d-s* of youth,
Jas 1:15 *d* has conceived, it gives birth
4:1 your *d-s* that battle within you

1Jn 2:17	The world and its *d-s* pass away,

desolate, -ion

Isa 54:1	are the children of the *d* woman
Jer 7:34	for the land will become *d*
Da 11:31	the abomination that causes *d-ion*
Mt 23:38	Look, your house is left to you *d*
24:15	'the abomination that causes *d-ion*'
Gal 4:27	are the children of the *d* woman

despair, -ed

Isa 61:3	instead of a spirit of *d*.
2Co 1:8	so that we *d-ed* even of life
4:8	perplexed, but not in *d*

despise, -s, -d

Ge 25:34	So Esau *d-d* his birthright
Job 42:6	Therefore I *d* myself and repent
Ps 51:17	O God, you will not *d*
Am 5:21	"I hate, I *d* your religious feasts;
Zec 4:10	"Who *d-s* the day of small things?
Mt 6:24	devoted to the one and *d* the other.
Tit 2:15	Do not let anyone *d* you

destined

Lk 2:34	child is *d* to cause the falling
1Co 2:7	God *d* for our glory before time
Col 2:22	These are all *d* to perish with use,
Heb 9:27	Just as man is *d* to die once,

destiny

Ps 73:17	then I understood their final *d*
Ecc 7:2	death is the *d* of every man;
Isa 65:11	and fill bowls of mixed wine for *D*
Php 3:19	Their *d* is destruction,

destitute

Ps 102:17	will respond to the prayer of the *d*
Pr 31:8	for the rights of all who are *d*
Heb 11:37	*d*, persecuted and ill-treated

destroy, -s, -ing, -ed

Ge 9:11	a flood to *d* the earth.
18:32	"For the sake of ten, I will not *d*
19:29	God *d-ed* the cities of the plain,
Est 9:24	plotted against the Jews to *d* them
Job 19:26	And after my skin has been *d-ed*,
Ps 5:6	You *d* those who tell lies;
Isa 11:9	nor *d* on all my holy mountain,
Jer 51:55	The LORD will *d* Babylon;
Da 2:44	a kingdom that will never be *d-ed*,
Mt 6:19	on earth, where moth and rust *d*,
10:28	One who can *d* both soul and body
Mk 1:24	Have you come to *d* us?
14:58	'I will *d* this man-made temple
Lk 6:9	to do evil, to save life or to *d* it
17:27	the flood came and *d-ed* them all
Jn 2:19	Jesus answered them, "*D* this
Ac 6:14	Jesus of Nazareth will *d* this place
8:3	But Saul began to *d* the church.
Ro 14:15	not by your eating *d* your brother
14:20	Do not *d* the work of God
1Co 3:17	If anyone *d-s* God's temple,
5:5	that the sinful nature may be *d-ed*
6:13	but God will *d* them both.
10:10	and were killed by the *d-ing* angel
15:26	The last enemy to be *d-ed* is death
Gal 1:13	the church of God and tried to *d* it
Eph 2:14	two one and has *d-ed* the barrier,
2Ti 1:10	Christ Jesus, who has *d-ed* death
Heb 2:14	so that by his death he might *d* him
2Pe 3:10	the elements will be *d-ed* by fire,
1Jn 3:8	appeared was to *d* the devil's work

destruction

Pr 16:18 Pride goes before *d*,
Hos 13:14 Where, O grave, is your *d*?
Mt 7:13 broad is the road that leads to *d*,
Jn 17:12 except the one doomed to *d*
Gal 6:8 from that nature will reap *d*;
2Th 2:3 the man doomed to *d*
2Pe 3:12 the *d* of the heavens by fire,

destructive

Ps 55:11 *D* forces are at work in the city;
Eze 5:16 my deadly and *d* arrows of famine,
2Pe 2:1 secretly introduce *d* heresies,

determine, -s, -d

Job 14:5 Man's days are *d-d*;
Ps 147:4 He *d-s* the number of the stars
Pr 16:9 but the LORD *d-s* his steps
Ac 17:26 and he *d-d* the times set for them
1Co 12:11 to each one, just as he *d-s*
15:38 God gives it a body as he has *d-d*,

detest, -s, -able

Dt 27:15 an idol—a thing *d-able* to the LORD
2Ch 15:8 He removed the *d-able* idols
Pr 6:16 seven that are *d-able* to him
8:7 for my lips *d* wickedness
12:22 The LORD *d-s* lying lips,
Lk 16:15 among men is *d-able* in God's sight
Tit 1:16 They are *d-able*, disobedient
1Pe 4:3 carousing and *d-able* idolatry

devil, -'s

Mt 4:1 the desert to be tempted by the *d*
4:8 the *d* took him to a very high
4:11 Then the *d* left him,
13:39 the enemy who sows them is the *d*.
25:41 the eternal fire prepared for the *d*
Lk 4:3 The *d* said to him, "If you are
8:12 then the *d* comes and takes away
Jn 6:70 Yet one of you is a *d*!
8:44 You belong to your father, the *d*,
13:2 the *d* had already prompted Judas
Ac 10:38 who were under the power of the *d*,
Eph 4:27 and do not give the *d* a foothold
6:11 your stand against the *d-'s* schemes
1Ti 3:6 under the same judgment as the *d*
Heb 2:14 the power of death—that is, the *d*
Jas 4:7 Resist the *d*, and he will flee
1Pe 5:8 Your enemy the *d* prowls around
1Jn 3:8 was to destroy the *d-'s* work
Rev 12:9 that ancient serpent called the *d*,
20:10 And the *d*, who deceived them,

devote, -d, -ion

1Ki 11:4 heart was not fully *d-d* to the LORD
1Ch 28:9 serve him with wholehearted *d-ion*
Ac 2:42 *d-d* themselves to the apostles'
Ro 12:10 Be *d-d* to one another in brotherly
2Co 11:3 sincere and pure *d-ion* to Christ
Col 4:2 *D* yourselves to prayer,
1Ti 4:13 *d* yourself to the public reading

devour, -s, -ing

2Sa 2:26 "Must the sword *d* for ever?
2Ch 7:13 or command locusts to *d*
Pr 21:20 but a foolish man *d-s* all he has
Lk 20:47 They *d* widows' houses
Gal 5:15 keep on biting and *d-ing* each other
1Pe 5:8 lion looking for someone to *d*

devout

Lk 2:25 Simeon, who was righteous and *d*.
Ac 10:2 his family were *d* and God-fearing;
13:43 the Jews and *d* converts to Judaism
22:12 He was a *d* observer of the law

die, -s, -d

Ge 2:17 you eat of it you will surely *d*
3:3 must not touch it, or you will *d*.'

3:4 “You will not surely *d*,”
Ex 11:5 Every firstborn son in Egypt will *d*
Ru 1:17 Where you *d* I will *d*, and there
2Sa 12:5 the man who did this deserves to *d*
1Ch 10:13 Saul *d-d* because he was unfaithful
Job 2:9 Curse God and *d*!
14:14 If a man *d-s*, will he live again?
Pr 10:21 but fools *d* for lack of judgment
Ecc 3:2 a time to be born and a time to *d*,
Isa 6:1 In the year that King Uzziah *d-d*,
22:13 you say, “for tomorrow we *d*!
66:24 their worm will not *d*
Eze 3:18 that wicked man will *d* for his sin,
18:4 soul who sins is the one who will *d*
18:31 Why will you *d*, O house of Israel
Jnh 4:9 “I am angry enough to *d*.
Mt 26:52 draw the sword will *d* by the sword
Mk 9:48 where “ ‘their worm does not *d*,
Jn 11:25 in me will live, even though he *d-s*
11:26 and believes in me will never *d*.
11:50 it is better for you that one man *d*
12:24 wheat falls to the ground and *d-s*,
Ro 5:6 Christ *d-d* for the ungodly
5:7 will anyone *d* for a righteous man
5:8 still sinners, Christ *d-d* for us
6:8 Now if we *d-d* with Christ,
6:10 The death he *d-d*, he died to sin
7:4 brothers, you also *d-d* to the law
14:8 and if we *d*, we die to the Lord.
1Co 15:3 that Christ *d-d* for our sins
15:22 For as in Adam all *d*, so in Christ
15:32 eat and drink, for tomorrow we *d*.
2Co 5:14 are convinced that one *d-d* for all
Php 1:21 to live is Christ and to *d* is gain
Col 2:20 Since you *d-d* with Christ
3:3 you *d-d*, and your life is now
1Th 4:14 We believe that Jesus *d-d* and rose
2Ti 2:11 If we *d-d* with him, we will also
Heb 9:27 Just as man is destined to *d* once,
1Pe 2:24 so that we might *d* to sins and live
3:18 Christ *d-d* for sins once for all,
Rev 2:8 who *d-d* and came to life again
14:13 the dead who *d* in the Lord

different, -nce

Ro 3:22 no *d-nce*, for all have sinned
12:6 *d* gifts, according to the grace
1Co 4:7 who makes you *d* from anyone else?
12:4 There are *d* kinds of gifts,
Gal 1:6 and are turning to a *d* gospel

differing

Dt 25:13 Do not have two *d* weights
Pr 20:23 The LORD detests *d* weights,

difficult, -ies

Ex 18:22 have them bring every *d* case to you
Dt 30:11 is not too *d* for you
2Ki 2:10 “You have asked a *d* thing,”
Ac 15:19 not make it *d* for the Gentiles
2Co 12:10 in persecutions, in *d-ies*.

diligent, -nce

Pr 10:4 but *d* hands bring wealth
21:5 The plans of the *d* lead to profit
1Ti 4:15 Be *d* in these matters;
Heb 6:11 each of you to show this same *d-nce*

Dinah

Daughter of Jacob by Leah (Ge 30:21; 46:15). Raped by Shechem; avenged by Simeon and Levi (Ge 34).

direct, -s, -ed

Ps 42:8 By day the LORD *d-s* his love,
119:35 *D* me in the path of your commands,
Pr 20:24 A man’s steps are *d-ed* by the LORD.
2Th 3:5 Lord *d* your hearts into God’s love

disappear, -s, -ed

Isa 2:18 and the idols will totally *d*
Hos 6:4 like the early dew that *d-s*
Lk 24:31 and he *d-ed* from their sight
1Co 13:10 perfection comes, the imperfect *d-s*
Heb 8:13 is obsolete and ageing will soon *d*
2Pe 3:10 The heavens will *d* with a roar;

disappoint, -ed

Ps 22:5 you they trusted and were not *d-ed*
Isa 49:23 who hope in me will not be *d-ed.*
Ro 5:5 And hope does not *d* us,

disarmed

Col 2:15 having *d* the powers and authorities

disaster

Ex 32:12 and do not bring *d* on your people
2Ki 22:16 I am going to bring *d* on this place
Ps 91:10 no *d* will come near your tent
Jer 17:17 you are my refuge in the day of *d*
42:10 for I am grieved over the *d*
Eze 7:5 An unheard-of *d* is coming

discern, -ment

Ps 19:12 Who can *d* his errors?
119:125 I am your servant; give me *d-ment*
Pr 17:10 A rebuke impresses a man of *d-ment*
Php 1:10 you may be able to *d* what is best

disciple, -s, -s'

Mt 10:1 He called his twelve *d-s* to him
10:42 little ones because he is my *d*,
26:26 broke it, and gave it to his *d-s*,
26:56 all the *d-s* deserted him and fled
28:19 go and make *d-s* of all nations,
Mk 4:34 when he was alone with his own *d-s*,
Lk 14:27 cross and follow me cannot be my *d*.
19:37 *d-s* began joyfully to praise God
22:11 I may eat the Passover with my *d-s*?
Jn 2:11 and his *d-s* put their faith in him
4:2 not Jesus who baptised, but his *d-s*
6:66 many of his *d-s* turned back
8:31 my teaching, you are really my *d-s*
12:16 At first his *d-s* did not understand
13:5 and began to wash his *d-s'* feet,
13:35 men will know that you are my *d-s*,
15:8 showing yourselves to be my *d-s*
19:26 the *d* whom he loved standing
19:38 a *d* of Jesus, but secretly
20:2 the other *d*, the one Jesus loved,
Ac 6:1 the number of *d-s* was increasing,
11:26 *d-s* were called Christians first
14:22 strengthening the *d-s*

discipline, -s, -d

Ps 94:12 Blessed is the man you *d*, O LORD,
Pr 3:12 the LORD *d-s* those he loves,
Tit 1:8 upright, holy and *d-d*
Heb 12:6 because the Lord *d-s* those he loves

discouraged

Dt 31:8 Do not be afraid; do not be *d*.
Jos 1:9 Do not be terrified; do not be *d*,
2Ch 20:15 or *d* because of this vast army.
Eph 3:13 to be *d* because of my sufferings
Col 3:21 children, or they will become *d*

discretion

1Ch 22:12 May the LORD give you *d*
Pr 1:4 knowledge and *d* to the young
2:11 *D* will protect you,
5:2 that you may maintain *d*

discuss, -ing, -ion

Mt 16:8 Aware of their *d-ion*, Jesus asked,
Mk 9:10 *d-ing* what "rising from the dead
Lk 24:17 asked them, "What are you *d-ing*

Ac 15:7 After much *d-ion*, Peter got up

disease, -s

Ps 103:3 and heals all your *d-s*,
Mt 4:23 and healing every *d* and sickness
8:17 and carried our *d-s*."
10:1 to heal every *d* and sickness
Lk 9:1 to cure *d-s*, and he sent them out

disgrace

Pr 11:2 When pride comes, then comes *d*,
14:34 but sin is a *d* to any people
Mt 1:19 not want to expose her to public *d*,
Lk 1:25 taken away my *d* among the people.
Ac 5:41 worthy of suffering *d* for the Name
Heb 6:6 and subjecting him to public *d*
11:26 regarded *d* for the sake of Christ
13:13 the camp, bearing the *d* he bore

dishonest

Lev 19:35 " 'Do not use *d* standards
Pr 11:1 The LORD abhors *d* scales,
Mic 6:11 Shall I acquit a man with *d* scales,
Lk 16:8 The master commended the *d* manager
16:10 and whoever is *d* with very little
Tit 1:7 not violent, not pursuing *d* gain

dishonour, -ed

Lev 18:7 " 'Do not *d* your father
Jn 8:49 I honour my Father and you *d* me
Ro 2:23 do you *d* God by breaking the law
1Co 4:10 You are honoured, we are *d-ed*
15:43 sown in *d*, it is raised in glory;

dismayed

Isa 28:16 the one who trusts will never be *d*
41:10 do not be *d*, for I am your God.
Jer 30:10 my servant; do not be *d*, O Israel,'

disobedient, -nce

Ne 9:26 "But they were *d* and rebelled
Ac 26:19 I was not *d* to the vision
Ro 5:19 just as through the *d-nce* of the one
10:21 hands to a *d* and obstinate people.
2Ti 3:2 proud, abusive, *d* to their parents,
Heb 4:6 not go in, because of their *d-nce*

disobey, -ed

Nu 14:22 who *d-ed* me and tested me ten times
Ro 1:30 doing evil; they *d* their parents
Heb 3:18 his rest if not to those who *d-ed*
1Pe 2:8 stumble because they *d* the message

disorder

1Co 14:33 not a God of *d* but of peace.
2Co 12:20 slander, gossip, arrogance and *d*
Jas 3:16 you find *d* and every evil practice

disown, -s

Pr 30:9 I may have too much and *d* you
Mt 10:33 But whoever *d-s* me before men,
26:34 you will *d* me three times.
2Ti 2:12 If we *d* him, he will also *d* us

display, -ed

Ex 14:31 saw the great power the LORD *d-ed*
Ps 19:2 night after night they *d* knowledge
45:4 let your right hand *d* awesome deeds
Eze 39:21 I will *d* my glory among the nations
1Co 4:9 God has put us apostles on *d*
1Ti 1:16 Christ Jesus might *d* his unlimited

dispute, -s

Ex 18:16 Whenever they have a *d*,
Jdg 4:5 to her to have their *d-s* decided
Lk 22:24 Also a *d* arose among them
Ac 17:18 philosophers began to *d* with him.

1Co 6:1 If any of you has a *d* with another,

disqualified

1Co 9:27 myself will not be *d* for the prize

dissension

Pr 10:12 Hatred stirs up *d*,
15:18 A hot-tempered man stirs up *d*,
Ro 13:13 debauchery, not in *d* and jealousy

distinguish, -ing

Lev 10:10 *d* between the holy and the common,
11:47 *d* between the unclean and the clean
1Ki 3:9 and to *d* between right and wrong.
1Co 12:10 to another *d-ing* between spirits,
2Th 3:17 the *d-ing* mark in all my letters.
Heb 5:14 themselves to *d* good from evil

distort

Jer 23:36 you *d* the words of the living God,
Ac 20:30 men will arise and *d* the truth
2Co 4:2 nor do we *d* the word of God.
2Pe 3:16 ignorant and unstable people *d*,

distress, -ed

1Sa 22:2 in *d* or in debt or discontented
Ps 120:1 I call on the LORD in my *d*,
Mt 24:21 For then there will be great *d*,
Mk 3:5 *d-ed* at their stubborn hearts,
Lk 12:50 how *d-ed* I am until it is completed
2Co 2:4 out of great *d* and anguish of heart
Jas 1:27 orphans and widows in their *d*
2Pe 2:7 who was *d-ed* by the filthy lives

distribute, -d, -ion

Mk 8:7 and told the disciples to *d* them
Jn 6:11 the loaves, gave thanks, and *d-d*
Ac 4:35 it was *d-d* to anyone as he had need
6:1 in the daily *d-ion* of food
Heb 2:4 gifts of the Holy Spirit *d-d*

divide, -ing, -d

Ex 14:21 The waters were *d-d*
Ps 22:18 They *d* my garments among them
78:13 He *d-d* the sea and led them through
Mt 12:25 "Every kingdom *d-d* against itself
Jn 19:23 they took his clothes, *d-ing* them
1Co 1:13 Is Christ *d-d*? Was Paul crucified
Eph 2:14 the *d-ing* wall of hostility
Heb 4:12 even to *d-ing* soul and spirit,

divination

Lev 19:26 "'Do not practise *d* or sorcery
Dt 18:10 who practises *d* or sorcery,
1Sa 15:23 For rebellion is like the sin of *d*,

divine

Ac 17:29 think that the *d* being is like gold
Ro 1:20 his eternal power and *d* nature—
9:4 theirs the *d* glory, the covenants,
2Co 10:4 *d* power to demolish strongholds
2Pe 1:3 His *d* power has given us everything
1:4 you may participate in the *d* nature

division, -s

Lk 12:51 on earth? No, I tell you, but *d*
Ro 16:17 watch out for those who cause *d-s*
1Co 1:10 that there may be no *d-s* among you
11:18 a church, there are *d-s* among you,

divisive

Tit 3:10 Warn a *d* person once,

divorce, -s

Dt 24:1 he writes her a certificate of *d*,
Mal 2:16 "I hate *d*," says the LORD God
Mt 1:19 he had in mind to *d* her quietly

5:31 It has been said, 'Anyone who *d-s*
19:8 "Moses permitted you to *d*
1Co 7:11 And a husband must not *d* his wife
7:27 Are you married? Do not seek a *d*.

doctor
Mt 9:12 It is not the healthy who need a *d*
Col 4:14 Our dear friend Luke, the *d*,

doctrine, -s
1Ti 1:3 certain men not to teach false *d-s*
1:10 contrary to the sound *d*
4:16 Watch your life and *d* closely.
2Ti 4:3 men will not put up with sound *d*.
Tit 2:1 what is in accord with sound *d*

dog, -s
Pr 26:11 As a *d* returns to its vomit,
Mt 15:27 "but even the *d-s* eat the crumbs
2Pe 2:22 "A *d* returns to its vomit,"

dominion
Ps 22:28 for *d* belongs to the LORD
145:13 your *d* endures through all
Da 7:14 everlasting *d* that will not pass
1Co 15:24 after he has destroyed all *d*,
Eph 1:21 all rule and authority, power and *d*
Col 1:13 rescued us from the *d* of darkness

donkey
Nu 22:30 The *d* said to Balaam,
Zec 9:9 gentle and riding on a *d*, on a colt
Mt 21:5 gentle and riding on a *d*, on a colt

door, -s
Ps 141:3 keep watch over the *d* of my lips
Mt 6:6 close the *d* and pray to your Father
7:7 knock and the *d* will be opened
Jn 20:19 with the *d-s* locked for fear of
1Co 16:9 a great *d* for effective work
Rev 3:20 I stand at the *d* and knock.

doorkeeper
Ps 84:10 I would rather be a *d* in the house

Dorcas
Also known as Tabitha. Disciple in Joppa, known for her good works (Ac 9:36,39). Died (Ac 9:37); raised to life by Peter (Ac 9:38–42).

double, -minded
1Sa 1:5 But to Hannah he gave a *d* portion
2Ki 2:9 a *d* portion of your spirit,"
Isa 40:2 the LORD's hand *d* for all her sins
1Ti 5:17 church well are worthy of *d* honour
Jas 1:8 he is a *d-minded* man, unstable

doubt, -s, -ing
Mt 14:31 he said, "why did you *d*?
21:21 if you have faith and do not *d*,
Lk 24:38 and why do *d-s* rise in your minds?
Jn 20:27 my side. Stop *d-ing* and believe.
Jas 1:6 who *d-s* is like a wave of the sea,
Jude :22 Be merciful to those who *d*

dough
Mt 13:33 until it worked all through the *d*.
Ro 11:16 If the part of the *d* offered
1Co 5:6 works through the whole batch of *d*

dove, -s
Ge 8:8 Then he sent out a *d* to see
Ps 55:6 "Oh, that I had the wings of a *d*!
SS 2:14 My *d* in the clefts of the rock,
Mt 3:16 Spirit of God descending like a *d*
Lk 2:24 a pair of *d-s* or two young pigeons

downcast
Ps 42:5 Why are you *d*, O my soul?
Lk 24:17 They stood still, their faces *d*

2Co 7:6 But God, who comforts the *d*,

dragon
Rev 12:3 an enormous red *d* with seven heads
12:7 and his angels fought against the *d*
20:2 the *d*, that ancient serpent,

draw, -s
Isa 12:3 With joy you will *d* water
Jn 6:44 the Father who sent me *d-s* him,
12:32 the earth, will *d* all men to myself
Heb 10:22 *d* near to God with a sincere heart

dread, -ful
Dt 8:15 through the vast and *d-ful* desert,
Joel 2:31 great and *d-ful* day of the LORD
Mt 24:19 How *d-ful* it will be in those days
Heb 10:31 *d-ful* thing to fall into the hands

dream, -s
Ge 28:12 He had a *d* in which he saw
37:5 Joseph had a *d*, and when he told it
40:5 were being held in prison—had a *d*
Da 2:24 and I will interpret his *d* for him.
Joel 2:28 your old men will *d d-s*,
Mt 1:20 of the Lord appeared to him in a *d*
2:13 appeared to Joseph in a *d*.
27:19 suffered a great deal today in a *d*
Ac 2:17 your old men will *d d-s*

dress
Jer 6:14 They *d* the wound of my people
1Ti 2:9 I also want women to *d* modestly,

drift
Heb 2:1 so that we do not *d* away

drink, -s, -ing
Ex 17:2 Give us water to *d*." Moses replied
32:6 they sat down to eat and *d*
Pr 5:15 *D* water from your own cistern,
25:21 he is thirsty, give him water to *d*
Mt 6:25 your life, what you will eat or *d*;
11:19 Son of Man came eating and *d-ing*,
20:22 *d* the cup I am going to drink?"
25:37 thirsty and give you something to *d*
26:27 saying, "*D* from it, all of you
27:48 and offered it to Jesus to *d*
Mk 14:25 I will not *d* again of the fruit
Lk 5:30 *d* with tax collectors and 'sinners'
12:19 Take life easy; eat, *d* and be merry
Jn 4:14 whoever *d-s* the water I give him
6:54 and *d-s* my blood has eternal life,
7:37 let him come to me and *d*
18:11 Shall I not *d* the cup the Father
1Co 10:4 and drank the same spiritual *d*;
10:7 "The people sat down to eat and *d*
11:27 or *d-s* the cup of the Lord
12:13 were all given the one Spirit to *d*
Php 2:17 being poured out like a *d* offering
Rev 14:10 will *d* of the wine of God's fury,
21:6 him who is thirsty I will give to *d*

drive, -s
Ex 23:30 Little by little I will *d* them out
Jdg 1:19 they were unable to *d* the people
Mt 10:1 authority to *d* out evil spirits
12:28 But if I *d* out demons by the Spirit
Jn 6:37 comes to me I will never *d* away
1Jn 4:18 But perfect love *d-s* out fear,

drop, -s
Pr 17:14 so *d* the matter before a dispute
Isa 40:15 nations are like a *d* in a bucket;

Lk 22:44	and his sweat was like *d-s* of blood

dross

Ps 119:119	of the earth you discard like *d*;
Isa 1:22	Your silver has become *d*,

drown, -ed

Ex 15:4	best of Pharaoh's officers are *d-ed*
Mt 8:25	"Lord, save us! We're going to *d*!
18:6	to be *d-ed* in the depths of the sea
Mk 5:13	bank into the lake and were *d-ed*

drunk, -ard

Ge 9:21	he became *d* and lay uncovered
1Sa 1:13	Eli thought she was *d*
Ac 2:15	These men are not *d*, as you suppose
1Co 5:11	a slanderer, a *d-ard* or a swindler.
Eph 5:18	Do not get *d* on wine, which leads

drunkenness

Lk 21:34	weighed down with dissipation, *d*
Ro 13:13	in the daytime, not in orgies and *d*
Gal 5:21	and envy; *d*, orgies, and the like.
Tit 1:7	not given to *d*, not violent,
1Pe 4:3	living in debauchery, lust, *d*,

dry

Ge 1:10	God called the *d* ground "land"
Ex 14:16	go through the sea on *d* ground
Jos 3:17	completed the crossing on *d* ground
Jdg 6:40	Only the fleece was *d*;
Pr 17:1	Better a *d* crust with peace
Isa 53:2	like a root out of *d* ground.
Eze 37:4	*D* bones, hear the word of the LORD.
Lk 23:31	what will happen when it is *d*?

dull

Mt 15:16	Are you still so *d*?" Jesus asked
2Co 3:14	But their minds were made *d*,

dust

Ge 2:7	the man from the *d* of the ground
3:14	and you will eat *d* all the days
3:19	for *d* you are and to *d* you will
Ps 22:15	you lay me in the *d* of death
90:3	"Return to *d*, O sons of men.
103:14	he remembers that we are *d*
113:7	He raises the poor from the *d*
Mt 10:14	shake the *d* off your feet
Ac 13:51	So they shook the *d* from their feet
1Co 15:47	The first man was of the *d*

duty

Mt 17:25	the kings of the earth collect *d*
Lk 17:10	servants; we have only done our *d*.'
Ac 23:1	I have fulfilled my *d* to God
1Co 7:3	fulfil his marital *d* to his wife,

dwell, -ing, -ings

Dt 12:11	will choose as a *d-ing* for his Name
2Sa 7:5	the one to build me a house to *d* in
1Ki 8:27	"But will God really *d* on earth?
Ps 15:1	LORD, who may *d* in your sanctuary?
23:6	I will *d* in the house of the LORD
Lk 16:9	be welcomed into eternal *d-ings*
Jn 5:38	nor does his word *d* in you,
2Co 5:2	be clothed with our heavenly *d-ing*
Eph 3:17	that Christ may *d* in your hearts
Col 1:19	to have all his fulness *d* in him
3:16	Let the word of Christ *d* in you
Rev 21:3	"Now the *d-ing* of God is with men,

dwelling-place

Ps 84:1	How lovely is your *d*, O LORD
90:1	Lord, you have been our *d*

E

eager

Pr 31:13	works with *e* hands
Ro 1:15	I am so *e* to preach the gospel
8:19	creation waits in *e* expectation

1Co 14:39 be *e* to prophesy,
1Ti 6:10 Some people, *e* for money,
1Pe 5:2 for money, but *e* to serve

eagle, -'s, -s, -s'
Ex 19:4 how I carried you on *e-s'* wings
Ps 103:5 youth is renewed like the *e-'s*
Isa 40:31 will soar on wings like *e-s*;
Da 4:33 like the feathers of an *e*

ear, -s
Ex 21:6 pierce his *e* with an awl.
2Ch 6:40 your *e-s* attentive to the prayers
Job 42:5 My *e-s* have heard you
Ps 40:6 my *e-s* you have pierced;
44:1 We have heard with our *e-s*, O God;
Isa 6:10 make their *e-s* dull and close
Mt 11:15 He who has *e-s*, let him hear
Ac 28:27 they hardly hear with their *e-s*,
1Co 2:9 "No eye has seen, no *e* has heard,
12:16 And if the *e* should say,
2Ti 4:3 their itching *e-s* want to hear
Rev 2:7 He who has an *e*, let him hear

earnest, -ly
Ps 63:1 my God, *e-ly* I seek you;
Lk 22:44 in anguish, he prayed more *e-ly*,
Ac 12:5 the church was *e-ly* praying to God
Heb 11:6 he rewards those who *e-ly* seek him
Jas 5:17 prayed *e-ly* that it would not rain

earth, -'s, -ly
Ge 1:1 God created the heavens and the *e*
1:28 fill the *e* and subdue it.
7:24 The waters flooded the *e*
8:22 *e* endures, seedtime and harvest,
Jos 23:14 to go the way of all the *e*.
1Ki 8:27 will God really dwell on *e*?
Job 38:4 when I laid the *e-'s* foundation?
Ps 2:8 the ends of the *e* your possession
8:1 majestic is your name in all the *e*!
24:1 The *e* is the LORD's,
46:2 though the *e* give way
96:13 he comes to judge the *e*.
97:1 LORD reigns, let the *e* be glad;
103:11 as the heavens are above the *e*,
Isa 6:3 the whole *e* is full of his glory.
40:22 enthroned above the circle of the *e*
45:22 be saved, all you ends of the *e*;
55:9 the heavens are higher than the *e*,
65:17 create new heavens and a new *e*.
Hab 2:14 For the *e* will be filled
Mt 6:10 be done on *e* as it is in heaven.
16:19 whatever you bind on *e* will be
24:35 Heaven and *e* will pass away,
28:18 All authority in heaven and on *e*
Lk 2:14 and on *e* peace to men
Jn 3:12 have spoken to you of *e-ly* things
12:32 when I am lifted up from the *e*,
1Co 10:26 "The *e* is the Lord's
15:40 there are *e-ly* bodies;
Eph 3:15 in heaven and on *e* derives its name
4:9 to the lower, *e-ly* regions
6:5 Slaves, obey your *e-ly* masters
Php 2:10 in heaven, and on *e*
3:19 Their mind is on *e-ly* things
Col 3:2 things above, not on *e-ly* things
3:5 belongs to your *e-ly* nature:
Heb 9:1 and also an *e-ly* sanctuary
Jas 3:15 heaven but is *e-ly*, unspiritual,
1Pe 4:2 *e-ly* life for evil human desires,
2Pe 3:13 a new heaven and a new *e*,
Rev 20:11 *E* and sky fled from his presence,
21:1 Then I saw a new heaven and a new *e*

earthquake, -s
1Ki 19:11 an *e*, but the LORD was not in the
Eze 38:19 shall be a great *e* in the land
Mt 24:7 famines and *e-s* in various places
28:2 There was a violent *e*, for an angel
Rev 6:12 There was a great *e*.

east
Ge 2:8 planted a garden in the *e*,
Ps 103:12 as far as the *e* is from the west,
Jnh 4:8 God provided a scorching *e* wind,

Mt 2:1 Magi from the *e* came to Jerusalem
24:27 lightning that comes from the *e*
Rev 7:2 another angel coming up from the *e*,

easy, -ier, -ily
Mt 9:5 Which is *e-ier*: to say,
11:30 my yoke is *e* and my burden is light
19:24 it is *e-ier* for a camel to go
Lk 12:19 Take life *e*; eat, drink
Heb 12:1 the sin that so *e-ily* entangles,

eat, -s, -ing
Ge 2:16 free to *e* from any tree
2:17 *e* from the tree of the knowledge
3:14 *e* dust all the days of your life
Lev 7:27 If anyone *e-s* blood, that person
Dt 8:16 gave you manna to *e* in the desert,
1Ki 19:5 "Get up and *e*.
Ps 22:26 The poor will *e* and be satisfied;
Pr 25:21 enemy is hungry, give him food to *e*
Isa 51:8 moth will *e* them up like a garment;
55:1 have no money, come, buy and *e*!
65:25 lion will *e* straw like the ox,
Eze 3:1 "Son of man, *e* what is before you
Da 4:25 you will *e* grass like cattle
Mt 6:25 what you will *e* or drink;
14:16 You give them something to *e*.
24:38 before the flood, people were *e-ing*
25:35 you gave me something to *e*,
26:26 "Take and *e*; this is my body."
Jn 4:32 food to *e* that you know nothing
6:31 gave them bread from heaven to *e*.'
6:52 this man give us his flesh to *e*?
6:54 *e-s* my flesh and drinks my blood
Ro 14:2 One man's faith allows him to *e*
14:17 not a matter of *e-ing* and drinking,
1Co 5:11 With such a man do not even *e*
8:13 if what I *e* causes my brother to
10:31 So whether you *e* or drink or
11:20 it is not the Lord's Supper you *e*
11:26 whenever you *e* this bread and drink
15:32 "Let us *e* and drink, for tomorrow
Col 2:16 judge you by what you *e* or drink,
2Th 3:10 will not work, he shall not *e*.
Rev 3:20 I will come in and *e* with him,

Ebenezer
1Sa 4:1 The Israelites camped at *E*,
7:12 He named it *E*, saying, "Thus far

Eden
Ge 2:8 a garden in the east, in *E*;
3:23 banished him from the Garden of *E*
Eze 28:13 You were in *E*, the garden of God;

edge
Jer 31:29 the children's teeth are set on *e*.
Mt 9:20 touched the *e* of his cloak
Heb 11:34 escaped the *e* of the sword;

edict
Da 6:7 the king should issue an *e*
Heb 11:23 not afraid of the king's *e*

edification
Ro 14:19 leads to peace and to mutual *e*

edify, -ies, -ied
1Co 14:4 speaks in a tongue *e-ies* himself
14:5 so that the church may be *e-ied*
14:17 the other man is not *e-ied*

Edom
1. Another name for *Esau*. **2.** Nation descended from Esau (Ge 36).

effect, -ive
Ac 7:53 put into *e* through angels
1Co 15:10 his grace to me was not without *e*.
16:9 door for *e-ive* work has opened
Heb 9:17 it never takes *e* while the one
Jas 5:16 righteous man is powerful and *e-ive*

effort

Lk 13:24 “Make every *e* to enter through
Ro 9:16 desire or *e*, but on God's mercy
Eph 4:3 Make every *e* to keep the unity
Heb 4:11 Let us, therefore, make every *e*
12:14 Make every *e* to live in peace

Egypt, -ians

Ge 12:10 Abram went down to *E* to live there
15:18 the river of *E* to the great river,
Ex 1:15 of *E* said to the Hebrew midwives,
3:7 seen the misery of my people in *E*.
3:12 brought the people out of *E*,
7:5 *E-ians* will know that I am the
10:22 total darkness covered all *E*
12:40 people lived in *E* was 430 years
20:2 God, who brought you out of *E*,
Nu 11:18 We were better off in *E*!”
14:4 choose a leader and go back to *E*.
Dt 5:15 Remember that you were slaves in *E*
2Ki 18:21 you are depending on *E*,
Ps 80:8 You brought a vine out of *E*;
Isa 19:23 a highway from *E* to Assyria.
31:1 Woe to those who go down to *E*
Hos 11:1 out of *E* I called my son
Mt 2:13 his mother and escape to *E*.
2:15 “Out of *E* I called my son.
2:19 a dream to Joseph in *E*
Heb 11:27 By faith he left *E*,
11:29 but when the *E-ians* tried to do so,

Eleazar

Third son of Aaron (Ex 6:23; Nu 3:2; 1Ch 6:3–4); anointed as priest (Lev 8–9; Nu 3:2–4); leader of Levites, responsible for care of sanctuary (Nu 3:32; 4:16). Succeeded Aaron (Nu 20:28; Dt 10:6); assisted Moses (Nu 26:1–4,63; 27:2; 31:12; 32:2). With Joshua, apportioned land (Nu 32:28; 34:17; Jos 14:1; 19:51). Death (Jos 24:33).

elder, -s

Nu 11:16 “Bring me seventy of Israel's *e-s*
Mt 15:2 break the tradition of the *e-s*?
Ac 4:8 “Rulers and *e-s* of the people
14:23 Paul and Barnabas appointed *e-s*
15:4 church and the apostles and *e-s*,
20:17 Paul sent to Ephesus for the *e-s*
1Ti 5:17 The *e-s* who direct the affairs
5:19 an accusation against an *e*
Tit 1:6 An *e* must be blameless,
Jas 5:14 He should call the *e-s*
Rev 4:4 on them were twenty-four *e-s*.
7:13 Then one of the *e-s* asked me,
19:4 The twenty-four *e-s* and the four

elect, -ion

Mt 24:22 for the sake of the *e* those days
24:24 even the *e*—if that were possible
Ro 9:11 God's purpose in *e-ion* might stand
2Ti 2:10 everything for the sake of the *e*,
2Pe 1:10 to make your calling and *e-ion*

elementary

Heb 5:12 to teach you the *e* truths
6:1 leave the *e* teachings about Christ

elements

2Pe 3:10 the *e* will be destroyed by fire,
3:12 and the *e* will melt in the heat

Eli

Priest at Shiloh; blessed Hannah (1Sa 1:9–17), who brought Samuel to him (1Sa 1:24–27); raised Samuel (1Sa 2:11,18–21,26). Wickedness of sons (1Sa 2:12–17,22–25); rebuked by prophet (1Sa 2:27–36). Directed Samuel to the Lord (1Sa 3). Death of Eli and his sons (1Sa 4:10–18).

Elihu

See *Job* **2**.

Elijah

Prophet; predicted drought in Israel (1Ki 17:1; Lk 4:25; Jas 5:17). Fed by ravens at brook Kerith (1Ki 17:2–6), and by widow of Zarephath (1Ki 17:9–16); raised widow's son (1Ki 17:17–24). Contest with prophets of Baal on Mt Carmel (1Ki 18:18–46). Fled from Jezebel to Horeb (1Ki 19); called Elisha (1Ki 19:19–21). Denounced Ahab over Naboth's vineyard (1Ki 21:17–29). Prophesied God's judgment on Ahaziah and called down fire (2Ki 1:1–17). Divided Jordan (2Ki 2:7–8); taken up to heaven in chariot of fire and whirlwind (2Ki 2:11–12); mantle taken by Elisha (2Ki 2:9–10,13–15). Appeared with Moses at Jesus' transfiguration (Mt 17:2–3; Mk 9:2–4; Lk 9:28–31). Return prophesied (Mal 4:5–6; Mt 17:10; Mk 9:11); identified with John the Baptist (Mt 11:13–14; 17:11–13; Mk 9:12–13; Lk 1:17).

Eliphaz
See *Job* **2**.

Elisha
Prophet; succeeded Elijah (1Ki 19:16–21); took his cloak and divided Jordan (2Ki 2:13–14). Purified bad water (2Ki 2:19–22); cursed youths who mocked him (2Ki 2:23–25); helped defeat Moab (2Ki 3:11–19); provided oil for widow (2Ki 4:1–7); raised Shunammite woman's son (2Ki 4:8–37); purified food (2Ki 4:38–41); fed 100 men with 20 loaves (2Ki 4:42–44); healed Naaman (2Ki 5); made axe-head float (2Ki 6:1–7). Captured Arameans (2Ki 6:8–23). Life threatened (2Ki 6:31–33). Prophesied end of siege of Samaria (2Ki 7:1–2). Visit to Damascus (2Ki 8:7–15). Sent prophet to anoint Jehu as king (2Ki 9:1–3). Death (2Ki 13:14–20); miracle with bones (2Ki 13:21).

Elizabeth
Wife of Zechariah; mother of John the Baptist (Lk 1:5–25,57–60). Related to Mary (Lk 1:36); blessed Mary when she visited (Lk 1:39–45).

Eloi
Mt 27:46 cried out in a loud voice, "*E*,

eloquent
Ex 4:10 "O Lord, I have never been *e*,

embitter
Col 3:21 Fathers, do not *e* your children,

empty, -ied
Ge 1:2 Now the earth was formless and *e*,
Isa 55:11 It will not return to me *e*,
Lk 1:53 has sent the rich away *e*
1Co 1:17 lest the cross of Christ be *e-ied*

Eph 5:6 no-one deceive you with *e* words,
1Pe 1:18 redeemed from the *e* way of life

enable, -s, -d
Ps 18:33 he *e-s* me to stand on the heights
Jn 6:65 unless the Father has *e-d* him.
Ac 2:4 tongues as the Spirit *e-d* them
Php 3:21 by the power that *e-s* him

encourage, -ing, -d, -ment
Ac 4:36 Barnabas (which means Son of *E-ment*
9:31 *e-d* by the Holy Spirit,
11:23 *e-d* them all to remain true
14:22 *e-ing* them to remain true
Ro 1:12 mutually *e-d* by each other's faith
12:8 if it is *e-ing*, let him *e*;
15:4 through endurance and the *e-ment*
Php 2:1 any *e-ment* from being united
1Th 4:18 *e* each other with these words
5:14 *e* the timid, help the weak,
2Ti 4:2 *e*—with great patience
Heb 3:13 But *e* one another daily,
10:25 let us *e* one another—
12:5 forgotten that word of *e-ment*

end, -s
Job 19:25 Redeemer lives, and that in the *e*
Ps 2:8 inheritance, the *e-s* of the earth
46:9 He makes wars cease to the *e-s*
Pr 16:25 but in the *e* it leads to death
Ecc 12:12 making many books there is no *e*,
Isa 9:7 there will be no *e*. He will reign
40:28 Creator of the *e-s* of the earth.
45:22 be saved, all you *e-s* of the earth;
Mt 13:39 The harvest is the *e* of the age,
24:13 stands firm to the *e* will be saved
Jn 11:4 This sickness will not *e* in death.
Ro 10:4 Christ is the *e* of the law
1Co 15:24 Then the *e* will come,
Heb 3:14 if we hold firmly till the *e*

Rev 21:6 the Beginning and the *E*.

endure, -s, -ing, -d, -ance

Ge 8:22 long as the earth *e-s*, seedtime
2Sa 7:16 your kingdom shall *e* for ever
Ps 107:1 his love *e-s* for ever
Da 4:3 his dominion *e-s* from generation
Mal 3:2 who can *e* the day of his coming?
Jn 6:27 for food that *e-s* to eternal life,
Ro 15:4 so that through *e-ance* and the
2Ti 2:3 *E* hardship with us like a good
2:10 Therefore I *e* everything for
Heb 12:2 joy set before him *e-d* the cross,
13:14 here we do not have an *e-ing* city,

enemy, -ies

Nu 10:35 May your *e-ies* be scattered;
Jos 5:13 for us or for our *e-ies*?
1Ki 21:20 you have found me, my *e*!"
Ps 8:2 praise because of your *e-ies*,
23:5 me in the presence of my *e-ies*.
69:4 many are my *e-ies* without cause,
110:1 I make your *e-ies* a footstool
Pr 24:17 Do not gloat when your *e* falls;
25:21 *e* is hungry, give him food to eat;
La 3:52 my *e-ies* without cause
Mic 7:8 Do not gloat over me, my *e*!
Mt 5:43 Love your neighbour and hate your *e*
10:36 a man's *e-ies* will be the members
13:25 his *e* came and sowed weeds
13:28 'An *e* did this,' he replied.
22:44 I put your *e-ies* under your feet."
Lk 1:71 salvation from our *e-ies*
10:19 overcome all the power of the *e*;
Ro 5:10 God's *e-ies*, we were reconciled
12:20 "If your *e* is hungry, feed him;
1Co 15:25 all his *e-ies* under his feet
15:26 last *e* to be destroyed is death
Gal 4:16 Have I now become your *e*
Php 3:18 many live as *e-ies* of the cross
Col 1:21 *e-ies* in your minds because
Heb 1:13 I make your *e-ies* a footstool
Jas 4:4 the world becomes an *e* of God
1Pe 5:8 Your *e* the devil prowls around

energy

Col 1:29 his *e*, which so powerfully works

engaged

1Co 7:36 towards the virgin he is *e* to,

engraved

Isa 49:16 I have *e* you on the palms
Jer 17:1 sin is *e* with an iron tool,
2Co 3:7 which was *e* in letters on stone,

enjoy, -ment

Dt 6:2 so that you may *e* long life
Ecc 9:9 *E* life with your wife,
Eph 6:3 may *e* long life on the earth.
1Ti 6:17 everything for our *e-ment*
Heb 11:25 to *e* the pleasures of sin

enlighten, -ed

Isa 40:14 did the LORD consult to *e* him,
Eph 1:18 eyes of your heart may be *e-ed*
Heb 6:4 those who have once been *e-ed*,

enmity

Ge 3:15 put *e* between you and the woman,

Enoch

1. Cain's first son; city named after him (Ge 4:17–18). **2.** Descendant of Seth; father of Methuselah (Ge 5:18–21). Prophesied (Jude 14–15); walked with God, and taken by him (Ge 5:22–24).

entangle, -s, -d

Ps 18:4 The cords of death *e-d* me;
35:8 may the net they hid *e* them,
Heb 12:1 the sin that so easily *e-s*,
2Pe 2:20 again *e-d* in it and overcome,

enter, -s, -ed

Ps 73:17 I *e-ed* the sanctuary of God;
95:11 "They shall never *e* my rest.
100:4 *E* his gates with thanksgiving
Isa 51:11 They will *e* Zion with singing;
Mt 5:20 not *e* the kingdom of heaven
7:13 and many *e* through it
7:21 'Lord, Lord,' will *e* the kingdom

12:29	how can anyone *e* a strong man's
15:17	whatever *e-s* the mouth goes into
18:8	It is better for you to *e* life
19:23	for a rich man to *e* the kingdom
Mk 9:43	to *e* life maimed
Lk 24:26	to suffer these things and then *e*
Jn 3:4	*e* a second time into his mother's
10:1	man who does not *e* the sheep pen
Ac 14:22	many hardships to *e* the kingdom
Ro 5:12	sin *e-ed* the world through one man
Heb 3:11	'They shall never *e* my rest.'
9:12	did not *e* by means of the blood
9:24	Christ did not *e* a man-made
10:19	confidence to *e* the Most Holy

entertain

Jdg 16:25	"Bring out Samson to *e* us."
Mt 9:4	"Why do you *e* evil thoughts
1Ti 5:19	*e* an accusation against an elder
Heb 13:2	Do not forget to *e* strangers,

enthrone, -d

1Sa 4:4	*e-d* between the cherubim.
Ps 2:4	The One *e-d* in heaven laughs;
9:11	praises to the LORD, *e-d* in Zion;
Isa 40:22	*e-d* above the circle of the earth

entice, -s, -d

Dt 11:16	Be careful, or you will be *e-d*
13:6	closest friend secretly *e-s* you,
Job 31:9	my heart has been *e-d* by a woman,
Pr 1:10	if sinners *e* you,
Jas 1:14	he is dragged away and *e-d*

entrance

Ge 18:1	was sitting at the *e* to his tent
Mt 27:60	in front of the *e* to the tomb
Jn 11:38	with a stone laid across the *e*
20:1	stone had been removed from the *e*
Ac 12:13	Peter knocked at the outer *e*,

entrusted

Mt 25:20	'you *e* me with five talents.
Lk 12:48	*e* with much, much more will be
Jn 5:22	has *e* all judgment to the Son
Ro 6:17	teaching to which you were *e*
2Ti 1:12	to guard what I have *e* to him
1Pe 2:23	he *e* himself to him who judges
Jude :3	once for all *e* to the saints

envy, -ious

Ps 37:1	or be *e-ious* of those who do wrong;
Pr 3:31	Do not *e* a violent man or choose
23:17	Do not let your heart *e* sinners,
Mk 7:22	deceit, lewdness, *e*, slander,
Ro 1:29	full of *e*, murder, strife, deceit
1Co 13:4	love is kind. It does not *e*,
Gal 5:21	and *e*; drunkenness, orgies,
Jas 3:14	bitter *e* and selfish ambition

Epaphroditus

Christian from Philippi; brought gifts from Philippians to Paul (Php 4:18); fellow-worker with Paul; almost died serving Christ (Php 2:25–29).

Ephesus

Ac 18:19	at *E*, where Paul left Priscilla
20:17	Paul sent to *E* for the elders
1Co 15:32	If I fought wild beasts in *E*
Eph 1:1	To the saints in *E*, the faithful
Rev 2:1	angel of the church in *E* write:

Ephraim

1. Joseph's second son (Ge 41:52); blessed by Jacob as firstborn (Ge 48:13–20). **2.** Tribe descended from Ephraim. Blessed by Moses (Dt 33:13–17). Included in census (Nu 1:32–33; 26:35–37). Apportioned land (Jos 16:1–9; Eze 48:5); unable to take full possession (Jos 16:10; Jdg 1:29). Occupied prestigious position among tribes (Jdg 8:2–3). **3.** Became synonym for northern kingdom (Ps 78:9–16,67–68; Isa 7:1–17; Jer 7:15; Hos 5; 11).

equal

Isa 40:25	who is my *e*?" says the Holy One
Mt 20:12	you have made them *e* to us
Jn 5:18	making himself *e* with God

2Co 2:16 And who is *e* to such a task

equip, -ped

2Ti 3:17 thoroughly *e-ped* for every good
Heb 13:21 *e* you with everything good

error, -s

Ps 19:12 Who can discern his *e-s*?
Mt 22:29 are in *e* because you do not know
Jas 5:20 a sinner from the *e* of his way
2Pe 3:17 away by the *e* of lawless men
Jude :11 rushed for profit into Balaam's *e*;

Esau

Also known as Edom (Ge 25:30). Son of Isaac; older twin of Jacob (Ge 25:24–26); hunter, favoured by Isaac (Ge 25:27–28). Sold birthright (Ge 25:29–34; Heb 12:6); lost blessing as eldest son (Ge 27). Married foreign wives (Ge 26:34–35; 28:8–9; 36:2–3). Reconciled to Jacob (Ge 32:3–21; 33:1–16). Occupied land of Seir (Ge 36:8; Dt 2:4–12); ancestor of Edomites (Ge 36:9–43). Rejection by God contrasted with gracious choice of Jacob (Mal 1:2–3; Ro 9:13).

escape, -ing, -d

Ro 2:3 think you will *e* God's judgment
1Co 3:15 as one *e-ing* through the flames
1Th 5:3 and they will not *e*
Heb 2:3 how shall we *e* if we ignore such
12:25 not *e* when they refused him
2Pe 1:4 *e* the corruption in the world
2:20 If they have *e-d* the corruption

establish, -es, -ed

Ge 6:18 I will *e* my covenant with you,
2Sa 3:10 *e* David's throne over Israel
Ps 9:7 has *e-ed* his throne for judgment
96:10 The world is firmly *e-ed*,
Isa 2:2 the LORD's temple will be *e-ed*
62:7 no rest till he *e-es* Jerusalem
Mt 18:16 'every matter may be *e-ed*
Ro 13:1 except that which God has *e-ed*.
Gal 3:15 covenant that has been duly *e-ed*,
Eph 3:17 being rooted and *e-ed* in love

Esther

Jewess living in Persia, also called Hadassah; brought up by cousin Mordecai (Est 2:7). Became Xerxes' queen (Est 2:8–18). Persuaded by Mordecai to help foil Haman's plot to destroy Jews (Est 3–4); risked life by approaching Xerxes (Est 4:9–11; 5:1–8); revealed Haman's plans (Est 7). Encouraged Jews to slaughter enemies; initiated feast of Purim in celebration (Est 9).

eternal

Ge 21:33 name of the LORD, the *E* God
Dt 33:27 The *e* God is your refuge,
Ps 16:11 *e* pleasures at your right hand
119:89 Your word, O LORD, is *e*;
Da 4:3 His kingdom is an *e* kingdom;
Mt 18:8 and be thrown into *e* fire
19:16 good thing must I do to get *e*
25:41 the *e* fire prepared for the devil
Jn 3:16 shall not perish but have *e* life
4:14 water welling up to *e* life.
6:54 and drinks my blood has *e* life,
10:28 I give them *e* life,
17:3 Now this is *e* life:
Ac 13:48 appointed for *e* life believed
Ro 6:23 the gift of God is *e* life
2Co 4:17 achieving for us an *e* glory
4:18 but what is unseen is *e*
Eph 3:11 according to his *e* purpose
1Ti 1:17 the King *e*, immortal, invisible,
Heb 5:9 became the source of *e* salvation
9:14 through the *e* Spirit offered
13:20 through the blood of the *e* covenant
1Jn 5:11 God has given us *e* life,

eternity

Ps 93:2 you are from all *e*
Pr 8:23 I was appointed from *e*,
Ecc 3:11 *e* in the hearts of men;

Ethiopian

Jer 13:23 Can the *E* change his skin

eunuch, -s

Mt 19:12 are *e-s* because they were born
Ac 8:27 he met an Ethiopian *e*,

evangelist, -s

Ac 21:8	Philip the *e*, one of the Seven
Eph 4:11	some to be *e-s*, and some
2Ti 4:5	do the work of an *e*,

Eve

First woman; created from Adam as wife and helper (Ge 2:20–24). Deceived by serpent (Ge 3:1–6; 2Co 11:3; 1Ti 2:13–14). Punished (Ge 3:16). Mother of Cain and Abel (Ge 4:1–2).

evening

Ge 1:5	was *e*, and there was morning—
Isa 17:14	In the *e*, sudden terror!
Lk 24:29	for it is nearly *e*;
Jn 20:19	*e* of that first day of the week,

everlasting

Ge 9:16	remember the *e* covenant
17:7	*e* covenant between me and you
Dt 33:27	underneath are the *e* arms.
Ps 103:17	*e* to *e* the LORD's love
Isa 9:6	Counsellor, Mighty God, *E* Father,
Jer 31:3	"I have loved you with an *e* love
Jn 6:47	he who believes has *e* life
2Th 1:9	punished with *e* destruction
Jude :6	bound with *e* chains for judgment

evidence, -nt

Mt 26:59	looking for false *e* against Jesus
Jn 14:11	believe on the *e* of the miracles
Ac 11:23	saw the *e* of the grace of God,
Gal 2:17	it becomes *e-nt* that we ourselves
Php 4:5	your gentleness be *e-nt* to all.

evil

Ge 2:9	of the knowledge of good and *e*
3:5	like God, knowing good and *e*.
6:5	heart was only *e* all the time
Jdg 2:11	Israelites did *e* in the eyes of
1Sa 16:14	an *e* spirit from the LORD
1Ki 11:6	Solomon did *e* in the eyes
Job 1:1	he feared God and shunned *e*
Ps 23:4	I will fear no *e*,
51:4	done what is *e* in your sight,
52:3	You love *e* rather than good,
Pr 3:7	fear the LORD and shun *e*
Isa 1:13	I cannot bear your *e* assemblies
5:20	Woe to those who call *e* good
55:7	wicked forsake his way and the *e*
Hab 1:13	eyes are too pure to look on *e*;
Mt 5:11	falsely say all kinds of *e* against
6:13	deliver us from the *e* one.
7:11	If you, then, though you are *e*,
Jn 3:19	light because their deeds were *e*
5:29	those who have done *e* will rise
Ro 1:29	wickedness, *e*, greed and depravity.
6:12	mortal body so that you obey its *e*
7:19	the *e* I do not want to do—this
12:9	Hate what is *e*;
12:17	Do not repay anyone *e* for evil.
1Co 13:6	Love does not delight in *e*
Eph 5:16	because the days are *e*
1Th 5:22	Avoid every kind of *e*
1Ti 6:10	money is a root of all kinds of *e*.
1Pe 1:14	do not conform to the *e* desires
2:16	freedom as a cover-up for *e*;
1Jn 2:13	you have overcome the *e* one.

exact

Mt 2:7	the *e* time the star had appeared
Jn 4:53	*e* time at which Jesus had said
Ac 17:26	*e* places where they should live
Heb 1:3	the *e* representation of his being,

exalt, -s, -ed

Ex 15:1	LORD, for he is highly *e-ed*.
Ps 30:1	I will *e* you, O LORD,
46:10	I will be *e-ed* among the nations,
Pr 14:34	Righteousness *e-s* a nation,
Isa 6:1	on a throne, high and *e-ed*,
Mt 23:12	*e-s* himself will be humbled,
Ac 5:31	God *e-ed* him to his own right hand
Php 2:9	God *e-ed* him to the highest place
Heb 7:26	*e-ed* above the heavens

examine, -s, -d

Ps 11:5	The LORD *e-s* the righteous,
26:2	try me, *e* my heart and my mind

Ac 17:11 *e-d* the Scriptures every day
1Co 11:28 A man ought to *e* himself
2Co 13:5 *E* yourselves to see whether you

example, -s
Jn 13:15 I have set you an *e*
1Co 10:6 Now these things occurred as *e-s*
11:1 Follow my *e*, as I follow
Php 3:17 with others in following my *e*,
1Pe 5:3 but being *e-s* to the flock

exasperate
Eph 6:4 Fathers, do not *e* your children;

excel
1Co 14:12 *e* in gifts that build up
2Co 8:7 just as you *e* in everything—

excellent
Lk 1:3 account for you, most *e* Theophilus
Ac 24:3 most *e* Felix, we acknowledge
1Co 12:31 I will show you the most *e* way
Php 4:8 if anything is *e* or praiseworthy—
1Ti 3:13 served well gain an *e* standing
Tit 3:8 These things are *e* and profitable

exchange, -d
Ps 106:20 They *e-d* their Glory for an image
Jer 2:11 my people have *e-d* their Glory
Mt 16:26 can a man give in *e* for his soul
Ro 1:23 *e-d* the glory of the immortal God
1:26 their women *e-d* natural relations

excuse, -s
Ps 25:3 who are treacherous without *e*
Lk 14:18 they all alike began to make *e-s*.
Jn 15:22 they have no *e* for their sin
Ro 1:20 so that men are without *e*
2:1 You, therefore, have no *e*,

exile, -s
2Ki 17:23 their homeland into *e* in Assyria,
25:11 into *e* the people who remained
Ezr 6:21 returned from the *e* ate it,
Eze 1:1 among the *e-s* by the Kebar River,
11:24 brought me to the *e-s* in Babylonia

exist, -s, -ed
Ro 13:1 The authorities that *e* have been
Heb 2:10 through whom everything *e-s*,
11:6 believe that he *e-s* and that he
2Pe 3:5 God's word the heavens *e-ed*

expect, -ed, -ation
Mt 11:3 or should we *e* someone else?
20:10 they *e-ed* to receive more.
24:44 an hour when you do not *e* him
Ro 8:19 creation waits in eager *e-ation*

expense, -ive
Mt 26:7 jar of very *e-ive* perfume,
Lk 7:25 those who wear *e-ive* clothes
1Co 9:7 serves as a soldier at his own *e*?
1Ti 2:9 gold or pearls or *e-ive* clothes

expert
Mt 22:35 One of them, an *e* in the law,
1Co 3:10 a foundation as an *e* builder,

explain, -s, -d
Mt 13:36 "*E* to us the parable of the weeds
Lk 24:27 all the Prophets, he *e-d* to them
Jn 4:25 he will *e* everything to us.
Ac 8:31 "unless someone *e-s* it to me?
18:26 *e-d* to him the way of God
Heb 5:11 hard to *e* because you are slow

exploit, -ing, -ed
Pr 22:22 Do not *e* the poor
Isa 58:3 and *e* all your workers
2Co 7:2 we have *e-ed* no-one
Jas 2:6 the rich who are *e-ing* you?
2Pe 2:3 teachers will *e* you with stories

expose, -d
Mt 1:19 to *e* her to public disgrace,
Jn 3:20 fear that his deeds will be *e-d*
1Co 4:5 *e* the motives of men's hearts.

Eph 5:11 deeds of darkness, but rather *e*

express, -ing

Ro 8:26 with groans that words cannot *e*
1Co 2:13 *e-ing* spiritual truths in
Gal 5:6 faith *e-ing* itself through love

extol

Ps 34:1 I will *e* the LORD at all times;
109:30 I will greatly *e* the LORD;
115:18 it is we who *e* the LORD,
145:2 I will praise you and *e* your name

eye, -s

Ge 3:5 your *e-s* will be opened,
Ex 21:24 *e* for *e*, tooth for tooth,
Dt 32:10 guarded him as the apple of his *e*,
Jdg 16:21 gouged out his *e-s*
Job 42:5 now my *e-s* have seen you
Ps 19:8 giving light to the *e-s*
33:18 the *e-s* of the LORD are on those
118:23 and it is marvellous in our *e-s*
121:1 I lift up my *e-s* to the hills—
SS 1:15 Your *e-s* are doves
Isa 5:21 who are wise in their own *e-s*
6:10 ears dull and close their *e-s*.
35:5 the *e-s* of the blind be opened
40:26 your *e-s* and look to the heavens:
64:4 ear has perceived, no *e* has seen
Hab 1:13 Your *e-s* are too pure to look
Mal 2:17 evil are good in the *e-s*
Mt 5:29 your right *e* causes you to sin,
5:38 '*E* for *e*, and tooth for tooth.
6:22 "The *e* is the lamp of the body.
7:3 sawdust in your brother's *e*
18:9 to have two *e-s* and be thrown
19:24 to go through the *e* of a needle
21:42 and it is marvellous in our *e-s*'
Lk 2:30 my *e-s* have seen your salvation
Jn 4:35 open your *e-s* and look
9:15 "He put mud on my *e-s*,"
12:40 "He has blinded their *e-s*
Ac 1:9 taken up before their very *e-s*,
9:18 like scales fell from Saul's *e-s*,
Ro 3:18 no fear of God before their *e-s*.
1Co 2:9 "No *e* has seen, no ear has heard
12:16 "Because I am not an *e*,
15:52 in the twinkling of an *e*,
Eph 1:18 that the *e-s* of your heart
6:6 favour when their *e* is on you,
Heb 4:13 laid bare before the *e-s* of him
12:2 Let us fix our *e-s* on Jesus,
1Pe 3:12 For the *e-s* of the Lord are on
1Jn 1:1 which we have seen with our *e-s*,
Rev 1:7 every *e* will see him,
1:14 his *e-s* were like blazing fire
7:17 every tear from their *e-s*.

eye-witnesses

Lk 1:2 *e* and servants of the word
2Pe 1:16 but we were *e* of his majesty

Ezekiel

Member of priestly family; deported to Babylon with Jehoiachin (Eze 1:1–3). Vision and call to be prophet to exiles (Eze 1:4–28; 2–3). Listened to, but words not acted upon (Eze 8:1; 14:1; 20:1; 33:30–32). Sudden death of wife (Eze 24:15–18). Visions: idolatry of Jerusalem (Eze 8–11); valley of dry bones (Eze 37); new temple (Eze 40–47). Prophetic symbolism (Eze 4–5; 12). Oracles: against Israel (Eze 13–24; 33); against nations (Eze 25–32; 35; 38–39); of restoration (Eze 34; 36).

Ezra

Priest and teacher of the Law of Moses (Ezr 7:6,10–28); commissioned by Artaxerxes to lead a return of exiles to Jerusalem, to provide resources for temple worship and to establish observance of Law (Ezr 7–8). Addressed problem of intermarriage (Ezr 9–10); read Law at Feast of Tabernacles (Ne 8); took part in dedication of city walls (Ne 12:36).

F

face, -s

Ge 32:30 "It is because I saw God *f* to *f*
Ex 3:6 At this, Moses hid his *f*,
33:11 LORD would speak to Moses *f* to *f*
33:20 "you cannot see my *f*
34:30 saw Moses, his *f* was radiant,
Nu 6:25 the LORD make his *f* shine upon you
1Ch 16:11 seek his *f* always
2Ch 7:14 and pray and seek my *f* and turn

Ps 27:8	My heart says of you, "Seek his *f*!
44:22	for your sake we *f* death all day
Pr 15:13	A happy heart makes the *f* cheerful,
Isa 50:7	have I set my *f* like flint,
54:8	I hid my *f* from you for a moment,
59:2	your sins have hidden his *f*
Mt 17:2	His *f* shone like the sun,
18:10	always see the *f* of my Father
Jn 19:3	And they struck him in the *f*
Ro 8:36	"For your sake we *f* death all day
1Co 13:12	then we shall see *f* to face.
2Co 3:18	who with unveiled *f-s* all reflect
4:6	the glory of God in the *f* of Christ
Rev 1:16	His *f* was like the sun shining
22:4	They will see his *f*, and his name

factions

2Co 12:20	outbursts of anger, *f*, slander,
Gal 5:20	selfish ambition, dissensions, *f*

fade, -ing

Isa 28:4	*f-ing* flower, his glorious beauty,
2Co 3:13	while the radiance was *f-ing* away
Jas 1:11	the rich man will *f* away
1Pe 1:4	that can never perish, spoil or *f*
5:4	crown of glory that will never *f*

fail, -s, -ings, -ed

Jos 23:14	been fulfilled; not one has *f-ed*
2Ch 6:16	'You shall never *f* to have a man
Ps 89:28	my covenant with him will never *f*
La 3:22	for his compassions never *f*
Lk 22:32	Simon, that your faith may not *f*.
Ro 15:1	to bear with the *f-ings* of the weak
1Co 13:8	Love never *f-s*.

faint

Ps 6:2	Be merciful to me, LORD, for I am *f*
SS 5:8	Tell him I am *f* with love
Isa 40:31	they will walk and not be *f*
Jer 31:25	refresh the weary and satisfy the *f*
Lk 21:26	Men will *f* from terror,

faith

Isa 7:9	If you do not stand firm in your *f*,
Hab 2:4	the righteous will live by his *f*
Mt 6:30	O you of little *f*?
8:10	anyone in Israel with such great *f*.
9:22	"your *f* has healed you."
15:28	"Woman, you have great *f*!
17:20	"Because you have so little *f*.
21:21	if you have *f* and do not doubt,
Mk 11:22	Have *f* in God," Jesus answered
Lk 17:6	*f* as small as a mustard seed,
18:8	will he find *f* on the earth?
Jn 2:11	his disciples put their *f* in him
Ac 3:16	By *f* in the name of Jesus,
6:5	Stephen, a man full of *f*
11:24	full of the Holy Spirit and *f*,
15:9	for he purified their hearts by *f*
26:18	those who are sanctified by *f* in me
Ro 1:5	the obedience that comes from *f*
1:17	a righteousness that is by *f*
3:25	through *f* in his blood.
3:26	justifies those who have *f* in Jesus
4:5	his *f* is credited as righteousness
4:12	the *f* that our father Abraham had
4:16	Therefore, the promise comes by *f*,
5:1	we have been justified through *f*,
10:17	*f* comes from hearing the message,
12:6	use it in proportion to his *f*.
14:1	Accept him whose *f* is weak,
1Co 12:9	to another *f* by the same Spirit,
13:2	a *f* that can move mountains,
13:13	three remain: *f*, hope and love.
15:14	is useless, and so is your *f*.
2Co 10:15	as your *f* continues to grow,
Gal 2:20	I live by *f* in the Son of God,
3:11	"The righteous will live by *f*.
3:26	You are all sons of God through *f*

Eph 2:8 you have been saved, through *f*
3:17 may dwell in your hearts through *f*.
4:5 one Lord, one *f*, one baptism;
4:13 until we all reach unity in the *f*
6:16 take up the shield of *f*,
Php 1:27 contending as one man for the *f*
Col 1:23 if you continue in your *f*,
1Th 3:10 supply what is lacking in your *f*
1Ti 4:1 some will abandon the *f*
4:6 brought up in the truths of the *f*
6:11 pursue righteousness, godliness, *f*,
6:12 Fight the good fight of the *f*.
6:21 so doing have wandered from the *f*.
2Ti 1:5 reminded of your sincere *f*,
3:15 salvation through *f* in Christ Jesus
4:7 I have kept the *f*
Heb 4:14 hold firmly to the *f* we profess
11:1 *f* is being sure of what we hope for
11:6 And without *f* it is impossible
Jas 2:26 so *f* without deeds is dead
1Pe 1:9 receiving the goal of your *f*,
2Pe 1:5 add to your *f* goodness;
1Jn 5:4 has overcome the world, even our *f*
Jude :3 and urge you to contend for the *f*
Rev 2:19 I know your deeds, your love and *f*,

faithful, -ness

Dt 7:9 the *f* God, keeping his covenant
2Sa 22:26 To the *f* you show yourself *f*
Ps 57:10 your *f-ness* reaches to the skies
85:10 Love and *f-ness* meet together;
100:5 his *f-ness* continues through all
145:13 The LORD is *f* to all his promises
Pr 3:3 Let love and *f-ness* never leave you
Isa 55:3 my *f* love promised to David
La 3:23 every morning; great is your *f-ness*
Mt 25:21 'Well done, good and *f* servant!
Ro 12:12 patient in affliction, *f* in prayer
1Co 10:13 God is *f*;
Gal 5:22 kindness, goodness, *f-ness*
1Th 5:24 The one who calls you is *f*
Heb 3:5 Moses was *f* as a servant
3:6 But Christ is *f* as a son
1Jn 1:9 confess our sins, he is *f* and just
Rev 2:10 Be *f*, even to the point of death,

faithless

Ps 101:3 The deeds of *f* men I hate;
Jer 3:12 " 'Return, *f* Israel,'
Ro 1:31 senseless, *f*, heartless, ruthless
2Ti 2:13 we are *f*, he will remain faithful

fall, -s, -ing, -en

Dt 32:2 Let my teaching *f* like rain
2Sa 1:27 "How the mighty have *f-en*!
Ps 37:24 though he stumble, he will not *f*,
46:5 God is within her, she will not *f*;
69:9 of those who insult you *f* on me
Pr 11:14 For lack of guidance a nation *f-s*,
16:18 a haughty spirit before a *f*
Isa 14:12 How you have *f-en* from heaven,
40:7 The grass withers and the flowers *f*
Eze 33:21 to me and said, "The city has *f-en*!
Da 3:5 must *f* down and worship the image
Hos 10:8 and to the hills, "*F* on us!
Mt 11:6 does not *f* away on account of me.
13:21 he quickly *f-s* away
26:31 This very night you will all *f* away
Lk 8:13 in the time of testing they *f* away
10:18 "I saw Satan *f* like lightning
23:30 say to the mountains, "*F* on us!"
Ro 3:23 and *f* short of the glory of God
14:21 that will cause your brother to *f*
15:3 who insult you have *f-en* on me.
1Co 10:12 be careful that you don't *f*
Gal 5:4 you have *f-en* away from grace
Heb 10:31 *f* into the hands of the living God

1Pe 1:24 the grass withers and the flowers *f*
Jude :24 who is able to keep you from *f-ing*
Rev 14:8 "*F-en*! *F-en* is Babylon the Great,

false, -ly, -hood
Ex 20:16 "You shall not give *f* testimony
La 2:14 The visions of your prophets were *f*
Mt 7:15 "Watch out for *f* prophets.
19:18 do not give *f* testimony
24:24 *f* Christs and false prophets
Mk 14:56 Many testified *f-ly* against him,
2Co 11:26 in danger from *f* brothers
Eph 4:25 put off *f-hood* and speak truthfully
1Ti 1:3 not to teach *f* doctrines any longer
1Jn 4:1 many *f* prophets have gone out
4:6 of truth and the spirit of *f-hood*

familiar
Ps 139:3 you are *f* with all my ways
Isa 53:3 and *f* with suffering.

family, -ies
Ge 7:1 into the ark, you and your whole *f*,
Ps 68:6 God sets the lonely in *f-ies*,
Pr 15:27 greedy man brings trouble to his *f*
31:15 she provides food for her *f*
Mk 3:21 When his *f* heard about this,
5:19 "Go home to your *f* and tell them
Lk 9:61 go back and say good-bye to my *f*.
12:52 in one *f* divided against each other
Jn 7:42 the Christ will come from David's *f*
Ac 10:2 He and all his *f* were devout
16:33 he and all his *f* were baptised
16:34 believe in God—he and his whole *f*
Gal 6:10 who belong to the *f* of believers
Eph 3:15 his whole *f* in heaven and on earth
1Ti 3:4 He must manage his own *f* well
5:4 by caring for their own *f*
5:8 and especially for his immediate *f*,
Heb 2:11 who are made holy are of the same *f*
1Pe 4:17 judgment to begin with the *f* of God

famine, -s
Ge 12:10 Now there was a *f* in the land,
41:30 seven years of *f* will follow them.
1Ki 18:2 Now the *f* was severe in Samaria
Am 8:11 *f* of hearing the words of the LORD
Mt 24:7 There will be *f-s* and earthquakes
Ro 8:35 hardship or persecution or *f*

fast[1]
Dt 13:4 serve him and hold *f* to him
Jos 22:5 obey his commands, to hold *f* to him
Ps 119:31 I hold *f* to your statutes, O LORD;
139:10 your right hand will hold me *f*
1Pe 5:12 true grace of God. Stand *f* in it

fast[2], -ing, -ed
Ne 1:4 For some days I mourned and *f-ed*
Isa 58:4 Your *f-ing* ends in quarrelling
Mt 4:2 After *f-ing* for forty days
6:16 "When you *f*, do not look sombre
9:14 but your disciples do not *f*?
Lk 18:12 I *f* twice a week and give a tenth
Ac 13:2 worshipping the Lord and *f-ing*,
13:3 So after they had *f-ed* and prayed,
14:23 with prayer and *f-ing*, committed

father, -'s, -s
Ge 2:24 a man will leave his *f* and mother
17:4 You will be the *f* of many nations
Ex 20:12 "Honour your *f* and your mother,

21:17 "Anyone who curses his *f* or mother
Dt 1:31 carried you, as a *f* carries his son
27:16 who dishonours his *f* or his mother.
32:6 Is he not your *F*, your Creator,
2Sa 7:14 I will be his *f*, and he shall be
2Ki 2:12 "My *f*! My *f*! The chariots
1Ch 22:10 will be my son, and I will be his *f*
Job 29:16 I was a *f* to the needy;
Ps 2:7 my Son; today I have become your *F*
27:10 Though my *f* and mother forsake me,
68:5 A *f* to the fatherless,
89:26 'You are my *F*, my God, the Rock
103:13 As a *f* has compassion
Pr 10:1 A wise son brings joy to his *f*,
23:22 Listen to your *f*, who gave you life
Isa 9:6 Everlasting *F*, Prince of Peace
51:2 look to Abraham, your *f*,
63:16 But you are our *F*, though Abraham
Jer 3:4 'My *F*, my friend from my youth
31:9 because I am Israel's *f*,
Eze 18:2 " 'The *f-s* eat sour grapes,
18:18 his *f* will die for his own sin,
Mal 1:6 If I am a *f*, where is the honour
4:6 hearts of the *f-s* to their children
Mt 3:9 'We have Abraham as our *f*.'
5:16 praise your *F* in heaven
6:9 you should pray: " 'Our *F* in heaven
6:26 yet your heavenly *F* feeds them.
10:37 Anyone who loves his *f* or mother
11:27 no-one knows the *F* except the Son
15:4 'Honour your *f* and mother'
19:5 a man will leave his *f* and mother
19:19 honour your *f* and mother,
28:19 in the name of the *F* and of the Son
Lk 1:17 to turn the hearts of the *f-s*
2:49 I had to be in my *F-'s* house?
9:59 first let me go and bury my *f*."
11:11 "Which of you *f-s*, if your son
14:26 does not hate his *f* and mother,
15:12 '*F*, give me my share of the estate
15:21 '*F*, I have sinned against heaven
22:42 "*F*, if you are willing, take this
23:34 "*F*, forgive them, for they do not
Jn 1:14 who came from the *F*, full of grace
3:35 The *F* loves the Son and has placed
4:21 you will worship the *F* neither on
5:18 he was even calling God his own *F*,
5:20 For the *F* loves the Son
5:22 the *F* judges no-one, but
6:44 No-one can come to me unless the *F*
6:46 No-one has seen the *F* except
8:19 "You do not know me or my *F*,"
8:44 You belong to your *f*, the devil
10:29 My *F*, who has given them to me,
10:30 I and the *F* are one."
10:38 the *F* is in me, and I in the *F*
12:28 *F*, glorify your name!"
14:2 In my *F-'s* house are many rooms;
14:6 No-one comes to the *F* except
14:11 I am in the *F*
14:23 My *F* will love him,
15:9 "As the *F* has loved me, so have I
16:15 All that belongs to the *F* is mine.
16:27 the *F* himself loves you because
17:1 "*F*, the time has come.
17:11 Holy *F*, protect them by the power
20:17 'I am returning to my *F* and
Ac 1:4 wait for the gift my *F* promised,
Ro 4:11 he is the *f* of all who believe
8:15 by him we cry, "Abba, *F*"
Eph 5:31 a man will leave his *f* and mother
6:2 "Honour your *f* and mother"
6:4 *F-s*, do not exasperate your
Php 2:11 to the glory of God the *F*
Col 3:21 *F-s*, do not embitter your children

Heb 1:5 today I have become your *F*"?
7:3 Without *f* or mother, without
12:10 Our *f-s* disciplined us
1Pe 1:2 the foreknowledge of God the *F*,
1Jn 1:3 our fellowship is with the *F*
2:13 I write to you, *f-s*, because you
2:24 remain in the Son and in the *F*.
4:14 the *F* has sent his Son to be the
2Jn :3 Jesus Christ, the *F-'s* Son,
1:9 teaching has both the *F* and the Son
Jude :1 who are loved by God the *F*
Rev 14:1 his name and his *F-'s* name written

fatherless

Dt 10:18 He defends the cause of the *f*
Ps 10:14 you are the helper of the *f*
68:5 A father to the *f*, a defender
82:3 Defend the cause of the weak and *f*

fathom, -ed

Job 5:9 wonders that cannot be *f-ed*,
11:7 "Can you *f* the mysteries of God?
Ps 145:3 his greatness no-one can *f*
1Co 13:2 *f* all mysteries and all knowledge,

fattened

Pr 15:17 than a *f* calf with hatred
Lk 15:23 Bring the *f* calf and kill it.

fault, -s

Ps 19:12 Forgive my hidden *f-s*
Mt 18:15 go and show him his *f*,
Php 2:15 pure, children of God without *f*
Jas 1:5 generously to all without finding *f*
Jude :24 his glorious presence without *f*

favour

Ge 4:4 The LORD looked with *f* on Abel
6:8 But Noah found *f* in the eyes
Ex 32:11 But Moses sought the *f* of the LORD
Ne 5:19 Remember me with *f*, O my God,
Ps 30:5 but his *f* lasts a lifetime;
Lk 1:30 Mary, you have found *f* with God
2:14 peace to men on whom his *f* rests.
2:52 and in *f* with God and men

favouritism

Ex 23:3 and do not show *f* to a poor man
Ac 10:34 God does not show *f*
Ro 2:11 For God does not show *f*
Eph 6:9 and there is no *f* with him
Jas 2:9 But if you show *f*, you sin

fear, -s, -ed

Dt 6:13 *F* the LORD your God,
Job 1:9 "Does Job *f* God for nothing?"
28:28 'The *f* of the Lord—that is wisdom,
Ps 19:9 The *f* of the LORD is pure,
23:4 I will *f* no evil,
27:1 my salvation—whom shall I *f*?
34:4 he delivered me from all my *f-s*
76:7 You alone are to be *f-ed*.
103:13 compassion on those who *f* him
147:11 LORD delights in those who *f* him,
Pr 8:13 To *f* the LORD is to hate evil;
9:10 The *f* of the LORD is the beginning
Ecc 12:13 *F* God and keep his commandments,
Isa 11:3 will delight in the *f* of the LORD.
41:10 So do not *f*, for I am with you;
Lk 12:5 I will show you whom you should *f*:
Ac 5:11 Great *f* seized the whole church
9:31 living in the *f* of the Lord
Ro 8:15 that makes you a slave again to *f*,
2Co 5:11 we know what it is to *f* the Lord,
Php 2:12 your salvation with *f* and trembling
Heb 2:15 held in slavery by their *f* of death
1Pe 3:6 and do not give way to *f*
1Jn 4:18 But perfect love drives out *f*,

feast, -s

Ex 23:15 Celebrate the *F* of Unleavened Bread
23:16 "Celebrate the *F* of Harvest
34:22 "Celebrate the *F* of Weeks

Lev 23:2 'These are my appointed *f-s*,
Am 5:21 I despise your religious *f-s*;
Mt 26:5 "But not during the *F*," they said,
Lk 13:29 at the *f* in the kingdom of God
14:8 someone invites you to a wedding *f*,
14:15 eat at the *f* in the kingdom of God
15:23 Let's have a *f* and celebrate
Jn 7:37 the last and greatest day of the *F*,
Jude :12 blemishes at your love *f-s*,

feeble
Isa 35:3 Strengthen the *f* hands,
Heb 12:12 Therefore, strengthen your *f* arms

feed, -s
Isa 65:25 wolf and the lamb will *f* together,
Mt 6:26 yet your heavenly Father *f-s*
Jn 6:58 he who *f-s* on this bread will live
21:17 Jesus said, "*F* my sheep
Ro 12:20 "If your enemy is hungry, *f* him;

feet
2Sa 9:3 he is crippled in both *f*.
Ps 8:6 you put everything under his *f*
110:1 your enemies a footstool for your *f*
119:105 Your word is a lamp to my *f*
Isa 52:7 the *f* of those who bring good news,
Mt 10:14 shake the dust off your *f*
22:44 I put your enemies under your *f*."
Lk 10:39 Mary, who sat at the Lord's *f*
24:39 Look at my hands and my *f*. It is I
Jn 12:3 she poured it on Jesus' *f* and wiped
13:5 and began to wash his disciples' *f*,
Ac 2:35 your enemies a footstool for your *f*
3:7 man's *f* and ankles became strong
13:51 So they shook the dust from their *f*
Ro 10:15 "How beautiful are the *f* of those
16:20 will soon crush Satan under your *f*.
1Co 12:21 And the head cannot say to the *f*,
Eph 1:22 God placed all things under his *f*
1Ti 5:10 washing the *f* of the saints,
Rev 1:15 His *f* were like bronze glowing

fellow-citizens
Eph 2:19 but *f* with God's people and members

fellowship
Ac 2:42 apostles' teaching, and to the *f*,
1Co 1:9 into *f* with his Son Jesus Christ
2Co 6:14 what *f* can light have with darkness
13:14 and the *f* of the Holy Spirit
Gal 2:9 the right hand of *f*
Php 2:1 if any *f* with the Spirit,
3:10 the *f* of sharing in his sufferings,
1Jn 1:3 And our *f* is with the Father
1:7 we have *f* with one another,

female
Ge 1:27 male and *f* he created them
Mt 19:4 the Creator 'made them male and *f*'
Gal 3:28 slave nor free, male nor *f*,

fervour
Ac 18:25 he spoke with great *f* and taught
Ro 12:11 but keep your spiritual *f*,

festival
Ex 23:14 you are to celebrate a *f* to me
Hos 9:5 on the *f* days of the LORD
1Co 5:8 Therefore let us keep the *F*,
Col 2:16 or with regard to a religious *f*,

fever
Job 30:30 my body burns with *f*
Mt 8:14 mother-in-law lying in bed with a *f*
Jn 4:52 "The *f* left him yesterday
Ac 28:8 suffering from *f* and dysentery.

field, -s
Ge 4:8 Abel, "Let's go out to the *f*."
Lev 19:19 'Do not plant your *f* with two kinds
Ps 103:15 flourishes like a flower of the *f*

Isa 40:6 glory is like the flowers of the *f*
Hab 3:17 and the *f-s* produce no food,
Mt 6:28 See how the lilies of the *f* grow.
9:38 workers into his harvest *f*.
13:24 a man who sowed good seed in his *f*
13:38 The *f* is the world,
24:40 Two men will be in the *f*;
27:10 used them to buy the potter's *f*,
Mk 10:30 sisters, mothers, children and *f-s*—
13:16 Let no-one in the *f* go back
Lk 2:8 shepherds living out in the *f-s*
14:18 said, 'I have just bought a *f*,
Jn 4:35 open your eyes and look at the *f-s*
Ac 1:18 Judas bought a *f*; there he fell
4:37 sold a *f* he owned and brought
1Co 3:9 you are God's *f*, God's building
2Co 10:13 the *f* God has assigned to us,

fig, -s
Ge 3:7 so they sewed *f* leaves together
Lk 6:44 do not pick *f-s* from thorn-bushes,
Jas 3:12 or a grapevine bear *f-s*?
Rev 6:13 as late *f-s* drop from a fig-tree

fig-tree
1Ki 4:25 each man under his own vine and *f*
Hab 3:17 Though the *f* does not bud
Mt 21:20 "How did the *f* wither so quickly?
24:32 "Now learn this lesson from the *f*
Lk 13:7 coming to look for fruit on this *f*
Jn 1:48 while you were still under the *f*

fight, -s, -ing
Ex 2:13 went out and saw two Hebrews *f-ing*.
14:14 The LORD will *f* for you;
2Ch 20:17 You will not have to *f* this battle.
Ne 4:20 Our God will *f* for us!
Ps 35:1 *f* against those who *f* against
Jn 18:36 If it were, my servants would *f*
Ac 5:39 find yourselves *f-ing* against God.
1Co 9:26 I do not *f* like a man beating
2Co 10:4 The weapons we *f* with are not
1Ti 6:12 Fight the good *f* of the faith.
2Ti 4:7 I have fought the good *f*,
Jas 4:1 What causes *f-s* and quarrels among

fill, -s, -ed
Ge 1:28 increase in number; *f* the earth
1Ki 8:11 glory of the LORD *f-ed* his temple
Ps 16:11 you will *f* me with joy
81:10 Open wide your mouth and I will *f*
107:9 and *f-s* the hungry with good things
Hab 2:14 earth ... *f-ed* with the knowledge
Mt 5:6 for they will be *f-ed*
Lk 3:5 Every valley shall be *f-ed* in,
Jn 2:7 servants, "*F* the jars with water"
Ac 2:4 were *f-ed* with the Holy Spirit
2:28 you will *f* me with joy
4:31 were all *f-ed* with the Holy Spirit
9:17 and be *f-ed* with the Holy Spirit.
13:52 the disciples were *f-ed* with joy
14:17 food and *f-s* your hearts with joy.
Ro 15:13 May the God of hope *f* you with
Eph 1:23 fulness of him who *f-s* everything
4:10 in order to *f* the whole universe.
5:18 Instead, be *f-ed* with the Spirit
Col 1:9 to *f* you with the knowledge
1:24 and I *f* up in my flesh

filth, -y
Isa 64:6 righteous acts are like *f-y* rags
Col 3:8 malice, slander and *f-y* language
Jas 1:21 get rid of all moral *f* and the evil

find, -s
Ge 18:26 "If I *f* fifty righteous people
Nu 32:23 your sin will *f* you out
Dt 4:29 you will *f* him if you look for him
Ps 36:7 *f* refuge in the shadow of your
62:5 *F* rest, O my soul, in God alone;

Pr 8:17 and those who seek me *f* me
8:35 For whoever *f-s* me *f-s* life
Ecc 11:1 after many days you will *f* it again
Jer 6:16 and you will *f* rest for your souls.
29:13 You will seek me and *f* me
Mt 2:8 As soon as you *f* him, report to me,
7:7 seek and you will *f*; knock
7:8 who asks receives; he who seeks *f-s*
7:14 leads to life, and only a few *f* it
10:39 Whoever *f-s* his life will lose it,
11:29 and you will *f* rest for your souls
12:43 seeking rest and does not *f* it
Lk 2:12 You will *f* a baby wrapped in cloths
18:8 will he *f* faith on the earth?
24:3 they did not *f* the body of the Lord
Jn 7:34 look for me, but you will not *f* me
10:9 come in and go out, and *f* pasture.
21:6 of the boat and you will *f* some."
Eph 5:10 *f* out what pleases the Lord
2Ti 1:18 that he will *f* mercy from the Lord

finger, -s

Ex 8:19 to Pharaoh, "This is the *f* of God.
Dt 9:10 tablets inscribed by the *f* of God.
Ps 8:3 your heavens, the work of your *f-s*,
Lk 11:20 I drive out demons by the *f* of God,
Jn 8:6 to write on the ground with his *f*
20:27 "Put your *f* here; see my hands.

finish, -ed

Ge 2:2 God had *f-ed* the work
1Ki 9:1 When Solomon had *f-ed* building
Jn 4:34 him who sent me and to *f* his work
19:30 Jesus said, "It is *f-ed*."
Ac 20:24 if only I may *f* the race
2Co 8:11 Now *f* the work, so that your eager
2Ti 4:7 I have *f-ed* the race,
Heb 4:3 And yet his work has been *f-ed*
Jas 1:4 Perseverance must *f* its work

fire

Ex 3:2 LORD appeared to him in flames of *f*
13:22 the pillar of *f* by night
29:18 an offering made to the LORD by *f*
Dt 4:12 the LORD spoke to you out of the *f*.
1Ki 18:38 Then the *f* of the LORD fell
19:12 but the LORD was not in the *f*.
2Ki 2:11 a chariot of *f* and horses of *f*
2Ch 7:1 *f* came down from heaven
Isa 43:2 When you walk through the *f*,
Jer 23:29 "Is not my word like *f*,"
Da 3:25 four men walking around in the *f*,
Mal 3:2 For he will be like a refiner's *f*
Mt 3:11 with the Holy Spirit and with *f*
5:22 in danger of the *f* of hell
7:19 cut down and thrown into the *f*
25:41 eternal *f* prepared for the devil
Lk 9:54 to call *f* down from heaven
12:49 I have come to bring *f* on the earth
16:24 because I am in agony in this *f*.
Jn 15:6 thrown into the *f* and burned
Ac 2:3 saw what seemed to be tongues of *f*
1Co 3:13 and the *f* will test the quality
1Th 5:19 Do not put out the Spirit's *f*
2Th 1:7 revealed from heaven in blazing *f*
Heb 1:7 his servants flames of *f*.
12:29 for our "God is a consuming *f*.
Jas 3:6 The tongue also is a *f*,
2Pe 3:10 the elements will be destroyed by *f*
Jude :7 suffer the punishment of eternal *f*
1:23 snatch others from the *f* and save
Rev 1:14 and his eyes were like blazing *f*
20:14 The lake of *f* is the second death

firm, -ly

Ex 14:13 "Do not be afraid. Stand *f* and you
2Ch 20:17 stand *f* and see the deliverance
Ps 93:1 The world is *f-ly* established;

Isa 7:9	If you do not stand *f* in your faith
Lk 21:19	By standing *f* you will gain life
1Co 15:2	you are saved, if you hold *f-ly*
2Co 1:24	it is by faith you stand *f*
Eph 6:14	Stand *f* then, with the belt of
1Th 3:8	you are standing *f* in the Lord
Heb 4:14	let us hold *f-ly* to the faith
1Pe 5:10	make you strong, *f* and steadfast
2Pe 1:12	*f-ly* established in the truth

first

Ge 1:5	and there was morning—the *f* day
Isa 44:6	I am the *f* and I am the last;
Mt 5:24	*F* go and be reconciled
6:33	But seek *f* his kingdom
7:5	hypocrite, *f* take the plank out
10:2	the twelve apostles: *f*, Simon
19:30	But many who are *f* will be last,
20:27	wants to be *f* must be your slave
22:38	the *f* and greatest commandment
Jn 8:7	let him be the *f* to throw a stone
20:1	Early on the *f* day of the week,
Ac 11:26	were called Christians *f* at Antioch
20:7	On the *f* day of the week
Ro 1:16	*f* for the Jew, then for the Gentile
1Co 12:28	God has appointed *f* of all apostles,
15:45	"The *f* man Adam became a living
16:2	On the *f* day of every week,
Eph 1:12	who were the *f* to hope in Christ,
6:2	the *f* commandment with a promise
1Th 4:16	and the dead in Christ will rise *f*
1Ti 2:13	For Adam was formed *f*, then Eve
Heb 10:9	He sets aside the *f* to establish
1Jn 4:19	We love because he *f* loved us
3Jn :9	Diotrephes, who loves to be *f*,
Rev 1:17	I am the *F* and the Last
2:4	You have forsaken your *f* love

firstborn

Ex 13:2	"Consecrate to me every *f* male.
Lk 2:23	"Every *f* male is to be consecrated
Ro 8:29	might be the *f* among many brothers
Col 1:15	the *f* over all creation
1:18	and the *f* from among the dead,
Heb 1:6	God brings his *f* into the world,
12:23	to the church of the *f*,
Rev 1:5	the *f* from the dead,

firstfruits

Ex 23:16	the Feast of Harvest with the *f*
Ro 8:23	who have the *f* of the Spirit,
1Co 15:20	the *f* of those who have fallen
Jas 1:18	kind of *f* of all he created
Rev 14:4	offered as *f* to God and the Lamb

fish, -ers

Ge 1:26	let them rule over the *f* of the sea
Jnh 1:17	But the LORD provided a great *f*
Mt 4:19	"and I will make you *f-ers* of men.
Lk 11:11	if your son asks for a *f*,
Jn 21:11	It was full of large *f*, 153,

fishermen

Mt 4:18	into the lake, for they were *f*
13:48	When it was full, the *f* pulled it
Lk 5:2	the *f*, who were washing their nets

fitting

Ps 147:1	how pleasant and *f* to praise him
1Co 14:40	done in a *f* and orderly way
Col 3:18	as is *f* in the Lord
Heb 2:10	it was *f* that God,

fix, -ed

Ps 141:8	But my eyes are *f-ed* on you,
Pr 4:25	*f* your gaze directly before you
Jer 33:25	the *f-ed* laws of heaven and earth
2Co 4:18	we *f* our eyes not on what is seen,
Heb 3:1	*f* your thoughts on Jesus,

12:2 Let us *f* our eyes on Jesus,

flame, -s, -ing
Ex 3:2 in *f-s* of fire from within a bush.
1Co 13:3 and surrender my body to the *f-s*,
Eph 6:16 the *f-ing* arrows of the evil one
2Ti 1:6 fan into *f* the gift of God,

flash
Job 37:15 and makes his lightning *f*
Lk 9:29 as bright as a *f* of lightning
1Co 15:52 in a *f*, in the twinkling of an eye,

flatter, -ing, -y
Ps 12:2 *f-ing* lips speak with deception
Ro 16:18 smooth talk and *f-y* they deceive
1Th 2:5 You know we never used *f-y*,
Jude :16 *f* others for their own advantage

flawless
2Sa 22:31 the word of the LORD is *f*.
Ps 12:6 And the words of the LORD are *f*,
Pr 30:5 "Every word of God is *f*;
SS 5:2 my darling, my dove, my *f* one.

fled
Ps 104:7 But at your rebuke the waters *f*,
Mt 26:56 the disciples deserted him and *f*
Mk 14:52 he *f* naked, leaving his garment
16:8 women went out and *f* from the tomb.
Rev 20:11 Earth and sky *f* from his presence,

flee
Ps 139:7 Where can I *f* from your presence?
Jnh 1:3 for Tarshish to *f* from the LORD
Mt 24:16 who are in Judea *f* to the mountains
1Co 6:18 *F* from sexual immorality.
10:14 my dear friends, *f* from idolatry
2Ti 2:22 *F* the evil desires of youth,
Jas 4:7 Resist the devil, and he will *f*

fleece
Jdg 6:37 look, I will place a wool *f*

flesh
Ge 2:23 bone of my bones and *f* of my *f*;
2:24 and they will become one *f*
Mt 19:5 and the two will become one *f*
Jn 1:14 The Word became *f*
6:51 This bread is my *f*,
6:55 For my *f* is real food
1Co 6:16 "The two will become one *f*.
15:39 All *f* is not the same:
2Co 12:7 there was given me a thorn in my *f*,
1Jn 4:2 that Jesus Christ has come in the *f*

flies
Ex 8:21 I will send swarms of *f* on you
Ps 78:45 He sent swarms of *f* that devoured
Ecc 10:1 As dead *f* give perfume a bad smell,

flock, -s
2Sa 7:8 from following the *f* to be ruler
Ps 77:20 You led your people like a *f*
Isa 40:11 He tends his *f* like a shepherd:
Jer 31:10 watch over his *f* like a shepherd.
Eze 34:16 I will shepherd the *f* with justice
Mt 26:31 sheep of the *f* will be scattered.
Lk 2:8 keeping watch over their *f-s*
12:32 "Do not be afraid, little *f*,
Jn 10:16 shall be one *f* and one shepherd
Ac 20:28 all the *f* of which the Holy Spirit
1Co 9:7 Who tends a *f* and does not drink
1Pe 5:2 God's *f* that is under your care,
5:3 but being examples to the *f*

flog, -ged
Dt 25:3 If he is *f-ged* more than that,
Mt 10:17 and *f* you in their synagogues
20:19 be mocked and *f-ged* and crucified
27:26 But he had Jesus *f-ged*,
Ac 5:40 the apostles in and had them *f-ged*.

22:25 Is it legal for you to *f* a Roman

flood, -gates
Ge 7:17 For forty days the *f* kept coming
Ps 29:10 The LORD sits enthroned over the *f*;
Mal 3:10 throw open the *f-gates* of heaven
Mt 24:38 For in the days before the *f*,
Lk 6:48 When the *f* came, the torrent struck
2Pe 2:5 brought the *f* on its ungodly people

flourish, -es
Ps 92:12 righteous will *f* like a palm tree,
103:15 he *f-es* like a flower of the field
Pr 12:12 but the root of the righteous *f-es*
Isa 66:14 and you will *f* like grass;

flow, -ing
Ex 3:8 a land *f-ing* with milk and honey—
Zec 14:8 water will *f* out from Jerusalem,
Jn 7:38 living water will *f* from within him
19:34 a sudden *f* of blood and water
2Co 1:5 of Christ *f* over into our lives,

flower, -s
Ps 103:15 he flourishes like a *f* of the field
SS 2:12 *F-s* appear on the earth;
Isa 40:6 and all their glory is like the *f-s*
40:8 The grass withers and the *f-s* fall,
1Pe 1:24 and all their glory is like the *f-s*

foal
Zec 9:9 on a colt, the *f* of a donkey
Mt 21:5 on a colt, the *f* of a donkey.'

follow, -s, -ing, -ed
Ex 23:2 "Do not *f* the crowd in doing wrong.
Lev 22:31 "Keep my commands and *f* them.
Nu 32:15 If you turn away from *f-ing* him,
Dt 5:1 Learn them and be sure to *f* them
1Ki 11:6 he did not *f* the LORD completely,
Ps 23:6 Surely goodness and love will *f* me
119:14 I rejoice in *f-ing* your statutes
Mt 4:19 "Come, *f* me," Jesus said,
4:20 they left their nets and *f-ed* him
8:22 But Jesus told him, "*F* me,
9:9 and Matthew got up and *f-ed* him
16:24 and take up his cross and *f* me
Mk 10:52 received his sight and *f-ed* Jesus
Lk 9:61 "I will *f* you, Lord; but first
18:28 "We have left all we had to *f* you!
Jn 6:66 turned back and no longer *f-ed* him
8:12 *f-s* me will never walk in darkness,
10:4 his sheep *f* him because they know
10:27 I know them, and they *f* me
12:26 Whoever serves me must *f* me;
13:36 "Where I am going, you cannot *f*
21:22 what is that to you? You must *f* me.
1Co 1:12 "I *f* Paul"; ... "I *f* Apollos
11:1 *F* my example, as I *f*
14:1 *F* the way of love
2Th 3:7 know how you ought to *f* our example
1Ti 4:6 good teaching that you have *f-ed*
5:15 already turned away to *f* Satan
1Pe 2:21 that you should *f* in his steps
Jude :16 they *f* their own evil desires;
Rev 14:4 They *f* the Lamb wherever he goes.

folly
Pr 14:29 but a quick-tempered man displays *f*
26:5 Answer a fool according to his *f*,
Ecc 10:1 a little *f* outweighs wisdom
Mk 7:22 envy, slander, arrogance and *f*
2Ti 3:9 their *f* will be clear to everyone

food, -s
Ge 1:30 I give every green plant for *f*."
9:3 that lives and moves will be *f*
Ps 104:21 and seek their *f* from God

111:5	provides *f* for those who fear him;
127:2	stay up late, toiling for *f* to eat—
Pr 9:5	"Come, eat my *f* and drink the wine
9:17	*f* eaten in secret is delicious!
22:9	for he shares his *f* with the poor
25:21	enemy is hungry, give him *f* to eat;
31:15	she provides *f* for her family
Isa 58:7	to share your *f* with the hungry
Mt 3:4	His *f* was locusts and wild honey
6:25	Is not life more important than *f*,
Mk 7:19	Jesus declared all *f-s* "clean".
Jn 4:34	"My *f*," said Jesus, "is to do
6:27	Do not work for *f* that spoils,
6:55	For my flesh is real *f* and my blood
Ac 15:29	abstain from *f* sacrificed to idols,
Ro 14:14	no *f* is unclean in itself.
1Co 3:2	I gave you milk, not solid *f*,
8:1	Now about *f* sacrificed to idols:
8:8	But *f* does not bring us near to God
Heb 5:14	But solid *f* is for the mature,

fool, -s

Ps 14:1	The *f* says in his heart,
Pr 1:7	*f-s* despise wisdom and discipline
Mt 5:22	But anyone who says, 'You *f*!'
23:17	You blind *f-s*! Which is greater:
Lk 12:20	"But God said to him, 'You *f*!
1Co 3:18	he should become a "*f*"
4:10	We are *f-s* for Christ,

foolish, -ness

1Co 1:18	the message of the cross is *f-ness*
1:20	God made *f* the wisdom of the world
1:27	God chose the *f* things of the world
Tit 3:9	But avoid *f* controversies

foot

Ps 121:3	He will not let your *f* slip—
Pr 25:17	Seldom set *f* in your neighbour's
Mt 4:6	not strike your *f* against a stone.'
Mk 9:45	And if your *f* causes you to sin,
1Co 12:15	If the *f* should say,
Heb 10:29	trampled the Son of God under *f*,

foothold

Eph 4:27	and do not give the devil a *f*

footstool

Ps 110:1	until I make your enemies a *f*
132:7	let us worship at his *f*
Isa 66:1	and the earth is my *f*.
Mt 5:35	or by the earth, for it is his *f*;
Ac 7:49	and the earth is my *f*.
Heb 10:13	for his enemies to be made his *f*

forbid

1Sa 26:11	the LORD *f* that I should lay a hand
1Co 14:39	and do not *f* speaking in tongues
1Ti 4:3	They *f* people to marry

force, -s, -ing, -d, -ful, -fully

Mt 5:41	If someone *f-s* you to go one mile,
11:12	*f-fully* advancing, and *f-ful* men
27:32	and they *f-d* him to carry the cross
Lk 16:16	everyone is *f-ing* his way into it
Jn 6:15	to come and make him king by *f*,
2Co 10:10	"His letters are weighty and *f-ful*
Eph 6:12	against the spiritual *f-s* of evil

forefathers

Ex 13:11	promised on oath to you and your *f*
Dt 4:31	or forget the covenant with your *f*,
10:22	Your *f* who went down into Egypt
Zec 1:4	Do not be like your *f*,
Mt 23:32	the measure of the sin of your *f*
Jn 6:49	Your *f* ate the manna in the desert

Heb 1:1 In the past God spoke to our *f*

foreign, -er, -ers

Ex 18:3 I have become an alien in a *f* land
Ru 2:10 that you notice me—a *f-er*?
Ps 137:4 songs of the LORD while in a *f* land
Isa 28:11 with *f* lips and strange tongues God
Mal 2:11 by marrying the daughter of a *f* god
Lk 17:18 give praise to God except this *f-er*
1Co 14:21 through the lips of *f-ers* I will
Eph 2:12 and *f-ers* to the covenants
2:19 you are no longer *f-ers* and aliens,

foreknew

Ro 8:29 For those God *f* he also predestined
11:2 not reject his people, whom he *f*.

foreknowledge

Ac 2:23 to you by God's set purpose and *f*;
1Pe 1:2 chosen according to the *f* of God

foresaw

Gal 3:8 Scripture *f* that God would justify

forfeit

Mk 8:36 the whole world, yet *f* his soul
Lk 9:25 and yet lose or *f* his very self

forgave

Ps 32:5 and you *f* the guilt of my sin.
65:3 you *f* our transgressions
78:38 he *f* their iniquities
85:2 You *f* the iniquity of your people
Eph 4:32 just as in Christ God *f* you
Col 2:13 with Christ. He *f* us all our sins
3:13 Forgive as the Lord *f* you

forget, -ting, -got, -gotten

Dt 4:23 Be careful not to *f* the covenant
6:12 careful that you do not *f* the LORD
1Sa 12:9 "But they *f-got* the LORD their God
Ps 103:2 and *f* not all his benefits
137:5 If I *f* you, O Jerusalem,
Isa 49:15 "Can a mother *f* the baby
Lk 12:6 not one of them is *f-gotten* by God
Php 3:13 *F-ting* what is behind and straining
Heb 6:10 not unjust; he will not *f* your work
13:2 Do not *f* to entertain strangers,

forgive, -s, -ing, -n, -ness

Ex 34:7 *f-ing* wickedness, rebellion and sin
Nu 14:18 abounding in love and *f-ing* sin
2Ch 7:14 and will *f* their sin and will heal
Ps 19:12 *F* my hidden faults
32:1 he whose transgressions are *f-n*,
103:3 who *f-s* all your sins and heals
Jer 31:34 "For I will *f* their wickedness
Mt 6:12 *F* us our debts, as we also have
6:15 But if you do not *f* men their sins
12:31 against the Spirit will not be *f-n*.
18:21 many times shall I *f* my brother
18:35 *f* your brother from your heart.
26:28 for many for the *f-ness* of sins
Mk 2:7 Who can *f* sins but God alone?
Lk 6:37 *F*, and you will be *f-n*
23:34 Jesus said, "Father, *f* them,
Jn 20:23 If you *f* anyone his sins,
Ac 2:38 for the *f-ness* of your sins.
Ro 4:7 they whose transgressions are *f-n*,
Eph 1:7 his blood, the *f-ness* of sins,
Col 1:14 redemption, the *f-ness* of sins.
3:13 Bear with each other and *f*
Heb 9:22 shedding of blood ... no *f-ness*
1Jn 1:9 faithful and just and will *f* us

form, -ed

Ge 2:7 God *f-ed* the man from the dust
Ps 95:5 and his hands *f-ed* the dry land
103:14 for he knows how we are *f-ed*,
Jer 1:5 "Before I *f-ed* you in the womb
Gal 4:19 until Christ is *f-ed* in you
Col 2:9 of the Deity lives in bodily *f*
2Ti 3:5 having a *f* of godliness but denying

forsake, -n

Dt 31:6	he will never leave you nor *f* you.
2Ch 15:2	if you *f* him, he will *f* you
Ps 22:1	my God, why have you *f-n* me?
27:10	Though my father and mother *f* me,
Mk 15:34	my God, why have you *f-n* me?
Heb 13:5	never will I *f* you.
Rev 2:4	You have *f-n* your first love

fortress

2Sa 22:2	my rock, my *f* and my deliverer
Ps 18:2	my rock, my *f* and my deliverer;
91:2	"He is my refuge and my *f*, my God,

forty

Ge 7:4	on the earth for *f* days and *f*
Ex 24:18	on the mountain *f* days and *f*
1Ki 19:8	he travelled for *f* days and *f*
Ps 95:10	For *f* years I was angry with that
Mt 4:2	fasting for *f* days and *f* nights
Ac 1:3	to them over a period of *f* days
Heb 3:17	with whom was he angry for *f* years?

fought

1Co 15:32	If I *f* wild beasts in Ephesus
2Ti 4:7	I have *f* the good fight,

found

Ge 2:20	for Adam no suitable helper was *f*
6:8	But Noah *f* favour
39:4	Joseph *f* favour in his eyes
Ru 2:10	"Why have I *f* such favour
1Sa 10:21	looked for him, he was not to be *f*
2Ki 22:8	"I have *f* the Book of the Law
1Ch 28:9	you seek him, he will be *f* by you;
Job 28:12	"But where can wisdom be *f*?
Isa 55:6	Seek the LORD while he may be *f*;
65:1	I was *f* by those who did not seek
Da 5:27	weighed on the scales and *f* wanting
Mt 8:10	I have not *f* anyone in Israel
13:44	When a man *f* it, he hid it again,
Lk 1:30	Mary, you have *f* favour with God
2:46	After three days they *f* him
15:6	I have *f* my lost sheep.
15:24	alive again; he was lost and is *f*.'
Ac 4:12	Salvation is *f* in no-one else,
Ro 10:20	"I was *f* by those who did not seek
Php 2:8	And being *f* in appearance as a man,
3:9	and be *f* in him,
Col 2:17	reality, however, is *f* in Christ
Heb 3:3	Jesus has been *f* worthy
11:5	he could not be *f*, because God had

foundation

1Ki 6:37	The *f* of the temple of the LORD
Ezr 3:10	builders laid the *f* of the temple
1Co 3:10	I laid a *f* as an expert builder,
Eph 2:20	the *f* of the apostles and prophets,
1Ti 3:15	the pillar and *f* of the truth

fountain

Ps 36:9	For with you is the *f* of life;
Pr 14:27	The fear of the LORD is a *f* of life
Zec 13:1	"On that day a *f* will be opened

fragrance, -nt

SS 1:3	Pleasing is the *f* of your perfumes
2Co 2:14	the *f* of the knowledge of him
Eph 5:2	as a *f-nt* offering and sacrifice
Php 4:18	a *f-nt* offering, an acceptable

free, -ly

Ge 2:16	"You are *f* to eat from any tree
Ps 119:32	for you have set my heart *f*
146:7	The LORD sets prisoners *f*
Mt 10:8	*F-ly* you have received, *f-ly* give
Jn 8:32	and the truth will set you *f*.
8:36	So if the Son sets you *f*,
Ro 6:18	You have been set *f* from sin
8:2	*f* from the law of sin and death
Gal 3:28	slave nor *f*, male nor female,

freedom

Isa 61:1	to proclaim *f* for the captives
Lk 4:18	to proclaim *f* for the prisoners

Ro 8:21 glorious *f* of the children of God
2Co 3:17 Spirit of the Lord is, there is *f*.
Gal 5:1 for *f* that Christ has set us free.
5:13 But do not use your *f* to indulge
Jas 1:25 the perfect law that gives *f*,
1Pe 2:16 do not use your *f* as a cover-up

friend, -s, -ship

Ex 33:11 as a man speaks with his *f*.
Pr 16:28 and a gossip separates close *f-s*
18:24 *f* who sticks closer than a brother
27:6 Wounds from a *f* can be trusted,
Isa 41:8 you descendants of Abraham my *f*
Zec 13:6 was given at the house of my *f-s*.
Mt 11:19 *f* of tax collectors and "sinners"
Lk 11:8 him the bread because he is his *f*,
Jn 15:13 lay down his life for his *f-s*
15:14 You are my *f-s* if you do what I
Jas 2:23 and he was called God's *f*
4:4 *f-ship* with the world is hatred
3Jn :14 The *f-s* here send their greetings.

frogs

Ex 8:2 plague your whole country with *f*
Ps 78:45 and *f* that devastated them
105:30 Their land teemed with *f*,
Rev 16:13 evil spirits that looked like *f*;

fruit, -ful

Ge 1:22 "Be *f-ful* and increase in number
Ps 1:3 which yields its *f* in season
Isa 11:1 from his roots a Branch will bear *f*
32:17 *f* of righteousness will be peace;
Mt 3:8 *f* in keeping with repentance
7:17 good *f*, but a bad tree bears bad *f*
26:29 not drink of this *f* of the vine
Jn 15:5 and I in him, he will bear much *f*;
15:16 go and bear *f*—*f* that will last
Gal 5:22 But the *f* of the Spirit is love,
Php 1:22 this will mean *f-ful* labour for me
Col 1:6 gospel is bearing *f* and growing,
1:10 bearing *f* in every good work,
Heb 13:15 the *f* of lips that confess his name
Rev 22:2 yielding its *f* every month.

frustration

Ro 8:20 For the creation was subjected to *f*

fulfil, -led, -ment

Ps 116:14 I will *f* my vows to the LORD
Jer 25:12 when the seventy years are *f-led*,
Mt 1:22 to *f* what the Lord had said
2:17 the prophet Jeremiah was *f-led*
5:17 not come to abolish them but to *f*
8:17 This was to *f* what was spoken
13:14 *f-led* the prophecy of Isaiah:
27:9 by Jeremiah the prophet was *f-led*:
Lk 4:21 "Today this scripture is *f-led*
24:44 be *f-led* that is written about me
Jn 15:25 to *f* what is written in their Law:
19:28 that the Scripture would be *f-led*,
Ac 13:27 yet in condemning him they *f-led*
Ro 13:10 love is the *f-ment* of the law
Gal 6:2 you will *f* the law of Christ

full, -y, -ness

1Ki 8:61 your hearts must be *f-y* committed
Ps 127:5 the man whose quiver is *f* of them.
130:7 and with him is *f* redemption
Isa 6:3 the whole earth is *f* of his glory.
Mt 6:2 have received their reward in *f*
Lk 4:1 Jesus, *f* of the Holy Spirit,
5:7 so *f* that they began to sink
10:21 *f* of joy through the Holy Spirit,
Jn 1:14 *f* of grace and truth
10:10 have life, and have it to the *f*
13:1 the *f* extent of his love
Ac 6:5 *f* of faith and of the Holy Spirit;

Gal 4:4	But when the time had *f-y* come,
Eph 1:23	the *f-ness* of him who fills
3:19	all the *f-ness* of God
4:13	measure of the *f-ness* of Christ
Col 1:19	to have all his *f-ness* dwell in him
2:9	all the *f-ness* of the Deity lives
Heb 10:22	in *f* assurance of faith,

furnace

Dt 4:20	the iron-smelting *f*, out of Egypt,
Isa 48:10	tested you in the *f* of affliction
Da 3:6	be thrown into a blazing *f*.
Mt 13:42	will throw them into the fiery *f*,
Rev 9:2	like the smoke from a gigantic *f*.

fury, -ious

Pr 27:4	Anger is cruel and *f* overwhelming,
Mt 2:16	he was *f-ious*, and he gave orders
Rev 14:10	will drink of the wine of God's *f*,
19:15	the *f* of the wrath of God Almighty

futile, -lity

Mal 3:14	have said, 'It is *f* to serve God
Ro 1:21	but their thinking became *f*
1Co 3:20	that the thoughts of the wise are *f*
15:17	not been raised, your faith is *f*;
Eph 4:17	in the *f-lity* of their thinking

future

Ps 37:37	there is a *f* for the man of peace
Pr 23:18	There is surely a *f* hope for you,
Jer 29:11	plans to give you hope and a *f*
Ro 8:38	neither the present nor the *f*,
1Co 3:22	or death or the present or the *f*—

G

Gabriel

Angel; sent to Daniel to interpret vision (Da 8:15–26) and deliver prophetic message (Da 9:20–27); announced birth of John the Baptist (Lk 1:11–20) and of Jesus (Lk 1:26–38).

Gad

1. Son of Jacob by Zilpah (Ge 30:9–11; 35:26); blessed by Jacob (Ge 49:19). **2.** Tribe descended from Gad. Blessed by Moses (Dt 33:20–21). Included in census (Nu 1:24–25); 26:15–18). Apportioned land east of Jordan (Nu 32; 34:14–15; Jos 18:7; 22); crossed into Canaan to fight alongside other tribes (Nu 32:16–32). Place in restored land (Eze 48:27–28). **3.** Seer at David's court (1Sa 22:5; 2Sa 24:11–19).

gain, -s, -ed

Ps 60:12	With God we shall *g* the victory,
Ecc 1:3	does man *g* from all his labour
Mt 16:26	if he *g-s* the whole world,
1Co 13:3	have not love, I *g* nothing
15:32	human reasons, what have I *g-ed*?
Php 1:21	to live is Christ and to die is *g*
1Ti 3:8	not pursuing dishonest *g*

Galatia

Ac 16:6	region of Phrygia and *G*,
18:23	*G* and Phrygia, strengthening all
Gal 1:2	To the churches in *G*

Galilean, -s

Mk 14:70	are one of them, for you are a *G*.
Lk 13:1	*G-s* whose blood Pilate had mixed
Ac 2:7	these men who are speaking *G-s*

Galilee

Isa 9:1	he will honour *G* of the Gentiles,
Mt 3:13	Jesus came from *G* to the Jordan
26:32	I will go ahead of you into *G*.
Jn 2:1	wedding took place at Cana in *G*.
7:41	"How can the Christ come from *G*
Ac 1:11	"Men of *G*," they said, "why

Gamaliel

1. Leader from Manasseh; helped Moses with census (Nu 1:10; 2:20; 7:54–59; 10:23). **2.** Pharisee and respected Rabbi and teacher of the law who intervened in trial of apostles (Ac 5:34–40). Acknowledged by Paul as his teacher (Ac 22:3).

garden

Ge 2:8 God had planted a *g* in the east,
SS 5:1 I have come into my *g*, my sister,
Eze 28:13 You were in Eden, the *g* of God;
Jn 19:41 Jesus was crucified, there was a *g*,

garment, -s

Ge 3:21 The LORD God made *g-s* of skin
Ru 3:9 "Spread the corner of your *g* over
Ps 22:18 They divide my *g-s* among them
102:26 they will all wear out like a *g*.
Isa 61:10 clothed me with *g-s* of salvation
Joel 2:13 Rend your heart and not your *g-s*.
Mt 9:16 unshrunk cloth on an old *g*,
Jn 19:24 "They divided my *g-s* among them

gate, -s

Ps 24:7 Lift up your heads, O you *g-s*;
100:4 Enter his *g-s* with thanksgiving
Pr 31:23 husband is respected at the city *g*,
Eze 43:4 entered the temple through the *g*
Mt 7:13 "Enter through the narrow *g*.
16:18 *g-s* of Hades will not overcome it
Lk 16:20 At his *g* was laid a beggar
Jn 10:1 not enter the sheep pen by the *g*,
10:7 I am the *g* for the sheep
Ac 3:2 to the temple *g* called Beautiful,
16:13 outside the city *g* to the river,
Heb 13:12 suffered outside the city *g*
Rev 21:25 will its *g-s* ever be shut,

gather, -ed

Ps 2:2 rulers *g* together against the LORD
Ecc 3:5 time to *g* them, a time to embrace
Isa 11:12 and *g* the exiles of Israel;
Jer 3:17 all nations will *g* in Jerusalem
23:3 "I myself will *g* the remnant
Zep 3:20 At that time I will *g* you;
Mt 12:30 who does not *g* with me scatters
13:30 then *g* the wheat and bring it
23:37 I have longed to *g* your children
24:31 *g* his elect from the four winds,
25:32 nations will be *g-ed* before him,
Lk 17:37 the vultures will *g*.
Ac 4:26 rulers *g* together against the Lord
14:27 they *g-ed* the church together

gave

Ge 2:20 man *g* names to all the livestock,
3:6 She also *g* some to her husband,
35:12 The land I *g* to Abraham and Isaac
Ne 9:20 You *g* your good Spirit
Job 1:21 The LORD *g* and the LORD has taken
Ps 106:15 he *g* them what they asked for,
Ecc 12:7 the spirit returns to God who *g* it
Da 1:17 God *g* knowledge and understanding
Mt 1:25 And he *g* him the name Jesus.
25:35 you *g* me something to eat,
26:26 took bread, *g* thanks and broke it,
27:50 he *g* up his spirit
Jn 1:12 he *g* the right to become children
3:16 he *g* his one and only Son,
6:31 'He *g* them bread from heaven
17:4 completing the work you *g* me
19:30 his head and *g* up his spirit
Ro 1:24 Therefore God *g* them over
8:32 Son, but *g* him up for us all
2Co 5:18 *g* us the ministry of reconciliation
8:5 they *g* themselves first to the Lord
Gal 1:4 who *g* himself for our sins
2:20 who loved me and *g* himself for me
Eph 4:8 captives in his train and *g* gifts
5:25 loved the church and *g* himself
1Ti 2:6 who *g* himself as a ransom
1Jn 3:24 We know it by the Spirit he *g* us

gaze

Ps 27:4	to *g* upon the beauty of the LORD
Pr 23:31	Do not *g* at wine when it is red,
Rev 11:9	*g* on their bodies and refuse them

Gehazi

Elisha's servant. Suggested Shunammite woman be rewarded with a son (2Ki 4:14); obtained money from Naaman falsely, contracted leprosy as punishment (2Ki 5:19–27); recounted Elisha's raising of Shunammite's son (2Ki 8:1–6). May be unnamed servant (2Ki 4:43; 6:15).

genealogy, -ies

Mt 1:1	A record of the *g* of Jesus Christ
1Ti 1:4	to myths and endless *g-ies.*
Tit 3:9	foolish controversies and *g-ies*
Heb 7:3	without *g*, without beginning

generation, -s

Ge 9:12	a covenant for all *g-s* to come
Ps 24:6	the *g* of those who seek him,
90:1	dwelling-place throughout all *g-s*
145:4	One *g* will commend your works
Mt 12:39	"A wicked and adulterous *g* asks
24:34	this *g* will certainly not pass
Mk 8:38	in this adulterous and sinful *g*,
Lk 1:48	all *g-s* will call me blessed
Php 2:15	in a crooked and depraved *g*,

generous, -ly

Pr 11:25	A *g* man will prosper;
Ro 12:8	let him give *g-ly*;
2Co 9:6	whoever sows *g-ly* will also reap
Tit 3:6	he poured out on us *g-ly*
Jas 1:5	he should ask God, who gives *g-ly*

Gentile, -s

Isa 42:6	a light for the *G-s*
Lk 2:32	a light for revelation to the *G-s*
Ac 9:15	to carry my name before the *G-s*
Ro 1:16	first for the Jew, then for the *G*
2:14	when *G-s*, who do not have the law,
3:9	Jews and *G-s* alike are all under
11:13	I am the apostle to the *G-s*
11:25	full number of the *G-s* has come in
1Co 1:23	Jews and foolishness to *G-s*
Gal 2:7	preaching the gospel to the *G-s*
2:8	an apostle to the *G-s*
3:8	God would justify the *G-s* by faith
Eph 2:11	formerly you who are *G-s* by birth
3:6	*G-s* are heirs together with Israel,
Col 1:27	to make known among the *G-s*

gentle, -ness

1Ki 19:12	after the fire came a *g* whisper
Pr 15:1	A *g* answer turns away wrath,
Mt 11:29	I am *g* and humble in heart,
2Co 10:1	the meekness and *g-ness* of Christ,
Gal 5:23	*g-ness* and self-control.
Php 4:5	Let your *g-ness* be evident to all.
1Ti 3:3	not violent but *g*, not quarrelsome,

genuine

2Co 6:8	*g*, yet regarded as impostors
1Pe 1:7	refined by fire—may be proved *g*

Gethsemane

Mt 26:36	disciples to a place called *G*,

ghost

Mt 14:26	they were terrified. "It's a *g*,"
Lk 24:37	frightened, thinking they saw a *g*
24:39	a *g* does not have flesh and bones,

Gideon

Judge, called to save Israel from Midianites (Jdg 6:11–24). Broke down altar of Baal (Jdg 6:25–32). Sign of fleece (Jdg 6:36–40); army reduced to 300 (Jdg 7:2–8); defeated Midianites (Jdg 7:16–8:28). Refused throne (Jdg 8:22–23); ephod made from spoil became source of idolatry (Jdg 8:24–27). Death (Jdg 8:32).

gift, -s

Ps 68:18 you received *g-s* from men,
Mt 2:11 *g-s* of gold and of incense
5:23 offering your *g* at the altar
7:11 give good *g-s* to your children,
Jn 4:10 "If you knew the *g* of God and who
Ac 2:38 receive the *g* of the Holy Spirit
Ro 6:23 the *g* of God is eternal life
1Co 12:1 about spiritual *g-s*, brothers,
2Co 9:15 God for his indescribable *g*
Eph 2:8 it is the *g* of God
4:8 train and gave *g-s* to men.
1Ti 4:14 Do not neglect your *g*,
Jas 1:17 good and perfect *g* is from above,
1Pe 4:10 whatever *g* he has received to serve
Rev 22:17 the free *g* of the water of life

Gilead

Jer 8:22 Is there no balm in *G*?

girl

Job 31:1 eyes not to look lustfully at a *g*
Mt 9:24 The *g* is not dead but asleep."
26:69 and a servant *g* came to him.
Ac 12:13 a servant *g* named Rhoda

give, -s, -ing, -n, -r

Ex 20:16 "You shall not *g* false testimony
33:14 I will *g* you rest.
Nu 6:26 face towards you and *g* you peace.
Ps 7:17 I will *g* thanks to the LORD
19:8 *g-ing* joy to the heart.
37:4 *g* you the desires of your heart
100:4 with praise; *g* thanks to him
107:1 *G* thanks to the LORD, for he is
119:130 unfolding of your words *g-s* light;
146:8 the LORD *g-s* sight to the blind,
Pr 2:6 For the LORD *g-s* wisdom,
3:34 *g-s* grace to the humble
28:27 *g-s* to the poor will lack nothing,
Ecc 6:2 God *g-s* a man wealth,
Isa 7:14 Lord himself will *g* you a sign:
9:6 to us a son is *g-n*,
40:29 He *g-s* strength to the weary
42:8 I will not *g* my glory to another
Eze 36:26 I will *g* you a new heart
Da 2:21 He *g-s* wisdom to the wise
7:14 He was *g-n* authority, glory and
Mt 6:4 your *g-ing* may be in secret.
6:11 *G* us today our daily bread.
6:33 these things will be *g-n* to you
7:7 "Ask and it will be *g-n* to you;
10:8 Freely you have received, freely *g*.
10:42 anyone *g-s* even a cup of cold water
13:12 Whoever has will be *g-n* more,
15:36 had *g-n* thanks, he broke them
21:43 away from you and *g-n* to a people
22:21 "*G* to Caesar what is Caesar's,
28:18 on earth has been *g-n* to me
Lk 6:38 *G*, and it will be *g-n* to you.
12:48 everyone who has been *g-n* much,
22:19 "This is my body *g-n* for you;
Jn 1:9 light that *g-s* light to every man
3:34 God *g-s* the Spirit without limit
5:27 *g-n* him authority to judge because
6:37 All that the Father *g-s* me will
6:63 The Spirit *g-s* life;
10:28 I *g* them eternal life,
10:29 My Father, who has *g-n* them to me,
14:27 give to you as the world *g-s*.
17:22 I have *g-n* them the glory
Ac 4:12 name under heaven *g-n* to men
17:25 he himself *g-s* all men life and
17:31 has *g-n* proof of this to all men
20:35 more blessed to *g* than to receive.
Ro 5:5 Holy Spirit, whom he has *g-n* us
12:6 according to the grace *g-n* us.
12:8 let him *g* generously;
13:7 *G* everyone what you owe him:
1Co 4:2 those who have been *g-n* a trust
12:7 Spirit is *g-n* for the common good
12:13 all *g-n* the one Spirit to drink.
15:57 He *g-s* us the victory through our
2Co 3:6 but the Spirit *g-s* life
4:11 *g-n* over to death for Jesus' sake,
9:7 for God loves a cheerful *g-r*
Eph 1:16 I have not stopped *g-ing* thanks

3:2	God's grace that was *g-n* to me
3:8	this grace was *g-n* me: to preach
4:7	each one of us grace has been *g-n*
5:20	always *g-ing* thanks to God
Php 4:13	through him who *g-s* me strength
Col 1:12	*g-ing* thanks to the Father,
2:10	have been *g-n* fulness in Christ,
1Ti 6:13	God, who *g-s* life to everything,
Jas 1:15	it *g-s* birth to sin; and sin,
1:25	the perfect law that *g-s* freedom,
4:6	But he *g-s* us more grace.
1Pe 1:3	he has *g-n* us new birth
5:5	but *g-s* grace to the humble.
2Pe 1:3	divine power has *g-n* us everything
1Jn 5:11	God has *g-n* us eternal life,
Rev 6:4	rider was *g-n* power to take peace
6:11	each of them was *g-n* a white robe,
13:4	he had *g-n* authority to the beast,
13:7	He was *g-n* power to make war
21:23	for the glory of God *g-s* it light,

glad

1Sa 19:5	you saw it and were *g*.
Ps 46:4	streams make *g* the city of God,
97:1	LORD reigns, let the earth be *g*;
118:24	let us rejoice and be *g* in it
Isa 25:9	rejoice and be *g* in his salvation.
Mt 5:12	be *g*, because great is your reward
Lk 15:32	*g*, because this brother of yours
Jn 8:56	he saw it and was *g*.
Gal 4:27	"Be *g*, O barren woman, who bears

glorify, -ies, -ing, -ied

Ps 34:3	*G* the LORD with me: let us exalt
Lk 1:46	"My soul *g-ies* the Lord
2:20	The shepherds returned, *g-ing*
Jn 7:39	since Jesus had not yet been *g-ied*
11:4	God's Son may be *g-ied* through it.
12:23	for the Son of Man to be *g-ied*
17:1	that your Son may *g* you
Ac 3:13	has *g-ied* his servant Jesus.
Ro 1:21	they neither *g-ied* him as God
8:30	those he justified, he also *g-ied*
1Pe 2:12	see your good deeds and *g* God

glorious

Ps 87:3	*G* things are said of you, O city
Isa 12:5	for he has done *g* things;
Mt 19:28	Son of Man sits on his *g* throne,
Ac 2:20	the great and *g* day of the Lord
Ro 8:21	*g* freedom of the children of God
Eph 3:16	I pray that out of his *g* riches
Php 3:21	they will be like his *g* body
4:19	his *g* riches in Christ Jesus
1Ti 1:11	the *g* gospel of the blessed God,
1Pe 1:8	an inexpressible and *g* joy
Jude :24	present you before his *g* presence

glory, -ies

Ex 16:7	you will see the *g* of the LORD,
24:16	the *g* of the LORD settled on Mount
33:18	"Now show me your *g*."
33:22	When my *g* passes by, I will put
40:34	the *g* of the LORD filled the
Nu 14:10	Then the *g* of the LORD appeared
Jos 7:19	"My son, give *g* to the LORD,
1Sa 4:21	"The *g* has departed from Israel"
Ps 8:1	set your *g* above the heavens
8:5	crowned him with *g* and honour
19:1	The heavens declare the *g* of God;
24:7	that the King of *g* may come in
29:2	Ascribe to the LORD the *g* due
73:24	afterwards you will take me into *g*
96:7	ascribe to the LORD *g* and strength
Isa 6:3	the whole earth is full of his *g*.
40:5	*g* of the LORD will be revealed,
Eze 1:28	appearance of the likeness of the *g*
Da 7:14	given authority, *g* and sovereign
Hag 2:9	The *g* of this present house will be

Mt 16:27 in his Father's *g* with his angels,
24:30 with power and great *g*
Lk 2:9 *g* of the Lord shone around them,
2:14 "*G* to God in the highest,
24:26 these things and then enter his *g*?
Jn 1:14 We have seen his *g*, the *g* of
2:11 He thus revealed his *g*,
17:4 I have brought you *g* on earth
17:5 *g* I had with you before the world
17:24 where I am, and to see my *g*,
Ac 7:2 The God of *g* appeared to our father
Ro 1:23 *g* of the immortal God for images
3:23 fall short of the *g* of God
5:2 rejoice in the hope of the *g* of God
8:18 not worth comparing with the *g*
9:4 theirs the divine *g*,
9:23 to make the riches of his *g* known
1Co 2:8 crucified the Lord of *g*
10:31 do it all for the *g* of God
11:7 he is the image and *g* of God;
15:43 it is raised in *g*; it is sown
2Co 3:18 faces all reflect the Lord's *g*,
4:17 achieving for us an eternal *g*
Eph 1:12 might be for the praise of his *g*
Php 2:11 to the *g* of God the Father
Col 1:27 Christ in you, the hope of *g*
1Ti 3:16 in the world, was taken up in *g*
Heb 1:3 Son is the radiance of God's *g*
2:7 you crowned him with *g* and honour
1Pe 1:11 sufferings of Christ and the *g-ies*
5:1 share in the *g* to be revealed
5:10 called you to his eternal *g*
Jude :25 to the only God our Saviour be *g*,
Rev 4:11 to receive *g* and honour and power,

gnashing

Mt 8:12 will be weeping and *g* of teeth.
13:42 will be weeping and *g* of teeth
24:51 will be weeping and *g* of teeth

gnat, -s

Ex 8:17 *g-s* came upon men and animals.
Mt 23:24 strain out a *g* but swallow a camel

goads

Ac 26:14 for you to kick against the *g*.

goal

2Co 5:9 we make it our *g* to please him,
Gal 3:3 attain your *g* by human effort?
Php 3:14 I press on towards the *g* to win
1Ti 1:5 The *g* of this command is love,
1Pe 1:9 receiving the *g* of your faith,

goat, -s

Lev 16:10 *g* chosen by lot as the scapegoat
Nu 7:16 one male *g* for a sin offering
Job 39:1 when the mountain *g-s* give birth?
Isa 11:6 leopard will lie down with the *g*,
Mt 25:32 separates the sheep from the *g-s*
Heb 9:13 The blood of *g-s* and bulls
10:4 bulls and *g-s* to take away sins

God, -'s

Ge 1:1 In the beginning *G* created
1:3 *G* said, "Let there be light,"
1:26 *G* said, "Let us make man
2:3 *G* blessed the seventh day
2:22 Then the LORD *G* made a woman
5:24 Enoch walked with *G*;
6:2 sons of *G* saw that the daughters
14:19 "Blessed be Abram by *G* Most High,
17:1 "I am *G* Almighty;
20:11 no fear of *G* in this place,
22:8 "*G* himself will provide the lamb
32:30 because I saw *G* face to face,
35:11 *G* said to him, "I am *G* Almighty;
39:9 and sin against *G*?
46:3 "I am *G*, the *G* of your father
50:20 but *G* intended it for good
Ex 2:24 *G* heard their groaning
3:6 "I am the *G* of your father,

8:19	"This is the finger of *G*."
20:1	*G* spoke all these words
20:5	the LORD your *G*, am a jealous *G*
20:7	the name of the LORD your *G*,
20:10	a Sabbath to the LORD your *G*.
34:14	for the LORD ... is a jealous *G*
Lev 19:2	I, the LORD your *G*, am holy
Nu 22:38	speak only what *G* puts in my mouth
23:19	*G* is not a man, that he should lie
Dt 4:24	LORD your *G* is a consuming fire,
6:4	The LORD our *G*, the LORD is one.
6:5	Love the LORD your *G* with all
6:16	Do not test the LORD your *G*
9:10	inscribed by the finger of *G*.
10:20	Fear the LORD your *G*
11:22	to love the LORD your *G*,
14:2	a people holy to the LORD your *G*.
18:15	*G* will raise up for you a prophet
31:6	the LORD your *G* goes with you;
32:39	There is no *g* beside me
33:27	The eternal *G* is your refuge,
Jos 1:9	your *G* will be with you wherever
14:8	LORD my *G* wholeheartedly
23:14	promises the LORD your *G* gave you
24:19	He is a holy *G*; he is a jealous
Jdg 13:8	let the man of *G* you sent to us
13:22	"We have seen *G*!
Ru 1:16	my people and your *G* my *G*
1Sa 2:2	there is no Rock like our *G*
4:11	The ark of *G* was captured,
12:9	they forgot the LORD their *G*;
14:44	"May *G* deal with me,
17:26	defy the armies of the living *G*?
30:6	found strength in the LORD his *G*
2Sa 6:6	took hold of the ark of *G*,
22:30	with my *G* I can scale a wall
22:31	"As for *G*, his way is perfect;
1Ki 8:27	But will *G* really dwell on earth?
17:24	I know that you are a man of *G*
18:21	If the LORD is *G*, follow him;
18:24	answers by fire—he is *G*."
18:39	"The LORD—he is *G*!
19:10	zealous for the LORD *G* Almighty.

2Ki 1:3	because there is no *G* in Israel
17:39	worship the LORD your *G*;
1Ch 17:20	there is no *G* but you,
2Ch 5:14	of the LORD filled the temple of *G*
6:18	will *G* really dwell on earth
Ezr 5:13	to rebuild this house of *G*
7:9	gracious hand of his *G* was on him
8:22	"The gracious hand of our *G*
Ne 1:5	*G* of heaven, the great and awesome
2:20	*G* of heaven will give us success.
Job 1:1	he feared *G* and shunned evil
1:5	cursed *G* in their hearts."
1:9	"Does Job fear *G* for nothing?"
2:9	Curse *G* and die!
2:10	Shall we accept good from *G*,
13:3	to argue my case with *G*
19:6	*G* has wronged me
19:26	in my flesh I will see *G*
25:4	can a man be righteous before *G*?
Ps 5:4	a *G* who takes pleasure in evil;
9:17	all the nations that forget *G*
14:1	in his heart, "There is no *G*."
18:2	my *G* is my rock,
18:30	As for *G*, his way is perfect;
19:1	heavens declare the glory of *G*;
22:1	my *G*, why have you forsaken me?
33:12	the nation whose *G* is the LORD,
36:1	no fear of *G* before his eyes
40:8	I desire to do your will, O my *G*;
42:1	so my soul pants for you, O *G*
43:5	Put your hope in *G*,
45:6	throne, O *G*, will last for ever
45:7	*G*, your *G*, has set you above
46:1	*G* is our refuge and strength,
46:4	streams make glad the city of *G*,
46:10	Be still, and know that I am *G*;
51:1	Have mercy on me, O *G*,
51:10	Create in me a pure heart, O *G*,
53:1	in his heart, "There is no *G*."
57:7	O *G*, my heart is steadfast;
63:1	O *G*, you are my God,
68:20	Our *G* is a God who saves;
73:1	Surely *G* is good to Israel,
73:17	I entered the sanctuary of *G*;
73:26	but *G* is the strength of my heart

81:10 I am the LORD your *G*,
84:2 cry out for the living *G*
84:10 a doorkeeper in the house of my *G*
90:2 to everlasting you are *G*
100:3 Know that the LORD is *G*.
139:23 Search me, O *G*,
Ecc 5:4 When you make a vow to *G*,
12:13 Fear *G* and keep his commandments,
Isa 9:6 Wonderful Counsellor, Mighty *G*,
40:1 comfort my people, says your *G*
40:3 a highway for our *G*
40:8 the word of our *G* stands for ever.
40:18 To whom, then, will you compare *G*?
40:28 The LORD is the everlasting *G*,
41:10 do not be dismayed, for I am your *G*
45:22 I am *G*, and there is no other
52:7 "Your *G* reigns!
53:4 we considered him stricken by *G*,
55:7 to our *G*, for he will freely pardon
57:21 "There is no peace," says my *G*
59:2 separated you from your *G*;
61:2 the day of vengeance of our *G*,
Jer 30:22 I will be your *G*.'
Eze 1:1 I saw visions of *G*
11:20 and I will be their *G*
Da 2:19 Daniel praised the *G* of heaven
2:28 *G* in heaven who reveals mysteries.
3:17 the *G* we serve is able to save us
6:16 "May your *G*, whom you serve
6:22 My *G* sent his angel,
9:4 O Lord, the great and awesome *G*,
Hos 1:10 'sons of the living *G*'
Jnh 1:9 worship the LORD, the *G* of heaven,
4:2 a gracious and compassionate *G*,
Mic 6:8 to walk humbly with your *G*
7:18 Who is a *G* like you,
Hab 3:18 I will be joyful in *G* my Saviour
Zec 4:7 shouts of '*G* bless it!
Mal 3:8 Will a man rob *G*? Yet you rob me.
3:14 'It is futile to serve *G*.
Mt 1:23 Immanuel" ... means "*G* with us
3:16 he saw the Spirit of *G* descending
4:3 "If you are the Son of *G*,
4:4 that comes from the mouth of *G*.'
5:8 pure in heart, for they will see *G*
5:9 for they will be called sons of *G*
6:24 You cannot serve both *G* and Money
12:28 drive out demons by the Spirit of *G*
14:33 "Truly you are the Son of *G*.
15:3 why do you break the command of *G*
16:16 Christ, the Son of the living *G*.
19:6 what *G* has joined together,
19:24 rich man to enter the kingdom of *G*
22:21 Caesar's, and to *G* what is *G-'s*.
22:29 the Scriptures or the power of *G*
22:37 Love the Lord your *G* with all your
27:43 He trusts in *G*. Let *G* rescue him
27:46 my *G*, why have you forsaken me?
Mk 1:15 "The kingdom of *G* is near.
2:7 Who can forgive sins but *G* alone?
9:47 enter the kingdom of *G* with one eye
10:6 creation *G* 'made them male
10:18 "No-one is good—except *G* alone
11:22 "Have faith in *G*," Jesus answered
12:27 He is not the *G* of the dead,
12:29 the Lord our *G*, the Lord is one.
16:19 he sat at the right hand of *G*
Lk 1:19 I stand in the presence of *G*,
1:30 Mary, you have found favour with *G*
1:37 For nothing is impossible with *G*.
1:47 my spirit rejoices in *G* my Saviour,
2:14 "Glory to *G* in the highest,
3:6 mankind will see *G-'s* salvation.'

9:60 proclaim the kingdom of *G*.
9:62 for service in the kingdom of *G*.
11:20 drive out demons by the finger of *G*
11:42 you give *G* a tenth of your mint,
12:20 "But *G* said to him, 'You fool!
12:28 how *G* clothes the grass
13:29 feast in the kingdom of *G*
17:21 the kingdom of *G* is within you.
23:40 "Don't you fear *G*,"
Jn 1:1 and the Word was *G*.
1:1 the Word was with *G*,
1:2 He was with *G* in the beginning
1:6 a man who was sent from *G*;
1:12 the right to become children of *G*
1:18 No-one has ever seen *G*,
1:29 "Look, the Lamb of *G*,
1:49 "Rabbi, you are the Son of *G*;
3:3 no-one can see the kingdom of *G*
3:16 "For *G* so loved the world
3:17 For *G* did not send his Son
4:24 *G* is spirit,
6:28 the works *G* requires?
6:33 bread of *G* is he who comes down
8:42 "If *G* were your Father,
9:31 *G* does not listen to sinners.
11:40 you would see the glory of *G*?
13:31 *G* is glorified in him
14:1 Trust in *G*; trust also in me
20:28 "My Lord and my *G*!
Ac 2:24 But *G* raised him from the dead,
2:39 whom the Lord our *G* will call.
3:15 but *G* raised him from the dead.
3:19 Repent, then, and turn to *G*,
5:4 You have not lied to men but to *G*.
5:29 "We must obey *G* rather than men
7:2 The *G* of glory appeared
7:55 saw the glory of *G*, and Jesus
10:46 speaking in tongues and praising *G*.
13:30 But *G* raised him from the dead
15:8 *G*, who knows the heart,
17:23 inscription: TO AN UNKNOWN *G*
17:24 "The *G* who made the world
17:30 past *G* overlooked such ignorance,
20:28 Be shepherds of the church of *G*,
22:14 *G* of our fathers has chosen you
26:20 repent and turn to *G*
Ro 1:4 with power to be the Son of *G*,
1:16 it is the power of *G*
1:17 righteousness from *G* is revealed,
1:18 The wrath of *G* is being revealed
1:20 world *G*-*'s* invisible qualities
1:23 the glory of the immortal *G*
1:24 Therefore *G* gave them over
3:4 Let *G* be true,
3:18 "There is no fear of *G*
3:21 a righteousness from *G*, apart
3:23 fall short of the glory of *G*
5:8 *G* demonstrates his own love for us
6:23 the gift of *G* is eternal life
8:7 the sinful mind is hostile to *G*.
8:28 in all things *G* works for the good
8:29 For those *G* foreknew
8:39 separate us from the love of *G*
11:33 wisdom and knowledge of *G*!
1Co 1:25 the foolishness of *G* is wiser
2:9 *G* has prepared for those who love
3:6 but *G* made it grow.
6:20 Therefore honour *G* with your body
10:13 *G* is faithful;
10:31 do it all for the glory of *G*.
15:10 by the grace of *G* I am what I am,
2Co 2:17 peddle the word of *G* for profit.
4:4 Christ, who is the image of *G*
5:19 *G* was reconciling the world
9:7 for *G* loves a cheerful giver
Gal 3:6 He believed *G*, and it was credited
4:4 *G* sent his Son, born of a woman,
Eph 2:4 *G*, who is rich in mercy
4:6 one *G* and Father of all,
4:30 do not grieve the Holy Spirit of *G*
Php 2:6 Who, being in very nature *G*,
4:19 And my *G* will meet all your needs

Col 1:15	He is the image of the invisible *G*,
1Th 1:9	how you turned to *G* from idols
1Ti 1:17	immortal, invisible, the only *G*,
2:5	there is one *G* and one mediator
4:4	For everything *G* created is good,
2Ti 1:6	fan into flame the gift of *G*,
Heb 1:1	In the past *G* spoke
1:8	"Your throne, O *G*, will last
10:22	let us draw near to *G*
10:31	into the hands of the living *G*
Jas 1:13	should say, "*G* is tempting me."
4:8	Come near to *G* and he will come
1Pe 2:4	rejected by men but chosen by *G*
3:18	to bring you to *G*.
5:2	Be shepherds of *G-'s* flock
2Pe 1:21	but men spoke from *G* as they were
1Jn 1:5	*G* is light; in him there is no
4:9	*G* showed his love among us:
4:16	rely on the love *G* has for us.
Jude :21	Keep yourselves in *G-'s* love
Rev 7:10	"Salvation belongs to our *G*,
19:10	Worship *G*!
19:13	his name is the Word of *G*
22:19	*G* will take away from him

God-breathed

2Ti 3:16	All Scripture is *G* and is useful

godless, -ness

Job 20:5	joy of the *g* lasts but a moment
Pr 11:9	mouth the *g* destroys his neighbour
Ro 1:18	the *g-ness* and wickedness of men
1Ti 4:7	Have nothing to do with *g* myths
2Ti 2:16	Avoid *g* chatter,
Heb 12:16	immoral, or is *g* like Esau,

godly, -iness

Mal 2:15	Because he was seeking *g* offspring.
Ac 3:12	as if by our own power or *g-iness*
2Co 7:10	*G* sorrow brings repentance
7:11	this *g* sorrow has produced in you:
1Ti 2:2	lives in all *g-iness* and holiness
3:16	the mystery of *g-iness* is great:
6:6	But *g-iness* with contentment
2Ti 3:5	a form of *g-iness* but denying
3:12	everyone who wants to live a *g*

gods

Ge 31:19	stole her father's household *g*
Ex 15:11	"Who among the *g* is like you,
20:3	shall have no other *g* before me
Ps 82:6	"I said, 'You are "*g*";
86:8	Among the *g* there is none like you,
Da 2:47	"Surely your God is the God of *g*
3:25	looks like a son of the *g*.
Jn 10:34	'I have said you are *g*'
Ac 14:11	*g* have come down to us in human
17:18	seems to be advocating foreign *g*."
1Co 8:5	even if there are so-called *g*,

Gog

Rev 20:8	*G* and Magog—to gather them

gold

Ge 44:8	why would we steal silver or *g*
Ex 11:2	for articles of silver and *g*.
25:17	an atonement cover of pure *g*—
32:31	have made themselves gods of *g*
1Ki 20:3	'Your silver and *g* are mine,
Ezr 5:14	from the temple of Babylon the *g*
Job 23:10	I shall come forth as *g*
Ps 19:10	They are more precious than *g*,
Pr 11:22	Like a *g* ring in a pig's snout
SS 5:11	His head is purest *g*;
Da 3:1	Nebuchadnezzar made an image of *g*,
Zec 13:9	like silver and test them like *g*.
Mal 3:3	refine them like *g* and silver.
Mt 2:11	presented him with gifts of *g*
Ac 3:6	"Silver or *g* I do not have,
1Co 3:12	builds on this foundation using *g*,
Jas 2:2	wearing a *g* ring and fine clothes,
1Pe 1:7	faith—of greater worth than *g*,
1:18	silver or *g* that you were redeemed

Rev 3:18 I counsel you to buy from me *g*
14:14 with a crown of *g* on his head
21:21 street of the city was of pure *g*,

Golgotha

Mt 27:33 *G* ... means The Place of the Skull)

Goliath

Philistine giant (1Sa 17:4–7); challenged Israel (1Sa 17:8–11,23–26); killed by David (1Sa 17:32–50). Sword kept at sanctuary at Nob; given to David (1Sa 21:9).

Gomorrah

See *Sodom*.

good, -ness

Ge 1:4 God saw that the light was *g*,
1:31 God saw ... made, and it was very *g*
2:18 not *g* for the man to be alone.
1Ki 8:56 failed of all the *g* promises
1Ch 16:34 for he is *g*; his love endures
Ne 9:20 You gave your *g* Spirit
Job 2:10 Shall we accept *g* from God,
Ps 14:1 there is no-one who does *g*
16:2 apart from you I have no *g* thing.
23:6 Surely *g-ness* and love will follow
27:13 I will see the *g-ness* of the LORD
34:8 Taste and see that the LORD is *g*;
73:1 Surely God is *g* to Israel,
84:11 no *g* thing does he withhold
100:5 LORD is *g* and his love endures
Pr 15:30 *g* news gives health to the bones
22:1 A *g* name is more desirable
Isa 52:7 feet of those who bring *g* news,
61:1 to preach *g* news to the poor.
La 3:25 The LORD is *g* to those whose hope
Mic 6:8 showed you, O man, what is *g*.
Mt 4:23 preaching the *g* news of the
5:45 sun to rise on the evil and the *g*,
7:11 to give *g* gifts to your children,
13:8 Still other seed fell on *g* soil,
16:26 What *g* will it be for a man
19:17 "There is only One who is *g*.
Mk 3:4 the Sabbath: to do *g* or to do evil,
Jn 1:46 Can anything *g* come from there?"
5:29 those who have done *g* will rise
10:11 "I am the *g* shepherd.
Ac 10:38 he went around doing *g*
Ro 2:7 persistence in doing *g* seek glory,
3:8 Let us do evil that *g* may result
3:12 no-one who does *g*, not even one.
5:7 though for a *g* man someone might
7:18 I know that nothing *g* lives in me,
8:28 in all things God works for the *g*
12:2 his *g*, pleasing and perfect will.
12:9 cling to what is *g*.
1Co 7:1 It is *g* for a man not to marry
12:7 Spirit is given for the common *g*
15:33 "Bad company corrupts *g* character.
2Co 5:10 in the body, whether *g* or bad
Gal 5:7 You were running a *g* race.
5:22 kindness, *g-ness*, faithfulness
6:9 Let us not become weary in doing *g*,
6:10 let us do *g* to all people,
Eph 2:10 created in Christ Jesus to do *g*
Php 1:6 he who began a *g* work in you will
1Ti 1:8 We know that the law is *g*
4:4 everything God created is *g*,
6:12 Fight the *g* fight of the faith.
2Ti 3:17 equipped for every *g* work
4:7 I have fought the *g* fight,
Heb 10:1 The law is only a shadow of the *g*
10:24 on towards love and *g* deeds
13:21 everything *g* for doing his will,
Jas 1:17 Every *g* and perfect gift
2:14 What *g* is it, my brothers,
1Pe 2:3 have tasted that the Lord is *g*
2Pe 1:5 to add to your faith *g-ness*;
3Jn :11 imitate what is evil but what is *g*.

gospel

Mt 24:14 this *g* of the kingdom will be
Mk 1:1 The beginning of the *g* about Jesus

8:35 for me and for the *g* will save it
Ro 1:16 I am not ashamed of the *g*,
1Co 9:16 when I preach the *g*, I cannot boast
15:2 By this *g* you are saved,
2Co 4:3 And even if our *g* is veiled,
Gal 1:8 preach a *g* other than the one
2:14 in line with the truth of the *g*,
Eph 3:6 *g* the Gentiles are heirs together
Php 1:27 manner worthy of the *g* of Christ.
Col 1:6 All over the world this *g*
1Th 1:5 *g* came to you not simply
1Ti 1:11 the glorious *g* of the blessed God,
2Ti 1:10 immortality to light through the *g*
2:8 descended from David. This is my *g*
1Pe 4:17 who do not obey the *g* of God
Rev 14:6 he had the eternal *g* to proclaim

gossip

Pr 11:13 A *g* betrays a confidence,
2Co 12:20 factions, slander, *g*, arrogance

govern, -ment

Isa 9:6 *g-ment* will be on his shoulders.
Ro 12:8 let him *g* diligently;

grace

Jn 1:14 full of *g* and truth
1:17 *g* and truth came through Jesus
Ac 4:33 much *g* was upon them all.
13:43 them to continue in the *g* of God.
15:11 through the *g* of our Lord Jesus
Ro 3:24 justified freely by his *g*
5:2 this *g* in which we now stand.
5:15 how much more did God's *g*
5:20 *g* increased all the more,
5:21 so also *g* might reign through
6:1 sinning, so that *g* may increase?
6:14 you are not under law, but under *g*
11:5 there is a remnant chosen by *g*
1Co 15:10 by the *g* of God I am what I am,
2Co 8:9 the *g* of our Lord Jesus Christ,
12:9 "My *g* is sufficient for you,
13:14 May the *g* of the Lord Jesus Christ,
Gal 2:21 I do not set aside the *g* of God,
5:4 you have fallen away from *g*
Eph 1:6 to the praise of his glorious *g*,
1:7 with the riches of God's *g*
2:5 it is by *g* you have been saved
2:7 the incomparable riches of his *g*,
2:8 it is by *g* you have been saved,
4:7 to each one of us *g* has been given
Col 4:6 conversation be always full of *g*,
2Ti 2:1 strong in the *g* that is in Christ
Tit 3:7 having been justified by his *g*,
Heb 2:9 *g* of God he might taste death
4:16 approach the throne of *g* with
Jas 4:6 But he gives us more *g*.
1Pe 1:10 spoke of the *g* that was to come
5:5 "God opposes the proud but gives *g*
5:10 And the God of all *g*,
2Pe 3:18 But grow in the *g* and knowledge

gracious, -ly

Ex 34:6 LORD, the compassionate and *g* God,
Isa 30:18 Yet the LORD longs to be *g* to you;
Jer 33:14 I will fulfil the *g* promise
Jnh 4:2 you are a *g* and compassionate God,
Ro 8:32 *g-ly* give us all things?

grafted

Ro 11:19 broken off so that I could be *g* in.
11:23 *g* in, for God is able to graft
11:24 *g* into a cultivated olive tree,

grain

Ge 41:35 store up the *g* under the authority
Ex 29:41 *g* offering and its drink offering
Dt 25:4 ox while it is treading out the *g*
Mk 4:7 so that they did not bear *g*
4:28 then the full *g* in the ear
Lk 6:1 in their hands and eat the *g*
17:35 women will be grinding *g* together;
Jn 12:24 unless a *g* of wheat falls
1Co 9:9 ox while it is treading out the *g*.

1Ti 5:18 ox while it is treading out the *g*.

grandchildren

Ex 10:2 tell your children and *g*
1Ti 5:4 if a widow has children or *g*,

grandmother

2Ti 1:5 first lived in your *g* Lois

grapes

Ge 40:11 I took the *g*, squeezed them into
Jer 31:29 'The fathers have eaten sour *g*,
Hab 3:17 there are no *g* on the vines,
Mt 7:16 Do people pick *g* from thornbushes,

grasp, -ing, -ed

Ge 25:26 with his hand *g-ing* Esau's heel;
Jn 10:39 seize him, but he escaped their *g*
Eph 3:18 to *g* how wide and long and high
Php 2:6 with God something to be *g-ed*

grass

Ps 90:5 like the new *g* of the morning
103:15 As for man, his days are like *g*,
Isa 40:6 "All men are like *g*,
Da 4:25 you will eat *g* like cattle
Mt 6:30 God clothes the *g* of the field,
1Pe 1:24 For, "All men are like *g*,

grasshoppers

Nu 13:33 We seemed like *g* in our own eyes,
Isa 40:22 its people are like *g*.

gratify, -ing

Ro 13:14 how to *g* the desires of the sinful
Gal 5:16 you will not *g* the desires
Eph 2:3 *g-ing* the cravings of our sinful

grave, -s

Nu 16:33 They went down alive into the *g*,
Ps 5:9 Their throat is an open *g*;
16:10 you will not abandon me to the *g*,
49:15 God will redeem my life from the *g*;
Isa 53:9 was assigned a *g* with the wicked,
Mt 23:29 decorate the *g-s* of the righteous
Jn 5:28 all who are in their *g-s* will hear
Ac 2:27 you will not abandon me to the *g*,
Ro 3:13 "Their throats are open *g-s*;

great, -er, -est, -ly, -ness

Ge 12:2 "I will make you into a *g* nation
15:1 your shield, your very *g* reward.
1Ch 16:25 For *g* is the LORD and most worthy
Ps 19:11 in keeping them there is *g* reward
48:1 *G* is the LORD, and most worthy
51:1 according to your *g* compassion blot
126:3 LORD has done *g* things for us,
Jer 31:34 least of them to the *g-est*,"
33:3 tell you *g* and unsearchable things
45:5 seek *g* things for yourself?
La 3:22 LORD's *g* love we are not consumed,
3:23 *g* is your faithfulness
Jnh 1:17 a *g* fish to swallow Jonah,
Na 1:3 slow to anger and *g* in power;
Zep 1:14 "The *g* day of the LORD is near—
Mal 4:5 *g* and dreadful day of the LORD
Mt 2:18 weeping and *g* mourning, Rachel
4:16 in darkness have seen a *g* light;
5:12 because *g* is your reward in heaven,
12:6 one *g-er* than the temple is here
13:46 When he found one of *g* value,
18:1 "Who is the *g-est* in the kingdom
19:22 because he had *g* wealth
22:36 which is the *g-est* commandment
Jn 1:50 shall see *g-er* things than that.
4:12 Are you *g-er* than our father
10:29 *g-er* than all; no-one can snatch
13:16 no servant is *g-er* than his master,
14:28 for the Father is *g-er* than I
15:13 *G-er* love has no-one than this,

1Co 12:31 eagerly desire the *g-er* gifts.
13:13 But the *g-est* of these is love
Php 3:8 surpassing *g-ness* of knowing Christ
Heb 6:13 no-one *g-er* for him to swear by,
7:7 person is blessed by the *g-er*
1Pe 1:6 In this you *g-ly* rejoice,
1:7 faith—of *g-er* worth than gold,
1Jn 3:20 For God is *g-er* than our hearts,
3Jn :4 I have no *g-er* joy than to hear

greed, -y

Mt 23:25 inside they are full of *g* and
1Co 5:11 but is sexually immoral or *g-y*,
Eph 5:3 any kind of impurity, or of *g*,
1Pe 5:2 *g-y* for money, but eager to serve
2Pe 2:14 experts in *g*—an accursed brood

Greek, -s

Jn 19:20 written in Aramaic, Latin and *G*
Ac 18:4 trying to persuade Jews and *G-s*
20:21 declared to both Jews and *G-s*
Ro 1:14 I am bound both to *G-s* and
1Co 1:22 signs and *G-s* look for wisdom
Gal 3:28 There is neither Jew nor *G*, slave

green

Ps 23:2 makes me lie down in *g* pastures,
37:35 flourishing like a *g* tree
Pr 11:28 righteous will thrive like a *g* leaf
Lk 23:31 when the tree is *g*, what will

grew

Isa 53:2 He *g* up before him like a tender
Mt 13:7 which *g* up and choked the plants
Lk 2:52 Jesus *g* in wisdom and stature,

grief

Jn 16:6 you are filled with *g*
16:20 but your *g* will turn to joy
1Pe 1:6 suffer *g* in all kinds of trials

grieve, -d

Ge 6:6 LORD was *g-d* that he had made man
Isa 63:10 rebelled and *g-d* his Holy Spirit.
Eph 4:30 do not *g* the Holy Spirit of God,
1Th 4:13 or to *g* like the rest of men,

groan, -s, -ing

Ex 2:24 God heard their *g-ing* and he
Ro 8:22 whole creation has been *g-ing*
8:26 intercedes for us with *g-s*
2Co 5:2 we *g*, longing to be clothed

ground

Ge 1:10 God called the dry *g* "land",
2:7 the man from the dust of the *g*
3:17 "Cursed is the *g* because of you;
Ex 3:5 where you are standing is holy *g*.
Ecc 12:7 dust returns to the *g* it came
Isa 40:4 the rough *g* shall become level,
Hos 10:12 break up your unploughed *g*;
Mt 10:29 not one of them will fall to the *g*
Jn 8:6 to write on the *g* with his finger
12:24 wheat falls to the *g* and dies,
Eph 6:13 you may be able to stand your *g*,

grow, -ing

Isa 40:28 He will not *g* tired or weary,
40:31 they will run and not *g* weary,
Mt 6:28 how the lilies of the field *g*.
13:30 both *g* together until the harvest.
24:12 the love of most will *g* cold
1Co 3:6 but God made it *g*
Col 1:6 gospel is bearing fruit and *g-ing*,
Heb 12:3 will not *g* weary and lose heart
2Pe 3:18 But *g* in the grace and knowledge

grumble, -ing, -d

Ex 15:24 So the people *g-d* against Moses,
Jn 6:43 "Stop *g-ing* among yourselves,"
1Co 10:10 do not *g*, as some of them did—
Jas 5:9 Don't *g* against each other,

1Pe 4:9 to one another without *g-ing*

guarantee, -ing
2Co 1:22 a deposit, *g-ing* what is to come
Eph 1:14 a deposit *g-ing* our inheritance
Heb 7:22 Jesus has become the *g* of a better

guard, -s
Ps 91:11 angels concerning you to *g* you
141:3 Set a *g* over my mouth, O LORD;
Pr 4:23 Above all else, *g* your heart,
13:3 who *g-s* his lips guards his life,
Mal 2:15 So *g* yourself in your spirit,
Lk 4:10 angels concerning you to *g* you
11:21 a strong man, fully armed, *g-s*
Ac 20:31 So be on your *g*! Remember
1Co 16:13 Be on your *g*; stand firm
Php 4:7 *g* your hearts and your minds
1Ti 6:20 *g* what has been entrusted
2Ti 1:12 able to *g* what I have entrusted
1:14 *G* the good deposit that was

guidance
1Ch 10:13 even consulted a medium for *g*
Pr 11:14 For lack of *g* a nation falls,
20:18 if you wage war, obtain *g*

guide, -s
Ex 13:21 a pillar of cloud to *g* them
Ps 23:3 *g-s* me in paths of righteousness
25:5 *g* me in your truth and teach me,
139:10 even there your hand will *g* me,
Isa 58:11 The LORD will *g* you always;
Mt 23:24 blind *g-s*! You strain out a gnat
Jn 16:13 he will *g* you into all truth.

guilt, -y
Ex 23:7 I will not acquit the *g-y*
34:7 does not leave the *g-y* unpunished;
Lev 5:15 It is a *g* offering
Ps 38:4 My *g* has overwhelmed me
Isa 6:7 your *g* is taken away and your sin
53:10 LORD makes his life a *g* offering,
Mk 3:29 he is *g-y* of an eternal sin.
Jn 8:46 any of you prove me *g-y* of sin?
16:8 he will convict the world of *g*
1Co 11:27 *g-y* of sinning against the body
Heb 10:22 cleanse us from a *g-y* conscience
Jas 2:10 stumbles at just one point is *g-y*

H

Habakkuk
Prophet to Judah (Hab 1:1; 3:1).

habit
1Ti 5:13 they get into the *h* of being idle
Heb 10:25 as some are in the *h* of doing,

Hades
Mt 16:18 gates of *H* will not overcome it
Rev 1:18 I hold the keys of death and *H*
20:13 death and *H* gave up the dead
20:14 death and *H* were thrown into

Hagar
Sarah's Egyptian maidservant given to Abraham as his wife (Ge 16:1–3). Became pregnant; fled from Sarah (Ge 16:4–8); encouraged by God (Ge 16:9–14). Gave birth to Ishmael (Ge 16:15–16; 25:12); driven away by Sarah (Ge 21:9–21). Symbol of those in slavery through dependence on law for justification (Gal 4:21–31).

Haggai
Prophet; encouraged returned exiles to continue rebuilding temple (Ezr 5:1; 6:14; Hag 1:1–11; 2).

hail
Ex 9:22 that *h* will fall all over Egypt—
9:24 *h* fell and lightning flashed back
Rev 8:7 came *h* and fire mixed with blood,

hair, -s
Jdg 16:22 *h* on his head began to grow again
Pr 20:29 grey *h* the splendour of the old
Mt 10:30 *h-s* of your head are all numbered
Lk 7:44 wiped them with her *h*
21:18 not a *h* of your head will perish.
1Co 11:15 woman has long *h*, it is her glory?

1Ti 2:9 not with braided *h* or gold

half

1Ki 3:25 living child in two and give *h*
Est 5:3 Even up to *h* the kingdom,
Da 12:7 a time, times and *h* a time.
Mk 6:23 give you, up to *h* my kingdom.
Lk 19:8 *h* of my possessions to the poor,

hallelujah

Rev 19:1 "*H*! Salvation and glory and power
19:3 "*H*! The smoke from her goes up
19:4 And they cried: "Amen, *H*!
19:6 "*H*! For our Lord God Almighty

hallowed

Mt 6:9 *h* be your name

Ham

Son of Noah (Ge 5:32; 6:10; 1Ch 1:4). Saved in ark (Ge 7:13; 9:18–19). Father of Canaan, Cush (Ethiopia), Put (Libya) and Mizraim (Egypt) (Ge 9:18; 10:6; 1Ch 1:8). Dishonoured Noah by looking at his nakedness; brought curse on Canaan (Ge 9:20–27). Associated with Egypt (Ps 78:51; 105:23,27; 106:22).

Haman

Agagite, honoured by Xerxes (Est 3:1–2). Angered by Mordecai's defiance (Est 3:3–5; 5:9–14); planned to exterminate Jewish people (Est 3:6–15). Ordered to honour Mordecai (Est 6:1–12). Plot exposed by Esther (Est 7:1–7); hanged on gallows built for Mordecai (Est 7:9–10).

hand, -s, -ed

Ex 3:20 I will stretch out my *h*
6:1 Because of my mighty *h*
6:8 I swore with uplifted *h*
7:19 stretch out your *h* over the waters
17:11 As long as Moses held up his *h-s*,
33:22 rock and cover you with my *h*
Dt 4:34 by a mighty *h* and an outstretched
1Ki 18:44 "A cloud as small as a man's *h*
1Ch 13:9 his *h* to steady the ark,
Ezr 8:18 gracious *h* of our God was on us,
Job 1:11 But stretch out your *h* and strike
40:14 your own right *h* can save you
Ps 16:8 Because he is at my right *h*,
16:11 eternal pleasures at your right *h*
19:1 skies proclaim the work of his *h-s*
22:16 pierced my *h-s* and my feet
24:4 clean *h-s* and a pure heart,
31:5 Into your *h-s* I commit my spirit;
31:15 My times are in your *h-s*;
47:1 Clap your *h-s*, all you nations;
73:23 you hold me by my right *h*
89:21 My *h* will sustain him;
90:17 establish the work of our *h-s*
98:8 Let the rivers clap their *h-s*,
102:25 heavens are the work of your *h-s*
110:1 "Sit at my right *h* until
110:5 The Lord is at your right *h*;
121:5 your shade at your right *h*
144:1 who trains my *h-s* for war,
Pr 6:10 little folding of the *h-s* to rest
10:4 Lazy *h-s* make a man poor,
21:1 heart is in the *h* of the LORD;
31:13 flax and works with eager *h-s*
Ecc 9:10 Whatever your *h* finds to do,
Isa 6:6 with a live coal in his *h*,
11:8 child put his *h* into the viper's
35:3 Strengthen the feeble *h-s*,
36:6 pierces a man's *h* and wounds him
40:2 received from the LORD's *h* double
40:12 the waters in the hollow of his *h*,
41:10 you with my righteous right *h*
49:16 engraved you on the palms of my *h-s*
Jer 32:21 mighty *h* and an outstretched arm
La 2:15 clap their *h-s* at you;
Eze 10:21 looked like the *h-s* of a man
Da 5:5 fingers of a human *h* appeared
Am 7:7 with a plumb-line in his *h*
Zec 2:1 with a measuring line in his *h*
Mt 3:12 His winnowing fork is in his *h*,
5:30 if your right *h* causes you to sin,
6:3 do not let your left *h* know
9:25 and took the girl by the *h*,
12:10 man with a shrivelled *h* was there.

15:2	They don't wash their *h-s* before
22:44	"Sit at my right *h* until
24:9	be *h-ed* over to be persecuted
26:45	betrayed into the *h-s* of sinners
26:64	Son of Man sitting at the right *h*
Lk 9:62	who puts his *h* to the plough
24:40	he showed them his *h-s* and feet
Jn 3:35	placed everything in his *h-s*
10:12	The hired *h* is not the shepherd
10:28	can snatch them out of my *h*
20:20	he showed them his *h-s* and side.
20:25	see the nail marks in his *h-s*
Ac 2:23	This man was *h-ed* over to you
2:33	Exalted to the right *h* of God,
2:34	to my Lord: "Sit at my right *h*
7:55	standing at the right *h* of God
17:24	live in temples built by *h-s*
Ro 8:34	is at the right *h* of God
10:21	held out my *h-s* to a disobedient
1Co 5:5	*h* this man over to Satan,
12:15	"Because I am not a *h*,
2Co 5:1	in heaven, not built by human *h-s*
Eph 1:20	seated him at his right *h*
Col 3:1	Christ is seated at the right *h*
1Ti 2:8	to lift up holy *h-s* in prayer,
5:22	hasty in the laying on of *h-s*,
2Ti 1:6	through the laying on of my *h-s*
Heb 1:3	the right *h* of the Majesty
10:12	he sat down at the right *h* of God
10:31	fall into the *h-s* of the living God
1Pe 5:6	under God's mighty *h*,
1Jn 1:1	looked at and our *h-s* have touched—
Rev 1:16	right *h* he held seven stars,
6:5	holding a pair of scales in his *h*

handle, -s

Col 2:21	"Do not *h*! Do not taste! Do not
2Ti 2:15	correctly *h-s* the word of truth

hang, -ing, -ed

Ge 40:19	and *h* you on a tree.
Mt 22:40	Law and the Prophets *h* on these
27:5	he went away and *h-ed* himself
Ac 10:39	killed him by *h-ing* him on a tree

Hannah

Wife of Elkanah; childless (1Sa 1:1–8). Prayed for a child (1Sa 1:9–18); gave birth to Samuel (1Sa 1:19–20); dedicated Samuel to God (1Sa 1:21–28). Her prayer (1Sa 2:1–10). Blessed with other children (1Sa 2:19–21).

happy, -ier

Pr 15:13	A *h* heart makes the face cheerful,
Ecc 3:12	than to be *h* and do good
Mt 18:13	he is *h-ier* about that one sheep
Jas 5:13	Is anyone *h*? Let him sing

hard, -er, -ship, -ships

Ge 18:14	Is anything too *h* for the LORD?
Ex 7:13	Yet Pharaoh's heart became *h*
Mt 19:8	because your hearts were *h*.
19:23	it is *h* for a rich man to enter
25:24	'I knew that you are a *h* man,
Jn 6:60	"This is a *h* teaching.
Ac 14:22	"We must go through many *h-ships*
26:14	It is *h* for you to kick against
Ro 8:35	Shall trouble or *h-ship* or
1Co 15:10	I worked *h-er* than all of them
2Ti 2:3	Endure *h-ship* with us
Heb 12:7	Endure *h-ship* as discipline;
1Pe 4:18	"If it is *h* for the righteous
2Pe 3:16	things that are *h* to understand,

harden, -s, -ing, -ed

Ex 4:21	But I will *h* his heart
8:15	he *h-ed* his heart
Ps 95:8	do not *h* your hearts as you did
Mk 6:52	their hearts were *h-ed*
Ro 9:18	he *h-s* whom he wants to *h*
11:7	elect did. The others were *h-ed*
Eph 4:18	due to the *h-ing* of their hearts
Heb 3:8	do not *h* your hearts as you did

harm

Ge 50:20	*h* me, but God intended it for good
Ps 121:6	the sun will not *h* you by day,
Lk 10:19	nothing will *h* you
Ac 16:28	"Don't *h* yourself! We are all here

Ro 13:10 Love does no *h* to its neighbour.
1Co 11:17 your meetings do more *h* than good

harmony
Ro 12:16 Live in *h* with one another.
2Co 6:15 What *h* is there between Christ
1Pe 3:8 live in *h* with one another;

harp, -s
Ps 137:2 on the poplars we hung our *h-s*
150:3 praise him with the *h* and lyre

harsh
Pr 15:1 but a *h* word stirs up anger
Mal 3:13 You have said *h* things against me,
2Co 13:10 I may not have to be *h*
Col 3:19 love your wives and do not be *h*
1Pe 2:18 but also to those who are *h*

harvest
Ge 8:22 seedtime and *h*, cold and heat,
Jer 8:20 *h* is past, the summer has ended,
Mt 9:37 *h* is plentiful but the workers
13:30 Let both grow together until the *h*.
13:39 The *h* is the end of the age,
Gal 6:9 reap a *h* if we do not give up
Jas 3:18 peace raise a *h* of righteousness

haste, -y
Ex 12:11 Eat it in *h*; it is the LORD's
1Ti 5:22 Do not be *h-y* in the laying on of

hate, -s, -ing, -d, -red
Ex 20:5 generation of those who *h* me
Ps 5:5 you *h* all who do wrong
69:4 Those who *h* me without reason
139:21 Do I not *h* those who *h* you,
Pr 6:16 There are six things the LORD *h-s*,
13:24 He who spares the rod *h-s* his son,
15:17 than a fattened calf with *h-red*.
Ecc 3:8 a time to love and a time to *h*,
Isa 1:14 appointed feasts my soul *h-s*.
Mal 1:3 but Esau I have *h-d*,
2:16 "I *h* divorce," says the LORD God
Mt 5:43 'Love your neighbour and *h*
10:22 All men will *h* you because of me,
Lk 14:26 does not *h* his father and mother,
Jn 3:20 Everyone who does evil *h-s* the
7:7 The world cannot *h* you,
15:18 If the world *h-s* you, keep in mind
Ro 9:13 "Jacob I loved, but Esau I *h-d*.
Gal 5:20 idolatry and witchcraft; *h-red*,
Eph 5:29 no-one ever *h-d* his own body,
Jas 4:4 friendship with the world is *h-red*
1Jn 2:9 in the light but *h-s* his brother
4:20 yet *h-s* his brother, he is a liar.
Jude :23 *h-ing* even the clothing stained by

haughty
2Sa 22:28 your eyes are on the *h*
Ps 131:1 O LORD, my eyes are not *h*;
Pr 16:18 a *h* spirit before a fall

head, -s
Ge 3:15 he will crush your *h*,
Jdg 13:5 No razor may be used on his *h*,
Ps 22:7 hurl insults, shaking their *h-s*
23:5 You anoint my *h* with oil;
24:7 Lift up your *h-s*, O you gates;
133:2 like precious oil poured on the *h*,
Pr 25:22 will heap burning coals on his *h*,
Isa 59:17 helmet of salvation on his *h*;
Mt 5:36 do not swear by your *h*,
8:20 Son of Man has nowhere to lay his *h*
10:30 hairs of your *h* are all numbered
14:8 the *h* of John the Baptist.
27:29 thorns and set it on his *h*.
Jn 13:9 my hands and my *h* as well!
Ac 18:6 "Your blood be on your own *h-s*!
Ro 12:20 will heap burning coals on his *h*.
1Co 11:3 the *h* of every man is Christ,
11:4 prophesies with his *h* covered
11:10 have a sign of authority on her *h*
Eph 1:10 together under one *h*, even Christ

1:22 *h* over everything for the church
5:23 the husband is the *h* of the wife
Col 1:18 And he is the *h* of the body,
2:10 who is the *H* over every power
2Ti 4:5 keep your *h* in all situations,
Rev 4:4 crowns of gold on their *h-s*
10:1 with a rainbow above his *h*;
13:3 One of the *h-s* of the beast
19:12 and on his *h* are many crowns.

heal, -s, -ing, -ed

Ex 15:26 I am the LORD, who *h-s* you.
2Ch 7:14 forgive their sin ... *h* their land
Job 5:18 he injures, but his hands also *h*
Ps 103:3 and *h-s* all your diseases
147:3 He *h-s* the broken-hearted
Ecc 3:3 a time to kill and a time to *h*,
Isa 6:10 and turn and be *h-ed*.
Mal 4:2 rise with *h-ing* in its wings.
Mt 4:23 *h-ing* every disease and sickness
8:8 my servant will be *h-ed*
9:21 touch his cloak, I will be *h-ed*.
10:1 to *h* every disease and sickness.
Lk 4:23 'Physician, *h* yourself!
Jn 12:40 nor turn—and I would *h* them.
1Co 12:9 to another gifts of *h-ing*
Jas 5:16 so that you may be *h-ed*.
1Pe 2:24 by his wounds you have been *h-ed*
Rev 22:2 for the *h-ing* of the nations

health, -y, -ier

Ps 73:4 their bodies are *h-y* and strong
Da 1:15 looked *h-ier* and better nourished
Mt 9:12 not the *h-y* who need a doctor,

hear, -s, -ing, -d

Ge 3:10 "I *h-d* you in the garden,
Ex 2:24 God *h-d* their groaning
Dt 6:4 *H*, O Israel: The LORD our God,
1Sa 15:14 this lowing of cattle that I *h*?
1Ki 8:30 and when you *h*, forgive
Job 42:5 My ears had *h-d* of you
Ps 18:6 From his temple he *h-d* my voice;
19:3 where their voice is not *h-d*
34:2 let the afflicted *h* and rejoice
34:6 and the LORD *h-d* him;
80:1 *H* us, O Shepherd of Israel,
95:7 Today, if you *h* his voice
Isa 6:9 "'Be ever *h-ing*, but never
29:18 the deaf will *h* the words
30:21 will *h* a voice behind you
40:28 Have you not *h-d*? The LORD
42:18 "*H*, you deaf; look, you blind
59:1 nor his ear too dull to *h*
Jer 31:15 "A voice is *h-d* in Ramah,
Eze 34:7 shepherds, *h* the word of the LORD
Hab 3:2 LORD, I have *h-d* of your fame;
Mal 3:16 the LORD listened and *h-d*.
Mt 2:18 "A voice is *h-d* in Ramah,
5:21 "You have *h-d* that it was said
7:24 who *h-s* these words of mine
11:15 He who has ears, let him *h*
12:19 no-one will *h* his voice
13:13 though *h-ing*, they do not *h*
13:20 the man who *h-s* the word
24:6 You will *h* of wars and rumours
Mk 12:29 '*H*, O Israel, the Lord our God,
Lk 4:21 is fulfilled in your *h-ing*.
8:10 *h-ing*, they may not understand.
11:28 those who *h* the word of God
Jn 3:8 You *h* its sound, but you cannot
3:29 he *h-s* the bridegroom's voice.
3:32 to what he has seen and *h-d*,
5:24 whoever *h-s* my word and believes
5:25 when the dead will *h* the voice
Ac 2:8 *h-s* them in his own native language
19:2 *h-d* that there is a Holy Spirit.
28:26 ever *h-ing* but never understanding;
Ro 10:14 one of whom they have not *h-d*?
10:17 faith comes from *h-ing* the message,
1Co 2:9 "No eye has seen, no ear has *h-d*,
Heb 3:7 "Today, if you *h* his voice
5:7 was *h-d* because of his reverent
Jas 1:25 not forgetting what he has *h-d*,
2Pe 1:18 We ourselves *h-d* this voice
1Jn 1:1 which we have *h-d*,
5:14 according to his will, he *h-s* us
Rev 1:3 blessed are those who *h* it
2:7 let him *h* what the Spirit says
3:20 If anyone *h-s* my voice

21:3 I *h-d* a loud voice from the throne
22:17 let him who *h-s* say, "Come!"

heart, -'s, -s

Ge 6:5 thoughts of his *h* was only evil
Ex 4:21 I will harden his *h* so
8:32 Pharaoh hardened his *h* and would
Lev 19:17 Do not hate your brother in your *h*
Dt 4:29 look for him with all your *h*
6:5 God with all your *h* and
1Sa 1:13 Hannah was praying in her *h*,
13:14 sought out a man after his own *h*
16:7 but the LORD looks at the *h*."
1Ki 3:9 give your servant a discerning *h*
8:17 in his *h* to build a temple
8:39 you alone know the *h-s* of all men)
Ps 7:9 God, who searches minds and *h-s*,
13:5 my *h* rejoices in your salvation
14:1 The fool says in his *h*,
19:14 the meditation of my *h* be pleasing
37:4 will give you the desires of your *h*
45:1 My *h* is stirred by a noble theme
51:10 Create in me a pure *h*, O God,
51:17 a broken and contrite *h*, O God,
66:18 If I had cherished sin in my *h*,
73:1 to those who are pure in *h*
73:26 My flesh and my *h* may fail,
84:2 my *h* and my flesh cry out
86:11 give me an undivided *h*,
95:8 do not harden your *h-s* as you did
119:11 I have hidden your word in my *h*
139:23 Search me, O God, and know my *h*;
Pr 3:5 Trust in the LORD with all your *h*
4:23 Above all else, guard your *h*,
12:25 An anxious *h* weighs a man down,
17:3 but the LORD tests the *h*
19:21 Many are the plans in a man's *h*,
SS 3:1 I looked for the one my *h* loves;
Isa 14:13 You said in your *h*, "I will ascend
40:11 and carries them close to his *h*;
Jer 17:9 The *h* is deceitful above all things
31:33 write it on their *h-s*.
Eze 36:26 I will give you a new *h*
Hos 10:2 Their *h* is deceitful,
Joel 2:13 Rend your *h* and not your garments.
Mal 4:6 He will turn the *h-s* of the fathers
Mt 5:8 Blessed are the pure in *h*,
5:28 adultery with her in his *h*
6:21 there your *h* will be also
11:29 I am gentle and humble in *h*,
12:34 overflow of the *h* the mouth speaks
13:15 people's *h* has become calloused
15:8 their *h-s* are far from me
15:19 For out of the *h* come evil thoughts
22:37 Lord your God with all your *h*
Lk 24:32 Were not our *h-s* burning within us
Jn 14:1 "Do not let your *h-s* be troubled.
Ac 16:14 The Lord opened her *h* to respond
Ro 1:21 their foolish *h-s* were darkened
10:1 Brothers, my *h-'s* desire and prayer
10:6 say in your *h*, 'Who will ascend
10:9 believe in your *h* that God raised
2Co 3:15 a veil covers their *h-s*
4:6 made his light shine in our *h-s*
Eph 3:17 Christ may dwell in your *h-s*
6:6 doing the will of God from your *h*.
Col 3:1 set your *h-s* on things above,
3:15 peace of Christ rule in your *h-s*,
Heb 3:8 do not harden your *h-s*
3:12 a sinful, unbelieving *h*
10:16 I will put my laws in their *h-s*,
10:22 having our *h-s* sprinkled
1Pe 3:15 in your *h-s* set apart Christ
1Jn 3:20 whenever our *h-s* condemn us.

heaven, -s, -ly

Ge 1:1 God created the *h-s* and the earth
14:19 Creator of *h* and earth
2Sa 22:10 He parted the *h-s* and came down;
1Ki 8:27 The *h-s*, even the highest *h*,
2Ki 1:12 "may fire come down from *h*
1Ch 29:11 everything in *h* and earth is yours.
2Ch 7:14 will I hear from *h* and will forgive
Ps 2:4 The One enthroned in *h* laughs;
8:3 When I consider your *h-s*,
8:5 a little lower than the *h-ly* beings
19:1 The *h-s* declare the glory of God;
73:25 Whom have I in *h* but you?
103:11 For as high as the *h-s* are above
119:89 it stands firm in the *h-s*
139:8 up to the *h-s*, you are there;
Isa 14:12 How you have fallen from *h*,
40:22 He stretches out the *h-s*
55:9 "As the *h-s* are higher than
64:1 Oh, that you would rend the *h-s*
66:1 "*H* is my throne, and the earth is
66:22 "As the new *h-s* and the new earth
Mal 3:10 throw open the floodgates of *h*
Mt 3:2 for the kingdom of *h* is near.
3:17 And a voice from *h* said,
5:3 theirs is the kingdom of *h*
5:18 until *h* and earth disappear,
5:34 Do not swear at all: either by *h*,
5:45 may be sons of your Father in *h*.
6:9 you should pray: "'Our Father in *h*
13:33 "The kingdom of *h* is like yeast
16:19 bind on earth will be bound in *h*,
24:35 *H* and earth will pass away,
26:64 coming on the clouds of *h*.
28:18 "All authority in *h* and on earth
Lk 10:20 that your names are written in *h*.
15:7 there will be more rejoicing in *h*
Jn 1:32 "I saw the Spirit come down from *h*
12:28 a voice came from *h*,
Ac 2:2 a violent wind came from *h*
2:19 I will show wonders in the *h* above
4:12 no other name under *h*
7:56 "I see *h* open and the Son of Man
Ro 1:18 is being revealed from *h*
1Co 15:49 the man from *h*
2Co 5:2 clothed with our *h-ly* dwelling
12:2 caught up to the third *h*.
Gal 1:8 if we or an angel from *h*
Php 3:20 our citizenship is in *h*.
1Th 4:16 will come down from *h*,
Heb 1:3 right hand of the Majesty in *h*
4:14 who has gone through the *h-s*,
9:24 he entered *h* itself, now to appear
11:16 a better country—a *h-ly* one.
1Pe 1:4 kept in *h* for you
2Pe 3:5 by God's word the *h-s* existed
3:13 looking forward to a new *h* and
Rev 4:1 a door standing open in *h*.
21:1 Then I saw a new *h* and a new earth,
21:2 coming down out of *h* from God,

Hebrew, -s

Ge 39:17 "That *H* slave you brought us
Ex 2:13 saw two *H-s* fighting.
Jnh 1:9 "I am a *H* and I worship the LORD,
2Co 11:22 Are they *H-s*? So am I.
Php 3:5 tribe of Benjamin, a *H* of *H-s*;

heel

Ge 3:15 and you will strike his *h*.
25:26 his hand grasping Esau's *h*;
Ps 41:9 has lifted up his *h* against me
Hos 12:3 womb he grasped his brother's *h*;
Jn 13:18 has lifted up his *h* against me.

height

1Sa 16:7 consider his appearance or his *h*,
Ro 8:39 *h* nor depth, nor anything else
Rev 2:5 the *h* from which you have fallen!

heir, -s

Ge 15:3 in my household will be my *h*.
Mt 21:38 'This is the *h*. Come, let's kill

Ro 8:17 children, then we are *h-s*—
Gal 3:29 *h-s* according to the promise
4:1 as long as the *h* is a child,
Eph 3:6 the Gentiles are *h-s* together
Heb 1:2 he appointed *h* of all things,
1Pe 3:7 *h-s* with you of the gracious gift

held
Ex 17:11 As long as Moses *h* up his hands,
Isa 65:2 All day long I have *h* out my hands
Ro 3:19 whole world *h* accountable to God
10:21 All day long I have *h* out my hands
Gal 3:23 we were *h* prisoners by the law,
Eph 4:16 whole body, joined and *h* together
Heb 2:15 *h* in slavery by their fear

hell
Mt 5:22 in danger of the fire of *h*
5:29 whole body to be thrown into *h*
10:28 destroy both soul and body in *h*
18:9 thrown into the fire of *h*
23:15 as much a son of *h* as you are
23:33 escape being condemned to *h*?
Lk 16:23 In *h*, where he was in torment,
Jas 3:6 and is itself set on fire by *h*
2Pe 2:4 but sent them to *h*,

helmet
Isa 59:17 the *h* of salvation on his head;
Eph 6:17 Take the *h* of salvation
1Th 5:8 the hope of salvation as a *h*

help, -s, -ing, -ed, -less, -er
Ge 2:18 will make a *h-er* suitable for him.
Dt 33:29 He is your shield and *h-er*
Ps 18:29 *h* I can advance against a troop;
46:1 an ever-present *h* in trouble
121:1 where does my *h* come from?
Mt 9:36 they were harassed and *h-less*,
15:5 'Whatever *h* you might otherwise
15:25 "Lord, *h* me!" she said.
25:44 in prison, and did not *h* you?
Mk 9:24 believe; *h* me overcome my unbelief!
Lk 1:54 He has *h-ed* his servant Israel,
Ac 4:20 *h* speaking about what we have seen
9:36 doing good, and *h-ing* the poor.
16:9 "Come over to Macedonia and *h* us.
20:35 we must *h* the weak, remembering
Ro 8:26 the Spirit *h-s* us in our weakness.
1Co 12:28 those able to *h* others,
2Co 6:2 in the day of salvation I *h-ed* you.
1Th 5:14 encourage the timid, *h* the weak
Heb 2:18 to *h* those who are being tempted
4:16 grace to *h* us in our time of need
13:6 "The Lord is my *h-er*; I will not

hen
Mt 23:37 as a *h* gathers her chicks

heritage
Ps 119:111 Your statutes are my *h* for ever;
127:3 Sons are a *h* from the LORD,

Hermon
Ps 133:3 as if the dew of *H* were falling

Herod
1. Herod the Great. King of Judea at time of Jesus' birth (Mt 2:1; Lk 1:5). Received Magi (Mt 2:1–8); slaughtered infants in attempt to kill Jesus (Mt 2:16–18). **2.** Son of Herod the Great, also called Antipas. Tetrarch of Galilee. Arrested and executed John the Baptist (Mt 14:1–12; Mk 6:14–29; Lk 3:19–20; 9:7–9); questioned Jesus (Lk 23:6–12,15). **3.** See *Agrippa*.

Herodias
Granddaughter of Herod the Great. Divorced Philip to marry his brother Herod Antipas, bringing condemnation from John the Baptist (Mt 14:3–4; Mk 6:17–19); prompted daughter to ask for John's head (Mt 14:6–12; Mk 6:21–29).

Hezekiah
King of Judah; outstanding for piety (2Ki 18:5–6; 2Ch 31:20–21). Reformed Judah's

religious life (2Ki 18:3–4; 2Ch 29–31). Rebelled against Assyria (2Ki 18:7); sought and received help from God (2Ki 19:1–4,14–37; Isa 37:1–7,14–38). Healed (2Ki 20:1–11; Isa 38:1–22; 2Ch 32:24). Built up Jerusalem's defences (2Ch 32:2–5,30). Isaiah challenged dependence on human resources (Isa 22:8–11) and pride in displaying wealth to envoys from Babylon (2Ki 20:12–18; 2Ch 32:31; Isa 39:1–8); repented (2Ch 32:26). Included in Jesus' genealogy (Mt 1:9–10).

hid, -den

Ge 3:8	they *h* from the LORD God
Ps 19:12	Forgive my *h-den* faults
119:11	I have *h-den* your word in my heart
Isa 59:2	sins have *h-den* his face from you,
Mt 5:14	A city on a hill cannot be *h-den*
10:26	*h-den* that will not be made known
11:25	*h-den* these things from the wise
13:44	like treasure *h-den* in a field.
25:18	ground and *h* his master's money
Ac 1:9	a cloud *h* him from their sight
Ro 16:25	mystery *h-den* for long ages past
1Co 2:7	wisdom that has been *h-den*
Eph 3:9	ages past was kept *h-den* in God,
Col 1:26	mystery that has been kept *h-den*
2:3	*h-den* all the treasures of wisdom
Heb 4:13	Nothing in all creation is *h-den*

hide, -s

Ge 18:17	"Shall I *h* from Abraham what
Ex 2:3	when she could *h* him no longer,
Job 14:13	only you would *h* me in the grave
Ps 10:1	Why do you *h* yourself in times
51:9	*H* your face from my sins
Isa 45:15	you are a God who *h-s* himself,
50:6	I did not *h* my face from mocking
53:3	one from whom men *h* their faces
Lk 8:16	"No-one lights a lamp and *h-s* it
Rev 6:16	"Fall on us and *h* us from the face

hiding-place

Ps 32:7	You are my *h*; you will protect me

high, -est

Ge 14:18	He was priest of God Most *H*
14:19	"Blessed be Abram by God Most *H*,
Lev 26:30	I will destroy your *h* places,
2Ch 2:6	*h-est* heavens, cannot contain him?
Ps 50:14	fulfil your vows to the Most *H*
68:18	When you ascended on *h*, you led
91:1	in the shelter of the Most *H*
103:11	For as *h* as the heavens are above
Isa 6:1	the Lord seated on a throne, *h*
Mt 26:51	the *h* priest, cutting off his ear
26:57	took him to Caiaphas, the *h* priest,
Mk 5:7	Jesus, Son of the Most *H* God?
Lk 1:32	be called the Son of the Most *H*.
1:35	power of the Most *H* will overshadow
24:49	clothed with power from on *h*.
Ac 7:48	the Most *H* does not live in houses
16:17	men are servants of the Most *H* God,
Eph 4:8	he ascended on *h*, he led captives
Php 2:9	God exalted him to the *h-est* place
Heb 2:17	a merciful and faithful *h* priest
3:1	Jesus, the apostle and *h* priest
4:15	have a *h* priest who is unable
5:1	Every *h* priest is selected
6:20	He has become a *h* priest for ever,
8:1	We do have such a *h* priest,

highway

Pr 15:19	the path of the upright is a *h*
Isa 35:8	*h* will be there; it will be called
40:3	in the wilderness a *h* for our God

hill, -s

Ps 2:6 my King on Zion, my holy *h*.
24:3 Who may ascend the *h* of the LORD?
50:10 and the cattle on a thousand *h-s*
121:1 I lift up my eyes to the *h-s*—
Isa 40:4 every mountain and *h* made low;
Mt 5:14 A city on a *h* cannot be hidden
Lk 3:5 every mountain and *h* made low.
23:30 and to the *h-s* "Cover us!"
Ac 1:12 the *h* called the Mount of Olives,
Rev 17:9 seven *h-s* on which the woman sits

hinder, -s, -ed

1Sa 14:6 Nothing can *h* the LORD from saving,
Mt 19:14 do not *h* them, for the kingdom
Lk 11:52 have *h-ed* those who were entering.
Heb 12:1 throw off everything that *h-s*
1Pe 3:7 so that nothing will *h* your prayers

hip

Ge 32:25 touched the socket of Jacob's *h*

Hiram

King of Tyre. Helped with building of David's palace (2Sa 5:11–12; 1Ch 14:1). Made treaty with Solomon (1Ki 5:12); provided materials and expertise for building temple (1Ki 5; 2Ch 2) and navy (1Ki 9:26–27; 2Ch 8:18; 1Ki 10:22; 2Ch 9:21).

hired

Lk 15:15 and *h* himself out to a citizen
Jn 10:12 The *h* hand is not the shepherd

hold, -s

Ps 73:23 you *h* me by my right hand
Mt 11:12 and forceful men lay *h* of it
Ac 2:24 for death to keep its *h* on him
1Co 15:2 if you *h* firmly to the word
Php 2:16 as you *h* out the word of life—
1Ti 6:12 Take *h* of the eternal life
Heb 2:14 him who *h-s* the power of death—
4:14 let us *h* firmly to the faith
Rev 2:1 him who *h-s* the seven stars
2:4 Yet I *h* this against you:

hole, -s

Eze 8:7 I looked, and I saw a *h* in the wall
Mt 8:20 "Foxes have *h-s* and birds
25:18 dug a *h* in the ground and hid

holiness

Ex 15:11 Who is like you—majestic in *h*,
Ps 96:9 LORD in the splendour of his *h*;
Ro 1:4 who through the Spirit of *h*
1Co 1:30 righteousness, *h* and redemption
2Co 7:1 perfecting *h* out of reverence
Eph 4:24 God in true righteousness and *h*
Heb 12:14 without *h* no-one will see the Lord

holy

Ge 2:3 the seventh day and made it *h*,
Ex 3:5 you are standing is *h* ground.
20:8 Sabbath day by keeping it *h*
26:33 *H* Place from the Most *H* Place.
Lev 10:3 I will show myself *h*;
11:45 be *h*, because I am *h*
Dt 7:6 a people *h* to the LORD your God.
Jos 5:15 where you are standing is *h*."
1Sa 2:2 "There is no-one *h* like the LORD;
Ps 2:6 my King on Zion, my *h* hill.
16:10 will you let your *H* One see decay
Isa 6:3 *H*, *h*, *h* is the LORD Almighty
40:25 who is my equal?" says the *H* One
Zec 14:5 and all the *h* ones with him
14:20 *H* TO THE LORD will be inscribed
Mk 1:24 you are—the *H* One of God!
Ac 2:27 will you let your *H* One see decay
Ro 1:2 his prophets in the *H* Scripture
7:12 So then, the law is *h*,
12:1 sacrifices, *h* and pleasing to God
1Co 1:2 Christ Jesus and called to be *h*,
Eph 1:4 to be *h* and blameless in his sight.
1Th 4:7 be impure, but to live a *h* life.
1Ti 2:8 to lift up *h* hands in prayer,
2Ti 1:9 and called us to a *h* life—

3:15 you have known the *h* Scriptures,
Heb 7:26 one who is *h*, blameless, pure,
10:14 those who are being made *h*
10:19 to enter the Most *H* Place
12:14 peace with all men and to be *h*;
1Pe 1:16 "Be *h*, because I am *h*.
2:9 a royal priesthood, a *h* nation,
2Pe 3:11 You ought to live *h* and godly lives
Rev 4:8 "*H*, *h*, *h* is the Lord God
21:2 the *H* City, the new Jerusalem,

home, -s
Dt 6:7 Talk about them when you sit at *h*
Ps 84:3 Even the sparrow has found a *h*,
Mt 10:12 *h*, give it your greeting
13:57 "Only in his *h* town
Mk 10:29 "no-one who has left *h* or brothers
Lk 15:30 *h*, you kill the fattened calf
18:14 went *h* justified before God.
Jn 14:23 to him and make our *h* with him
Ac 2:46 They broke bread in their *h-s*
16:15 she invited us to her *h*.
1Co 11:22 Don't you have *h-s* to eat
14:35 ask their own husbands at *h*;
2Co 5:6 at *h* in the body we are away
5:8 body and at *h* with the Lord
Tit 2:5 to be busy at *h*,
2Pe 3:13 new earth, the *h* of righteousness

homosexual
1Co 6:9 male prostitutes nor *h* offenders

honest
Ge 42:11 servants are *h* men, not spies.
Lev 19:36 Use *h* scales and honest weights,
Pr 24:26 An *h* answer is like a kiss

honey
Ex 3:8 a land flowing with milk and *h*—
Ps 19:10 they are sweeter than *h*,
119:103 sweeter than *h* to my mouth
Pr 5:3 the lips of an adulteress drip *h*,
Mt 3:4 His food was locusts and wild *h*

honour, -s
Ex 20:12 "*H* your father and your mother,
1Sa 2:30 Those who *h* me I will *h*,
Ps 8:5 crowned him with glory and *h*
Mal 1:6 "A son *h-s* his father,
Mt 13:57 own house is a prophet without *h*.
15:4 For God said, '*H* your father
15:8 These people *h* me with their lips,
Jn 5:23 that all may *h* the Son just as
12:26 My Father will *h* the one
Ro 2:7 seek glory, *h* and immortality,
12:10 *H* one another above yourselves
1Co 6:20 Therefore *h* God with your body
Eph 6:2 "*H* your father and mother"—
Heb 2:7 you crowned him with glory and *h*

hope, -s, -d
Job 13:15 slay me, yet will I *h* in him;
Ps 25:3 No-one whose *h* is in you will ever
42:5 Put your *h* in God,
71:14 as for me, I shall always have *h*;
130:7 O Israel, put your *h* in the LORD,
Pr 13:12 *H* deferred makes the heart sick,
Isa 40:31 who *h* in the LORD will renew
Mt 12:21 the nations will put their *h*.
Lk 24:21 we had *h-d* that he was the one
Ac 26:6 my *h* in what God has promised
Ro 4:18 Against all *h*, Abraham in *h*
5:2 in the *h* of the glory of God
5:4 character; and character, *h*.
8:24 Who *h-s* for what he already has
12:12 joyful in *h*, patient in affliction,
15:4 the Scriptures we might have *h*
15:13 May the God of *h* fill you with
15:13 so that you may overflow with *h*
1Co 13:13 three remain: faith, *h* and love.
15:19 for this life we have *h* in Christ,
Eph 1:12 were the first to *h* in Christ,
2:12 without *h* and without God
Col 1:23 not moved from the *h* held out

1:27	Christ in you, the *h* of glory
1Th 4:13	the rest of men, who have no *h*
5:8	the *h* of salvation as a helmet.
1Ti 4:10	have put our *h* in the living God,
Tit 2:13	we wait for the blessed *h*—
Heb 6:19	this *h* as an anchor for the soul,
10:23	unswervingly to the *h* we profess,
11:1	faith is being sure of what we *h*
1Pe 1:3	new birth into a living *h*
3:15	the reason for the *h* that you have.
1Jn 3:3	this *h* in him purifies himself,

Horeb

Ex 17:6	at *H*. Strike the rock,
1Ki 19:8	he reached *H*, the mountain of God
Ps 106:19	At *H* they made a calf

horn, -s

Ge 22:13	he saw a ram caught by its *h-s*.
Ps 18:2	shield and the *h* of my salvation,
Da 7:7	beasts, and it had ten *h-s*
8:3	before me was a ram with two *h-s*,
Rev 5:6	He had seven *h-s* and seven eyes,
12:3	ten *h-s* and seven crowns

horse

Ex 15:1	*h* and its rider he has hurled into
Ps 33:17	*h* is a vain hope for deliverance;
Zec 1:8	a man riding a red *h*!
Rev 6:2	there before me was a white *h*!
6:5	there before me was a black *h*!
19:11	there before me was a white *h*,

Hosanna

Mt 21:9	"*H* to the Son of David!"
Jn 12:13	"*H*!" "Blessed is he who comes

Hosea

Prophet to Israel. Relationship with unfaithful wife, Gomer, and readiness to forgive her mirrored relationship between God and unfaithful Israel (Hos 1–3).

Hoshea

1. Former name of *Joshua*. **2.** Last king of Israel. Assassinated and succeeded Pekah (2Ki 15:30). Imprisoned when withheld tribute from Assyria; Israel was invaded and king and people exiled (2Ki 17:3–6; 18:9–12).

hospitable

1Ti 3:2	respectable, *h*, able to teach
Tit 1:8	*h*, one who loves what is good,

hospitality

Ro 12:13	who are in need. Practise *h*
1Pe 4:9	*h* to one another without grumbling
3Jn :8	We ought therefore to show *h*

hostile, -ity

Ro 8:7	the sinful mind is *h* to God.
Eph 2:14	the dividing wall of *h-ity*
2:16	he put to death their *h-ity*

hot-tempered

Pr 15:18	A *h* man stirs up dissension,
22:24	Do not make friends with a *h* man,

hour

Ecc 9:12	no man knows when his *h* will come:
Mt 6:27	can add a single *h* to his life
24:44	Son of Man will come at an *h*
Jn 12:23	"The *h* has come for the Son of Man
12:27	this very reason I came to this *h*.

house, -s, -hold

Ge 28:17	none other than the *h* of God;
Ex 20:17	not covet your neighbour's *h*.
Jos 24:15	as for me and my *h-hold*,
2Sa 7:13	who will build a *h* for my Name,
23:5	"Is not my *h* right with God?
1Ch 17:12	the one who will build a *h* for me,
Ps 23:6	dwell in the *h* of the LORD
27:4	I may dwell in the *h* of the LORD
69:9	zeal for your *h* consumes me,
84:10	a doorkeeper in the *h* of my God
122:1	"Let us go to the *h* of the LORD.
127:1	Unless the LORD builds the *h*,
Pr 25:24	share a *h* with a quarrelsome wife
Jer 18:2	"Go down to the potter's *h*,

Hag 1:4 to be living in your panelled *h-s*,
2:9 'The glory of this present *h*
Mt 7:24 a wise man who built his *h*
10:36 the members of his own *h-hold*.
12:25 city or *h-hold* divided against
12:29 anyone enter a strong man's *h*
12:44 'I will return to the *h* I left.'
21:13 "'My *h* will be called a house
Lk 2:4 to the *h* and line of David
2:49 I had to be in my Father's *h*?
11:17 *h* divided against itself will fall.
19:5 I must stay at your *h* today.
20:47 They devour widows' *h-s*
Jn 2:17 "Zeal for your *h* will consume me.
14:2 In my Father's *h* are many rooms;
Ac 2:2 heaven and filled the whole *h*
7:48 Most High does not live in *h-s*
16:31 be saved—you and your *h-hold*.
Ro 16:5 church that meets at their *h*.
2Co 5:1 an eternal *h* in heaven,
Eph 2:19 members of God's *h-hold*
1Ti 3:12 manage his children and his *h-hold*
2Ti 2:20 In a large *h* there are articles
Heb 3:3 builder of a *h* has greater honour
3:6 faithful as a son over God's *h*.
10:21 a great priest over the *h* of God
1Pe 2:5 being built into a spiritual *h*

hovering
Ge 1:2 Spirit of God was *h* over the waters

human, -ity
Da 2:34 a rock was cut out, but not by *h*
Ro 1:3 *h* nature was a descendant of David
1Co 1:17 not with words of *h* wisdom,
Php 2:7 being made in *h* likeness
Heb 2:14 he too shared in their *h-ity*

humble, -s, -d, -y
2Ch 7:14 will *h* themselves and pray
Isa 66:2 he who is *h* and contrite in spirit,
Mic 6:8 to love mercy and to walk *h-y*
Mt 11:29 I am gentle and *h* in heart,
18:4 whoever *h-s* himself like this child
Eph 4:2 Be completely *h* and gentle;
Php 2:8 he *h-d* himself and became obedient
Jas 4:6 the proud but gives grace to the *h*.
1Pe 5:6 *H* yourselves, therefore, under

humility
Pr 11:2 but with *h* comes wisdom
Php 2:3 but in *h* consider others better
Col 2:18 false *h* and the worship of angels
1Pe 5:5 clothe yourselves with *h*

hung
Dt 21:23 *h* on a tree is under God's curse.
Mt 18:6 large millstone *h* around his neck
Lk 23:39 One of the criminals who *h* there
Gal 3:13 "Cursed is everyone who is *h*

hunger, -y
Pr 25:21 If your enemy is *h-y*,
Mt 5:6 Blessed are those who *h* and thirst
25:35 was *h-y* and you gave me something
Jn 6:35 who comes to me will never go *h-y*,
Ro 12:20 "If your enemy is *h-y*, feed him;

husband, -s
Isa 54:5 your Maker is your *h*—
Hos 2:2 and I am not her *h*.
Jn 4:16 "Go, call your *h* and come back.
Ro 7:2 a married woman is bound to her *h*
1Co 7:3 *h* should fulfil his marital duty
Eph 5:22 submit to your *h-s* as to the Lord
5:23 the *h* is the head of the wife
5:25 *H-s*, love your wives, just as
1Ti 3:2 the *h* of but one wife,
1Pe 3:7 *H-s*, in the same way
Rev 21:2 beautifully dressed for her *h*

hymn, -s
Mt 26:30 When they had sung a *h*,
Ac 16:25 praying and singing *h-s* to God,
Ro 15:9 I will sing *h-s* to your name.

1Co 14:26 come together, everyone has a *h*,
Eph 5:19 psalms, *h-s* and spiritual songs.
Col 3:16 psalms, *h-s* and spiritual songs

hypocrisy
Mt 23:28 you are full of *h* and wickedness
Mk 12:15 But Jesus knew their *h*.
Lk 12:1 yeast of the Pharisees, which is *h*
1Pe 2:1 malice and all deceit, *h*, envy,

hypocrite, -s
Mt 6:2 as the *h-s* do in the synagogues
6:5 do not be like the *h-s*,
7:5 You *h*, first take the plank
15:7 You *h-s*! Isaiah was right
23:25 you *h-s*! You clean the outside

hyssop
Ps 51:7 Cleanse me with *h*, and I shall

I

idle, -ness
Pr 31:27 does not eat the bread of *i-ness*
1Th 5:14 warn those who are *i*,
2Th 3:6 away from every brother who is *i*
3:11 some among you are *i*.
1Ti 5:13 they get into the habit of being *i*

idol, -s
Ex 20:4 not make for yourself an *i*
32:4 an *i* cast in the shape of a calf,
1Ch 16:26 the gods of the nations are *i-s*,
Ps 115:4 their *i-s* are silver and gold,
Isa 40:19 As for an *i*, a craftsman casts it,
Jer 2:11 their Glory for worthless *i-s*
Ac 15:20 abstain from food polluted by *i-s*,
17:16 the city was full of *i-s*
1Co 8:1 Now about food sacrificed to *i-s*:
2Co 6:16 between the temple of God and *i-s*?
1Th 1:9 how you turned to God from *i-s*
1Jn 5:21 keep yourselves from *i-s*

idolater, -s
1Co 5:10 the greedy and swindlers, or *i-s*.
6:9 immoral nor *i-s* nor adulterers
10:7 not be *i-s*, as some of them were;
Eph 5:5 greedy person—such a man is an *i*—

idolatry
1Co 10:14 my dear friends, flee from *i*
1Pe 4:3 carousing and detestable *i*

ignorant, -nce
Ac 17:30 past God overlooked such *i-nce*,
Ro 11:25 I do not want you to be *i* of this
1Co 10:1 I do not want you to be *i*
1Th 4:13 not want you to be *i* about those
2Pe 3:16 which *i* and unstable people distort

ignore, -s
Pr 10:17 *i-s* correction leads others astray
Heb 2:3 how shall we escape if we *i* such

ill
Da 8:27 lay *i* for several days.
Mt 4:24 brought to him all who were *i*
Php 2:26 because you heard he was *i*

ill-treat, -ed
Ex 22:21 "Do not *i* an alien or oppress him,
Lk 6:28 pray for those who *i* you
Heb 11:25 *i-ed* along with the people of God

illegitimate
Jn 8:41 "We are not *i* children,"
Heb 12:8 then you are *i* children and not

image, -s
Ge 1:26 "Let us make man in our *i*,
Isa 40:18 What *i* will you compare him
Da 3:1 Nebuchadnezzar made an *i* of gold,
Ro 1:23 glory of the immortal God for *i-s*
2Co 4:4 Christ, who is the *i* of God

indestructible
Heb 7:16 the power of an *i* life

inexpressible
2Co 12:4 paradise. He heard *i* things,
1Pe 1:8 filled with an *i* and glorious joy

infant, -s
Ps 8:2 From the lips of children and *i-s*
Mt 21:16 'From the lips of children and *i-s*
1Co 14:20 In regard to evil be *i-s*,
Eph 4:14 Then we will no longer be *i-s*,
Heb 5:13 lives on milk, being still an *i*,

infirmities
Isa 53:4 Surely he took up our *i*
Mt 8:17 "He took up our *i* and carried

influential
1Co 1:26 not many were *i*;

inherit
Ps 37:11 But the meek will *i* the land
Mt 5:5 meek, for they will *i* the earth
Mk 10:17 "what must I do to *i* eternal life?
1Co 6:9 the wicked will not *i* the kingdom
15:50 cannot *i* the kingdom of God,

inheritance
Ge 21:10 share in the *i* with my son Isaac.
Ex 32:13 it will be their *i* for ever.'
Ps 2:8 I will make the nations your *i*,
33:12 the people he chose for his *i*
Mt 21:38 let's kill him and take his *i*.
25:34 blessed by my Father; take your *i*,
Lk 12:13 tell my brother to divide the *i*
Gal 3:18 if the *i* depends on the law,
Eph 1:14 a deposit guaranteeing our *i*
1:18 his glorious *i* in the saints
Heb 9:15 receive the promised eternal *i*—
1Pe 1:4 into an *i* that can never perish,

iniquity, -ies
Ps 25:11 forgive my *i*, though it is great
51:2 Wash away all my *i* and cleanse me
103:10 repay us according to our *i-ies*
Isa 53:6 laid on him the *i* of us all
59:2 your *i-ies* have separated you

injustice
2Ch 19:7 God there is no *i* or partiality
Ps 58:2 in your heart you devise *i*,

inn
Lk 2:7 no room for them in the *i*
10:34 brought him to an *i* and took care

innocent
Job 4:7 Who, being *i*, has ever perished?
Pr 16:2 All a man's ways seem *i* to him,
Mt 10:16 shrewd as snakes and as *i* as doves
27:4 "for I have betrayed *i* blood."
27:19 anything to do with that *i* man,
27:24 "I am *i* of this man's blood,"
Ac 20:26 I am *i* of the blood of all men
1Co 4:4 that does not make me *i*.

inscription
Mt 22:20 portrait is this? And whose *i*?
Ac 17:23 with this *i*: TO AN UNKNOWN GOD.
2Ti 2:19 stands firm, sealed with this *i*:

instruct, -ed, -ion, -ions
Ex 12:24 these *i-ions* as a lasting ordinance
Ne 9:20 gave your good Spirit to *i* them.
Pr 1:8 Listen ... to your father's *i-ion*
9:9 *I* a wise man and he will be wiser
Isa 40:13 or *i-ed* him as his counsellor?
Ac 1:2 *i-ions* through the Holy Spirit
Ro 15:14 competent to *i* one another.
1Co 2:16 the Lord that he may *i* him?"
Gal 6:6 Anyone who receives *i-ion* in the
Eph 6:4 the training and *i-ion* of the Lord
1Ti 1:18 I give you this *i-ion* in keeping

instrument, -s
Ac 9:15 This man is my chosen *i*
Ro 6:13 body to sin, as *i-s* of wickedness,
2Ti 2:21 he will be an *i* for noble purposes,

insult, -s, -ed

Ps 22:7 they hurl *i-s*, shaking their heads
Mt 5:11 Blessed are you when people *i* you,
27:39 Those who passed by hurled *i-s*
Ro 15:3 "The *i-s* of those who insult you
1Pe 2:23 When they hurled their *i-s* at him,
4:14 *i-ed* because of the name of Christ,

intelligence

Isa 29:14 *i* of the intelligent will vanish.
1Co 1:19 the *i* of the intelligent I will

intended

Ge 50:20 You *i* to harm me, but God
Ro 7:10 commandment that was *i* to bring

intercede, -s, -ing

1Sa 2:25 who will *i* for him?"
Ro 8:26 the Spirit himself *i-s* for us
8:34 and is also *i-ing* for us
Heb 7:25 he always lives to *i* for them

intercession

Isa 53:12 and made *i* for the transgressors
1Ti 2:1 that requests, prayers, *i*

interest[1]

Dt 23:19 Do not charge your brother *i*,
Pr 28:8 *i* amasses it for another,
Mt 25:27 would have received it back with *i*

interest[2], -s

1Co 7:34 and his *i-s* are divided.
Php 2:20 takes a genuine *i* in your welfare
2:21 everyone looks out for his own *i-s*,
1Ti 6:4 an unhealthy *i* in controversies

interpret, -er

Ge 41:15 a dream, and no-one can *i* it.
Da 2:6 tell me the dream and *i* it for me.
Mt 16:3 to *i* the appearance of the sky,
1Co 12:30 Do all speak in tongues? Do all *i*
14:28 If there is no *i-er*, the speaker

interpretation

1Co 12:10 still another the *i* of tongues
2Pe 1:20 came about by the prophet's own *i*

invented

2Pe 1:16 did not follow cleverly *i* stories

invisible

Ro 1:20 God's *i* qualities—his eternal
Col 1:15 He is the image of the *i* God,
1Ti 1:17 immortal, *i*, the only God,
Heb 11:27 because he saw him who is *i*

invite, -d

Mt 22:3 who had been *i-d* to the banquet
22:14 many are *i-d*, but few are chosen.
25:35 I was a stranger and you *i-d* me in
Lk 14:13 you give a banquet, *i* the poor,
Rev 19:9 'Blessed are those who are *i-d*

iron

2Ki 6:5 the *i* axe-head fell into the water.
Ps 2:9 will rule them with an *i* sceptre;
Pr 27:17 As *i* sharpens *i*, so one man
Da 2:33 its legs of *i*, its feet partly
1Ti 4:2 seared as with a hot *i*
Rev 19:15 will rule them with an *i* sceptre."

Isaac

Son of Abraham and Sarah. Birth announced by God (Ge 17:15–19; 18:10–15; 21:1–7); heir through whom God's promises to Abraham continued (Ge 17:19, 21; 21:12; 26:2–5; Ro 9:6–9; Heb 11:9); patriarch (Ge 50:24; Ex 3:6; Dt 29:13; Mt 8:11).
Offered by Abraham (Ge 22; Heb 11:17–19; Jas 2:21). Married Rebekah (Ge 24); father of Esau and Jacob (Ge 25:21–26; 1Ch 1:34). In Gerar, passed Rebekah off as his sister (Ge 26:6–11). Made treaty with Abimelech (Ge 26:26–31). Deceived by Rebekah; blessed Jacob as firstborn (Ge 27:1–29; 28:1–4). Death (Ge 35:28–29).

Isaiah

Prophet to Judah (Isa 1:1); commissioned by God (Isa 6). Married prophetess (Isa 8:3), had two sons whose names were clues to message (Isa 7:3; 8:3). Warned Ahaz; gave sign of Immanuel (Isa 7). Called for trust in God rather than human resources (Isa 7:9; 22:7–11; 31:1); rebuked Hezekiah's pride (2Ki 20:12–18; 2Ch 32:31; Isa 39:1–8). Announced deliverance from Assyria (Isa 10:12–19,24–27; 14:24–27; 36–37; 2Ki 19). Hezekiah's sickness and recovery (2Ki 20:1–11; 2Ch 32:24–26; Isa 38). Recorded Judah's history (2Ch 26:22; 32:32).

Ishmael

1. Son of Abraham by Hagar (Ge 16:15; 1Ch 1:28); circumcised (Ge 17:23–26); blessed by God, but not as heir of promise (Ge 17:19–21; 21:10–13; Gal 4:21–30). Hostility towards Isaac (Ge 16:12; 21:9; 25:18; Gal 4:29); driven away by Sarah (Ge 21:10–14); cry heard by God (Ge 21:15–21). With Isaac, buried Abraham (Ge 25:9). Children (Ge 25:12–16; 1Ch 1:29–31). Death (Ge 25:17).
2. Son of Nethaniah; killed Gedaliah, governor of Judah, and his followers (2Ki 25:22–26; Jer 40:7–9; 41:1–16). Pursued by Johanan; escaped to Ammon (Jer 41:10–15).

Israel

1. See *Jacob.*
2. In the sense of Israel as the people of God, united kingdom or northern kingdom.

Ex 4:22	*I* is my firstborn son
5:2	obey him and let *I* go?
14:30	LORD saved *I* from the hands
24:10	and saw the God of *I*.
Nu 32:13	The LORD's anger burned against *I*
Dt 6:4	Hear, O *I*: The LORD our God,
Jos 10:14	the LORD was fighting for *I*
Jdg 21:25	In those days *I* had no king;
1Sa 4:22	"The glory has departed from *I*,
15:26	rejected you as king over *I*!
15:29	He who is the Glory of *I*
17:46	there is a God in *I*
2Sa 3:18	I will rescue my people *I*
7:8	to be ruler over my people *I*
20:1	Every man to his tent, O *I*!
1Ki 9:5	royal throne over *I* for ever,
17:1	"As the LORD, the God of *I*, lives,
18:18	"I have not made trouble for *I*,"
22:17	"I saw all *I* scattered
2Ki 1:3	because there is no God in *I*
2:12	The chariots and horsemen of *I*!"
2Ch 18:16	"I saw all *I* scattered
Ezr 3:11	his love to *I* endures for ever."
Ps 14:7	that salvation for *I* would come
22:3	you are the praise of *I*
73:1	Surely God is good to *I*,
78:41	they vexed the Holy One of *I*
80:1	Hear us, O Shepherd of *I*,
118:2	Let *I* say: "His love endures
149:2	Let *I* rejoice in their Maker;
Isa 41:8	"But you, O *I*, my servant, Jacob
54:5	Holy One of *I* is your Redeemer;
Jer 3:11	"Faithless *I* is more righteous
3:23	God is the salvation of *I*
50:17	"*I* is a scattered flock
50:19	bring *I* back to his own pasture
Eze 3:17	a watchman for the house of *I*;
8:4	the glory of the God of *I*,
12:6	a sign to the house of *I*.
18:31	Why will you die, O house of *I*
21:2	Prophesy against the land of *I*
34:2	against the shepherds of *I*;
39:23	*I* went into exile for their sin,
39:29	my Spirit on the house of *I*,
Hos 8:14	*I* has forgotten his Maker
10:1	*I* was a spreading vine;
11:1	"When *I* was a child, I loved him,
14:5	I will be like the dew to *I*;
Am 2:6	"For three sins of *I*, even
Mic 5:2	one who will be ruler over *I*,
Mt 2:6	the shepherd of my people *I*.'
8:10	I have not found anyone in *I*
10:6	Go rather to the lost sheep of *I*
19:28	judging the twelve tribes of *I*.
Mk 12:29	Hear, O *I*, the Lord our God,
15:32	Christ, this King of *I*,
Lk 2:25	waiting for the consolation of *I*,
4:25	many widows in *I* in Elijah's time,
24:21	one who was going to redeem *I*.
Jn 1:31	he might be revealed to *I*.
1:49	you are the King of *I*.
12:13	"Blessed is the King of *I*!
Ac 1:6	to restore the kingdom to *I*?
5:31	forgiveness of sins to *I*
Ro 9:4	the people of *I*. Theirs is

9:6	who are descended from *I* are *I*.
9:31	*I*, who pursued a law of
11:26	And so all *I* will be saved,
Gal 6:16	even to the *I* of God
Eph 3:6	heirs together with *I*,
Heb 8:8	new covenant with the house of *I*

Israelite, -s

Ex 1:7	the *I-s* were fruitful
3:15	Moses, "Say to the *I-s*,
14:22	the *I-s* went through the sea
29:45	I will dwell among the *I-s*
Lev 25:42	the *I-s* are my servants,
Nu 14:2	the *I-s* grumbled against Moses
20:13	where the *I-s* quarrelled
Dt 34:8	The *I-s* grieved for Moses
Jos 7:1	But the *I-s* acted unfaithfully
Jdg 2:11	the *I-s* did evil in the eyes
1Sa 9:2	without equal among the *I-s*—
1Ki 8:9	made a covenant with the *I-s*
19:10	*I-s* have rejected your covenant,
2Ki 17:7	because the *I-s* had sinned
Eze 2:3	I am sending you to the *I-s*,
Hos 3:1	as the LORD loves the *I-s*,
3:5	the *I-s* will return
Ro 9:27	the *I-s* be like the sand
10:1	prayer to God for the *I-s* is
2Co 3:7	the *I-s* could not look steadily
11:22	Are they *I-s*? So am I.

Issachar

1. Son of Jacob by Leah (Ge 30:17–18; 35:23); blessed by Jacob (Ge 49:14–15). **2.** Tribe descended from Issachar. Blessed by Moses (Dt 33:18–19). Included in census (Nu 1:28–29; 26:23–25). Apportioned land (Jos 19:17–23; Eze 48:25).

itching

2Ti 4:3	what their *i* ears want to hear

J

Jacob

Son of Isaac; younger twin of Esau (Ge 25:21–26). Favoured by Rebekah (Ge 25:27–28). Bought birthright from Esau (Ge 25:29–34); tricked Isaac into blessing him as firstborn (Ge 27); fled to Haran (Ge 27:41–28:5).

Dream at Bethel (Ge 28:10–22); heir to promises of Abrahamic covenant (Ge 28:13–15; 48:3–4; Lev 26:42; Heb 11:9); patriarch (Ex 3:15–16; Jer 33:26; Mt 22:32; Mk 12:26). Gracious choice by God contrasted with rejection of Esau (Mal 1:2–3; Ro 9:13).

Worked for Laban to win Rachel; tricked into marrying Leah; married Rachel in return for further labour (Ge 29:16–30). Children (Ge 29:31–30:24; 35:23–26; 1Ch 2–9). Wealth increased (Ge 30:25–43); returned to Canaan (Ge 31); wrestled with God; called Israel (Ge 32:22–32); reconciled to Esau (Ge 33). Returned to Bethel (Ge 35:1–15).

Showed favouritism to Joseph (Ge 37:3–4). Sent sons to Egypt for food (Ge 42:1–5). Settled in Egypt with family (Ge 46; Ex 1:1–5). Blessed Ephraim and Manasseh (Ge 48:8–20; Heb 11:21); blessed sons (Ge 49:1–28). Death (Ge 49:29–33); burial in Canaan (Ge 50:1–14).

Jael

Wife of Heber the Kenite; killed Sisera, commander of Canaanite army, after his defeat by Deborah and Barak (Jdg 4:17–22; 5:24–27).

Jairus

Synagogue ruler whose daughter was raised to life by Jesus (Mt 9:18–26; Mk 5:22–43; Lk 8:41–56).

James

1. Apostle; son of Zebedee, brother of John (Mt 4:21–22; 10:2; Mk 1:19–20; 3:17; Lk 5:10). With Peter and John, especially close to Jesus: at raising of Jairus' daughter (Mk 5:37; Lk 8:51); transfiguration (Mt 17:1–2; Mk 9:2; Lk 9:28–29); in Gethsemane (Mt 26:36–38; Mk 14:32–34). Mother's request (Mt 20:20–28; Mk 10:35–45). Killed by Herod (Ac 12:2). **2.** Apostle; son of Alphaeus (Mt 10:3; Mk 3:18; Lk 6:15; Ac 1:13). **3.** Brother of Jesus and Jude (Mt 13:55; Mk 6:3; Gal 1:19; Jude 1); saw risen Lord (1Co 15:7) and with disciples before Pentecost (Ac 1:13); leader of church in Jerusalem (Ac 12:17; 15:13–21; 21:18; Gal 2:9); wrote letter (Jas 1:1).

Japheth

Son of Noah (Ge 5:32; 6:10; 1Ch 1:4). Saved in ark (Ge 7:13; 9:18–19). Blessed by Noah

(Ge 9:27); descendants (Ge 10:2–5; 1Ch 1:5–7).

jar, -s

1Ki 17:14	The *j* of flour will not be used up
Mt 25:4	The wise, however, took oil in *j-s*
Mk 14:3	a woman came with an alabaster *j*
Lk 8:16	lights a lamp and hides it in a *j*
Jn 2:6	Nearby stood six stone water *j-s*,
2Co 4:7	this treasure in *j-s* of clay

jealous, -y

Ex 20:5	I, the LORD your God, am a *j* God,
Ps 78:58	aroused his *j-y* with their idols
SS 8:6	its *j-y* unyielding as the grave.
2Co 11:2	am *j* for you with a godly *j-y*
Gal 5:20	*j-y*, fits of rage, selfish

Jehoiachin

King of Judah; succeeded father, Jehoiakim; after three months taken as captive to Babylon (2Ki 24:8–17; 2Ch 36:8–10); removed from prison to royal palace (2Ki 25:27–30; Jer 52:31–34).

Jehoiakim

King of Judah. Son of Josiah, formerly called Eliakim; made king by Pharaoh Neco (2Ki 23:33–36; 2Ch 36:4). Killed prophet Uriah (Jer 26:20–23; burned Jeremiah's scroll (Jer 36). Became Babylonian vassal; subsequent rebellion brought invasion; died on way into captivity (2Ki 24:1–4; 2Ch 36:5–8; Da 1:1–2).

Jehoshaphat

King of Judah; son of Asa (1Ki 22:41). Devoted to God; removed idols; sent officials to teach Law (2Ch 17:3–9). Strengthened kingdom (2Ch 17:2,10–19). Allied with Israel (1Ki 22:44; 2Ch 18:1; 20:35–36); helped Ahab against Aram (1Ki 22:1–33; 2Ch 18:1–19:1) and Joram against Moab (2Ki 3). Alliances rebuked (2Ch 19:1–2; 2Ch 20:35–37). Appointed judges (2Ch 19:4–11). Trusted God for victory over Moab and Ammon (2Ch 20:1–30). Death (2Ch 21:1).

Jehu

1. Prophet; rebuked Baasha (1Ki 16:1–7) and Jehoshaphat (2Ch 19:1–2). **2.** King of Israel. Choice by God announced to Elijah (1Ki 19:16–17); anointed by servant of Elisha; instructed to destroy Ahab's house (2Ki 9:1–13). Killed Joram, Ahaziah (2Ki 9:14–29), Jezebel (2Ki 9:30–37), Ahab's family (2Ki 10:1–17), ministers of Baal (2Ki 10:18–29). Succession promised for four generations (2Ki 10:30). Death (2Ki 10:34–36).

Jephthah

Judge. Social outcast, called on to deliver Israel from Ammonites (Jdg 11:1–32). Rash vow led to sacrifice of daughter (Jdg 11:30–40). Victory over Ephraim (Jdg 12:1–6). Death (Jdg 12:7). Example of faith (Heb 11:32–34).

Jeremiah

Prophet to Judah (Jer 1:1–3). Called by God while still young (Jer 1). Persecuted (Jer 11:18–23; 12:6; 18:18); put in stocks (Jer 20:2); threatened with death (Jer 26:7–11); scroll burned (Jer 36); imprisoned (Jer 37); thrown into cistern (Jer 38:6–13). Warned of Babylonian exile (Jer 25:8–11; 34:1–3); challenged false prophets (Jer 6:10–15; 23:9–40; 28). Promised restoration (Jer 25:12–14; 30; 33); announced new covenant (Jer 31); bought field (Jer 32). Taken to Egypt with fleeing remnant (Jer 43).

Jeroboam

1. Israel's first king. Former official of Solomon; rebelled and fled to Egypt (1Ki 11:26–40). After Solomon's death, led northern tribes in rebellion against Rehoboam (1Ki 12:1–20; 2Ch 10). Established idolatrous worship (1Ki 12:25–33); set evil example for successors (1Ki 15:34; 16:19,26,31; 22:52). Rebuked by prophets (1Ki 13–14). Death (2Ch 13:20). **2.** Jeroboam II. Son of Jehoash. Restored Israel's boundaries; brought economic prosperity (2Ki 14:23–29). Spiritual decay challenged by Amos (Am 1:1; 2:6–8; 5:21–24; 6:1–8; 7:9–11).

Jerusalem

Jos 15:63 the Jebusites, who were living in *J*
2Sa 5:6 The king and his men marched to *J*
2Ki 21:12 going to bring such disaster on *J*
23:27 I will reject *J*, the city I chose,
24:14 He carried into exile all *J*:
2Ch 9:1 she came to *J* to test him
12:7 wrath will not be poured out on *J*
33:4 "My Name will remain in *J* for ever
36:19 and broke down the wall of *J*;
Ezr 7:13 who wish to go to *J* with you,
Ne 1:3 The wall of *J* is broken down,
11:2 who volunteered to live in *J*
Ps 51:18 build up the walls of *J*
79:1 they have reduced *J* to rubble
122:3 *J* is built like a city
122:6 Pray for the peace of *J*:
128:5 may you see the prosperity of *J*
137:5 If I forget you, O *J*,
SS 3:5 Daughters of *J*, I charge you
Isa 2:3 the word of the LORD from *J*
40:2 Speak tenderly to *J*,
65:19 I will rejoice over *J*
Jer 26:18 *J* will become a heap of rubble,
Eze 16:2 "Son of man, confront *J*
24:2 king of Babylon has laid siege to *J*
Joel 2:32 in *J* there will be deliverance,
3:17 *J* will be holy;
Mic 4:2 the word of the LORD from *J*
Zec 8:8 I will bring them back to live in *J*
Mt 2:1 Magi from the east came to *J*
3:5 People went out to him from *J*
21:10 When Jesus entered *J*, the whole
23:37 "O *J*, *J*, you who kill
Mk 10:33 "We are going up to *J*," he said,
Lk 2:22 Mary took him to *J* to present him
2:43 the boy Jesus stayed behind in *J*,
19:41 As he approached *J* and saw the city
21:20 "When you see *J* being surrounded
21:24 *J* will be trampled on
24:47 to all nations, beginning at *J*
Jn 4:20 where we must worship is in *J*.
5:1 Jesus went up to *J* Jews
Ac 1:8 and you will be my witnesses in *J*,
11:2 So when Peter went up to *J*,
Ro 15:26 for the poor among the saints in *J*
1Co 16:3 and send them with your gift to *J*
Gal 1:18 after three years, I went up to *J*
4:26 But the *J* that is above is free,
Heb 12:22 Mount Zion, to the heavenly *J*,
Rev 21:2 I saw the Holy City, the new *J*,

Jesse

From Bethlehem; father of David (Ru 4:17,22; 1Sa 16; 17:12–20; 1Ch 2:12–17; Isa 11:1,10; Ro 15:12).

Jesus

LIFE: Genealogy (Mt 1:1–17; Lk 3:23–38); birth (Mt 1:18–2:12; Lk 1:26–38; 2:1–20); presented in temple (Lk 2:21–40); fled to Egypt (Mt 2:13–18). Brought up in Nazareth (Mt 2:19–23); visited Jerusalem temple (Lk 2:41–52).
Baptised by John (Mt 3:13–17; Mk 1:9–11; Lk 3:21–23; Jn 1:29–34); tempted (Mt 4:1–11; Mk 1:12–13; Lk 4:1–13); began public ministry (Mt 4:12–17; Mk 1:14–15; Lk 4:14–30); called first disciples (Mt 4:18–22; Mk 1:16–20; Lk 5:2–11; Jn 1:35–51); preached in Galilee (Mt 4:23–25; Mk 1:39). Appointed and sent out disciples (Mt 9:35–10:16; Mk 3:13–18; 6:7–11; Lk 9:1–6; 10:1–17).
Acknowledged by Peter as Christ (Mt 16:13–23; Mk 8:27–33; Lk 9:18–22). Transfigured (Mt 17:1–8; Mk 9:2–8; Lk 9:28–36). Set out for Jerusalem (Mt 16:21; 20:17–19; Mk 10:32–34; Lk 18:31–34).
Last week in Jerusalem: entered city (Mt 21:1–11; Mk 11:1–11; Lk 19:29–44; Jn 12:12–15); cleared temple (Mt 21:12–13; Mk 11:15–19; Lk 19:45–48; Jn 2:13–16); anointed at Bethany (Mt 26:6–13; Mk 14:3–9); shared Last Supper (Mt 26:17–30; Mk 14:12–26; Lk 22:7–23); washed disciples' feet (Jn 13:1–17); prayed in Gethsemane (Mt 26:36–46; Mk 14:32–42; Lk 22:40–46); arrested and tried (Mt 26:47–68; 27:11–26; Mk 14:43–65; 15:1–15; Lk 22:47–53; 22:66–23:25; Jn 18:1–19:16); crucified and buried (Mt 27:27–66; Mk 15:16–47; Lk 23:26–56; Jn 19:17–42).
Raised to life; appeared to followers (Mt 28; Mk 16; Lk 24; Jn 20–21; Ac 1:1–4;

1Co 15:1–8); commissioned disciples (Mt 28:16–20; Ac 1:4–8); ascended (Lk 24:50–53; Ac 1:9).
MIRACLES: Healed: crowds (Mt 4:23–24; 8:16; Mk 1:32–34; Lk 4:40–41; Mt 14:14; Lk 9:11; Mt 15:29–31; Lk 6:17–18); those with leprosy (Mt 8:2–4; Mk 1:40–45; Lk 5:12–16; Lk 17:11–19); centurion's servant (Mt 8:5–13; Lk 7:1–10); Peter's mother-in-law (Mt 8:14–15; Mk 1:29–31; Lk 4:38–39); demon-possessed (Mt 8:28–34; Mk 5:1–20; Lk 8:26–39; Mt 9:32–34; 12:22; Lk 11:14; Mt 17:14–18; Mk 9:17–27; Lk 9:38–43; Mk 1:23–26; Lk 4:33–35); paralysed man (Mt 9:1–8; Mk 2:3–12; Lk 5:18–26); woman with bleeding (Mt 9:20–22; Mk 5:25–34; Lk 8:43–48); blind (Mt 9:27–31; 20:29–34; Mk 10:46–52; Lk 18:35–43; Mk 8:22–26; Jn 9:1–7); man with shrivelled hand (Mt 12:9–14; Mk 3:1–6; Lk 6:6–11); deaf mute (Mk 7:31–37); crippled woman (Lk 13:10–17); man with dropsy (Lk 14:1–4); high priest's servant (Lk 22:50–51); official's son (Jn 4:46–54); man at pool of Bethesda (Jn 5:1–9).
Raised to life: Jairus' daughter (Mt 9:18–26; Mk 5:22–43; Lk 8:41–56); widow of Nain's son (Lk 7:11–17); Lazarus (Jn 11:1–44).
Stilled storm (Mt 8:23–27; Mk 4:35–41; Lk 8:22–25); fed 5,000 (Mt 14:15–21; Mk 6:35–44; Lk 9:12–17; Jn 6:5–13); walked on water (Mt 14:25–33; Mk 6:47–52; Jn 6:18–20); fed 4,000 (Mt 15:32–39; Mk 8:1–10); money from fish (Mt 17:24–27); cursed fig-tree (Mt 21:18–19; Mk 11:12–14,20–22); catches of fish (Lk 5:1–11; Jn 21:4–6); changed water to wine (Jn 2:1–11).
TEACHING: Announced God's kingdom (Mt 4:17; 10:7; 12:24–29; Lk 11:14–22; Mt 16:28; Mk 9:1; Mk 1:15; Lk 4:43; 9:11); Sermon on the Mount (Mt 5–7; Lk 6:20–49); pronounced woe on Pharisees (Mt 23; Lk 11:37–54); signs of the end of the age (Mt 24; Mk 13; Lk 21); conversations with Nicodemus (Jn 3), Samaritan woman (Jn 4); the bread of life (Jn 6:25–58); the good shepherd (Jn 10:1–20); discourse in Upper Room (Jn 13–17).
PARABLES: wise and foolish builders (Mt 7:24–27; Lk 6:47–49); sower (Mt 13:3–23; Mk 4:2–20; Lk 8:4–8); weeds (Mt 13:24–30); mustard seed and yeast (Mt 13:31–33; Mk 4:30–32; Lk 13:18–21); hidden treasure, pearl, net, houseowner (Mt 13:44–52); lost sheep (Mt 18:12–14; Lk 15:4–7); unmerciful servant (Mt 18:23–34); workers in vineyard (Mt 20:1–16); two sons (Mt 21:28–32); tenants (Mt 21:33–41; Mk 12:1–9; Lk 20:9–16); banquet (Mt 22:2–14; Lk 14:16–24); ten virgins (Mt 25:1–13); talents (Mt 25:14–30; Lk 19:12–27); sheep and goats (Mt 25:31–46); growing seed (Mk 4:26–29); good Samaritan (Lk 10:30–37); rich fool (Lk 12:16–21); cost of discipleship (Lk 14:28–33); lost coin, lost son (Lk 15:8–32); shrewd manager (Lk 16:1–8); rich man and Lazarus (Lk 16:19–31); persistent widow (Lk 18:2–8); Pharisee and tax collector (Lk 18:10–14).

Jethro

Father-in-law of Moses (Ex 3:1; 4:18), also called Reuel (Ex 2:18). Visited Moses at Horeb; advised him to delegate administration of justice (Ex 18).

Jew, -s

Ezr 4:12	the *J-s* who came up to us
6:14	the elders of the *J-s*
Ne 4:1	He ridiculed the *J-s*
Est 3:13	kill and annihilate all the *J-s*—
4:14	deliverance for the *J-s* will arise
Da 3:8	came forward and denounced the *J-s*
Mt 2:2	who has been born king of the *J-s*?
27:11	"Are you the king of the *J-s*?"
27:29	"Hail, king of the *J-s*!"
Jn 4:9	*J-s* do not associate with Samaritans
4:22	for salvation is from the *J-s*
8:31	To the *J-s* who had believed him,
12:11	the *J-s* were going over to Jesus
Ac 10:28	for a *J* to associate with a Gentile
14:1	number of *J-s* and Gentiles believed
17:12	Many of the *J-s* believed,
18:4	trying to persuade *J-s* and Greeks
21:39	"I am a *J*, from Tarsus in Cilicia,
Ro 1:16	first for the *J*, then for
2:29	a man is a *J* if he is one inwardly;
3:29	Is God the God of *J-s* only?

10:12	no difference between *J* and Gentile
15:8	has become a servant of the *J-s*
1Co 1:23	a stumbling-block to *J-s*
9:20	To the *J-s* I became like a *J*,
Gal 2:8	Peter as an apostle to the *J-s*,
3:28	There is neither *J* nor Greek,
Rev 3:9	claim to be *J-s* though they are not

jewel, -s

Pr 20:15	that speak knowledge are a rare *j*
Isa 61:10	a bride adorns herself with her *j-s*
Zec 9:16	in his land like *j-s* in a crown
Rev 21:11	was like that of a very precious *j*,

jewellery

1Pe 3:3	wearing of gold *j* and fine clothes

Jezebel

1. Daughter of Sidonian king; wife of Ahab (1Ki 16:31). Encouraged his sin (1Ki 21:25): promoted worship of native god, Baal (1Ki 16:32–33; 18:19); killed LORD's prophets (1Ki 18:4,13); threatened Elijah (1Ki 19:1–2); had Naboth killed (1Ki 21). Death prophesied by Elijah (1Ki 21:23); killed by Jehu (2Ki 9:30–37). **2.** Designation of prophetess in church at Thyatira who was leading believers astray (Rev 2:20).

Joab

Nephew of David; brother of Abishai and Asahel (1Ch 2:16). Led David's army against Abner (2Sa 2:13–32); killed Abner to avenge death of Asahel (2Sa 3:26–27,30). Led attack on Jerusalem (1Ch 11:4–6); made commander-in-chief (2Sa 8:16; 18:2; 20:23). Defeated Ammon (2Sa 10:7–14; 1Ch 19:8–15), Rabbah (2Sa 12:26–27). Followed David's order to kill Uriah (2Sa 11:14–17); killed Absalom (2Sa 18:14–15); killed Amasa (2Sa 20:9–10). Supported Adonijah (1Ki 1:17–19); killed by Benaiah (1Ki 2:5–6,28–34).

Joash

1. Father of Gideon (Jdg 6:11,29–31; 8:32). **2.** King of Judah; son of Ahaziah. Hidden from Athaliah (2Ki 11:1–3; 2Ch 22:10–12); crowned king by Jehoida (2Ki 11:4–21; 2Ch 23). Repaired temple (2Ki 12; 2Ch 24:1–14); returned to idolatry after Jehoiada's death (2Ch 24:17–24). Defeated by Aram (2Ch 24:23–24); murdered by officials (2Ki 12:20; 2Ch 24:25).

Job

1. Wealthy, God-fearing man from Uz (Job 1:1–8). Uprightness tested by Satan, with God's permission (Job 1:6–12; 2:1–6). Suffered loss of family and wealth (Job 1:13–19), and physical affliction (Job 2:7–8). Remained patient (Job 1:20–22; 2:9–10); protested when innocence challenged by friends (Job 3–31). Rebuked by the LORD (Job 38–41); finally vindicated, healed and restored to greater wealth (Job 42:7–17). **2.** Job's friends: Eliphaz (Job 4–5; 15; 22), Bildad (Job 8; 18; 25) Zophar (Job 11; 20) and Elihu (Job 32–37). Came to offer sympathy (Job 2:11–13); tried and failed to explain Job's suffering in terms of conventional wisdom.

Joel

Prophet (Joel 1:1). Saw plague of locusts as depiction of God's judgment (Joel 1:2–2:12); called for repentance (Joel 2:13–17). Future blessing included pouring out of Spirit (Joel 2:18–32; Ac 2:16–21).

John

1. The Baptist; son of Zechariah and Elizabeth (Lk 1:5–25,57–80). Prepared way for Jesus (Mt 3:1–12; Mk 1:3–8; Lk 3:2–17; Jn 1:6–8,15,19–36; 3:27–30); baptised Jesus (Mt 3:13–15; Mk 1:9; Lk 3:21). Opposed Herod's marriage to Herodias; arrested (Mt 14:3–5; Mk 6:17–18); reassured and commended by Jesus (Mt 11:2–19; Lk 7:18–35). Executed (Mt 14:6–12; Mk 6:21–29). Identified with Elijah (Mt 11:14; 17:11–13; Mk 9:12–13; Lk 1:17). **2.** Apostle; son of Zebedee; brother of James. With Peter and James, especially close to Jesus: at raising of Jairus' daughter (Mk 5:37; Lk 8:51); transfiguration (Mt 17:1–2; Mk 9:2; Lk 9:28–29); in Gethsemane (Mt 26:36–38; Mk 14:32–34). Mother's request (Mt 20:20–28; Mk 10:35–45). Called "the disciple whom Jesus loved": close to Jesus at Last Supper (Jn 13:23; 21:20); at crucifixion (Jn 19:25–27). Leader in Jerusalem church (Gal 2:9; 2Jn 1; 3Jn 1). Wrote fourth gospel, letters, book of

Revelation (Rev 1:1,9; 22:8; Jn 20:2; 21:7,24). **3.** See *Mark.*

join, -ed

Zec 2:11	nations will be *j-ed* with the LORD
Mt 19:6	what God has *j-ed* together,
Ac 1:14	*j-ed* together constantly in prayer
Ro 15:30	to *j* me in my struggle by praying
Eph 2:21	the whole building is *j-ed* together

joint, -s

Ps 22:14	all my bones are out of *j.*
Heb 4:12	soul and spirit, *j-s* and marrow;

Jonah

Prophet during reign of Jeroboam II (2Ki 14:25). Ran from God's call to preach against Nineveh (Jnh 1:2–3,10). God sent storm; thrown overboard; swallowed by fish (Jnh 1:4–17). Prayed; disgorged onto dry land (Jnh 2); deliverance a "sign" prefiguring Jesus' death and resurrection (Mt 12:39–41; Lk 11:29–32). Obeyed second call (Jnh 3); response to Nineveh's repentance rebuked (Jnh 4).

Jonathan

Eldest son of Saul (1Sa 13:16; 14:49; 1Ch 8:33). Courageous warrior (1Sa 14:1–23; 2Sa 1:22–23). Violated Saul's oath (1Sa 14:24–45). Friendship with David (1Sa 18:1–4; 19–20; 23:16–18; 2Sa 1:26). Killed (1Sa 31:1–2); mourned by David (2Sa 1:19–27).

Jordan

Nu 35:10	'When you cross the *J* into Canaan
Dt 3:25	and see the good land beyond the *J*—
3:27	you are not going to cross this *J*
Jos 3:17	dry ground in the middle of the *J*,
4:3	stones from the middle of the *J*
4:22	'Israel crossed the *J* on dry ground
2Ki 5:10	wash yourself seven times in the *J*,
Mt 3:6	baptised by him in the *J* River

Joseph

1. Son of Jacob by Rachel (Ge 30:22–24; 35:24; 1Ch 2:2). Father's favouritism aroused brothers' hostility (Ge 37:3–4). Dreams (Ge 37:5–11). Sold by brothers (Ge 37:12–36); became slave of Potiphar (Ge 39:1–6). Resisted attentions of Potiphar's wife; falsely accused; imprisoned (Ge 39:7–23). Interpreted dreams of cupbearer and baker (Ge 40); Pharaoh (Ge 41:1–36). Put in charge of Egypt (Ge 41:37–57). Tested brothers when came to buy grain (Ge 42–44); made himself known (Ge 45:1–15); settled family in Egypt (Ge 45:16–47:12). Sons blessed (Ge 48); received Jacob's blessing (Ge 49:22–26). Death (Ge 50:22–26; Ex 13:19; Jos 24:32; Heb 11:22). Descendants divided into tribes of Ephraim and Manasseh (Jos 14:4; 16–17; Eze 47:13); blessed by Moses (Dt 33:13–17). **2.** Husband of Jesus' mother, Mary (Mt 1:16,18–25; Lk 1:27); descendant of David (Lk 2:4); carpenter (Mt 13:55). Dreams (Mt 1:20–23; 2:13,19–20). **3.** Disciple from Arimathea; member of Jewish council. Asked for Jesus' body; gave tomb for burial (Mt 27:57–60; Mk 15:42–46; Lk 23:50–54; Jn 19:38–42). **4.** See *Barnabas.*

Joshua

1. Son of Nun, formerly called Hoshea (Nu 13:8,16; 1Ch 7:27). Fought Amalekites (Ex 17:9–14). Moses' assistant: on Sinai (Ex 24:13; 32:17); at tent of meeting (Ex 33:11). One of spies sent to explore Canaan (Nu 13:8); with Caleb encouraged people to go in (Nu 14:6–9); so allowed to enter land (Nu 26:65; 32:12). Succeeded Moses (Dt 1:38; 3:28; 31:1–8; 34:9). Commissioned and encouraged by God (Jos 1:1–9). crossed Jordan (Jos 3–4). Victory at Jericho (Jos 5:13–6:27); defeat then victory at Ai (Jos 7–8); renewed covenant at Mt Ebal (Jos 8:30–35); deceived by Gibeonites (Jos 9); sun stood still to enable victory over five kings at Gibeon (Jos 10); conquered southern Canaan (Jos 10:29–43), northern Canaan (Jos 11). Apportioned land among tribes (Jos 13–22). Gave final instructions (Jos 23); renewed covenant at Shechem (Jos 24:1–27); death (Jos 24:29–31; Jdg 2:8–9). **2.** High priest at time of restoration (Hag 1:1); encouraged by Haggai to finish work on temple (Hag 1:12–2:9). Representative of sinful Israel saved by God's grace (Zec 3); crowning foreshadowed reign of Messiah (Zec 6:9–15).

Josiah

King of Judah; son of Amon (2Ki 21:26; 1Ch 3:14; 2Ch 33:25). Birth prophesied (1Ki 13:2). Godliness commended (2Ki 22:2; 2Ch 34:2–3; Jer 22:15–16). Removed idols (2Ch 34:3–7); repaired temple (2Ki 22:3–7; 2Ch 34:8–13). Repented, following discovery of Book of the Law (2Ki 22:8–20; 2Ch 34:14–28); renewed covenant (2Ki 23:1–3; 2Ch 34:29–32); purified temple (2Ki 23:4–12); destroyed high places (2Ki 23:13–20,24–25; 2Ch 34:33). Celebrated Passover (2Ki 23:21–23; 2Ch 35:1–19). Killed fighting Pharaoh Neco (2Ki 23:29–30; 2Ch 35:20–27).

journey

Ge 24:27	the LORD has led me on the *j*
Jos 24:17	He protected us on our entire *j*
Ezr 8:21	a safe *j* for us and our children,
Mt 25:14	it will be like a man going on a *j*,

joy, -ful

Ne 8:10	the *j* of the LORD is your strength
Ps 16:11	fill me with *j* in your presence,
51:12	the *j* of your salvation
98:4	Shout for *j* to the LORD,
Isa 12:3	With *j* you will draw water
55:12	You will go out in *j*
Lk 6:23	Rejoice in that day and leap for *j*
Jn 15:11	so that my *j* may be in you
16:20	but your grief will turn to *j*
Ro 14:17	peace and *j* in the Holy Spirit
Gal 4:15	What has happened to all your *j*?
5:22	the fruit of the Spirit is love, *j*,
Php 1:4	I always pray with *j*
1:26	your *j* in Christ Jesus
1Th 1:6	with the *j* given by the Holy Spirit
5:16	Be *j-ful* always
Heb 12:2	who for the *j* set before him
1Pe 1:8	an inexpressible and glorious *j*
1Jn 1:4	this to make our *j* complete
Jude :24	without fault and with great *j*

jubilee

Lev 25:11	fiftieth year shall be a *j* for you
27:21	When the field is released in the *J*

Judah

1. Son of Jacob by Leah (Ge 29:35; 35:23; 1Ch 2:1). Urged brothers to sell, not kill, Joseph (Ge 37:26–27). Father of Perez and Zerah, by daughter-in-law, Tamar (Ge 38). Offered himself in place of Benjamin (Ge 44:18–34). Blessed by Jacob as ruler (Ge 49:8–12). **2.** Tribe descended from Judah. Blessed by Moses (Dt 33:7). Included in census (Nu 1:26–27; 26:19–22). Apportioned land (Jos 15; Eze 48:7); unable to take full possession (Jos 15:63; Jdg 1:1–20). Anointed David as king (2Sa 2:4); remained loyal to Davidic kings (1Ki 12:21; 2Ch 11:12). Tribe of Jesus (Mt 1:3; Heb 7:14). **3.** In the sense of Judah as the southern kingdom.

2Sa 3:10	David's throne over Israel and *J*
1Ki 1:35	ruler over Israel and *J*.
4:20	The people of *J* and Israel
14:22	*J* did evil in the eyes of the LORD.
2Ch 11:14	and came to *J* and Jerusalem
11:17	They strengthened the kingdom of *J*
12:12	Indeed, there was some good in *J*
17:9	They taught throughout *J*,
24:18	God's anger came upon *J*
24:24	Because *J* had forsaken the LORD,
25:22	*J* was routed by Israel,
28:19	The LORD had humbled *J*
29:21	for the sanctuary and for *J*.
Ne 6:7	'There is a king in *J*!'
Ps 60:7	*J* my sceptre
76:1	In *J* God is known;
78:68	but he chose the tribe of *J*,
114:2	*J* became God's sanctuary,
Isa 3:8	Jerusalem staggers, *J* is falling;
7:17	since Ephraim broke away from *J*
11:12	assemble the scattered people of *J*
37:31	a remnant of the house of *J*
40:9	say to the towns of *J*,
Jer 3:7	her unfaithful sister *J* saw it

14:19	Have you rejected *J* completely?
23:6	In his days *J* will be saved
24:5	I regard as good the exiles from *J*,
30:3	I will bring my people Israel and *J*
31:24	People will live together in *J*
33:7	I will bring *J* and Israel back
La 1:3	*J* has gone into exile.
1:15	trampled the Virgin Daughter of *J*
Eze 48:7	"*J* will have one portion;
Da 1:6	Among these were some from *J*:
Hos 1:7	I will show love to the house of *J*;
6:4	What can I do with you, *J*?
Am 2:5	I will send fire upon *J*
Zec 2:12	LORD will inherit *J* as his portion
14:14	*J* too will fight at Jerusalem.
Mal 2:11	*J* has broken faith.

Judaism

Ac 2:11	(both Jews and converts to *J*);
13:43	devout converts to *J* followed Paul
Gal 1:13	my previous way of life in *J*,

Judas

1. Brother of Jesus (Mt 13:55; Mk 6:3); also called Jude, author of letter (Jude 1). **2.** Apostle; son of James (Lk 6:16; Jn 14:22; Ac 1:13); also known as Thaddaeus (Mt 10:3; Mk 3:18). **3.** Apostle; also called Iscariot; known as Jesus' betrayer (Mt 10:4; Mk 3:19; Lk 6:16; Jn 6:71; 12:4); treasurer for disciples (Jn 12:6; 13:29). Agreed to betray Jesus for 30 silver pieces (Mt 26:14–16; Mk 14:10–11; Lk 22:3–6); kissed Jesus to identify him (Mt 26:47–49; Mk 14:43–45; Lk 22:47–48); filled with remorse; committed suicide (Mt 27:3–5; Ac 1:16–25). **4.** Prophet; also called Barsabbas. Sent, with Silas, by apostles in Jerusalem to Antioch with decision about circumcision (Ac 15:22–34).

Jude

See *Judas* 1.

judge, -s, -ing, -d

Ge 18:25	Will not the *J* of all the earth
Ex 2:14	"Who made you ruler and *j* over us?
Dt 1:17	Do not show partiality in *j-ing*;
Jdg 2:16	Then the LORD raised up *j-s*,
Ps 98:9	for he comes to *j* the earth.
Isa 11:4	but with righteousness he will *j*
Mt 7:1	Do not *j*, or you too will be *j-d*
Lk 18:2	"In a certain town there was a *j*
Jn 7:24	Stop *j-ing* by mere appearances,
Ro 2:16	day when God will *j* men's secrets
14:10	why do you *j* your brother?
1Co 6:2	the saints will *j* the world?
11:32	When we are *j-d* by the Lord,
Gal 2:6	does not *j* by external appearance—
2Ti 4:1	who will *j* the living and the dead,
Heb 12:23	have come to God, the *j* of all men,
1Pe 4:5	ready to *j* the living and the dead
Rev 20:12	dead were *j-d* according to what

judgment

Pr 6:32	a man who commits adultery lacks *j*;
Mt 11:24	bearable for Sodom on the day of *j*
Jn 5:22	has entrusted all *j* to the Son,
9:39	Jesus said, "For *j* I have come
12:31	Now is the time for *j* on this world
16:8	to sin and righteousness and *j*:
Ro 14:13	stop passing *j* on one another.
1Co 11:29	eats and drinks *j* on himself
2Co 5:10	appear before the *j* seat of Christ,
1Ti 3:6	fall under the same *j* as the devil
Heb 9:27	die once, and after that to face *j*
1Pe 4:17	*j* to begin with the family of God;
2Pe 3:7	being kept for the day of *j*
Rev 14:7	because the hour of his *j* has come.

just, -ly, -ice

Ps 37:28	For the LORD loves the *j*
140:12	the LORD secures *j-ice* for the poor
Pr 17:23	to pervert the course of *j-ice*
Isa 42:1	he will bring *j-ice* to the nations

Am 5:24 But let *j-ice* roll on like a river,
Mic 6:8 To act *j-ly* and to love mercy
Mt 12:18 will proclaim *j-ice* to the nations
Lk 11:42 neglect *j-ice* and the love of God.
Jn 5:30 my judgment is *j*, for I seek not
Ac 17:31 he will judge the world with *j-ice*
Ro 3:25 did this to demonstrate his *j-ice*,
1Jn 1:9 he is faithful and *j*

justification
Ro 4:25 and was raised to life for our *j*
5:16 many trespasses and brought *j*
5:18 *j* that brings life for all men

justify, -ies, -ied
Ps 51:4 and *j-ied* when you judge
Isa 53:11 my righteous servant will *j* many,
Lk 10:29 But he wanted to *j* himself,
18:14 went home *j-ied* before God.
Ro 3:24 and are *j-ied* freely by his grace
4:5 trusts God who *j-ies* the wicked,
5:1 we have been *j-ied* through faith,
5:9 have now been *j-ied* by his blood,
8:30 those he called, he also *j-ied*;
8:33 It is God who *j-ies*
10:10 that you believe and are *j-ied*,
Gal 2:16 not *j-ied* by observing the law,
3:8 God would *j* the Gentiles by faith,
Tit 3:7 having been *j-ied* by his grace,

K

keep, -ing, -er
Ge 4:9 "Am I my brother's *k-er*?
31:49 the LORD *k* watch between you and me
Ex 20:6 who love me and *k* my commandments
20:8 the Sabbath day by *k-ing* it holy
Nu 6:24 "The LORD bless you and *k* you
2Ki 23:3 follow the LORD and *k* his commands,
1Ch 10:13 he did not *k* the word of the LORD,
Ps 17:8 *K* me as the apple of your eye;
19:11 in *k-ing* them there is great reward
34:13 *k* your tongue from evil
119:9 How can a young man *k* his way pure?
121:7 The LORD will *k* you from all harm—
Ecc 12:13 Fear God and *k* his commandments,
Isa 26:3 You will *k* in perfect peace
Jer 17:22 but *k* the Sabbath day holy,
Mt 10:10 for the worker is worth his *k*
24:42 "Therefore *k* watch,
26:40 "Could you men not *k* watch with me
Lk 17:33 Whoever tries to *k* his life
Jn 12:25 will *k* it for eternal life
12:47 hears my words but does not *k* them,
Ac 20:28 *K* watch over yourselves
1Co 1:8 He will *k* you strong to the end,
Gal 5:25 let us *k* in step with the Spirit
Eph 4:3 to *k* the unity of the Spirit
Heb 13:1 *K* on loving each other as brothers
1Jn 5:21 *k* yourselves from idols
Jude :21 *K* yourselves in God's love
1:24 who is able to *k* you from falling
Rev 22:9 all who *k* the words of this book.

kept
Dt 7:8 the LORD loved you and *k* the oath
1Ki 8:20 "The LORD has *k* the promise he made
11:11 not *k* my covenant and my decrees,
Ps 130:3 If you, O LORD, *k* a record of sins,
Lk 18:21 these I have *k* since I was a boy,"
2Ti 4:7 I have *k* the faith
Heb 13:4 and the marriage bed *k* pure,
1Pe 1:4 *k* in heaven for you
Rev 3:8 yet you have *k* my word
14:4 for they *k* themselves pure.

key, -s
Isa 22:22 the *k* to the house of David;
33:6 the fear of the LORD is the *k*

Mt 16:19 I will give you the *k-s*
Rev 1:18 I hold the *k-s* of death and Hades
3:7 who holds the *k* of David.

kill, -s, -ed

Ge 4:8 his brother Abel and *k-ed* him
37:18 they plotted to *k* him
Ex 2:15 he tried to *k* Moses, but Moses fled
13:15 LORD *k-ed* every firstborn in Egypt,
Lev 24:21 *k-s* a man must be put to death
2Ki 5:7 Can I *k* and bring back to life?
Ecc 3:3 a time to *k* and a time to heal,
Jer 18:23 all their plots to *k* me.
Mt 2:16 to *k* all the boys in Bethlehem
Mk 3:4 or to do evil, to save life or to *k*
12:7 This is the heir. Come, let's *k* him
Lk 12:4 do not be afraid of those who *k*
13:34 Jerusalem, you who *k* the prophets
Jn 7:19 Why are you trying to *k* me?
10:10 The thief comes only to steal and *k*
Ac 3:15 You *k-ed* the author of life,
10:13 "Get up, Peter. *K* and eat.
10:39 *k-ed* him by hanging him on a tree
16:27 and was about to *k* himself
2Co 3:6 for the letter *k-s*, but the Spirit
6:9 beaten, and yet not *k-ed*
1Th 2:15 who *k-ed* the Lord Jesus

kind[1], -s

Ge 1:12 bearing seed according to their *k-s*
1:24 creatures according to their *k-s*:
7:2 seven of every *k* of clean animal,
Isa 58:6 the *k* of fasting I have chosen:
Mt 8:27 "What *k* of man is this?
Mk 9:29 This *k* can come out only by prayer
Jn 18:32 the *k* of death he was going to die
1Co 12:4 different *k-s* of gifts,
15:38 to each *k* of seed he gives its own

kind[2], -ness, -nesses

Ex 1:20 God was *k* to the midwives
Ru 1:8 May the LORD show *k-ness* to you,
Pr 19:17 He who is *k* to the poor lends to
Isa 63:7 tell of the *k-nesses* of the LORD,
Hos 11:4 with cords of human *k-ness*,
Lk 6:35 because he is *k* to the ungrateful
Ro 2:4 his *k-ness*, tolerance and patience,
11:22 the *k-ness* and sternness of God:
1Co 13:4 Love is patient, love is *k*.
Gal 5:22 peace, patience, *k-ness*, goodness,
Eph 4:32 Be *k* and compassionate
1Th 5:15 always try to be *k* to each

king, -'s, -s

Ge 14:18 Melchizedek *k* of Salem
Dt 7:24 will give their *k-s* into your hand,
28:36 the *k* you set over you
Jos 8:23 they took the *k* of Ai alive
Jdg 17:6 In those days Israel had no *k*;
1Sa 8:5 now appoint a *k* to lead us,
10:24 people shouted, "Long live the *k*!
12:2 Now you have a *k* as your leader.
12:12 though the LORD your God was your *k*
15:17 The LORD anointed you *k* over Israel
15:23 he has rejected you as *k*.
24:20 I know that you will surely be *k*
2Sa 2:4 and there they anointed David *k*
1Ki 1:30 Solomon your son shall be *k*
Ps 2:6 "I have installed my *K* on Zion,
10:16 The LORD is *K* for ever and ever;
20:9 O LORD, save the *k*!
24:7 that the *K* of glory may come in
47:2 the great *K* over all the earth
48:2 the city of the Great *K*
72:1 Endow the *k* with your justice,
72:11 All *k-s* will bow down to him
74:12 you, O God, are my *k* from of old;
95:3 the great *K* above all gods
Pr 14:35 A *k* delights in a wise servant,

16:13	*K-s* take pleasure in honest lips;
19:12	A *k-'s* rage is like the roar
20:28	Love and faithfulness keep a *k* safe
24:21	Fear the LORD and the *k*, my son,
Isa 6:5	and my eyes have seen the *K*,
44:6	Israel's *K* and Redeemer,
52:15	*k-s* will shut their mouths because
Jer 10:10	he is the living God, the eternal *K*
Da 1:19	so they entered the *k-'s* service
Zec 9:9	See, your *k* comes to you,
14:9	LORD will be *k* over the whole earth
Mt 2:2	who has been born *k* of the Jews?
21:5	'See, your *k* comes to you,
25:40	"The *K* will reply, 'I tell you
27:37	JESUS, THE *K* OF THE JEWS.
Lk 14:31	suppose a *k* is about to go to war
19:38	"Blessed is the *k* who comes
Jn 18:37	"You are right in saying I am a *k*.
Ac 4:26	*k-s* of the earth take their stand
9:15	before the Gentiles and their *k-s*
13:21	Then the people asked for a *k*,
1Ti 1:17	the *K* eternal, immortal, invisible,
2:2	for *k-s* and all those in authority
6:15	the *K* of *k-s* and Lord of lords
Heb 7:2	name means "*k* of righteousness"
1Pe 2:17	fear God, honour the *k*
Rev 19:16	*K* OF *K-S* AND LORD OF LORDS.
21:24	and the *k-s* of the earth will bring

kingdom

Ex 19:6	you will be for me a *k* of priests
2Sa 7:12	and I will establish his *k*
1Ch 29:11	Yours, O LORD, is the *k*;
Ps 145:13	Your *k* is an everlasting *k*,
Da 7:27	His *k* will be an everlasting *k*,
Mt 3:2	Repent, for the *k* of heaven is near
5:3	for theirs is the *k* of heaven
6:10	your *k* come, your will be done
6:33	But seek first his *k*
7:21	Lord,' will enter the *k* of heaven,
13:24	The *k* of heaven is like a man who
18:1	the greatest in the *k* of heaven?
19:24	a rich man to enter the *k* of God.
24:14	gospel of the *k* will be preached
26:29	anew with you in my Father's *k*.
Mk 9:1	see the *k* of God come with power.
Lk 8:1	the good news of the *k* of God.
Jn 3:3	no-one can see the *k* of God unless
18:36	"My *k* is not of this world.
Ac 8:12	the good news of the *k* of God
14:22	hardships to enter the *k* of God,"
Ro 14:17	For the *k* of God is not a matter
1Co 6:9	will not inherit the *k* of God?
15:50	blood cannot inherit the *k* of God,
Col 1:13	brought us into the *k* of the Son
2Ti 4:18	bring me safely to his heavenly *k*.
Heb 12:28	receiving a *k* that cannot be shaken
2Pe 1:11	a rich welcome into the eternal *k*
Rev 1:6	has made us to be a *k* and priests
12:10	the power and the *k* of our God,

kinsman-redeemer

Ru 3:9	over me, since you are a *k*.
4:14	has not left you without a *k*.

kiss, -es

Ps 2:12	*K* the Son, lest he be angry
SS 1:2	Let him *k* me with the *k-es*
Lk 22:48	betraying the Son of Man with a *k*?
1Co 16:20	Greet one another with a holy *k*

knee, -s

1Ki 19:18	*k-s* have not bowed down to Baal
Da 6:10	he got down on his *k-s* and prayed,

Php 2:10 that at the name of Jesus every *k*
Heb 12:12 your feeble arms and weak *k-s*!

kneel
Est 3:2 But Mordecai would not *k* down
Ps 95:6 let us *k* before the LORD our Maker
Eph 3:14 I *k* before the Father

knew
Dt 34:10 whom the LORD *k* face to face
Mt 7:23 'I never *k* you. Away from me,
12:25 Jesus *k* their thoughts
Jn 2:25 for he *k* what was in a man
Ro 1:21 For although they *k* God,

knock, -ing
SS 5:2 Listen! My lover is *k-ing*:
Mt 7:7 *k* and the door will be opened
Rev 3:20 I stand at the door and *k*.

know, -s, -ing, -n
Ge 3:5 like God, *k-ing* good and evil.
22:12 Now I *k* that you fear God,
Ex 14:18 Egyptians will *k* that I am the LORD
Dt 7:9 *K* therefore that the LORD your God
1Sa 3:7 Now Samuel did not yet *k* the LORD:
2Ch 20:12 We do not *k* what to do, but our
Ps 46:10 "Be still, and *k* that I am God;
51:3 For I *k* my transgressions,
73:11 They say, "How can God *k*?
90:11 Who *k-s* the power of your anger?
94:11 The LORD *k-s* the thoughts of man;
100:3 *K* that the LORD is God.
139:1 you have searched me and you *k* me
139:23 Search me, O God, and *k* my heart;
Isa 1:3 The ox *k-s* his master,
40:21 Do you not *k*? Have you not heard?
Jer 24:7 I will give them a heart to *k* me,
29:11 For I *k* the plans I have for you,"
Eze 6:10 And they will *k* that I am the LORD;
Mt 6:3 do not let your left hand *k* what
6:8 for your Father *k-s* what you need
9:4 *K-ing* their thoughts, Jesus said,
9:6 *k* that the Son of Man has authority
11:27 No-one *k-s* the Son except the
22:29 because you do not *k* the Scriptures
24:36 "No-one *k-s* about that day or hour
25:12 I tell you the truth, I don't *k* you
26:72 with an oath: "I don't *k* the man!
Lk 9:33 (He did not *k* what he was saying.
12:2 or hidden that will not be made *k-n*
18:20 You *k* the commandments:
23:34 they do not *k* what they are doing.
Jn 3:11 we speak of what we *k*,
6:64 Jesus had *k-n* from the beginning
7:29 but I *k* him because I am from him
8:32 Then you will *k* the truth,
10:14 I *k* my sheep and my sheep *k* me
14:4 You *k* the way to the place where
16:15 what is mine and make it *k-n* to you
17:3 eternal life: that they may *k* you,
21:17 Lord, you *k* all things; you *k*
21:24 We *k* that his testimony is true
Ro 8:26 We do not *k* what we ought to pray
8:28 we *k* that in all things God works
11:34 "Who has *k-n* the mind of the Lord?
1Co 13:9 For we *k* in part and we prophesy
14:16 he does not *k* what you are saying
2Co 6:9 *k-n*, yet regarded as unknown;
8:9 For you *k* the grace of our Lord
Gal 4:9 you *k* God—or rather are *k-n* by
Eph 1:17 so that you may *k* him better

3:19	and to *k* this love that surpasses
4:20	did not come to *k* Christ that way
Php 3:10	I want to *k* Christ and the power
Col 1:27	to make *k-n* among the Gentiles
2:2	that they may *k* the mystery of God,
2Ti 1:12	because I *k* whom I have believed,
3:15	you have *k-n* the holy Scriptures,
Tit 1:16	They claim to *k* God,
1Jn 2:4	The man who says, "I *k* him,"
2:5	This is how we *k* we are in him
3:24	how we *k* that he lives in us:
4:7	born of God and *k-s* God
5:13	*k* that you have eternal life
Rev 2:2	I *k* your deeds, your hard work

knowledge

Ge 2:9	the tree of the *k* of good and evil
Ps 139:6	Such *k* is too wonderful for me,
Lk 11:52	you have taken away the key to *k*.
1Co 8:1	*K* puffs up, but love builds up.
12:8	to another the message of *k*
13:8	where there is *k*, it will pass away
2Co 4:6	light of the *k* of the glory of God
Col 1:10	growing in the *k* of God
1Ti 2:4	and to come to a *k* of the truth
2Pe 3:18	grow in the grace and *k* of our Lord

Korah

1. Son of Esau; Edomite chief (Ge 36:5,14,18). **2.** Grandson of Kohath (1Ch 6:22); ancestor of group of musicians (Ps 42; 44–49; 84; 85; 87; 88) and temple gatekeepers (1Ch 9:19; 26:1,19); led rebellion against Moses; killed by God (Nu 16; 26:9–11; Jude 11). **3.** Son of Hebron (1Ch 2:43).

L

Laban

Brother of Rebekah (Ge 24:29); gave permission for sister to marry Isaac (Ge 24:50–51). Received Jacob (Ge 29:13–14); gave daughters, Leah and Rachel, in exchange for service (Ge 29:15–30). Deceived by Jacob (Ge 30:25–31:21); pursued and made covenant with him (Ge 31:22–55).

labour

Ex 1:11	to oppress them with forced *l*,
20:9	Six days you shall *l*
Ps 127:1	the house, its builders *l* in vain.
1Co 15:58	your *l* in the Lord is not in vain
Php 1:22	this will mean fruitful *l* for me.
1Th 1:3	your *l* prompted by love,
Rev 14:13	"they will rest from their *l*,

lack, -s, -ing

Pr 28:27	gives to the poor will *l* nothing,
Mt 13:58	because of their *l* of faith
Mk 10:21	"One thing you *l*," he said. "Go,
1Th 3:10	supply what is *l-ing* in your faith
Jas 1:5	If any of you *l-s* wisdom,

laid

Ge 22:9	son Isaac and *l* him on the altar
Nu 27:23	Then he *l* his hands on him
Isa 53:6	the LORD has *l* on him the iniquity
Mk 6:29	took his body and *l* it in a tomb
15:47	mother of Joses saw where he was *l*
16:6	See the place where they *l* him
Lk 12:19	good things *l* up for many years.
23:53	one in which no-one had yet been *l*
23:55	tomb and how his body was *l* in it
Ac 6:6	prayed and *l* their hands on them
1Ti 4:14	body of elders *l* their hands on you
1Jn 3:16	Jesus Christ *l* down his life for us

lake

Mt 4:18 They were casting a net into the *l*,
14:25 went out to them, walking on the *l*
16:5 When they went across the *l*,
Rev 19:20 into the fiery *l* of burning sulphur
20:14 The *l* of fire is the second death

lamb, -'s, -s

Ge 22:8 "God himself will provide the *l*
Ex 12:21 and slaughter the Passover *l*
2Ch 30:15 They slaughtered the Passover *l*
Isa 11:6 The wolf will live with the *l*,
53:7 was led like a *l* to the slaughter
Lk 22:7 the Passover *l* had to be sacrificed
Jn 1:29 *L* of God, who takes away the sin
21:15 Jesus said, "Feed my *l-s*.
Ac 8:32 as a *l* before the shearer is silent
1Co 5:7 our Passover *l*, has been sacrificed
1Pe 1:19 Christ, a *l* without blemish
Rev 5:6 Then I saw a *L*, looking
5:12 "Worthy is the *L*, who was slain,
7:17 the *L* at the centre of the throne
21:27 written in the *L-'s* book of life

lamp

1Sa 3:3 The *l* of God had not yet gone out,
Ps 18:28 You, O LORD, keep my *l* burning;
119:105 Your word is a *l* to my feet
Mt 5:15 light a *l* and put it under a bowl.
6:22 "The eye is the *l* of the body.
Rev 21:23 and the Lamb is its *l*.

lampstand, -s

Ex 25:31 "Make a *l* of pure gold
Heb 9:2 In its first room were the *l*,
Rev 2:1 walks among the seven golden *l-s*
2:5 and remove your *l* from its place

land, -s

Ge 1:10 God called the dry ground "*l*",
1:11 "Let the *l* produce vegetation:
1:24 Let the *l* produce living creatures
12:1 go to the *l* I will show you
15:18 "To your descendants I give this *l*,
17:8 The whole *l* of Canaan,
Ex 3:8 a *l* flowing with milk and honey
Lev 25:19 Then the *l* will yield its fruit,
25:24 provide for the redemption of the *l*
Nu 35:33 Do not pollute the *l* where you are.
Dt 1:8 See, I have given you this *l*.
8:7 God is bringing you into a good *l*—
11:9 you may live long in the *l*
26:1 When you have entered the *l*
29:27 LORD's anger burned against this *l*,
30:5 He will bring you to the *l*
34:1 the LORD showed him the whole *l*—
Jos 1:11 take possession of the *l*
2:2 come here tonight to spy out the *l*.
2:9 the LORD has given this *l* to you
2:24 given the whole *l* into our hands;
13:2 "This is the *l* that remains:
14:5 So the Israelites divided the *l*,
14:15 Then the *l* had rest from war
2Ch 7:14 and will heal their *l*
36:21 The *l* enjoyed its sabbath rests;
Ezr 9:11 'The *l* you are entering to possess
Ps 37:11 But the meek will inherit the *l*
41:2 he will bless him in the *l*
60:2 You have shaken the *l*
63:1 in a dry and weary *l*
65:9 You care for the *l* and water it;
67:6 Then the *l* will yield its harvest,
80:9 and it took root and filled the *l*
Eze 37:21 bring them back into their own *l*
Mt 4:16 the *l* of the shadow of death
23:15 You travel over *l* and sea
27:45 darkness came over all the *l*
Ac 4:34 those who owned *l-s* or houses

language

Ge 11:1 Now the whole world had one *l*
Ac 2:6 heard them speaking in his own *l*
Col 3:8 slander and filthy *l* from your lips
Rev 5:9 men for God from every tribe and *l*

Laodicea

Rev 3:14 "To the angel of the church in *L*

last[1]

2Sa 23:1 These are the *l* words of David:
Isa 2:2 In the *l* days the mountain
44:6 I am the first and I am the *l*;
Mt 19:30 But many who are first will be *l*,
Mk 15:37 Jesus breathed his *l*
Jn 6:40 I will raise him up at the *l* day.
1Co 15:26 *l* enemy to be destroyed is death
Rev 1:17 I am the First and the *L*

last[2]

Ps 45:6 Your throne, O God, will *l* for ever
Mk 4:17 they *l* only a short time.
Jn 15:16 and bear fruit—fruit that will *l*.
1Co 9:25 to get a crown that will not *l*;

laugh, -ed, -ter

Ge 18:12 So Sarah *l-ed* to herself
21:6 "God has brought me *l-ter*,
Lk 6:21 you who weep now, for you will *l*
6:25 Woe to you who *l* now, for you will
Jas 4:9 Change your *l-ter* to mourning

lavished

Eze 16:15 You *l* your favours on anyone
Eph 1:8 that he *l* on us with all wisdom
1Jn 3:1 the love the Father has *l* on us,

law, -s

Dt 1:5 Moses began to expound this *l*,
4:44 This is the *l* Moses set before
2Ki 22:8 "I have found the Book of the *L*
Ezr 7:6 a teacher well versed in the *L*
Ne 8:9 they listened to the words of the *L*
Ps 1:2 But his delight is in the *l*
19:7 The *l* of the LORD is perfect,
37:31 The *l* of his God is in his heart;
40:8 your *l* is within my heart.
119:18 may see wonderful things in your *l*
119:97 Oh, how I love your *l*!
Isa 2:3 The *l* will go out from Zion,
8:20 To the *l* and to the testimony!
Jer 31:33 "I will put my *l* in their minds
Da 6:8 the *l-s* of the Medes and Persians,
Mt 5:17 to abolish the *L* or the Prophets;
7:12 sums up the *L* and the Prophets
22:36 the greatest commandment in the *L*?
23:15 "Woe to you, teachers of the *l*
Lk 2:23 it is written in the *L* of the Lord,
Jn 1:17 For the *l* was given through Moses;
Ro 2:12 All who sin apart from the *l*
3:20 through the *l* we become conscious
3:28 by faith apart from observing the *l*
3:31 Not at all! Rather, we uphold the *l*
4:15 because *l* brings wrath.
5:20 *l* was added so that the trespass
6:15 not under *l* but under grace?
7:7 Is the *l* sin? Certainly not!
7:14 We know that the *l* is spiritual;
8:2 *l* of the Spirit of life set me free
8:3 For what the *l* was powerless to do
10:4 Christ is the end of the *l*
13:10 love is the fulfilment of the *l*
1Co 9:20 I became like one under the *l*
15:56 and the power of sin is the *l*
Gal 2:16 not justified by observing the *l*,
3:13 redeemed us from the curse of the *l*
3:24 the *l* was put in charge to lead us
4:4 born of a woman, born under *l*
5:14 *l* is summed up in a single command:
6:2 you will fulfil the *l* of Christ
1Ti 1:8 *l* is good if one uses it properly
Heb 7:19 (for the *l* made nothing perfect),

8:10 I will put my *l-s* in their minds
10:1 The *l* is only a shadow of the good
Jas 1:25 the perfect *l* that gives freedom,
1Jn 3:4 Everyone who sins breaks the *l*;

lawful
Mt 12:4 which was not *l* for them to do,
12:12 it is *l* to do good on the Sabbath.
14:4 "It is not *l* for you to have her.
19:3 "Is it *l* for a man to divorce

lawless, -ness
2Th 2:3 and the man of *l-ness* is revealed,
2:8 then the *l* one will be revealed,
Heb 10:17 and *l* acts I will remember no more.
2Pe 3:17 carried away by the error of *l* men
1Jn 3:4 in fact, sin is *l-ness*

lay, -ing
Ge 4:1 Adam *l* with his wife Eve,
Ru 3:14 So she *l* at his feet until morning,
1Sa 3:15 Samuel *l* down until morning
Ps 5:3 in the morning I *l* my requests
Isa 28:16 I *l* a stone in Zion, a tested stone
52:10 The LORD will *l* bare his holy arm
Mt 8:20 of Man has nowhere to *l* his head.
28:6 Come and see the place where he *l*.
Jn 10:15 and I *l* down my life for the sheep.
15:13 he *l* down his life for his friends.
Ro 9:33 "See, I *l* in Zion a stone
2Ti 1:6 through the *l-ing* on of my hands
1Pe 2:6 I *l* a stone in Zion, a chosen
Rev 4:10 *l* their crowns before the throne

Lazarus
1. Beggar in Jesus' parable (Lk 16:19–31). 2. Brother of Mary and Martha; raised to life by Jesus (Jn 11:1–12:11).

lazy
Pr 10:4 *L* hands make a man poor,
26:15 too *l* to bring it back to his mouth
Tit 1:12 liars, evil brutes, *l* gluttons.
Heb 6:12 We do not want you to become *l*,

lead, -s
Dt 3:28 for he will *l* this people across
1Sa 8:5 now appoint a king to *l* us,
2Ch 1:10 that I may *l* this people,
Ps 23:2 he *l-s* me beside quiet waters
27:11 O LORD; *l* me in a straight path
Eze 13:10 'Because they *l* my people astray,
Mt 6:13 And *l* us not into temptation,
7:14 narrow the road that *l-s* to life,
Jn 12:50 his command *l-s* to eternal life.
Ro 2:4 kindness *l-s* you towards repentance
2Co 7:10 repentance that *l-s* to salvation
Tit 1:1 the truth that *l-s* to godliness
1Jn 3:7 do not let anyone *l* you astray.

leader, -s
Ex 18:25 and made them *l-s* of the people,
1Sa 9:16 Anoint him *l* over my people Israel;
2Sa 7:11 I appointed *l-s* over my people
2Ch 13:12 God is with us; he is our *l*.
Heb 13:7 Remember your *l-s*, who spoke
13:17 Obey your *l-s* and submit

leadership
Nu 33:1 under the *l* of Moses and Aaron
Ac 1:20 'May another take his place of *l*.
Ro 12:8 if it is *l*, let him govern

Leah
Daughter of Laban; wife of Jacob (Ge 29:16–23); bore six sons and one daughter (Ge 29:31–35; 30:16–21; 34:1; 35:23).

leap, -s, -ing, -ed
2Sa 6:16 *l-ing* and dancing before the LORD,
Ps 28:7 My heart *l-s* for joy
Isa 35:6 Then will the lame *l* like a deer,
Lk 1:44 the baby in my womb *l-ed* for joy

6:23	Rejoice in that day and *l* for joy,

learn, -ing, -ed

Dt 14:23	that you may *l* to revere the LORD
Mt 11:29	Take my yoke upon you and *l* from me
Jn 7:15	"How did this man get such *l-ing*
Php 4:9	Whatever you have *l-ed* or received
2Ti 3:14	continue in what you have *l-ed*
Heb 5:8	he was a son, he *l-ed* obedience
5:11	because you are slow to *l*

least

Mt 5:19	one of the *l* of these commandments
11:11	who is *l* in the kingdom of heaven
25:40	for one of the *l* of these brothers
1Co 15:9	For I am the *l* of the apostles

led

Ge 24:27	the LORD has *l* me on the journey
1Ki 11:3	and his wives *l* him astray
2Ch 26:16	his pride *l* to his downfall.
Ps 68:18	you *l* captives in your train;
77:20	You *l* your people like a flock
Isa 53:7	*l* like a lamb to the slaughter,
Hos 11:4	*l* them with cords of human kindness
Mt 4:1	Then Jesus was *l* by the Spirit
2Co 7:9	your sorrow *l* you to repentance.
Gal 5:18	But if you are *l* by the Spirit,
Eph 4:8	he *l* captives in his train

left

Ge 7:23	Only Noah was *l*, and those with him
25:5	Abraham *l* everything he owned
39:12	But he *l* his cloak in her hand
Dt 16:3	because you *l* Egypt in haste—
Jos 11:15	he *l* nothing undone of all that
Ru 1:3	and she was *l* with her two sons
1Sa 18:12	LORD was with David but had *l* Saul
1Ki 19:10	I am the only one *l*, and now they
2Ch 32:31	God *l* him to test him and to know
Hag 2:3	'Who of you is *l* who saw this house
Mt 4:20	they *l* their nets and followed him
8:15	the fever *l* her, and she got up
Mk 1:42	Immediately the leprosy *l* him
10:28	We have *l* everything to follow you
Lk 5:11	*l* everything and followed him
17:34	one will be taken and the other *l*
Jn 6:12	Gather the pieces that are *l* over.
Ac 16:18	At that moment the spirit *l* her

legion

Mk 5:9	"My name is *L*,"
5:15	possessed by the *l* of demons,

lend, -s

Lev 25:37	must not *l* him money at interest
Dt 15:8	be open-handed and freely *l* him
Ps 37:26	are always generous and *l* freely;
Pr 19:17	kind to the poor *l-s* to the LORD,
Lk 6:35	*l* to them without expecting to get

length

Ps 90:10	The *l* of our days is seventy years—
Pr 10:27	The fear of the LORD adds *l* to life
Rev 21:16	found it to be 12,000 stadia in *l*,

leopard

Isa 11:6	the *l* will lie down with the goat,
Jer 13:23	his skin or the *l* its spots?

leprosy, -ous

Nu 12:10	stood Miriam—*l-ous*, like snow.
2Ki 5:1	a valiant soldier, but he had *l*
5:27	he was *l-ous*, as white as snow
2Ch 26:21	Uzziah had *l* until the day he died.
Mt 8:2	A man with *l* came and knelt

Lk 17:12 ten men who had *l* met him.

letter, -s

Jer 29:1 *l* that the prophet Jeremiah sent
Mt 5:18 not the smallest *l*, not the least
2Co 3:3 you are a *l* from Christ,
3:6 *l* kills, but the Spirit gives life.
Gal 6:11 See what large *l-s* I use
2Pe 3:16 the same way in all his *l-s*,

level

Ps 26:12 My feet stand on *l* ground;
143:10 good Spirit lead me on *l* ground
Pr 4:26 Make *l* paths for your feet
Heb 12:13 "Make *l* paths for your feet,"

Levi

1. Son of Jacob by Leah (Ge 29:34; 35:23); with Simeon killed Shechemites to avenge rape of sister Dinah (Ge 34); blessed by Jacob (Ge 49:5–7). 2. Tribe descended from Levi. Blessed by Moses (Dt 33:8–11). Numbered separately (Nu 1:47–49; 3:14–39; 26:57–62); responsible for tabernacle (Nu 1:50–53; 3:14–37; 4; 8; 18:2–4); dedicated to God in place of firstborn (Nu 3:11–13,40–41). Given towns (Nu 35; Jos 21) but not land (Nu 18:20–24; 26:62; Dt 10:9; Jos 13:14); allocated land in new division (Eze 48:13–14). 3. See *Matthew.*

Leviathan

Job 41:1 "Can you pull in the *l* with a
Ps 104:26 the *l*, which you formed to frolic
Isa 27:1 *L* the coiling serpent;

Levite, -s

Ex 4:14 your brother, Aaron the *L*?
Nu 3:9 Give the *L-s* to Aaron and his sons;
8:14 you are to set the *L-s* apart
Dt 10:9 *L-s* have no share or inheritance
12:19 Be careful not to neglect the *L-s*
1Ch 15:2 the *L-s* may carry the ark of God,
Mal 3:3 he will purify the *L-s* and refine
Lk 10:32 a *L*, when he came to the place
Ac 4:36 Joseph, a *L* from Cyprus,

liar, -s

Ps 63:11 the mouths of *l-s* will be silenced
Pr 19:22 better to be poor than a *l*
Jn 8:55 I would be a *l* like you,
Ro 3:4 Let God be true, and every man a *l*.
Tit 1:12 Cretans are always *l-s*, evil brutes
1Jn 4:20 yet hates his brother, he is a *l*.

lie[1]

Lev 18:22 "'Do not *l* with a man
Dt 6:7 when you *l* down and when you get up
1Sa 3:5 I did not call; go back and *l* down
Ps 4:8 I will *l* down and sleep in peace,
23:2 makes me *l* down in green pastures,

lie[2], -s, -d

Nu 23:19 God is not a man, that he should *l*,
Ps 88:7 Your wrath *l-s* heavily upon me;
Jer 5:31 The prophets prophesy *l-s*,
23:14 They commit adultery and live a *l*.
Ac 5:3 you have *l-d* to the Holy Spirit
5:4 You have not *l-d* to men but to God.
Ro 1:25 exchanged the truth of God for a *l*,
Heb 6:18 it is impossible for God to *l*,
1Jn 1:6 yet walk in the darkness, we *l*
Rev 14:5 No *l* was found in their mouths;

life

Ge 2:9 of the garden were the tree of *l*
Ex 21:23 you are to take *l* for *l*
Dt 30:15 I set before you today *l* and
30:15 See, I set before you today *l*
Ps 16:11 made known to me the path of *l*;
49:15 God will redeem my *l* from the grave
91:16 With long *l* will I satisfy him
Pr 19:23 The fear of the LORD leads to *l*:
Isa 53:12 he poured out his *l* unto death,
Da 12:2 will awake: some to everlasting *l*,

lift, -ed

light[1]

Ac 9:3 suddenly a *l* from heaven flashed
13:47 have made you a *l* for the Gentiles
2Co 4:6 *l* of the knowledge of the glory
6:14 what fellowship can *l* have with
11:14 masquerades as an angel of *l*
Eph 5:8 Live as children of *l*
1Ti 6:16 and who lives in unapproachable *l*,
1Pe 2:9 of darkness into his wonderful *l*
1Jn 1:5 God is *l*;
1:7 But if we walk in the *l*, as he is
Rev 22:5 for the Lord God will give them *l*.

light²

Mt 11:30 my yoke is easy and my burden is *l*.
2Co 4:17 our *l* and momentary troubles

lightning

Da 10:6 face like *l*, his eyes like flaming
Mt 24:27 For as *l* that comes from the east
28:3 His appearance was like *l*,
Lk 10:18 I saw Satan fall like *l* from heaven
Rev 4:5 From the throne came flashes of *l*,

likeness

Ge 1:26 make man in our image, in our *l*,
Ro 8:3 his own Son in the *l* of sinful man
2Co 3:18 are being transformed into his *l*
Php 2:7 of a servant, being made in human *l*

lilies

Mt 6:28 See how the *l* of the field grow.

lion, -'s, -s, -s'

Jdg 14:6 so that he tore the *l* apart
Ps 22:21 Rescue me from the mouth of the *l-s*
Pr 28:1 the righteous are as bold as a *l*
Isa 11:7 the *l* will eat straw like the ox
Da 6:7 shall be thrown into the *l-s'* den
7:4 "The first was like a *l*,
Am 3:8 The *l* has roared—who will not fear
2Ti 4:17 I was delivered from the *l-'s* mouth
Heb 11:33 who shut the mouths of *l-s*
1Pe 5:8 prowls around like a roaring *l*
Rev 5:5 the *L* of the tribe of Judah,

lips

Ps 8:2 From the *l* of children and infants
51:15 O Lord, open my *l*, and my mouth
141:3 keep watch over the door of my *l*
Pr 13:3 He who guards his *l* guards his life
Isa 6:5 For I am a man of unclean *l*,
28:11 with foreign *l* and strange tongues
Mt 15:8 These people honour me with their *l*
21:16 'From the *l* of children and infants
1Co 14:21 and through the *l* of foreigners
Col 3:8 filthy language from your *l*
Heb 13:15 fruit of *l* that confess his name

listen, -s, -ing, -ed

Ge 3:17 "Because you *l-ed* to your wife
1Sa 3:10 Speak, for your servant is *l-ing*.
1Ki 4:34 came to *l* to Solomon's wisdom,
2Ki 21:9 But the people did not *l*.
Ne 8:9 they *l-ed* to the words of the Law
Ps 81:11 "But my people would not *l* to me;
86:6 O LORD; *l* to my cry for mercy
Pr 12:15 but a wise man *l-s* to advice
13:1 but a mocker does not *l* to rebuke
Mt 18:17 If he refuses to *l* to them,
Mk 9:7 my Son, whom I love. *L* to him!
Lk 8:18 consider carefully how you *l*.
10:16 "He who *l-s* to you *l-s* to me;
10:39 who sat at the Lord's feet *l-ing*
Jn 6:45 Everyone who *l-s* to the Father
10:27 My sheep *l* to my voice;
Jas 1:19 Everyone should be quick to *l*,

1:22	Do not merely *l* to the word,

live, -s, -ing

Ge 2:7	and the man became a *l-ing* being
3:22	and *l* for ever.
Ex 20:12	so that you may *l* long in the land
33:20	for no-one may see me and *l*.
Nu 21:8	bitten can look at it and *l*.
Dt 8:3	man does not *l* on bread alone
2Sa 22:47	The LORD *l-s*! Praise be to my Rock!
2Ch 23:11	and shouted, "Long *l* the king!
Job 14:14	If a man dies, will he *l* again?
19:25	I know that my Redeemer *l-s*,
28:13	in the land of the *l-ing*
Ps 15:1	Who may *l* on your holy hill?
18:46	The LORD *l-s*! Praise be
118:17	I will not die but *l*,
133:1	when brothers *l* together in unity
Pr 21:9	Better to *l* on a corner of the roof
Ecc 9:4	a *l* dog is better off than a dead
9:5	the *l-ing* know that they will die,
Isa 6:5	I *l* among a people of unclean lips,
11:6	The wolf will *l* with the lamb,
26:19	But your dead will *l*;
55:3	hear me, that your soul may *l*.
Jer 10:10	the *l-ing* God, the eternal King.
Eze 18:4	For every *l-ing* soul belongs to me,
20:11	man who obeys them will *l* by them
37:3	"Son of man, can these bones *l*?"
Am 5:6	Seek the LORD and *l*,
Hab 2:4	the righteous will *l* by his faith
Zec 2:11	I will *l* among you
Mt 4:4	'Man does not *l* on bread alone,
4:16	the people *l-ing* in darkness
16:16	the Son of the *l-ing* God.
22:32	God of the dead but of the *l-ing*.
Lk 10:28	"Do this and you will *l*.
Jn 4:50	"You may go. Your son will *l*."
5:25	and those who hear will *l*
6:51	I am the *l-ing* bread
6:57	and I *l* because of the Father,
7:38	streams of *l-ing* water will flow
14:17	for he *l-s* with you
Ac 2:26	my body also will *l* in hope
17:28	'For in him we *l* and move
Ro 1:17	"The righteous will *l* by faith.
6:8	we believe that we will also *l*
6:10	the life he *l-s*, he *l-s* to God
8:11	his Spirit, who *l-s* in you
12:1	your bodies as *l-ing* sacrifices,
12:16	*L* in harmony with one another.
14:8	If we *l*, we *l* to the Lord;
14:9	Lord of both the dead and the *l-ing*
1Co 3:16	and that God's Spirit *l-s* in you
7:15	God has called us to *l* in peace
2Co 5:7	We *l* by faith, not by sight
6:16	God has said: "I will *l* with them
Gal 2:20	I no longer *l*, but Christ *l-s* in me
3:11	"The righteous will *l* by faith.
5:25	Since we *l* by the Spirit,
Eph 4:17	must no longer *l* as the Gentiles do
5:15	Be very careful, then, how you *l*—
Php 1:21	For to me, to *l* is Christ
Col 1:10	you may *l* a life worthy of the Lord
1Th 1:9	to serve the *l-ing* and true God
4:1	how to *l* in order to please God,
5:13	*L* in peace with each other
1Ti 2:2	we may *l* peaceful and quiet *l-s*
6:16	who *l-s* in unapproachable light,
2Ti 1:14	the Holy Spirit who *l-s* in us
2:11	we will also *l* with him
3:12	to *l* a godly life in Christ Jesus
Heb 4:12	word of God is *l-ing* and active.
7:24	because Jesus *l-s* for ever,
7:25	he always *l-s* to intercede for them
9:14	that we may serve the *l-ing* God
10:31	into the hands of the *l-ing* God
10:38	my righteous one will *l* by faith.
12:14	Make every effort to *l* in peace
1Pe 1:17	live your *l-s* as strangers here
2:4	come to him, the *l-ing* Stone—
2:12	*L* such good *l-s* among the pagans
2:24	die to sins and *l* for righteousness

4:5 to judge the *l-ing* and the dead
2Pe 3:11 ought to *l* holy and godly *l-s*
1Jn 2:6 Whoever claims to *l* in him
2:10 Whoever loves his brother *l-s*
2:14 the word of God *l-s* in you,
3:16 lay down our *l-s* for our brothers
3:24 who obey his commands *l* in him,
4:13 We know that we *l* in him
4:16 Whoever *l-s* in love *l-s* in God,
Rev 1:18 I am the *L-ing* One;
10:6 he swore by him who *l-s* for ever
12:11 they did not love their *l-s* so much
21:3 and he will *l* with them.

load
Lk 11:46 you *l* people down with burdens
Gal 6:5 for each one should carry his own *l*

loaf, -ves
Mt 14:17 five *l-ves* of bread and two fish,"
16:10 seven *l-ves* for the four thousand,
Lk 11:5 'Friend, lend me three *l-ves*
1Co 10:17 Because there is one *l*,

locusts
Ex 10:4 I will bring *l* into your country
2Ch 7:13 or command *l* to devour the land
Joel 2:25 for the years the *l* have eaten—
Mt 3:4 His food was *l* and wild honey

lonely
Ps 25:16 be gracious to me, for I am *l*
68:6 God sets the *l* in families,
Mk 1:45 but stayed outside in *l* places.
Lk 5:16 Jesus often withdrew to *l* places

long[1]
Ge 8:22 "As *l* as the earth endures,
Ex 17:11 As *l* as Moses held up his hands,
20:12 so that you may live *l* in the land
1Ki 3:14 I will give you a *l* life.
1Ch 29:28 enjoyed *l* life, wealth and honour.
Ps 6:3 How *l*, O LORD, how *l*
44:22 your sake we face death all day *l*;
63:4 I will praise you as *l* as I live,
91:16 With *l* life will I satisfy him
Isa 65:2 All day *l* I have held out my hands
Mt 5:21 it was said to the people *l* ago,
24:48 'My master is staying away a *l* time
Lk 15:20 while he was still a *l* way off
Jn 9:4 As *l* as it is day,
Ro 8:36 your sake we face death all day *l*;
10:21 All day *l* I have held out my hands
1Co 11:14 if a man has *l* hair,
Eph 3:18 how wide and *l* and high and deep
6:3 and that you may enjoy *l* life
Heb 3:13 as *l* as it is called Today,

long[2], -s, -ing, -ed
Ps 61:4 I *l* to dwell in your tent for ever
119:20 consumed with *l-ing* for your laws
119:174 I *l* for your salvation, O LORD,
Pr 13:12 a *l-ing* fulfilled is a tree of life
Isa 30:18 the LORD *l-s* to be gracious to you;
Mt 13:17 righteous men *l-ed* to see what you
23:37 I have *l-ed* to gather your children
Ro 15:23 *l-ing* for many years to see you
2Co 5:2 we groan, *l-ing* to be clothed
Php 1:8 God can testify how I *l* for all
4:1 brothers, you whom I love and *l* for
2Ti 4:8 all who have *l-ed* for his appearing
Heb 11:16 were *l-ing* for a better country—
1Pe 1:12 angels *l* to look into these things

look, -s, -ing, -ed
Ge 4:4 The LORD *l-ed* with favour on Abel
19:26 But Lot's wife *l-ed* back,
Ex 2:25 So God *l-ed* on the Israelites
3:6 because he was afraid to *l* at God
Dt 4:29 you will find him if you *l* for him
1Sa 16:7 but the LORD *l-s* at the heart."

Job 31:1	not to *l* lustfully at a girl.
Ps 34:5	Those who *l* to him are radiant;
105:4	*L* to the LORD and his strength;
145:15	The eyes of all *l* to you,
Pr 15:30	cheerful *l* brings joy to the heart,
Isa 42:18	"Hear, you deaf; *l*, you blind,
51:1	*L* to the rock from which you were
Jer 6:16	"Stand at the crossroads and *l*;
Da 8:15	stood one who *l-ed* like a man
Hab 1:13	Your eyes are too pure to *l* on evil
Zec 12:10	*l* on me, the one they have pierced,
Mt 5:28	anyone who *l-s* at a woman lustfully
6:16	"When you fast, do not *l* sombre
18:10	"See that you do not *l* down on one
18:12	to *l* for the one that wandered off
25:36	I was sick and you *l-ed* after me,
28:5	I know that you are *l-ing* for Jesus
Mk 1:37	"Everyone is *l-ing* for you!
7:34	He *l-ed* up to heaven
10:21	Jesus *l-ed* at him and loved him.
13:21	'*L*, here is the Christ!' or, '*L*,
16:6	are *l-ing* for Jesus the Nazarene
Lk 2:45	back to Jerusalem to *l* for him
13:6	and he went to *l* for fruit on it,
18:13	He would not even *l* up to heaven,
22:61	turned and *l-ed* straight at Peter.
24:5	you *l* for the living among the dead
24:39	*L* at my hands and my feet.
Jn 1:36	he said, "*L*, the Lamb of God!
6:40	everyone who *l-s* to the Son
7:34	You will *l* for me, but you will not
12:45	When he *l-s* at me, he sees the one
19:37	*l* on the one they have pierced.
20:15	Who is it you are *l-ing* for?"
Ac 1:11	you stand here *l-ing* into the sky?
Ro 14:10	why do you *l* down on your brother?
Heb 13:14	*l-ing* for the city that is to come
Jas 1:23	man who *l-s* at his face in a mirror
1Jn 1:1	which we have *l-ed* at and our hands
Rev 5:6	Then I saw a Lamb, *l-ing* as if it

LORD, -'s (Yahweh)

Ge 2:4	When the *L* God made the earth
2:7	the *L* God formed the man
2:22	Then the *L* God made a woman
3:1	the wild animals the *L* God had made
4:26	began to call on the name of the *L*
10:9	He was a mighty hunter before the *L*
15:6	Abram believed the *L*,
18:14	Is anything too hard for the *L*?
Ex 3:2	the angel of the *L* appeared to him
3:15	'The *L*, the God of your fathers-
6:3	but by my name the *L* I did not
9:12	But the *L* hardened Pharaoh's heart
9:29	know that the earth is the *L-'s*
10:2	that you may know that I am the *L*.
15:2	The *L* is my strength and my song;
15:3	the *L* is his name
20:2	"I am the *L* your God, who brought
20:5	I, the *L* your God, am a jealous God
20:7	shall not misuse the name of the *L*
29:46	will know that I am the *L* their God
Lev 19:2	I, the *L* your God, am holy
25:38	I am the *L* your God, who brought
Nu 6:24	"The *L* bless you and keep you
14:18	'The *L* is slow to anger,
15:41	I am the *L* your God, who brought
22:22	angel of the *L* stood in the road
Dt 1:32	you did not trust in the *L* your God
1:36	he followed the *L* wholeheartedly.
4:24	*L* your God is a consuming fire,
4:31	the *L* your God is a merciful God;

5:2 The *L* our God made a covenant
6:4 The *L* our God, the *L* is one
6:5 Love the *L* your God
10:20 Fear the *L* your God and serve him.
11:1 Love the *L* your God
28:1 If you fully obey the *L* your God
31:6 for the *L* your God goes with you;
31:8 The *L* himself goes before you
Jos 1:9 the *L* your God will be with you
23:10 the *L* your God fights for you,
Jdg 6:10 I said to you, 'I am the *L* your God
7:18 'For the *L* and for Gideon.'
1Sa 1:28 So now I give him to the *L*.
7:12 "Thus far has the *L* helped us.
2Sa 22:7 In my distress I called to the *L*;
22:32 For who is God besides the *L*?
1Ki 5:5 a temple for the Name of the *L*
18:21 If the *L* is God, follow him;
18:24 I will call on the name of the *L*.
1Ch 16:8 thanks to the *L*, call on his name;
16:29 ascribe to the *L* the glory
17:20 "There is no-one like you, O *L*,
17:26 O *L*, you are God!
Ezr 3:11 they sang to the *L*: "He is good;
Job 1:8 Then the *L* said to Satan,
1:21 *L* gave and the *L* has taken away;
Ps 1:2 his delight is in the law of the *L*,
16:8 I have set the *L* always before me.
18:2 The *L* is my rock, my fortress
19:7 The law of the *L* is perfect,
19:14 O *L*, my Rock and my Redeemer
21:13 Be exalted, O *L*, in your strength;
23:1 The *L* is my shepherd,
23:6 dwell in the house of the *L* for
24:1 The earth is the *L-'s*,
25:1 To you, O *L*, I lift up my soul
27:8 Your face, *L*, I will seek
31:23 Love the *L*, all his saints!
34:3 Glorify the *L* with me:
46:7 The *L* Almighty is with us;
92:1 It is good to praise the *L*
95:3 For the *L* is the great God,
96:1 Sing to the *L* a new song;
96:7 Ascribe to the *L*,
96:9 Worship the *L* in the splendour
97:1 The *L* reigns, let the earth be glad
98:1 Sing to the *L* a new song,
99:1 *L* reigns, let the nations tremble;
100:2 Worship the *L* with gladness;
103:1 Praise the *L*, O my soul;
110:1 The *L* says to my Lord:
111:10 The fear of the *L* is the beginning
115:1 Not to us, O *L*, not to us
118:14 The *L* is my strength and my song;
118:24 This is the day the *L* has made;
118:26 he who comes in the name of the *L*.
121:2 My help comes from the *L*,
139:1 O *L*, you have searched me
Pr 1:7 The fear of the *L* is the beginning
6:16 six things the *L* hates,
8:13 To fear the *L* is to hate evil;
11:1 The *L* abhors dishonest scales,
15:3 The eyes of the *L* are everywhere,
16:9 the *L* determines his steps
16:20 blessed is he who trusts in the *L*
18:10 The name of the *L* is a strong tower
Isa 6:3 Holy, holy, holy is the *L* Almighty
11:2 Spirit of the *L* will rest on him-
25:8 The Sovereign *L* will wipe away
40:3 prepare the way for the *L*;
43:3 For I am the *L*, your God,
45:5 I am the *L*, and there is no other;
50:5 The Sovereign *L* has opened my ears,
51:11 The ransomed of the *L* will return.
51:15 For I am the *L* your God,
55:6 Seek the *L* while he may be found;
59:1 the arm of the *L* is not too short
59:19 men will fear the name of the *L*,
60:1 the glory of the *L* rises upon you

Jer 9:24 I am the *L*, who exercises kindness,
17:10 "I the *L* search the heart
17:13 O *L*, the hope of Israel,
32:27 "I am the *L*, the God of all mankind
La 3:25 The *L* is good to those whose hope
Eze 7:27 Then they will know that I am the *L*
23:49 will know that I am the Sovereign *L*
Hos 6:1 "Come, let us return to the *L*.
10:12 for it is time to seek the *L*,
Joel 1:15 the day of the *L* is near;
Am 1:2 "The *L* roars from Zion
5:8 the *L* is his name
5:18 you who long for the day of the *L*!
Jnh 1:9 "I am a Hebrew and I worship the *L*
Mic 6:8 And what does the *L* require of you?
Na 1:3 The *L* is slow to anger and great
Hab 1:12 O *L*, are you not from everlasting?
Zec 14:20 HOLY TO THE *L* will be inscribed
Mal 1:2 "I have loved you," says the *L*.
3:6 "I the *L* do not change.

lord, -'s, -s

Ge 18:31 so bold as to speak to the *L*,
Ex 4:13 "O *L*, please send someone else
Dt 10:17 God of gods and *L* of *l-s*,
Jos 3:13 the LORD—the *L* of all the earth
Ne 4:14 Remember the *L*, who is great
Ps 8:1 O LORD, our *L*, how majestic is
16:2 I said to the LORD, "You are my *L*;
90:1 *L*, you have been our dwelling-place
110:1 The LORD says to my *L*:
Isa 6:1 I saw the *L* seated on a throne,
7:14 the *L* himself will give you a sign:
Da 2:47 God of gods and the *L* of kings
9:4 "O *L*, the great and awesome God,
Mic 4:13 the *L* of all the earth
Zec 4:14 serve the *L* of all the earth.
Mt 3:3 'Prepare the way for the *L*,
4:7 not put the *L* your God to the test.
7:21 everyone who says to me, '*L*, *L*,
12:8 the Son of Man is *L* of the Sabbath.
22:37 'Love the *L* your God with all your
22:44 " 'The *L* said to my *L*:
Lk 1:28 The *L* is with you.
4:12 not put the *L* your God to the test.
6:46 "Why do you call me, '*L*, *L*,'
10:39 Mary, who sat at the *L-'s* feet
19:34 They replied, "The *L* needs it."
24:34 "It is true! The *L* has risen and
Ac 2:21 calls on the name of the *L* will be
2:25 " 'I saw the *L* always before me.
2:34 " 'The *L* said to my *L*:
9:5 "Who are you, *L*?" Saul asked.
9:42 and many people believed in the *L*
16:31 "Believe in the *L* Jesus,
Ro 10:9 with your mouth, "Jesus is *L*,"
11:34 "Who has known the mind of the *L*?
1Co 1:31 "Let him who boasts boast in the *L*
4:5 wait till the *L* comes.
8:5 many "gods" and many "*l-s*"
8:6 there is but one *L*, Jesus Christ,
11:20 it is not the *L-'s* Supper you eat
11:23 The *L* Jesus, on the night he was
11:26 you proclaim the *L-'s* death
12:3 "Jesus is *L*,"
15:57 victory through our *L* Jesus Christ
16:22 If anyone does not love the *L*—
2Co 1:14 in the day of the *L* Jesus
3:17 Now the *L* is the Spirit,
5:6 in the body we are away from the *L*
12:1 visions and revelations from the *L*
Eph 4:5 one *L*, one faith, one baptism
5:10 find out what pleases the *L*
6:10 Finally, be strong in the *L*
Php 2:11 confess that Jesus Christ is *L*,
4:1 how you should stand firm in the *L*,
4:4 Rejoice in the *L* always.
Col 1:10 live a life worthy of the *L*
3:17 all in the name of the *L* Jesus
3:24 It is the *L* Christ you are serving.

4:17	work you have received in the *L*.
1Th 3:12	May the *L* make your love increase
4:16	For the *L* himself will come down
5:2	day of the *L* will come like a thief
5:28	The grace of our *L* Jesus Christ
2Th 2:1	the coming of our *L* Jesus Christ
3:3	But the *L* is faithful,
1Ti 6:15	King of kings and *L* of *l-s*
2Ti 2:19	"The *L* knows those who are his,
4:22	The *L* be with your spirit.
Heb 12:14	holiness no-one will see the *L*.
13:6	"The *L* is my helper;
Jas 4:10	Humble yourselves before the *L*,
1Pe 1:25	the word of the *L* stands for ever.
3:15	your hearts set apart Christ as *L*.
2Pe 1:11	the eternal kingdom of our *L*
1:16	coming of our *L* Jesus Christ,
3:9	The *L* is not slow in keeping his
Jude :14	the *L* is coming with thousands
Rev 1:10	On the *L-'s* Day I was in the Spirit
4:8	holy, holy is the *L* God Almighty,
19:16	KING OF KINGS AND *L* OF *L-S*.
22:20	Come, *L* Jesus

lose, -s

Mt 5:13	But if the salt *l-s* its saltiness,
10:39	Whoever finds his life will *l* it,
2Co 4:16	Therefore we do not *l* heart.
Heb 12:5	do not *l* heart when he rebukes you

loss

Jn 11:19	to comfort them in the *l*
1Co 3:15	it is burned up, he will suffer *l*;
Php 3:8	I consider everything a *l* compared
Heb 6:6	to their *l* they are crucifying

lost

Ps 119:176	I have strayed like a *l* sheep.
Mt 10:6	Go rather to the *l* sheep of Israel
Lk 15:6	I have found my *l* sheep.
15:24	he was *l* and is found.'
19:10	came to seek and to save what was *l*
Jn 18:9	I have not *l* one of those you gave

Lot

Nephew of Abraham (Ge 11:27); accompanied him from Haran (Ge 12:4–5; 13:1). Settled in Sodom (Ge 13:5–13); rescued by Abraham (Ge 14), and by two angels (Ge 19; 2Pe 2:7–8). Wife became pillar of salt (Ge 19:26). Fathered Ammon and Moab by his two daughters (Ge 19:30–38).

lot, -s

Nu 26:55	the land is distributed by *l*.
1Ch 25:8	cast *l-s* for their duties
Est 3:7	they cast the pur (that is, the *l*)
Ps 22:18	and cast *l-s* for my clothing
Mt 27:35	up his clothes by casting *l-s*
Jn 19:24	and cast *l-s* for my clothing."
Ac 1:26	they cast *l-s*, and the *l* fell

love, -s, -ing, -d

Ge 22:2	your only son, Isaac, whom you *l*,
Lev 19:18	but *l* your neighbour as yourself.
Dt 6:5	*L* the LORD your God with all your
7:8	it was because the LORD *l-d* you
30:16	I command you today to *l* the LORD
1Ch 16:34	his *l* endures for ever
Ne 9:17	slow to anger and abounding in *l*.
Ps 13:5	But I trust in your unfailing *l*;
26:3	for your *l* is ever before me,
31:23	*L* the LORD, all his saints!
57:10	For great is your *l*,
63:3	Because your *l* is better than life,
92:2	to proclaim your *l* in the morning
106:1	he is good; his *l* endures for ever
116:1	I *l* the LORD, for he heard my voice
136:1	*His* l *endures for ever.*
145:8	slow to anger and rich in *l*
Pr 10:12	*l* covers over all wrongs

SS 2:4 and his banner over me is *l*
8:7 Many waters cannot quench *l*;
Isa 5:1 I will sing for the one I *l* a song
Jer 31:3 *l-d* you with an everlasting *l*;
Hos 6:4 Your *l* is like the morning mist,
11:1 When Israel was a child, I *l-d* him
Joel 2:13 slow to anger and abounding in *l*,
Mic 6:8 To act justly and to *l* mercy
Mal 1:2 "I have *l-d* you," says the LORD.
Mt 3:17 "This is my Son, whom I *l*;
5:44 But I tell you: *L* your enemies
5:46 If you *l* those who love you,
17:5 "This is my Son, whom I *l*;
22:37 *L* the Lord your God with all your
22:39 '*L* your neighbour as yourself.
Lk 10:27 "'*L* the Lord your God
Jn 3:16 "For God so *l-d* the world
11:36 "See how he *l-d* him!
13:23 the disciple whom Jesus *l-d*,
13:34 command I give you: *L* one another.
13:35 my disciples, if you *l* one another.
14:15 "If you *l* me, you will obey
14:21 He who *l-s* me will be *l-d*
15:9 "As the Father has *l-d* me,
15:12 *L* each other as I have *l-d* you.
15:13 Greater *l* has no-one than this,
21:17 "Simon son of John, do you *l* me?"
Ro 5:5 because God has poured out his *l*
5:8 God demonstrates his own *l* for us
8:28 for the good of those who *l* him,
8:37 conquerors through him who *l-d* us.
8:39 to separate us from the *l* of God
12:9 *L* must be sincere.
13:9 "*L* your neighbour as yourself.
1Co 2:9 God has prepared for those who *l*
8:3 the man who *l-s* God is known by God
13:4 *L* is patient, *l* is kind.
13:13 But the greatest of these is *l*.
16:14 Do everything in *l*
2Co 5:14 For Christ's *l* compels us,
9:7 for God *l-s* a cheerful giver
Gal 2:20 faith in the Son of God, who *l-d* me
5:6 faith expressing itself through *l*
5:22 the fruit of the Spirit is *l*,
Eph 1:4 In *l* he predestined us
2:4 because of his great *l* for us, God
3:18 high and deep is the *l* of Christ,
4:15 speaking the truth in *l*,
5:25 Husbands, *l* your wives,
5:25 just as Christ *l-d* the church
Php 1:9 that your *l* may abound more
Col 1:8 your *l* in the Spirit
3:14 And over all these virtues put on *l*
1Ti 6:10 For the *l* of money is a root of
2Ti 4:10 because he *l-d* this world, has
Heb 13:1 Keep on *l-ing* each other
Jas 2:8 "*L* your neighbour as yourself,"
1Pe 1:8 you have not seen him, you *l* him;
2:17 *L* the brotherhood of believers,
4:8 Above all, *l* each other deeply,
4:8 *l* covers over a multitude of sins.
2Pe 1:17 "This is my Son, whom I *l*;
1Jn 3:1 How great is the *l* the Father
3:16 This is how we know what *l* is:
4:8 God is *l*.
4:10 This is *l*: not that we *l-d* God,
4:19 We *l* because he first *l-d* us.
5:3 This is *l* for God: to obey
Jude :21 Keep yourselves in God's *l*
Rev 2:4 You have forsaken your first *l*
3:19 whom I *l* I rebuke and discipline.

lovely

Ge 29:17 Rachel was *l* in form, and beautiful
Est 2:7 Esther, was *l* in form and features,
Ps 84:1 How *l* is your dwelling-place,
SS 1:5 Dark am I, yet *l*,
2:14 voice is sweet, and your face is *l*
Php 4:8 whatever is pure, whatever is *l*,

lover, -s

SS 2:16 My *l* is mine and I am his;
1Ti 3:3 not quarrelsome, not a *l* of money
2Ti 3:4 *l-s* of pleasure rather than *l-s*

lower
Ps 8:5 You made him a little *l* than
Eph 4:9 descended to the *l*, earthly regions
Heb 2:7 made him a little *l* than the angels

lowly
Ps 138:6 he looks upon the *l*,
Pr 16:19 Better to be *l* in spirit
1Co 1:28 He chose the *l* things of this world
Php 3:21 will transform our *l* bodies

loyal
1Ch 29:18 and keep their hearts *l* to you
Ps 78:37 their hearts were not *l* to him,
Php 4:3 Yes, and I ask you, *l* yokefellow,

Luke
Doctor; co-worker and close companion of Paul (Col 4:14; 2Ti 4:11; Phm 24). Writer of third Gospel and Acts.

lukewarm
Rev 3:16 you are *l*—neither hot nor cold-

lust, -s
Nu 15:39 after the *l-s* of your own hearts
Pr 6:25 Do not *l* in your heart
Ro 1:27 inflamed with *l* for one another.
Col 3:5 impurity, *l*, evil desires and greed
1Pe 4:3 *l*, drunkenness, orgies, carousing
1Jn 2:16 the *l* of his eyes and the boasting

Lydia
God-fearing woman living in Philippi; accepted Paul's message; baptised; offered hospitality (Ac 16:14–15,40).

lying
Ps 120:2 Save me, O LORD, from *l* lips
Pr 12:22 The LORD detests *l* lips,
26:28 A *l* tongue hates those it hurts,

M

Macedonia
Ac 16:9 Paul had a vision of a man of *M*

made
Ge 1:7 So God *m* the expanse
1:16 God *m* two great lights-
1:31 God saw all that he had *m*,
2:3 the seventh day and *m* it holy,
2:22 Then the LORD God *m* a woman
3:1 animals the LORD God had *m*.
6:6 grieved that he had *m* man
9:6 the image of God has God *m* man
15:18 the LORD *m* a covenant
Ex 20:11 six days the LORD *m* the heavens
24:8 that the LORD has *m* with you
32:4 *m* it into an idol cast
Lev 16:34 Atonement is to be *m* once a year
Dt 32:6 who *m* you and formed you
2Ki 19:15 You have *m* heaven and earth
2Ch 2:12 God of Israel, who *m* heaven
Job 31:1 "I *m* a covenant with my eyes
Ps 8:5 You *m* him a little lower
73:28 I have *m* the Sovereign LORD my
95:5 The sea is his, for he *m* it,
98:2 LORD has *m* his salvation known
100:3 the LORD is God. It is he who *m* us,
118:24 This is the day that the LORD has *m*
139:14 I am fearfully and wonderfully *m*;
145:10 All you have *m* will praise you,
Ecc 3:11 He has *m* everything beautiful
Isa 43:7 whom I formed and *m*.
Jer 11:10 broken the covenant I *m*
32:17 you have *m* the heavens
Eze 33:7 I have *m* you a watchman
Mal 2:15 Has not {the LORD} *m* them one?
Mt 5:13 how can it be *m* salty again?
19:4 Creator '*m* them male and female'
Mk 2:27 "The Sabbath was *m* for man,

Lk 3:5	every mountain and hill *m* low.
Jn 1:3	Through him all things were *m*;
1:10	the world was *m* through him,
1:18	Father's side, has *m* him known
Ac 17:24	"The God who *m* the world
17:26	From one man he *m* every nation
Ro 1:23	immortal God for images *m* to look
1Co 3:6	but God *m* it grow
12:14	the body is not *m* up of one part
Heb 1:2	through whom he *m* the universe.
2:7	You *m* him a little lower
2:9	Jesus, who was *m* a little lower
Jas 3:9	been *m* in God's likeness
Rev 14:7	Worship him who *m* the heavens,

Magi

Mt 2:1	*M* from the east came to Jerusalem
2:7	Herod called the *M* secretly
2:16	outwitted by the *M*, he was furious,

magic, -ians

Ex 7:11	Egyptian *m-ians* also did the same
Eze 13:20	I am against your *m* charms
Da 2:2	So the king summoned the *m-ians*,
Ac 8:11	for a long time with his *m*
Rev 9:21	their murders, their *m* arts,
21:8	immoral, those who practise *m*

magnificent

1Ki 8:13	built a *m* temple for you,
Isa 28:29	wonderful in counsel and *m*
Mk 13:1	massive stones! What *m* buildings!

Magog

Eze 38:2	against Gog, of the land of *M*,
Rev 20:8	and *M*—to gather them for battle.

maiden

Ge 24:43	if a *m* comes out to draw water
Pr 30:19	and the way of a man with a *m*
Isa 62:5	As a young man marries a *m*,
Jer 2:32	Does a *m* forget her jewellery,

maimed

Lev 22:22	the blind, the injured or the *m*,
Mt 18:8	to enter life *m* or crippled

majestic

Ex 15:6	hand, O LORD, was *m* in power.
15:11	Who is like you—*m* in holiness,
Job 37:4	he thunders with his *m* voice.
Ps 8:1	our Lord, how *m* is your name
111:3	Glorious and *m* are his deeds,
2Pe 1:17	voice came to him from the *M* Glory,

majesty

Ps 93:1	The LORD reigns, he is robed in *m*;
Isa 2:19	LORD and the splendour of his *m*,
53:2	He had no beauty or *m* to attract
2Th 1:9	Lord and from the *m* of his power
Heb 1:3	the right hand of the *M* in heaven
2Pe 1:16	we were eye-witnesses of his *m*
Jude :25	God our Saviour be glory, *m*, power

make, -s, -ing

Ge 1:26	"Let us *m* man in our image,
2:18	I will *m* a helper suitable
9:12	sign of the covenant I am *m-ing*
12:2	"I will *m* you into a great nation
28:3	bless you and *m* you fruitful
Ex 6:3	the LORD I did not *m* myself known
20:4	shall not *m* for yourself an idol
20:23	Do not *m* any gods to be
25:17	"*M* an atonement cover of pure gold
32:10	I will *m* you into a great nation.
32:23	'*M* us gods who will go before us.
34:10	"I am *m-ing* a covenant with you.
Lev 17:11	the blood that *m-s* atonement
20:8	the LORD, who *m-s* you holy

Nu 6:25 Lord *m* his face shine upon you
21:8 "*M* a snake and put it up
Ps 2:8 I will *m* the nations
4:8 for you alone, O Lord, *m* me dwell
19:7 *m-ing* wise the simple
23:2 *m-s* me lie down in green pastures,
46:4 streams *m* glad the city of God,
106:8 to *m* his mighty power known
110:1 until I *m* your enemies a footstool
139:8 if I *m* my bed in the depths,
Ecc 5:4 When you *m* a vow to God,
Isa 6:10 *m* their ears dull and close
8:14 a rock that *m-s* them fall.
40:3 *m* straight in the wilderness
44:9 All who *m* idols are nothing,
49:6 *m* you a light for the Gentiles,
Jer 31:31 I will *m* a new covenant
32:40 I will *m* an everlasting covenant
Hos 13:2 they *m* idols for themselves
Joel 2:19 will I *m* you an object of scorn
Hab 3:2 in our time *m* them known;
Mal 3:17 I *m* up my treasured possession.
Mt 3:3 *m* straight paths for him.'
4:19 I will *m* you fishers of men.
15:11 mouth does not *m* him 'unclean',
Lk 20:43 until I *m* your enemies a footstool
Jn 1:23 '*M* straight the way for the Lord.'
5:18 *m-ing* himself equal with God
Ac 2:35 I *m* your enemies a footstool
Ro 9:23 *m* the riches of his glory known
1Co 3:7 God, who *m-s* things grow
2Co 5:9 we *m* it our goal to please him,
2Ti 3:15 able to *m* you wise for salvation
Heb 1:7 "He *m-s* his angels winds,
1:13 until I *m* your enemies a footstool
1Pe 2:8 a rock that *m-s* them fall."

maker

Job 4:17 Can a man be more pure than his *M*
Ps 95:6 let us kneel before the Lord our *M*;
121:2 My help comes from the Lord, the *M*
Pr 14:31 poor shows contempt for their *M*,
Isa 17:7 that day men will look to their *M*
54:5 For your *M* is your husband—

Malachi

Prophet; name means "my messenger" (Mal 1:1).

male

Ge 1:27 *m* and female he created them
17:10 *m* among you shall be circumcised
Ex 13:2 Consecrate to me every firstborn *m*
Mt 19:4 the Creator 'made them *m* and
Lk 2:23 firstborn *m* is to be consecrated
1Co 6:9 nor adulterers nor *m* prostitutes
Gal 3:28 slave nor free, *m* nor female,
Rev 12:5 gave birth to a son, a *m* child,

malice, -ious

Pr 17:4 a liar pays attention to a *m-ious*
Mk 7:22 greed, *m*, deceit, lewdness, envy,
Ro 1:29 murder, strife, deceit and *m*.
Eph 4:31 along with every form of *m*
1Ti 3:11 women worthy of respect, not *m-ious*
1Pe 2:1 rid yourselves of all *m*

man, -'s

Ge 1:26 "Let us make *m* in our image,
2:7 formed the *m* from the dust
2:15 The Lord God took the *m*
2:18 not good for the *m* to be alone.
2:20 So the *m* gave names to
2:24 For this reason a *m* will leave
2:25 *m* and his wife were both naked,
6:5 Lord saw how great *m-'s* wickedness
Nu 23:19 God is not a *m*, that he should lie
Dt 8:5 as a *m* disciplines his son,
1Sa 2:25 If a *m* sins against another *m*,
2Sa 12:7 to David, "You are the *m*!
1Ki 18:44 "A cloud as small as a *m's* hand
Job 5:7 Yet *m* is born to trouble

14:1 "*M* born of woman is of few days
14:14 If a *m* dies, will he live again?
Ps 1:1 Blessed is the *m* who does not
8:4 what is *m* that you are mindful
22:6 I am a worm and not a *m*,
32:2 Blessed is the *m* whose sin
119:9 How can a young *m* keep his way
Pr 14:12 a way that seems right to a *m*,
27:17 so one *m* sharpens another
Ecc 7:28 I found one (upright) *m* among
Isa 6:5 For I am a *m* of unclean lips,
53:3 rejected by men, a *m* of sorrows,
55:7 the evil *m* his thoughts.
Eze 18:21 if a wicked *m* turns away
37:3 "Son of *m*, can these bones live?
Da 7:13 was one like a son of *m*, coming
Hos 11:9 I am God, and not *m*—
Mal 3:8 "Will a *m* rob God?
Mt 1:19 her husband was a righteous *m*
4:4 '*M* does not live on bread alone,
7:24 a wise *m* who built his house
10:35 to turn " 'a *m* against his father,
11:6 Blessed is the *m* who does not
12:29 enter a strong *m-'s* house
16:26 for a *m* if he gains the whole
19:3 "Is it lawful for a *m* to divorce
19:23 it is hard for a rich *m*
19:26 "With *m* this is impossible,
Mk 2:27 "The Sabbath was made for *m*,
9:38 "we saw a *m* driving out demons
Lk 5:8 I am a sinful *m*!
16:22 The rich *m* also died
Jn 1:6 came a *m* who was sent from God;
1:9 that gives light to every *m*
2:25 for he knew what was in a *m*.
4:18 the *m* you now have is not
4:29 see a *m* who told me everything
10:1 *m* who does not enter the sheep
11:1 a *m* named Lazarus was sick.
Ac 12:22 voice of a god, not of a *m*.
17:26 From one *m* he made every nation
Ro 1:23 images made to look like mortal *m*
3:28 a *m* is justified by faith
4:8 Blessed is the *m* whose sin
5:7 anyone die for a righteous *m*,
5:12 entered the world through one *m*,
7:24 What a wretched *m* I am!
9:20 But who are you, O *m*,
1Co 1:20 Where is the wise *m*?
11:8 *m* did not come from woman,
11:28 A *m* ought to examine himself
13:11 I became a *m*, I put childish
15:21 since death came through a *m*,
Gal 2:16 that a *m* is not justified
6:7 A *m* reaps what he sows
Eph 5:31 "For this reason a *m* will leave
Php 2:8 found in appearance as a *m*,
2Th 2:3 the *m* of lawlessness is revealed,
3:10 "If a *m* will not work,
1Ti 2:5 the *m* Christ Jesus
Heb 2:6 "What is *m* that you are mindful
9:27 Just as *m* is destined to die once,
Jas 2:14 if a *m* claims to have faith
5:17 Elijah was a *m* just like us.
1Pe 1:17 a Father who judges each *m's* work
Rev 1:13 someone "like a son of *m*",

manage, -r

Lk 12:42 then is the faithful and wise *m-r*,
16:8 master commended the dishonest *m-r*
1Ti 3:4 He must *m* his own family well
3:12 must *m* his children
5:14 to have children, to *m* their homes

Manasseh

1. Joseph's elder son (Ge 41:51; 46:20); blessed by Jacob but not as firstborn (Ge 48:13–20). **2.** Tribe descended from Manasseh. Blessed by Moses (Dt 33:13–17). Included in census (Nu 1:34–35; 26:29–34). Apportioned land on both sides of Jordan: east (Nu 32:33,39–42; Jos 13:8,29–31); west (Jos 17:1–11; Eze 48:4); failed to fully possess (Jos 17:12–13). **3.** King of Judah; son of Hezekiah (2Ki 20:21; 2Ch 32:33). Led Israel into idolatry (2Ki 21:2–9; 2Ch 33:2–9); sin held responsible for exile (2Ki 21:10–15; Jer 15:3–4;). Deported to Babylon; repented; carried out limited reform (2Ch 33:10–19). Death (2Ki 21:18; 2Ch 33:20).

manger

Isa 1:3	the donkey his owner's *m*,
Lk 2:7	in cloths and placed him in a *m*,
2:12	wrapped in cloths and lying in a *m*.

mankind

Ge 6:7	I will wipe *m*, whom I have created
Ps 33:13	the LORD looks down and sees all *m*
Isa 45:12	the earth and created *m* upon it.
Lk 3:6	all *m* will see God's salvation.'

manna

Ex 16:31	Israel called the bread *m*.
16:35	Israelites ate *m* for forty years,
Nu 11:7	The *m* was like coriander seed
Jn 6:31	Our forefathers ate the *m* in
Rev 2:17	I will give some of the hidden *m*.

Mark

Also called John (Ac 12:12). Cousin of Barnabas (Col 4:10). Accompanied Paul and Barnabas (Ac 12:25) but later deserted them (Ac 13:13). Cause of disagreement (Ac 15:37–39). Reconciled to Paul (2Ti 4:11) and a fellow-worker (Phm 24); close to Peter (1Pe 5:13). Wrote second Gospel.

mark, -s

Ge 4:15	Then the LORD put a *m* on Cain
Jn 20:25	"Unless I see the nail *m-s*
2Co 12:12	The things that *m* an apostle-
Gal 6:17	I bear on my body the *m-s* of Jesus
Rev 14:9	receives his *m* on the forehead

marriage

Mal 2:14	the wife of your *m* covenant
Mt 19:12	renounced *m* because of the kingdom
22:30	neither marry nor be given in *m*;
24:38	giving in *m*, up to the day Noah
Ro 7:2	she is released from the law of *m*
Heb 13:4	*M* should be honoured by all, and

marry, -ies, -ied

Ezr 10:10	you have *m-ied* foreign women,
Isa 62:4	and your land will be *m-ied*
Hos 1:3	So he *m-ied* Gomer
Mt 1:18	pledged to be *m-ied* to Joseph,
5:32	anyone who *m-ies* the divorced woman
19:9	and *m-ies* another woman commits
22:25	The first one *m-ied* and died,
Lk 14:20	'I have just got *m-ied*, so
Ro 7:2	*m-ied* woman is bound to her husband
1Co 7:1	It is good for a man not to *m*
7:27	*m-ied*? Do not seek a divorce.
7:33	a *m-ied* man is concerned about
1Ti 4:3	They forbid people to *m*
5:14	So I counsel younger widows to *m*,

Martha

Sister of Mary and Lazarus (Lk 10:38–39; Jn 11). Concerned with practical things (Lk 10:40–41; Jn 12:2).

marvel, -led, -lous

Ps 72:18	who alone does *m-lous* deeds
98:1	for he has done *m-lous* things
118:23	and it is *m-lous* in our eyes
Mt 21:42	it is *m-lous* in our eyes'?
Lk 2:33	*m-led* at what was said about him
Rev 15:3	Great and *m-lous* are your deeds.

Mary

1. Mother of Jesus; husband of Joseph (Mt 1:16–25; Lk 1–2). Visited by Gabriel (Lk 1:26–38); praised God (Lk 1:46–55). With Jesus at wedding in Cana (Jn 2:1–11). Witnessed crucifixion (Jn 19:25); entrusted to John's care (Jn 19:26–27). With disciples after resurrection (Ac 1:14). **2.** Magdalene. Demoniac delivered by Jesus (Lk 8:2; Mk 16:9). At crucifixion (Mt 27:55–56; Mk 15:40–41,47; Jn 19:25); visited tomb (Mt 28:1; Mk 16:1; Lk 24:1–10; Jn 20:1); met by risen Jesus (Jn 20:10–18). **3.** Sister of Martha and Lazarus (Lk 10:38–39; Jn 11); commended for devotion (Lk 10:39–42); anointed Jesus' feet (Jn 12:3; 11:2). **4.** Mother of James and Joses; wife of Clopas. At crucifixion (Mt 27:55–56;

Mk 15:40–41,47; Jn 19:25); visited tomb (Mt 28:1; Mk 16:1; Lk 24:1–10). **5.** Mother of John Mark whose home used by one Jerusalem church (Ac 12:12–17). **6.** Believer in Rome (Ro 16:6).

master, -'s, -s, -s', -ed

Ge 4:7	to have you, but you must *m* it.
2Ki 2:3	to take your *m* from you today?"
Isa 1:3	The ox knows his *m*, the donkey
Mal 1:6	his father, and a servant his *m*.
Mt 6:24	"No-one can serve two *m-s*.
10:24	nor a servant above his *m*
15:27	that fall from their *m-s'* table.
23:8	for you have only one *M*
24:46	that servant whose *m* finds him
Jn 13:16	no servant is greater than his *m*,
15:15	a servant does not know his *m-'s*
Ro 6:14	For sin shall not be your *m*,
14:4	To his own *m* he stands or falls.
1Co 6:12	I will not be *m-ed* by anything
Eph 6:5	Slaves, obey your earthly *m-s*
Col 3:22	your earthly *m-s* in everything;

Matthew

Apostle; tax collector, also called Levi (Mt 9:9–13; Mk 2:14–17; Lk 5:27–32; Mt 10:3; Mk 3:18; Ac 1:13). Wrote first Gospel.

mature, -ity

1Co 2:6	a message of wisdom among the *m*,
Eph 4:13	the Son of God and become *m*,
Php 3:15	All of us who are *m* should take
Heb 5:14	But solid food is for the *m*,
6:1	go on to *m-ity*, not laying again

meal

Pr 15:17	Better a *m* of vegetables
Jn 13:4	he got up from the *m*, took off
1Co 10:27	some unbeliever invites you to a *m*
Heb 12:16	Esau, who for a single *m* sold his

meaningless

Ecc 1:2	"*M*! *M*!" says the Teacher.
4:7	I saw something *m* under the sun
Isa 1:13	Stop bringing *m* offerings!

measure, -s, -d

Pr 20:10	differing *m-s*—the LORD detests
Isa 40:12	has *m-d* the waters in the hollow
Mt 7:2	judged, and with the *m* you use,
Lk 6:38	A good *m*, pressed down, shaken
Eph 3:19	filled to the *m* of all the fulness
Rev 11:1	"Go and *m* the temple of God

meat

Ge 9:4	not eat *m* that has its lifeblood
1Ki 17:6	The ravens brought him bread and *m*
Ro 14:6	He who eats *m*, eats to the Lord,
1Co 8:13	I will never eat *m* again,
10:25	Eat anything sold in the *m* market

mediator

Gal 3:19	through angels by a *m*
1Ti 2:5	one God and one *m* between God
Heb 8:6	the covenant of which he is *m*
9:15	Christ is the *m* of a new covenant,
12:24	Jesus the *m* of a new covenant,

meditate, -s, -d, -ion

Jos 1:8	*m* on it day and night,
Ps 1:2	on his law he *m-s* day and night
19:14	my mouth and the *m-ion* of my heart
39:3	and as I *m-d*, the fire burned;
145:5	I will *m* on your wonderful works

medium, -s

Lev 19:31	'Do not turn to *m-s* or seek out
1Sa 28:3	Saul had expelled the *m-s*
28:7	"Find me a woman who is a *m*,
Isa 8:19	When men tell you to consult *m-s*

meek, -ness

Ps 37:11	But the *m* will inherit the land
Zep 3:12	leave within you the *m* and humble,
Mt 5:5	Blessed are the *m*, for they will

2Co 10:1 By the *m-ness* and gentleness

meet, -s, -ing, -ings

Ex 19:17 out of the camp to *m* with God,
28:43 they enter the Tent of *M-ing*
1Ki 18:19 Israel to *m* me on Mount Carmel.
Ps 42:2 When can I go and *m* with God
Am 4:12 prepare to *m* your God, O Israel.
Mt 25:1 went out to *m* the bridegroom
Mk 5:2 came from the tombs to *m* him
Jn 12:13 out to *m* him, shouting, "Hosanna!
Ac 2:46 to *m* together in the temple courts.
4:31 where they were *m-ing* was shaken.
Ro 16:5 the church that *m-s* at their house.
1Co 11:17 your *m-ings* do more harm than good
Php 4:19 And my God will *m* all your needs
1Th 4:17 in the clouds to *m* the Lord
Heb 10:25 Let us not give up *m-ing* together,
Jas 2:2 Suppose a man comes into your *m-ing*

Melchizedek

King of Salem and priest of God Most High who blessed Abraham and received tithe from him (Ge 14:18–20; Heb 7:1–10). Presented as a type of Christ (Ps 110:4; Heb 5:6,10; 6:20; 7:11–17).

melt, -s

Ps 46:6 he lifts his voice, the earth *m-s*
68:2 as wax *m-s* before the fire,
97:5 The mountains *m* like wax
2Pe 3:12 the elements will *m* in the heat

member, -s

Mic 7:6 a man's enemies are the *m-s* of his
Mt 10:25 much more the *m-s* of his household
10:36 a man's enemies will be the *m-s* of
Ro 7:23 law at work in the *m-s* of my body,
1Co 6:15 your bodies are *m-s* of Christ
Eph 2:19 *m-s* of God's household
5:30 for we are *m-s* of his body.

men, -'s

Ge 4:26 At that time *m* began to call
6:2 daughters of *m* were beautiful,
Ps 5:6 deceitful *m* the LORD abhors
27:2 When evil *m* advance against me
68:18 you received gifts from *m*,
90:3 You turn *m* back to dust, saying,
126:1 we were like *m* who dreamed
Pr 20:29 glory of young *m* is their strength,
Isa 29:13 rules taught by *m*
40:6 "All *m* are like grass,
40:30 young *m* stumble and fall
Da 1:17 young *m* God gave knowledge
3:25 I see four *m* walking around
4:17 sovereign over the kingdoms of *m*
Joel 2:28 your old *m* will dream dreams,
Mt 4:19 I will make you fishers of *m*.
5:16 let your light shine before *m*,
6:14 if you forgive *m* when they sin
9:17 Neither do *m* pour new wine
10:22 All *m* will hate you because of me,
15:9 but rules taught by *m*.'
Lk 2:14 earth peace to *m* on whom
5:10 from now on you will catch *m*.
18:11 I am not like other *m*—robbers,
21:17 All *m* will hate you because of me
Jn 1:4 that life was the light of *m*
3:19 but *m* loved darkness instead of
12:32 will draw all *m* to myself.
Ac 1:10 suddenly two *m* dressed in white
2:17 your young *m* will see visions,
2:23 with the help of wicked *m*,
4:12 to *m* by which we must be saved.
5:29 "We must obey God rather than *m*
17:27 God did this so that *m* would seek
Ro 1:18 godlessness and wickedness of *m*
9:33 a stone that causes *m* to stumble
11:32 For God has bound all *m* over
1Co 2:5 might not rest on *m-'s* wisdom,
13:1 the tongues of *m* and of angels,

15:19	to be pitied more than all *m*
2Co 5:11	we try to persuade *m*.
Eph 4:8	and gave gifts to *m*.
Php 2:29	and honour *m* like him
1Th 2:4	we speak as *m* approved by God
4:13	to grieve like the rest of *m*,
1Ti 1:3	you may command certain *m*
2:4	who wants all *m* to be saved
2:5	one mediator between God and *m*,
2:6	as a ransom for all *m*—
4:10	who is the Saviour of all *m*,
1Pe 1:24	"All *m* are like grass,
2Pe 1:21	but *m* spoke from God
Rev 2:2	you cannot tolerate wicked *m*,
5:9	with your blood you purchased *m*
21:3	the dwelling of God is with *m*,

Mephibosheth

1. Son of Jonathan; also called Merib-Baal (1Ch 8:34; 9:40). Crippled by a fall (2Sa 4:4); shown kindness by David (2Sa 9:1–13). Slandered by Ziba (2Sa 16:1–4); reconciled to David (2Sa 19:24–30). **2.** Son of Saul, executed by the Gibeonites (2Sa 21:8–9).

merchant

Hos 12:7	The *m* uses dishonest scales;
Mt 13:45	the kingdom of heaven is like a *m*

mercy, -iful

Ex 33:19	have *m* on whom I will have *m*,
Dt 4:31	the LORD your God is a *m-iful* God;
Ps 40:11	Do not withhold your *m* from me,
51:1	Have *m* on me, O God,
Da 9:9	our God is *m-iful* and forgiving,
Hos 6:6	For I desire *m*, not sacrifice,
Mic 6:8	To act justly and to love *m*
Mt 5:7	for they will be shown *m*
9:13	'I desire *m*, not sacrifice.'
Lk 1:50	*m* extends to those who fear him,
18:13	'God, have *m* on me, a sinner.'
Ro 9:15	I will have *m* on whom I have *m*
9:16	desire or effort, but on God's *m*
11:32	so that he may have *m* on them all
12:1	brothers, in view of God's *m*,
Eph 2:4	God, who is rich in *m*
Heb 4:16	we may receive *m* and find grace
Jas 2:13	judgment without *m* will be shown
1Pe 1:3	great *m* he has given us new birth
Jude :22	Be *m-iful* to those who doubt;

merry

Lk 12:19	eat, drink and be *m*."

Meshach

Formerly Mishael; member of Jewish nobility taken to Babylon with Daniel, Shadrach and Abednego (Da 1:3–7). Refused unclean food (Da 1:8–16); appointed as administrator (Da 2:49). Refused to worship golden image; kept safe in fiery furnace (Da 3).

message

Isa 53:1	Who has believed our *m* and to whom
Mt 13:19	hears the *m* about the kingdom
Jn 12:38	"Lord, who has believed our *m*
Ro 10:16	"Lord, who has believed our *m*?
10:17	faith comes from hearing the *m*,
1Co 1:18	the *m* of the cross is foolishness
2:4	My *m* and my preaching were not
2:6	a *m* of wisdom among the mature,
2Co 1:18	*m* to you is not "Yes" and "No"
5:19	to us the *m* of reconciliation
Heb 2:2	the *m* spoken by angels was binding,

messenger

Mal 3:1	I will send my *m*, who will prepare
Mt 11:10	'I will send my *m* ahead of you,
2Co 12:7	a *m* of Satan, to torment me

Messiah

Jn 1:41	"We have found the *M*"
4:25	"I know that *M*" (called Christ)

Methuselah
Son of Enoch; grandfather of Noah; lived to be 969 (Ge 5:21–27; 1Ch 1:3; Lk 3:36–37).

Micah
1. Prophet from Moresheth (Jer 26:18–19; Mic 1:1) **2.** Ephraimite whose idols and priest were taken by migrating Danites (Jdg 17–18). **3.** Micaiah. Prophet (1Ki 22:4–28; 2Ch 18:1–27).

Michael
Archangel (Jude 9). Heavenly guardian of Israel against power of Greece and Persia (Da 10:13,21; 12:1). Defeated Satan and cast him from heaven (Rev 12:7–9).

Michal
Daughter of Saul (1Sa 14:49). Became David's wife (1Sa 18:20–29); warned him of Saul's plot (1Sa 19:11–17). Given to Paltiel (1Sa 25:44); returned to David (2Sa 3:13–16). Despised David (2Sa 6:16–23; 1Ch 15:29).

midwives
Ex 1:17 The *m*, however, feared God

might, -y
Ge 10:9 a *m-y* hunter before the LORD;
Dt 10:17 the great God, *m-y* and awesome,
2Sa 1:25 How the *m-y* have fallen in battle!
Ps 24:8 The LORD strong and *m-y*,
29:1 Ascribe to the LORD, O *m-y* ones,
106:2 proclaim the *m-y* acts of the LORD
Isa 9:6 Wonderful Counsellor, *M-y* God,
62:8 right hand and by his *m-y* arm:
Da 11:3 Then a *m-y* king will appear,
Zep 3:17 he is *m-y* to save.
Zec 4:6 'Not by *m* nor by power, but by
Mt 26:64 at the right hand of the *M-y* One
Lk 1:49 the *M-y* One has done great things
1:51 He has performed *m-y* deeds with
Ac 13:17 with *m-y* power he led them out
Eph 1:19 the working of his *m-y* strength
6:10 in the Lord and in his *m-y* power
Col 1:11 according to his glorious *m*
1Pe 5:6 under God's *m-y* hand,
Rev 5:2 I saw a *m-y* angel proclaiming

mile
Mt 5:41 If someone forces you to go one *m*,

milk
Ex 3:8 a land flowing with *m* and honey—
Isa 55:1 Come, buy wine and *m* without money
1Co 3:2 I gave you *m*, not solid food,
1Pe 2:2 crave pure spiritual *m*,

millstone
Mt 18:6 a large *m* hung around his neck

mind, -s, -ful
Nu 23:19 that he should change his *m*.
1Sa 15:29 does not lie or change his *m*;
Ps 8:4 man that you are *m-ful* of him,
110:4 sworn and will not change his *m*:
Isa 26:3 keep in perfect peace, him whose *m*
40:13 understood the *m* of the LORD,
Mt 22:37 all your soul and with all your *m*.
Ro 1:28 he gave them over to a depraved *m*,
8:6 The *m* of sinful man is death,
8:7 the sinful *m* is hostile to God.
11:34 "Who has known the *m* of the Lord?
12:2 by the renewing of your *m*.
1Co 2:9 no *m* has conceived what God
2:16 who has known the *m* of the Lord
2Co 4:4 blinded the *m-s* of unbelievers,
Php 3:19 Their *m* is on earthly things.
4:7 guard your hearts and your *m-s*
Col 3:2 Set your *m-s* on things above,
Heb 2:6 "What is man that you are *m-ful*
7:21 sworn and will not change his *m*:

minister, -s, -ing

Ps 134:1 who *m* by night in the house of
2Co 3:6 competent as *m-s* of a new covenant—
1Ti 4:6 you will be a good *m* of Christ
Heb 1:14 Are not all angels *m-ing* spirits
13:10 those who *m* at the tabernacle

ministry

Ac 6:2 neglect the *m* of the word of God
2Co 3:8 will not the *m* of the Spirit be
5:18 gave us the *m* of reconciliation
2Ti 4:5 discharge all the duties of your *m*
Heb 8:6 But the *m* Jesus has received is

miracle, -s, -ulous

Ps 77:14 You are the God who performs *m-s*;
Mt 7:22 demons and perform many *m-s*?
12:39 generation asks for a *m-ulous* sign!
Jn 2:11 the first of his *m-ulous* signs,
6:30 "What *m-ulous* sign then will you
14:11 believe on the evidence of the *m-s*
Ac 2:22 accredited by God to you by *m-s*,
4:30 to heal and perform *m-ulous* signs
5:12 apostles performed many *m-ulous*
19:11 God did extraordinary *m-s* through
Ro 15:19 by the power of signs and *m-s*,
1Co 1:22 Jews demand *m-ulous* signs
12:10 to another *m-ulous* powers,
12:29 Are all teachers? Do all work *m-s*
2Co 12:12 apostle—signs, wonders and *m-s*—
Gal 3:5 his Spirit and work *m-s* among you
2Th 2:9 all kinds of counterfeit *m-s*,
Heb 2:4 signs, wonders and various *m-s*,
Rev 13:13 performed great and *m-ulous* signs,

Miriam

Sister of Moses and Aaron (Nu 25:59; 1Ch 6:3). Watched Moses in bulrushes; suggested mother as nurse (Ex 2:4–8). Prophetess; led dancing and sang at Red Sea (Ex 15:20–21); criticised Moses, became leprous (Nu 12:1–15; Dt 24:9). Death (Nu 20:1).

mirror

1Co 13:12 but a poor reflection as in a *m*;
Jas 1:23 who looks at his face in a *m*

misery

Ex 3:7 "I have indeed seen the *m*
Ro 3:16 ruin and *m* mark their ways
Jas 5:1 weep and wail because of the *m*

mist

Isa 44:22 your sins like the morning *m*.
Hos 6:4 Your love is like the morning *m*,
Jas 4:14 What is your life? You are a *m*

misuse

Ex 20:7 *m* the name of the LORD your God,
Ps 139:20 your adversaries *m* your name

mock, -s, -ing, -ed, -er

Ps 22:7 who see me *m* me; they hurl insults,
119:51 arrogant *m* me without restraint,
Pr 3:34 *m-s* proud mockers but gives grace
20:1 Wine is a *m-er* and beer
Isa 50:6 I did not hide my face from *m-ing*
Mt 20:19 *m-ed* and flogged and crucified.
27:29 *m-ed* him. "Hail, king of the Jews!
Gal 6:7 God cannot be *m-ed*.

model

1Th 1:7 became a *m* to all the believers
2Th 3:9 ourselves a *m* for you to follow

modest, -ly, -y

1Co 12:23 are treated with special *m-y*
1Ti 2:9 I also want women to dress *m-ly*,

moment, -ary

Job 20:5 joy of the godless lasts but a *m*
Ps 2:12 his wrath can flare up in a *m*.

30:5	his anger lasts only a *m*,
Isa 54:7	"For a brief *m* I abandoned you,
Mt 27:51	At that *m* the curtain of the
2Co 4:17	For our light and *m-ary* troubles
Gal 2:5	did not give in to them for a *m*,

money

Pr 13:11	Dishonest *m* dwindles away,
Ecc 5:10	loves *m* never has money enough;
Isa 55:1	you who have no *m*, come, buy
55:2	Why spend *m* on what is not bread,
Mt 6:24	You cannot serve both God and *M*
26:9	sold at a high price and the *m*
Lk 3:14	"Don't extort *m* and don't accuse
Jn 2:14	sitting at tables exchanging *m*
12:6	as keeper of the *m* bag,
Ac 4:37	*m* and put it at the apostles' feet
8:20	"May your *m* perish with you,
1Co 16:2	*m* in keeping with his income,
1Ti 3:3	not quarrelsome, not a lover of *m*
6:10	For the love of *m* is a root
Heb 13:5	lives free from the love of *m*
1Pe 5:2	not greedy for *m*, but eager to

month, -s

Ex 12:2	"This *m* is to be for you the first
Lk 1:26	In the sixth *m*, God sent the angel
Jn 4:35	'Four *m-s* more and then the harvest
Gal 4:10	observing special days and *m-s*
Rev 11:2	trample on the holy city for 42 *m-s*

moon

Ge 37:9	*m* and eleven stars were bowing
Jos 10:13	stood still, and the *m* stopped,
Ps 8:3	your fingers, the *m* and the stars,
121:6	nor the *m* by night
Joel 2:31	to darkness and the *m* to blood
Mt 24:29	and the *m* will not give its light;
Ac 2:20	to darkness and the *m* to blood
Rev 6:12	the whole *m* turned blood red

moral

Jas 1:21	get rid of all *m* filth

Mordecai

1. Benjamite exile; brought up cousin, Esther, as own daughter (Est 2:5–7,15,20). Reported plot to kill Xerxes (Est 2:21–23). Refused to bow to Haman resulting in plot against Jews (Est 3:1–6); mourned; persuaded Esther to help (Est 4). Honoured (Est 6); given Haman's position as next in rank to king (Est 8:1–2; 10). Saved Jews; instituted feast of Purim (Est 8–9). **2.** Jewish exile who returned with Zerubbabel (Ezr 2:2; Ne 7:7).

Moriah

Ge 22:2	region of *M*. Sacrifice him there
2Ch 3:1	*M*, where the LORD had appeared

morning

Ge 1:5	and there was *m*—the first day
Ex 12:10	Do not leave any of it till *m*;
Job 38:7	while the *m* stars sang together
Ps 30:5	but rejoicing comes in the *m*
Isa 14:12	fallen from heaven, O *m* star,
La 3:23	They are new every *m*; great is
Mt 16:3	in the *m*, 'Today it will be stormy,
Ac 2:15	It's only nine in the *m*
2Pe 1:19	the *m* star rises in your hearts
Rev 22:16	and the bright *M* Star.

mortal

Ge 6:3	he is *m*; his days will be
Job 4:17	Can a *m* be more righteous than God?
Ps 56:4	What can *m* man do to me?
Ro 6:12	do not let sin reign in your *m* body
8:11	give life to your *m* bodies
1Co 15:54	and the *m* with immortality,
2Co 5:4	*m* may be swallowed up by life

Moses

Levite; brother of Aaron (Ex 6:20; 1Ch 6:3). Put into Nile in basket; found and raised by Pharaoh's daughter; killed Egyptian; fled to Midian; married Zipporah (Ex 2; Ac 7:20–29). Called by God at burning bush (Ex 3–4; Ac 7:30–36); confronted Pharaoh

(Ex 5:1–4; 7:1–13); plagues (Ex 7–11; Ps 105:26–36). Led people out of Egypt (Ex 12–13), through Red Sea (Ex 14). Brought water from rock (Ex 17:1–7); raised hands to enable victory over Amalekites (Ex 17:8–16); appointed judges (Ex 18; Dt 1:9–18). Given Law on Mt Sinai (Ex 19–23); spoke to people; confirmed covenant (Ex 19:7–8; 24:1–11; Heb 9:19); returned to mountain to receive stone tablets (Ex 24:12–18; 31:18). Broke tablets over golden calf (Ex 32:15–19; Dt 9:7–17); interceded for people (Ex 32:10–14; Dt 9:25–29). Saw God's glory (Ex 33:18–23); given new tablets (Ex 34; Dt 10:1–5); face shone (Ex 34:29–35).

Supervised building of tabernacle (Ex 35–40; Heb 8:5); consecrated Aaron and sons as priests (Ex 28–29; Lev 8–9). Took census (Nu 1–4; 26). Opposed by Aaron and Miriam (Nu 12), Korah (Nu 16; Jude 11). Sent spies into Canaan (Nu 13; Dt 1:19–25). Forbidden to enter Canaan for striking rock (Nu 20:12; 27:12–14; Dt 3:27; 32:48–52). Lifted up bronze snake (Nu 21:4–9). Allocated land east of Jordan (Nu 32). Last words to Israel (Dt 31–33); death (Dt 34); succeeded by Joshua (Dt 3:28; 34:9; Jos 1:1–9). Faithfulness as God's servant commended (Heb 3:3–5). Prayer of Moses (Ps 90); songs of Moses (Ex 15:1–18; Dt 32; Rev 15:3–4).

moth

Ps 39:11 consume their wealth like a *m*—
Isa 51:8 For the *m* will eat them up
Mt 6:19 earth, where *m* and rust destroy,

mother, -'s, -s

Ge 2:24 man will leave his father and *m*
3:20 become the *m* of all the living
Ex 20:12 "Honour your father and your *m*,
Job 1:21 "Naked I came from my *m-'s* womb,
Ps 27:10 Though my father and *m* forsake me,
51:5 from the time my *m* conceived me
139:13 knit me together in my *m-'s* womb
Isa 49:15 "Can a *m* forget the baby at
66:13 As a *m* comforts her child,
Mt 1:18 *m* Mary was pledged to be married
10:35 a daughter against her *m*,
10:37 loves his father or *m* more than me
12:48 "Who is my *m*, and who
15:4 'Honour your father and *m*'
19:5 man will leave his father and *m*
Jn 3:4 a second time into his *m-'s* womb
19:27 the disciple, "Here is your *m*."
Eph 5:31 a man will leave his father and *m*
6:2 "Honour your father and *m*"—
1Ti 5:2 older women as *m-s*, and younger
Heb 7:3 Without father or *m*,

mother-in-law

Mt 8:14 he saw Peter's *m* lying in bed
10:35 a daughter-in-law against her *m*

motives

Pr 16:2 but *m* are weighed by the LORD
1Co 4:5 expose the *m* of men's hearts.
Php 1:18 whether from false *m* or true,
Jas 4:3 because you ask with wrong *m*,

mountain, -s

Ge 8:4 ark came to rest on the *m-s*
Ps 18:7 the foundations of the *m-s* shook;
90:2 Before the *m-s* were born
Isa 40:4 every *m* and hill made low;
40:12 weighed the *m-s* on the scales
52:7 beautiful on the *m-s* are the feet
Da 2:35 struck the statue became a huge *m*
Hos 10:8 say to the *m-s*, "Cover us!"
Mic 4:1 the last days the *m* of the LORD's
Mt 4:8 devil took him to a very high *m*
17:1 led them up a high *m* by themselves
17:20 you can say to this *m*,
24:16 in Judea flee to the *m-s*
Jn 4:20 Our fathers worshipped on this *m*,
1Co 13:2 I have a faith that can move *m-s*,

Heb 12:18 come to a *m* that can be touched
Rev 6:16 called to the *m-s* and the rocks,

mourn
Ecc 3:4 a time to *m* and a time to dance
Isa 61:2 our God, to comfort all who *m*
Mt 5:4 Blessed are those who *m*,
Ro 12:15 *m* with those who *m*.
1Co 7:30 those who *m*, as if they did not;
Rev 1:7 earth will *m* because of him.

mouth, -s
Ps 19:14 May the words of my *m* and
22:15 tongue sticks to the roof of my *m*;
40:3 He put a new song in my *m*,
119:103 sweeter than honey to my *m*
Isa 40:5 For the *m* of the LORD has spoken.
53:7 yet he did not open his *m*;
55:11 my word that goes out from my *m*:
Eze 3:3 tasted as sweet as honey in my *m*
Da 6:22 he shut the *m-s* of the lions.
Mt 4:4 that comes from the *m* of God.'
12:34 overflow of the heart the *m* speaks
13:35 "I will open my *m* in parables,
15:11 man's *m* does not make him 'unclean'
Ac 11:8 or unclean has ever entered my *m*.
Ro 3:14 "Their *m-s* are full of cursing
10:9 That if you confess with your *m*,
Jas 3:10 Out of the same *m* come praise and
1Pe 2:22 no deceit was found in his *m*.
Rev 1:16 *m* came a sharp double-edged sword.
3:16 I am about to spit you out of my *m*

move, -s, -d
Ge 9:3 that lives and *m-s* will be food
Ex 14:19 The pillar of cloud also *m-d*
Dt 19:14 Do not *m* your neighbour's boundary
Ps 93:1 established; it cannot be *m-d*
Mt 17:20 mountain, '*M* from here to there'
Ac 17:28 in him we live and *m* and have
1Co 13:2 a faith that can *m* mountains, but
15:58 Let nothing *m* you.
Col 1:23 not *m-d* from the hope held out

multitude, -s
Ps 42:4 how I used to go with the *m*,
Da 10:6 his voice like the sound of a *m*
12:2 *M-s* who sleep in the dust
Jas 5:20 cover over a *m* of sins
1Pe 4:8 love covers over a *m* of sins
Rev 7:9 great *m* that no-one could count,

murder, -er, -ers, -ous
Ex 20:13 "You shall not *m*.
Mt 5:21 to the people long ago, 'Do not *m*,
15:19 heart come evil thoughts, *m*,
Jn 8:44 He was a *m-er* from the beginning,
Ac 9:1 Saul was still breathing out *m-ous*
1Ti 1:9 *m-ers*, for adulterers and perverts,
1Jn 3:15 hates his brother is a *m-er*,

music
Ps 27:6 I will sing and make *m* to the LORD
95:2 extol him with *m* and song.
Lk 15:25 he heard *m* and dancing
Eph 5:19 Sing and make *m* in your heart

mustard
Mt 13:31 kingdom of heaven is like a *m* seed,
17:20 faith as small as a *m* seed,

mute
Isa 35:6 the *m* tongue shout for joy.
Mt 9:33 the man who had been *m* spoke.
12:22 man who was blind and *m*,

muzzle
Dt 25:4 Do not *m* an ox while
1Co 9:9 "Do not *m* an ox while
1Ti 5:18 "Do not *m* the ox while

myrrh
SS 5:5 my hands dripped with *m*,
Mt 2:11 gold and of incense and of *m*
Mk 15:23 offered him wine mixed with *m*,

Jn 19:39 Nicodemus brought a mixture of *m*

mystery, -ies

Job 11:7 "Can you fathom the *m-ies* of God?
1Co 13:2 fathom all *m-ies* and all knowledge,
15:51 Listen, I tell you a *m*:
Eph 1:9 made known to us the *m* of his will
Col 1:26 the *m* that has been kept hidden
1:27 this *m*, which is Christ in you,
1Ti 3:16 the *m* of godliness is great:

myths

1Ti 1:4 nor to devote themselves to *m*
4:7 Have nothing to do with godless *m*

N

Naaman

Commander-in-chief of Aramaean army; leprosy healed by Elisha (2Ki 5).

Naboth

Jezreelite, killed by Jezebel so Ahab could take possion of his vineyard (1Ki 21:1–16).

Nahum

Prophet; spoke against Nineveh (Na 1:1).

nail, -ing

Ac 2:23 put him to death by *n-ing* him
Col 2:14 *n-ing* it to the cross

naked

Ge 2:25 man and his wife were both *n*,
Job 1:21 "*N* I came from my mother's womb,
Mk 14:52 he fled *n*, leaving his garment
2Co 5:3 we will not be found *n*
Rev 3:17 pitiful, poor, blind and *n*

name, -'s, -s

Ge 2:19 to see what he would *n* them;
12:2 I will make your *n* great,
12:8 called on the *n* of the LORD
Ex 3:13 they ask me, 'What is his *n*?'
20:7 not misuse the *n* of the LORD
Dt 18:19 the prophet speaks in my *n*,
32:3 I will proclaim the *n* of the LORD.
Jdg 13:18 "Why do you ask my *n*? It is beyond
2Sa 7:9 Now I will make your *n* great,
7:13 who will build a house for my *N*,
1Ki 5:5 a temple for the *N* of the LORD
2Ki 21:4 "In Jerusalem I will put my *N*.
1Ch 16:29 the glory due to his *n*.
Job 1:21 may the *n* of the LORD be praised.
Ps 8:1 how majestic is your *n* in all
23:3 righteousness for his *n-'s* sake.
29:2 LORD the glory due to his *n*;
34:3 let us exalt his *n* together
102:15 will fear the *n* of the LORD,
103:1 inmost being, praise his holy *n*
Pr 18:10 *n* of the LORD is a strong tower;
22:1 A good *n* is more desirable than
30:9 so dishonour the *n* of my God
Isa 59:19 men will fear the *n* of the LORD,
Da 2:20 Praise be to the *n* of God for ever
12:1 everyone whose *n* is found written
Joel 2:32 who calls on the *n* of the LORD
Mal 1:11 *n* will be great among the nations,
Mt 1:21 you are to give him the *n* Jesus,
6:9 hallowed be your *n*
7:22 did we not prophesy in your *n*,
18:5 in my *n* welcomes me
18:20 two or three come together in my *n*,
28:19 baptising them in the *n* of
Jn 1:12 to those who believed in his *n*,
3:18 in the *n* of God's one and only Son
5:43 I have come in my Father's *n*,
10:3 He calls his own sheep by *n*
12:28 Father, glorify your *n*!"
14:14 ask me for anything in my *n*,
14:26 the Father will send in my *n*,
20:31 you may have life in his *n*
Ac 2:21 everyone who calls on the *n* of
3:6 In the *n* of Jesus Christ
3:16 It is Jesus' *n* and the faith that
4:12 there is no other *n* under heaven
5:41 suffering disgrace for the *N*
9:15 to carry my *n* before the Gentiles
10:43 forgiveness of sins through his *n*.

Ro 10:13	“Everyone who calls on the *n* of
1Co 1:2	call on the *n* of our Lord Jesus
Php 2:9	him the *n* that is above every *n*
2:10	at the *n* of Jesus every knee
Col 3:17	all in the *n* of the Lord Jesus,
2Ti 2:19	who confesses the *n* of the Lord
Heb 1:4	the *n* he has inherited is superior
2:12	will declare your *n* to my brothers;
12:23	whose *n-s* are written in heaven.
1Jn 2:12	forgiven on account of his *n*
3:23	his command: to believe in the *n*
Rev 2:3	have endured hardships for my *n*,
20:15	anyone’s *n* was not found written
21:27	*n-s* are written in the Lamb’s

Naomi

Mother-in-law of Ruth. With husband Elimelech, moved from Bethlehem to Moab during famine; returned with Ruth after death of husband and sons (Ru 1). Encouraged Ruth’s marriage to Boaz (Ru 2:19–3:6); nursed Ruth’s son (Ru 4:16–17).

Naphtali

1. Son of Jacob by Bilhah (Ge 30:8; 35:25; 1Ch 2:2). Blessed by Jacob (Ge 49:21). **2.** Tribe descended from Naphtali. Blessed by Moses (Dt 33:23). Included in census (Nu 1:42–43; 26:48–50). Apportioned land (Jos 19:32–39; Eze 48:3); unable to take full possession (Jdg 1:33).

narrow

Mt 7:13	“Enter through the *n* gate.
Lk 13:24	to enter through the *n* door,

Nathan

1. Prophet; announced God’s promise to David of lasting dynasty (2Sa 7:1–17; 1Ch 17:1–15); rebuked David’s sin with Bathsheba (2Sa 12:1–14). Supported Solomon’s succession (1Ki 1:8–40). Chronicled reigns of David and Solomon (1Ch 29:29; 2Ch 9:29) **2.** Son of David (2Sa 5:14; Zec 12:12); included in Jesus’ genealogy (Lk 3:31).

Nathanael

Apostle from Cana in Galilee; brought to Jesus by Philip (Jn 1:45–51; 21:2). Possibly to be identified with Bartholomew, who is also linked with Philip (Mt 10:3).

nation, -s

Ge 12:2	“I will make you into a great *n*
18:18	all *n-s* on earth will be blessed
Ex 34:24	I will drive out *n-s* before you
Dt 17:14	king over us like all the *n-s*
28:64	will scatter you among all *n-s*,
1Sa 8:5	such as all the other *n-s* have.
Ps 2:1	Why do the *n-s* conspire
2:8	Ask of me, and I will make the *n-s*
22:28	and he rules over the *n-s*
33:12	Blessed is the *n* whose God is
46:10	I will be exalted among the *n-s*,
67:2	your salvation among all *n-s*
99:1	The LORD reigns, let the *n-s*
Pr 11:14	For lack of guidance a *n* falls,
Isa 14:12	you who once laid low the *n-s*
40:15	*n-s* are like a drop in a bucket;
63:6	I trampled the *n-s* in my anger;
65:1	a *n* that did not call on my name,
Jer 1:5	you as a prophet to the *n-s*.
2:11	Has a *n* ever changed its gods?
6:22	a great *n* is being stirred up
29:14	will gather you from all the *n-s*
Eze 11:17	I will gather you from the *n-s*
39:21	display my glory among the *n-s*,
Hag 2:7	I will shake all *n-s*,
Zec 14:2	I will gather all the *n-s*
Mal 1:11	name will be great among the *n-s*,
3:12	all the *n-s* will call you blessed,
Mt 12:18	will proclaim justice to the *n-s*
24:7	*N* will rise against *n*,
24:9	you will be hated by all *n-s*
24:14	as a testimony to all *n-s*,
24:30	the *n-s* of the earth will mourn.
25:32	All the *n-s* will be gathered
28:19	go and make disciples of all *n-s*,
Mk 11:17	a house of prayer for all *n-s*’?
Jn 11:51	Jesus would die for the Jewish *n*
Ac 2:5	Jews from every *n* under heaven
4:25	“ ‘Why do the *n-s* rage
10:35	accepts men from every *n*

14:16	he let all *n-s* go their own way
17:26	From one man he made every *n*
Ro 4:17	made you a father of many *n-s.*"
16:26	so that all *n-s* might believe
Gal 3:8	"All *n-s* will be blessed
1Ti 3:16	was preached among the *n-s*,
1Pe 2:9	a royal priesthood, a holy *n*,
Rev 5:9	language and people and *n*

natural

Jn 1:13	children born not of *n* descent,
Ro 1:26	their women exchanged *n* relations
1:27	men also abandoned *n* relations
9:8	not the *n* children who are God's
11:21	God did not spare the *n* branches,
1Co 15:44	it is sown a *n* body,

nature

Ro 1:3	his Son, who as to his human *n*
1:20	his eternal power and divine *n*—
2:14	by *n* things required by the law,
7:5	controlled by the sinful *n*,
8:5	live according to the sinful *n*
1Co 5:5	the sinful *n* may be destroyed
Gal 5:16	the desires of the sinful *n*
Php 2:6	Who, being in very *n* God,
Col 2:11	putting off of the sinful *n*,
2Pe 1:4	participate in the divine *n*

Nazarene

Mt 2:23	"He will be called a *N*.
Mk 14:67	"You also were with that *N*, Jesus,
16:6	"You are looking for Jesus the *N*,

Nazareth

Mt 2:23	lived in a town called *N*.
Mk 1:24	do you want with us, Jesus of *N*?
Lk 18:37	"Jesus of *N* is passing by.
Jn 1:46	"*N*! Can anything good come

Nazirite

Nu 6:2	of separation to the LORD as a *N*,
Jdg 13:7	boy will be a *N* of God from birth

Nebuchadnezzar

King of Babylon. Defeated Egyptians at Carchemish (Jer 46:2); invaded and subdued Judah; took exiles to Babylon; destroyed Jerusalem (2Ki 24–25; 2Ch 36; Jer 39; Da 1:1–5). Dreams interpreted by Daniel (Da 2; 4); fiery furnace (Da 3); madness and restoration; worshipped God (Da 3:28–29; 4:34–35).

necessary

Ac 1:21	it is *n* to choose one of the men
Php 1:24	it is more *n* for you that I remain
Heb 9:16	In the case of a will, it is *n*
9:23	It was *n*, then, for the copies

Neco

Pharaoh. Reluctantly fought and killed Josiah, who opposed support for Assyria (2Ki 23:29–30; 2Ch 35:20–25). Deposed Jehoahaz, appointed Jehoiakim as vassal (2Ki 23:31–35; 2Ch 36:2–4). Defeated by Nebuchadnezzar at Carchemish (Jer 46:2).

need, -s, -ed, -y

Ps 40:17	Yet I am poor and *n-y*;
Pr 14:21	he who is kind to the *n-y*
Isa 11:4	will judge the *n-y*,
58:11	he will satisfy your *n-s*
Am 8:6	the *n-y* for a pair of sandals,
Mt 6:2	"So when you give to the *n-y*,
6:8	your Father knows what you *n*
Ac 2:45	they gave to anyone as he had *n*
17:25	as if he *n-ed* anything,
Ro 12:8	contributing to the *n-s* of others,
1Co 12:21	say to the hand, "I don't *n* you!"
Eph 4:28	something to share with those in *n*
Php 4:19	my God will meet all your *n-s*
1Jn 3:17	sees his brother in *n* and has no

needle

Mt 19:24	eye of a *n* than for a rich man

neglect, -ed

SS 1:6	my own vineyard I have *n-ed*
Mt 23:23	you have *n-ed* the more important

Ac 6:2 to *n* the ministry of the word
1Ti 4:14 Do not *n* your gift,

Nehemiah

Cupbearer to Artaxerxes (Ne 1:10). Prayed over state of Jerusalem (Ne 1); allowed to return to rebuild city walls (Ne 2–6); appointed governor (Ne 5:14; 8:9). Called Ezra to read Law (Ne 8); confessed nation's sin (Ne 9); dedicated wall (12:27–47); made other reforms (Ne 13).

neighbour, -'s

Ex 20:16 false testimony against your *n*
20:17 not covet your *n-'s* house.
Lev 19:18 love your *n* as yourself.
Jer 31:34 No longer will a man teach his *n*,
Mt 5:43 'Love your *n* and hate your enemy.
19:19 'love your *n* as yourself.'
Lk 10:29 he asked Jesus, "And who is my *n*?
Ro 13:10 Love does no harm to its *n*.
Gal 5:14 "Love your *n* as yourself."
Heb 8:11 No longer will a man teach his *n*,

net, -s

Mt 4:20 At once they left their *n-s*
13:47 kingdom of heaven is like a *n*
Jn 21:6 "Throw your *n* on the right side

new

Ps 40:3 He put a *n* song in my mouth,
90:5 like the *n* grass of the morning
96:1 Sing to the LORD a *n* song;
Ecc 1:9 there is nothing *n* under the sun
Isa 43:19 See, I am doing a *n* thing!
65:17 create *n* heavens and a new earth.
Jer 31:31 "when I will make a *n* covenant
Eze 11:19 put a *n* spirit in them;
36:26 I will give you a *n* heart
Mt 9:17 pour *n* wine into old wineskins.
Lk 22:20 "This cup is the *n* covenant
Jn 13:34 "A *n* command I give you:
1Co 11:25 "This cup is the *n* covenant
2Co 5:17 in Christ, he is a *n* creation;
Gal 6:15 what counts is a *n* creation
Eph 4:24 put on the *n* self, created to be
Heb 8:8 I will make a *n* covenant
9:15 the mediator of a *n* covenant,
2Pe 3:13 to a *n* heaven and a new earth,
1Jn 2:8 I am writing you a *n* command;
Rev 21:1 I saw a *n* heaven and a *n* earth,
21:2 the Holy City, the *n* Jerusalem,
21:5 "I am making everything *n*!"

newborn

1Pe 2:2 Like *n* babies, crave pure

news

2Ki 7:9 This is a day of good *n*
Pr 15:30 good *n* gives health to the bones.
Isa 52:7 feet of those who bring good *n*,
61:1 anointed me to preach good *n*
Mt 4:23 the good *n* of the kingdom,
Mk 1:14 proclaiming the good *n* of God
1:15 Repent and believe the good *n*!"
Lk 2:10 I bring you good *n* of great joy
Ac 17:18 *n* about Jesus and the resurrection
Ro 10:15 feet of those who bring good *n*!

Nicodemus

Pharisee, member of Sanhedrin who visited Jesus at night (Jn 3:1–15). Argued against condemning Jesus without a hearing (Jn 7:50–51). With Joseph anointed and buried Jesus (Jn 19:38–42).

night, -s

Ge 1:5 the darkness he called "*n*".
7:4 for forty days and forty *n-s*,
Ex 13:21 and by *n* in a pillar of fire
34:28 forty *n-s* without eating bread
1Ki 19:8 forty *n-s* until he reached Horeb,
Ps 1:2 on his law he meditates day and *n*
19:2 *n* after night they display
30:5 weeping may remain for a *n*,
90:4 or like a watch in the *n*
121:6 harm you by day, nor the moon by *n*
Mt 4:2 and forty *n-s*, he was hungry
12:40 and three *n-s* in the belly
24:43 time of *n* the thief was coming,
Lk 12:20 This very *n* your life will be
Jn 3:2 He came to Jesus at *n* and said,
1Co 11:23 Jesus, on the *n* he was betrayed,
2Co 6:5 hard work, sleepless *n-s* and hunger

1Th 2:9	we worked *n* and day in order not
5:2	will come like a thief in the *n*
2Ti 1:3	*n* and day I constantly remember
Rev 14:11	There is no rest day or *n* for
22:5	There will be no more *n*.

Nineveh

Jnh 1:2	"Go to the great city of *N*
Mt 12:41	*N* will stand up at the judgment

Noah

Righteous man (Ge 6:8–9; 7:1; Eze 14:14,20; Heb 11:7). Obeyed God's command to build ark (Ge 6:11–22). God's covenant with (Ge 6:18; 9:8–17). Planted vineyard; became drunk, dishonoured by Ham (Ge 9:20–23); cursed Canaan; blessed Shem and Japheth (Ge 9:24–27). Death (Ge 9:28–29).

noble

Pr 31:10	A wife of *n* character who can find?
Ac 17:11	Bereans were of more *n* character
Ro 9:21	some pottery for *n* purposes
1Co 1:26	not many were of *n* birth
Php 4:8	whatever is true, whatever is *n*,

nothing

Job 1:9	"Does Job fear God for *n*?"
Ps 34:9	for those who fear him lack *n*
49:17	will take *n* with him when he dies,
73:25	earth has *n* I desire besides you
Ecc 1:9	there is *n* new under the sun
Isa 40:17	all the nations are as *n*;
53:2	*n* in his appearance that we should
Jer 32:17	*N* is too hard for you
La 1:12	"Is it *n* to you, all you who
Mt 10:26	There is *n* concealed that will not
Lk 1:37	For *n* is impossible with God.
23:41	But this man has done *n* wrong.
Jn 1:3	without him *n* was made that has
1:47	in whom there is *n* false.
6:63	the flesh counts for *n*.
15:5	apart from me you can do *n*.
Ac 20:24	I consider my life worth *n* to me,
Ro 7:18	I know that *n* good lives in me,
1Co 2:2	know *n* while I was with you except
13:2	but have not love, I am *n*
Php 2:7	made himself *n*, taking the very
1Ti 6:7	For we brought *n* into the world,
Heb 4:13	*N* in all creation is hidden
Rev 21:27	*N* impure will ever enter it,

nullify

Mt 15:6	Thus you *n* the word of God
Ro 3:31	*n* the law by this faith?
1Co 1:28	to *n* the things that are

numerous

Ge 22:17	as *n* as the stars in the sky
Heb 11:12	as *n* as the stars in the sky

nurse, -ing, -d

Ex 2:7	Hebrew women to *n* the baby for you?
Mt 24:19	pregnant women and *n-ing* mothers
Lk 11:27	who gave you birth and *n-d* you.
23:29	the breasts that never *n-d*!

O

oath

Ex 33:1	the land I promised on *o* to Abraham
1Ch 16:16	the *o* he swore to Isaac
Ps 95:11	So I declared on *o* in my anger,
132:11	The LORD swore an *o* to David,
Mt 5:33	long ago, 'Do not break your *o*,
23:16	the temple, he is bound by his *o*.
26:72	He denied it again, with an *o*:
Lk 1:73	*o* he swore to our father Abraham

Obadiah

1. Official in charge of Ahab's palace; believer; hid 100 prophets from Jezebel (1Ki 18:1–16). **2.** Prophet; spoke against Edom (Ob 1).

obedient, -nce

Lk 2:51	with them and was *o* to them.
Ac 6:7	priests became *o* to the faith
Ro 1:5	to the *o-nce* that comes from faith

Php 2:8 he humbled himself and became *o*
Heb 5:8 a son, he learned *o-nce* from what
1Pe 1:14 As *o* children, do not conform to

obey, -ing, -ed

Ex 12:24 "*O* these instructions as a lasting
Lev 18:4 You must *o* my laws and be careful
Dt 11:32 be sure that you *o* all the decrees
28:2 if you *o* the LORD your God:
Jos 1:7 Be careful to *o* all the law
1Sa 15:22 To *o* is better than sacrifice,
2Ki 18:12 because they had not *o-ed* the LORD
Ps 119:57 I have promised to *o* your words
Mt 8:27 Even the winds and the waves *o* him!
19:17 to enter life, *o* the commandments.
28:20 to *o* everything I have commanded
Mk 1:27 orders to evil spirits and they *o*
Jn 14:15 "If you love me, you will *o* what I
17:6 and they have *o-ed* your word.
Ac 5:29 "We must *o* God rather than men!"
5:32 whom God has given to those who *o*
Ro 2:13 but it is those who *o* the law
6:12 so that you *o* its evil desires
6:17 you wholeheartedly *o-ed* the form of
Gal 5:7 and kept you from *o-ing* the truth
Eph 6:1 Children, *o* your parents
Heb 5:9 eternal salvation for all who *o* him
13:17 *O* your leaders and submit
1Jn 5:3 love for God: to *o* his commands.

observe, -ing

Ex 31:13 'You must *o* my Sabbaths.
Ps 37:37 the blameless, *o* the upright;
Mk 7:4 And they *o* many other traditions,
Ro 3:28 justified by faith apart from *o-ing*

obsolete

Heb 8:13 he has made the first one *o*;

obstinate

Isa 65:2 held out my hands to an *o* people,
Ac 19:9 But some of them became *o*;
Ro 10:21 hands to a disobedient and *o* people

obtain, -ed

Jn 5:44 yet make no effort to *o* the praise
Ro 9:30 pursue righteousness, have *o-ed* it,
11:7 sought so earnestly it did not *o*,
Php 3:12 Not that I have already *o-ed* all
2Ti 2:10 that they too may *o* the salvation
Heb 9:12 having *o-ed* eternal redemption

obvious

Mt 6:18 so that it will not be *o* to men
Gal 5:19 The acts of the sinful nature are *o*
1Ti 5:24 The sins of some men are *o*,
5:25 In the same way, good deeds are *o*,

offence, -s

Pr 17:9 who covers over an *o* promotes love,
19:11 it is to his glory to overlook an *o*
Isa 44:22 I have swept away your *o-s*
Mt 13:57 they took *o* at him. But Jesus said
Gal 5:11 the *o* of the cross

offend, -ed, -ers

Pr 18:19 An *o-ed* brother is more unyielding
Mt 15:12 Pharisees were *o-ed* when they heard
Jn 6:61 said to them, "Does this *o* you?
1Co 6:9 prostitutes nor homosexual *o-ers*

offensive

Job 19:17 My breath is *o* to my wife;
Ps 139:24 See if there is any *o* way in me,
Jer 6:10 The word of the LORD is *o* to them;

offer, -ing, -ings, -ed

Ge 8:20 he sacrificed burnt *o-ings* on it
22:7 is the lamb for the burnt *o-ing*?
31:54 He *o-ed* a sacrifice there
2Sa 24:24 burnt *o-ings* that cost me nothing.
Ps 4:5 *O* right sacrifices and trust
40:6 Sacrifice and *o-ing* you did not
51:16 not take pleasure in burnt *o-ings*
Isa 1:13 Stop bringing meaningless *o-ings*!
53:10 LORD makes his life a guilt *o-ing*,
Hos 14:2 that we may *o* the fruit of our lips
Mal 3:8 we rob you?' "In tithes and *o-ings*
Mt 5:23 if you are *o-ing* your gift
26:27 gave thanks and *o-ed* it to them,
27:34 There they *o-ed* Jesus wine to drink
Ro 6:13 Do not *o* the parts of your body
12:1 *o* your bodies as living sacrifices,
15:16 become an *o-ing* acceptable to God,
1Co 9:18 gospel I may *o* it free of charge,
10:20 of pagans are *o-ed* to demons,
Eph 5:2 fragrant *o-ing* and sacrifice to God
Php 2:17 poured out like a drink *o-ing*
4:18 They are a fragrant *o-ing*,
2Ti 4:6 being poured out like a drink *o-ing*
Heb 5:1 to *o* gifts and sacrifices for sins
5:7 he *o-ed* up prayers and petitions
7:27 once for all when he *o-ed* himself
9:14 who through the eternal Spirit *o-ed*
10:5 he said: "Sacrifice and *o-ing*
13:15 continually *o* to God a sacrifice
Jas 2:21 he *o-ed* his son Isaac on the altar
5:15 And the prayer *o-ed* in faith

officer

1Sa 29:3 David, who was an *o* of Saul
2Ki 3:11 An *o* of the king of Israel answered
1Ch 26:24 the *o* in charge of the treasuries
Mt 5:25 judge may hand you over to the *o*,
2Ti 2:4 he wants to please his commanding *o*

offspring

Ge 3:15 and between your *o* and hers;
12:7 "To your *o* I will give this land.
21:12 it is through Isaac that your *o*
Ac 17:29 "Therefore since we are God's *o*,
Ro 9:7 "It is through Isaac that your *o*
Heb 11:18 "It is through Isaac that your *o*
Rev 22:16 I am the Root and the *O* of David,

Oholiab

See *Bezalel*.

oil

Ex 29:7 Take the anointing *o* and anoint him
1Sa 16:13 took the horn of *o* and anointed him
1Ki 1:39 Zadok the priest took the horn of *o*
17:16 and the jug of *o* did not run dry,
Ps 23:5 You anoint my head with *o*;
45:7 by anointing you with the *o* of joy
89:20 my sacred *o* I have anointed him
133:2 like precious *o* poured on the head,
Mt 6:17 when you fast, put *o* on your head
25:4 The wise, however, took *o* in jars
Mk 6:13 anointed many sick people with *o*
Lk 7:46 You did not put *o* on my head,
10:34 bandaged his wounds, pouring on *o*
Jas 5:14 pray over him and anoint him with *o*

olive, -s

Ge 8:11 was a freshly plucked *o* leaf!
Ps 52:8 But I am like an *o* tree flourishing
Zec 14:4 feet will stand on the Mount of *O-s*
Mt 24:3 was sitting on the Mount of *O-s*,

Jn 18:26	I see you with him in the *o* grove?
Ac 1:12	the hill called the Mount of *O-s*,
Ro 11:17	and you, though a wild *o* shoot,
Jas 3:12	brothers, can a fig-tree bear *o-s*,

Omega

Rev 1:8	"I am the Alpha and the *O*,"
21:6	I am the Alpha and the *O*,

Omri

King of Israel; father of Ahab (1Ki 16:30). Army commander, appointed king after Zimri assassinated Baasha (1Ki 16:15–28). Sinned against God (1Ki 16:25–26).

one

Ge 2:24	and they will become *o* flesh
11:1	Now the whole world had *o* language
Dt 6:4	The LORD our God, the LORD is *o*
Ps 27:4	*O* thing I ask of the LORD,
Ecc 4:9	Two are better than *o*,
Isa 40:26	brings out the starry host *o* by *o*
43:15	I am the LORD, your Holy *O*,
47:4	is the Holy *O* of Israel
Eze 34:23	I will place over them *o* shepherd,
37:17	Join them together into *o* stick
39:7	I the LORD am the Holy *O* in Israel
Mt 19:17	"There is only *O* who is good.
Mk 12:29	the Lord our God, the Lord is *o*.
15:27	*o* on his right and *o* on his left
Lk 23:35	the Christ of God, the Chosen *O*.
Jn 1:18	but God the *O* and Only,
6:69	you are the Holy *O* of God.
17:22	that they may be *o* as we are *o*
19:36	Not *o* of his bones will be broken,
Ac 1:17	he was *o* of our number
3:14	the Holy and Righteous *O*
4:32	*o* in heart and mind.
13:35	not let your Holy *O* see decay.
17:26	From *o* man he made every nation
Ro 5:15	the trespass of the *o* man,
12:5	we who are many form *o* body,
1Co 10:17	Because there is *o* loaf,
12:13	baptised by *o* Spirit
12:20	many parts, but *o* body
12:26	If *o* part suffers,
2Co 5:14	*o* died for all, and therefore all
Gal 3:28	for you are all *o* in Christ Jesus.
Eph 2:15	*o* new man out of the two,
4:4	*o* body and *o* Spirit—
4:5	*o* Lord, *o* faith, *o* baptism
4:6	*o* God and Father of all,
5:31	and the two will become *o* flesh."
Php 2:2	*o* in spirit and purpose
3:13	But *o* thing I do:
1Th 5:24	The *o* who calls you is faithful
1Ti 2:5	there is *o* God and *o* mediator
Heb 11:17	to sacrifice his *o* and only son
1Jn 2:20	anointing from the Holy *O*,
Rev 11:17	the *O* who is and who was,

Onesimus

Runaway slave belonging to Philemon; converted by Paul and dear to him (Col 4:9; Phm 10–16).

open, -s, -ed

Ge 3:7	the eyes of both of them were *o-ed*,
30:22	listened to her and *o-ed* her womb
1Ki 8:29	your eyes be *o* towards this temple
Ps 51:15	O Lord, *o* my lips,
81:10	*O* wide your mouth and I will fill
119:18	*O* my eyes that I may see
Pr 31:20	She *o-s* her arms to the poor
Mt 7:7	and the door will be *o-ed* to you
13:35	"I will *o* my mouth in parables,
Lk 10:38	Martha *o-ed* her home to him
24:31	eyes were *o-ed* and they recognised
24:45	Then he *o-ed* their minds
Jn 9:10	"How then were your eyes *o-ed*?"
Ac 7:56	I see heaven *o* and the Son of Man
10:11	He saw heaven *o-ed*
16:14	The Lord *o-ed* her heart to respond
26:18	to *o* their eyes and turn them
Ro 3:13	"Their throats are *o* graves;
2Co 2:12	the Lord had *o-ed* a door for me

Col 4:3 God may *o* a door for our message,
Heb 10:20 a new and living way *o-ed* for us
Rev 3:20 hears my voice and *o-s* the door,
5:2 to break the seals and *o* the scroll

opinions
1Ki 18:21 will you waver between two *o*?
Pr 18:2 but delights in airing his own *o*

opportunity
Mt 26:16 Judas watched for an *o*
Ro 7:8 But sin, seizing the *o*
Gal 6:10 as we have *o*, let us do good
Eph 5:16 making the most of every *o*,
Col 4:5 make the most of every *o*
1Ti 5:14 to give the enemy no *o* for slander

oppose, -s
Mk 3:26 And if Satan *o-s* himself
Ac 11:17 was I to think that I could *o* God?
Jas 4:6 God *o-s* the proud but gives grace
1Pe 5:5 God *o-s* the proud but gives grace

opposition
Nu 16:42 gathered in *o* to Moses and Aaron
20:2 the people gathered in *o* to Moses
Ac 6:9 *O* arose, however, from members
1Th 2:2 his gospel in spite of strong *o*
Heb 12:3 who endured such *o* from sinful men,

oppress, -ed, -ion
Ex 1:11 slave masters over them to *o* them
23:9 "Do not *o* an alien;
1Ch 16:21 He allowed no man to *o* them;
Ps 82:3 the rights of the poor and *o-ed*
Isa 53:7 He was *o-ed* and afflicted,
Lk 4:18 for the blind, to release the *o-ed*
Ac 7:34 the *o-ion* of my people in Egypt.

ordained
Lev 21:10 *o* to wear the priestly garments,
Nu 3:3 who were *o* to serve as priests
Ps 8:2 and infants you have *o* praise
139:16 All the days *o* for me were written
Isa 37:26 Have you not heard? Long ago I *o* it
Mt 21:16 and infants you have *o* praise'?

order, -s, -ly
Ex 1:22 Then Pharaoh gave this *o* to all
Job 38:12 you ever given *o-s* to the morning,
Ps 110:4 for ever, in the *o* of Melchizedek.
Isa 38:1 the LORD says: Put your house in *o*,
Mt 2:16 he gave *o-s* to kill all the boys
Mk 9:9 Jesus gave them *o-s* not to tell
Lk 1:3 to write an *o-ly* account for you,
4:36 he gives *o-s* to evil spirits
11:25 the house swept clean and put in *o*
Ac 5:28 We gave you strict *o-s* not to teach
1Co 14:40 be done in a fitting and *o-ly* way
Col 2:5 and delight to see how *o-ly* you are
Heb 5:6 for ever, in the *o* of Melchizedek.
Rev 21:4 the old *o* of things has passed away

orgies
Ro 13:13 not in *o* and drunkenness,
Gal 5:21 envy; drunkenness, *o*, and the like.
1Pe 4:3 lust, drunkenness, *o*, carousing

origin, -s
Mic 5:2 whose *o-s* are from of old,
Ac 5:38 purpose or activity is of human *o*,
2Pe 1:21 For prophecy never had its *o*

orphan, -s
Ex 22:22 advantage of a widow or an *o*
Jer 49:11 Leave your *o-s*; I will protect
Jn 14:18 I will not leave you as *o-s*;

Jas 1:27 to look after *o-s* and widows

outcome
Da 12:8 what will the *o* of all this be?
Heb 13:7 Consider the *o* of their way of life
1Pe 4:17 the *o* be for those who do not obey

outsiders
Col 4:5 wise in the way you act towards *o*;
1Th 4:12 may win the respect of *o*
1Ti 3:7 a good reputation with *o*,

outstanding
SS 5:10 *o* among ten thousand
Da 5:14 insight, intelligence and *o* wisdom
Ac 4:16 they have done an *o* miracle,
Ro 13:8 Let no debt remain *o*, except
16:7 They are *o* among the apostles,

outstretched
Ex 6:6 I will redeem you with an *o* arm
Dt 4:34 by a mighty hand and an *o* arm,
1Ki 8:42 your mighty hand and your *o* arm—
Ps 136:12 with a mighty hand and *o* arm;
Jer 27:5 With my great power and *o* arm

outward, -ly
1Sa 16:7 Man looks at the *o* appearance,
Ro 2:28 not a Jew if he is only one *o-ly*,
2Co 4:16 Though *o-ly* we are wasting away,
Gal 6:12 to make a good impression *o-ly*
1Pe 3:3 should not come from *o* adornment,

outweighs
Ecc 10:1 a little folly *o* wisdom and honour
2Co 4:17 eternal glory that far *o* them all

overbearing
Tit 1:7 he must be blameless—not *o*,

overboard
Jnh 1:15 they took Jonah and threw him *o*,
Ac 27:18 they began to throw the cargo *o*

overcome, -s, -came
Ge 32:28 with God and with men and have *o*.
Hos 12:4 with the angel and *o-came* him;
Mt 16:18 the gates of Hades will not *o* it
Mk 9:24 I do believe; help me *o* my unbelief
Jn 16:33 But take heart! I have *o* the world.
Ro 12:21 but *o* evil with good
1Jn 2:13 because you have *o* the evil one.
5:4 victory that has *o* the world, even
Rev 2:7 To him who *o-s*, I will give the
12:11 *o-came* him by the blood of the Lamb

overflow, -s
Ps 23:5 anoint my head with oil; my cup *o-s*
119:171 May my lips *o* with praise,
Mt 12:34 For out of the *o* of the heart
Ro 15:13 so that you may *o* with hope by
2Co 1:5 through Christ our comfort *o-s*
1Th 3:12 Lord make your love increase and *o*

overjoyed
Mt 2:10 When they saw the star, they were *o*
Jn 20:20 The disciples were *o* when they saw
1Pe 4:13 may be *o* when his glory is revealed

overseer, -s
Ac 20:28 the Holy Spirit has made you *o-s*.
1Ti 3:1 sets his heart on being an *o*,
Tit 1:7 an *o* is entrusted with God's work,
1Pe 2:25 to the Shepherd and *O* of your souls
5:2 under your care, serving as *o-s*—

overshadow, -ing
Ex 25:20 *o-ing* the cover with them.
Lk 1:35 power of the Most High will *o* you.

Heb 9:5	*o-ing* the atonement cover.

overthrow, -n

Ge 19:21	I will not *o* the town you speak of
2Ch 25:8	God will *o* you before the enemy,
Pr 12:7	Wicked men are *o-n* and are no more,
Jer 1:10	tear down, to destroy and *o*,
2Th 2:8	whom the Lord Jesus will *o*

overwhelm, -ed

Ps 18:4	the torrents of destruction *o-ed* me
38:4	My guilt has *o-ed* me like a burden
SS 6:5	Turn your eyes from me; they *o* me.
Mt 26:38	"My soul is *o-ed* with sorrow
2Co 2:7	not be *o-ed* by excessive sorrow

owe, -d

Mt 18:28	who *o-d* him a hundred denarii.
Lk 16:5	'How much do you *o* my master?
Ro 13:7	Give everyone what you *o* him:
Phm :19	you *o* me your very self

ox

Dt 25:4	Do not muzzle an *o*
Isa 1:3	The *o* knows his master,
11:7	the lion will eat straw like the *o*
Eze 1:10	and on the left the face of an *o*;
Lk 13:15	on the Sabbath untie his *o*
1Co 9:9	Law of Moses: "Do not muzzle an *o*
1Ti 5:18	"Do not muzzle the *o*
Rev 4:7	the second was like an *o*,

P

pagan, -s

Mt 6:7	do not keep on babbling like *p-s*,
6:32	the *p-s* run after all these things,
18:17	treat him as you would a *p*
1Co 5:1	that does not occur even among *p-s*:
12:2	You know that when you were *p-s*,
1Pe 2:12	Live such good lives among the *p-s*

paid

Zec 11:12	they *p* me thirty pieces of silver
Mt 5:26	until you have *p* the last penny

pain, -s, -ful

Ge 3:16	increase your *p-s* in childbearing;
6:6	and his heart was filled with *p*
Ps 38:7	My back is filled with searing *p*;
Ro 8:22	as in the *p-s* of childbirth
2Co 2:1	another *p-ful* visit to you
Gal 4:19	am again in the *p-s* of childbirth
Rev 21:4	death or mourning or crying or *p*,

palace

2Sa 5:11	and they built a *p* for David
7:2	Here I am, living in a *p* of cedar,
2Ch 2:12	a temple for the LORD and a *p*
Ps 45:15	they enter the *p* of the king
Jer 22:5	that this *p* will become a ruin.'
22:13	builds his *p* by unrighteousness
Da 1:4	qualified to serve in the king's *p*.
4:29	the roof of the royal *p* of Babylon
Mk 15:16	led Jesus away into the *p*
Php 1:13	throughout the whole *p* guard

pale

Jer 30:6	every face turned deathly *p*
Da 5:6	His face turned *p*
Rev 6:8	and there before me was a *p* horse!

palm, -s

Dt 34:3	Jericho, the City of *P-s*,
Isa 49:16	I have engraved you on the *p-s*
Jn 12:13	They took *p* branches and went out
Rev 7:9	holding *p* branches in their hands

parable, -s

Ps 78:2	I will open my mouth in *p-s*,
Mt 13:3	he told them many things in *p-s*,

13:35 “I will open my mouth in *p-s*,
Mk 4:13 “Don’t you understand this *p*?

paradise
Lk 23:43 today you will be with me in *p*.
2Co 12:4 was caught up to *p*.
Rev 2:7 the tree of life, which is in the *p*

paralytic
Mt 9:2 Some men brought to him a *p*,
Ac 9:33 Aeneas, a *p* who had been bedridden

pardon, -s
2Ch 30:18 the LORD, who is good, *p* everyone
Isa 55:7 for he will freely *p*
Mic 7:18 Who is a God like you, who *p-s* sin

parents
Mt 10:21 children will rebel against their *p*
Lk 2:41 Every year his *p* went to Jerusalem
21:16 You will be betrayed even by *p*,
Jn 9:3 Neither this man nor his *p* sinned,
Eph 6:1 obey your *p* in the Lord,
2Ti 3:2 disobedient to their *p*,

partake
1Co 10:17 for we all *p* of the one loaf

partiality
Lev 19:15 do not show *p* to the poor
Dt 1:17 Do not show *p* in judging;
16:19 Do not pervert justice or show *p*.
2Ch 19:7 no injustice or *p* or bribery.
Job 34:19 who shows no *p* to princes
1Ti 5:21 keep these instructions without *p*,

participate, -ion
1Co 10:16 a *p-ion* in the blood of Christ?
1Pe 4:13 you *p* in the sufferings of Christ,
2Pe 1:4 you may *p* in the divine nature

partner, -s, -ship
Pr 2:17 who has left the *p* of her youth
2Co 8:23 my *p* and fellow-worker among you;
Eph 5:7 Therefore do not be *p-s* with them
Php 1:5 your *p-ship* in the gospel
1Pe 3:7 with respect as the weaker *p*

pass, -ing, -ed
Ex 12:13 I see the blood, I will *p* over you.
34:6 And he *p-ed* in front of Moses,
Ps 84:6 they *p* through the Valley of Baca
90:9 our days *p* away under your wrath;
Isa 43:2 When you *p* through the waters,
La 1:12 Is it nothing to you, all you who *p*
Mt 24:35 but my words will never *p* away
27:39 Those who *p-ed* by hurled insults
Lk 10:31 he *p-ed* by on the other side
18:37 “Jesus of Nazareth is *p-ing* by.
Ro 15:24 to visit you while *p-ing* through
1Co 10:1 they all *p-ed* through the sea
13:8 there is knowledge, it will *p* away
15:3 what I received I *p-ed* on to you
Jas 1:10 he will *p* away like a wild flower
1Jn 3:14 we have *p-ed* from death to life,
Rev 21:4 old order of things has *p-ed* away.

passion, -s, -ate
Ro 7:5 the sinful *p-s* aroused by the law
1Co 7:9 better to marry than to burn with *p*
Gal 5:24 the sinful nature with its *p-s*
1Th 4:5 not in *p-ate* lust like the heathen,
Tit 2:12 to ungodliness and worldly *p-s*
3:3 enslaved by all kinds of *p-s*

Passover
Ex 12:11 Eat it in haste; it is the LORD’s *P*
Jos 5:10 the Israelites celebrated the *P*
Ezr 6:19 the exiles celebrated the *P*
Mt 26:2 As you know, the *P* is two days away
Jn 6:4 The Jewish *P* Feast was near

1Co 5:7	Christ, our *P* lamb,

past

SS 2:11	The winter is *p*; the rains are over
Isa 43:18	do not dwell on the *p*
Ro 16:25	the mystery hidden for long ages *p*
Heb 1:1	In the *p* God spoke

pastors

Eph 4:11	and some to be *p* and teachers

pasture, -s

Ps 23:2	He makes me lie down in green *p-s*,
95:7	and we are the people of his *p*,
Eze 34:14	I will tend them in a good *p*,
Jn 10:9	will come in and go out, and find *p*

patch

Jer 10:5	Like a scarecrow in a melon *p*,
Mt 9:16	"No-one sews a *p* of unshrunk cloth

path, -s

Ps 16:11	made known to me the *p* of life;
23:3	guides me in *p-s* of righteousness
25:4	O LORD, teach me your *p-s*
Isa 2:3	so that we may walk in his *p-s*."
Jer 6:16	ask for the ancient *p-s*,
Ac 2:28	made known to me the *p-s* of life;
Ro 11:33	and his *p-s* beyond tracing out
Heb 12:13	"Make level *p-s* for your feet,"

patient, -ly, -nce

Ps 40:1	I waited *p-ly* for the LORD;
Pr 14:29	A *p* man has great understanding,
Isa 7:13	Will you try the *p-nce* of my God
Ro 2:4	his kindness, tolerance and *p-nce*,
8:25	we wait for it *p-ly*
1Co 13:4	Love is *p*, love is kind.
Gal 5:22	fruit of the Spirit is ... *p-nce*,
Eph 4:2	be *p*, bearing with one another
1Th 5:14	help the weak, be *p* with everyone.
Jas 5:7	Be then, brothers, until the
1Pe 3:20	God waited *p-ly* in the days of Noah
2Pe 3:15	our Lord's *p-nce* means salvation,
Rev 13:10	This calls for *p* endurance

pattern

Ex 25:40	the *p* shown you on the mountain
Ro 5:14	Adam, who was a *p* of the one
12:2	any longer to the *p* of this world,
Php 3:17	live according to the *p* we gave you
2Ti 1:13	keep as the *p* of sound teaching,
Heb 8:5	the *p* shown you on the mountain.

Paul

Apostle (Gal 1:1); also called Saul (Ac 13:9). From Tarsus (Ac 9:11; 21:39; 22:3; Php 3:5); Pharisee (Ac 23:6; 26:5; Php 3:5); taught by Gamaliel (Ac 22:3).

Approved of Stephen's death (Ac 7:58; 8:1); persecuted church (Ac 8:3; 9:1–2; 1Co 15:9; Gal 1:13). Saw Jesus on Damascus road (Ac 9:3–9; 22:6–11; 26:12–18); healed and baptised by Ananias (Ac 9:17–19; 22:12–16). Into Arabia (Gal 1:17); escaped from Damascus in a basket (Ac 9:23–25; 2Co 11:32–33). Introduced to apostles in Jerusalem by Barnabas; sent to Tarsus (Ac 9:26–30; Gal 1:18–21).

Brought to Antioch by Barnabas (Ac 11:22–26). Visited Jerusalem; message and commission confirmed by apostles (Ac 11:30; Gal 2:1–10). First missionary journey, with Barnabas, (Ac 13–14). Stoned at Lystra (Ac 14:19–20). At Council of Jerusalem (Ac 15). Disagreed with Barnabas over Mark (Ac 15:36–39). Second missionary journey, with Silas (Ac 15:40–18:22). Called to Macedonia (Ac 16:9–10); miraculously released from prison in Philippi (Ac 16:16–40); in Athens (Ac 17:16–34); in Corinth (Ac 18). Third missionary journey (Ac 18:23). In Ephesus (Ac 19); raised Eutychus to life (Ac 20:7–12); farewell to Ephesian elders (Ac 20:13–37). Travelled to Jerusalem (Ac 21); arrested (Ac 21:27–36); appealed as Roman citizen (Ac 22:25–29); before Sanhedrin (Ac 22:30–23:10). Taken to Caesarea (Ac 23:12–35); before Felix, Festus and Agrippa

(Ac 24–26). Journeyed to Rome (Ac 27–28); shipwrecked on Malta (Ac 27:27–28:10); under house arrest in Rome; preached gospel (Ac 28:16–31).
Letters: Romans, 1 & 2 Corinthians, Galatians, Ephesians, Philippians, Colossians, 1 & 2 Thessalonians, 1 & 2 Timothy, Titus, Philemon.

pay, -ment

Ge 23:13	I will *p* the price of the field.
Ex 30:12	*p* the LORD a ransom for his life
Lev 26:43	They will *p* for their sins
Mt 17:24	your teacher *p* the temple tax?
18:34	until he should *p* back all he owed
20:2	He agreed to *p* them a denarius
22:17	Is it right to *p* taxes to Caesar
Lk 3:14	be content with your *p*.
19:8	I will *p* back four times the amount
23:2	opposes *p-ment* of taxes to Caesar
Ac 22:28	to *p* a big price for my citizenship
Ro 13:7	If you owe taxes, *p* taxes;

peace, -loving

Nu 6:26	his face towards you and give you *p*
Jdg 6:24	and called it The LORD is *P*.
1Ch 22:9	son who will be a man of *p*
Ps 29:11	the LORD blesses his people with *p*
37:37	there is a future for the man of *p*
119:165	Great *p* have they who love your law
122:6	Pray for the *p* of Jerusalem:
Isa 9:6	Everlasting Father, Prince of *P*
26:3	You will keep in perfect *p* him
48:22	"There is no *p* ... for the wicked.
Jer 6:14	'*P, p*,' they say, when there
Mt 10:34	I did not come to bring *p*,
Lk 2:14	and on earth *p* to men on whom
2:29	now dismiss your servant in *p*.
Jn 14:27	*P* I leave with you; my *p* I give
16:33	so that in me you may have *p*.
20:19	Jesus ... said, "*P* be with you!"
Ro 5:1	*p* with God through our Lord Jesus
8:6	by the Spirit is life and *p*;
12:18	live at *p* with everyone.
1Co 7:15	God has called us to live in *p*
Gal 5:22	love, joy, *p*, patience, kindness,
Eph 2:14	For he himself is our *p*,
6:15	that comes from the gospel of *p*.
Php 4:7	And the *p* of God, which transcends
Col 1:20	by making *p* through his blood,
3:15	Let the *p* of Christ rule in your
1Th 5:13	Live in *p* with each other
Heb 12:14	Make every effort to live in *p*
13:20	May the God of *p*, who through
Jas 3:17	first of all pure; then *p-loving*,
1Pe 3:11	he must seek *p* and pursue it

peacemakers

Mt 5:9	Blessed are the *p*,
Jas 3:18	*P* who sow in peace raise a harvest

pearl, -s

Mt 7:6	do not throw your *p-s* to pigs.
13:45	a merchant looking for fine *p-s*
1Ti 2:9	gold or *p-s* or expensive clothes
Rev 21:21	The twelve gates were twelve *p-s*,

peddle

2Co 2:17	we do not *p* the word of God

pen

Ps 45:1	tongue is the *p* of a skilful writer
Isa 8:1	and write on it with an ordinary *p*:
Mt 5:18	not the least stroke of a *p*,
3Jn :13	not want to do so with *p* and ink

penetrates

Heb 4:12	*p* even to dividing soul and spirit,

penny

Mt 5:26	until you have paid the last *p*
10:29	Are not two sparrows sold for a *p*?
Mk 12:42	worth only a fraction of a *p*

Pentecost

Ac 2:1	When the day of *P* came,
20:16	if possible, by the day of *P*

1Co 16:8 I will stay on at Ephesus until *P*

people, -s

Ge 12:1 "Leave your country, your *p*
49:33 and was gathered to his *p*
Ex 3:7 the misery of my *p* in Egypt.
7:16 Let my *p* go,
33:3 you are a stiff-necked *p*
Nu 22:11 'A *p* that has come out of Egypt
Dt 7:6 For you are a *p* holy to the LORD
32:9 For the LORD's portion is his *p*,
2Ki 15:29 and deported the *p* to Assyria
1Ch 17:21 And who is like your *p* Israel—
2Ch 2:11 "Because the LORD loves his *p*,
7:5 and all the *p* dedicated the temple
7:14 if my *p*, who are called by my name,
36:16 the LORD was aroused against his *p*
Ps 2:1 and the *p-s* plot in vain
28:8 The LORD is the strength of his *p*,
44:12 You sold your *p* for a pittance,
57:9 I will sing of you among the *p-s*
67:5 May the *p-s* praise you, O God;
77:14 display your power among the *p-s*
77:20 You led your *p* like a flock
94:14 For the LORD will not reject his *p*;
95:7 and we are the *p* of his pasture,
96:10 he will judge the *p-s* with equity
100:3 and we are his; we are his *p*,
111:9 He provided redemption for his *p*;
Pr 14:34 sin is a disgrace to any *p*
Isa 5:13 Therefore my *p* will go into exile
6:5 I live among a *p* of unclean lips,
6:10 Make the heart of this *p* calloused;
9:2 The *p* walking in darkness
11:12 he will assemble the scattered *p*
12:6 sing for joy, *p* of Zion,
29:13 "These *p* come near to me
40:1 Comfort, comfort my *p*,
40:7 Surely the *p* are grass
49:13 For the LORD comforts his *p*
52:6 Therefore my *p* will know my name;
53:8 for the transgression of my *p*
62:12 They will be called the Holy *P*,
Jer 4:22 "My *p* are fools; they do not know
4:25 I looked, and there were no *p*;
31:7 'O LORD, save your *p*, the remnant
32:38 They will be my *p*, and I will be
33:6 I will heal my *p*
Eze 39:7 my holy name among my *p* Israel.
Da 5:21 He was driven away from *p*
7:27 the *p* of the Most High.
11:32 but the *p* who know their God will
Hos 1:10 said to them, 'You are not my *p*',
2:23 will say to those called 'Not my *p*'
Am 9:14 I will bring back my exiled *p*
Hag 2:4 Be strong, all you *p* of the land,'
Zec 2:11 and will become my *p*.
Mk 5:20 And all the *p* were amazed
7:6 'These *p* honour me with their lips,
8:24 "I see *p*; they look like trees
10:13 *P* were bringing little children
Lk 1:17 to make ready a *p* prepared
1:68 he has come and has redeemed his *p*
2:10 joy that will be for all the *p*
Jn 11:50 that one man die for the *p*
Ac 7:3 'Leave your country and your *p*,'
7:51 "You stiff-necked *p*,
15:14 from the Gentiles a *p* for himself
18:10 because I have many *p* in this city.
28:26 " 'Go to this *p* and say,
Ro 10:21 to a disobedient and obstinate *p*.
11:1 Did God reject his *p*? By no means!
12:13 Share with God's *p* who are in need.
12:16 associate with *p* of low position.
15:10 "Rejoice, O Gentiles, with his *p*.
15:11 sing praises to him, all you *p-s*.

1Co 10:7	"The *p* sat down to eat and drink
2Co 4:15	reaching more and more *p*
6:16	and they will be my *p*.
Tit 2:14	a *p* that are his very own,
Heb 2:17	atonement for the sins of the *p*
4:9	a Sabbath-rest for the *p* of God
5:3	as well as for the sins of the *p*
10:30	"The Lord will judge his *p*.
13:12	to make the *p* holy
1Pe 2:9	But you are a chosen *p*,
2:10	but now you are the *p* of God;
2Pe 3:11	what kind of *p* ought you to be?
Rev 13:7	every tribe, *p*, language and nation
18:4	"Come out of her, my *p*,
21:3	They will be his *p*,

perceive, -ing

Ps 139:2	you *p* my thoughts from afar
Isa 6:9	be ever seeing, but never *p-ing*.
43:19	Now it springs up; do you not *p* it?
Mt 13:14	will be ever seeing but never *p-ing*
Ac 28:26	will be ever seeing but never *p-ing*

perfect, -ing, -ion, -er

Dt 32:4	He is the Rock, his works are *p*,
2Sa 22:31	"As for God, his way is *p*;
Ps 19:7	The law of the LORD is *p*,
Isa 26:3	You will keep in *p* peace
Mt 5:48	Be *p*, therefore,
Ro 12:2	his good, pleasing and *p* will
1Co 13:10	but when *p-ion* comes,
2Co 7:1	*p-ing* holiness out of reverence for
12:9	for my power is made *p* in weakness.
Php 3:12	or have already been made *p*, but
Col 1:28	we may present everyone *p* in Christ
Heb 7:19	(for the law made nothing *p*),
7:28	Son, who has been made *p* for ever
9:11	the greater and more *p* tabernacle
10:14	by one sacrifice he has made *p*
12:2	the author and *p-er* of our faith,
12:23	the spirits of righteous men made *p*

Jas 1:25	who looks intently into the *p* law
1Jn 4:18	But *p* love drives out fear,

perform, -s, -ed

Ex 3:20	all the wonders that I will *p*
1Ch 17:21	and to *p* great and awesome wonders
Ps 77:14	You are the God who *p-s* miracles;
Lk 1:51	has *p-ed* mighty deeds with his arm
Jn 3:2	no-one could *p* the miraculous signs

perfume

Ru 3:3	Wash and *p* yourself,
Ecc 7:1	A good name is better than fine *p*,
10:1	As dead flies give *p* a bad smell,
SS 1:3	your name is like *p* poured out.
Mt 26:7	alabaster jar of very expensive *p*,
Lk 7:46	but she has poured *p* on my feet

perish, -ing, -able

Ge 6:17	Everything on earth will *p*
Ps 1:6	but the way of the wicked will *p*
Lk 13:3	you repent, you too will all *p*.
21:18	But not a hair of your head will *p*
Jn 3:16	shall not *p* but have eternal life
10:28	and they shall never *p*;
1Co 1:18	foolishness to those who are *p-ing*,
15:42	The body that is sown is *p-able*,
2Co 4:3	it is veiled to those who are *p-ing*
2Pe 3:9	not wanting anyone to *p*,

perjurers

Mal 3:5	against sorcerers, adulterers and *p*
1Ti 1:10	for slave traders and liars and *p*—

permanent

Jn 8:35	slave has no *p* place in the family,
Heb 7:24	for ever, he has a *p* priesthood

permissible
1Co 6:12 "Everything is *p* for me"—but not
10:23 "Everything is *p*"—but not

permit, -ted
Mt 19:8 "Moses *p-ted* you to divorce
2Co 12:4 that man is not *p-ted* to tell
1Ti 2:12 I do not *p* a woman to teach

persecute, -d, -ion
Mt 5:10 Blessed are those who are *p-d*
5:44 and pray for those who *p* you
10:23 When you are *p-d* in one place,
13:21 or *p-ion* comes because of the word,
Jn 15:20 If they *p-d* me, they will *p* you
Ac 8:1 *p-ion* broke out against the church
9:4 "Saul, Saul, why do you *p* me?
22:4 I *p-d* the followers of this Way
Ro 8:35 Shall trouble or hardship or *p-ion*
12:14 Bless those who *p* you;
2Ti 3:12 life in Christ Jesus will be *p-d*,

persevere, -s, -ing, -ance
Lk 8:15 and by *p-ing* produce a crop
Ro 5:3 suffering produces *p-ance*
1Co 13:7 trusts, always hopes, always *p-s*
Heb 12:1 let us run with *p-ance* the race
Jas 1:12 Blessed is the man who *p-s*
Rev 2:2 your hard work and your *p-ance*.

persistence
Ro 2:7 who by *p* in doing good seek glory,

persuade, -d
Ac 17:4 Some of the Jews were *p-d*
26:28 you can *p* me to be a Christian?
2Co 5:11 we try to *p* men.

pervert, -s, -sion
Ex 23:2 do not *p* justice
Pr 17:23 to *p* the course of justice
Ro 1:27 the due penalty for their *p-sion*
Gal 1:7 trying to *p* the gospel of Christ
1Ti 1:10 for adulterers and *p-s*,
Jude :7 to sexual immorality and *p-sion*.

Peter
Name means "rock"; in Aramaic, Cephas (Jn 1:42). Apostle; brother of Andrew, also called Simon (Mt 4:18; Mk 1:16–18; Lk 5:3–11; Jn 1:40–42; Mt 10:2; Mk 3:16; Lk 6:14; Ac 1:13). With James and John, especially close to Jesus at raising of Jairus' daughter (Mk 5:37; Lk 8:51); transfiguration (Mt 17:1–2; Mk 9:2; Lk 9:28–29); in Gethsemane (Mt 26:36–38; Mk 14:32–34). Confessed Jesus as Christ (Mt 16:13–20; Mk 8:27–30; Lk 9:18–21). Caught fish with coin (Mt 17:24–27). Denial predicted (Mt 26:33–35; Mk 14:29–31; Lk 22:31–34; Jn 13:37–38). Followed Jesus after arrest (Mt 26:58; Mk 14:54; Jn 18:15); denied Jesus (Mt 26:69–75; Mk 14:66–72; Lk 22:54–62; Jn 18:17–27). Commissioned by Jesus after resurrection (Jn 21).
Exercised leadership in early church (Ac 1:15; 2:14; 5:3–11). Preached on day of Pentecost (Ac 2). Healed lame man at temple gate (Ac 3); before Sanhedrin (Ac 4). In Samaria (Ac 8:14–25). Received vision; went to Cornelius (Ac 10); supported Gentile mission (Ac 11; 15:7–11); lapsed and rebuked by Paul at Antioch (Gal 2:11–21). Miraculously released from prison (Ac 12). Wrote 1 & 2 Peter.

petition, -s
1Ch 16:4 to make *p*, to give thanks,
Jer 11:14 nor offer any plea or *p* for them,
Da 9:17 the prayers and *p-s* of your servant
Php 4:6 by prayer and *p*, with thanksgiving,
Heb 5:7 he offered up prayers and *p-s*

Pharaoh, -'s
Ge 12:15 And when *P*'s officials saw her,
41:1 *P* had a dream: He was standing
41:14 So *P* sent for Joseph,
44:18 you are equal to *P* himself
47:10 Then Jacob blessed *P* and went out
Ex 1:19 The midwives answered *P*,
2:5 *P-'s* daughter went down to the Nile
3:10 I am sending you to *P*
7:1 See, I have made you like God to *P*

7:13 Yet *P-'s* heart became hard
9:12 But the LORD hardened *P-'s* heart
14:17 And I will gain glory through *P*
1Ki 3:1 Solomon made an alliance with *P*
Ps 135:9 against *P* and all his servants
Ac 7:13 and *P* learned about Joseph's family
7:21 *P-'s* daughter took him and brought

Pharisee, -s
Mt 5:20 surpasses that of the *P-s*
9:14 How is it that we and the *P-s* fast,
12:14 But the *P-s* went out and plotted
23:2 and the *P-s* sit in Moses' seat
Ac 15:5 belonged to the party of the *P-s*
23:8 but the *P-s* acknowledge them all.
Php 3:5 in regard to the law, a *P*

Philemon
Co-worker with Paul (Phm 1); owner of runaway slave, Onesimus (Phm 8–11).

Philip
1. Apostle (Mt 10:3; Mk 3:18; Lk 6:14; Ac 1:13); from Bethsaida; brought Nathaniel to Jesus (Jn 1:43–45). **2.** Deacon (Ac 6:1–7). Evangelist (Ac 21:8); in Samaria (Ac 8:4–13); spoke to Ethiopian official (Ac 8:26–40).

Philippi
Mt 16:13 came to the region of Caesarea *P*,
Ac 16:12 From there we travelled to *P*,
Php 1:1 the saints in Christ Jesus at *P*

Philistine, -s
Ge 21:34 stayed in the land of the *P-s*
Jdg 3:31 who struck down six hundred *P-s*
14:1 and saw there a young *P* woman
16:9 "Samson, the *P-s* are upon you!"
16:30 "Let me die with the *P-s*!"
1Sa 4:1 went out to fight against the *P-s*.
4:17 "Israel fled before the *P-s*,
13:5 The *P-s* assembled to fight Israel,
17:4 Goliath ... came out of the *P* camp.
23:2 "Shall I go and attack these *P-s*?"
2Sa 5:19 "Shall I go and attack the *P-s*?
8:1 David defeated the *P-s* and subdued
2Ch 26:6 He went to war against the *P-s*
Isa 2:6 practise divination like the *P-s*

philosophy, -er
1Co 1:20 Where is the *p-er* of this age?
Col 2:8 through hollow and deceptive *p*,

Phinehas
1. Son of Eleazar; grandson of Aaron (Ex 6:25). Priest (Nu 31:6; Jdg 20:28). Held back God's judgment by killing Israelite and pagan Midianite woman (Nu 25:6–11; Ps 106:28–31); zeal rewarded by everlasting covenant of priesthood (Nu 26:12–13). In charge of temple gatekeepers (1Ch 9:20). **2.** Disreputable son of Eli (1Sa 1:3; 2:12–17). Condemned with his brother (1Sa 2:34). Both died in battle (1Sa 4:11).

phylacteries
Mt 23:5 They make their *p* wide

physical
Da 1:4 young men without any *p* defect,
Ro 2:28 circumcision merely outward and *p*
Col 1:22 reconciled you by Christ's *p* body
1Ti 4:8 For *p* training is of some value,
Jas 2:16 but does nothing about his *p* needs,

physician
Jer 8:22 Is there no *p* there?
Lk 4:23 proverb to me: '*P*, heal yourself!

piece, -s
Ps 2:9 will dash them to *p-s* like pottery.
Jer 23:29 a hammer that breaks a rock in *p-s*
Zec 11:12 they paid me thirty *p-s* of silver
Lk 12:46 He will cut him to *p-s*
Jn 6:12 Gather the *p-s* that are left over.

19:23 woven in one *p* from top to bottom
Rev 2:27 will dash them to *p-s* like pottery'

pierce, -d
Ex 21:6 and *p* his ear with an awl.
Ps 22:16 they have *p-d* my hands and my feet
40:6 but my ears you have *p-d*;
Isa 53:5 he was *p-d* for our transgressions,
Lk 2:35 a sword will *p* your own soul too.
Jn 19:37 will look on the one they have *p-d*.
Rev 1:7 see him, even those who *p-d* him;

pig, -'s, -s
Dt 14:8 The *p* is also unclean;
Pr 11:22 Like a gold ring in a *p-'s* snout
Isa 66:17 those who eat the flesh of *p-s*
Mt 7:6 do not throw your pearls to *p-s*.
8:30 a large herd of *p-s* was feeding
Lk 15:15 sent him to his fields to feed *p-s*

pigeons
Lev 12:8 to bring two doves or two young *p*,
Lk 2:24 "a pair of doves or two young *p*"

Pilate
Roman governor of Judea (Lk 3:1). Questioned Jesus (Mt 27:11–14; Mk 15:2–5; Lk 23:2–5; Jn 18:33–38); gave way to crowds: freed Barabbas; washed hands and gave Jesus up to be crucified (Mt 27:15–26; Mk 15:6–15; Lk 23:13–25; Jn 19). Released Jesus' body to Joseph (Mt 27:57–58; Mk 15:43–46; Lk 23:50–54); allowed guard on tomb (Mt 27:62–66).

pillar, -s
Ge 19:26 and she became a *p* of salt
Ex 13:21 in a *p* of cloud to guide them
Pr 9:1 she has hewn out its seven *p-s*
Gal 2:9 and John, those reputed to be *p-s*,
1Ti 3:15 the *p* and foundation of the truth
Rev 3:12 make a *p* in the temple of my God.

pit
Ps 40:2 He lifted me out of the slimy *p*,
103:4 who redeems your life from the *p*
Jnh 2:6 you brought my life up from the *p*,
Mt 12:11 it falls into a *p* on the Sabbath,
15:14 both will fall into a *p*.

pity, -ied
2Ch 36:15 because he had *p* on his people
Lk 10:33 when he saw him, he took *p* on him
17:13 "Jesus, Master, have *p* on us!
1Co 15:19 to be *p-ied* more than all men

plague, -s
Ex 8:2 I will *p* your whole country
Nu 14:12 I will strike them down with a *p*
2Sa 24:15 So the LORD sent a *p* on Israel
2Ch 20:9 sword of judgment, or *p* or famine,
Ps 106:30 intervened, and the *p* was checked
Jer 14:12 with the sword, famine and *p*.
Hos 13:14 Where, O death, are your *p-s*?
Rev 22:18 the *p-s* described in this book

plain[1]
Ge 11:2 they found a *p* in Shinar
19:29 God destroyed the cities of the *p*,
Isa 40:4 become level, the rugged places a *p*

plain[2]
Ro 1:19 what may be known about God is *p*
Eph 3:9 and to make *p* to everyone

plan, -s, -ned
Ex 26:30 to the *p* shown you on the mountain
Pr 12:5 The *p-s* of the righteous are just,
16:9 a man *p-s* his course, but the LORD
Isa 46:11 what I have *p-ned*, that will I do
Jer 29:11 For I know the *p-s* I have for you,
Eph 1:11 *p* of him who works out everything
Heb 11:40 God had *p-ned* something better

plank
Mt 7:3 attention to the *p* in your own eye

plant, -s, -ed
Ge 1:11 seed-bearing *p-s* and trees
9:20 proceeded to *p* a vineyard
Ps 1:3 He is like a tree *p-ed* by streams
80:15 the root your right hand has *p-ed*,
Jer 1:10 and overthrow, to build and to *p*.
17:8 like a tree *p-ed* by the water
Mt 13:6 sun came up, the *p-s* were scorched,
15:13 "Every *p* that my heavenly Father
1Co 3:8 man who *p-s* and the man who waters
15:37 you do not *p* the body that will be,
Jas 1:21 humbly accept the word *p-ed* in you,

platter
Mt 14:8 on a *p* the head of John the Baptist

play, -ed
Ge 4:21 the father of all who *p* the harp
Mt 11:17 "'We *p-ed* the flute for you,

plea
1Ki 9:3 "I have heard the prayer and *p*
Ps 17:1 Hear, O LORD, my righteous *p*;
55:1 O God, do not ignore my *p*
102:17 he will not despise their *p*

plead, -ed
2Sa 12:16 David *p-ed* with God for the child.
1Ki 8:47 repent and *p* with you in the land
Ac 2:40 warned them; and he *p-ed* with them,
2Co 12:8 Three times I *p-ed* with the Lord

pleasant
Ps 16:6 have fallen for me in *p* places;
106:24 Then they despised the *p* land;
133:1 How good and *p* it is when brothers
147:1 how *p* and fitting to praise him
Heb 12:11 No discipline seems *p* at the time,

please, -s, -ing, -d
Lev 1:9 an aroma *p-ing* to the LORD
1Ki 3:10 The Lord was *p-d* that Solomon
Ps 104:34 May my meditation be *p-ing* to him,
115:3 he does whatever *p-s* him
Pr 15:8 the prayer of the upright *p-s* him
Jer 6:20 your sacrifices do not *p* me.
Mic 6:7 Will the LORD be *p-d* with thousands
Mt 3:17 whom I love; with him I am well *p-d*
Jn 3:8 The wind blows wherever it *p-s*.
5:30 for I seek not to *p* myself but him
Ro 12:1 sacrifices, holy and *p-ing* to God—
15:2 Each of us should *p* his neighbour
1Co 7:32 how he can *p* the Lord
2Co 5:9 So we make it our goal to *p* him,
Gal 1:10 Or am I trying to *p* men?
6:8 who sows to *p* the Spirit,
Eph 5:10 find out what *p-s* the Lord.
Php 4:18 acceptable sacrifice, *p-ing* to God
Col 1:19 God was *p-d* to have all his fulness
1Th 2:4 We are not trying to *p* men but God,
Heb 11:6 faith it is impossible to *p* God,
13:21 work in us what is *p-ing* to him,
2Pe 1:17 whom I love; with him I am well *p-d*

pleasure, -s
Ps 16:11 with eternal *p-s* at your right hand
Eze 18:32 I take no *p* in the death of anyone,
Mt 11:26 Father, for this was your good *p*
Eph 1:5 in accordance with his *p* and will

2Ti 3:4 lovers of *p* rather than lovers of

plenty, -iful

Ps 37:19 in days of famine they will enjoy *p*
Mt 9:37 "The harvest is *p-iful* but
Lk 12:19 I'll say to myself, "You have *p*
2Co 8:14 your *p* will supply what they need,
Php 4:12 and I know what it is to have *p*.

plot

Ps 2:1 and the peoples *p* in vain
Mk 3:6 Pharisees went out and began to *p*
Ac 4:25 and the peoples *p* in vain
20:3 the Jews made a *p* against him

plough, -shares

Isa 2:4 beat their swords into *p-shares*
Joel 3:10 Beat your *p-shares* into swords
Mic 4:3 beat their swords into *p-shares*
Lk 9:62 "No-one who puts his hand to the *p*

pluck

Mk 9:47 eye causes you to sin, *p* it out.

plunder, -ed

Ex 3:22 And so you will *p* the Egyptians.
2Ch 14:13 carried off a large amount of *p*
Est 8:11 to *p* the property of their enemies
Isa 42:22 this is a people *p-ed* and looted,
Jer 30:16 Those who plunder you will be *p-ed*;

pods

2Ki 6:25 cab of seed *p* for five shekels
Lk 15:16 the *p* that the pigs were eating,

poison

Dt 29:18 that produces such bitter *p*
32:32 Their grapes are filled with *p*,
Job 6:4 my spirit drinks in their *p*;
Ps 140:3 the *p* of vipers is on their lips.
Am 6:12 But you have turned justice into *p*
Ro 3:13 "The *p* of vipers is on their lips.

Jas 3:8 a restless evil, full of deadly *p*

pole, -s

Ex 25:13 Then make *p-s* of acacia wood
Dt 12:3 burn their Asherah *p-s* in the fire;
1Ki 8:8 *p-s* were so long that their ends
14:23 and Asherah *p-s* on every high hill

pollute, -s, -d

Nu 35:33 'Do not *p* the land where you are.
35:33 Bloodshed *p-s* the land,
Ezr 9:11 a land *p-d* by the corruption
Pr 25:26 Like a muddied spring or a *p-d* well
Ac 15:20 to abstain from food *p-d* by idols,
Jas 1:27 from being *p-d* by the world
Jude :8 these dreamers *p* their own bodies,

ponder, -ed

Ps 64:9 and *p* what he has done
111:2 *p-ed* by all who delight in them
119:95 but I will *p* your statutes
Lk 2:19 and *p-ed* them in her heart

pool

Ps 114:8 who turned the rock into a *p*,
Jn 5:2 near the Sheep Gate a *p*,
5:7 I have no-one to help me into the *p*
9:7 "wash in the *P* of Siloam"

poor

Dt 15:11 There will always be *p* people
Ps 34:6 *p* man called, and the LORD heard
82:3 maintain the rights of the *p*
113:7 He raises the *p* from the dust
Pr 19:17 is kind to the *p* lends to the LORD,
31:20 She opens her arms to the *p*
Isa 25:4 You have been a refuge for the *p*,
61:1 to preach good news to the *p*.
Am 2:7 They trample on the heads of the *p*
Mt 5:3 "Blessed are the *p* in spirit,
11:5 the good news is preached to the *p*
26:11 he *p* you will always have with you

Lk 4:18 to preach good news to the *p*.
2Co 8:9 yet for your sakes he became *p*,
Gal 2:10 should continue to remember the *p*,

portion

Dt 32:9 For the LORD's *p* is his people,
1Sa 1:5 But to Hannah he gave a double *p*
2Ki 2:9 inherit a double *p* of your spirit,
La 3:24 I say to myself, "The LORD is my *p*

position, -s

Est 4:14 to royal *p* for such a time as this?
Ecc 10:6 Fools are put in many high *p-s*,
Da 2:48 the king placed Daniel in a high *p*
Ro 12:16 to associate with people of low *p*.

possess, -ing, -ed, -ion, -ions

Ge 15:7 this land to take *p-ion* of it.
17:8 I will give as an everlasting *p-ion*
Ex 19:5 you will be my treasured *p-ion*.
Dt 1:8 Go in and take *p-ion* of the land
8:1 and may enter and *p* the land that
1Ch 28:8 that you may *p* this good land
Da 7:18 the kingdom and will *p* it for ever
Mt 19:21 go, sell your *p-ions* and give
Mk 1:23 who was *p-ed* by an evil spirit
Lk 12:15 in the abundance of his *p-ions*.
19:8 give half of my *p-ions* to the poor,
Jn 10:21 sayings of a man *p-ed* by a demon.
1Co 13:3 If I give all I *p* to the poor
2Co 6:10 nothing, and yet *p-ing* everything
12:14 what I want is not your *p-ions* but
Heb 10:34 had better and lasting *p-ions*
1Jn 3:17 If anyone has material *p-ions*

possible

Mt 19:26 but with God all things are *p*.
26:39 and prayed, "My Father, if it is *p*,
Mk 9:23 *p* for him who believes.
13:22 deceive the elect—if that were *p*
1Co 9:19 to win as many as *p*
9:22 by all *p* means I might save some

pot

2Ki 4:40 there is death in the *p*!"
Jer 22:28 Jehoiachin a despised, broken *p*,
Eze 11:3 This city is a cooking *p*,

Potiphar

Egyptian official who bought Joseph (Ge 37:36; 39:1) and made him chief steward (Ge 39:2–6). Sent him to prison (Ge 39:7–20).

potter, -'s, -y

Ps 2:9 will dash them to pieces like *p-y*.
Isa 64:8 We are the clay, you are the *p*;
Jer 18:6 can I not do with you as this *p*
Mt 27:7 the money to buy the *p-'s* field
Ro 9:21 Does not the *p* have the right
Rev 2:27 will dash them to pieces like *p-y*

pour, -s, -ed

1Sa 10:1 oil and *p-ed* it on Saul's head
2Ki 3:11 to *p* water on the hands of Elijah.
Ps 22:14 I am *p-ed* out like water,
62:8 *p* out your hearts to him,
133:2 like precious oil *p-ed* on the head,
Isa 53:12 he *p-ed* out his life unto death,
Eze 39:29 I will *p* out my Spirit on the house
Joel 2:28 I will *p* out my Spirit on all
Mt 26:28 which is *p-ed* out for many
Lk 5:37 And no-one *p-s* new wine into old
Ac 2:17 I will *p* out my Spirit on all
Ro 5:5 because God has *p-ed* out his love
2Ti 4:6 *p-ed* out like a drink offering,
Tit 3:6 whom he *p-ed* out on us generously
Rev 16:1 Go, *p* out the seven bowls of God's

poverty

Pr 14:23 but mere talk leads only to *p*
30:8 give me neither *p* nor riches,

Lk 21:4 out of her *p* put in all she had
2Co 8:2 *p* welled up in rich generosity
8:9 you through his *p* might become rich
Rev 2:9 I know your afflictions and your *p*

power, -s, -ful, -less

Ex 9:16 that I might show you my *p*
Jdg 14:19 of the LORD came upon him in *p*.
1Ch 29:11 greatness and the *p* and the glory
2Ch 20:6 *P* and might are in your hand,
Ps 63:2 and beheld your *p* and your glory
90:11 Who knows the *p* of your anger?
Isa 11:2 the Spirit of counsel and of *p*,
Zec 4:6 nor by *p*, but by my Spirit,'
Mt 24:30 Son of Man coming ... with *p*
Mk 5:30 Jesus realised that *p* had gone out
Lk 1:35 *p* of the Most High will overshadow
4:14 to Galilee in the *p* of the Spirit,
24:49 been clothed with *p* from on high.
Ac 1:8 receive *p* when the Holy Spirit
4:33 With great *p* the apostles continued
Ro 1:16 the *p* of God for the salvation
5:6 we were still *p-less*, Christ died
8:38 present nor the future, nor any *p-s*
9:17 that I might display my *p* in you
1Co 1:18 are being saved it is the *p* of God.
1:24 Christ the *p* of God and the wisdom
6:14 By his *p* God raised the Lord
2Co 4:7 this all-surpassing *p* is from God
12:9 my *p* is made perfect in weakness."
13:4 weakness, yet he lives by God's *p*.
Eph 1:19 his incomparably great *p* for us
6:12 against the *p-s* of this dark world
Php 3:10 and the *p* of his resurrection
Col 2:15 disarmed the *p-s* and authorities,
1Th 1:5 simply with words, but also with *p*,
2Ti 3:5 form of godliness but denying its *p*
Heb 1:3 all things by his *p-ful* word.
7:16 the *p* of an indestructible life
1Pe 1:5 who ... are shielded by God's *p*
Jude :25 be glory, majesty, *p* and authority,
Rev 4:11 to receive glory and honour and *p*,
5:12 Worthy is the Lamb ... to receive *p*
20:6 The second death has no *p* over them

practice, -s

Lev 18:3 Do not follow their *p-s*
Zec 1:4 your evil ways and your evil *p-s*.'
Mt 7:24 words of mine and puts them into *p*
Lk 8:21 hear God's word and put it into *p*.
1Ti 5:4 to put their religion into *p*

practise, -d

Lev 19:26 "'Do not *p* divination or sorcery
Mt 23:3 for they do not *p* what they preach
Ac 19:19 A number who had *p-d* sorcery
Ro 1:32 also approve of those who *p* them
12:13 *P* hospitality.

praise, -ing, -d

Ex 15:2 He is my God, and I will *p* him
Dt 10:21 He is your *p*; he is your God,
2Sa 22:47 "The LORD lives! *P* be to my Rock!
1Ch 16:25 is the LORD and most worthy of *p*;
29:10 David *p-d* the LORD in the presence
2Ch 20:22 As they began to sing and *p*,
Ne 8:6 Ezra *p-d* the LORD, the great God;
Job 1:21 may the name of the LORD be *p-d*.
Ps 8:2 and infants you have ordained *p*
22:3 Holy One; you are the *p* of Israel.

51:15 and my mouth will declare your *p*
96:4 is the LORD and most worthy of *p*;
100:4 thanksgiving and his courts with *p*
103:1 my inmost being, *p* his holy name
108:3 *p* you, O LORD, among the nations;
135:3 LORD is good; sing *p* to his name,
144:1 *P* be to the LORD my Rock,
146:2 I will *p* the LORD all my life;
150:6 that has breath *p* the LORD.
Pr 27:21 man is tested by the *p* he receives
Isa 61:3 and a garment of *p* instead of
Da 2:19 Then Daniel *p-d* the God of heaven
Mt 5:16 and *p* your Father in heaven
11:25 "I *p* you Father, Lord of heaven
21:16 and infants you have ordained *p*'?
Lk 2:13 appeared with the angel, *p-ing* God
Jn 12:43 *p* from men more than *p* from God
Ac 10:46 speaking in tongues and *p-ing* God.
Ro 2:29 Such a man's *p* is not from men,
1Co 4:5 each will receive his *p* from God
2Co 1:3 *P* be to the God and Father of our
Eph 1:6 to the *p* of his glorious grace,
1:12 might be for the *p* of his glory.
Heb 13:15 offer to God a sacrifice of *p*—
Jas 5:13 happy? Let him sing songs of *p*
1Pe 2:9 declare the *p-s* of him who called
Rev 5:13 and to the Lamb be *p* and honour

pray, -s, -ing, -ed

Ge 20:17 Then Abraham *p-ed* to God,
Nu 21:7 So Moses *p-ed* for the people
Dt 4:7 God is near us whenever we *p* to him
Jdg 16:28 Then Samson *p-ed* to the LORD,
2Sa 15:31 So David *p-ed*, "O LORD, turn
1Ki 8:30 when they *p* towards this place.
18:36 Elijah stepped forward and *p-ed*:
2Ch 7:1 When Solomon finished *p-ing*,
7:14 humble themselves and *p* and seek
Da 6:13 He still *p-s* three times a day.
Mt 6:5 "And when you *p*, do not be like
6:9 "This, then, is how you should *p*:
26:36 while I go over there and *p*.
26:41 "Watch and *p* so that you will not
Lk 6:12 and spent the night *p-ing* to God
11:1 Jesus was *p-ing* in a certain place.
18:1 should always *p* and not give up.
18:10 Two men went up to the temple to *p*,
Ac 10:9 Peter went up on the roof to *p*
12:5 the church was earnestly *p-ing*
Ro 8:26 do not know what we ought to *p* for,
1Co 14:14 For if I *p* in a tongue,
Eph 6:18 be alert and always keep on *p-ing*
1Th 5:17 *p* continually;
Jas 5:14 elders of the church to *p* over him
Jude :20 and *p* in the Holy Spirit

prayer, -s

2Ch 7:12 I have heard your *p* and have chosen
Ps 61:1 Hear my cry, O God; listen to my *p*
Mk 9:29 This kind can come out only by *p*.
Lk 19:46 'My house will be a house of *p*';
Ac 2:42 to the breaking of bread and to *p*
2Co 1:11 as you help us by your *p-s*.
Php 4:6 in everything, by *p* and petition,
Col 4:2 Devote yourselves to *p*,
1Th 1:2 mentioning you in our *p-s*
1Ti 2:1 *p-s* ... be made for everyone
Jas 5:16 *p* of a righteous man is powerful

Rev 5:8 which are the *p-s* of the saints

preach, -ing, -ed

Ezr 6:14 the *p-ing* of Haggai the prophet
Isa 61:1 to *p* good news to the poor.
Mt 4:17 From that time on Jesus began to *p*,
11:5 the good news is *p-ed* to the poor
24:14 gospel of the kingdom will be *p-ed*
Lk 4:18 to *p* good news to the poor.
Ro 1:15 why I am so eager to *p* the gospel
10:14 can they hear without someone *p-ing*
1Co 1:21 foolishness of what was *p-ed* to
1:23 but we *p* Christ crucified:
9:16 Woe to me if I do not *p* the gospel!
1Th 2:9 we *p-ed* the gospel of God to you
1Ti 4:13 devote yourself ... to *p-ing* and
5:17 whose work is *p-ing* and teaching
2Ti 4:2 *P* the Word;

precepts

Ps 19:8 The *p* of the LORD are right,
111:7 all his *p* are trustworthy

precious

Ps 116:15 *P* in the sight of the LORD
139:17 *p* to me are your thoughts, O God!
Isa 28:16 a tested stone, a *p* cornerstone
1Pe 1:19 but with the *p* blood of Christ,
2:6 in Zion, a chosen and *p* cornerstone
2:7 to you who believe, this stone is *p*

predestined

Ro 8:29 For those God foreknew he also *p*
8:30 And those he *p*, he also called;
Eph 1:5 he *p* us to be adopted as his sons
1:11 having been *p* according to the plan

predict, -ed

Ac 7:52 killed those who *p-ed* the coming
11:28 and through the Spirit *p-ed*
16:16 who had a spirit by which she *p-ed*
1Pe 1:11 he *p-ed* the sufferings of Christ

pregnant

Mt 24:19 for *p* women and nursing mothers
Rev 12:2 She was *p* and cried out in pain

preparation, -s

1Ch 22:5 Therefore I will make *p-s* for it."
Mt 26:17 *p-s* for you to eat the Passover?
Lk 10:40 distracted by all the *p-s*
Jn 19:14 the day of *P* of Passover Week,

prepare, -d

Ex 23:20 bring you to the place I have *p-d*
Ps 23:5 You *p* a table before me
Isa 40:3 calling: "In the desert *p* the way
Mal 3:1 my messenger, who will *p* the way
Mt 3:3 '*P* the way for the Lord,
11:10 who will *p* your way before you.
25:34 *p-d* for you since the creation
26:12 she did it to *p* me for burial
Jn 14:3 And if I go and *p* a place for you,
1Co 2:9 what God has *p-d* for those who love
Eph 2:10 which God *p-d* in advance for us
2Ti 4:2 be *p-d* in season and out of season;
Heb 10:5 but a body you *p-d* for me
1Pe 1:13 Therefore, *p* your minds for action;
3:15 Always be *p-d* to give an answer

presence

Ge 4:16 So Cain went out from the LORD's *p*
Ex 25:30 Put the bread of the *P*
1Sa 2:21 Samuel grew up in the *p* of the LORD
Ps 16:11 you will fill me with joy in your *p*
23:5 in the *p* of my enemies.
51:11 Do not cast me from your *p*
139:7 Where can I flee from your *p*

Lk 1:19 Gabriel. I stand in the *p* of God,
Ac 2:28 you will fill me with joy in your *p*
1Th 3:13 holy in the *p* of our God and Father
2Ti 4:1 In the *p* of God and of Christ Jesus
Heb 2:12 in the *p* of the congregation
9:24 now to appear for us in God's *p*
1Jn 3:19 we set our hearts at rest in his *p*
Jude :24 before his glorious *p* without fault
Rev 20:11 Earth and sky fled from his *p*,

present[1]
Ps 56:12 I will *p* my thank-offerings to you
Isa 41:21 "*P* your case," says the LORD.
2Co 11:2 that I might *p* you as a pure virgin
Col 1:28 we may *p* everyone perfect in Christ
2Ti 2:15 *p* yourself to God as one approved,
Jude :24 *p* you before his glorious presence

present[2]
Ro 8:18 I consider that our *p* sufferings
8:38 neither the *p* nor the future,
Eph 1:21 *p* age but also in the one to come
Col 2:5 absent from you in body, I am *p*
1Ti 4:8 the *p* life and the life to come

preserve
Ge 45:7 to *p* for you a remnant on earth
Ps 36:6 O LORD, you *p* both man and beast
119:25 *p* my life according to your word
Pr 3:21 *p* sound judgment and discernment,
Lk 17:33 whoever loses his life will *p* it

press, -ed, -ure
Hos 6:3 let us *p* on to acknowledge him.
Lk 6:38 *p-ed* down, shaken together
2Co 4:8 We are hard *p-ed* on every side,
11:28 face daily the *p-ure* of my concern
Php 3:14 I *p* on towards the goal to win

price
Ge 23:9 for the full *p* as a burial site
1Ch 21:24 "No, I insist on paying the full *p*
Zec 11:13 handsome *p* at which they priced me!
Mt 27:9 the thirty silver coins, the *p* set
1Co 6:20 you were bought at a *p*.

pride
2Ch 26:16 his *p* led to his downfall.
Pr 8:13 I hate *p* and arrogance,
16:18 *P* goes before destruction,
Gal 6:4 Then he can take *p* in himself,
Jas 1:9 to take *p* in his high position

priest, -s, -hood
Ge 14:18 He was *p* of God Most High
Ex 3:1 his father-in-law, the *p* of Midian,
19:6 a kingdom of *p-s* and a holy nation.
28:1 so that they may serve me as *p-s*
Lev 21:7 because *p-s* are holy to their God
Nu 10:8 the *p-s*, are to blow the trumpets.
Jos 3:8 the *p-s* who carry the ark
1Sa 1:3 the two sons of Eli, were *p-s*
2:35 raise up for myself a faithful *p*,
Ezr 7:12 Ezra the *p*, a teacher of the Law
Ps 99:6 Moses and Aaron were among his *p-s*,
132:9 *p-s* be clothed with righteousness;
Mt 8:4 But go, show yourself to the *p*
26:3 Then the chief *p-s* and the elders
Ac 9:14 with authority from the chief *p-s*
Heb 3:1 Jesus, the apostle and high *p*
4:14 since we have a great high *p*
6:20 He has become a high *p* for ever,
7:1 king of Salem and *p* of God
7:17 declared: "You are a *p* for ever,
7:26 Such a high *p* meets our need—
9:11 When Christ came as high *p*
10:21 a great *p* over the house of God

13:11	The high *p* carries the blood
1Pe 2:5	spiritual house to be a holy *p-hood*
2:9	a chosen people, a royal *p-hood*,
Rev 1:6	a kingdom and *p-s* to serve his God
20:6	but they will be *p-s* of God

prince, -s

Ge 23:6	You are a mighty *p* among us.
Ezr 1:8	Sheshbazzar the *p* of Judah
Ps 146:3	Do not put your trust in *p-s*,
Pr 8:16	by me *p-s* govern,
Isa 9:6	Everlasting Father, *P* of Peace
Da 12:1	"At that time Michael, the great *p*
Mt 9:34	"It is by the *p* of demons that he
Jn 12:31	*p* of this world will be driven out
Ac 5:31	own right hand as *P* and Saviour

principle, -s

Gal 4:3	under the basic *p-s* of the world
4:9	those weak and miserable *p-s*?
Col 2:8	and the basic *p-s* of this world
2:20	to the basic *p-s* of this world,

Priscilla

Also called Prisca. Wife of Aquila. Disciples from Rome (Ac 18:2); co-workers with Paul (Ro 16:3; 1Co 16:19; 2Ti 4:19), accompanied him to Ephesus (Ac 18:18–19); instructed Apollos (Ac 18:26).

prison, -ers

Ps 142:7	Set me free from my *p*,
146:7	The LORD sets *p-ers* free
Isa 42:7	to free captives from *p*
Mt 25:36	I was in *p* and you came to visit me
Lk 4:18	to proclaim freedom for the *p-ers*
Ac 16:23	flogged, they were thrown into *p*,
Gal 3:23	we were held *p-ers* by the law,
Heb 13:3	Remember those in *p*
1Pe 3:19	and preached to the spirits in *p*
Rev 2:10	the devil will put some of you in *p*

prize

1Co 9:24	but only one gets the *p*?
9:27	will not be disqualified for the *p*
Php 3:14	the *p* for which God has called me
Col 2:18	disqualify you for the *p*.

procession

Ne 12:36	Ezra the scribe led the *p*
Ps 42:4	leading the *p* to the house of God,
118:27	join in the festal *p*
Isa 60:11	their kings led in triumphal *p*
1Co 4:9	on display at the end of the *p*,
2Co 2:14	who always leads us in triumphal *p*

proclaim, -ed

Ex 33:19	and I will *p* my name, the LORD,
2Sa 1:20	*p* it not in the streets of Ashkelon
Ps 19:1	the skies *p* the work of his hands
Isa 52:7	who bring good news, who *p* peace,
61:1	to *p* freedom for the captives
Mt 12:18	he will *p* justice to the nations
Lk 4:18	to *p* freedom for the prisoners
Ac 13:38	forgiveness of sins is *p-ed* to you
Ro 15:19	fully *p-ed* the gospel of Christ
1Co 11:26	*p* the Lord's death until he comes
Col 1:28	We *p* him, admonishing and teaching
4:3	that we may *p* the mystery of Christ
1Jn 1:3	We *p* to you what we have seen

produce, -s, -d

Ge 1:11	"Let the land *p* vegetation:
3:18	will *p* thorns and thistles for you,
Lk 3:8	*P* fruit in keeping with repentance.
2Co 7:11	See what this godly sorrow has *p-d*
Heb 6:8	land that *p-s* thorns and thistles
12:11	it *p-s* a harvest of righteousness

profane, -d

Lev 18:21 you must not *p* the name of your God
21:6 must not *p* the name of their God.
Jer 34:16 have turned round and *p-d* my name;
Eze 39:7 no longer let my holy name be *p-d*,
Mal 2:10 Why do we *p* the covenant

profess

1Ti 2:10 for women who *p* to worship God
Heb 4:14 hold firmly to the faith we *p*
10:23 hold unswervingly to the hope we *p*,

profit, -able

Pr 3:14 for she is more *p-able* than silver
21:5 The plans of the diligent lead to *p*
Isa 44:10 an idol, which can *p* him nothing
2Co 2:17 not peddle the word of God for *p*.
Php 3:7 But whatever was to my *p*
Tit 3:8 excellent and *p-able* for everyone

profound

Ps 92:5 O LORD, how *p* your thoughts
Eph 5:32 This is a *p* mystery—

prolong

Dt 5:33 and *p* your days in the land
Ps 85:5 Will you *p* your anger
Pr 3:2 they will *p* your life many years
Isa 53:10 see his offspring and *p* his days,
La 4:22 he will not *p* your exile.

promise, -s, -d

Ge 21:1 LORD did for Sarah what he had *p-d*
50:24 the land he *p-d* on oath to Abraham,
Ex 3:17 And I have *p-d* to bring you up
Dt 6:18 good land that the LORD *p-d* on oath
Jos 23:15 every good *p* of the LORD your God
2Sa 7:25 keep for ever the *p* you have made
1Ki 6:12 the *p* I gave to David your father
Ps 119:116 Sustain me according to your *p*,
Lk 24:49 send you what my Father has *p-d*;
Ac 1:4 wait for the gift my Father *p-d*,
2:39 The *p* is for you and your children
Ro 4:16 Therefore, the *p* comes by faith,
9:8 but it is the children of the *p*
2Co 1:20 no matter how many *p-s* God has made
7:1 Since we have these *p-s*,
Gal 3:14 might receive the *p* of the Spirit.
Eph 1:13 with a seal, the *p-d* Holy Spirit
2:12 to the covenants of the *p*, without
Heb 6:15 Abraham received what was *p-d*
10:23 for he who *p-d* is faithful
2Pe 1:4 his very great and precious *p-s*,
3:9 Lord is not slow in keeping his *p*,
1Jn 2:25 what he *p-d* us—even eternal life

prompted

Jn 13:2 devil had already *p* Judas Iscariot,
1Th 1:3 your labour *p* by love,
2Th 1:11 and every act *p* by your faith

proper

Ecc 5:18 and *p* for a man to eat and drink,
Mt 3:15 it is *p* for us to do this to fulfil
24:45 give them their food at the *p* time
1Co 11:13 Judge for yourselves: Is it *p*
Gal 6:9 the *p* time we will reap a harvest

prophecy, -ies

1Co 12:10 miraculous powers, to another *p*,
13:2 If I have the gift of *p*
14:1 especially the gift of *p*
1Th 5:20 do not treat *p-ies* with contempt

2Pe 1:21 *p* never had its origin in the will
Rev 19:10 of Jesus is the spirit of *p*.
22:7 the words of the *p* in this book.

prophesy, -ies, -ing, -ied
Nu 11:25 Spirit rested on them, they *p-ied*,
1Ki 18:29 they continued their frantic *p-ing*
Eze 37:4 "*P* to these bones and say to them,
Mt 7:22 Lord, did we not *p* in your name,
26:68 "*P* to us, Christ. Who hit you?
Lk 1:67 with the Holy Spirit and *p-ied*
Jn 11:51 he *p-ied* that Jesus would die
Ac 2:17 Your sons and daughters will *p*,
21:9 four unmarried daughters who *p-ied*
1Co 13:9 we know in part and we *p* in part
14:4 but he who *p-ies* edifies the church

prophet, -'s, -s
Ge 20:7 for he is a *p*,
Ex 7:1 your brother Aaron will be your *p*
Nu 11:29 that all the LORD's people were *p-s*
Dt 13:5 *p* or dreamer must be put to death,
18:18 will raise up for them a *p* like you
34:10 no *p* has risen in Israel like Moses
1Sa 19:24 "Is Saul also among the *p-s*?
1Ki 19:10 and put your *p-s* to death
1Ch 16:22 do my *p-s* no harm.
2Ch 24:19 Although the LORD sent *p-s*
36:16 scoffed at his *p-s* until the wrath
Jer 1:5 appointed you as a *p* to the nations
7:25 I sent you my servants the *p-s*
14:14 *p-s* are prophesying lies in my name
29:19 and again by my servants the *p-s*.
Am 7:14 was neither a *p* nor a *p-'s* son
Zec 7:12 through the earlier *p-s*.
Mal 4:5 "See, I will send you the *p* Elijah
Mt 1:22 the Lord had said through the *p*
2:23 what was said through the *p-s*:
3:3 was spoken of through the *p* Isaiah:
5:12 they persecuted the *p-s* who were
5:17 come to abolish the Law or the *P-s*;
7:15 "Watch out for false *p-s*.
13:57 own house is a *p* without honour.
Ac 7:37 'God will send you a *p* like me
Ro 1:2 promised beforehand through his *p-s*
11:3 "Lord, they have killed your *p-s*
1Co 12:28 first of all apostles, second *p-s*,
12:29 Are all apostles? Are all *p-s*?
14:32 The spirits of *p-s* are subject
Eph 2:20 foundation of the apostles and *p-s*,
4:11 some to be apostles, some to be *p-s*
Tit 1:12 Even one of their own *p-s* has said,
Heb 1:1 through the *p-s* at many times
2Pe 3:2 spoken in the past by the holy *p-s*
1Jn 4:1 because many false *p-s* have gone
Rev 16:13 out of the mouth of the false *p*

prophetess
Ex 15:20 Then Miriam the *p*, Aaron's sister,
Jdg 4:4 Deborah, a *p*, the wife of Lappidoth
2Ki 22:14 went to speak to the *p* Huldah,
Ne 6:14 remember also the *p* Noadiah
Isa 8:3 Then I went to the *p*,
Lk 2:36 a *p*, Anna, the daughter of Phanuel,
Rev 2:20 Jezebel, who calls herself a *p*.

prosper, -s, -ed, -ity
Ge 39:2 LORD was with Joseph and he *p-ed*,
Dt 30:15 set before you today life and *p-ity*
2Ch 14:7 So they built and *p-ed*
Ps 73:3 when I saw the *p-ity* of the wicked
Pr 19:8 he who cherishes understanding *p-s*

Jer 29:7 the peace and *p-ity* of the city

prostitute, -s

Jos 2:1 the house of a *p* named Rahab
1Ki 3:16 Now two *p-s* came to the king
Pr 23:27 for a *p* is a deep pit
Mt 21:31 *p-s* are entering the kingdom of God
Lk 15:30 squandered your property with *p-s*
1Co 6:9 nor adulterers nor male *p-s*
6:16 that he who unites himself with a *p*
Rev 17:1 great *p*, who sits on many waters

prostrate

Dt 9:18 once again I fell *p* before the LORD
1Ki 18:39 they fell *p* and cried, "The LORD
Da 8:17 I was terrified and fell *p*.

protect, -s

Ps 32:7 You are my hiding-place; you will *p*
Jn 17:15 that you *p* them from the evil one
1Co 13:7 It always *p-s*, always trusts,
2Th 3:3 and *p* you from the evil one

proud

Pr 16:5 The LORD detests all the *p* of heart
Lk 1:51 he has scattered those who are *p*
Ro 12:16 Do not be *p*, but be willing to
1Co 13:4 it does not boast, it is not *p*
Jas 4:6 "God opposes the *p* but gives grace
1Pe 5:5 "God opposes the *p* but gives grace

prove, -ing, -d

Ps 51:4 you are *p-d* right when you speak
Mt 11:19 wisdom is *p-d* right by her actions
Ac 9:22 by *p-ing* that Jesus is the Christ
Ro 3:4 "So that you may be *p-d* right

provide, -s, -d

Ge 22:8 "God himself will *p* the lamb
22:14 that place The LORD Will *P*.
Jnh 1:17 But the LORD *p-d* a great fish
4:6 Then the LORD God *p-d* a vine
1Co 10:13 he will also *p* a way out
1Ti 5:8 anyone does not *p* for his relatives
6:17 hope in God, who richly *p-s* us
Heb 1:3 After he had *p-d* purification

prowls

1Pe 5:8 Your enemy the devil *p* around

prudent, -nce

Pr 8:5 You who are simple, gain *p-nce*;
12:16 but a *p* man overlooks an insult
14:15 a *p* man gives thought to his steps
15:5 heeds correction shows *p-nce*

pruning

Isa 2:4 their spears into *p* hooks.

psalms

Lk 20:42 declares in the Book of *P*:
24:44 Moses, the Prophets and the *P*.
Eph 5:19 Speak to one another with *p*,
Col 3:16 sing *p*, hymns and spiritual songs

public, -ly

Mt 1:19 to expose her to *p* disgrace,
Lk 1:80 until he appeared *p-ly* to Israel
1Ti 4:13 the *p* reading of Scripture,
Heb 10:33 you were *p-ly* exposed to insult

puffs

1Co 8:1 Knowledge *p* up, but love builds up
Col 2:18 and his unspiritual mind *p* him up

punish, -es, -ed, -ment

Ge 15:14 But I will *p* the nation they serve
2Sa 7:14 I will *p* him with the rod of men,
Ezr 9:13 you have *p-ed* us less than our sins
Pr 16:22 but folly brings *p-ment* to fools
Isa 13:11 I will *p* the world for its evil,
Jer 21:14 I will *p* you as your deeds deserve,
Am 3:2 therefore I will *p* you

Mt 25:46 they will go away to eternal *p-ment*
2Th 1:9 *p-ed* with everlasting destruction
Heb 12:6 and he *p-es* everyone he accepts
1Jn 4:18 because fear has to do with *p-ment*.
Jude :7 suffer the *p-ment* of eternal fire

purchased
Ps 74:2 Remember the people you *p* of old,
Rev 5:9 with your blood you *p* men for God

pure
2Sa 22:27 to the *p* you show yourself *p*,
Ps 19:9 The fear of the LORD is *p*,
51:10 Create in me a *p* heart, O God,
119:9 How can a young man keep his way *p*?
Hab 1:13 Your eyes are too *p* to look on evil
Mt 5:8 Blessed are the *p* in heart,
2Co 11:2 present you as a *p* virgin to him
Php 2:15 blameless and *p*, children of God
4:8 whatever is right, whatever is *p*,
Tit 1:15 To the *p*, all things are *p*,
Heb 13:4 and the marriage bed kept *p*,
Jas 3:17 comes from heaven is first of all *p*

purify, -ies, -ied
Ac 15:9 for he *p-ied* their hearts by faith
1Jn 1:9 and *p* us from all unrighteousness
3:3 *p-ies* himself, just as he is pure

Purim
Est 9:26 Therefore these days were called *P*

purity
2Co 6:6 in *p*, understanding, patience
1Ti 4:12 in life, in love, in faith and in *p*
5:2 women as sisters, with absolute *p*
1Pe 3:2 the *p* and reverence of your lives

purple
Lk 16:19 a rich man who was dressed in *p*
Jn 19:5 the crown of thorns and the *p* robe,
Ac 16:14 Lydia, a dealer in *p* cloth

purpose, -s
Ex 9:16 have raised you up for this very *p*,
Pr 20:5 *p-s* of a man's heart are deep
Isa 55:11 achieve the *p* for which I sent it
Ro 9:11 God's *p* in election might stand
9:17 "I raised you up for this very *p*,
2Co 5:5 God who has made us for this very *p*
Eph 3:11 according to his eternal *p*

purse
Hag 1:6 to put them in a *p* with holes in it
Lk 10:4 Do not take a *p* or bag or sandals;
22:36 "But now if you have a *p*, take it,

pursue, -s
Ps 34:14 and do good; seek peace and *p* it
Pr 21:21 He who *p-s* righteousness and love
Ro 9:30 who did not *p* righteousness,
2Ti 2:22 and *p* righteousness, faith, love
1Pe 3:11 he must seek peace and *p* it

Q

quail
Ex 16:13 That evening *q* came and covered
Nu 11:31 and drove *q* in from the sea.
Ps 105:40 They asked, and he brought them *q*

quality, -ies
Da 6:3 by his exceptional *q-ies* that
Ro 1:20 God's invisible *q-ies*—
1Co 3:13 will test the *q* of each man's work

2Pe 1:8 For if you possess these *q-ies*

quarrel, -s

1Co 1:11 that there are *q-s* among you
1Ti 6:4 *q-s* about words that result in envy
2Ti 2:24 the Lord's servant must not *q*;
Jas 4:1 What causes fights and *q-s*

queen

1Ki 10:1 *q* of Sheba heard about the fame
Est 1:9 *Q* Vashti also gave a banquet
Mt 12:42 The *Q* of the South will rise
Ac 8:27 Candace, *q* of the Ethiopians.

quench, -ed

SS 8:7 Many waters cannot *q* love;
Isa 66:24 die, nor will their fire be *q-ed*,
Mk 9:48 not die, and the fire is not *q-ed*.

quick, -ly

Ps 40:13 O LORD, come *q-ly* to help me
Pr 20:3 but every fool is *q* to quarrel
Ecc 4:12 of three strands is not *q-ly* broken
Mt 28:7 Then go *q-ly* and tell his disciples
Jn 13:27 "What you are about to do, do *q-ly*
Jas 1:19 *q* to listen, slow to speak

quiet, -ly, -ness

Ge 25:27 while Jacob was a *q* man,
1Ch 22:9 I will grant Israel peace and *q*
Ps 23:2 he leads me beside *q* waters
Isa 30:15 *q-ness* and trust is your strength,
La 3:26 to wait *q-ly* for the salvation
Mk 4:39 "*Q*! Be still!" Then the wind died
Lk 19:40 if they keep *q*, the stones will cry
1Th 4:11 your ambition to lead a *q* life,
1Ti 2:2 we may live peaceful and *q* lives

quiver

Ps 127:5 the man whose *q* is full of them.
La 3:13 my heart with arrows from his *q*

R

Rabbi

Mt 23:8 you are not to be called '*R*',
Mk 9:5 "*R*, it is good for us to be here.
10:51 "*R*, I want to see.
Jn 1:49 "*R*, you are the Son of God;
9:2 "*R*, who sinned, this man or

race

Ecc 9:11 The *r* is not to the swift
Ac 20:24 if only I may finish the *r*
1Co 9:24 in a *r* all the runners run,
Gal 2:2 running or had run my *r* in vain
5:7 You were running a good *r*.
2Ti 4:7 I have finished the *r*, I have kept
Heb 12:1 let us run with perseverance the *r*

Rachel

Daughter of Laban (Ge 29:9–13); became Jacob's wife (Ge 29:28); mother of Joseph and Benjamin (Ge 30:22–24; 35:16–18,24); died in childbirth; buried by Jacob (Ge 35:16–20; 48:7).

radiant, -nce

Ex 34:30 his face was *r*,
Ps 19:8 The commands of the LORD are *r*,
34:5 Those who look to him are *r*;
2Co 3:13 while the *r-nce* was fading away
Eph 5:27 her to himself as a *r* church,
Heb 1:3 The Son is the *r-nce* of God's glory

rage

Pr 19:12 A king's *r* is like the roar
Ac 4:25 "'Why do the nations *r*
Eph 4:31 Get rid of all bitterness, *r*

rags

Isa 64:6 righteous acts are like filthy *r*;
Jer 38:11 He took some old *r* and worn-out
1Co 4:11 hungry and thirsty, we are in *r*,

Rahab

1. Prostitute in Jericho; sheltered Israelite spies and helped them escape (Jos 2; Jas 2:25); spared when city fell (Jos 6:22–25;

Heb 11:31). Mother of Boaz (Mt 1:5). **2.** Female chaos monster (Job 26:12; Ps 89:10; Isa 51:9); figurative name for Egypt (Ps 87:4; Isa 30:7).

rain, -ed

Ge 2:5 God had not sent *r* on the earth
7:4 I will send *r* on the earth
1Ki 17:1 there will be neither dew nor *r*
Ps 78:24 he *r-ed* down manna for the people
Mt 5:45 sends *r* on the righteous
7:25 The *r* came down, the streams rose,
Heb 6:7 Land that drinks in the *r*
Jas 5:17 earnestly that it would not *r*,
Jude :12 They are clouds without *r*,

rainbow

Ge 9:13 I have set my *r* in the clouds,
Eze 1:28 Like the appearance of a *r*
Rev 4:3 A *r*, resembling an emerald,
10:1 He was robed in a cloud, with a *r*

raise, -ing, -d

Mt 10:8 Heal the sick, *r* the dead,
16:21 on the third day be *r-d* to life
27:52 who had died were *r-d* to life
Jn 2:19 I will *r* it again in three days.
6:40 I will *r* him up at the last day.
Ac 2:24 But God *r-d* him from the dead,
13:34 The fact that God *r-d* him
17:31 proof of this to all men by *r-ing*
Ro 4:24 who believe in him who *r-d* Jesus
4:25 to death for our sins and was *r-d*
8:11 the Spirit of him who *r-d* Jesus
10:9 believe in your heart that God *r-d*
1Co 15:4 he was buried, that he was *r-d*
15:14 And if Christ has not been *r-d*,
15:20 But Christ has indeed been *r-d*
15:35 "How are the dead *r-d*?
15:43 it is *r-d* in glory;
15:52 the dead will be *r-d* imperishable,
Eph 2:6 And God *r-d* us up with Christ

ram, -s

Ge 22:13 in a thicket he saw a *r*
Ex 29:18 burn the entire *r* on the altar.
1Sa 15:22 heed is better than the fat of *r-s*
Isa 1:11 enough of burnt offerings, of *r-s*
Da 8:3 before me was a *r* with two horns,
Mic 6:7 be pleased with thousands of *r-s*,

ran

Ge 39:12 he left his cloak in her hand and *r*
1Sa 17:24 they all *r* from him in great fear.
1Ki 19:3 was afraid and *r* for his life.
Jnh 1:3 But Jonah *r* away from the LORD
Mt 28:8 and *r* to tell his disciples.
Mk 10:17 a man *r* up to him and fell on his
Lk 15:20 he *r* to his son, threw his arms
24:12 Peter ... got up and *r* to the tomb
Ac 8:30 Then Philip *r* up to the chariot

ransom, -ed

Ps 49:7 or give to God a *r* for him
Isa 35:10 the *r-ed* of the LORD will return.
Mt 20:28 to give his life as a *r* for many.
1Ti 2:6 gave himself as a *r* for all men—
Heb 9:15 now that he has died as a *r*

rape, -s, -d

Ge 34:2 he took her and *r-d* her
Dt 22:25 pledged to be married and *r-s* her,
Jdg 19:25 they *r-d* her and abused her
2Sa 13:14 stronger than she, he *r-d* her

raven, -s

Ge 8:7 sent out a *r*,
1Ki 17:4 ordered the *r-s* to feed you there.
Job 38:41 Who provides food for the *r*
Lk 12:24 Consider the *r-s*: They do not sow

read, -s, -ing

Dt 17:19 he is to *r* it all the days
Da 5:7 "Whoever *r-s* this writing
Mt 12:3 "Haven't you *r* what David did
22:31 have you not *r* what God said
Lk 4:16 And he stood up to *r*
2Co 3:2 written on our hearts, known and *r*

1Ti 4:13 the public *r-ing* of Scripture,
Rev 1:3 Blessed is the one who *r-s*

real
Jn 6:55 my flesh is *r* food and my blood

reality, -ies
Col 2:17 the *r*, however, is found in Christ
Heb 10:1 not the *r-ies* themselves.

realm, -s
Eph 1:3 blessed us in the heavenly *r-s*
1:20 right hand in the heavenly *r-s*
2:6 in the heavenly *r-s* in Christ Jesus
3:10 authorities in the heavenly *r-s*
6:12 forces of evil in the heavenly *r-s*

reap, -s
Ps 126:5 Those who sow in tears will *r*
Hos 8:7 sow the wind and *r* the whirlwind.
Mt 6:26 they do not sow or *r* or store away
Jn 4:37 'One sows and another *r-s*' is true
2Co 9:6 sows sparingly will also *r*
Gal 6:7 A man *r-s* what he sows
6:9 proper time we will *r* a harvest

reason, -ed
Ge 2:24 For this *r* a man will leave
Ps 35:19 those who hate me without *r*
Isa 1:18 "Come now, let us *r* together,"
Mt 19:3 his wife for any and every *r*?
19:5 'For this *r* a man will leave
Ac 18:4 Sabbath he *r-ed* in the synagogue,
1Co 13:11 I *r-ed* like a child.
1Pe 3:15 to give the *r* for the hope
1Jn 3:1 The *r* the world does not know us

Rebekah
Sister of Laban (Ge 25:20); left Haran with Abraham's servant to marry Isaac (Ge 24). Mother of Esau and Jacob (Ge 25:21–26). In Gerar, pretended to be Isaac's sister (Ge 26:1–11). Helped Jacob deceive Jacob and steal blessing (Ge 27).

rebel, -s, -led, -lion
Dt 13:5 he preached *r-lion* against the LORD
1Sa 15:23 for *r-lion* is like the sin of
Ps 78:56 they put God to the test and *r-led*
Mt 10:21 children will *r* against their
26:55 "Am I leading a *r-lion*,
Ro 13:2 he who *r-s* against the authority
2Th 2:3 the *r-lion* occurs and the man of
Heb 3:8 hearts as you did in the *r-lion*,
3:16 Who were they who heard and *r-led*?
Jude :11 been destroyed in Korah's *r-lion*

rebirth
Tit 3:5 *r* and renewal by the Holy Spirit

rebuild
Ezr 5:2 *r* the house of God in Jerusalem.
Mt 26:61 destroy the temple of God and *r*
Ac 15:16 I will return and *r* David's

rebuke, -s, -ing, -d
Pr 27:5 Better is open *r* than
29:1 stiff-necked after many *r-s* will
Mt 8:26 he got up and *r-d* the winds
16:22 took him aside and began to *r* him.
1Ti 5:1 Do not *r* an older man harshly,
2Ti 3:16 and is useful for teaching, *r-ing*,
Heb 12:5 do not lose heart when he *r-s* you
Rev 3:19 whom I love I *r* and discipline.

receive, -s, -d
Mt 7:8 For everyone who asks *r-s*;
10:8 Freely you have *r-d*, freely give
10:40 "He who *r-s* you *r-s* me,
13:20 word and at once *r-s* it with joy
21:22 If you believe, you will *r*
Jn 1:12 Yet to all who *r-d* him, to those
16:24 Ask and you will *r*,
20:22 "*R* the Holy Spirit
Ac 2:38 you will *r* the gift of the Holy
19:2 "Did you *r* the Holy Spirit
20:35 more blessed to give than to *r*.'
Ro 5:11 we have now *r-d* reconciliation

8:15 you *r-d* the Spirit of sonship.
1Co 4:7 do you have that you did not *r*?
11:23 I *r-d* from the Lord what I also
Gal 3:2 Did you *r* the Spirit by observing
Col 2:6 as you *r-d* Christ Jesus as Lord,
Heb 4:16 we may *r* mercy and find grace
Jas 4:3 When you ask, you do not *r*,
1Pe 5:4 you will *r* the crown of glory

reckoning
Isa 10:3 What will you do on the day of *r*,

recognise, -ing
Mt 7:20 by their fruit you will *r* them
Lk 19:44 you did not *r* the time of God's
24:16 but they were kept from *r-ing* him.
Jn 1:10 the world did not *r* him
1Jn 4:2 how you can *r* the Spirit of God:

reconcile, -ing, -d
Mt 5:24 go and be *r-d* to your brother;
Ro 5:10 *r-d* to him through the death
2Co 5:18 All this is from God, who *r-d* us
5:19 that God was *r-ing* the world
5:20 Be *r-d* to God
Eph 2:16 in this one body to *r* both of them
Col 1:20 through him to *r* to himself

reconciliation
Ro 5:11 we have now received *r*
11:15 rejection is the *r* of the world,
2Co 5:18 gave us the ministry of *r*
5:19 committed to us the message of *r*

record, -ed
Job 19:23 "Oh, that my words were *r-ed*,
Ps 130:3 If you, O Lord, kept a *r* of sins,
Jn 20:30 which are not *r-ed* in this book
1Co 13:5 it keeps no *r* of wrongs

red
Ex 15:4 officers are drowned in the *R* Sea
Jos 2:10 dried up the water of the *R* Sea
Pr 23:31 Do not gaze at wine when it is *r*,
Isa 1:18 though they are *r* as crimson,
Zec 1:8 was a man riding a *r* horse!
Rev 6:4 another horse came out, a fiery *r*

redeem, -s, -ed, -er
Ex 6:6 *r* you with an outstretched arm
Job 19:25 I know that my *R-er* lives,
Ps 19:14 O Lord, my Rock and my *R-er*
49:7 No man can *r* the life of another
103:4 who *r-s* your life from the pit
Isa 41:14 your *R-er*, the Holy One of Israel
43:1 "Fear not, for I have *r-ed* you;
Lk 1:68 come and has *r-ed* his people
24:21 one who was going to *r* Israel.
Gal 3:13 Christ *r-ed* us from the curse
4:5 to *r* those under law,
1Pe 1:18 *r-ed* from the empty way of life

redemption
Ps 111:9 He provided *r* for his people;
Lk 2:38 forward to the *r* of Jerusalem.
21:28 because your *r* is drawing near.
Ro 3:24 freely by his grace through the *r*
8:23 the *r* of our bodies
1Co 1:30 our righteousness, holiness and *r*
Eph 1:7 we have *r* through his blood,
1:14 until the *r* of those who are God's
4:30 you were sealed for the day of *r*.
Col 1:14 in whom we have *r*,
Heb 9:12 having obtained eternal *r*

reed
Isa 42:3 A bruised *r* he will not break,
Mt 11:7 A *r* swayed by the wind
12:20 A bruised *r* he will not break,

refine, -d, -r's
Ps 12:6 silver *r-d* in a furnace of clay,
66:10 you *r-d* us like silver
Isa 48:10 See, I have *r-d* you,
Mal 3:2 he will be like a *r-r's* fire
1Pe 1:7 perishes even though *r-d* by fire—
Rev 3:18 buy from me gold *r-d* in the fire,

reflect, -s, -ion
Pr 27:19 As water *r-s* a face,
1Co 13:12 Now we see but a poor *r-ion*

2Co 3:18 faces all *r* the Lord's glory,

refresh, -ing, -ed

Ac 3:19 that times of *r-ing* may come
Ro 15:32 together with you be *r-ed*
1Co 16:18 For they *r-ed* my spirit and yours

refuge

Nu 35:6 will be cities of *r*,
Dt 33:27 The eternal God is your *r*,
2Sa 22:31 a shield for all who take *r* in him
Ps 2:12 Blessed are all who take *r* in him
9:9 The LORD is a *r* for the oppressed,
18:2 my rock, in whom I take *r*.
46:1 God is our *r* and strength,
Na 1:7 The LORD is good, a *r* in times

refuse, -s, -d

Mt 18:17 If he *r-s* to listen to them,
22:3 but they *r-d* to come
Jn 5:40 you *r* to come to me to have life
2Th 2:10 because they *r-d* to love the truth
Heb 11:35 tortured and *r-d* to be released,
Rev 16:9 they *r-d* to repent and glorify him

regulation, -s

Eph 2:15 law with its commandments and *r-s*.
Col 2:14 written code, with its *r-s*,
Heb 7:16 a priest not on the basis of a *r*
7:18 The former *r* is set aside

Rehoboam

Son of Solomon; succeeded him as king (1Ki 11:43; 2Ch 9:31). Refusal to ease burden on people led to breaking away of northern tribes under Jeroboam (1Ki 12; 2Ch 10). In his evil reign temple plundered by Egyptians (1Ki 14:21–28; 2Ch 12:9–16).

reign, -s, -ed

Ex 15:18 The LORD will *r* for ever and ever.
Ps 9:7 The LORD *r-s* for ever;
93:1 LORD *r-s*, he is robed in majesty;
97:1 LORD *r-s*, let the earth be glad;
99:1 LORD *r-s*, let the nations tremble;
Isa 9:7 He will *r* on David's throne
32:1 a king will *r* in righteousness
52:7 "Your God *r-s*!
Lk 1:33 *r* over the house of Jacob for ever;
Ro 5:14 death *r-ed* from the time of Adam
5:21 just as sin *r*ed in death,
6:12 not let sin *r* in your mortal body
1Co 15:25 For he must *r* until
2Ti 2:12 we will also *r* with him.
Rev 5:10 and they will *r* on the earth.

reject, -s, -ed

1Sa 8:7 it is not you they have *r-ed*,
15:23 the LORD, he has *r-ed* you as king.
2Ki 17:20 LORD *r-ed* all the people of Israel;
Ps 27:9 Do not *r* me or forsake me,
118:22 The stone the builders *r-ed*
Isa 53:3 He was despised and *r-ed* by men,
Mt 21:42 " 'The stone the builders *r-ed*
Mk 8:31 suffer many things and be *r-ed*
Jn 3:36 whoever *r-s* the Son will not see
Ac 4:11 " 'the stone you builders *r-ed*,
Ro 11:1 Did God *r* his people?
1Pe 2:7 "The stone the builders *r-ed*

rejoice, -s, -ing, -d

1Sa 2:1 "My heart *r-s* in the LORD;
Ps 13:5 my heart *r-s* in your salvation
Pr 5:18 *r* in the wife of your youth
Hab 3:18 yet I will *r* in the LORD,
Zec 9:9 *R* greatly, O Daughter of Zion!
Mt 5:12 *R* and be glad, because great
Lk 1:47 my spirit *r-s* in God my Saviour
10:20 do not *r* that the spirits submit
15:7 there will be more *r-ing* in heaven
Jn 8:56 Your father Abraham *r-d*
Ro 5:2 *r* in the hope of the glory of God
5:3 but we also *r* in our sufferings,
1Co 13:6 but *r-s* with the truth
Php 3:1 my brothers, *r* in the Lord!
4:4 *R* in the Lord always.

1Pe 1:6 In this you greatly *r*,

release, -d

Isa 61:1 *r* from darkness for the prisoners
Mt 27:17 "Which one do you want me to *r*
Lk 4:18 to *r* the oppressed
Ro 7:2 *r-d* from the law of marriage
7:6 we have been *r-d* from the law
Rev 20:7 Satan will be *r-d* from his prison

relent, -ed

Ex 32:14 Then the LORD *r-ed*
Ps 90:13 *R*, O LORD! How long will it be?
106:45 out of his great love he *r-ed*.
Jnh 3:9 Who knows? God may yet *r*

reliable

Jn 8:26 he who sent me is *r*,
2Ti 2:2 entrust to *r* men who will also

relief

1Sa 8:18 cry out for *r* from the king
Ps 4:1 Give me *r* from my distress;
La 2:18 give yourself no *r*,
2Th 1:7 give *r* to you who are troubled,

religion, -ious

Am 5:21 I despise your *r-ious* feasts;
Ac 17:22 in every way you are very *r-ious*
Col 2:16 with regard to a *r-ious* festival,
1Ti 5:4 to put their *r* into practice
Jas 1:26 his *r* is worthless
1:27 *R* that God our Father accepts

rely

Ro 2:17 if you *r* on the law and brag
2Co 1:9 that we might not *r* on ourselves
Gal 3:10 All who *r* on observing the law
1Jn 4:16 we know and *r* on the love God has

remain, -s, -ed

2Ch 33:4 "My Name will *r* in Jerusalem
Ps 30:5 weeping may *r* for a night,
Isa 62:1 for Jerusalem's sake I will not *r*
Hag 1:4 while this house *r-s* a ruin?
Mt 26:63 But Jesus *r-ed* silent.
Jn 1:32 as a dove and *r* on him
3:36 God's wrath *r-s* on him.
6:56 and drinks my blood *r-s* in me,
15:4 *R* in me, and I will *r* in you.
15:9 Now *r* in my love
Ac 3:21 He must *r* in heaven until
14:22 encouraging them to *r* true
Ro 13:8 Let no debt *r* outstanding,
1Co 7:20 Each one should *r* in the situation
13:13 three *r*: faith, hope and love.
14:34 women should *r* silent
Php 1:24 that I *r* in the body
2Ti 2:13 he will *r* faithful,
Heb 1:11 They will perish, but you *r*;
4:9 There *r-s*, then, a Sabbath-rest
Rev 2:13 Yet you *r* true to my name.

remember, -s, -ed

Ge 9:15 I will *r* my covenant
Ex 2:24 he *r-ed* his covenant with Abraham,
20:8 "*R* the Sabbath day
Ne 5:19 *R* me with favour, O my God,
Ps 6:5 No-one *r-s* you when he is dead.
42:4 I *r* as I pour out my soul:
63:6 On my bed I *r* you;
103:14 he *r-s* that we are dust.
137:1 wept when we *r-ed* Zion
Ecc 12:1 *R* your Creator in the days
Isa 17:10 you have not *r-ed* the Rock,
43:25 *r-s* your sins no more
64:9 do not *r* our sins for ever.
Hab 3:2 in wrath *r* mercy
Mt 5:23 at the altar and there *r* that
Lk 17:32 *R* Lot's wife!
23:42 *r* me when you come into your
2Ti 1:3 I constantly *r* you in my prayers
2:8 *R* Jesus Christ,
Heb 8:12 will *r* their sins no more.
13:7 *R* your leaders, who spoke
Rev 2:5 *R* the height from which

remembrance

Mal 3:16 A scroll of *r* was written
Lk 22:19 do this in *r* of me.
1Co 11:24 do this in *r* of me.

remind, -er

Jn 14:26 *r* you of everything I have said
1Co 15:1 I want to *r* you of the gospel
2Ti 1:6 I *r* you to fan into flame the gift

Heb 10:3 an annual *r-er* of sins

remnant

Isa 10:21 A *r* will return,
Jer 11:23 Not even a *r* will be left to them,
Mic 2:12 I will surely bring together the *r*
Ac 15:17 the *r* of men may seek the Lord,
Ro 9:27 only the *r* will be saved.
11:5 there is a *r* chosen by grace.

remorse

Mt 27:3 he was seized with *r*

remove, -d

Ps 103:12 has he *r-d* our transgressions
Isa 25:8 will *r* the disgrace of his people
54:10 be shaken and the hills be *r-d*,
Mt 7:5 to *r* the speck from your brother's
Jn 20:1 the stone had been *r-d*
2Co 3:14 It has not been *r-d*,

rend

Isa 64:1 Oh, that you would *r* the heavens
Joel 2:13 *R* your heart and not your garments.

renew, -ing, -ed, -al

Ps 51:10 *r* a steadfast spirit within me
103:5 youth is *r-ed* like the eagle's
Isa 40:31 will *r* their strength.
Hab 3:2 *R* them in our day,
Mt 19:28 at the *r-al* of all things,
Ro 12:2 by the *r-ing* of your mind.
2Co 4:16 inwardly we are being *r-ed*
Tit 3:5 the washing of rebirth and *r-al*

renounce, -s, -d

Pr 28:13 whoever confesses and *r-s* them
Mt 19:12 others have *r-d* marriage
2Co 4:2 we have *r-d* secret and shameful
Rev 2:13 You did not *r* your faith in me,

renown

Ge 6:4 the heroes of old, men of *r*
Ps 102:12 your *r* endures through all
Isa 55:13 This will be for the LORD's *r*,
63:12 to gain for himself everlasting *r*

repay

Dt 32:35 It is mine to avenge; I will *r*.
Ps 103:10 *r* us according to our iniquities
Jer 16:18 I will *r* them double
Ro 11:35 that God should *r* him?
12:17 Do not *r* anyone evil for evil.
12:19 "It is mine to avenge; I will *r*,
Heb 10:30 "It is mine to avenge; I will *r*,
1Pe 3:9 Do not *r* evil with evil

repent, -s, -ed

Job 42:6 *r* in dust and ashes.
Eze 14:6 what the Sovereign LORD says: *R*!
Mt 3:2 "*R*, for the kingdom of heaven
4:17 "*R*, for the kingdom of heaven
11:21 they would have *r-ed* long ago
12:41 *r-ed* at the preaching of Jonah,
21:32 you did not *r* and believe him
Mk 1:15 *R* and believe the good news!"
Lk 13:3 unless you *r*, you too
15:7 heaven over one sinner who *r-s*
17:3 if he *r-s*, forgive him
Ac 2:38 "*R* and be baptised,
17:30 all people everywhere to *r*
Rev 2:5 *R* and do the things you did at

repentance

Isa 30:15 In *r* and rest is your salvation,
Mt 3:8 Produce fruit in keeping with *r*
3:11 "I baptise you with water for *r*.
Lk 5:32 the righteous, but sinners to *r*.
24:47 *r* and forgiveness of sins will be
Ac 5:31 give *r* and forgiveness of sins
20:21 they must turn to God in *r*
Ro 2:4 God's kindness leads you towards *r*
2Co 7:10 Godly sorrow brings *r*
2Ti 2:25 that God will grant them *r*
Heb 6:1 laying again the foundation of *r*
6:6 to be brought back to *r*,
2Pe 3:9 but everyone to come to *r*

representation

Heb 1:3 the exact *r* of his being,

reproach

Jos 5:9 "Today I have rolled away the *r*
Ps 44:16 those who *r* and revile me,

Isa 51:7	Do not fear the *r* of men
1Ti 3:2	Now the overseer must be above *r*,

reputation

1Ti 3:7	a good *r* with outsiders,
Rev 3:1	you have a *r* of being alive,

requests

Ps 20:5	May the LORD grant all your *r*
Eph 6:18	with all kinds of prayers and *r*.
Php 4:6	present your *r* to God
1Ti 2:1	that *r*, prayers, intercession and

require, -d

Ps 40:6	sin offerings you did not *r*
Mic 6:8	And what does the LORD *r* of you?
Lk 3:13	any more than you are *r-d* to,"
Ro 2:14	by nature things *r-d* by the law,
1Co 4:2	Now it is *r-d* that those

rescue, -s, -d

Ps 22:8	let the LORD *r* him.
Da 3:17	he will *r* us from your hand,
6:16	whom you serve continually, *r* you!
6:27	He *r-s* and he saves;
Mt 27:43	Let God *r* him now
Ac 12:11	Lord sent his angel and *r-d* me
Ro 7:24	Who will *r* me from this body
Gal 1:4	gave himself for our sins to *r* us
Col 1:13	he has *r-d* us from the dominion
1Th 1:10	who *r-s* us from the coming wrath

resent, -s, -ful

Pr 3:11	and do not *r* his rebuke
15:12	A mocker *r-s* correction;
2Ti 2:24	able to teach, not *r-ful*

resist, -ed

Da 11:32	who know their God will firmly *r*
Mt 5:39	Do not *r* an evil person.
Ac 7:51	You always *r* the Holy Spirit
Heb 12:4	*r-ed* to the point of shedding
Jas 4:7	*R* the devil,

resolved

Ps 17:3	*r* that my mouth will not sin
1Co 2:2	For I *r* to know nothing

resounding

Ps 150:5	praise him with *r* cymbals
1Co 13:1	I am only a *r* gong or

respect, -ed

Pr 31:23	husband is *r-ed* at the city gate,
Mal 1:6	where is the *r* due to me?"
Mt 21:37	'They will *r* my son,'
Ro 13:7	if *r*, then *r*; if honour,
1Ti 3:8	men worthy of *r*,
1Pe 2:17	Show proper *r* to everyone:

response

Ro 8:31	What, then, shall we say in *r*
Gal 2:2	I went in *r* to a revelation

responsible, -ility

Mt 27:4	"That's your *r-ility*.
Lk 11:50	this generation will be held *r*
Ac 18:6	I am clear of my *r-ility*.
1Co 7:24	each man, as *r* to God,

rest, -s, -ed

Ge 2:2	on the seventh day he *r-ed*
8:4	ark came to *r* on the mountains
1Ki 5:4	God has given me *r* on every side,
Ps 62:1	My soul finds *r* in God alone;
91:1	*r* in the shadow of the Almighty
95:11	"They shall never enter my *r*.
Pr 6:10	little folding of the hands to *r*
Isa 11:2	Spirit of the LORD will *r* on him—
30:15	repentance and *r* is your salvation,
62:7	give him no *r* till he establishes
Mt 10:13	let your peace *r* on it;
11:28	I will give you *r*
11:29	you will find *r* for your souls
12:43	through arid places seeking *r*
Mk 6:31	to a quiet place and get some *r*."
Lk 2:14	to men on whom his favour *r-s*.
23:56	*r-ed* on the Sabbath in obedience
Ac 2:3	came to *r* on each of them
1Co 2:5	faith might not *r* on men's wisdom,
2Co 12:9	Christ's power may *r* on me
Heb 3:11	'They shall never enter my *r*.'
4:11	make every effort to enter that *r*,

Rev 14:13 "they will *r* from their labour,

restitution

Ex 22:3 "A thief must certainly make *r*,
Lev 6:5 make *r* in full, add a fifth

restore, -s, -d

Ps 14:7 When the LORD *r-s* the fortunes
23:3 he *r-s* my soul.
51:12 *R* to me the joy of your salvation
Mt 9:30 their sight was *r-d*.
17:11 Elijah comes and will *r* all things
Ac 1:6 to *r* the kingdom to Israel?
3:21 time comes for God to *r* everything,
Gal 6:1 you who are spiritual should *r* him

restraint

Ps 119:51 The arrogant mock me without *r*,
Pr 17:27 man of knowledge uses words with *r*,
29:18 the people cast off *r*;

resurrection

Mt 22:28 at the *r*, whose wife will she be
Lk 14:14 repaid at the *r* of the righteous.
Jn 11:24 he will rise again in the *r*
11:25 "I am the *r* and the life.
Ac 4:33 to testify to the *r* of the Lord
17:18 good news about Jesus and the *r*
Ro 1:4 Son of God, by his *r* from the dead:
6:5 united with him in his *r*
1Co 15:12 there is no *r* of the dead
15:21 the *r* of the dead comes also
Php 3:10 power of his *r* and the fellowship
2Ti 2:18 the *r* has already taken place,
Heb 11:35 that they might gain a better *r*
Rev 20:5 This is the first *r*

retaliate

1Pe 2:23 he did not *r*; when he suffered,

retribution

Isa 34:8 a day of vengeance, a year of *r*,
35:4 with divine *r* he will come to save
59:18 wrath to his enemies and *r* to
Jer 51:56 For the LORD is a God of *r*;

return, -s, -ing, -ed

Ge 3:19 *r* to the ground, since from it
1Ki 17:21 let this boy's life *r* to him!
Job 7:9 goes down to the grave does not *r*
Ps 9:17 The wicked *r* to the grave,
90:3 "*R* to dust, O sons of men.
126:6 will *r* with songs of joy,
Pr 26:11 As a dog *r-s* to its vomit,
Isa 10:21 A remnant will *r*,
35:10 the ransomed of the LORD will *r*.
55:11 It will not *r* to me empty,
Jer 3:12 "'*R*, faithless Israel,'
Hos 6:1 "Come, let us *r* to the LORD.
Joel 2:12 "*r* to me with all your heart,
Mal 3:7 and I will *r* to you,"
Mt 2:12 they *r-ed* to their country
10:13 let your peace *r* to you
24:46 finds him doing so when he *r-s*
Jn 13:3 from God and was *r-ing* to God
20:17 'I am *r-ing* to my Father
20:17 I have not yet *r-ed* to the Father.
1Pe 2:25 you have *r-ed* to the Shepherd
2Pe 2:22 "A dog *r-s* to its vomit,"

Reuben

1. Jacob's firstborn, by Leah (Ge 29:32; 35:23; 46:8). Wanted to save Joseph (Ge 37:19–30). Lost position because slept with Bilhah (Ge 35:22; 49:4). Blessed by Jacob (Ge 49:3–4). **2.** Tribe descended from Reuben. Blessed by Moses (Dt 33:6). Included in census (Nu 1:20–21; 26:5–11). Apportioned land east of Jordan (Nu 32; 34:14–15; Jos 18:7; 22); crossed into Canaan to fight alongside other tribes (Nu 32:16–31). Place restored in land (Eze 48:6).

reveal, -ed

Nu 12:6 I *r* myself to him in visions,
Isa 40:5 glory of the LORD will be *r-ed*,
53:1 has the arm of the LORD been *r-ed*
Mt 11:27 to whom the Son chooses to *r* him
Lk 10:21 and *r-ed* them to little children.
Jn 1:31 that he might be *r-ed* to Israel.
17:6 "I have *r-ed* you to those whom you

Ro 1:17 a righteousness from God is *r-ed*,
1:18 The wrath of God is being *r-ed*
8:19 for the sons of God to be *r-ed*
1Co 2:10 God has *r-ed* it to us
2Th 1:7 Lord Jesus is *r-ed* from heaven
2:3 man of lawlessness is *r-ed*,
1Pe 5:1 share in the glory to be *r-ed*

revelation, -s
Pr 29:18 Where there is no *r*, the people
Hab 2:2 Write down the *r* and make it plain
Lk 2:32 a light for *r* to the Gentiles
Ro 16:25 the *r* of the mystery hidden
1Co 14:6 I bring you some *r* or knowledge
14:26 a word of instruction, a *r*,
2Co 12:1 I will go on to visions and *r-s*
12:7 these surpassingly great *r-s*,
Gal 1:12 I received it by *r* from Jesus
Eph 3:3 the mystery made known to me by *r*,

revenge
Lev 19:18 "'Do not seek *r*
Ro 12:19 Do not take *r*, my friends,

revere
Lev 19:32 and *r* your God.
Ps 33:8 all the people of the world *r* him
Isa 59:19 they will *r* his glory.
Mal 4:2 But for you who *r* my name,

reverent, -nce
2Co 7:1 perfecting holiness out of *r-nce*
Eph 5:21 out of *r-nce* for Christ
Tit 2:3 teach the older women to be *r*
Heb 5:7 heard because of his *r* submission
12:28 worship God acceptably with *r-nce*
1Pe 3:2 the purity and *r-nce* of your lives

revive, -ing
Ps 19:7 perfect, *r-ing* the soul.
80:18 *r* us, and we will call
85:6 Will you not *r* us again,
Hos 6:2 After two days he will *r* us;

reward
Ge 15:1 your shield, your very great *r*.
Ps 19:11 in keeping them there is great *r*
127:3 children a *r* from him
Isa 40:10 See, his *r* is with him,
Mt 5:12 great is your *r* in heaven,
6:4 done in secret, will *r* you
16:27 he will *r* each person according to
1Co 3:14 he will receive his *r*.
Eph 6:8 the Lord will *r* everyone for
Col 3:24 inheritance from the Lord as a *r*.
Rev 22:12 My *r* is with me,

ribs
Ge 2:21 he took one of the man's *r*

rich, -es
Ps 49:6 boast of their great *r-es*
Pr 8:18 With me are *r-es* and honour,
22:1 more desirable than great *r-es*;
Isa 53:9 and with the *r* in his death,
Mt 19:24 for a *r* man to enter the kingdom
27:57 there came a *r* man from Arimathea,
Lk 1:53 but has sent the *r* away empty
8:14 choked by life's worries, *r-es* and
16:19 "There was a *r* man who was dressed
Ro 9:23 make the *r-es* of his glory known
11:33 Oh, the depth of the *r-es*
2Co 8:9 he was *r*, yet for your sakes
Eph 2:4 God, who is *r* in mercy
3:8 the unsearchable *r-es* of Christ,
Php 4:19 according to his glorious *r-es* in
Jas 2:6 Is it not the *r* who are exploiting

rid
Ge 21:10 "Get *r* of that slave woman
1Co 5:7 Get *r* of the old yeast
Gal 4:30 "Get *r* of the slave woman
Eph 4:31 Get *r* of all bitterness, rage
Jas 1:21 get *r* of all moral filth

ride, -ing, -r
Ex 15:1 horse and its *r-r* he has hurled
Zec 9:9 gentle and *r-ing* on a donkey,
Mt 21:5 gentle and *r-ing* on a donkey,
Rev 19:11 *r-r* is called Faithful and True.

ridicule, -d
Isa 37:4 has sent to *r* the living God,
Lk 14:29 everyone who sees it will *r* him

23:11 soldiers *r-d* and mocked him.

right[1], -s

Ge 18:25 the Judge of all the earth do *r*?"
Dt 12:25 what is *r* in the eyes of the LORD
2Sa 23:5 "Is not my house *r* with God?
Job 42:7 what is *r*, as my servant Job
Ps 9:4 For you have upheld my *r*
19:8 The precepts of the LORD are *r*,
51:4 you are proved *r* when you speak
Pr 16:25 a way that seems *r* to a man,
21:2 All a man's ways seem *r* to him,
Isa 7:15 reject the wrong and choose the *r*
Eze 18:21 just and *r*, he will surely live;
33:16 He has done what is just and *r*;
Da 4:37 everything he does is *r*
Hos 14:9 The ways of the LORD are *r*;
Jnh 4:4 "Have you any *r* to be angry?
Mt 11:19 wisdom is proved *r* by her actions.
15:7 Isaiah was *r* when he prophesied
20:15 I have the *r* to do what I want
Lk 7:29 acknowledged that God's way was *r*,
Jn 1:12 he gave the *r* to become children
8:16 if I do judge, my decisions are *r*,
18:37 "You are *r* in saying I am a king.
Ac 4:19 whether it is *r* in God's sight
6:2 "It would not be *r* for us
10:35 who fear him and do what is *r*
Ro 5:6 You see, at just the *r* time,
9:21 Does not the potter have the *r*
1Co 9:4 Don't we have the *r* to food
Gal 4:5 receive the full *r-s* of sons
Php 4:8 whatever is *r*, whatever is pure,
1Pe 2:14 to commend those who do *r*
3:14 should suffer for what is *r*,
1Jn 3:10 who does not do what is *r*

right[2]

Ex 15:6 "Your *r* hand, O LORD, was majestic
Dt 5:32 turn aside to the *r* or to
Ps 16:8 Because he is at my *r* hand,
16:11 eternal pleasures at your *r* hand
73:23 you hold me by my *r* hand
110:1 "Sit at my *r* hand until
110:5 The Lord is at your *r* hand;
139:10 your *r* hand will hold me fast
Isa 30:21 you turn to the *r* or to the left,
62:8 The LORD has sworn by his *r* hand
Zec 3:1 Satan standing at his *r* side
Mt 5:29 If your *r* eye causes you to sin,
5:39 strikes you on the *r* cheek,
6:3 left hand know what your *r* hand
22:44 "Sit at my *r* hand until
25:33 the sheep on his *r* and the goats
26:64 Son of Man sitting at the *r* hand
27:38 one on his *r* and one on his left.
Mk 10:37 "Let one of us sit at your *r*
Ac 2:25 Because he is at my *r* hand,
2:33 Exalted to the *r* hand of God,
2:34 "Sit at my *r* hand
5:31 God exalted him to his own *r* hand
7:56 Son of Man standing at the *r* hand
Ro 8:34 is at the *r* hand of God and
Gal 2:9 the *r* hand of fellowship
Eph 1:20 seated him at his *r* hand
Col 3:1 Christ is seated at the *r* hand
Heb 1:3 he sat down at the *r* hand
10:12 sins, he sat down at the *r* hand

righteous, -ness

Ge 6:9 Noah was a *r* man, blameless among
15:6 he credited it to him as *r-ness*
18:26 "If I find fifty *r* people
Job 9:2 how can a mortal be *r* before God
Ps 1:5 sinners in the assembly of the *r*
9:8 He will judge the world in *r-ness*;
17:15 in *r-ness* I shall see your face;
19:9 are sure and altogether *r*
23:3 He guides me in paths of *r-ness*
34:19 A *r* man may have many troubles,
37:25 I have never seen the *r* forsaken
85:10 *r-ness* and peace kiss each other
106:31 credited to him as *r-ness*
Pr 11:30 fruit of the *r* is a tree of life,

14:34 *R-ness* exalts a nation, but sin
18:10 the *r* run to it and are safe.
Isa 11:5 *R-ness* will be his belt
32:17 effect of *r-ness* will be quietness
41:10 uphold you with my *r* right hand
45:21 a *r* God and a Saviour;
59:17 put on *r-ness* as his breastplate,
61:10 arrayed me in a robe of *r-ness*,
64:6 our *r* acts are like filthy rags;
Jer 33:16 The LORD Our *R-ness*.'
Eze 33:13 *r* man that he will surely live,
Am 5:24 *r-ness* like a never-failing stream
Hab 2:4 the *r* will live by his faith
Mal 4:2 the sun of *r-ness* will rise
Mt 1:19 Joseph her husband was a *r* man
5:6 who hunger and thirst for *r-ness*,
5:20 unless your *r-ness* surpasses that
6:33 first his kingdom and his *r-ness*,
9:13 I have not come to call the *r*,
13:49 separate the wicked from the *r*
25:46 the *r* to eternal life.
Jn 16:8 guilt in regard to sin and *r-ness*
Ro 1:17 in the gospel a *r-ness* from God
3:10 "There is no-one *r*, not even one
3:21 But now a *r-ness* from God,
4:3 it was credited to him as *r-ness*.
4:13 the *r-ness* that comes by faith
5:7 will anyone die for a *r* man,
5:17 grace and of the gift of *r-ness*
5:19 the many will be made *r*
8:4 that the *r* requirements of the law
10:4 *r-ness* for everyone who believes
14:17 but of *r-ness*, peace and joy
1Co 1:30 our *r-ness*, holiness and
2Co 5:21 we might become the *r-ness* of God.
Gal 3:11 "The *r* will live by faith.
Eph 6:14 the breastplate of *r-ness* in place,
Php 3:9 not having a *r-ness* of my own
2Ti 3:16 correcting and training in *r-ness*
4:8 crown of *r-ness*, which the Lord,
Heb 10:38 my *r* one will live by faith.
Jas 2:23 it was credited to him as *r-ness*,
3:18 raise a harvest of *r-ness*
1Pe 3:18 the *r* for the unrighteous,
1Jn 3:7 He who does what is right is *r*,

ring
Pr 11:22 Like a gold *r* in a pig's snout
Hag 2:23 I will make you like my signet *r*,
Lk 15:22 Put a *r* on his finger
Jas 2:2 wearing a gold *r* and fine clothes,

riot
Mt 26:5 there may be a *r* among the people.
Ac 17:5 started a *r* in the city.

ripe
Jn 4:35 fields! They are *r* for harvest
Rev 14:15 the harvest of the earth is *r*.

rise, -s, -n
Nu 24:17 a sceptre will *r* out of Israel.
Ps 44:26 *R* up and help us; redeem us
127:2 In vain you *r* early and stay up
139:2 You know when I sit and when I *r*;
Isa 60:1 the glory of the LORD *r-s* upon you
Mal 4:2 the sun of righteousness will *r*
Mt 5:45 He causes his sun to *r* on the evil
11:11 not *r-n* anyone greater than John
24:7 Nation will *r* against nation,
27:63 'After three days I will *r* again.
28:6 He is not here; he has *r-n*,
Lk 16:31 even if someone *r-s* from the dead.
Jn 5:29 who have done good will *r* to live,
11:23 "Your brother will *r* again."
1Th 4:16 and the dead in Christ will *r* first
2Pe 1:19 the morning star *r-s* in your hearts

river, -s
Ge 2:10 A *r* watering the garden flowed
Ps 36:8 drink from your *r* of delights

46:4 a *r* whose streams make glad
98:8 Let the *r-s* clap their hands,
137:1 By the *r-s* of Babylon we sat
Eze 47:5 it was a *r* that I could not cross,
Am 5:24 let justice roll on like a *r*,
Rev 22:1 the *r* of the water of life,

road, -s
Nu 22:22 angel of the LORD stood in the *r*
Pr 26:13 "There is a lion in the *r*,
Mt 7:13 the gate and broad is the *r*
Mk 9:33 were you arguing about on the *r*?
Lk 3:5 crooked *r-s* shall become straight,
24:32 while he talked with us on the *r*

roar, -ing
Jer 25:30 " 'The LORD will *r* from on high;
1Pe 5:8 prowls around like a *r-ing* lion
2Pe 3:10 heavens will disappear with a *r*;
Rev 19:1 like the *r* of a great multitude

rob, -bed
Pr 17:12 to meet a bear *r-bed* of her cubs
Mal 3:8 "Will a man *r* God?
Mt 12:29 Then he can *r* his house.

robber, -s
Jer 7:11 become a den of *r-s* to you?
Mt 21:13 you are making it a 'den of *r-s*'.
27:38 Two *r-s* were crucified with him,
Lk 10:30 he fell into the hands of *r-s*.
Jn 10:1 is a thief and a *r*
10:8 thieves and *r-s*, but the sheep

robbery
Isa 61:8 love justice; I hate *r*

robe, -s, -d
1Sa 24:4 cut off a corner of Saul's *r*
Ps 93:1 LORD reigns, he is *r-d* in majesty;
Isa 6:1 train of his *r* filled the temple
61:10 arrayed me in a *r* of righteousness,
Mt 27:28 put a scarlet *r* on him
Lk 15:22 'Quick! Bring the best *r*
Heb 1:12 You will roll them up like a *r*;
Rev 22:14 are those who wash their *r-s*,

rock, -s
Ge 49:24 the Shepherd, the *R* of Israel
Ex 17:6 Strike the *r*, and water will come
33:22 in a cleft in the *r* and cover you
Dt 32:4 He is the *R*, his works are perfect,
32:18 You deserted the *R*, who fathered
32:31 their *r* is not like our *R*,
1Sa 2:2 there is no *R* like our God
Ps 18:2 The LORD is my *r*, my fortress
Isa 51:1 to the *r* from which you were cut
Jer 23:29 hammer that breaks a *r* in pieces
Da 2:34 a *r* was cut out, but not by human
Mt 7:24 who built his house on the *r*
16:18 Peter, and on this *r* I will build
27:60 tomb that he had cut out of the *r*.
Ro 9:33 and a *r* that makes them fall,
1Co 10:4 drank from the spiritual *r*
1Pe 2:8 and a *r* that makes them fall."
Rev 6:16 to the mountains and the *r-s*,

rod, -s
Ps 23:4 for you are with me; your *r* and
Pr 13:24 who spares the *r* hates his son,
23:14 Punish him with the *r* and save
2Co 11:25 Three times I was beaten with *r-s*,

roll, -ed
Jos 5:9 I have *r-ed* away the reproach
Isa 34:4 the sky *r-ed* up like a scroll;
Am 5:24 But let justice *r* on like a river,
Mt 27:60 He *r-ed* a big stone in front
Mk 16:3 "Who will *r* the stone away
Heb 1:12 You will *r* them up like a robe;

Roman
Lk 2:1 taken of the entire *R* world
Ac 11:28 spread over the entire *R* world.
16:37 even though we are *R* citizens,

Rome
Ac 19:21 "I must visit *R* also."
23:11 you must also testify in *R*.
28:16 we got to *R*, Paul was allowed

Ro 1:15	gospel also to you who are at *R*

roof, -s

Pr 25:24	to live on a corner of the *r*
Mt 8:8	under my *r*. But just say the word,
10:27	proclaim from the *r-s*
Mk 2:4	an opening in the *r* above Jesus

room, -s

Ps 10:4	thoughts there is no *r* for God
Mt 6:6	when you pray, go into your *r*,
Mk 14:15	He will show you a large upper *r*,
Lk 2:7	was no *r* for them in the inn
Jn 14:2	In my Father's house are many *r-s*;
21:25	the whole world would not have *r*
Ro 12:19	leave *r* for God's wrath,
Heb 9:7	high priest entered the inner *r*,

root, -s, -ed

Isa 11:1	his *r-s* a Branch will bear fruit
53:2	like a *r* out of dry ground.
Mt 3:10	The axe is already at the *r* of
13:6	withered because they had no *r*
Ro 15:12	"The *R* of Jesse will spring up,
Eph 3:17	being *r-ed* and established in love
1Ti 6:10	money is a *r* of all kinds of evil.
Heb 12:15	bitter *r* grows up to cause trouble

rose

Mk 16:9	Jesus *r* early on the first day
Ac 10:41	after he *r* from the dead
1Th 4:14	We believe that Jesus died and *r*

royal

1Ki 9:5	I will establish your *r* throne
Isa 62:3	a *r* diadem in the hand
Da 4:31	Your *r* authority has been taken
Jn 4:46	there was a certain *r* official
Ac 12:21	Herod, wearing his *r* robes,
Jas 2:8	keep the *r* law found in Scripture,
1Pe 2:9	chosen people, a *r* priesthood,

rubbish

Php 3:8	I consider them *r*, that I may gain

rubies

Job 28:18	the price of wisdom is beyond *r*
Pr 3:15	She is more precious than *r*;
8:11	wisdom is more precious than *r*,
31:10	She is worth far more than *r*

rudder

Jas 3:4	steered by a very small *r*

ruddy

1Sa 17:42	he was only a boy, *r* and handsome,
SS 5:10	My lover is radiant and *r*,

rude

1Co 13:5	is not *r*, it is not self-seeking,

ruin, -s, -ed

Ps 73:18	you cast them down to *r*
Pr 10:8	a chattering fool comes to *r*
18:24	come to *r*, but there is a friend
SS 2:15	little foxes that *r* the vineyards,
Isa 6:5	"Woe to me!" I cried. "I am *r-ed*!
Jer 9:11	I will make Jerusalem a heap of *r-s*
Hag 1:4	while this house remains a *r*?
Mt 12:25	divided against itself will be *r-ed*
Ac 15:16	Its *r-s* I will rebuild,
1Ti 6:9	plunge men into *r* and destruction

rule, -s, -r, -rs

Ge 1:26	let them *r* over the fish
3:16	husband, and he will *r* over you.
1Ki 8:16	chosen David to *r* my people Israel.
Ps 2:2	the *r-rs* gather together against
2:9	will *r* them with an iron sceptre;
8:6	You made him *r-r* over the works
Pr 8:15	By me kings reign and *r-rs*
Isa 29:13	made up only of *r-s* taught by men
Mic 5:2	who will be *r-r* over Israel,
Mt 2:6	least among the *r-rs* of Judah;
9:18	a *r-r* came and knelt before him
15:9	teachings are but *r-s* taught
20:25	the *r-rs* of the Gentiles lord it
Ro 13:9	summed up in this one *r*: "Love

8:1 Now about food *s-d* to idols:
Heb 7:27 He *s-d* for their sins once
9:28 Christ was *s-d* once to take away
10:5 said: "*S* and offering you did not
10:18 there is no longer any *s* for sin
11:4 Abel offered God a better *s*
1Pe 2:5 spiritual *s-s* acceptable to God
1Jn 2:2 the atoning *s* for our sins,

sad
Ne 2:1 I had not been *s* in his presence
Ecc 7:3 a *s* face is good for the heart.
Mt 19:22 went away *s*, because he had great
26:22 They were very *s* and began to say

Sadducees
Mt 16:6 the yeast of the Pharisees and *S*.
22:23 the *S*, who say there is no
Ac 23:8 (The *S* say that there is no

safe, -ty
Ps 4:8 O LORD, make me dwell in *s-ty*
Pr 18:10 righteous run to it and are *s*
Lk 11:21 his possessions are *s*
Jn 17:12 I protected them and kept them *s*
1Th 5:3 saying, "Peace and *s-ty*",

saints
1Sa 2:9 He will guard the feet of his *s*,
Ps 116:15 is the death of his *s*
Ro 8:27 the Spirit intercedes for the *s*
1Co 6:2 the *s* will judge the world?
2Co 1:1 together with all the *s*
Eph 1:18 his glorious inheritance in the *s*
Jude :3 once for all entrusted to the *s*
Rev 5:8 which are the prayers of the *s*
19:8 the righteous acts of the *s*.

salt
Ge 19:26 she became a pillar of *s*
Mt 5:13 "You are the *s* of the earth.
Jas 3:11 Can both fresh water and *s* water

salvation
Ex 15:2 he has become my *s*.
2Sa 22:3 my shield and the horn of my *s*.
Ps 13:5 my heart rejoices in your *s*
27:1 The LORD is my light and my *s*—
51:12 Restore to me the joy of your *s*
Isa 12:3 draw water from the wells of *s*
30:15 "In repentance and rest is your *s*,
59:17 the helmet of *s* on his head;
Jnh 2:9 *S* comes from the LORD.
Lk 1:69 He has raised up a horn of *s*
19:9 "Today *s* has come to this house,
Ac 4:12 *S* is found in no-one else,
Ro 1:16 it is the power of God for the *s*
2Co 6:2 now is the day of *s*.
Eph 6:17 Take the helmet of *s*
Php 2:12 work out your *s* with fear
2Ti 3:15 make you wise for *s* through faith
Tit 2:11 the grace of God that brings *s*
Heb 2:3 if we ignore such a great *s*?
1Pe 1:10 Concerning this *s*, the prophets,
2Pe 3:15 our Lord's patience means *s*,
Rev 7:10 "*S* belongs to our God,

Samaria
Jn 4:4 Now he had to go through *S*
Ac 8:5 Philip went down to a city in *S*

Samaritan
Lk 10:33 But a *S*, as he travelled,
17:16 thanked him—and he was a *S*
Jn 4:7 a *S* woman came to draw water,

Samson
Judge. Birth promised (Jdg 13:2–3); set apart as Nazirite (Jdg 13:4–7); great strength linked with uncut hair (Jdg 16:17,22). Married Philistine (Jdg 14); killed lion, 30 Philistines (Jdg 14:6,19). Took vengeance on Philistines when wife given away (Jdg 15); killed 1,000 with jaw-bone (Jdg 15:15–16). Carried off gates of Gaza (Jdg 16:1–3). Betrayed by Delilah and captured (Jdg 16:4–21); died when brought temple of Dagon down on Philistines (Jdg 16:23–30).

Samuel
Judge and prophet (Ac 3:24; 13:20). Born to Hannah, who vowed to dedicate him to God (1Sa 1:9–20). Taken to temple to be raised by Eli (1Sa 1:21–28; 2:11,18–21). Called by God (1Sa 3). Led Israel to victory

over Philistines (1Sa 7). Asked by people for a king (1Sa 8); anointed Saul (1Sa 9–10). Farewell speech (1Sa 12). Rebuked Saul (1Sa 13:8–14; 15); and announced his rejection by God (1Sa 13:13–14; 15:22–26). Anointed David (1Sa 16:1–13); protected David (1Sa 19:18–24). Death (1Sa 25:1). Spirit called up by Saul (1Sa 28:11–19).

Sanballat
Horonite; governor of Samaria; leading opponent of Nehemiah in his task to rebuild walls of Jerusalem (Ne 2:10,19; 4:1–9; 6).

sanctify, -ing, -ied
Jn 17:17 — *S* them by the truth;
Ac 20:32 — among all those who are *s-ied*
26:18 — *s-ied* by faith in me.
Ro 15:16 — *s-ied* by the Holy Spirit
1Co 6:11 — you were washed, you were *s-ied*,
7:14 — unbelieving husband has been *s-ied*
1Th 4:3 — will that you should be *s-ied*:
1Pe 1:2 — the *s-ing* work of the Spirit,

sanctuary
Ex 25:8 — have them make a *s* for me,
Ps 15:1 — LORD, who may dwell in your *s*?
73:17 — till I entered the *s* of God;
Heb 6:19 — It enters the inner *s*
8:2 — the *s*, the true tabernacle
9:24 — Christ did not enter a man-made *s*

sand
Ge 22:17 — as the *s* on the seashore.
Mt 7:26 — man who built his house on *s*
Ro 9:27 — be like the *s* by the sea,

sandal, -s
Ex 3:5 — "Take off your *s-s*, for the place
Mt 3:11 — whose *s-s* I am not fit to carry.
10:10 — or *s-s* or a staff; for the worker

sang
Job 38:7 — the morning stars *s* together
Mt 11:17 — you did not dance; we *s* a dirge,
Rev 5:9 — And they *s* a new song:
15:3 — and *s* the song of Moses

Sarah
Wife of Abraham; formerly Sarai; barren (Ge 11:29–30). Taken by Pharaoh when pretending to be Abraham's sister (Ge 12:10–20). Gave Hagar to Abraham (Ge 16:1–3). Name changed; promised a son (Ge 17:15–21; 18:9–10; Ro 9:9; Heb 11:11); laughed in disbelief (Ge 18:10–15). Taken by Abimelech when pretending to be Abraham's sister; returned (Ge 20:1–18). Gave birth to Isaac (Ge 21:1–7); sent away Hagar and Ishmael (Ge 21:8–14). Death and burial (Ge 23).

sat
Ps 137:1 — By the rivers of Babylon we *s* and
Mk 16:19 — up into heaven and he *s* at
Heb 1:3 — he *s* down at the right hand
Rev 3:21 — I overcame and *s* down
5:7 — right hand of him who *s*

Satan
Job 1:6 — *S* also came with them
Mt 4:10 — "Away from me, *S*!
12:26 — If *S* drives out *S*,
16:23 — said to Peter, "Get behind me, *S*!
Lk 10:18 — "I saw *S* fall like lightning
1Co 5:5 — hand this man over to *S*,
2Co 11:14 — *S* himself masquerades as an angel
12:7 — a messenger of *S*, to torment me

satisfy, -ies, -ied
Ps 17:15 — when I awake, I shall be *s-ied*
103:5 — who *s-ies* your desires with good
Isa 53:11 — the light (of life) and be *s-ied*;
55:2 — your labour on what does not *s*?
Mt 14:20 — They all ate and were *s-ied*,
Lk 6:21 — hunger now, for you will be *s-ied*.

Saul
1. Benjamite; Israel's first king. Chosen by God (1Sa 9:15–16); anointed by Samuel (1Sa 10:1); acknowledged publicly (1Sa 10:17–25). Defeated Ammonites (1Sa 11). Rebuked by Samuel, when offered sacrifices (1Sa 13) and for disobedience

(1Sa 15); rejected as king (1Sa 13:13–14; 15:23,26–28; 28:17). Defeated Philistines (1Sa 14). Troubled by evil spirit; soothed by David's playing (1Sa 16:14–23). Sent David to fight Goliath (1Sa 17). Gave David his daughter Michal as wife (1Sa 18:20–21). Became jealous; tried to kill David (1Sa 18:1–11; 19:1–10). Anger at Jonathan (1Sa 20:26–34). Pursued David; killed priests at Nob (1Sa 22); life spared by David (1Sa 24; 26). Consulted medium at Endor; rebuked by Samuel's spirit (1Sa 28). Defeated by Philistines on Mt Gilboa; wounded, took own life (1Sa 31; 1Ch 10). Mourned by David (2Sa 1:19–27). Children (1Sa 14:49–51; 1Ch 8). **2.** See *Paul.*

save, -s, -d

Ps 6:4 *s* me because of your unfailing love
39:8 *S* me from all my transgressions;
68:20 Our God is a God who *s-s*;
Isa 45:22 "Turn to me and be *s-d*,
59:1 LORD is not too short to *s*,
Da 3:17 God we serve is able to *s* us
Mt 1:21 because he will *s* his people
10:22 stands firm to the end will be *s-d*
16:25 to *s* his life will lose it,
19:25 "Who then can be *s-d*?
Lk 7:50 "Your faith has *s-d* you;
19:10 to seek and to *s* what was lost.
Jn 3:17 but to *s* the world through him
10:9 enters through me will be *s-d*.
Ac 4:12 by which we must be *s-d*.
16:31 be *s-d*—you and your household.
Ro 10:13 name of the Lord will be *s-d*.
1Co 1:18 to us who are being *s-d* it is the
3:15 he himself will be *s-d*,
9:22 possible means I might *s* some
Eph 2:5 it is by grace you have been *s-d*
1Ti 1:15 into the world to *s* sinners—
2:4 who wants all men to be *s-d*
Heb 7:25 he is able to *s* completely those

saviour

Dt 32:15 rejected the Rock his *S*
Ps 25:5 you are God my *S*,
Isa 43:11 apart from me there is no *s*
62:11 'See, your *S* comes! See, his reward
Lk 1:47 my spirit rejoices in God my *S*
2:11 town of David a *S* has been born
Jn 4:42 really is the *S* of the world.
Php 3:20 we eagerly await a *S* from there,
1Ti 1:1 by the command of God our *S*
2:3 good, and pleases God our *S*
4:10 God, who is the *S* of all men,
Tit 3:4 love of God our *S* appeared,
2Pe 1:1 our God and *S* Jesus Christ
1Jn 4:14 his Son to be the *S* of the world
Jude :25 to the only God our *S* be glory,

scales

Pr 16:11 Honest *s* and balances are from the
Isa 40:15 regarded as dust on the *s*;
Da 5:27 weighed on the *s* and found wanting
Ac 9:18 *s* fell from Saul's eyes,

scapegoat

Lev 16:8 LORD and the other for the *s*

scarlet

Jos 2:18 tied this *s* cord in the window
Isa 1:18 "Though your sins are like *s*,
Mt 27:28 put a *s* robe on him
Rev 17:3 saw a woman sitting on a *s* beast

scatter, -s, -ing, -ed

Isa 11:12 he will assemble the *s-ed* people
Mt 12:30 does not gather with me *s-s*
13:4 As he was *s-ing* the seed,
26:31 sheep of the flock will be *s-ed*.
Ac 8:1 all except the apostles were *s-ed*

sceptre

Ge 49:10 The *s* will not depart from Judah,
Ps 2:9 rule them with an iron *s*;
Heb 1:8 righteousness will be the *s*
Rev 2:27 rule them with an iron *s*;

schemes

2Co 2:11 we are not unaware of his *s*
Eph 6:11 stand against the devil's *s*

scoffers

Ac 13:41 "'Look, you *s*, wonder and perish,
2Pe 3:3 in the last days *s* will come,

Jude :18 last times there will be *s*

scripture, -s

Mt 22:29 because you do not know the *S-s*
26:54 how then would the *S-s* be
Lk 4:21 "Today this *s* is fulfilled
24:32 opened the *S-s* to us?
Jn 5:39 You diligently study the *S-s*
10:35 the *S* cannot be broken
Ac 1:16 the *S* had to be fulfilled
17:11 examined the *S-s* every day
Ro 15:4 encouragement of the *S-s*
1Co 15:3 for our sins according to the *S-s*
Gal 3:8 *S* foresaw that God would justify
1Ti 4:13 to the public reading of *S*,
2Ti 3:15 you have known the holy *S-s*,
3:16 All *S* is God-breathed and is useful
2Pe 1:20 no prophecy of *S* came about by

scroll

Ps 40:7 it is written about me in the *s*
Isa 34:4 the sky rolled up like a *s*;
Heb 10:7 it is written about me in the *s*—
Rev 5:2 break the seals and open the *s*?

scum

1Co 4:13 we have become the *s* of the earth,

sea

Ex 14:22 went through the *s* on dry ground,
Ps 107:23 Others went out on the *s* in ships;
139:9 I settle on the far side of the *s*
Isa 11:9 as the waters cover the *s*
Hab 2:14 as the waters cover the *s*
Mt 21:21 'Go, throw yourself into the *s*,'
23:15 land and *s* to win a single convert
1Co 10:1 they all passed through the *s*
Jas 1:6 doubts is like a wave of the *s*,
Jude :13 They are wild waves of the *s*,
Rev 20:13 The *s* gave up the dead
21:1 and there was no longer any *s*

seal, -s, -ed

Mt 27:66 tomb secure by putting a *s* on
Jn 6:27 God the Father has placed his *s*
2Co 1:22 set his *s* of ownership on us,
Eph 1:13 you were marked in him with a *s*,
4:30 with whom you were *s-ed*
Rev 5:2 "Who is worthy to break the *s-s*

search, -es, -ing, -ed

Ps 139:1 O LORD, you have *s-ed* me
139:23 *S* me, O God, and know my heart;
Jer 17:10 "I the LORD *s* the heart
Lk 2:49 "Why were you *s-ing* for me?"
Ro 8:27 he who *s-es* our hearts
1Co 2:10 The Spirit *s-es* all things,
1Pe 1:10 *s-ed* intently and with

seashore

Ge 22:17 as the sand on the *s*.
Heb 11:12 countless as the sand on the *s*

season, -s

Ps 1:3 which yields its fruit in *s*
Gal 4:10 special days and months and *s-s*
2Ti 4:2 prepared in *s* and out of season;

seasoned

Col 4:6 full of grace, *s* with salt,

seat, -s, -ed

Ps 1:1 or sit in the *s* of mockers
Isa 6:1 I saw the Lord *s-ed* on a throne,
Mt 23:6 important *s-s* in the synagogues
Jn 12:15 king is coming, *s-ed* on a donkey's
2Co 5:10 before the judgment *s* of Christ,
Eph 2:6 raised us up with Christ and *s-ed*
Col 3:1 things above, where Christ is *s-ed*
Rev 20:11 white throne and him who was *s-ed*

secret, -s, -ly

Dt 29:29 The *s* things belong to the LORD
Mt 6:4 your giving may be in *s*.
13:11 the *s-s* of the kingdom of heaven
Jn 19:38 a disciple of Jesus, but *s-ly*

Ro 2:16 God will judge men's *s-s* through
2Co 4:2 renounced *s* and shameful ways;
Php 4:12 learned the *s* of being content

see, -s, -ing, -n
Ge 16:13 "You are the God who *s-s* me,"
Ex 16:7 will *s* the glory of the LORD,
33:20 "you cannot *s* my face,
Jdg 13:22 "We have *s-n* God!
Job 19:26 in my flesh I will *s* God
Ps 27:13 I will *s* the goodness of the LORD
34:8 Taste and *s* that the LORD is good;
37:25 I have never *s-n* the righteous
119:18 that I may *s* wonderful things
139:24 *S* if there is any offensive way
Isa 6:5 my eyes have *s-n* the King,
6:9 be ever *s-ing*, but never perceiving
9:2 have *s-n* a great light;
52:10 will *s* the salvation of our God
53:10 he will *s* his offspring
Mt 4:16 have *s-n* a great light;
5:8 pure in heart, for they will *s* God
Lk 2:30 my eyes have *s-n* your salvation
Jn 1:14 We have *s-n* his glory,
1:18 No-one has ever *s-n* God,
17:24 and to *s* my glory,
20:29 "Because you have *s-n* me,
Ac 1:11 you have *s-n* him go into heaven.
2:31 nor did his body *s* decay.
Ro 8:24 hope that is *s-n* is no hope at all.
1Co 2:9 No eye has *s-n*, no ear has heard,
1Ti 3:16 was *s-n* by angels,
Heb 2:9 But we *s* Jesus,
1Jn 1:1 we have *s-n* with our eyes,
3:2 we shall *s* him as he is.

seed, -time
Ge 8:22 earth endures, *s-time* and harvest,
Mt 13:3 "A farmer went out to sow his *s*
13:31 heaven is like a mustard *s*,
1Co 3:6 I planted the *s*, Apollos watered it
Gal 3:16 spoken to Abraham and to his *s*.
1Pe 1:23 born again, not of perishable *s*,

seek, -s
Dt 4:29 if from there you *s* the LORD
2Ch 7:14 humble themselves and pray and *s*
Ps 27:8 Your face, LORD, I will *s*
Isa 55:6 *S* the LORD while he may be found;
65:1 found by those who did not *s* me.
Jer 45:5 Should you then *s* great things
Mt 6:33 But *s* first his kingdom
7:7 *s* and you will find;
Lk 19:10 Son of Man came to *s* and to save
Jn 4:23 worshippers the Father *s-s*
Ac 17:27 God did this so that men would *s*
Ro 3:11 no-one who *s-s* God
10:20 found by those who did not *s* me;

self-control, -led
Gal 5:23 gentleness and *s*. Against such
1Ti 3:2 temperate, *s-led*, respectable,
Tit 2:6 the young men to be *s-led*
1Pe 5:8 Be *s-led* and alert. Your enemy

self-discipline
2Ti 1:7 of power, of love and of *s*

self-seeking
Ro 2:8 those who are *s* and who reject
1Co 13:5 It is not rude, it is not *s*,

selfish
Pr 18:1 An unfriendly man pursues *s* ends;
Gal 5:20 fits of rage, *s* ambition,
Php 1:17 preach Christ out of *s* ambition,
2:3 Do nothing out of *s* ambition
Jas 3:16 you have envy and *s* ambition,

sell
Pr 23:23 Buy the truth and do not *s* it;
Am 2:6 They *s* the righteous for silver,
Mt 19:21 perfect, go, *s* your possessions

send, -s, -ing
Ps 43:3 *S* forth your light and your truth,
Isa 6:8 "Here am I. *S* me!"

Mal 3:1	"See, I will *s* my messenger,
Mt 5:45	*s-s* rain on the righteous
9:38	*s* out workers into his harvest
10:16	I am *s-ing* you out like sheep
Lk 24:49	*s* you what my Father has promised;
Jn 3:17	did not *s* his Son into the world
14:26	Spirit, whom the Father will *s*
16:7	I will *s* him to you
20:21	I am *s-ing* you.
Ro 8:3	God did by *s-ing* his own Son

Sennacherib

King of Assyria. Attacked Judah and laid siege to Jerusalem (2Ki 18:13–19:13; Isa 36:1–37:13; 2Ch 32). Pride brought God's judgment (Isa 10:12–19). Fall prophesied by Isaiah, following Hezekiah's prayer (2Ki 19:14–34; Isa 37:14–35); defeat and death (2Ki 19:35–37; Isa 37:36–38).

senses

Lk 15:17	"When he came to his *s*, he said,
1Co 15:34	Come back to your *s* as you ought,

sent

Ex 3:14	'I AM has *s* me to you.'
Isa 55:11	the purpose for which I *s* it.
61:1	He has *s* me to bind up
Da 3:28	has *s* his angel and rescued
Mt 10:40	receives the one who *s* me.
15:24	"I was *s* only to the lost sheep
22:3	He *s* his servants to those
Mk 9:37	welcome me but the one who *s* me.
Lk 1:26	God *s* the angel Gabriel
Jn 1:6	a man who was *s* from God;
6:44	the Father who *s* me draws him,
17:3	Jesus Christ, whom you have *s*.
Ro 10:15	preach unless they are *s*?
Gal 4:4	time had fully come, God *s* his Son,
2Pe 2:4	but *s* them to hell,
1Jn 4:10	he loved us and *s* his Son

separate, -s, -d

Pr 16:28	a gossip *s-s* close friends
Isa 59:2	have *s-d* you from your God;
Mt 19:6	joined together, let man not *s*.
25:32	will *s* the people one from another
Ro 8:35	Who shall *s* us from the love of
1Co 7:10	A wife must not *s* from her husband
Eph 2:12	time you were *s* from Christ,

seraphs

Isa 6:2	Above him were *s*, each with six
6:6	the *s* flew to me with a live coal

serpent, -'s

Ge 3:1	Now the *s* was more crafty
2Co 11:3	Eve was deceived by the *s-'s*
Rev 12:9	that ancient *s* called the devil,

servant, -s

1Sa 3:9	'Speak, LORD, for your *s*
2Sa 11:21	your *s* Uriah the Hittite is dead.'
2Ki 17:13	through my *s-s* the prophets.
Job 1:8	"Have you considered my *s* Job?
Ps 19:11	By them is your *s* warned;
34:22	The LORD redeems his *s-s*;
134:1	Praise the LORD, all you *s-s* of
Isa 41:9	'You are my *s*'; I have chosen you
42:1	"Here is my *s*, whom I uphold,
52:13	See, my *s* will act wisely;
53:11	my righteous *s* will justify many,
Am 3:7	revealing his plan to his *s-s*
Mal 1:6	and a *s* his master.
Mt 8:8	say the word, and my *s* will
10:24	nor a *s* above his master
12:18	"Here is my *s* whom I have chosen,
20:26	great among you must be your *s*
23:11	greatest among you will be your *s*
25:21	'Well done, good and faithful *s*!
26:51	struck the *s* of the high priest,
Lk 1:38	"I am the Lord's *s*,"
1:54	He has helped his *s* Israel,
16:13	"No *s* can serve two masters.
17:10	'We are unworthy *s-s*;
Jn 12:26	where I am, my *s* also will be.
13:16	no *s* is greater than his master,
15:15	I no longer call you *s-s*,
Ac 4:27	conspire against your holy *s* Jesus,
12:13	a *s* girl named Rhoda came to

Ro 13:4 he is God's *s* to do you good.
14:4 to judge someone else's *s*?
1Co 3:5 what is Paul? Only *s-s*,
4:1 to regard us as *s-s* of Christ
2Co 4:5 ourselves as your *s-s* for Jesus'
Php 2:7 taking the very nature of a *s*,
Col 1:23 I, Paul, have become a *s*
2Ti 2:24 the Lord's *s* must not quarrel;
Heb 1:7 his *s-s* flames of fire.
3:5 Moses was faithful as a *s*

serve, -s, -ing, -d

Ge 25:23 the older will *s* the younger.
Dt 6:13 Fear the LORD your God, *s* him only
Jos 24:15 this day whom you will *s*,
1Ki 18:15 the LORD Almighty lives, whom I *s*,
Ps 2:11 *S* the LORD with fear and rejoice
Da 3:17 the God we *s* is able to save us
Mt 4:10 Lord your God, and *s* him only.'
6:24 "No-one can *s* two masters.
20:28 Son of Man did not come to be *s-d*,
Ac 17:25 he is not *s-d* by human hands,
Ro 1:25 worshipped and *s-d* created things
9:12 "The older will *s* the younger.
12:7 If it is *s-ing*, let him *s*;
1Co 9:7 Who *s-s* as a soldier at his own
Col 3:24 the Lord Christ you are *s-ing*
1Th 1:9 to God from idols to *s* the living
1Ti 3:10 let them *s* as deacons
Heb 1:14 ministering spirits sent to *s*
7:13 has ever *s-d* at the altar
1Pe 4:10 gift he has received to *s* others,
Rev 22:3 his servants will *s* him

service

Lk 1:23 When his time of *s* was completed,
9:62 plough and looks back is fit for *s*
1Co 12:5 There are different kinds of *s*,
Eph 4:12 God's people for works of *s*,

settle

Ps 139:9 if I *s* on the far side of the sea
Mt 5:25 "*S* matters quickly with

seven, -s

Ge 7:2 Take with you *s* of every kind
Jos 6:4 march around the city *s* times,
Da 4:25 *S* times will pass by for you
9:24 "Seventy '*s-s*' are decreed
Mt 18:21 sins against me? Up to *s* times?
22:25 Now there were *s* brothers
Mk 16:9 out of whom he had driven *s* demons
Rev 1:12 I turned I saw *s* golden lampstands
6:1 opened the first of the *s* seals.
17:9 The *s* heads are *s* hills

seventh

Ge 2:2 By the *s* day God had finished
Ex 20:10 the *s* day is a Sabbath to the LORD
Rev 8:1 When he opened the *s* seal,

seventy

Nu 11:16 "Bring me *s* of Israel's elders
Ps 90:10 The length of our days is *s* years
Jer 25:12 when the *s* years are fulfilled,

sew, -s, -ed

Ge 3:7 they *s-ed* fig leaves together
Mt 9:16 "No-one *s-s* a patch of unshrunk

sexual, -ly

Ex 22:19 who has *s* relations with an animal
Lev 18:6 close relative to have *s* relations.
Mt 15:19 adultery, *s* immorality, theft,
Ro 1:24 to *s* impurity for the degrading
1Co 5:1 there is *s* immorality among you,
6:9 Neither the *s-ly* immoral
Eph 5:3 not be even a hint of *s* immorality,
1Th 4:3 you should avoid *s* immorality;
Heb 12:16 See that no-one is *s-ly* immoral,

shadow

Ps 17:8 hide me in the *s* of your wing
23:4 the valley of the *s* of death,
Isa 51:16 covered you with the *s* of my hand—
Mt 4:16 in the land of the *s* of death
Heb 10:1 The law is only a *s*

Shadrach

Formerly Hananiah; member of Jewish nobility taken to Babylon with Daniel,

Meshach and Abednego (Da 1:3–7). Refused unclean food (Da 1:8–16); appointed as administrator (Da 2:49). Refused to worship golden image; kept safe in fiery furnace (Da 3).

shake, -n

Ps 16:8	I shall not be *s-n*
Isa 54:10	Though the mountains be *s-n*
Mt 10:14	*s* the dust off your feet
24:29	the heavenly bodies will be *s-n*.
Ac 2:25	right hand, I will not be *s-n*
Heb 12:28	a kingdom that cannot be *s-n*,

shame, -ful

Ge 2:25	naked, and they felt no *s*
Ps 25:2	Do not let me be put to *s*,
Da 12:2	to *s* and everlasting contempt
Ro 1:26	God gave them over to *s-ful* lusts.
10:11	will never be put to *s*.
1Co 1:27	foolish things of the world to *s*
2Co 4:2	renounced secret and *s-ful* ways;
Php 3:19	their glory is in their *s*.
Heb 12:2	endured the cross, scorning its *s*,

share, -s, -ing, -d

Ge 21:10	slave woman's son will never *s*
Pr 21:9	*s* a house with a quarrelsome wife
Isa 58:7	Is it not to *s* your food
Mt 25:21	Come and *s* your master's happiness!
Lk 3:11	"The man with two tunics should *s*
15:12	'Father, give me my *s*
Jn 13:18	'He who *s-s* my bread has lifted up
Ac 4:32	they *s-d* everything they had
Ro 8:17	if indeed we *s* in his sufferings
Gal 4:30	slave woman's son will never *s*
6:6	must *s* all good things
Eph 4:28	he may have something to *s*
Php 3:10	the fellowship of *s-ing* in his
Col 1:12	you to *s* in the inheritance

Sharon

SS 2:1	I am a rose of *S*, a lily

sharpen, -s

Ps 64:3	They *s* their tongues like swords
Pr 27:17	As iron *s-s* iron,

sheaf, -ves

Ge 37:7	suddenly my *s* rose and stood
Ru 2:7	glean and gather among the *s-ves*
Ps 126:6	carrying *s-ves* with him

shearer, -s

Isa 53:7	a sheep before her *s-s* is silent,
Ac 8:32	a lamb before the *s* is silent,

Shechem

Son of Hamor, a ruling Hivite (Ge 34:2). Raped Jacob's daughter, Dinah, and asked to marry her (Ge 34:2–12). Shechemites treacherously killed by Simeon and Levi in revenge (Ge 34:13–31).

shed, -s, -ding

Ge 9:6	"Whoever *s-s* the blood of man,
Ac 22:20	blood of your martyr Stephen was *s*,
Col 1:20	through his blood, *s* on the cross
Heb 9:22	without the *s-ding* of blood

sheep, -'s

Nu 27:17	not be like *s* without a shepherd.
1Sa 15:14	"What then is this bleating of *s*
Ps 100:3	his people, the *s* of his pasture
Isa 53:6	We all, like *s*, have gone astray,
53:7	a *s* before her shearers is silent,
Zec 13:7	and the *s* will be scattered,
Mt 7:15	They come to you in *s-'s* clothing,
9:36	like *s* without a shepherd
10:6	to the lost *s* of Israel
25:33	He will put the *s* on his right
26:31	*s* of the flock will be scattered.
Jn 10:2	is the shepherd of his *s*
10:7	I am the gate for the *s*
10:11	lays down his life for the *s*
10:26	because you are not my *s*
21:17	"Feed my *s*
Ac 8:32	led like a *s* to the slaughter,
Ro 8:36	considered as *s* to be slaughtered.
Heb 13:20	that great Shepherd of the *s*

shelter, -s

Ps 91:1	dwells in the *s* of the Most High
Eze 17:23	they will find *s* in the shade

Mt 17:4 I will put up three *s-s*—

Shem

Son of Noah (Ge 5:32; 6:10; 1Ch 1:4). Saved in ark (Ge 7:13; 9:18–19). Blessed by Noah (Ge 9:26); descendants (Ge 10:21–31); ancestor of Abraham (Ge 11:10–32).

shepherd, -s

Ps 23:1 The LORD is my *s*,
80:1 Hear us, O *S* of Israel,
Isa 40:11 He tends his flock like a *s*:
Eze 34:2 prophesy against the *s-s* of Israel;
Lk 2:8 there were *s-s* living out
Jn 10:2 who enters by the gate is the *s*
10:11 "I am the good *s*.
Ac 20:28 Be *s-s* of the church of God,
Heb 13:20 that great *S* of the sheep
1Pe 5:4 And when the Chief *S* appears,

Shibboleth

Jdg 12:6 "All right, say '*S*'."

shield, -ed

Ge 15:1 I am your *s*, your very great
Ps 28:7 The LORD is my strength and my *s*;
Eph 6:16 take up the *s* of faith,
1Pe 1:5 through faith are *s-ed* by God's

shine

Nu 6:25 LORD make his face *s* upon you
Isa 60:1 "Arise, *s*, for your light
Mt 5:16 let your light *s* before men,
13:43 the righteous will *s* like the sun
2Co 4:6 "Let light *s* out of darkness,"
Php 2:15 you *s* like stars in the universe

ship, -s

Ps 107:23 went out on the sea in *s-s*;
Jnh 1:3 he found a *s* bound for that port.
Ac 27:22 only the *s* will be destroyed

shipwrecked

2Co 11:25 three times I was *s*,
1Ti 1:19 so have *s* their faith

shone

Mt 17:2 His face *s* like the sun,
Lk 2:9 glory of the Lord *s* around them,
Rev 21:11 It *s* with the glory of God,

shook

Ps 18:7 foundations of the mountains *s*;
Isa 6:4 thresholds *s* and the temple
Mt 27:51 The earth *s* and the rocks split
Ac 13:51 they *s* the dust from their feet
Heb 12:26 his voice *s* the earth,

shoot

Isa 11:1 A *s* will come up from the stump
53:2 grew up before him like a tender *s*,
Ro 11:17 and you, though a wild olive *s*,

short

Nu 11:23 "Is the LORD's arm too *s*?
Isa 59:1 LORD is not too *s* to save,
Mt 13:21 he lasts only a *s* time.
24:22 If those days had not been cut *s*,
Ro 3:23 sinned and fall *s* of the glory
Heb 11:25 pleasures of sin for a *s* time

shorten, -ed

Mt 24:22 elect those days will be *s-ed*

show, -ed, -n

Ex 33:18 "Now *s* me your glory.
Ps 18:25 To the faithful you *s* yourself
25:4 *S* me your ways, O LORD,
Joel 2:30 I will *s* wonders in the heavens
Mic 6:8 He has *s-ed* you, O man,
Mal 1:6 who *s* contempt for my name.
Mt 4:8 and *s-ed* him all the kingdoms
5:7 for they will be *s-n* mercy
18:15 go and *s* him his fault,
22:19 *S* me the coin used for paying
Lk 12:5 I will *s* you whom you should fear:
Jn 5:20 Son and *s-s* him all he does.
14:8 "Lord, *s* us the Father
Ac 2:19 I will *s* wonders in the heaven
Ro 9:22 choosing to *s* his wrath
1Co 12:31 I will *s* you the most excellent
Eph 2:7 might *s* the incomparable riches
Jas 2:18 I will *s* you my faith by what
1Pe 2:17 *S* proper respect to everyone:

shrewd, -ly

Mt 10:16 Therefore be as *s* as snakes
Lk 16:8 manager because he had acted *s-ly*.

shun, -s

Job 1:8 — a man who fears God and *s-s* evil.
Pr 3:7 — fear the LORD and *s* evil.
Isa 59:15 — whoever *s-s* evil becomes a prey.

shut

Isa 22:22 — what he opens no-one can *s*,
52:15 — kings will *s* their mouths
60:11 — will never be *s*, day or night,
Da 6:22 — he *s* the mouths of the lions.
Rev 3:7 — What he opens no-one can *s*,

sick, -ness

Pr 13:12 — Hope deferred makes the heart *s*,
Mt 9:12 — who need a doctor, but the *s*
25:36 — I was *s* and you looked after me,
Jn 11:4 — This *s-ness* will not end in death.
1Co 11:30 — many among you are weak and *s*,
Jas 5:14 — Is any one of you *s*?

side

Ps 91:7 — A thousand may fall at your *s*,
124:1 — If the LORD had not been on our *s*—
Lk 10:31 — he passed by on the other *s*
16:22 — angels carried him to Abraham's *s*.
Jn 1:18 — who is at the Father's *s*,
20:20 — he showed them his hands and *s*.
2Co 4:8 — We are hard pressed on every *s*,
2Ti 4:17 — But the Lord stood at my *s*

sift

Lk 22:31 — Satan has asked to *s* you as wheat

sigh, -ing, -ed

Isa 35:10 — sorrow and *s-ing* will flee away
Mk 7:34 — with a deep *s* said to him,
8:12 — He *s-ed* deeply and said,

sight

Ex 3:3 — go over and see this strange *s*—
Ps 19:14 — of my heart be pleasing in your *s*,
51:4 — done what is evil in your *s*,
90:4 — a thousand years in your *s*
116:15 — in the *s* of the LORD is the death
Mt 11:5 — The blind receive *s*, the lame walk,
Ac 4:19 — whether it is right in God's *s*
22:13 — 'Brother Saul, receive your *s*!'
Ro 3:20 — declared righteous in his *s*
2Co 5:7 — We live by faith, not by *s*.
Heb 4:13 — creation is hidden from God's *s*.

sign, -s

Ge 9:13 — it will be the *s* of the covenant
Isa 7:14 — Lord himself will give you a *s*:
Mt 12:39 — asks for a miraculous *s*!
16:3 — interpret the *s-s* of the times
24:3 — what will be the *s* of your coming
Jn 2:11 — the first of his miraculous *s-s*,
20:30 — Jesus did many other miraculous *s-s*
Ac 2:19 — wonders in the heaven above and *s-s*
1Co 1:22 — Jews demand miraculous *s-s*

Silas

Prophet and a leader in Jerusalem church; sent to Antioch from Council of Jerusalem (Ac 15:22–32). Accompanied Paul on second missionary journey (Ac 15:40–18:22; 2Co 1:19). Assisted Peter with first letter (1Pe 5:12); and Paul (1Th 1:1; 2Th 1:1).

silence, -d

Ro 3:19 — so that every mouth may be *s-d*
1Pe 2:15 — by doing good you should *s*
Rev 8:1 — there was *s* in heaven

silent

Pr 17:28 — is thought wise if he keeps *s*,
Isa 53:7 — a sheep before her shearers is *s*,
1Co 14:34 — should remain *s* in the churches.
1Ti 2:12 — she must be *s*

silver

Ps 115:4 — But their idols are *s* and gold,
Pr 8:10 — Choose my instruction instead of *s*,
22:1 — to be esteemed is better than *s*
Am 2:6 — They sell the righteous for *s*,
Hag 2:8 — 'The *s* is mine and the gold

Zec 11:12 they paid me thirty pieces of *s*
Mt 26:15 counted out for him thirty *s* coins
Lk 15:8 a woman has ten *s* coins and loses
Ac 3:6 "*S* or gold I do not have,
1Pe 1:18 with perishable things such as *s*

Simeon

1. Son of Jacob by Leah (Ge 29:33; 35:23; 1Ch 2:1). With Levi killed Shechemites to avenge rape of sister Dinah (Ge 34). Left in Egypt as hostage (Ge 42:24–43:23). Blessed by Jacob (Ge 49:5–7). **2.** Tribe descended from Simeon. Included in census (Nu 1:22–23; 26:12–14). Apportioned land within Judah (Jos 19:1–9). Given territory in restored land (Eze 48:24). **3.** Righteous and devout man in Jerusalem; recognised the child Jesus as the Messiah when he was brought into the temple (Lk 2:25–35).

Simon

1. See *Peter*. **2.** Apostle; called "the Zealot" (Mt 10:4; Mk 3:18; Lk 6:15; Ac 1:13). **3.** Brother of Jesus (Mt 13:55; Mk 6:3). **4.** Leper from Bethany, in whose house Jesus was anointed with oil (Mt 26:6; Mk 14:3). **5.** Pharisee, in whose house Jesus' feet were washed with tears (Lk 7:40). **6.** Man from Cyrene, forced to carry Jesus' cross (Mk 15:21). **7.** Sorcerer, who amazed Samaritans with his magic (Ac 8:9–11). Believed Philip and was baptised (Ac 8:12–13); rebuked by Peter for trying to buy spiritual power (Ac 8:18–24). **8.** Tanner, with whom Peter lodged (Ac 9:43).

simple, -y

Ps 19:7 making wise the *s*
Pr 1:4 giving prudence to the *s*,
1Th 1:5 came to you not *s-y* with words,

sin, -s, -ning, -ned, -ful

Ge 4:7 *s* is crouching at your door;
39:9 a wicked thing and *s* against God?
Nu 14:18 abounding in love and forgiving *s*
32:23 sure that your *s* will find you out
Dt 5:9 punishing the children for the *s*
2Ch 6:36 for there is no-one who does not *s*
7:14 forgive their *s* and will heal
Job 1:22 Job did not *s* by charging God
Ps 4:4 In your anger do not *s*;
19:13 servant also from wilful *s-s*;
32:1 whose *s-s* are covered
51:3 my *s* is always before me
51:4 Against you, you only, have I *s-ned*
66:18 If I had cherished *s* in my heart,
103:3 who forgives all your *s-s* and heals
103:10 not treat us as our *s-s* deserve
119:11 that I might not *s* against you
Isa 1:18 "Though your *s-s* are like scarlet,
6:7 taken away and your *s* atoned for.
53:12 For he bore the *s* of many,
59:2 your *s-s* have hidden his face
Jer 31:30 everyone will die for his own *s*;
Eze 18:20 The soul who *s-s* is the one
Mt 1:21 save his people from their *s-s*.
5:29 If your right eye causes you to *s*,
9:5 'Your *s-s* are forgiven,'
18:15 "If your brother *s-s* against you,
Lk 11:4 Forgive us our *s-s*,
15:18 Father, I have *s-ned*
Jn 1:29 who takes away the *s* of the world
8:7 "If any one of you is without *s*,
8:34 everyone who *s-s* is a slave to *s*
16:8 the world of guilt in regard to *s*
Ac 2:38 for the forgiveness of your *s-s*.
7:60 do not hold this *s* against them."
10:43 receives forgiveness of *s-s*
Ro 1:24 God gave them over in the *s-ful*
3:23 all have *s-ned* and fall short
5:12 just as *s* entered the world
6:1 Shall we go on *s-ning*,
6:12 do not let *s* reign
6:23 For the wages of *s* is death,
7:5 were controlled by the *s-ful* nature
8:2 free from the law of *s* and death
8:4 live according to the *s-ful* nature
8:9 not by the *s-ful* nature but by the
14:23 does not come from faith is *s*

1Co 15:56 The sting of death is *s*,
2Co 5:21 God made him who had no *s* to be *s*
Gal 5:19 of the *s-ful* nature are obvious:
5:24 have crucified the *s-ful* nature
Eph 2:1 dead in your transgressions and *s-s*
Heb 1:3 provided purification for *s-s*,
4:15 just as we are—yet was without *s*
8:12 will remember their *s-s* no more.
9:28 to take away the *ss* of many people;
Jas 5:16 Therefore confess your *s-s*
5:20 and cover over a multitude of *s-s*.
1Pe 2:22 "He committed no *s*,
2:24 He himself bore our *s-s* in his body
3:18 Christ died for *s-s* once for all,
4:8 covers over a multitude of *s-s*
1Jn 1:7 his Son, purifies us from all *s*
1:8 If we claim to be without *s*,
1:9 If we confess our *s-s*,
2:2 the atoning sacrifice for our *s-s*,
3:4 Everyone who *s-s* breaks the law;
3:5 And in him is no *s*.
3:9 born of God will continue to *s*,

Sinai
Ex 19:11 LORD will come down on Mount *S*
Gal 4:24 One covenant is from Mount *S*

sincere
Ro 12:9 Love must be *s*.
1Ti 1:5 a good conscience and a *s* faith
3:8 men worthy of respect, *s*,
Heb 10:22 draw near to God with a *s* heart

sing, -ing
Ex 15:1 "I will *s* to the LORD,
Ps 33:3 *S* to him a new song;
98:8 the mountains *s* together for joy
Isa 12:5 *S* to the LORD, for he has done
Ac 16:25 praying and *s-ing* hymns to God,
1Co 14:15 I will *s* with my spirit,
Eph 5:19 *S* and make music in your heart
Jas 5:13 Let him *s* songs of praise

sinner, -s
Ps 1:1 stand in the way of *s-s*
Mt 9:11 eat with tax collectors and '*s-s*'?
9:13 call the righteous, but *s-s*.
Lk 15:7 rejoicing in heaven over one *s*
18:13 'God, have mercy on me, a *s*.
Ro 5:8 While we were still *s-s*,
1Ti 1:15 into the world to save *s-s*—
1:16 in me, the worst of *s-s*,

sister, -s
SS 4:9 You have stolen my heart, my *s*,
Mt 12:50 is my brother and *s* and mother.
19:29 left houses or brothers or *s-s*
Lk 10:40 don't you care that my *s* has left
1Ti 5:2 women as *s-s*, with absolute purity
Jas 2:15 a brother or *s* is without clothes

sit, -s, -ting
Ps 1:1 or *s* in the seat of mockers
110:1 The LORD says to my Lord: "*S* at
139:2 You know when I *s* and
Isa 40:22 He *s-s* enthroned above the circle
Mt 19:28 Son of Man *s-s* on his glorious
22:44 'The Lord said to my Lord: "*S* at
26:64 see the Son of Man *s-ting*
Heb 1:13 angels did God ever say, "*S* at
Rev 5:13 "To him who *s-s* on the throne

skin
Job 19:20 by only the *s* of my teeth.
19:26 after my *s* has been destroyed,
Jer 13:23 Can the Ethiopian change his *s*
Mt 9:17 If they do, the *s* will burst,

skull
Mt 27:33 (which means The Place of the *S*)

sky
Ge 1:8 God called the expanse "*s*".
Isa 34:4 the *s* rolled up like a scroll;
Mt 16:2 fair weather, for the *s* is red,
24:30 Son of Man will appear in the *s*,

Ac 1:10 up into the *s* as he was going,
Rev 6:13 the stars in the *s* fell to earth,

slain
1Sa 18:7 "Saul has *s* his thousands,
Rev 5:6 Lamb, looking as if it had been *s*,
5:12 "Worthy is the Lamb, who was *s*,

slander, -ed
Lev 19:16 " 'Do not go about spreading *s*
Eph 4:31 rage and anger, brawling and *s*,
1Ti 5:14 the enemy no opportunity for *s*

slaughter, -ed
Ps 44:22 considered as sheep to be *s-ed*
Isa 53:7 led like a lamb to the *s*,
Ac 8:32 led like a sheep to the *s*,
Ro 8:36 considered as sheep to be *s-ed*.

slave, -s, -ry
Ge 21:10 "Get rid of that *s* woman
Dt 5:15 Remember that you were *s-s*
Mt 20:27 to be first must be your *s*
Jn 8:34 everyone who sins is a *s* to sin
Ro 6:6 we should no longer be *s-s* to sin
7:25 in my mind am a *s* to God's law,
1Co 9:27 I beat my body and make it my *s*
Gal 3:28 neither Jew nor Greek, *s* nor free,
4:30 rid of the *s* woman and her son,
5:1 burdened again by a yoke of *s-ry*
Eph 6:5 *S-s*, obey your earthly masters

slay
Job 13:15 Though he *s* me, yet will I hope
Ps 139:19 If only you would *s* the wicked,

sleep, -ing, -er
Ge 2:21 the man to fall into a deep *s*;
Ps 127:2 he grants *s* to those he loves
Pr 6:10 A little *s*, a little slumber,
Mt 26:40 disciples and found them *s-ing*.
1Co 15:51 We will not all *s*, but we will
Eph 5:14 Wake up, O *s-er*, rise from the dead
1Th 5:7 For those who *s*, *s* at night,

sling
1Sa 17:50 Philistine with a *s* and a stone;

slip, -ped
Ps 73:2 my feet had almost *s-ped*;
121:3 He will not let your foot *s*—

slow
Ex 34:6 gracious God, *s* to anger,
Ps 103:8 *s* to anger, abounding in love
Lk 24:25 how *s* of heart to believe
Jas 1:19 quick to listen, *s* to speak
2Pe 3:9 not *s* in keeping his promise,

sluggard
Pr 6:6 Go to the ant, you *s*;

slumber
Ps 121:3 your foot slip—he who watches
Pr 6:10 A little sleep, a little *s*,
Ro 13:11 to wake up from your *s*,

small, -est
1Ki 18:44 "A cloud as *s* as a man's hand
Mic 5:2 though you are *s* among the clans
Zec 4:10 despises the day of *s* things?
Mt 5:18 earth disappear, not the *s-est*
Rev 20:12 I saw the dead, great and *s*,

smell
1Co 12:17 where would the sense of *s* be?
2Co 2:16 To the one we are the *s* of death;

snake, -s
Nu 21:9 Moses made a bronze *s* and put it
Mt 7:10 a fish, will give him a *s*
10:16 as shrewd as *s-s* and as innocent
Mk 16:18 pick up *s-s* with their hands;
Jn 3:14 lifted up the *s* in the desert,

snatch, -es
Mt 13:19 the evil one comes and *s-es* away
Jn 10:28 no-one can *s* them out of my hand
Jude :23 *s* others from the fire and save

snow
Ps 51:7 I shall be whiter than *s*
Isa 1:18 they shall be as white as *s*;

Da 7:9	His clothing was as white as *s*;
Mt 28:3	his clothes were white as *s*
Rev 1:14	white like wool, as white as *s*,

soap

Job 9:30	if I washed myself with *s*
Mal 3:2	refiner's fire or a launderer's *s*

soar

Isa 40:31	They will *s* on wings like eagles;

sober

Ro 12:3	think of yourself with *s* judgment,

Sodom

Ge 19:24	burning sulphur on *S* and Gomorrah—
Mt 10:15	more bearable for *S* and Gomorrah
Ro 9:29	we would have become like *S*,
2Pe 2:6	if he condemned the cities of *S*

sold

Mt 10:29	two sparrows *s* for a penny?
13:44	in his joy went and *s* all he had
Heb 12:16	who for a single meal *s* his

soldier, -s

Mk 15:16	The *s-s* led Jesus away
1Co 9:7	serves as a *s* at his own expense?
2Ti 2:3	like a good *s* of Christ Jesus
2:4	No-one serving as a *s*

solid

1Co 3:2	I gave you milk, not *s* food,
2Ti 2:19	God's *s* foundation stands firm,
Heb 5:12	You need milk, not *s* food

Solomon

Third king of Israel; son of David and Bathsheba (2Sa 12:24). Appointed by David; anointed by Nathan and Zadok (1Ki 1; 1Ch 29:21–25). Given charge by David (1Ki 2:1–9); had Adonijah, Joab and Shimei killed (1Ki 2:13–46). Asked God for wisdom (1Ki 3:5–15; 2Ch 1:7–12); gave wise judgment (1Ki 3:16–28); noted for his wisdom (1Ki 4:29–34; 10:23–24). Wrote proverbs (1Ki 4:32; Pr 1:1; 10:1–22:16; 25–29); psalms (Ps 72:1; 127:1); Song of Songs (SS 1:1). Built temple (1Ki 5–7; 2Ch 2–4); brought ark; prayer of dedication (1Ki 8–9; 2Ch 5–7). Established trading fleet (1Ki 9:26–28; 2Ch 8:17). Visited by Queen of Sheba (1Ki 10:1–13; 2Ch 9:1–12; Mt 12:42; Lk 11:31). Acquired great wealth (1Ki 10:14–29; 2Ch 1:14–17; 9:13–28). Foreign wives turned his heart from God (1Ki 11:1–10), causing him to break covenant with God and so to lose part of kingdom (1Ki 11:11–13,29–39). Death (1Ki 11:41–43; 2Ch 9:29–31).

son, -s

Ge 17:19	Sarah will bear you a *s*,
22:2	"Take your *s*, your only *s*, Isaac
Ex 4:22	Israel is my firstborn *s*
11:5	Every firstborn *s* in Egypt will die
2Sa 19:4	"O my *s* Absalom! O Absalom,
Ps 2:7	"You are my *S*; today I have become
2:12	Kiss the *S*, lest he be angry
8:4	the *s* of man that you care for him?
127:3	*S-s* are a heritage from the LORD,
Pr 10:1	A wise *s* brings joy to his father,
Isa 7:14	to a *s*, and will call him Immanuel
9:6	to us a *s* is given,
Eze 37:3	"*S* of man, can these bones live?
Da 7:13	one like a *s* of man,
Hos 11:1	out of Egypt I called my *s*.
Joel 2:28	*s-s* and daughters will prophesy,
Mal 1:6	"A *s* honours his father,
Mt 1:21	She will give birth to a *s*,
2:15	"Out of Egypt I called my *s*.
3:17	"This is my *S*, whom I love;
4:3	"If you are the *S* of God,
5:9	they will be called *s-s* of God.
8:20	the *S* of Man has nowhere
9:6	you may know that the *S* of Man
9:27	"Have mercy on us, *S* of David!
10:37	anyone who loves his *s* or daughter
11:19	The *S* of Man came eating
11:27	No-one knows the *S* except the
12:8	*S* of Man is Lord of the Sabbath.
14:33	"Truly you are the *S* of God.
16:16	Christ, the *S* of the living God.

20:28 *S* of Man did not come to be served
22:42 the Christ? Whose *s* is he?"
24:27 the coming of the *S* of Man
25:31 the *S* of Man comes in his glory,
27:43 he said, 'I am the *S* of God.'
27:54 "Surely he was the *S* of God!"
Lk 1:31 with child and give birth to a *s*,
1:32 called the *S* of the Most High.
1:35 will be called the *S* of God
15:19 worthy to be called your *s*;
Jn 1:49 "Rabbi, you are the *S* of God;
3:14 the *S* of Man must be lifted up,
3:16 he gave his one and only *S*,
3:36 believes in the *S* has eternal life,
5:19 the *S* can do nothing by himself;
6:53 eat the flesh of the *S* of Man
8:36 So if the *S* sets you free,
10:36 because I said, 'I am God's *S*'
17:1 Glorify your *S*, that your *S*
20:31 Jesus is the Christ, the *S* of God,
Ac 2:17 *s-s* and daughters will prophesy,
7:56 I see heaven open and the *S* of Man
13:33 'You are my *S*; today I have become
Ro 8:3 God did by sending his own *S*
8:14 led by the Spirit of God are *s-s*
8:19 for the *s-s* of God to be revealed
8:23 eagerly for our adoption as *s-s*,
8:29 conformed to the likeness of his *S*,
8:32 He who did not spare his own *S*,
2Co 6:18 you will be my *s-s* and daughters,
Gal 2:20 I live by faith in the *S* of God,
3:26 You are all *s-s* of God
4:5 receive the full rights of *s-s*.
Eph 1:5 to be adopted as his *s-s*
1Th 1:10 to wait for his *S* from heaven,
Heb 1:2 he has spoken to us by his *S*,
1:3 *S* is the radiance of God's glory
12:5 "My *s*, do not make light
12:7 God is treating you as *s-s*.
1Jn 2:23 who denies the *S* has the Father;
4:9 his one and only *S* into the world
5:5 who believes that Jesus is the *S*
5:11 this life is in his *S*.
5:12 He who has the *S* has life;
Rev 1:13 someone "like a *s* of man",

song, -s
Ex 15:2 The LORD is my strength and my *s*;
Ps 40:3 He put a new *s* in my mouth,
96:1 Sing to the LORD a new *s*;
Eph 5:19 psalms, hymns and spiritual *s-s*.
Col 3:16 spiritual *s-s* with gratitude
Jas 5:13 Let him sing *s-s* of praise
Rev 5:9 And they sang a new *s*:

sonship
Ro 8:15 you received the Spirit of *s*.

sorcery
Lev 19:26 " 'Do not practise divination or *s*
Ac 8:9 Simon had practised *s* in the city
19:19 *s* brought their scrolls together

sores
Job 2:7 afflicted Job with painful *s*
Lk 16:21 the dogs came and licked his *s*

sorrow, -s
Ps 90:10 their span is but trouble and *s*,
Isa 53:3 rejected by men, a man of *s-s*,
53:4 infirmities and carried our *s-s*,
2Co 7:10 Godly *s* brings repentance

soul, -s
Dt 6:5 heart and with all your *s*
Ps 19:7 perfect, reviving the *s*.
23:3 he restores my *s*.
42:1 so my *s* pants for you, O God
42:11 Why are you downcast, O my *s*?
103:2 Praise the LORD, O my *s*,
Isa 53:11 After the suffering of his *s*,
Mt 10:28 body but cannot kill the *s*.
11:29 you will find rest for your *s-s*.
16:26 yet forfeits his *s*?
22:37 heart and with all your *s*
Lk 1:46 "My *s* glorifies the Lord
1Th 5:23 May your whole spirit, *s* and body
Heb 4:12 even to dividing *s* and spirit,

1Pe 1:9	the salvation of your *s-s*

sound[1]

Ex 32:18	"It is not the *s* of victory,
1Ch 14:15	the *s* of marching in the tops
Isa 6:4	At the *s* of their voices
Jn 3:8	You hear its *s*, but
Ac 2:2	*s* like the blowing of a violent
1Co 15:52	the trumpet will *s*,
Rev 1:15	like the *s* of rushing waters

sound[2]

1Ti 1:10	contrary to the *s* doctrine
2Ti 1:13	the pattern of *s* teaching,
Tit 2:2	self-controlled, and *s* in faith,

sovereign

Isa 28:16	*S* LORD says: "See, I lay a stone
61:1	The Spirit of the *S* LORD is on me,
Da 4:17	Most High is *s* over the kingdoms
Am 7:2	I cried out, "*S* LORD, forgive!
Lk 2:29	"*S* Lord, as you have promised,
Ac 4:24	in prayer to God. "*S* Lord,"
Jude :4	Jesus Christ our only *S* and Lord

sow, -s, -n

Ps 126:5	Those who *s* in tears
Mt 6:26	they do not *s* or reap
13:3	"A farmer went out to *s* his seed
Jn 4:37	'One *s-s* and another reaps'
1Co 15:42	The body that is *s-n* is perishable,
2Co 9:6	Whoever *s-s* sparingly will also
Gal 6:7	A man reaps what he *s-s*

spare, -s, -ingly

Pr 13:24	He who *s-s* the rod hates his son,
Ro 8:32	He who did not *s* his own Son,
2Co 9:6	Whoever sows *s-ingly* will also
2Pe 2:4	if God did not *s* angels

spark, -s

Job 5:7	as surely as *s-s* fly upward.
Jas 3:5	set on fire by a small *s*

sparrow, -s

Ps 84:3	Even the *s* has found a home,
Mt 10:29	Are not two *s-s* sold for a penny?
10:31	you are worth more than many *s-s*

spat

Mt 26:67	they *s* in his face
Mk 7:33	he *s* and touched the man's tongue
8:23	When he had *s* on the man's eyes

speak, -s, -ing

Ex 33:11	would *s* to Moses face to face,
Dt 18:20	a prophet who presumes to *s*
1Sa 3:10	"*S*, for your servant is listening.
Ps 73:15	If I had said, "I will *s* thus,"
Isa 65:24	still *s-ing* I will hear
Jer 1:6	"I do not know how to *s*;
Mt 12:34	of the heart the mouth *s-s*
13:13	why I *s* to them in parables:
Lk 6:26	Woe to you when all men *s* well
Jn 3:11	we *s* of what we know,
8:44	When he lies, he *s-s* his native
9:21	he will *s* for himself.
10:25	in my Father's name *s* for me
12:49	I did not *s* of my own accord,
Ac 2:4	began to *s* in other tongues
4:20	we cannot help *s-ing* about
10:46	they heard them *s-ing* in tongues
13:46	"We had to *s* the word of God
Ro 7:1	I am *s-ing* to men who know the law—
9:1	I *s* the truth in Christ—
1Co 2:6	We do, however, *s* a message
12:28	those *s-ing* in different kinds
13:1	If I *s* in the tongues of men
14:35	for a woman to *s* in the church
Eph 4:15	Instead, *s-ing* the truth in love,
5:19	*S* to one another with psalms,
Heb 11:4	by faith he still *s-s*,
12:24	blood that *s-s* a better word
1Jn 2:1	one who *s-s* to the Father

spear, -s

Ps 46:9	breaks the bow and shatters the *s*,
Isa 2:4	their *s-s* into pruning hooks.
Mic 4:3	their *s-s* into pruning hooks.
Jn 19:34	pierced Jesus' side with a *s*,

speck

Mt 7:3	do you look at the *s* of sawdust

spend
Pr 31:3 do not *s* your strength on women,
Isa 55:2 Why *s* money on what is not bread,
Jas 4:3 *s* what you get on your pleasures

spent
Mk 5:26 doctors and had *s* all she had,
Lk 15:14 After he had *s* everything,

spice, -s
Mt 23:23 You give a tenth of your *s-s*—
Mk 16:1 bought *s-s* so that they might
Jn 19:40 wrapped it, with the *s-s*,

spies
Lk 20:20 sent *s*, who pretended to be honest.
Heb 11:31 Rahab, because she welcomed the *s*,
Jas 2:25 she gave lodging to the *s*

spirit, -'s, -s
Ge 1:2 the *S* of God was hovering
6:3 "My *S* will not contend with man
1Sa 16:15 an evil *s* from God is tormenting
28:8 "Consult a *s* for me," he said,
1Ki 22:23 the LORD has put a lying *s*
2Ki 2:9 a double portion of your *s*,"
Ps 51:10 renew a steadfast *s* within me
51:11 or take your Holy *S* from me
139:7 Where can I go from your *S*?
Isa 42:1 I will put my *S* on him
57:15 him who is contrite and lowly in *s*,
61:1 *S* of the Sovereign LORD is on me,
Eze 36:26 new heart and put a new *s* in you;
Joel 2:28 I will pour out my *S* on all people.
Zec 4:6 but by my *S*, says the LORD
Mt 1:18 with child through the Holy *S*
3:11 baptise you with the Holy *S*
3:16 he saw the *S* of God descending
5:3 "Blessed are the poor in *s*,
12:31 blasphemy against the *S* will not
26:41 The *s* is willing, but
27:50 in a loud voice, he gave up his *s*.
28:19 of the Son and of the Holy *S*
Lk 1:17 in the *s* and power of Elijah,
1:35 The Holy *S* will come upon you,
2:26 revealed to him by the Holy *S*
4:1 Jesus, full of the Holy *S*,
4:18 "The *S* of the Lord is on me,
11:13 the Holy *S* to those who ask him!
Jn 1:32 "I saw the *S* come down from heaven
3:5 born of water and the *S*
3:34 God gives the *S* without limit
4:24 God is *s*, and his worshippers
14:26 the Counsellor, the Holy *S*,
16:13 when he, the *S* of truth, comes,
20:22 "Receive the Holy *S*
Ac 1:5 baptised with the Holy *S*.
1:8 receive power when the Holy *S*
2:4 them were filled with the Holy *S*
2:38 receive the gift of the Holy *S*
7:51 You always resist the Holy *S*!
15:28 It seemed good to the Holy *S*
19:2 "Did you receive the Holy *S*
Ro 5:5 into our hearts by the Holy *S*,
8:2 law of the *S* of life
8:6 the mind controlled by the *S*
8:9 does not have the *S* of Christ,
8:10 your *s* is alive because
8:16 The *S* himself testifies
8:26 the *S* helps us in our weakness.
14:17 peace and joy in the Holy *S*
1Co 2:4 a demonstration of the *S-'s* power
2:10 God has revealed it to us by his *S*.
2:11 the thoughts ... except the man's *s*
6:19 your body is a temple of the Holy *S*
12:3 speaking by the *S* of God says,
12:10 another distinguishing between *s-s*
12:13 we were all baptised by one *S*
14:14 if I pray in a tongue, my *s* prays,
2Co 1:22 his *S* in our hearts as a deposit,
3:6 letter kills, but the *S* gives life.
3:17 Now the Lord is the *S*,
Gal 4:6 God sent the *S* of his Son
5:16 live by the *S*,
5:22 the fruit of the *S* is love,

5:25 let us keep in step with the *S*.
Eph 1:13 a seal, the promised Holy *S*
4:30 do not grieve the Holy *S* of God,
6:17 and the sword of the *S*, which is
1Th 5:19 Do not put out the *S-'s* fire;
2Ti 1:7 God did not give us a *s* of timidity
Heb 9:14 who through the eternal *S* offered
1Pe 3:19 preached to the *s-s* in prison
2Pe 1:21 were carried along by the Holy *S*.
1Jn 4:1 do not believe every *s*, but test
Rev 22:17 The *S* and the bride say, "Come!"

spiritual, -ly

Ro 7:14 We know that the law is *s*;
12:1 this is your *s* act of worship.
12:11 keep your *s* fervour, serving the
1Co 1:7 you do not lack any *s* gift
2:13 expressing *s* truths in *s*
2:14 because they are *s-ly* discerned
12:1 Now about *s* gifts, brothers,
Gal 6:1 you who are *s* should restore him
Eph 1:3 every *s* blessing in Christ
6:12 against the *s* forces of evil
1Pe 2:2 crave pure *s* milk,

spit

Mk 10:34 who will mock him and *s* on him,
14:65 Then some began to *s* at him;
Rev 3:16 I am about to *s* you out

splendour

1Ch 16:29 LORD in the *s* of his holiness
Ps 104:1 clothed with *s* and majesty
Mt 6:29 not even Solomon in all his *s*

spoil, -s

Isa 53:12 divide the *s-s* with the strong,
Lk 11:22 divides up the *s-s*
Jn 6:27 Do not work for food that *s-s*,
1Pe 1:4 can never perish, *s* or fade—

spoke, -n

Ex 20:1 And God *s* all these words
Nu 12:2 LORD *s-n* only through Moses?"
Dt 5:4 LORD *s* to you face to face out
Job 40:6 LORD *s* to Job out of the storm
Ps 33:9 For he *s*, and it came to be;
Am 3:8 The Sovereign LORD has *s-n*—
Mt 3:3 This is he who was *s-n* of
22:1 Jesus *s* to them again in parables,
Lk 24:25 all that the prophets have *s-n*
Jn 7:46 "No-one ever *s* the way this man
12:41 he saw Jesus' glory and *s* about him
Ac 2:31 he *s* of the resurrection
18:9 the Lord *s* to Paul in a vision:
2Co 4:13 "I believed; therefore I have *s-n*.
Heb 1:2 he has *s-n* to us by his Son,
13:7 who *s* the word of God to you.
2Pe 1:21 men *s* from God

spots

Jer 13:23 his skin or the leopard its *s*?

sprang

Jnh 4:10 It *s* up overnight and died
Mt 13:5 It *s* up quickly, because the soil
Ro 7:9 sin *s* to life and I died.

spread, -s, -ing

Hos 10:1 Israel was a *s-ing* vine;
Mt 21:8 very large crowd *s* their cloaks
Jn 12:17 continued to *s* the word
Ac 6:7 So the word of God *s*.
12:24 continued to increase and *s*
2Co 2:14 *s-s* everywhere the fragrance

spring, -s

Isa 43:19 it *s-s* up; do you not perceive it?
Jer 2:13 forsaken me, the *s* of living water,
9:1 that my head were a *s* of water
Jn 4:14 *s* of water welling up to eternal
Ro 15:12 "The Root of Jesse will *s* up,
Jas 3:11 salt water flow from the same *s*
2Pe 2:17 These men are *s-s* without water

sprinkle, -ing, -d

Eze 36:25 I will *s* clean water on you,
Heb 10:22 having our hearts *s-d* to cleanse
12:24 to the *s-d* blood that speaks

1Pe 1:2 Christ and *s-ing* by his blood:

spy
Dt 1:22 "Let us send men ahead to *s* out
Jos 2:2 to *s* out the land.

staff
Ps 23:4 rod and your *s*, they comfort me
Mt 27:29 They put a *s* in his right hand

stain, -ed
Isa 63:1 with his garments *s-ed* crimson?
Eph 5:27 a radiant church, without *s*
Jude :23 clothing *s-ed* by corrupted flesh

stairway
Ge 28:12 he saw a *s* resting on the earth,

stand, -s, -ing
Ex 3:5 where you are *s-ing* is holy ground.
14:13 "Do not be afraid. *S* firm
Jos 10:12 "O sun, *s* still over Gibeon,
2Ch 20:17 *s* firm and see the deliverance
Ps 1:1 or *s* in the way of sinners
1:5 wicked will not *s* in the judgment,
2:2 kings of the earth take their *s*
24:3 Who may *s* in his holy place
119:89 it *s-s* firm in the heavens
130:3 sins, O Lord, who could *s*
Jer 6:16 "*S* at the crossroads and look;
Mal 3:2 Who can *s* when he appears?
Mt 4:5 had him *s* on the highest point
10:22 he who *s-s* firm to the end
12:25 divided against itself will not *s*
Lk 1:19 I *s* in the presence of God,
Jn 1:26 among you *s-s* one you do not know
3:18 does not believe *s-s* condemned
Ac 1:11 "why do you *s* here looking into
4:26 kings of the earth take their *s*
7:56 Son of Man *s-ing* at the right hand
Ro 5:2 this grace in which we now *s*.
9:11 God's purpose in election might *s*
14:4 To his own master he *s-s* or falls.
14:10 all *s* before God's judgment seat
1Co 10:12 if you think you are *s-ing* firm,
2Co 1:21 both us and you *s* firm in Christ.
Eph 6:11 take your *s* against the devil's
2Ti 2:19 God's solid foundation *s-s* firm,
1Pe 1:25 the word of the Lord *s-s* for ever."
5:9 Resist him, *s-ing* firm
Rev 3:20 I *s* at the door and knock.
5:6 *s-ing* in the centre of the throne,
6:17 wrath has come, and who can *s*?

star, -s
Ge 1:16 He also made the *s-s*
Job 38:7 the morning *s-s* sang together
Isa 14:12 fallen from heaven, O morning *s*,
Mt 2:2 We saw his *s* in the east
24:29 the *s-s* will fall from the sky,
2Pe 1:19 morning *s* rises in your hearts
Rev 22:16 and the bright Morning *S*.

statue
Da 2:32 the *s* was made of pure gold,
2:35 the rock that struck the *s*

stature
Lk 2:52 Jesus grew in wisdom and *s*,

steadfast
Ps 51:10 renew a *s* spirit within me
57:7 My heart is *s*, O God,
Isa 26:3 peace him whose mind is *s*,
1Pe 5:10 make you strong, firm and *s*

steal, -ing
Ex 20:15 "You shall not *s*
Pr 30:9 I may become poor and *s*,
Mt 6:19 where thieves break in and *s*
19:18 do not commit adultery, do not *s*,
27:64 may come and *s* the body
Jn 10:10 The thief comes only to *s*
Eph 4:28 been *s-ing* must *s* no longer,

step, -s
Pr 20:24 man's *s-s* are directed by the LORD.
Gal 5:25 let us keep in *s* with the Spirit

1Pe 2:21 you should follow in his *s-s*

Stephen

Deacon (Ac 6:5–6). Performed miracles; aroused opposition; arrested (Ac 6:8–15). Defence to Sanhedrin (Ac 7:1–53); killed by stoning (Ac 7:54–8:1; 22:20).

still

Jos 10:12 "O sun, stand *s* over Gibeon,
Ps 37:7 Be *s* before the LORD
46:10 "Be *s*, and know that I am God;

sting

1Co 15:55 Where, O death, is your *s*?
15:56 The *s* of death is sin,

stir, -s, -red

Ps 45:1 My heart is *s-red* by a noble theme
Pr 6:19 a man who *s-s* up dissension
Mk 15:11 chief priests *s-red* up the crowd

stole, -n

Pr 9:17 *S-n* water is sweet;
Mt 28:13 *s* him away while we were asleep.

stomach

Mt 15:17 goes into the *s* and then out
Lk 15:16 longed to fill his *s* with the pods
Php 3:19 their god is their *s*,
1Ti 5:23 a little wine because of your *s*

stone, -s

Ex 24:12 give you the tablets of *s*,
Dt 19:14 move your neighbour's boundary *s*
Jos 4:6 'What do these *s-s* mean?
1Sa 17:40 five smooth *s-s* from the stream,
Ps 91:12 strike your foot against a *s*
118:22 The *s* the builders rejected
Isa 8:14 a *s* that causes men to stumble
28:16 "See, I lay a *s* in Zion,
Mt 4:3 tell these *s-s* to become bread.
4:6 strike your foot against a *s*.'
7:9 asks for bread, will give him a *s*
21:42 " 'The *s* the builders rejected
Jn 8:7 the first to throw a *s* at her.
8:59 to *s* him, but Jesus hid himself,
Ac 4:11 'the *s* you builders rejected,
Ro 9:33 a *s* that causes men to stumble
2Co 3:3 not on tablets of *s* but on tablets
1Pe 2:4 the living *S*—rejected by men
2:7 who believe, this *s* is precious.
Rev 2:17 I will also give him a white *s*

stood

Nu 22:22 angel of the LORD *s* in the road
Jos 3:17 *s* firm on dry ground
10:13 So the sun *s* still,
Ps 33:9 he commanded, and it *s* firm
Lk 4:16 And he *s* up to read
18:11 The Pharisee *s* up and prayed
Jn 20:19 Jesus came and *s* among them
Ac 27:23 whom I serve *s* beside me
2Co 13:7 will see that we have *s* the test
2Ti 4:17 But the Lord *s* at my side
Heb 10:33 you *s* side by side with those
Jas 1:12 when he has *s* the test,

stoop

Mk 1:7 not worthy to *s* down and untie

stop, -ped

Mt 2:9 it *s-ped* over the place where
Mk 5:29 Immediately her bleeding *s-ped*
Lk 23:45 the sun *s-ped* shining.
Eph 1:16 I have not *s-ped* giving thanks
2Pe 2:14 they never *s* sinning;

store, -house

Mal 3:10 whole tithe into the *s-house*,
Mt 6:19 *s* up for yourselves treasures
Lk 12:18 I will *s* all my grain and my goods

stories

2Pe 1:16 follow cleverly invented *s*
2:3 exploit you with *s* they have made

storm

Job 38:1 LORD answered Job out of the *s*.
Mt 8:24 a furious *s* came up on the lake,
Heb 12:18 to darkness, gloom and *s*
2Pe 2:17 and mists driven by a *s*.

straight

Isa 40:3 make *s* in the wilderness a highway
Mt 3:3 make *s* paths for him.'

Lk 3:5 The crooked roads shall become *s*,
Jn 1:23 'Make *s* the way for the Lord.'
Ac 9:11 the house of Judas on *S* Street

strange
Ex 3:3 go over and see this *s* sight—
Isa 28:11 foreign lips and *s* tongues God
1Co 14:21 "Through men of *s* tongues
1Pe 4:12 something *s* were happening to you

stranger, -s
Ge 15:13 will be *s-s* in a country
Mt 25:35 I was a *s* and you invited me in
Jn 10:5 they will never follow a *s*;
Heb 11:9 like a *s* in a foreign country;
13:2 Do not forget to entertain *s-s*,
1Pe 1:17 as *s-s* here in reverent fear

straw
Ex 5:7 with *s* for making bricks;
Isa 11:7 lion will eat *s* like the ox
1Co 3:12 costly stones, wood, hay or *s*

stream, -s
Ps 42:1 deer pants for *s-s* of water,
Isa 44:3 and *s-s* on the dry ground;
Am 5:24 like a never-failing *s*
Mt 7:25 rain came down, the *s-s* rose,
Jn 7:38 *s-s* of living water will flow

street
Mt 6:5 the *s* corners to be seen by men.
22:9 Go to the *s* corners and invite

strength
Ex 15:2 The LORD is my *s* and my song;
1Sa 23:16 helped him to find *s* in God.
30:6 David found *s* in the LORD his God
Ne 8:10 the joy of the LORD is your *s*.
Ps 28:7 The LORD is my *s* and my shield;
46:1 God is our refuge and *s*,
Isa 12:2 the LORD, is my *s* and my song;
30:15 in quietness and trust is your *s*,
40:31 the LORD will renew their *s*.
Mk 12:30 your mind and with all your *s*.
1Co 1:25 God is stronger than man's *s*
Eph 1:19 the working of his mighty *s*
Php 4:13 through him who gives me *s*

strengthen
Isa 35:3 *S* the feeble hands,
Lk 22:32 *s* your brothers.
Eph 3:16 he may *s* you with power
Heb 12:12 *s* your feeble arms and weak knees

stretch, -es
Ex 3:20 I will *s* out my hand
7:19 'Take your staff and *s* out
Job 9:8 He alone *s-es* out the heavens
Isa 40:22 He *s-es* out the heavens
Mt 12:13 "*S* out your hand."

strike, -s
Ge 3:15 and you will *s* his heel.
Ex 7:17 I will *s* the water of the Nile,
Zec 13:7 "*S* the shepherd, and the sheep
Mt 4:6 not *s* your foot against a stone.'
5:39 If someone *s-s* you
26:31 "'I will *s* the shepherd,

strive
Ac 24:16 I *s* always to keep my conscience
1Ti 4:10 for this we labour and *s*

strong
Jos 1:6 "Be *s* and courageous,
Ps 24:8 The LORD *s* and mighty,
61:3 a *s* tower against the foe
Joel 3:10 Let the weakling say, "I am *s*!
Mt 12:29 enter a *s* man's house
Ro 15:1 We who are *s* ought to bear
1Co 1:8 He will keep you *s* to the end,
1:27 the world to shame the *s*
2Co 12:10 when I am weak, then I am *s*
Eph 6:10 Finally, be *s* in the Lord
2Ti 2:1 be *s* in the grace

stronghold, -s
2Sa 22:3 He is my *s*, my refuge and
Ps 9:9 a *s* in times of trouble
2Co 10:4 divine power to demolish *s-s*

struggle, -ing, -d
Ge 32:28 you have *s-d* with God
Eph 6:12 our *s* is not against flesh
Col 1:29 *s-ing* with all his energy,
Heb 12:4 In your *s* against sin,

stubborn, -ness
Ps 78:8 a *s* and rebellious generation,
Mk 3:5 distressed at their *s* hearts,

Ro 2:5 But because of your *s-ness*

student
Mt 10:24 "A *s* is not above his teacher,

study
Ezr 7:10 Ezra had devoted himself to the *s*
Ecc 12:12 much *s* wearies the body
Jn 5:39 You diligently *s* the Scriptures

stumble, -s
Isa 8:14 a stone that causes men to *s*
40:30 young men *s* and fall
Ro 9:33 a stone that causes men to *s*
1Co 10:32 Do not cause anyone to *s*,
1Pe 2:8 "A stone that causes men to *s*

stumbling-block
Mt 16:23 You are a *s* to me;
1Co 1:23 a *s* to Jews and foolishness
8:9 become a *s* to the weak
2Co 6:3 We put no *s* in anyone's path,

stump
Isa 11:1 come up from the *s* of Jesse;

subdue
Ge 1:28 fill the earth and *s* it.
Mk 5:4 No-one was strong enough to *s* him

submission
1Co 14:34 must be in *s*, as the Law says
1Ti 2:11 learn in quietness and full *s*
Heb 5:7 heard because of his reverent *s*

submissive
Jas 3:17 considerate, *s*, full of mercy
1Pe 3:1 be *s* to your husbands
3:5 They were *s* to their own husbands
5:5 be *s* to those who are older.

submit
Lk 10:17 the demons *s* to us in your name.
Ro 8:7 It does not *s* to God's law,
13:1 *s* himself to the governing
Eph 5:21 *S* to one another out of reverence
5:22 Wives, *s* to your husbands
Col 3:18 Wives, *s* to your husbands,
Heb 13:17 Obey your leaders and *s*
Jas 4:7 *S* yourselves, then, to God.
1Pe 2:13 *S* yourselves for the Lord's sake

succeed
Pr 15:22 with many advisers they *s*
16:3 and your plans will *s*.

success
Ge 24:12 give me *s* today,
39:3 the LORD gave him *s* in everything
1Sa 18:14 he had great *s*, because the LORD

suffer, -s, -ing, -ings, -ed
Isa 53:3 sorrows, and familiar with *s-ing*.
53:11 After the *s-ing* of his soul,
Mt 16:21 go to Jerusalem and *s* many things
Lk 24:26 Christ have to *s* these things
Ac 5:41 counted worthy of *s-ing* disgrace
Ro 5:3 we also rejoice in our *s-ings*,
8:18 our present *s-ings* are not worth
1Co 12:26 If one part *s-s*, every part
Heb 13:12 Jesus also *s-ed* outside the city
1Pe 2:20 if you *s* for doing good
4:16 if you *s* as a Christian,

sufficient
2Co 12:9 "My grace is *s* for you,
Php 1:20 will have *s* courage so that

sulphur
Ge 19:24 burning *s* on Sodom and Gomorrah—
Ps 11:6 fiery coals and burning *s*;
Rev 19:20 the fiery lake of burning *s*

summer
Ge 8:22 cold and heat, *s* and winter,
Pr 26:1 Like snow in *s* or rain in harvest,
Jer 8:20 harvest is past, the *s* has ended,
Mt 24:32 you know that *s* is near

sun
Jos 10:13 So the *s* stood still,
Ps 121:6 the *s* will not harm you by day,
Ecc 1:9 there is nothing new under the *s*
Isa 60:19 The *s* will no more be your light

Joel 2:31	The *s* will be turned to darkness
Mal 4:2	the *s* of righteousness will rise
Mt 5:45	He causes his *s* to rise
17:2	His face shone like the *s*,
24:29	"'the *s* will be darkened,
Ac 2:20	The *s* will be turned to darkness
Eph 4:26	*s* go down while you are still angry

superior

1Co 2:1	with eloquence or *s* wisdom
Heb 1:4	he became as much *s* to the angels
8:6	has received is as *s* to theirs

supervision

Gal 3:25	no longer under the *s* of the law

supper

Lk 22:20	after the *s* he took the cup,
1Co 11:20	it is not the Lord's *S* you eat
11:25	after *s* he took the cup,
Rev 19:9	to the wedding *s* of the Lamb!'"

supply, -ies, -ied

Ps 147:8	he *s-ies* the earth with rain
Ac 20:34	have *s-ied* my own needs
2Co 8:14	your plenty will *s* what they need,
Php 4:18	I am amply *s-ied*,
1Th 3:10	*s* what is lacking in your faith

support, -ing, -ed

Lk 8:3	to *s* them out of their own means
Eph 4:16	together by every *s-ing* ligament,
Col 2:19	the whole body, *s-ed* and held

supreme, -acy

Pr 4:7	Wisdom is *s*;
Col 1:18	everything he might have the *s-acy*
1Pe 2:13	the king, as the *s* authority

surpass, -es, -ing, -ed

Ps 150:2	for his *s-ing* greatness
Pr 31:29	but you *s* them all.
Mt 5:20	unless your righteousness *s-es* that
Jn 1:15	'He who comes after me has *s-ed* me
2Co 3:10	comparison with the *s-ing* glory
Eph 3:19	this love that *s-es* knowledge—
Php 3:8	compared to the *s-ing* greatness

surprise, -d

1Th 5:4	this day should *s* you like a thief
1Pe 4:12	do not be *s-d* at the painful trial
1Jn 3:13	Do not be *s-d*, my brothers,

surrender

1Co 13:3	*s* my body to the flames,

surround, -ed

Ps 5:12	you *s* them with your favour
Lk 21:20	Jerusalem being *s-ed* by armies,
Heb 12:1	*s-ed* by such a great cloud

sustain, -s, -ing

Ps 3:5	because the LORD *s-s* me
51:12	grant me a willing spirit, to *s* me.
55:22	on the LORD and he will *s* you;
Heb 1:3	*s-ing* all things by his powerful

swallow, -ed

Ge 41:7	The thin ears of corn *s-ed* up
Mt 23:24	You strain out a gnat but *s* a camel
1Co 15:54	Death has been *s-ed* up in victory.

swayed

Mt 11:7	A reed *s* by the wind
2Ti 3:6	*s* by all kinds of evil desires

swear, -s

Ge 22:16	"I *s* by myself, declares the LORD,
Mt 5:34	Do not *s* at all:
23:16	'If anyone *s-s* by the temple,
Heb 6:13	no-one greater for him to *s* by,
Jas 5:12	my brothers, do not *s*—

sweat

Ge 3:19	the *s* of your brow you will eat
Lk 22:44	his *s* was like drops of blood

swift, -er

Job 7:6	"My days are *s-er* than a weaver's
Pr 1:16	they are *s* to shed blood

Ecc 9:11 The race is not to the *s*
Ro 3:15 "Their feet are *s* to shed blood
2Pe 2:1 bringing *s* destruction

sword, -s
Ge 3:24 flaming *s* flashing back and forth
Jdg 7:14 other than the *s* of Gideon
1Sa 17:45 come against me with *s* and spear
Isa 2:4 beat their *s-s* into ploughshares
Joel 3:10 Beat your ploughshares into *s-s*
Mic 4:3 beat their *s-s* into ploughshares
Zec 13:7 "Awake, O *s*, against my shepherd,
Mt 10:34 come to bring peace, but a *s*
26:51 companions reached for his *s*,
Lk 2:35 a *s* will pierce your own soul too.
Ro 8:35 nakedness or danger or *s*
13:4 not bear the *s* for nothing.
Eph 6:17 and the *s* of the Spirit,
Heb 4:12 Sharper than any double-edged *s*,
Rev 1:16 came a sharp double-edged *s*.
19:15 Out of his mouth comes a sharp *s*

swore
Ex 6:8 the land I *s* with uplifted hand
Isa 54:9 I *s* that the waters of Noah
Mt 26:74 he *s* to them, "I don't know
Heb 6:13 he *s* by himself
Rev 10:6 he *s* by him who lives for ever

sworn
Ps 110:4 The LORD has *s* and will not
Isa 45:23 By myself I have *s*,
Heb 7:21 "The Lord has *s* and will not

sycamore-fig
Lk 19:4 climbed a *s* tree to see him,

sympathise, -d
Heb 4:15 unable to *s* with our weaknesses,
10:34 You *s-d* with those in prison

synagogue, -s
Mt 6:2 as the hypocrites do in the *s-s*
10:17 flog you in their *s-s*
23:6 important seats in the *s-s*
Lk 4:16 went into the *s*, as was his custom.
Jn 16:2 They will put you out of the *s*;
Ac 15:21 is read in the *s-s* on every Sabbath

T

tabernacle, -s
Ex 25:9 Make this *t* and all its furnishings
40:34 the glory of the LORD filled the *t*
Lev 23:34 the LORD's Feast of *T-s* begins,
Jn 7:2 the Jewish Feast of *T-s* was near
Ac 7:44 "Our forefathers had the *t*
Heb 8:2 the true *t* set up by the Lord,
9:11 the greater and more perfect *t*
Rev 15:5 that is, the *t* of the Testimony,

Tabitha
See *Dorcas*.

table, -s
Ex 25:23 "Make a *t* of acacia wood—
Ps 23:5 You prepare a *t* before me
78:19 "Can God spread a *t* in the desert?
Mt 15:27 that fall from their masters' *t*.
26:20 Jesus was reclining at the *t*
Mk 11:15 He overturned the *t-s*
Lk 22:30 you may eat and drink at my *t*
Ac 6:2 in order to wait on *t-s*
1Co 10:21 Lord's *t* and the *t* of demons

tablet, -s
Ex 24:12 I will give you the *t-s* of stone,
32:16 The *t-s* were the work of God;
1Ki 8:9 in the ark except the two stone *t-s*
Lk 1:63 He asked for a writing *t*,
2Co 3:3 not on *t-s* of stone but on *t-s*

take, -s, -n
Ge 2:15 and *t* care of it.
2:22 the rib he had *t-n* out of the man,
3:22 and *t* also from the tree of life
15:7 this land to *t* possession of it.
22:17 Your descendants will *t* possession
Ex 3:5 "*T* off your sandals,
21:23 you are to *t* life for life,

29:20 *t* some of its blood and put it
Lev 10:17 given to you to *t* away the guilt
14:24 The priest is to *t* the lamb
24:14 "*T* the blasphemer outside the camp
25:17 Do not *t* advantage of each other,
Dt 1:8 Go in and *t* possession of the land
12:32 do not add to it or *t* away from it.
31:26 "*T* this Book of the Law
Jos 6:6 "*T* up the ark of the covenant
Job 1:21 LORD gave and the LORD has *t-n* away
27:8 when God *t-s* away his life
Ps 5:4 You are not a God who *t-s* pleasure
16:1 for in you I *t* refuge.
25:18 and *t* away all my sins.
51:11 or *t* your Holy Spirit from me.
89:33 I will not *t* my love from him,
109:8 another *t* his place of leadership
Pr 23:11 he will *t* up their case against you
SS 2:4 He has *t-n* me to the banquet hall,
Isa 6:7 your guilt is *t-n* away
Jer 27:22 'They will be *t-n* to Babylon
Eze 36:24 I will *t* you out of the nations;
Jnh 4:3 Now, O LORD, *t* away my life,
Zec 3:4 "See, I have *t-n* away your sin,
Mt 1:20 do not be afraid to *t* Mary
2:20 Get up, *t* the child and his mother
9:6 *t* your mat and go home.
9:15 bridegroom will be *t-n* from them;
10:9 Do not *t* along any gold or silver
10:38 anyone who does not *t* his cross
11:29 *T* my yoke upon you and learn
13:12 what he has will be *t-n* from him
15:26 not right to *t* the children's bread
24:20 flight will not *t* place in winter
25:3 but did not *t* any oil with them.
26:26 "*T* and eat; this is my body."
26:42 for this cup to be *t-n* away unless
Mk 6:50 "*T* courage! It is I.
Lk 12:19 *T* life easy; eat, drink
17:35 one will be *t-n* and the other left.
24:51 and was *t-n* up into heaven.
Jn 1:29 Lamb of God, who *t-s* away the sin
10:18 No-one *t-s* it from me,
11:39 "*T* away the stone," he said.
16:15 the Spirit will *t* from what is mine
Ac 1:2 the day he was *t-n* up to heaven,
2Co 3:14 only in Christ is it *t-n* away.
12:8 pleaded with the Lord to *t* it away
Eph 6:16 *t* up the shield of faith,
6:17 *T* the helmet of salvation
Php 3:12 but I press on to *t* hold of that
1Ti 6:12 *T* hold of the eternal life
Heb 10:4 of bulls and goats to *t* away sins.
1Jn 3:5 so that he might *t* away our sins.
Rev 3:11 so that no-one will *t* your crown.
22:19 And if anyone *t-s* words away

talent, -s

Ex 25:39 A *t* of pure gold is to be used
Mt 25:15 To one he gave five *t-s* of money,

tales

1Ti 4:7 godless myths and old wives' *t*;

talk, -ing, -ed, -ers

Pr 4:24 keep corrupt *t* far from your lips
Mt 12:22 so that he could both *t* and see
Mk 9:4 Moses, who were *t-ing* with Jesus
Lk 7:15 The dead man sat up and began to *t*,
1Co 4:20 is not a matter of *t* but of power
13:11 I was a child, I *t-ed* like a child,
Eph 5:4 foolish *t* or coarse joking,
1Ti 6:4 envy, strife, malicious *t*,
Tit 1:10 mere *t-ers* and deceivers,

Tamar

1. Married in turn to Judah's sons Er and Onan (Ge 38:6–10). Pretended to be prostitute & became pregnant by Judah when he withheld third son (Ge 38:11–30). Mother of Perez and Zerah (Ge 38:27–30;

Ru 4:12). **2.** Daughter of David. Raped by Amnon; avenged by brother Absalom (2Sa 13).

tame

Jas 3:8 but no man can *t* the tongue.

Tarshish

Ps 48:7 You destroyed them like ships of *T*
Eze 27:25 "'The ships of *T* serve as carriers
Jnh 1:3 away from the LORD and headed for *T*

Tarsus

Ac 9:11 and ask for a man from *T* named Saul
11:25 Barnabas went to *T* to look for Saul
21:39 Paul answered, "I am a Jew, from *T*

task

Ac 20:24 the *t* the Lord Jesus has given me—
2Co 2:16 And who is equal to such a *t*?
1Ti 3:1 an overseer, he desires a noble *t*

taste, -d

Ps 34:8 *T* and see that the LORD is good;
119:103 How sweet are your words to my *t*,
Heb 2:9 he might *t* death for everyone
6:5 *t-d* the goodness of the word of God
1Pe 2:3 you have *t-d* that the Lord is good

taught

Isa 50:4 my ear to listen like one being *t*.
54:13 your sons will be *t* by the LORD,
Mt 7:29 he *t* as one who had authority,
Mk 4:2 He *t* them many things by parables,
Jn 6:45 'They will all be *t* by God.'

tax, -es

Mt 9:10 *t* collectors and "sinners" came
22:17 Is it right to pay *t-es* to Caesar
Lk 23:2 He opposes payment of *t-es*
Ro 13:7 If you owe *t-es*, pay *t-es*;

teach, -es, -ing, -ings

Dt 4:9 *T* them to your children
Ps 32:8 I will instruct you and *t* you
51:13 I will *t* transgressors your ways,
90:12 *T* us to number our days aright,
Isa 2:3 He will *t* us his ways,
Jer 31:34 No longer will a man *t* his
Mt 5:2 and he began to *t* them, saying:
28:20 and *t-ing* them to obey everything
Lk 11:1 "Lord, *t* us to pray,
12:12 for the Holy Spirit will *t* you
Jn 8:31 "If you hold to my *t-ing*,
14:26 will *t* you all things
Ro 12:7 if it is *t-ing*, let him *t*
Col 3:16 dwell in you richly as you *t*
2Th 2:15 hold to the *t-ings* we passed on
1Ti 2:12 I do not permit a woman to *t*
3:2 respectable, hospitable, able to *t*,
2Ti 3:16 and is useful for *t-ing*, rebuking,
Heb 8:11 No longer will a man *t* his
13:9 by all kinds of strange *t-ings*.
1Jn 2:27 But as his anointing *t-es* you
2Jn :9 continue in the *t-ing* of Christ

teacher, -s

Ps 119:99 I have more insight than all my *t-s*
Mt 10:24 "A student is not above his *t*,
23:10 for you have one *T*, the Christ
Jn 3:2 you are a *t* who has come from God.
13:13 "You call me '*T*' and 'Lord',
20:16 "Rabboni!" (which means *T*)
1Co 12:28 second prophets, third *t-s*,
Eph 4:11 and some to be pastors and *t-s*
Heb 5:12 by this time you ought to be *t-s*,
Jas 3:1 of you should presume to be *t-s*,
2Pe 2:1 there will be false *t-s* among you.

tear[1], -s

Ps 80:5 have fed them with the bread of *t-s*
126:5 Those who sow in *t-s* will reap
Jer 9:1 and my eyes a fountain of *t-s*!

Lk 7:44 but she wet my feet with her *t-s*
Heb 5:7 petitions with loud cries and *t-s*
Rev 7:17 God will wipe away every *t*

tear[2]
1Ki 11:11 *t* the kingdom away from you
Ecc 3:3 time to *t* down and a time to build
Mt 7:6 and then turn and *t* you to pieces
9:16 the garment, making the *t* worse
Lk 12:18 I will *t* down my barns

teeth
Job 19:20 escaped by only the skin of my *t*
Jer 31:29 the children's *t* are set on edge.
Mt 8:12 will be weeping and gnashing of *t*.

temper
Pr 16:32 a man who controls his *t* than one

temperate
1Ti 3:2 *t*, self-controlled, respectable,
3:11 but *t* and trustworthy in everything
Tit 2:2 Teach the older men to be *t*,

temple, -s
1Ki 6:1 he began to build the *t* of the LORD
6:9 So he built the *t* and completed it,
8:10 the cloud filled the *t* of the LORD
8:27 How much less this *t* I have built!
9:7 reject this *t* I have consecrated
2Ch 6:2 have built a magnificent *t* for you,
Ezr 1:2 to build a *t* for him at Jerusalem
6:15 The *t* was completed
Ps 5:7 I bow down towards your holy *t*
11:4 The LORD is in his holy *t*;
68:29 Because of your *t* at Jerusalem
Isa 37:14 he went up to the *t* of the LORD
64:11 Our holy and glorious *t*,
Jer 7:4 "This is the *t* of the LORD,
52:13 He set fire to the *t* of the LORD,
Eze 43:5 the glory of the LORD filled the *t*
Jnh 2:4 look again towards your holy *t*.
Hab 2:20 But the LORD is in his holy *t*;
Hag 2:18 foundation of the LORD's *t* was laid
Zec 6:12 and build the *t* of the LORD.
8:9 so that the *t* may be built.
Mal 3:1 you are seeking will come to his *t*;
Mt 4:5 on the highest point of the *t*.
12:6 one greater than the *t* is here.
23:16 You say, 'If anyone swears by the *t*
Mk 15:38 curtain of the *t* was torn in two
Lk 1:9 to go into the *t* of the Lord
2:37 She never left the *t*
2:46 they found him in the *t* courts,
18:10 "Two men went up to the *t* to pray,
19:45 he entered the *t* area and began
Jn 2:15 and drove all from the *t* area,
2:20 forty-six years to build this *t*,
2:21 the *t* he had spoken of was his body
Ac 3:1 to the *t* at the time of prayer—
5:25 in the *t* courts teaching the people
17:24 does not live in *t-s* built by hands
1Co 3:16 that you yourselves are God's *t*
6:19 your body is a *t* of the Holy Spirit
2Co 6:16 For we are the *t* of the living God.
Eph 2:21 to become a holy *t* in the Lord.
Rev 11:19 Then God's *t* in heaven was opened,
15:8 And the *t* was filled with smoke
21:22 I did not see a *t* in the city,

temporary
2Co 4:18 For what is seen is *t*,

tempt, -ed, -ation, -er
Mt 4:3 The *t-er* came to him and said,
6:13 And lead us not into *t-ation*,
26:41 that you will not fall into *t-ation*
1Co 7:5 so that Satan will not *t* you
10:13 he will not let you be *t-ed*
Heb 2:18 to help those who are being *t-ed*

4:15 *t-ed* in every way, just as we are
Jas 1:13 no-one should say, "God is *t-ing*

ten, -th

Ge 14:20 Abram gave him a *t-th* of everything
18:32 the sake of *t* I will not destroy
Ex 34:28 of the covenant—the *T* Commandments
Ps 91:7 *t* thousand at your right hand,
SS 5:10 ruddy, outstanding among *t* thousand
Da 7:24 The *t* horns are *t* kings
Mt 23:23 You give a *t-th* of your spices—
25:1 will be like *t* virgins who took
25:28 to the one who has the *t* talents
Lk 15:8 suppose a woman has *t* silver coins
17:12 *t* men who had leprosy met him.
Heb 7:2 and Abraham gave him a *t-th*
Rev 13:1 He had *t* horns and seven heads,

tenants

Lev 25:23 and you are but aliens and my *t*
SS 8:11 he let out his vineyard to *t*.
Mt 21:34 he sent his servants to the *t*

tent, -s, -maker

Ge 13:12 and pitched his *t-s* near Sodom
Ex 29:44 I will consecrate the *T* of Meeting
33:7 Moses used to take a *t* and pitch it
40:34 the cloud covered the *T* of Meeting,
Dt 31:15 Then the LORD appeared at the *T*
Jdg 4:21 Heber's wife, picked up a *t* peg
2Sa 7:2 while the ark of God remains in a *t*
2Ch 10:16 To your *t-s*, O Israel!
Ps 19:4 he has pitched a *t* for the sun
104:2 stretches out the heavens like a *t*
Isa 54:2 "Enlarge the place of your *t*,
Ac 18:3 and because he was a *t-maker*
2Co 5:4 For while we are in this *t*,
2Pe 1:13 as I live in the *t* of this body

terrible

Nu 20:5 up out of Egypt to this *t* place?
2Ti 3:1 will be *t* times in the last days

terrify, -ing, -ied

Mt 14:26 they were *t-ied*. "It's a ghost,"
17:6 fell face down to the ground, *t-ied*
27:54 they were *t-ied*, and exclaimed,
Heb 12:21 sight was so *t-ing* that Moses said,
Rev 11:13 survivors were *t-ied* and gave glory

terror

Ps 91:5 You will not fear the *t* of night,
Lk 21:26 Men will faint from *t*, apprehensive
Ro 13:3 For rulers hold no *t* for those who

test, -ed

Ge 22:1 Some time later God *t-ed* Abraham.
Dt 6:16 Do not *t* the LORD your God
Ps 95:9 your fathers *t-ed* and tried me,
139:23 *t* me, and know my anxious thoughts.
Mt 4:7 not put the Lord your God to the *t*.
19:3 Pharisees came to him to *t* him.
2Co 13:6 that we have not failed the *t*
1Th 5:21 *T* everything. Hold on to the good
Heb 3:9 your fathers *t-ed* and tried me
Jas 1:12 because when he has stood the *t*,
1Jn 4:1 but *t* the spirits to see whether

testify, -ies, -ing, -ied

Mk 14:56 Many *t-ied* falsely against him,
Jn 1:34 I *t* that this is the Son of God.
3:11 and we *t* to what we have seen,
15:26 Spirit of truth ... will *t* about me
15:27 you also must *t*, for you have
Ro 8:16 The Spirit himself *t-ies*
1Ti 6:13 while *t-ing* before Pontius Pilate

testimony

Ex 20:16 “You shall not give false *t*
Dt 17:6 On the *t* of two or three witnesses
Mt 15:19 immorality, theft, false *t*, slander
18:16 by the *t* of two or three witnesses.
Jn 21:24 We know that his *t* is true.
1Jn 5:9 but God’s *t* is greater because
Rev 1:2 and the *t* of Jesus Christ
12:11 and by the word of their *t*;

Thaddaeus

See *Judas* **2**.

thank, -s, -ful

1Ch 16:8 Give *t-s* to the LORD,
Ps 7:17 I will give *t-s* to the LORD
Mt 15:36 and when he had given *t-s*,
26:26 Jesus took bread, gave *t-s*
Ro 7:25 *T-s* be to God—through Jesus Christ
1Co 11:24 when he had given *t-s*, he broke it
15:57 But *t-s* be to God! He gives us the
2Co 2:14 *t-s* be to God, who always leads us
9:12 in many expressions of *t-s* to God
9:15 *T-s* be to God for his indescribable
Eph 5:20 always giving *t-s* to God the Father
1Th 5:18 give *t-s* in all circumstances,
Heb 12:28 let us be *t-ful*, and so worship God

thanksgiving

Ps 95:2 Let us come before him with *t*
100:4 Enter his gates with *t*
1Co 10:16 cup of *t* for which we give thanks
2Co 9:11 generosity will result in *t* to God.
Php 4:6 by prayer and petition, with *t*,
1Ti 2:1 prayers, intercession and *t*
4:3 God created to be received with *t*

theft, -s

Mt 15:19 adultery, sexual immorality, *t*,
Rev 9:21 sexual immorality or their *t-s*

Thessalonians

Ac 17:11 more noble character than the *T*,
1Th 1:1 To the church of the *T* in God

thief, -ves

Ex 22:3 A *t* must certainly make restitution
Mt 6:19 and where *t-ves* break in and steal
24:43 what time of night the *t* was coming
Jn 10:1 in by some other way, is a *t*
1Th 5:2 will come like a *t* in the night
2Pe 3:10 day of the Lord will come like a *t*.
Rev 3:3 I will come like a *t*,

think, -s, -ing

Ps 63:6 I *t* of you through the watches
144:3 the son of man that you *t* of him
Mt 22:42 “What do you *t* about the Christ?
Ro 12:3 Do not *t* of yourself more highly
1Co 14:20 Brothers, stop *t-ing* like children.
Gal 6:3 If anyone *t-s* he is something when
Eph 4:17 in the futility of their *t-ing*
Php 4:8 praiseworthy—*t* about such things
2Pe 3:1 to stimulate you to wholesome *t-ing*

thirst, -s, -y

Ps 63:1 my soul *t-s* for you,
69:21 and gave me vinegar for my *t*.
Isa 55:1 “Come, all you who are *t-y*,
Mt 5:6 who hunger and *t* for righteousness,
25:35 I was *t-y* and you gave me something
Jn 6:35 believes in me will never be *t-y*
7:37 If anyone is *t-y*, let him come to
19:28 Jesus said, “I am *t-y*.
Rev 22:17 Whoever is *t-y*, let him come;

thirty

Zec 11:12 So they paid me *t* pieces of silver
Mt 26:15 counted out for him *t* silver coins
27:9 “They took the *t* silver coins,

Thomas
Apostle (Mt 10:3; Mk 3:18; Lk 6:15; Ac 1:13); called Didymus, the Twin (Jn 11:16). Asked where Jesus was going (Jn 14:5). Doubted resurrection (Jn 20:24–25); saw Jesus alive; confessed him as Lord and God (Jn 20:26–29). Present at miraculous catch of fish after resurrection (Jn 21:2–14).

thongs
Mk 1:7 *t* of whose sandals I am not worthy

thorn, -s
Ge 3:18 It will produce *t-s* and thistles
Mt 27:29 twisted together a crown of *t-s*
Mk 4:7 Other seed fell among *t-s*,
2Co 12:7 there was given me a *t* in my flesh,

thought, -s
Ps 139:17 How precious to me are your *t-s*,
139:23 test me and know my anxious *t-s*
Isa 55:8 "For my *t-s* are not your *t-s*,
Mk 7:21 evil *t-s*, sexual immorality, theft,
Lk 11:17 Jesus knew their *t-s* and said
1Co 2:11 For who among men knows the *t-s*
13:11 I talked like a child, I *t* like a
2Co 10:5 and we take captive every *t*
Heb 4:12 it judges the *t-s* and attitudes

thousand, -s
Ex 34:7 maintaining love to *t-s*,
1Sa 21:11 'Saul has slain his *t-s*, and David
1Ki 19:18 Yet I reserve seven *t* in Israel—
Ps 50:10 and the cattle on a *t* hills
90:4 a *t* years in your sight are like
Mt 14:21 of those who ate was about five *t*
Heb 12:22 You have come to *t-s* upon *t-s*
2Pe 3:8 the Lord a day is like a *t* years,
Rev 5:11 angels, numbering *t-s* upon *t-s*
20:2 and bound him for a *t* years

three
Ge 6:10 Noah had *t* sons:
18:2 Abraham looked up and saw *t* men
Ex 23:14 *T* times a year you are to celebrate
Ecc 4:12 A cord of *t* strands
Da 6:13 He still prays *t* times a day.
Jnh 1:17 the fish *t* days and *t* nights
Mt 12:40 For as Jonah was *t* days and *t*
18:20 For where two or *t* come together
26:34 you will disown me *t* times.
27:40 the temple and build it in *t* days,
27:63 'After *t* days I will rise again.
Mk 9:5 Let us put up *t* shelters—
1Co 13:13 And now these *t* remain:
2Co 12:8 *T* times I pleaded with the Lord
1Ti 5:19 it is brought by two or *t* witnesses
Heb 10:28 the testimony of two or *t* witnesses
1Jn 5:7 For there are *t* that testify

threw
Dt 9:17 tablets and *t* them out of my hands,
Mt 27:5 Judas *t* the money into the temple
Lk 15:20 ran to his son, *t* his arms around
Rev 20:3 He *t* him into the Abyss,

throat, -s
Ps 5:9 Their *t* is an open grave;
69:3 my *t* is parched. My eyes fail,
Ro 3:13 "Their *t-s* are open graves;

throne, -s
2Sa 7:16 your *t* shall be established
Ps 93:2 Your *t* was established long ago;
Isa 6:1 I saw the Lord seated on a *t*,
9:7 He will reign on David's *t*
Mt 5:34 by heaven, for it is God's *t*
19:28 Son of Man sits on his glorious *t*,
19:28 me will also sit on twelve *t-s*,
Lk 1:32 give him the *t* of his father David
Heb 1:8 But about the Son he says, "Your *t*
4:16 approach the *t* of grace
Rev 4:9 thanks to him who sits on the *t*

20:11	Then I saw a great white *t*

throw, -n

Ex 4:3	The LORD said, "*T* it on the ground
Jos 24:23	"*t* away the foreign gods
Mal 3:10	if I will not *t* open the floodgates
Mt 4:6	*t* yourself down. For it is written:
5:30	cut it off and *t* it away.
7:6	do not *t* your pearls to pigs.
Jn 8:7	let him be the first to *t* a stone
9:35	heard that they had *t-n* him out
21:6	"*T* your net on the right side
Heb 10:35	So do not *t* away your confidence;
12:1	*t* off everything that hinders
Rev 20:15	he was *t-n* into the lake of fire

thwart

Isa 14:27	who can *t* him?

tidings

Isa 40:9	You who bring good *t* to Zion,
41:27	to Jerusalem a messenger of good *t*
52:7	proclaim peace, who bring good *t*,

tie, -s, -d

Hos 11:4	with *t-s* of love;
Mt 21:2	you will find a donkey *t-d* there,
Mk 3:27	he first *t-s* up the strong man.
Ac 21:11	*t-d* his own hands and feet with it

time, -s

Ge 4:26	At that *t* men began to call
2Sa 11:1	at the *t* when kings go off to war,
Est 4:14	for such a *t* as this?
Ps 9:9	a stronghold in *t-s* of trouble.
10:1	you hide yourself in *t-s* of trouble
21:9	At the *t* of your appearing
31:15	My *t-s* are in your hands;
34:1	I will extol the LORD at all *t-s*;
59:16	my refuge in *t-s* of trouble.
119:164	Seven *t-s* a day I praise you
Pr 17:17	A friend loves at all *t-s*,
Ecc 3:1	There is a *t* for everything,
3:2	a *t* to be born and a time to die,
Da 2:21	He changes *t-s* and seasons;
6:13	He still prays three *t-s* a day.
8:17	vision concerns the *t* of the end.
12:4	until the *t* of the end.
12:7	for a *t*, *t-s* and half a *t*.
Mic 5:2	from of old, from ancient *t-s*.
Mt 13:21	he lasts only a short *t*.
16:3	interpret the signs of the *t-s*.
24:10	At that *t* many will turn away
25:5	bridegroom was a long *t* in coming,
26:34	you will disown me three *t-s*.
Mk 1:15	"The *t* has come," he said.
Lk 19:8	I will pay back four *t-s* the amount
21:24	until the *t-s* of the Gentiles.
Jn 2:4	"My *t* has not yet come."
12:31	Now is the *t* for judgment
Ac 1:7	"It is not for you to know the *t-s*
3:19	that *t-s* of refreshing may come
3:21	the *t* comes for God to restore
26:28	Do you think that in such a short *t*
Ro 5:6	You see, at just the right *t*,
9:9	"At the appointed *t* I will return
2Co 6:2	In the *t* of my favour I heard you,
Gal 4:4	But when the *t* had fully come,
2Th 2:6	he may be revealed at the proper *t*.
1Ti 6:15	God will bring about in his own *t*—
2Ti 3:1	terrible *t-s* in the last days.
Heb 9:28	and he will appear a second *t*,
10:12	offered for all *t* one sacrifice
1Pe 1:5	to be revealed in the last *t*.
1:20	but was revealed in these last *t-s*
Rev 12:14	for a *t*, *t-s* and half a *t*,

timid, -ity

2Co 10:1	Paul, who am "*t*" when face to
1Th 5:14	encourage the *t*, help the weak,
2Ti 1:7	did not give us a spirit of *t-ity*,

Timothy

Disciple from Lystra (Ac 16:1); convert of Paul (1Ti 1:2), probably during first missionary journey (2Ti 3:10–11). Circumcised by Paul and taken with him on second missionary journey (Ac 16:2–18:22; 2Co 1:19). Ministry confirmed by prophetic utterances (1Ti 1:18) and laying on of hands

(1Ti 4:14; 2Ti 1:6). Sent by Paul to Thessalonica (1Th 3:2); Macedonia (Ac 19:22); Corinth (1Co 4:17). Accompanied Paul to Jerusalem (Ac 20:4–16). Remained in Ephesus to give leadership to church (1Ti 1:3). Imprisoned and released (Heb 13:23).
Timid (1Co 16:10–11; 2Ti 1:7), needing encouragement (1Ti 4:12; 2Ti 1:8; 2:1); but warmly commended by Paul as co-worker and son in the faith (Ro 16:21; 1Co 4:17; Php 2:19–22; 1Th 3:2; 2Ti 1:1–5).
Associated with Paul in the writing of the letters to the Thessalonians (1Th 1:1; 2Th 1:1) and to Philemon (Phm 1).

tire, -d

Ex 17:12 When Moses' hands grew *t-d*,
Isa 40:30 Even youths grow *t-d* and weary,
Jn 4:6 and Jesus, *t-d* as he was
2Th 3:13 never *t* of doing what is right

tithe, -s

Lev 27:30 'A *t* of everything from the land,
Ne 10:37 the Levites who collect the *t-s*
13:12 All Judah brought the *t-s* of grain,
Mal 3:10 Bring the whole *t* into

Titus

Gentile convert and companion of Paul (Tit 1:4; 2Ti 4:10; 2Co 8:23). Accompanied Paul and Barnabas to Jerusalem (Gal 2:1–3). Sent to Corinth to deal with difficulties; brought good news to Paul in Macedonia (2Co 7:6–16). In Corinth again to complete collection (2Co 8:6,16–17). Left by Paul in Crete to consolidate work (Tit 1:5).

today

Dt 27:1 these commands that I give you *t*
30:15 See, I set before you *t* life
Ps 2:7 *t* I have become your Father.
95:7 *T*, if you hear his voice,
Mt 6:11 Give us *t* our daily bread
Lk 2:11 *T* in the town of David a Saviour
12:28 which is here *t*, and tomorrow is
23:43 *t* you will be with me in paradise.
Heb 1:5 *t* I have become your Father"?
3:7 "*T*, if you hear his voice,
3:13 as long as it is called *T*,
13:8 same yesterday and *t* and for ever.
Jas 4:13 listen, you who say, "*T* or tomorrow

toil, -ing, -ed

Ge 3:17 through painful *t* you will eat
Ps 127:2 up late, *t-ing* for food to eat—
Ecc 2:22 What does a man get for all the *t*
2Co 11:27 I have laboured and *t-ed*
1Th 2:9 our *t* and hardship; we worked night
2Th 3:8 night and day, labouring and *t-ing*

tolerate

Hab 1:13 you cannot *t* wrong. Why then
Rev 2:2 I know that you cannot *t* wicked men
2:20 You *t* that woman Jezebel,

tomb, -s

Mt 23:27 You are like whitewashed *t-s*,
27:60 and placed it in his own new *t*
28:1 Mary went to look at the *t*.
Jn 12:17 he called Lazarus from the *t*

tomorrow

Isa 22:13 drink," you say, "for *t* we die!
Mt 6:34 Therefore do not worry about *t*,
1Co 15:32 Let us eat and drink, for *t* we die.
Jas 4:14 not even know what will happen *t*.

tongue, -s

Ps 137:6 my *t* cling to the roof of my mouth
Pr 10:19 but he who holds his *t* is wise.
Isa 28:11 with foreign lips and strange *t-s*
45:23 by me every *t* will swear.
Ac 2:4 and began to speak in other *t-s*
1Co 12:10 another the interpretation of *t-s*.
13:1 If I speak in the *t-s* of men
14:2 anyone who speaks in a *t* does not
14:21 "Through men of strange *t-s*
14:39 and do not forbid speaking in *t-s*.

Php 2:11	every *t* confess that Jesus Christ
Jas 3:6	The *t* also is a fire,
1Pe 3:10	must keep his *t* from evil

took

Ge 2:15	The LORD God *t* the man and put him
2:21	he *t* one of the man's ribs
5:24	was no more, because God *t* him away
2Sa 6:6	reached out and *t* hold of the ark
7:8	I *t* you from the pasture and from
Isa 53:4	Surely he *t* up our infirmities
Mt 2:14	got up, *t* the child and his mother
4:5	the devil *t* him to the holy city
8:17	"He *t* up our infirmities
26:26	Jesus *t* bread, gave thanks
26:27	Then he *t* the cup, gave thanks
Mk 9:36	*t* a little child and had him stand
Lk 24:1	the women *t* the spices
Jn 6:11	Jesus then *t* the loaves, gave
19:27	this disciple *t* her into his home
1Co 11:23	the night he was betrayed, *t* bread
11:25	after supper he *t* the cup,
Php 3:12	for which Christ Jesus *t* hold of me
Col 2:14	*t* it away, nailing it to the cross

tooth

Ex 21:24	eye for eye, *t* for *t*,
Pr 25:19	Like a bad *t* or a lame foot
Mt 5:38	'Eye for eye, and *t* for *t*.'

torment, -ed

1Sa 16:14	evil spirit from the LORD *t-ed* him
Lk 16:23	In hell, where he was in *t*,
2Co 12:7	a messenger of Satan, to *t* me.
Rev 20:10	They will be *t-ed* day and night

torn

1Sa 15:28	LORD has *t* the kingdom of Israel
Mk 1:10	he saw heaven being *t* open
15:38	curtain of the temple was *t* in two
Php 1:23	I am *t* between the two:

torture, -d

Mt 8:29	"Have you come here to *t* us
18:34	over to the jailers to be *t-d*,
Mk 5:7	Swear to God that you won't *t* me!
Heb 11:35	were *t-d* and refused to be released

touch, -es, -ed

Ge 3:3	you must not *t* it, or you will die.
Ex 29:37	and whatever *t-es* it will be holy
Nu 4:15	they must not *t* the holy things
Mt 8:3	Jesus reached out his hand and *t-ed*
8:15	He *t-ed* her hand and the fever
Lk 8:45	"Who *t-ed* me?" Jesus asked.
24:39	It is I myself! *T* me and see;
Col 2:21	Do not taste! Do not *t*!"
Heb 12:18	to a mountain that can be *t-ed*
1Jn 1:1	looked at and our hands have *t-ed*—

towel

Jn 13:4	and wrapped a *t* round his waist.

tower

Ge 11:4	a *t* that reaches to the heavens,
Ps 61:3	a strong *t* against the foe.
Pr 18:10	The name of the LORD is a strong *t*
SS 7:4	Your neck is like an ivory *t*.
Lk 13:4	when the *t* in Siloam fell on them—

town, -s

Nu 35:2	to give the Levites *t-s* to live in
35:11	*t-s* to be your cities of refuge,
Mt 10:11	"Whatever *t* or village you enter,
13:57	in his home *t* and in his own house
Tit 1:5	appoint elders in every *t*,

tradition, -s

2Ch 35:25	These became a *t* in Israel
Mic 6:16	and you have followed their *t-s*.
Mt 15:2	"Why do your disciples break the *t*
15:6	word of God for the sake of your *t*.

Gal 1:14 zealous for the *t-s* of my fathers.
Col 2:8 which depends on human *t*

train[1]
Ps 68:18 you led captives in your *t*;
Isa 6:1 the *t* of his robe filled the temple
Eph 4:8 he led captives in his *t*

train[2]**, -s, -ing, -ed**
2Sa 22:35 He *t-s* my hands for battle;
Pr 22:6 *T* a child in the way he should go,
Lk 6:40 but everyone who is fully *t-ed*
Ac 22:3 I was thoroughly *t-ed* in the law
1Co 9:25 in the games goes into strict *t-ing*
Eph 6:4 *t-ing* and instruction of the Lord.
1Ti 4:8 For physical *t-ing* is of some value
2Ti 3:16 and *t-ing* in righteousness,
Tit 2:4 Then they can *t* the younger women

traitor, -s
Ps 59:5 show no mercy to wicked *t-s*.
Lk 6:16 and Judas Iscariot, who became a *t*.
Jn 18:5 (And Judas the *t* was standing there

trample, -d
Am 8:4 Hear this, you who *t* the needy
Lk 10:19 given you authority to *t* on snakes
21:24 Jerusalem will be *t-d* on
Heb 10:29 has *t-d* the Son of God under foot,

trance
Ac 10:10 being prepared, he fell into a *t*
11:5 and in a *t* I saw a vision.
22:17 at the temple, I fell into a *t*

transcends
Php 4:7 which *t* all understanding,

transfigured
Mt 17:2 There he was *t* before them.

transform, -ed
Ro 12:2 *t-ed* by the renewing of your mind.
2Co 3:18 are being *t-ed* into his likeness
Php 3:21 will *t* our lowly bodies

transgression, -s,
Ps 103:12 far has he removed our *t-s* from us.
Isa 53:5 But he was pierced for our *t-s*,
Ro 4:15 where there is no law there is no *t*
Eph 2:1 you were dead in your *t-s* and sins

trap
Mt 22:15 laid plans to *t* him in his words.
Ro 11:9 their table become a snare and a *t*,
2Ti 2:26 and escape from the *t* of the devil,

tread, -s, -ing
Dt 25:4 while it is *t-ing* out the grain.
1Co 9:9 while it is *t-ing* out the grain."
1Ti 5:18 while it is *t-ing* out the grain,"
Rev 19:15 He *t-s* the winepress of the fury

treasure, -s, -d
Ex 19:5 you will be my *t-d* possession.
Mt 2:11 Then they opened their *t-s*
6:19 for yourselves *t-s* on earth, where
6:21 where your *t* is, there your heart
13:44 kingdom of heaven is like *t* hidden
Lk 2:19 But Mary *t-d* up all these things
2Co 4:7 But we have this *t* in jars of clay
Col 2:3 in whom are hidden all the *t-s*

treasury, -ies
Jos 6:24 into the *t* of the LORD's house.
1Ch 26:20 Levites were in charge of the *t-ies*
Lk 21:1 putting their gifts in the temple *t*
Ac 8:27 in charge of all the *t* of Candace,

treat, -ing
Ps 103:10 does not *t* us as our sins deserve
Mt 18:17 *t* him as you would a pagan
18:35 how my heavenly Father will *t* each

1Ti 5:1 — *T* younger men as brothers,
Heb 12:7 — God is *t-ing* you as sons.

treaty
Ex 34:12 — careful not to make a *t* with those
Dt 7:2 — Make no *t* with them,
1Ki 5:12 — and the two of them made a *t*.

tree, -s
Ge 2:9 — the *t* of life
2:17 — *t* of the knowledge of good and evil
Dt 21:23 — hung on a *t* is under God's curse.
Ps 1:3 — He is like a *t* planted by streams
Pr 3:18 — She is a *t* of life to those
Isa 55:12 — all the *t-s* of the field will clap
Jer 17:8 — like a *t* planted by the water
Mt 3:10 — axe is ... at the root of the *t-s*
7:18 — A good *t* cannot bear bad fruit,
Mk 8:24 — they look like *t-s* walking around.
Ac 5:30 — had killed by hanging him on a *t*.
13:29 — they took him down from the *t*
Gal 3:13 — is everyone who is hung on a *t*.
1Pe 2:24 — bore our sins in his body on the *t*,
Rev 2:7 — the right to eat from the *t* of life
22:2 — of the river stood the *t* of life,

tremble, -s, -ing, -d
Ex 19:16 — Everyone in the camp *t-d*.
1Ch 16:30 — *T* before him, all the earth!
Ezr 9:4 — Then everyone who *t-d* at the words
Ps 18:7 — The earth *t-d* and quaked,
119:161 — but my heart *t-s* at your word.
2Co 7:15 — with fear and *t-ing*.
Heb 12:21 — Moses said, "I am *t-ing* with fear.

trespass
Ro 5:15 — But the gift is not like the *t*.
5:17 — For if, by the *t* of the one man,
5:18 — result of one *t* was condemnation

trial
Mk 13:11 — you are arrested and brought to *t*,
Ac 27:24 — You must stand *t* before Caesar;
Jas 1:12 — the man who perseveres under *t*,
1Pe 4:12 — not be surprised at the painful *t*

tribe, -s
Ge 49:28 — these are the twelve *t-s* of Israel,
Mt 19:28 — judging the twelve *t-s* of Israel.
Rev 5:5 — See, the Lion of the *t* of Judah,
7:9 — nation, *t*, people and language,

tribulation
Rev 7:14 — who have come out of the great *t*;

tried
Ps 73:16 — When I *t* to understand all this,
95:9 — where your fathers tested and *t* me,
Ac 9:26 — he *t* to join the disciples,
Heb 3:9 — where your fathers tested and *t* me

triumph, -s, -ing, -al
Ps 25:2 — nor let my enemies *t* over me
118:7 — I will look in *t* on my enemies.
2Co 2:14 — always leads us in *t-al* procession
Col 2:15 — *t-ing* over them by the cross.
Jas 2:13 — Mercy *t-s* over judgment!

trouble, -s, -d
Jos 7:25 — Why have you brought this *t* on us?
1Sa 1:15 — "I am a woman who is deeply *t-d*.
Job 5:7 — Yet man is born to *t* as surely as
Mt 6:34 — Each day has enough *t* of its own.
26:37 — he began to be sorrowful and *t-d*.
Jn 14:1 — "Do not let your hearts be *t-d*.
16:33 — In this world you will have *t*.
Ro 8:35 — Shall *t* or hardship or persecution
2Co 1:4 — who comforts us in all our *t-s*,
4:17 — For our light and momentary *t-s*
Php 4:14 — was good of you to share in my *t-s*.
Heb 12:15 — no bitter root grows up to cause *t*

Jas 5:13 Is any one of you in *t*?

true

Ps 119:160 All your words are *t*;
Lk 24:34 "It is *t*! The Lord has risen
Jn 15:1 "I am the *t* vine,
17:3 they may know you, the only *t* God,
Ro 3:4 Let God be *t*, and every man a liar.
Php 4:8 whatever is *t*, whatever is noble,
1Th 1:9 to serve the living and *t* God,
1Jn 5:20 so that we may know him who is *t*.
Rev 19:9 "These are the *t* words of God."

trumpet, -s

Jos 6:4 with the priests blowing the *t-s*.
Ps 150:3 him with the sounding of the *t*
Mt 6:2 do not announce it with *t-s*,
24:31 send his angels with a loud *t* call,
1Co 14:8 if the *t* does not sound a clear
15:52 the *t* will sound, the dead will be
1Th 4:16 and with the *t* call of God,
Rev 8:7 The first angel sounded his *t*,

trust, -s, -ed

Ps 22:8 "He *t-s* in the Lord; let the Lord
125:1 Those who *t* in the Lord are like
Pr 3:5 *T* in the Lord with all your heart
Isa 26:3 steadfast, because he *t-s* in you.
28:16 one who *t-s* will never be dismayed
30:15 in quietness and *t* is your strength
Mt 27:43 He *t-s* in God. Let God rescue him
Lk 16:10 can be *t-ed* with very little can
Jn 14:1 *T* in God; *t* also in me.
Ro 4:5 *t-s* God who justifies the wicked,
10:11 "Anyone who *t-s* in him will never
1Co 9:17 discharging the *t* committed to me.
13:7 It always protects, always *t-s*,
Heb 2:13 And again, "I will put my *t* in him
1Pe 2:6 the one who *t-s* in him will never

trustworthy

Pr 11:13 a *t* man keeps a secret.
Lk 19:17 *t* in a very small matter,
1Ti 1:15 Here is a *t* saying
Rev 22:6 "These words are *t* and true.

truth, -s

Ps 51:6 you desire *t* in the inner parts;
Jn 3:21 whoever lives by the *t* comes into
4:23 worship the Father in spirit and *t*
8:32 know the *t*, and the *t* will set
14:6 I am the way and the *t* and the life
16:13 he will guide you into all *t*.
17:17 your word is *t*.
18:38 "What is *t*?" Pilate asked.
Ro 1:25 exchanged the *t* of God for a lie,
1Co 5:8 the bread of sincerity and *t*.
13:6 in evil but rejoices with the *t*.
Eph 4:15 speaking the *t* in love,
6:14 belt of *t* buckled round your waist,
1Ti 3:15 the pillar and foundation of the *t*.
2Ti 2:15 correctly handles the word of *t*.
3:7 but never able to acknowledge the *t*
Heb 5:12 the elementary *t-s* of God's word
Jas 5:19 one of you should wander from the *t*
1Jn 1:8 and the *t* is not in us.
2:20 and all of you know the *t*.

try, -ing

Ps 26:2 Test me, O Lord, and *t* me,
Lk 12:58 *t* hard to be reconciled to him
13:24 many, I tell you, will *t* to enter
1Th 2:4 We are not *t-ing* to please men
5:15 always *t* to be kind to each other

tunic, -s

Lk 3:11 "The man with two *t-s* should share
6:29 do not stop him from taking your *t*.

9:3 no bread, no money, no extra *t*.

turn, -s, -ing, -ed

Ex 32:12 *T* from your fierce anger; relent
Lev 19:4 "'Do not *t* to idols or make gods
19:31 "'Do not *t* to mediums
Dt 5:32 do not *t* aside to the right
30:10 and *t* to the LORD your God with all
2Sa 22:29 the LORD *t-s* my darkness into light
2Ki 13:6 they did not *t* away from the sins
2Ch 7:14 and *t* from their wicked ways,
7:19 "But if you *t* away and forsake
12:12 the LORD's anger *t-ed* from him,
Ps 25:16 *T* to me and be gracious to me,
30:11 You *t-ed* my wailing into dancing;
34:14 *T* from evil and do good;
Pr 15:1 A gentle answer *t-s* away wrath,
22:6 he is old he will not *t* from it
Isa 6:10 and *t* and be healed.
45:22 "*T* to me and be saved,
53:6 each of us has *t-ed* to his own way
55:7 Let him *t* to the LORD, and he will
La 5:15 our dancing has *t-ed* to mourning.
Eze 3:19 he does not *t* from his wickedness
18:21 "But if a wicked man *t-s* away
Mal 4:6 He will *t* the hearts of the fathers
Mt 10:35 I have come to *t* "'a man against
13:15 and *t*, and I would heal them.'
Lk 1:17 to *t* the hearts of the fathers
6:29 on one cheek, *t* to him the other
Jn 6:66 many of his disciples *t-ed* back
16:20 but your grief will *t* to joy.
Ac 3:19 Repent, then, and *t* to God,
15:19 the Gentiles who are *t-ing* to God
28:27 and *t*, and I would heal them.'
2Co 3:16 But whenever anyone *t-s* to the Lord
1Th 1:9 how you *t-ed* to God from idols

twelve

Ge 35:22 Jacob had *t* sons:
49:28 these are the *t* tribes of Israel,
Mt 10:2 the names of the *t* apostles:
Mk 6:43 *t* basketfuls of broken pieces
Rev 21:14 the *t* apostles of the Lamb.

twin, -s

Ge 25:24 there were *t* boys in her womb.
Ac 28:11 the *t* gods Castor and Pollux.
Ro 9:11 Yet, before the *t-s* were born

twinkling

1Co 15:52 in the *t* of an eye,

U

unapproachable

1Ti 6:16 immortal and who lives in *u* light,

unaware

Ro 1:13 I do not want you to be *u*,
2Co 2:11 For we are not *u* of his schemes.

unbelief, -ving, -vers

Mt 17:17 "O *u-ving* and perverse generation,
Mk 9:24 I do believe; help me overcome by *u*
Ro 11:20 they were broken off because of *u*,
1Co 7:14 *u-ving* husband has been sanctified
2Co 6:14 not be yoked together with *u-vers*.
1Ti 1:13 because I acted in ignorance and *u*.
Heb 3:19 to enter, because of their *u*.
Rev 21:8 the *u-ving*, the vile, the murderers

unblemished

Heb 9:14 offered himself *u* to God,

uncertain

1Ti 6:17 hope in wealth, which is so *u*,

unchangeable

Heb 6:18 by two *u* things in which

uncircumcised

1Sa 17:26	Who is this *u* Philistine that he
Ac 7:51	stiff-necked people, with *u* hearts
11:3	"You went into the house of *u* men
Col 3:11	no Greek or Jew, circumcised or *u*,

uncircumcision

1Co 7:19	is nothing and *u* is nothing.
Gal 6:15	Neither circumcision nor *u* means

unclean

Ge 7:2	and two of every kind of *u* animal,
Lev 10:10	between the *u* and the clean,
11:4	it is ceremonially *u* for you.
Isa 6:5	For I am a man of *u* lips,
52:11	Touch no *u* thing! Come out from it
Mt 15:20	These are what make a man '*u*';
Ac 10:28	should not call any man impure or *u*
Ro 14:14	that no food is *u* in itself.
2Co 6:17	Touch no *u* thing,

unclothed

2Co 5:4	because we do not wish to be *u*

uncovered

Ge 9:21	he became drunk and lay *u*
Ru 3:7	Ruth approached quietly, *u* his feet
1Co 11:5	or prophesies with her head *u*
Heb 4:13	Everything is *u* and laid bare

underneath

Dt 33:27	and *u* are the everlasting arms.

understand, -s, -ing, -ood

Job 42:3	I spoke of things I did not *u*,
Ps 32:9	or the mule, which have no *u-ing*
73:16	When I tried to *u* all this,
Pr 2:2	applying your heart to *u-ing*,
3:5	lean not on your own *u-ing*;
Isa 6:9	'Be ever hearing, but never *u-ing*;
11:2	the Spirit of wisdom and of *u-ing*,
40:13	Who has *u-ood* the mind of the LORD,
40:28	and his *u-ing* no-one can fathom.
Mt 13:13	hearing, they do not hear or *u*.
Lk 24:45	opened their minds so they could *u*
Ac 8:30	"Do you *u* what you are reading?"
Ro 7:15	I do not *u* what I do.
1Co 14:2	no-one *u-s* him; he utters mysteries
2Co 6:6	in purity, *u-ing*, patience
Eph 4:18	They are darkened in their *u-ing*
5:17	but *u* what the Lord's will is
Php 4:7	which transcends all *u-ing*,
Col 2:2	the full riches of complete *u-ing*,
Heb 11:3	By faith we *u*
Jas 3:13	Who is wise and *u-ing* among you?
2Pe 2:12	blaspheme in matters they do not *u*.
3:16	some things that are hard to *u*,
1Jn 5:20	has come and has given us *u-ing*,

undivided

Ps 86:11	give me an *u* heart,
Eze 11:19	I will give them an *u* heart
1Co 7:35	in *u* devotion to the Lord.

undone

Jos 11:15	he left nothing *u*
Lk 11:42	without leaving the former *u*.

undying

Eph 6:24	Lord Jesus Christ with an *u* love.

unequalled

Mt 24:21	*u* from the beginning of the world

unfading

1Pe 3:4	of your inner self, the *u* beauty

unfailing

Ps 13:5	But I trust in your *u* love;
33:5	the earth is full of his *u* love.
48:9	we meditate on your *u* love.
La 3:32	so great is his *u* love.

Hos 10:12 reap the fruit of *u* love,

unfaithful, -ness

Lev 6:2 If anyone sins and is *u* to the LORD
1Ch 10:13 Saul died because he was *u*
Mt 5:32 except for marital *u-ness*,
19:9 except for marital *u-ness*,

unfruitful

Mt 13:22 choke it, making it *u*.
1Co 14:14 my spirit prays, but my mind is *u*.

ungodly, -iness

Isa 9:17 for everyone is *u* and wicked,
Ro 5:6 Christ died for the *u*.
Tit 2:12 teaches us to say "No" to *u-iness*
Jude :18 will follow their own *u* desires.

unintentionally

Lev 4:2 'When anyone sins *u* and does what
Dt 4:42 if he had *u* killed his neighbour
Jos 20:3 kills a person accidentally and *u*

union

Mt 1:25 But he had no *u* with her until

unite, -d

Ge 2:24 and be *u-d* to his wife,
Mt 19:5 and be *u-d* to his wife,
Ro 6:5 If we have been *u-d* with him
Eph 5:31 and be *u-d* to his wife,
Php 2:1 from being *u-d* with Christ,

unity

Ps 133:1 when brothers live together in *u*!
Jn 17:23 May they be brought to complete *u*
Ro 15:5 a spirit of *u* among yourselves
Eph 4:3 effort to keep the *u* of the Spirit
4:13 until we all reach *u* in the faith
Col 3:14 them all together in perfect *u*.

universe

1Co 4:9 a spectacle to the whole *u*,
Eph 4:10 in order to fill the whole *u*.
Php 2:15 you shine like stars in the *u*
Heb 1:2 and through whom he made the *u*.
11:3 the *u* was formed at God's command,

unknown

Ac 17:23 this inscription: TO AN *U* GOD.
2Co 6:9 known, yet regarded as *u*; dying,

unlawful

Mt 12:2 doing what is *u* on the Sabbath.
Ac 16:21 advocating customs *u* for us Romans

unleavened

Ex 12:17 "Celebrate the Feast of *U* Bread,
Nu 9:11 with *u* bread and bitter herbs.
2Ch 30:13 to celebrate the Feast of *U* Bread

unlimited

1Ti 1:16 might display his *u* patience

unmarried

Ac 21:9 four *u* daughters who prophesied.
1Co 7:8 Now to the *u* and the widows I say:
7:32 An *u* man is concerned about

unpunished

Ex 34:7 Yet he does not leave the guilty *u*;
Pr 6:29 no-one who touches her will go *u*.
19:5 A false witness will not go *u*,
Jer 30:11 I will not let you go entirely *u*.
Na 1:3 LORD will not leave the guilty *u*.
Ro 3:25 the sins committed beforehand *u*.

unquenchable

Jer 17:27 will kindle an *u* fire in the gates
Mt 3:12 burning up the chaff with *u* fire.

unrepentant

Ro 2:5 your stubbornness and your *u* heart,

unrighteous, -ness
Jer 22:13 who builds his palace by *u-ness,*
Mt 5:45 rain on the righteous and the *u.*
Ro 3:5 But if our *u-ness* brings out
1Pe 3:18 for all, the righteous for the *u,*
2Pe 2:9 hold the *u* for the day of judgment,
1Jn 1:9 and purify us from all *u-ness.*

unsearchable
Pr 25:3 so the hearts of kings are *u.*
Jer 33:3 great and *u* things you do not know.
Ro 11:33 How *u* his judgments, and his paths
Eph 3:8 the *u* riches of Christ,

unseen
Mt 6:6 and pray to your Father, who is *u.*
2Co 4:18 but what is *u* is eternal.

unspiritual
Ro 7:14 but I am *u,* sold as a slave to sin.
Col 2:18 and his *u* mind puffs him up
Jas 3:15 but is earthly, *u,* of the devil.

unstable
Jas 1:8 double-minded man, *u* in all he does
2Pe 2:14 they seduce the *u;*
3:16 which ignorant and *u* people distort

untie
Isa 58:6 and *u* the cords of the yoke,
Mt 21:2 *U* them and bring them to me.
Mk 1:7 I am not worthy to stoop down and *u*
Lk 13:15 on the Sabbath *u* his ox or donkey

unveiled
2Co 3:18 we, who with *u* faces all reflect

unworthy
Lk 17:10 'We are *u* servants; we have only
1Co 11:27 the cup of the Lord in an *u* manner

uphold, -s
Dt 27:26 does not *u* the words of this law
32:51 because you did not *u* my holiness
1Ki 8:45 and their plea, and *u* their cause.
Ps 37:17 but the LORD *u-s* the righteous.
41:12 In my integrity you *u* me
140:12 and *u-s* the cause of the needy.
145:14 The LORD *u-s* all those who fall
Isa 42:1 "Here is my servant, whom I *u,*
Ro 3:31 Not at all! Rather, we *u* the law.

upper
Ps 104:3 lays the beams of his *u* chambers
104:13 the mountains from his *u* chambers;
Mk 14:15 He will show you a large *u* room,

upright
Ps 119:7 I will praise you with an *u* heart
Lk 1:6 were *u* in the sight of God,
23:50 a good and *u* man,
Tit 1:8 who is self-controlled, *u,* holy

Ur
Ge 11:28 Haran died in *U* of the Chaldeans,
15:7 the LORD, who brought you out of *U*
Ne 9:7 and brought him out of *U*

urge, -d
Lk 24:29 But they *u-d* him strongly,
Jn 4:31 Meanwhile his disciples *u-d* him,
Ac 21:4 Through the Spirit they *u-d* Paul
2Co 6:1 As God's fellow-workers we *u* you

Uriah
Hittite. Husband of Bathsheba; killed on David's order (2Sa 11).

useful
Eph 4:28 something *u* with his own hands,
2Ti 2:21 made holy, *u* to the Master
3:16 and is *u* for teaching, rebuking,

Phm :11 has become *u* both to you and to me
Heb 6:7 that produces a crop *u* to those

useless
1Co 15:14 not been raised, our preaching is *u*
Phm :11 Formerly he was *u* to you,
Heb 7:18 set aside because it was weak and *u*
Jas 2:20 that faith without deeds is *u*?

usury
Ne 5:10 But let the exacting of *u* stop!
Ps 15:5 who lends his money without *u*
Eze 22:12 you take *u* and excessive interest

Uzziah
Also called Azariah. King of Judah; son of Amaziah (2Ki 14:21–22; 15:1–2; 2Ch 26:1–3). Commended, though failed to remove high places (2Ki 15:3–4; 2Ch 26:4–5). Extended power and prestige; strengthened Jerusalem's defences (2Ch 26:6–15). Pride in assuming priestly authority led to affliction with leprosy and isolation (2Ki 15:5; 2Ch 26:16–21). Death (1Ki 15:7; 2Ch 26:23; Isa 6:1).

V

vain
Mt 15:9 They worship me in *v*;
1Co 15:2 Otherwise, you have believed in *v*.
15:58 your labour in the Lord is not in *v*
2Co 6:1 not to receive God's grace in *v*.
Php 2:3 of selfish ambition or *v* conceit,

valid
Jn 5:32 his testimony about me is *v*,
8:14 my testimony is *v*, for I know
8:17 the testimony of two men is *v*.

valley, -s
2Sa 15:23 The king also crossed the Kidron *V*
Ps 23:4 the *v* of the shadow of death,
84:6 As they pass through the *V* of Baca
SS 2:1 rose of Sharon, a lily of the *v-s*.
Isa 40:4 Every *v* shall be raised up,
Joel 3:14 multitudes in the *v* of decision!
Zec 14:5 You will flee by my mountain *v*,
Lk 3:5 Every *v* shall be filled in,
Jn 18:1 and crossed the Kidron *V*.

value, -able
Pr 10:2 Ill-gotten treasures are of no *v*,
Mt 6:26 Are you not much more *v-able*
13:46 When he found one of great *v*,
Gal 5:2 Christ will be of no *v* to you
1Ti 4:8 but godliness has *v* for all things
Heb 11:26 the sake of Christ as of greater *v*

various
Ge 1:11 according to their *v* kinds."
Mt 4:24 who were ill with *v* diseases,
24:7 and earthquakes in *v* places
Heb 1:1 at many times and in *v* ways,
2:4 signs, wonders and *v* miracles,
1Pe 4:10 God's grace in its *v* forms.

Vashti
Queen of Persia; wife of Xerxes. Deposed for refusal to appear at banquet (Est 1). Replaced by Esther (Est 2:1–17).

vegetables
Pr 15:17 Better a meal of *v* where
Da 1:12 Give us nothing but *v* to eat
Ro 14:2 whose faith is weak, eats only *v*.

veil, -ed
Ex 34:33 he put a *v* over his face.
2Co 3:13 like Moses, who would put a *v*
3:16 to the Lord, the *v* is taken away.
4:3 And even if our gospel is *v-ed*,

vengeance
Isa 61:2 and the day of *v* of our God,
Jer 51:6 It is time for the LORD's *v*;

verdict
Jdg 20:7 speak up and give your *v*.
Jn 3:19 This is the *v*: Light has come

victory

Ex 32:18 replied: "It is not the sound of *v*
2Sa 8:6 LORD gave David *v* wherever he went.
1Co 15:55 "Where, O death, is your *v*?
15:57 He gives us the *v* through our Lord
1Jn 5:4 the *v* that has overcome the world,

vindicate, -d

Ge 30:6 Then Rachel said, "God has *v-d* me;
Ps 43:1 *V* me, O God, and plead my cause
135:14 For the LORD will *v* his people
1Ti 3:16 in a body, was *v-d* by the Spirit,

vine, -yard

Ge 9:20 proceeded to plant a *v-yard*.
1Ki 21:2 Naboth, "Let me have your *v-yard*
Ps 80:8 You brought a *v* out of Egypt;
Isa 5:7 The *v-yard* of the LORD Almighty
Mt 20:1 to hire men to work in his *v-yard*.
21:28 go and work today in the *v-yard*.
21:33 a landowner who planted a *v-yard*.
26:29 not drink of this fruit of the *v*
Jn 15:5 I am the *v*; you are the branches.

vinegar

Nu 6:3 and must not drink *v* made from wine
Ru 2:14 bread and dip it in the wine *v*."
Ps 69:21 and gave me *v* for my thirst.
Pr 25:20 or like *v* poured on soda,
Mt 27:48 a sponge. He filled it with wine *v*,

violent, -nce

Ge 6:11 in God's sight and was full of *v-nce*
Ps 140:1 protect me from men of *v-nce*,
1Ti 1:13 and a persecutor and a *v* man,
3:3 not *v* but gentle, not quarrelsome,

vipers

Ps 140:3 the poison of *v* is on their lips.
Mt 3:7 "You brood of *v*! Who warned you
12:34 You brood of *v*, how can you
Ro 3:13 "The poison of *v* is on their lips.

virgin, -s

Isa 7:14 *v* will be with child
Mt 1:23 "The *v* will be with child
Lk 1:34 asked the angel, "since I am a *v*?
1Co 7:25 Now about *v-s*:
2Co 11:2 present you as a pure *v* to him.

virtues

Col 3:14 And over all these *v* put on love,

visible

Eph 5:14 it is light that makes everything *v*
Col 1:16 and on earth, *v* and invisible,
Heb 11:3 was not made out of what was *v*.

vision, -s

Ge 15:1 of the LORD came to Abram in a *v*:
1Sa 3:1 there were not many *v-s*.
Eze 1:1 heavens were opened and I saw *v-s*
40:2 In *v-s* of God he took me
Da 1:17 And Daniel could understand *v-s*
7:2 Daniel said: "In my *v* at night
Lk 24:23 they had seen a *v* of angels,
Ac 2:17 your young men will see *v-s*,
9:10 The Lord called to him in a *v*,
10:3 in the afternoon he had a *v*.
16:9 During the night Paul had a *v*
26:19 I was not disobedient to the *v*
2Co 12:1 I will go on to *v-s* and revelations
Rev 9:17 horses and riders I saw in my *v*

voice

Ps 19:4 Their *v* goes out into all the earth
95:7 Today, if you hear his *v*,
Isa 6:8 Then I heard the *v* of the Lord
30:21 your ears will hear a *v* behind you
40:3 A *v* of one calling: "In the desert

Ac 9:25 basket through an opening in the *w*.
23:3 strike you, you whitewashed *w*!
Eph 2:14 the dividing *w* of hostility,
Rev 21:14 The *w* of the city had twelve

wander, -s, -ed
Mt 18:12 one of them *w-s* away,
1Ti 6:10 have *w-ed* from the faith
Jas 5:19 should *w* from the truth

want, -s, -ing, -ed
1Sa 8:19 "We *w* a king over us.
Ps 23:1 I shall not be in *w*.
Da 5:27 scales and found *w-ing*.
Jn 17:24 I *w* those you have given me
21:18 went where you *w-ed*;
Ro 1:13 I do not *w* you to be unaware,
7:16 I do what I do not *w* to do,
9:18 whom he *w-s* to have mercy,
Php 3:10 I *w* to know Christ
1Th 4:13 we do not *w* you to be ignorant
1Ti 2:4 who *w-s* all men to be saved
2Ti 3:12 who *w-s* to live a godly life
Jas 4:2 You *w* something but don't get it.
2Pe 3:9 not *w-ing* anyone to perish,

war, -s
Ps 46:9 He makes *w-s* cease to the ends
Da 9:26 *W* will continue until the end,
Mt 24:6 *w-s* and rumours of *w-s*,
Lk 14:31 a king is about to go to *w*
Ro 7:23 waging *w* against the law of
2Co 10:3 we do not wage *w* as the world
Rev 12:7 And there was *w* in heaven.
17:14 make *w* against the Lamb,

warn, -ing, -ings, -ed
Ps 19:11 By them is your servant *w-ed*;
Mt 2:12 been *w-ed* in a dream
3:7 Who *w-ed* you to flee from
Ac 20:31 I never stopped *w-ing* each of you
1Co 10:11 written down as *w-ings* for us,
1Th 5:14 *w* those who are idle,

wash, -ing, -ed
Ps 51:7 *w* me, and I shall be whiter
Mt 6:17 oil on your head and *w* your face,
15:2 They don't *w* their hands before
27:24 he took water and *w-ed* his hands
Jn 13:5 began to *w* his disciples' feet,
Ac 22:16 be baptised and *w* your sins away,
1Co 6:11 were *w-ed*, you were sanctified,
Eph 5:26 cleansing her by the *w-ing*
Tit 3:5 through the *w-ing* of rebirth
Rev 7:14 they have *w-ed* their robes

waste, -ing, -d
Ps 32:3 my bones *w-d* away
Mt 26:8 "Why this *w*?" they asked.
2Co 4:16 outwardly we are *w-ing* away,

watch, -es, -ful, -man
Ps 1:6 the LORD *w-es* over the way of
90:4 or like a *w* in the night.
121:4 he who *w-es* over Israel
Eze 33:6 if the *w-man* sees the sword
Mt 7:15 "*W* out for false prophets.
24:42 "Therefore keep *w*, because
26:41 "*W* and pray so that you will not
Lk 2:8 keeping *w* over their flocks
Jn 10:3 The *w-man* opens the gate
Ac 20:28 Keep *w* over yourselves and all
Php 3:2 *W* out for those dogs,
Col 4:2 being *w-ful* and thankful
1Ti 4:16 *W* your life and doctrine closely.
Heb 13:17 They keep *w* over you as men who

water, -s, -ed
Ex 7:20 struck the *w* of the Nile,
14:16 to divide the *w* so that
Ps 1:3 a tree planted by streams of *w*,
23:2 he leads me beside quiet *w-s*,
42:1 deer pants for streams of *w*,
Ecc 11:1 Cast your bread upon the *w-s*,
SS 8:7 Many *w-s* cannot quench love;
Isa 12:3 draw *w* from the wells of salvation.
32:2 like streams of *w* in the desert
40:12 measured the *w-s* in the hollow
43:2 When you pass through the *w-s*,
55:1 who are thirsty, come to the *w-s*;
58:11 a spring whose *w-s* never fail.
Eze 36:25 I will sprinkle clean *w* on you,
Hab 2:14 as the *w-s* cover the sea.
Mt 3:11 I baptise you with *w* for repentance

14:29 walked on the *w* and came towards
27:24 he took *w* and washed his hands
Mk 9:41 gives you a cup of *w* in my name
Lk 16:24 dip the tip of his finger in *w*
Jn 1:26 "I baptise with *w*," John replied
3:5 born of *w* and the Spirit.
4:11 Where can you get this living *w*?
4:14 drinks the *w* I give him will
5:7 when the *w* is stirred.
7:38 streams of living *w* will flow
19:34 a sudden flow of blood and *w*.
1Co 3:6 Apollos *w-ed* it, but God made
Eph 5:26 washing with *w* through the word,
1Ti 5:23 Stop drinking only *w*,
Heb 10:22 our bodies washed with pure *w*.
1Pe 3:21 this *w* symbolises baptism
2Pe 2:17 These men are springs without *w*
3:5 the earth was formed out of *w*
1Jn 5:6 the one who came by *w* and blood—
Rev 1:15 like the sound of rushing *w-s*.
22:17 the free gift of the *w* of life.

wave, -s

Mt 8:26 rebuked the winds and the *w-s*,
Eph 4:14 tossed back and forth by the *w-s*,
Jas 1:6 he who doubts is like a *w*
Jude :13 They are wild *w-s* of the sea,

way, -s

Ex 33:13 teach me your *w-s* so that I may
Dt 1:33 and to show you the *w* you should go
32:4 and all his *w-s* are just.
1Sa 12:23 I will teach you the *w* that is good
2Sa 22:31 As for God, his *w* is perfect;
Ps 1:1 stand in the *w* of sinners or sit
1:6 the LORD watches over the *w* of the
25:9 right and teaches them his *w*.
32:8 teach you in the *w* you should go;
37:5 Commit your *w* to the LORD;
51:13 I will teach transgressors your *w-s*
119:9 How can a young man keep his *w* pure?
139:3 you are familiar with all my *w-s*
139:24 if there is any offensive *w* in me,
Pr 3:6 in all your *w-s* acknowledge him,
14:12 *w* that seems right to a man, but
22:6 Train a child in the *w* he should go
30:19 the *w* of an eagle in the sky,
Isa 30:21 "This is the *w*; walk in it."
40:27 "My *w* is hidden from the LORD;
53:6 each of us has turned to his own *w*;
55:7 Let the wicked forsake his *w*
55:8 neither are your *w-s* my *w-s*,
Eze 33:11 turn from their *w-s* and live.
Mt 3:3 'Prepare the *w* for the Lord, make
Jn 14:6 "I am the *w* and the truth and the
Ac 9:2 any there who belonged to the *W*,
1Co 10:13 he will also provide a *w* out
12:31 will show you the most excellent *w*.
Col 1:10 and may please him in every *w*:
Heb 4:15 tempted in every *w*, just as we are
10:20 by a new and living *w* opened for us
Jas 3:2 We all stumble in many *w-s*.

weak, -er, -ness, -nesses

Ps 82:3 cause of the *w* and fatherless;
Mt 26:41 is willing, but the body is *w*.
Ac 20:35 of hard work we must help the *w*,
Ro 8:26 Spirit helps us in our *w-ness*.
14:1 Accept him whose faith is *w*,
1Co 1:27 chose the *w* things of the world
9:22 To the *w* I became *w*,
11:30 many among you are *w* and sick,
15:43 it is sown in *w-ness*,
2Co 12:9 my power is made perfect in *w-ness*.

Heb 4:15 to sympathise with our *w-nesses*,
1Pe 3:7 with respect as the *w-er* partner

weaken, -ing, -ed
Ro 4:19 Without *w-ing* in his faith,
8:3 it was *w-ed* by the sinful nature,

wealth
Ps 49:6 who trust in their *w* and boast
Pr 3:9 Honour the LORD with your *w*,
Mt 13:22 the deceitfulness of *w* choke it,
19:22 sad, because he had great *w*.
Jas 5:2 Your *w* has rotted,
Rev 3:17 I have acquired *w* and do not need

weaned
1Sa 1:22 After the boy is *w*, I will take him
Ps 131:2 like a *w* child is my soul

weapon, -s
2Co 6:7 *w-s* of righteousness in the right
10:4 The *w-s* we fight with are not

wear
Ps 102:26 all *w* out like a garment.
Mt 6:25 your body, what you will *w*.
Heb 1:11 all *w* out like a garment.
Rev 3:18 and white clothes to *w*,

weary
Isa 40:28 He will not grow tired or *w*,
40:30 Even youths grow tired and *w*,
50:4 know the word that sustains the *w*.
Mt 11:28 all you who are *w* and burdened,
Gal 6:9 Let us not become *w* in doing good,
Heb 12:3 will not grow *w* and lose heart.

wedding
Mt 22:2 prepared a *w* banquet for his son.
Lk 14:8 someone invites you to a *w* feast,
Jn 2:1 a *w* took place at Cana
Rev 19:7 the *w* of the Lamb has come,

weeds
Mt 13:25 came and sowed *w* among the wheat,
13:30 First collect the *w* and tie them

week
Mt 28:1 at dawn on the first day of the *w*,
Jn 20:1 Early on the first day of the *w*,
1Co 16:2 On the first day of every *w*,

weep, -ing
Ps 6:6 I flood my bed with *w-ing*
30:5 *w-ing* may remain for a night,
Ecc 3:4 a time to *w* and a time to laugh,
Mt 2:18 Ramah, *w-ing* and great mourning,
8:12 be *w-ing* and gnashing of teeth.
Lk 6:25 for you will mourn and *w*.
23:28 "Daughters of Jerusalem, do not *w*
Rev 5:5 "Do not *w*! See, the Lion

weigh, -s, -ed, -ts
Pr 20:23 The LORD detests differing *w-ts*,
Isa 40:15 he *w-s* the islands as though
Da 5:27 You have been *w-ed* on the scales
1Co 14:29 should *w* carefully what is said

welcome, -s
Mt 10:14 If anyone will not *w* you
18:5 whoever *w-s* a little child
Lk 9:53 the people there did not *w* him,
15:2 "This man *w-s* sinners,
2Pe 1:11 a rich *w* into the eternal kingdom
2Jn :10 take him into your house or *w* him.

well[1], -s
Isa 12:3 water from the *w-s* of salvation.
Lk 14:5 falls into a *w* on the Sabbath
Jn 4:11 to draw with and the *w* is deep.

well[2]
Mt 3:17 with him I am *w* pleased."
Mk 7:37 "He has done everything *w*,"
Lk 17:19 your faith has made you *w*."

Eph 6:3 "that it may go *w* with you
1Ti 3:13 Those who have served *w* gain
5:17 direct the affairs of the church *w*

wept

Ps 137:1 rivers of Babylon we sat and *w*
Mt 26:75 he went outside and *w* bitterly.
Lk 19:41 saw the city, he *w* over it
Jn 11:35 Jesus *w*.

wheat

Mt 13:25 came and sowed weeds among the *w*,
Lk 22:31 Satan has asked to sift you as *w*.
Jn 12:24 unless a grain of *w* falls

wheels

Eze 1:16 and structure of the *w*:

whirlwind

2Ki 2:1 Elijah up to heaven in a *w*,
Isa 40:24 a *w* sweeps them away like chaff.

whisper, -ed

1Ki 19:12 after the fire came a gentle *w*.
Mt 10:27 what is *w-ed* in your ear,

white, -r

Ps 51:7 I shall be *w-r* than snow.
Isa 1:18 they shall be as *w* as snow;
Mt 17:2 clothes became as *w* as the light.
Rev 1:14 His head and hair were *w* like wool
7:9 They were wearing *w* robes
20:11 I saw a great *w* throne

whole

Ex 19:5 the *w* earth is mine.
Nu 14:21 glory of the LORD fills the *w* earth
Ps 48:2 the joy of the *w* earth.
72:19 may the *w* earth be filled
Isa 6:3 the *w* earth is full of his glory.
Mal 3:10 the *w* tithe into the storehouse,
Mt 5:29 your *w* body to be thrown into hell.
6:22 your *w* body will be full of light.
16:26 if he gains the *w* world,
24:14 be preached in the *w* world
Mk 15:33 darkness came over the *w* land
Ac 20:27 to proclaim to you the *w* will
Ro 3:19 *w* world held accountable to God.
8:22 the *w* creation has been groaning
1Co 5:6 yeast works through the *w* batch
Gal 3:22 the *w* world is a prisoner of sin,
5:3 he is required to obey the *w* law.
Eph 2:21 the *w* building is joined together
3:15 his *w* family in heaven
1Th 5:23 May your *w* spirit, soul and body
Jas 2:10 whoever keeps the *w* law
1Jn 2:2 for the sins of the *w* world.
5:19 the *w* world is under the control

wholehearted, -ly

Nu 14:24 spirit and follows me *w-ly*,
32:12 they followed the LORD *w-ly*.
Ro 6:17 you *w-ly* obeyed the form
Eph 6:7 Serve *w-ly*, as if you were

wick

Isa 42:3 a smouldering *w* he will not snuff
Mt 12:20 a smouldering *w* he will not snuff

wicked, -ness

Ge 6:5 how great man's *w-ness*
2Sa 13:12 Don't do this *w* thing.
Ps 1:1 walk in the counsel of the *w*
1:6 the way of the *w* will perish.
5:4 with you the *w* cannot dwell.
9:17 The *w* return to the grave,
73:3 when I saw the prosperity of the *w*.
Pr 10:27 the years of the *w* are cut short.
Isa 48:22 peace," says the LORD, "for the *w*
53:9 assigned a grave with the *w*,
55:7 Let the *w* forsake his way
Eze 3:18 a *w* man, 'You will surely die,'
Mt 12:39 "A *w* and adulterous generation
12:45 other spirits more *w* than itself,
13:49 separate the *w* from the righteous

24:12 *w-ness*, the love of most will grow
Ac 24:15 of both the righteous and the *w*.
Ro 1:18 the godlessness and *w-ness* of men
4:5 trusts God who justifies the *w*,
1Co 5:8 the yeast of malice and *w-ness*,
6:9 the *w* will not inherit the kingdom
2Ti 2:19 Lord must turn away from *w-ness*.
Tit 2:14 to redeem us from all *w-ness*
Heb 1:9 righteousness and hated *w-ness*;
8:12 I will forgive their *w-ness*
Rev 2:2 you cannot tolerate *w* men,

wide

Ps 81:10 Open *w* your mouth and I will fill
Mt 7:13 For *w* is the gate and broad
2Co 6:13 open *w* your hearts also.
Eph 3:18 to grasp how *w* and long and high
Rev 21:16 as long as it was *w*.

widow, -s, -s'

Dt 10:18 the fatherless and the *w*,
Isa 1:17 plead the case of the *w*.
Mt 22:24 his brother must marry the *w*
Mk 12:40 They devour *w-s'* houses
12:42 *w* came and put in two very small
Lk 18:5 this *w* keeps bothering me,
Ac 6:1 their *w-s* were being overlooked
1Co 7:8 to the unmarried and the *w-s* I say:
1Ti 5:3 those *w-s* who are really in need.
Jas 1:27 to look after orphans and *w-s*

wife

Ge 2:24 united to his *w*,
38:8 "Lie with your brother's *w*
Ex 20:17 covet your neighbour's *w*,
Ps 128:3 Your *w* will be like a fruitful vine
Pr 5:18 rejoice in the *w* of your youth.
27:15 A quarrelsome *w* is like a constant
31:10 A *w* of noble character
Ecc 9:9 Enjoy life with your *w*,
Mal 2:15 faith with the *w* of your youth.
Mt 1:20 to take Mary home as your *w*,
5:31 'Anyone who divorces his *w*
19:3 for a man to divorce his *w*
22:28 whose *w* will she be of the seven,
Lk 17:32 Remember Lot's *w*!
18:29 left home or *w* or brothers
1Co 5:1 A man has his father's *w*.
7:3 fulfil his marital duty to his *w*,
7:14 sanctified through his *w*,
Eph 5:23 husband is the head of the *w*
1Ti 3:2 the husband of but one *w*,
Rev 21:9 the bride, the *w* of the Lamb.

wild

Ge 3:1 crafty than any of the *w* animals
Mt 3:4 His food was locusts and *w* honey.
Mk 1:13 He was with the *w* animals,
Lk 15:13 squandered his wealth in *w* living.
Ro 11:17 though a *w* olive shoot,
1Co 15:32 I fought *w* beasts in Ephesus

will

Ps 40:8 desire to do your *w*, O my God;
Isa 53:10 it was the LORD's *w* to crush him
Mt 6:10 your kingdom come, you *w* be done
7:21 he who does the *w* of my Father
26:39 Yet not as I *w*, but as you *w*.
Lk 12:47 servant who knows his master's *w*
Jn 1:13 a husband's *w*, but born of God.
4:34 to do the *w* of him who sent me
Ac 4:28 *w* had decided beforehand
Ro 8:20 the *w* of the one who subjected it,
12:2 to test and approve what God's *w* is
Eph 1:11 with the purpose of his *w*,
5:17 understand what the Lord's *w* is.
Php 2:13 it is God who works in you to *w*
1Th 4:3 It is God's *w* that you should be
Heb 10:7 I have come to do your *w*, O God.'
Jas 4:15 say, "If it is the Lord's *w*,
2Pe 1:21 had its origin in the *w* of man

1Jn 2:17 does the *w* of God lives for ever.

willing

Mt 8:2 "Lord, if you are *w*, you can
18:14 Father in heaven is not *w* that
23:37 her wings, but you were not *w*.
26:41 The spirit is *w*, but the body

win, -s

Pr 11:30 he who *w-s* souls is wise.
Mt 23:15 to *w* a single convert,
1Co 9:19 to *w* as many as possible.
Gal 1:10 trying to *w* the approval of men,
4:17 zealous to *w* you over,
Php 3:14 to *w* the prize for which God

wind, -s

Ex 14:21 sea back with a strong east *w*
Ps 1:4 chaff that the *w* blows away.
103:16 *w* blows over it and it is gone,
Ecc 2:11 a chasing after the *w*;
Hos 8:7 sow the *w* and reap the whirlwind.
Mt 7:25 the *w-s* blew and beat against
8:26 rebuked the *w-s* and the waves,
11:7 A reed swayed by the *w*?
Jn 3:8 The *w* blows wherever it pleases.
Ac 2:2 the blowing of a violent *w*
Eph 4:14 blown here and there by every *w*
Heb 1:7 "He makes his angels *w-s*,
Jas 1:6 blown and tossed by the *w*.

wine, -press, -skins

Ps 60:3 given us *w* that makes us stagger.
104:15 *w* that gladdens the heart of man,
Pr 20:1 *W* is a mocker and beer
23:31 Do not gaze at *w* when it is red,
Isa 55:1 buy *w* and milk without money
Mt 9:17 pour new *w* into old *w-skins*.
21:33 a wall around it, dug a *w-press*
27:34 they offered Jesus *w* to drink,
Jn 2:9 water that had been turned into *w*.
Ac 2:13 "They have had too much *w*."
Ro 14:21 not to eat meat or drink *w*
Eph 5:18 Do not get drunk on *w*,
1Ti 3:8 not indulging in much *w*,
Rev 14:10 drink of the *w* of God's fury,

wings

Ex 19:4 I carried you on eagles' *w*
Ps 36:7 refuge in the shadow of your *w*.
55:6 "Oh, that I had the *w* of a dove!
139:9 If I rise on the *w* of the dawn,
Isa 6:2 seraphs, each with six *w*:
40:31 They will soar on *w* like eagles;
Mal 4:2 will rise with healing in its *w*.
Mt 23:37 gathers her chicks under her *w*,

winter

Ge 8:22 cold and heat, summer and *w*,
Mt 24:20 will not take place in *w*

wipe, -d

Lk 7:38 Then she *w-d* them with her hair,
Jn 11:2 and *w-d* his feet with her hair.
Ac 3:19 so that your sins may be *w-d* out,
Rev 7:17 And God will *w* away every tear

wisdom

1Ki 4:29 God gave Solomon *w*
Job 28:28 fear of the Lord—that is *w*,
Ps 90:12 that we may gain a heart of *w*.
111:10 LORD is the beginning of *w*;
Pr 3:13 Blessed is the man who finds *w*,
4:5 Get *w*, get understanding;
Isa 11:2 Spirit of *w* and of understanding,
Mt 11:19 *w* is proved right by her actions.
Lk 2:52 Jesus grew in *w* and stature,
Ac 6:3 full of the Spirit and *w*.
Ro 11:33 the riches of the *w* and knowledge
1Co 1:20 made foolish the *w* of the world?
1:22 signs and Greeks look for *w*,
1:30 who has become for us *w* from God
12:8 through the Spirit the message of *w*
Eph 1:17 may give you the Spirit of *w* and
Col 2:3 treasures of *w* and knowledge.
Jas 1:5 If any of you lacks *w*,

3:17	the *w* that comes from heaven is

wise, -r, -ly

1Ki 3:12	give you a *w* and discerning heart,
Ps 19:7	making *w* the simple.
119:98	make me *w-r* than my enemies,
Pr 9:8	rebuke a *w* man and he will love you
11:30	and he who wins souls is *w*.
Isa 5:21	those who are *w* in their own eyes
52:13	my servant will act *w-ly*;
Mt 7:24	like a *w* man who built his house on
11:25	hidden these things from the *w*
25:2	foolish and five were *w*.
Ro 1:22	Although they claimed to be *w*,
1Co 1:19	I will destroy the wisdom of the *w*;
1:26	Not many of you were *w* by human
2:4	not with *w* and persuasive words,
2Ti 3:15	to make you *w* for salvation

witchcraft

Gal 5:20	idolatry and *w*; hatred, discord,

withdrew

Mt 2:22	he *w* to the district of Galilee.
Lk 5:16	Jesus often *w* to lonely places
Jn 6:15	*w* again to a mountain by himself

wither, -s, -ed

Ps 1:3	whose leaf does not *w*.
Isa 40:7	grass *w-s* and the flowers fall,
Mt 13:6	they *w-ed* because they had no root.
21:19	Immediately the tree *w-ed*.
1Pe 1:24	grass *w-s* and the flowers fall,

withhold, -held

Ge 22:12	not *w-held* from me your son,
Ps 84:11	no good thing does he *w* from those
Pr 23:13	Do not *w* discipline from a child;

witness, -es

Isa 43:10	"You are my *w-es*," declares
Mt 18:16	testimony of two or three *w-es*.
26:60	many false *w-es* came forward.
Jn 1:7	a *w* to testify concerning
Ac 1:8	you will be my *w-es* in Jerusalem,
1Co 15:15	found to be false *w-es* about God,
Heb 12:1	such a great cloud of *w-es*,

wives

Mt 19:8	permitted you to divorce your *w*
1Co 7:29	those who have *w* should live
Eph 5:22	*W*, submit to your husbands
5:25	Husbands, love your *w*,
1Pe 3:1	by the behaviour of their *w*,

woe

Isa 6:5	"*W* to me!" I cried. "I am ruined
Mt 18:7	but *w* to the man through whom
26:24	*w* to that man who betrays the Son
1Co 9:16	*W* to me if I do not preach

wolf, -ves

Isa 11:6	The *w* will live with the lamb,
Mt 7:15	inwardly they are ferocious *w-ves*.
10:16	like sheep among *w-ves*.
Jn 10:12	when he sees the *w* coming,
Ac 20:29	savage *w-ves* will come in

woman, -en

Ge 2:22	LORD God made a *w* from the rib
3:15	put enmity between you and the *w*,
Ru 3:11	you are a *w* of noble character.
Job 2:10	"You are talking like a foolish *w*.
Pr 31:29	"Many *w-en* do noble things, but
Isa 54:1	"Sing, O barren *w*,
Joel 2:29	*w-en*, I will pour out my Spirit
Mt 5:28	anyone who looks at a *w* lustfully
5:32	marries the divorced *w* commits
9:20	*w* who had been subject to bleeding
15:28	"*W*, you have great faith!

24:41 Two *w-en* will be grinding
28:5 The angel said to the *w-en*,
Lk 1:42 "Blessed are you among *w-en*,
Jn 2:4 "Dear *w*, why do you involve me?"
4:7 Samaritan *w* came to draw water,
8:3 a *w* caught in adultery.
19:26 "Dear *w*, here is your son,"
20:13 "*W*, why are you crying?"
Ac 2:18 *w-en*, I will pour out my Spirit
8:12 baptised, both men and *w-en*.
Ro 1:26 *w-en* exchanged natural relations
7:2 by law a married *w* is bound
1Co 7:2 and each *w* her own husband.
11:3 the head of the *w* is man,
14:34 *w-en* should remain silent
Gal 4:4 born of a *w*, born under law,
1Ti 2:9 I also want *w-en* to dress modestly,
2:12 I do not permit a *w* to teach
Tit 2:4 train the younger *w-en*
1Pe 3:5 the way the holy *w-en* of the past
Rev 2:20 You tolerate that *w* Jezebel,
17:3 a *w* sitting on a scarlet beast

womb
Ge 25:23 "Two nations are in your *w*,
Job 1:21 "Naked I came from my mother's *w*,
Ps 139:13 knit me together in my mother's *w*.
Lk 1:41 the baby leaped in her *w*,

wonder, -s, -ful, -fully
Ex 7:3 miraculous signs and *w-s* in Egypt,
Ps 119:18 see *w-ful* things in your law.
139:14 I am fearfully and *w-fully* made;
Isa 9:6 he will be called *W-ful* Counsellor,
Joel 2:30 show *w-s* in the heavens
Mt 21:15 saw the *w-ful* things he did
Ac 2:11 the *w-s* of God in our own tongues!
2:19 I will show *w-s* in the heaven
2Co 12:12 that mark an apostle—signs, *w-s*
2Th 2:9 counterfeit miracles, signs and *w-s*
Heb 2:4 testified to it by signs, *w-s*
1Pe 2:9 darkness into his *w-ful* light.

wood
Ge 22:7 "The fire and *w* are here,"
Dt 4:28 man-made gods of *w* and stone,
Pr 26:20 Without *w* a fire goes out;
Isa 44:16 Half of the *w* he burns
1Co 3:12 costly stones, *w*, hay or straw,
2Ti 2:20 also of *w* and clay;

wool
Pr 31:13 She selects *w* and flax
Isa 1:18 they shall be like *w*.
Da 7:9 head was white like *w*.
Rev 1:14 hair were white like *w*,

word, -s
Ge 15:1 the *w* of the LORD came to Abram
Ex 20:1 God spoke all these *w-s*:
Dt 8:3 live on bread alone but on every *w*
30:14 No, the *w* is very near you;
1Sa 3:1 the *w* of the LORD was rare;
1Ki 8:56 Not one *w* has failed
Job 19:23 "Oh, that my *w-s* were recorded,
Ps 12:6 the *w-s* of the LORD are flawless,
19:14 May the *w-s* of my mouth
119:9 By living according to your *w*.
119:11 hidden your *w* in my heart
119:89 Your *w*, O LORD, is eternal;
119:130 unfolding of your *w-s* gives light;
Pr 25:11 A *w* aptly spoken is like apples of
Ecc 5:2 so let your *w-s* be few.
Isa 8:20 speak according to this *w*,
40:8 the *w* of our God stands for ever.
55:11 my *w* that goes out from my mouth:
66:2 and trembles at my *w*.
Jer 23:29 "Is not my *w* like fire,"
Mal 2:17 wearied the LORD with your *w-s*.
Mt 4:4 every *w* that comes from the mouth
7:24 who hears these *w-s* of mine
12:32 speaks a *w* against the Son of Man
12:37 by your *w-s* you will be acquitted,

13:20	the man who hears the *w*
24:35	my *w-s* will never pass away.
Mk 7:13	you nullify the *w* of God
Jn 1:1	In the beginning was the *W*,
1:14	The *W* became flesh
5:24	whoever hears my *w* and believes
6:68	You have the *w-s* of eternal life.
8:51	if anyone keeps my *w*,
8:55	I do know him and keep his *w*.
15:3	already clean because of the *w*
15:7	and my *w-s* remain in you, ask
17:14	I have given them your *w*
17:17	your *w* is truth.
Ac 6:2	neglect the ministry of the *w*
13:49	The *w* of the Lord spread
Ro 3:2	entrusted with the very *w-s* of God.
9:6	not as though God's *w* had failed.
10:8	"The *w* is near you;
1Co 1:17	not with *w-s* of human wisdom,
14:19	rather speak five intelligible *w-s*
2Co 2:17	we do not peddle the *w* of God
Eph 1:13	when you heard the *w* of truth,
5:26	washing with water through the *w*,
6:17	the Spirit, which is the *w* of God.
Php 2:16	hold out the *w* of life—
Col 1:5	heard about in the *w* of truth,
3:16	the *w* of Christ dwell in you richly
1Th 1:5	not simply with *w-s*,
4:15	According to the Lord's own *w*,
4:18	each other with these *w-s*.
2Ti 2:9	But God's *w* is not chained.
2:15	correctly handles the *w* of truth.
4:2	Preach the *W*;
Heb 1:3	all things by his powerful *w*.
4:12	the *w* of God is living and active.
12:24	speaks a better *w* than the blood
Jas 1:18	birth through the *w* of truth,
1:22	Do not merely listen to the *w*,
1Pe 1:25	the *w* of the Lord stands for ever.
3:1	any of them do not believe the *w*,
2Pe 1:19	we have the *w* of the prophets
3:5	long ago by God's *w* the heavens
1Jn 1:1	proclaim concerning the *W* of life.
2:14	the *w* of God lives in you,
Rev 1:2	that is, the *w* of God
3:8	yet you have kept my *w*
12:11	by the *w* of their testimony;
22:19	takes *w-s* away from this book of

work, -s, -ing, -er, -ers

Ge 2:2	God had finished the *w*
2:15	in the Garden of Eden to *w* it
29:18	"I'll *w* for you seven years
Ex 20:9	labour and do all your *w*,
Dt 5:14	On it you shall not do any *w*,
32:4	the Rock, his *w-s* are perfect,
Ps 8:3	heavens, the *w* of your fingers,
8:6	ruler over the *w-s* of your hands;
19:1	skies proclaim the *w* of his hands.
46:8	Come and see the *w-s* of the LORD,
90:17	establish the *w* of our hands
104:23	Then man goes out to his *w*,
107:24	They saw the *w-s* of the LORD,
139:14	your *w-s* are wonderful,
145:4	commend your *w-s* to another;
Pr 8:22	forth as the first of his *w-s*,
Ecc 5:19	his lot and be happy in his *w*
Mt 9:37	but the *w-ers* are few.
10:10	the *w-er* is worth his keep.
20:4	go and *w* in my vineyard,
Lk 13:14	"There are six days for *w*.
Jn 4:34	and to finish his *w*.
5:17	"My Father is always at his *w*
6:27	Do not *w* for food that spoils,
6:29	"The *w* of God is this: to believe
17:4	by completing the *w* you gave me
Ro 4:2	Abraham was justified by *w-s*,
4:4	Now when a man *w-s*,
7:21	So I find this law at *w*:
8:28	in all things God *w-s* for the good
11:6	then it is no longer by *w-s*;
1Co 3:13	his *w* will be shown for what it is,
12:11	the *w* of one and the same Spirit,
12:29	Do all *w* miracles?

15:58 fully to the *w* of the Lord,
2Co 4:12 death is at *w* in us,
Gal 3:5 his Spirit and *w* miracles
Eph 1:11 the plan of him who *w-s* out
1:19 the *w-ing* of his mighty strength,
2:2 the spirit who is now at *w*
2:9 gift of God—not by *w-s*,
2:10 in Christ Jesus to do good *w-s*,
4:12 God's people for *w-s* of service,
Php 1:6 he who began a good *w* in you
2:12 continue to *w* out your salvation
Col 3:23 *w* at it with all your heart,
2Th 2:7 lawlessness is already at *w*;
3:10 "If a man will not *w*,
1Ti 5:17 those whose *w* is preaching
5:18 "The *w-er* deserves his wages."
2Ti 3:17 equipped for every good *w*.
4:5 do the *w* of an evangelist,
Heb 1:10 heavens are the *w* of your hands.
1Jn 3:8 to destroy the devil's *w*.
Rev 2:2 I know your deeds, your hard *w*

workman, -men, -ship

2Co 11:13 false apostles, deceitful *w-men*,
Eph 2:10 For we are God's *w-ship*,
2Ti 2:15 *w* who does not need to be ashamed
Jas 5:4 wages you failed to pay the *w-men*

world, -ly

Ge 11:1 the whole *w* had one language
Ps 9:8 judge the *w* in righteousness;
24:1 the *w*, and all who live in it;
50:12 *w* is mine, and all that is in it.
Mt 4:8 all the kingdoms of the *w*
5:14 "You are the light of the *w*.
16:26 if he gains the whole *w*,
24:14 preached in the whole *w*
Mk 16:15 "Go into all the *w* and preach
Lk 2:1 taken of the entire Roman *w*.
Jn 1:10 He was in the *w*,
1:29 who takes away the sin of the *w*
3:16 "For God so loved the *w*
4:42 the Saviour of the *w*."
8:12 "I am the light of the *w*.
14:30 the prince of this *w* is coming.
15:18 "If the *w* hates you, keep in mind
16:33 In this *w* you will have trouble.
17:11 I will remain in the *w* no longer,
17:16 They are not of the *w*, even as I
17:18 As you sent me into the *w*, I have
17:21 be in us so that the *w* may believe
18:36 "My kingdom is not of this *w*.
Ac 17:6 have caused trouble all over the *w*
17:24 "The God who made the *w*
17:31 will judge the *w* with justice
Ro 1:20 creation of the *w* God's invisible
5:12 sin entered the *w* through one man,
1Co 3:19 the wisdom of this *w* is foolishness
6:2 the saints will judge the *w*?
2Co 5:19 God was reconciling the *w*
Eph 1:4 before the creation of the *w*
6:12 against the powers of this dark *w*
1Ti 1:15 Jesus came into the *w* to save
6:7 we brought nothing into the *w*,
2Ti 4:10 because he loved this *w*,
Tit 2:12 "No" to ungodliness and *w-ly*
Heb 9:26 since the creation of the *w*.
Jas 4:4 friendship with the *w* is hatred
1Pe 1:20 before the creation of the *w*,
2Pe 3:6 the *w* of that time was deluged
1Jn 2:2 also for the sins of the whole *w*.
2:15 Do not love the *w* or anything in
2:17 The *w* and its desires pass away,
Rev 11:15 "The kingdom of the *w* has become
13:8 slain from the creation of the *w*.

worm

Ps 22:6 I am a *w* and not a man,
Isa 66:24 their *w* will not die,
Mk 9:48 "'their *w* does not die,

worry, -ies

Mt 6:25 do not *w* about your life,
6:34 do not *w* about tomorrow,
13:22 the *w-ies* of this life

Lk 21:14 not to *w* beforehand

worship, -s, -ped

Ge 22:5 We will *w* and then
Ex 7:16 they may *w* me in the desert.
20:5 not bow down to them or *w* them;
1Ch 16:29 *w* the LORD in the splendour of his
Ps 29:2 *w* the LORD in the splendour
95:6 Come, let us bow down in *w*,
100:2 *W* the LORD with gladness;
Isa 44:17 he bows down to it and *w-s*.
Da 3:6 Whoever does not fall down and *w*
Mt 2:2 have come to *w* him.
4:9 if you will bow down and *w* me."
15:9 They *w* me in vain;
28:17 they *w-ped* him; but some doubted.
Jn 4:21 a time is coming when you will *w*
Ro 1:25 and *w-ped* and served created
12:1 this is your spiritual act of *w*.
Php 3:3 we who *w* by the Spirit of God,
Heb 1:6 "Let all God's angels *w* him."

worth, -y

Ps 48:1 LORD, and most *w-y* of praise,
Pr 31:10 She is *w* far more than rubies.
Mt 10:10 the worker is *w* his keep.
10:31 you are *w* more than many sparrows.
10:37 mother more than me is not *w-y*
Mk 1:7 sandals I am not *w-y* to stoop down
Lk 15:19 *w-y* to be called your son;
Ro 8:18 sufferings are not *w* comparing
Eph 4:1 to live a life *w-y* of the calling
Php 1:27 conduct yourselves in a manner *w-y*
1Ti 3:8 men *w-y* of respect, sincere,
5:17 *w-y* of double honour,
1Pe 1:7 faith—of greater *w* than gold,
Rev 4:11 "You are *w-y*, our Lord and God,
5:12 "*W-y* is the Lamb, who was slain

wound, -s

Pr 27:6 *W-s* from a friend can be trusted,
Isa 53:5 by his *w-s* we are healed.
1Pe 2:24 by his *w-s* you have been healed

woven

Ps 139:15 I was *w* together in the depths
Jn 19:23 seamless, *w* in one piece

wrath

Ps 2:12 his *w* can flare up in a moment.
90:11 your *w* is as great as the fear
Pr 15:1 A gentle answer turns away *w*,
Isa 63:3 trod them down in my *w*;
Eze 7:19 in the day of the LORD's *w*.
Hab 3:2 in *w* remember mercy.
Zep 2:2 of the LORD's *w* comes upon you.
Mt 3:7 to flee from the coming *w*?
Jn 3:36 God's *w* remains on him."
Ro 1:18 The *w* of God is being revealed
5:9 saved from God's *w* through him!
Eph 2:3 by nature objects of *w*.
1Th 1:10 rescues us from the coming *w*.
5:9 God did not appoint us to suffer *w*
Rev 6:16 from the *w* of the Lamb!
19:15 fury of the *w* of God Almighty.

wrestle, -ing, -d

Ge 32:24 a man *w-d* with him till daybreak.
Col 4:12 always *w-ing* in prayer for you,

wretched

Ro 7:24 What a *w* man I am!
Rev 3:17 you are *w*, pitiful, poor, blind

write, -ten, -r

Dt 6:9 *W* them on the door-frames
10:4 tablets what he had *w-ten* before,
28:58 which are *w-ten* in this book,
Jos 1:8 to do everything *w-ten* in it.
23:6 to obey all that is *w-ten*
Ps 40:7 it is *w-ten* about me in the scroll.
45:1 tongue is the pen of a skilful *w-r*
Pr 7:3 *w* them on the tablet of your heart.
Jer 31:33 and *w* it on their hearts.
Da 12:1 name is found *w-ten* in the book—
Mal 3:16 A scroll of remembrance was *w-ten*

Lk 10:20	your names are *w-ten* in heaven."
24:44	fulfilled that is *w-ten* about me
Jn 8:6	Jesus bent down and started to *w*
20:31	are *w-ten* that you may believe
Ro 2:15	requirements of the law are *w-ten*
1Co 10:11	were *w-ten* down as warnings for us
2Co 3:3	*w-ten* not with ink
Col 2:14	cancelled the *w-ten* code,
Heb 10:7	it is *w-ten* about me in the scroll
10:16	I will *w* them on their minds."
12:23	whose names are *w-ten* in heaven.
Jude :4	whose condemnation was *w-ten* about
Rev 1:19	"*W*, therefore, what you have seen
2:17	with a new name *w-ten* on it,
21:27	names are *w-ten* in the Lamb's

wrong, -s, -ed, -doing

Ex 23:2	Do not follow the crowd in doing *w*.
Job 1:22	by charging God with *w-doing*.
Ps 119:104	I hate every *w* path.
Lk 23:41	this man has done nothing *w*."
Ro 13:4	if you do *w*, be afraid,
1Co 6:7	Why not rather be *w-ed*?
13:5	it keeps no record of *w-s*.
Gal 2:11	he was clearly in the *w*.
Heb 8:7	nothing *w* with that first covenant,
1Pe 2:20	you receive a beating for doing *w*

wrote

Ex 34:28	he *w* on the tablets
Jn 1:45	the one Moses *w* about
5:46	believe me, for he *w* about me.
2Pe 3:15	Paul also *w* to you

X

Xerxes

King of Persia (Ezr 4:6; Est 1:1–2); father of Darius (Da 9:1). Deposed Vashti; married Esther (Est 1–2). Assassination attempt uncovered by Mordecai (Est 2:21–23). Gave assent to Haman's edict to kill Jews (Est 3); allowed Esther to see him without being called (Est 5:1–8); hanged Haman (Est 7). Exalted Mordecai (Est 8:1–2; 9:4; 10); allowed Jews to defend themselves (Est 8–9).

Y

year, -s

Ge 6:3	a hundred and twenty *y-s*.
41:29	Seven *y-s* of great abundance
Lev 16:34	Atonement is to be made once a *y*
25:11	fiftieth *y* shall be a jubilee
Ps 90:4	a thousand *y-s* in your sight
90:10	length of our days is seventy *y-s*—
Isa 6:1	In the *y* that King Uzziah died,
61:2	to proclaim the *y* of the LORD's
Joel 2:25	the *y-s* the locusts have eaten—
Lk 4:19	the *y* of the Lord's favour."
12:19	good things laid up for many *y-s*.
13:8	'leave it alone for one more *y*,
Heb 9:7	and that only once a *y*,
10:1	repeated endlessly *y* after *y*,
Jas 4:13	a *y* there, carry on business
2Pe 3:8	a day is like a thousand *y-s*,
Rev 20:4	with Christ for a thousand *y-s*.

yeast

Ex 12:15	eat bread made without *y*.
Mt 13:33	"The kingdom of heaven is like *y*
16:6	"Be on your guard against the *y*
1Co 5:6	a little *y* works through
Gal 5:9	"A little *y* works through

yesterday

Heb 13:8	Jesus Christ is the same *y*

yoke, -d

Mt 11:30	my *y* is easy and my burden
2Co 6:14	*y-d* together with unbelievers.
Gal 5:1	again by a *y* of slavery.

young, -er

Ps 37:25	I was *y* and now I am old,
119:9	How can a *y* man keep his way pure?
Pr 20:29	glory of *y* men is their strength,
Isa 40:30	*y* men stumble and fall;
La 3:27	to bear the yoke while he is *y*.

Lk 15:13 the *y-er* son got together
Ac 2:17 your *y* men will see visions,
Ro 9:12 "The older will serve the *y-er.*"
1Ti 4:12 down on you because you are *y*,
5:1 Treat *y-er* men as brothers,
1Pe 5:5 *Y* men, in the same way

youth, -s

Ps 25:7 Remember not the sins of my *y*
103:5 your *y* is renewed like the eagle's.
Pr 5:18 rejoice in the wife of your *y.*
Ecc 12:1 Creator in the days of your *y*,
Isa 40:30 Even *y-s* grow tired and weary,
Mal 2:15 faith with the wife of your *y.*
2Ti 2:22 Flee the evil desires of *y*,

Z

Zacchaeus

Tax collector; climbed tree to see Jesus (Lk 19:2–10).

Zadok

Priest; descendant of Aaron (1Ch 6:3–8). With Abiathar, served David (2Sa 8:17; 1Ch 15:11; 16:39–40); in charge of ark (2Sa 15:24–29). Anointed Solomon as David's successor when Abiathar supported Adonijah (1Ki 1:8,32–48). Descendants served as chief priests (2Ch 31:10; Eze 40:46; 43:19; 44:15).

zeal, -ous

1Ki 19:10 been very *z-ous* for the LORD
Ps 69:9 *z* for your house consumes me,
Pr 19:2 good to have *z* without knowledge,
Jn 2:17 "*Z* for your house will consume me.
Ro 10:2 they are *z-ous* for God,
12:11 Never be lacking in *z*,

Zebulun

1. Son of Jacob by Leah (Ge 30:20; 35:23; 1Ch 2:1). Blessed by Jacob (Ge 49:13). **2.** Tribe descended from Zebulun. Blessed by Moses (Dt 33:18–19). Included in census (Nu 1:30–31; 26:26–27). Apportioned land (Jos 19:10–16; Eze 48:26); unable to take full possession (Jdg 1:30).

Zechariah

1. King of Israel; son of Jeroboam II; assassinated (2Ki 14:29; 15:8–12). **2.** Prophet who, with Haggai, encouraged rebuilding of temple (Ezr 5:1; 6:14; Zec 1:1). **3.** Priest; father of John the Baptist; struck dumb because of unbelief at the angel Gabriel's announcement of the birth of a son (Lk 1:5–22,59–79).

Zedekiah

1. Last king of Judah. Son of Josiah, formerly Mattaniah. Installed by Nebuchadnezzar (2Ki 24:17–18). Evil denounced (Jer 24:8–10; Eze 21:25); dealings with Jeremiah (2Ch 36:12; Jer 37; 38:14–28). Rebellion and broken oath led to fall of Jerusalem (2Ki 24:20–25:7; 2Ch 36:13–21; Jer 39; Eze 17:12–15). **2.** Leader of false prophets at Ahab's court (1Ki 22:11–24; 2Ch 18:10–23).

Zephaniah

Prophet during reign of Josiah; descended from Hezekiah (Zep 1:1).

Zerubbabel

Leader of returning exiles (Ne 12:1; Hag 1:1; 2:2); began work on temple (Ezr 3); after delay, encouraged to continue by Haggai (Ezr 5:1–2; Hag 1:2–15; 2) and Zechariah (Zec 4:6–10).

Zion

Ps 2:6 installed my King on *Z*,
50:2 From *Z*, perfect in beauty,
137:3 "Sing us one of the songs of *Z!*"
Isa 28:16 "See, I lay a stone in *Z*,
Mt 21:5 "Say to the Daughter of *Z*,
Ro 9:33 "See, I lay in *Z* a stone
Heb 12:22 you have come to Mount *Z*,
1Pe 2:6 "See, I lay a stone in *Z*,
Rev 14:1 the Lamb, standing on Mount *Z*,

Zipporah

Daughter of Jethro; wife of Moses (Ex 2:21–22; 18:2); circumcised son to save Moses' life (Ex 4:20–26).

Zophar

See *Job* **2**.

The Bible in One Year

New International Version

An excellent way to read through the Bible methodically in one year.

A unique arrangement of the Bible into 365 daily readings. Each day's selection includes text from both the Old and New Testaments, as well as a reading from either Psalms or Proverbs. Enables a structured but varied reading of the full Bible text in one year.

FEATURES

- Old and New Testament readings in chronological order
- readings begin on 1st January although the reader can start at any time during the year
- text from Psalms or Proverbs is included each day
- a time chart and 5 black and white Bible maps
- *What is the Bible?* section providing a helpful introduction to Bible reading
- a summary of each Bible book
- index to well known passages

ISBN 0 340 41917 2

NIV Bible Commentary

Edited by Alister McGrath

The highly acclaimed one-volume guide to God's Word.

A one-volume commentary written in a clear, accessible style with the minimum of theological jargon. Ideal for those just starting out on serious Bible study and wanting to gain a firmly established understanding of Scripture. Clearly introduces leading Bible themes, offering succinct and informative comment for your everyday reading of the Bible.

FEATURES

- introductory articles: *Why a Commentary? What's in the Bible? Where do I start?* and *Referring to Biblical Books*
- an introduction to each book
- commentary broken down into easy-to-manage sections with headings and verse references
- black and white maps and charts throughout
- suggestions for further reading

"Probably the most user friendly Bible commentary yet produced, designed to be used with the New International Version, but equally helpful with any translation."

Home and Family

ISBN 0 340 66142 9